DIVE TRUK LAGOON

Published by
Whittles Publishing Ltd,
Dunbeath,
Caithness, KW6 6EG,
Scotland, UK

www.whittlespublishing.com

© 2023 Rod Macdonald

ISBN 978-184995-541-6

Printed and bound in the UK
by Halstan Printing Group, Amersham

DIVE TRUK LAGOON

2nd edition

THE JAPANESE WWII PACIFIC SHIPWRECKS

ROD MACDONALD

Whittles Publishing

About the Author

Rod Macdonald is one of the world's pre-eminent shipwreck explorers and an international best-selling author of a number of classic diving books. He lives in Stonehaven, a small fishing town on the rugged north east coast of Scotland.

A graduate from Aberdeen University School of Law, he retired from law in 2010 to concentrate on writing professionally. He has appeared in numerous international television documentaries on shipwrecks with National Geographic, BBC and Channel 5 - such as Equinox, Timewatch and Drain the Oceans

An RYA Advanced Powerboat Instructor and seasoned yachtsman, he served as lifeboat crew for several years on the Stonehaven Lifeboat - before being appointed RNLI Lifeboat Operations Manager, responsible for setting up and running the new Stonehaven Lifeboat service in 2013.

Rod is a motivational speaker, a Fellow of the Explorers Club of New York and a Patron of the GB and Ireland Chapter of the Explorers Club.

Also, by Rod Macdonald:
Diving books
Wreck guides
Dive Scapa Flow
Dive Scotland's Greatest Wrecks
Dive England's Greatest Wrecks
Great British Shipwrecks - a personal adventure
Force Z Shipwrecks of the South China Sea - HMS *Prince of Wales* & HMS *Repulse*
Dive Truk Lagoon - the Japanese WWII Pacific Shipwrecks
Dive Palau - the Shipwrecks
Shipwrecks of Truk Lagoon
The Diving Trilogy
Vol I.   *Into the Abyss – Diving to Adventure in the Liquid World*
Vol II.   *The Darkness Below*
Vol III.   *Deeper into the Darkness*
Military History
TASK FORCE 58 – the US Navy's Fast Carrier Strike Force that won the War in the Pacific
PEARL HARBOR'S REVENGE: How the Devastated U.S. Battleships Returned to War
HMS Hampshire 100 Survey Report 2016 with Ben Wade, Emily Turton, Paul Haynes, David Crofts & Prof Chris Rowland.
HMS K-4 & K-17 Survey report 2023

www.rod-macdonald.com   Twitter: @divescapa
Facebook: Rod Macdonald page   YouTube: Rod Macdonald channel

CONTENTS

Acknowledgements vii

Introduction xi

Explanatory Notes xix

PART 1

1 Prelude to War in the Pacific 1
2 Operation HAILSTONE 12

PART 2   THE SHIPWRECKS OF TRUK LAGOON

1. Aikoku Maru 51
2. Amagisan Maru 66
3. Eisen No 761 75
4. Eisen (unkown) 77
5. Fujikawa Maru 81
6. Fujisan Maru 92
7. Fumizuki 103
8. Futagami 115
9. Gosei Maru 118
10. Hanagawa Maru 124
11. Heian Maru 131
12. Hino Maru No 2 143
13. Hoki Maru (ex-Hauraki) 147
14. Hokuyo Maru 155
15. Hoyo Maru 162
16. I-169 170
17. Inter-Island Supply vessel 178
18. Katsuragisan Maru 179
19. Kensyo Maru 185
20. Kikukawa Maru 195
21. Kiyosumi Maru 201
22. The Lighter 209
23. Momokawa Maru 211
24. Nagano Maru 218

25. Nippo Maru 224
26. IJN Oite 238
27. Ojima 249
28. Patrol Boat No 34 (ex-IJN Susuki) 253
29. Reiyo Maru 258
30. Rio de Janeiro Maru 264
31. San Francisco Maru 275
32. Sankisan Maru 285
33. Sapporo Maru 293
34. Seiko Maru 296
35. Sinkoku Maru 302
36. Shotan Maru 313
37. Taiho Maru 322
38. Unkai Maru No 6 (ex-Venus) 326
39. Yamagiri Maru 334
40. Yubae Maru 342

Japanese Aircraft Wrecks Of Truk Lagoon 346
Us Task Force 58 Strike Aircraft 364

Bibliography 371
Index 373

Gas mask (Author)

ACKNOWLEDGEMENTS

My thanks go to Rob Ward, a talented artist who in 2013 created the wonderful illustrations of the most popular Truk wrecks for the 1st edition. Rob and I started out more than 30 years ago in 1989 creating the illustrations of the German WWI High Seas Fleet wrecks for my first book *Dive Scapa Flow* - and since then Rob has illustrated all my other books. Rob is not a diver and almost amazingly has never seen any of the almost 100 wrecks he has illustrated for me over the years.

Much though I would have liked to do so, there are so many wrecks in the Chuuk lagoon that it was simply economically impossible for me to prepare illustrations of them all for that 1st edition. I had to cherry pick and select the wrecks that divers were most likely to visit on a week or two's dive expedition.

Since publication however, there have been a number of significant changes to some of the wrecks. As anyone who dives shipwrecks knows, wrecks decay and collapse naturally over time, the rate of degradation becoming almost exponential once a wreck is old and has lost its structural integrity.

Ships are designed to cope with the stresses of seafaring in their normal upright position. However, when ships sink and end up lying on their beam ends (their sides), they are subjected to stresses and strains that they were not designed to withstand. As a general rule, shipwrecks that lie on their beam ends degrade faster than wrecks that sit upright in their natural design position.

Thus, no sooner had the 1st edition been published in 2014, there were a few examples of significant collapsing of sections of several of the major wrecks. The beautiful former liner *Rio de Janeiro Maru*, one of Chuuk's most famous wrecks, lies on its starboard side. Its superstructure and smokestack were largely pristine in the years I dived it until 2013 – but almost as soon as the book was published, the superstructure and smokestack sagged and began its inexorable collapse down towards the seabed.

The atmospheric wreck of the requisitioned passenger cargo vessel *Fujikawa Maru* sits upright in about 35 metres of water. She is a big ship, so much so that her superstructure and smokestack had risen (since the war) to just 10 metres short of the surface. You can usually see her upper works from above in your dive boat. Sadly, just shortly after the 1st edition was published, the smokestack and upper bridge superstructure collapsed.

In addition, in 2018, the wreck of a 300-tonne IJN *Zatsueki-sen* fleet tug was located off Weno Island by Truk Stop Dive Center. Although we know that the tug was built by

Kawasaki in Kobe, its actual identity still has not been established and there are no known archive photos of it – so Rob has illustrated this new wreck for me. Its identity will no doubt be revealed at some point – although I do quite like that the sea keeps some of its secrets.

This new 2nd edition therefore brings new illustrations by Rob Ward of previously unillustrated wrecks – and has updates to existing 1st edition wreck illustrations to cater for significant changes. It has been great fun working with such a consummate professional as Rob again – and I am very grateful to him for his time. As I mentioned in the 1st edition, this book is and always will be, a work in progress. Rob may well be busy again with the Truk wrecks in a few year's time!

There are two basic ways to dive Truk Lagoon: either from a bespoke liveaboard dive vessel such as the fine *Truk Odyssey* or the M/Y *Truk Master*, or by booking onto one of the two main onshore dive centres, the *Truk Stop Hotel & Dive Center* and the *Blue Lagoon Resort*, both on the west shore of Weno. From the shore-based dive centres you will go out daily in small, fast, covered dive boats – it's usually a run out of about an hour to most of the wrecks. You dive - and are then back ashore for lunch - and then out again for a 2nd dive in the afternoon.

I have used both Truk Stop and Blue Lagoon over the years, but more often stay at the smaller Truk Stop - who look after me fabulously. They know my specific quirky needs, to visit particular wrecks on particular days and particular times. My trips are mostly a bit outside the mainstream of standard dive trips, but Truk Stop are usually able to give my group our own boat, skipper and guide.

The Truk Stop Hotel & Dive Center is set right on the water's edge of the lagoon and has its own jetty where the dive boats leave from. It caters for both sport and technical divers like myself – and is particularly well set up for Closed Circuit Rebreather divers. A row of large lockable wet gear lockers, able to take all your dive kit, is just a few feet away from the

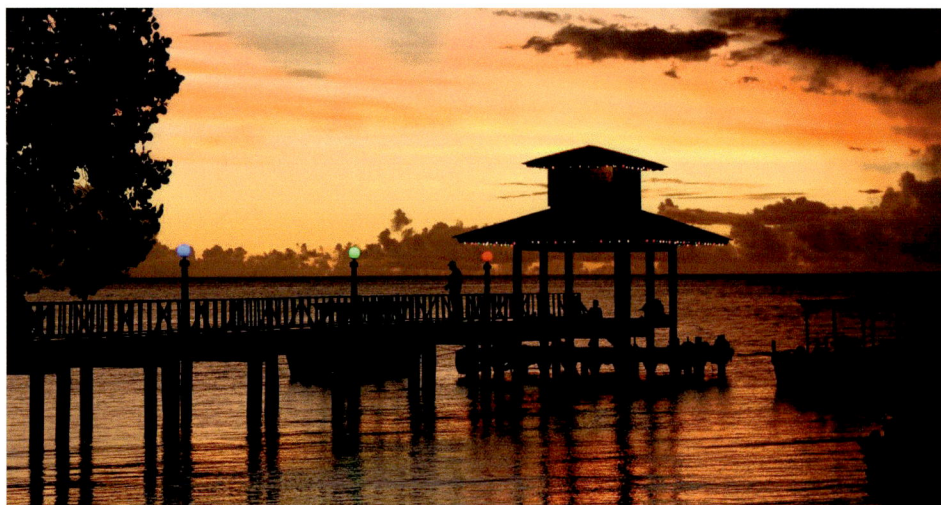

Tropical sunset over a jetty on Truk lagoon. (Author)

edge of the lagoon. Right beside the gear lockers is a row of sturdy kit preparation tables for building up your dive kit and rebreathers (CCR's). For the CCR divers I usually travel with, any combination of 2-3 litre diluent and oxygen cylinders is usually available - as is sofnalime (carbon dioxide scrubber for rebreathers). Any sort of stage cylinder, and breathing gas, we needed was available; all suitably banded with clips. Truk Stop caters extremely well for recreational divers with nitrox available for the suitably qualified. There is also an open-air bar right on the edge of the lagoon, which plays the coolest sunset music - so once the day's diving is done, you can sit and relax with a beer or one of those strange coloured things, often seen with a paper umbrella in it, and watch the sun set on the lagoon.

The Blue Lagoon Resort is equally a fantastic place to stay. It was the first dive centre on Truk back in the day – and was the only dive centre when I made my first pilgrimage to Truk back in 1990. Today it is much bigger, with more rooms and more divers milling about. Fine restaurants, an atmospheric outdoor bar and a great dive set up make it also a great base for your dive trip.

Ewan Rowell has always been into underwater photography - and is getting really good at it, despite his vehement denials. On that first trip in 2013, he worked extremely hard taking more than 100 photographs on each dive, continuously marshalling my buddies and myself into the right place and position to get *that* shot. He came up with some awesome photographs for the book, for which I am very grateful.

The irrepressible and charismatic Pete Mesley runs his wonderful Lust4Rust wreck diving trips to Chuuk from the Blue Lagoon Resort. He also runs fabulous dive trips to Bikini, and many other destinations such as the Galapagos. Pete is a great underwater photographer and has devoted countless hours underwater to photographing the Truk wrecks. He has kindly let me use some of his shots in this book. Many thanks as well to Mike Boring for allowing me to include his wonderful shot of the iconic oil flow inspection panel on *Kensyo Maru*.

My daughter Nicola works in London in the PR and media world. She is far more expert in IT than me, so she sprang into action by working on Rob Ward's illustrations and adding labels to points of interest, so that the illustrations have essentially become mini dive-briefs. I hope this work helps bring out features of interest in the illustrations, which may otherwise be missed by the casual reader.

In this book, all tonnages and dimensions for ships built pre-war are taken from the Lloyd's Register entry for the year of construction. Tonnages often varied in the years following construction, when ships were altered or refitted – so it is not unusual to see tonnages differing throughout a ship's life.

During the late 1930's, as war became more likely, the Japanese authorities denied Lloyd's agents access to shipyards and documentation. Then as war erupted, many ships were built that were unknown to the Allies - and obviously for which there are no Lloyds records. For these ship's I have used a variety of sources, such as the wartime U.S. Intelligence document *Japanese Merchant Ships - Recognition Manual ONI 208-J*. For Imperial Japanese Navy warships a number of sources have been used - such as *Warships of the Imperial Japanese Navy, 1869-1945* by Hansgeorg Jentschura, Dieter Jung and Peter Mickel (Arms & Armour Press 1977).

Finally, I must acknowledge the amazing website CombinedFleet.com founded by Jonathan Parshall and developed over many years with a wealth of detailed information about the IJN, its warships and requisitioned merchant vessels. The detail in this website is incredible – and I would refer any student of this era who wants to learn more about the IJN and its ships to it, here: www.combinedfleet.com

Fair winds and following seas

Rod Macdonald

INTRODUCTION

The lagoon at Chuuk atoll, as Truk has been known since 1990, is a great natural harbour ringed by a protective barrier reef some 140 miles in circumference and almost 50 miles in diameter at its widest.

Rising up from the deep blue oceanic depths of the western Pacific, Chuuk State is one of the Federated States of Micronesia, an independent sovereign island nation formed in 1979 that consists of four states, Yap, Chuuk, Pohnpei and Kosrae. Together the four states comprise some 607 islands scattered over almost 1,700 miles just north of the equator, to the north east of New Guinea. Micronesia forms part of the larger archipelago of the Caroline Islands, which span a distance of more than 2,000 miles from the Palauan islands in the west, to Kosrae, far to the east of Chuuk.

Seized by Japan from Germany during WWI, Truk was administered by the Japanese until their defeat in 1945 - when Truk became one of the six districts of the Trust Territory of the Pacific Islands administered by the United States under charter from the United Nations until 1986.

The fortification of Truk by Japan before the war, was carried out in the utmost secrecy. No foreigners had been allowed anywhere near the islands and as war loomed, the Allies had no idea of the scale of the operation at Truk. But they knew of its excellent natural defences – Truk became known as the "Gibraltar of the Pacific."

Looking south across the azure lagoon towards Weno (Moen) left with Tonoas (Dublon) centre and Fefan to the right (Author)

In 1939, Truk became the Imperial Japanese Navy's (IJN) Fourth Fleet Base. On 5 November 1941, Truk was designated as a supply base for Admiral Isoroku Yamamoto's IJN Combined Fleet – just in time for the initial offensive phase of the planned Pacific war the following month, December 1941 - when amongst a number of bold operations, all eight battleships of the U.S. Navy Pacific Fleet at Pearl Harbor were sunk or damaged. Subsequently, Truk became the main forward naval base from 1942 until 1944 for the IJN Combined Fleet.

The 140 miles of barrier coral reef around the Truk lagoon have five entrance channels that are wide enough and deep enough for large vessels to safely navigate as they entered and left the lagoon. During the war, these five Passes were heavily defended - flanked by Coastal Defence guns set on the islands either side of the Pass. With the exception of North Pass and South Pass (used by the Japanese), the other Passes were mined and closed off to shipping. The atoll islands of Truk held a number of airfields and seaplane bases that bristled with hundreds of fighters, dive bombers, torpedo and high-altitude bombers and reconnaissance float planes.

Truk served from 1942 onwards as a safe, sheltered and well protected forward base for the IJN Combined Fleet. In addition to the front-line warships, a large number of naval auxiliary transport ships, often civilian passenger/cargo vessels that had been requisitioned and converted, worked as tenders for the fleet and its submarines, carrying naval shells,

A WWII Japanese 14 cm (6-inch) coastal defence gun stands guard above
Weno (Moen) airfield in tunnels hewn from the bare rock (Author)

ammunition, torpedoes, stores, spares - and everything else needed to keep a battle fleet operational.

The tide of war turned in the summer of 1942 when the Japanese expansion was halted at the battles of the Coral Sea and Midway. The Allies began their own offensive in the Solomon Islands in August 1942 and then in late 1943, began to advance west across the Pacific towards the Philippines. As Truk became threatened - the Imperial Japanese Army began to fortify Truk's defences against an Allied assault. Beach defences of reinforced concrete pill boxes and blockhouses were established at the shoreline, supplemented by mine fields. Numerous anti–aircraft gun positions were established and eventually there would be over eighty 25mm and 12cm AA guns in emplacements, along with many lighter AA weapons. *Kaiten* manned suicide torpedo bases were established on the outer islands and Daihatsu landing craft were converted into torpedo boats. More heavy naval coastal defence guns were set in caves on strategic island peaks and promontories. Anti-submarine netting was placed around docks and key anchorages.

The Allies invaded and seized Kwajalein and Majuro in the Marshall Islands in late January 1944. It was clear that the major Japanese base at Truk, 1,100 miles to the west would be next in line – and so the pace of fortification increased. Auxiliary transport vessels, usually requisitioned freighters and cargo vessels, arrived continuously at Truk. Their deep cargo holds were filled with munitions, tanks, trucks, land artillery, beach mines, ammunition and the like – all destined to be offloaded to fortify Truk's defences against the anticipated land invasion by the Allies. Other ships served as troop transports, each carrying hundreds of troops. Convoys of transport ships, escorted by destroyers or submarine chasers, stopped over at Truk to refuel, replenish and regroup, before heading off in convoy to reinforce and resupply other outlying Japanese island garrisons that were now threatened.

As Japanese forces were pushed back in the Gilberts and Marshalls between November 1943 and early 1944, much of the IJN Combined Fleet retreated and gathered in their perceived stronghold of Truk - amidst the intense work ashore to fortify Truk's defences. A significant portion of the Imperial Japanese Navy was based there - battleships, carriers, cruisers, destroyers, oilers, tankers, naval auxiliary transport ships, tugs, gun boats, mine sweepers, sub chasers and submarines all thronged the lagoon. By early February 1944, Truk had been heavily fortified with a military infrastructure of roads, trenches, bunkers, caves, five airstrips, seaplane bases, a torpedo boat station, submarine repair centres, a communications centre and a radar station. The Japanese garrison now consisted of almost 17,000 Imperial Japanese Army (IJA) troops in addition to the IJN personnel present.

The scene was set for the showdown.

On the evening of 3 February 1944, two U.S. Marine, long-range Consolidated PB4Y-1 Liberator photo-reconnaissance planes rose into the air from their Stirling Island airfield in the Solomon Islands for a 2,000-mile round trip to overfly the secretive Japanese base at Truk - and photograph Japanese shipping and land fortifications. The two PB4Y-1 reconnaissance aircraft arrived undetected over Truk atoll and were able to spend more than 20 minutes unopposed, overflying and photographing shipping in the lagoon and land fortifications, before turning unscathed to head back to their distant Solomon Islands airbase at full speed.

The U.S. reconnaissance overflight was enough to convince the Japanese that an attack by the Americans was now imminent and that the battleships, aircraft carriers, cruisers and submarines of the IJN Combined Fleet - the main fighting strength of the Imperial Japanese Navy - was in danger. Japan knew that the Allies could not bypass Truk without attacking: Truk could not be left to the rear, able to mount air attacks from behind the Allied front, for its submarines to put to sea, for its warships to attack Allied shipping. On the day of the Truk overflight, a first group of battleships and cruisers departed Truk for Palau, more than 1,000 miles west.

A few days later, on 10 February 1944, the super-battleship *Musashi* departed for Japan along with escort cruisers, destroyers and several fleet supply ships. Four carriers and their escorts departed Truk, heading to safety far to the west - to the great harbour of Singapore. The super-battleship *Yamato* and a number of escort cruisers and destroyers left Truk soon after the carriers.

The Commander-in-Chief of the IJN Combined Fleet, Admiral Mineichi Koga, ordered the Fourth Fleet underway from its anchorage to the east of Dublon Island. The Fourth Fleet operated in the Japanese held island territories of the South Pacific such as the Caroline Islands, Marshall Islands, Mariana Islands and the Palaus - and formed part of the IJN Combined Fleet. But not all of the ship's captains were immediately given their sailing orders. Many requisitioned transport ships lingered in the anchorage, all busily engaged in off-loading their war supplies, before they could leave. Their escort destroyers and sub chasers had to wait for them. Other ships that had been damaged in attacks elsewhere (and were in Truk for repair) were simply not fit to leave for the open sea.

When the U.S. aerial reconnaissance photographs were safely returned and analysed, they revealed the land fortifications of the Japanese stronghold of Truk in astounding detail and permitted the drawing up of a well-coordinated plan of attack. Suddenly, from not knowing what shipping was at Truk before the overflight, it now became instantly clear that nearly all of the IJN Combined Fleet had been there. U.S. High Command immediately advanced plans to attack shipping in Truk – the original plan had been for an attack on 15 April 1944.

The Americans were unaware however that following the reconnaissance overflight, the majority of the IJN warships had almost immediately left the lagoon, leaving only a few lighter IJN escort warships along with almost 50 naval auxiliaries, tenders, cargo vessels, oilers and tankers. Most of the vessels at anchor in Truk were lightly armed merchantmen.

The twelve fast carriers of Task Force 58, which was screened by battleships, cruisers, destroyers and submarines and protected by its own combat air patrols and anti-submarine patrols, sortied from Majuro on 12-13 February for the first independent carrier strike of that size of the war. Nine of the carriers were headed for Truk, whilst the remaining three carriers would head for Eniwetok atoll, which would simultaneously be invaded as Truk was neutralised.

Every day, unaware of the clandestine approach of the huge American carrier force, more Japanese naval transport ships were arriving from Japan, some destined for, or returning from, other Japanese island strongholds. Such was the pace of the war that supply ships, setting off from Japan to reinforce island outposts, reached Truk en route - only to learn that the Allies had overrun their final destinations.

The carriers of Task Force 58 arrived on station 94 miles north east of Truk, in darkness, on the evening of 16 February 1944. The scene was set for the great 2-day raid – codenamed Operation HAILSTONE. It would commence just before dawn the following day, 17 February 1944.

Operation HAILSTONE began with a dawn initial fighter sweep of Truk by 72 Grumman F6F Hellcats - designed to destroy Japanese air power and win air superiority. Although at the beginning of the war the iconic Japanese Mitsubishi A6M Zero naval fighter had outclassed all Allied aircraft, by now, towards the end of the war, new faster and more powerful Allied aircraft such as the F6F Hellcat had in turn out classed the Zero. The Zero – or Zeke (to give it its Allied reporting code name) was no match for the carrier-based F6F Hellcats that swept over the lagoon.

The initial fighter sweep by the 72 F6F Hellcats was so swift and unexpected that, with uncanny parallels with the Japanese attack on Pearl Harbor, many of the Japanese aircraft were caught by surprise and destroyed on the ground. Others scrambled to get airborne - but with insufficient time, many were shot down as they lifted off. Today, Japanese aircraft lie all around the lagoon – some in shallow water just 100's of yards from the end of their airstrips. Those that did get airborne were shot out of the sky in one of the largest aerial dogfights of WWII.

With U.S. air superiority quickly established, throughout 17 February and into the following day, 18 February, the Task Force 58 carriers launched wave after wave of dive-bombers and torpedo-bombers, escorted by Hellcat fighters, to attack the now vulnerable shipping and land fortifications. They met limited AA fire from the lightly armed merchant ships below and from the island land defences. It was a one-sided battle – and more then 40 ships were sent to the bottom of the lagoon over the two days of Operation HAILSTONE. Truk had been smashed.

After the war, the sunken Japanese ships were left to rust on the bottom. The world moved on and tried to rebuild - and the ships lying at the bottom of the Truk lagoon were forgotten about by the outside world. The local Trukese islanders however could not forget the ships – they had to deal with the toxic legacy of a war they had never sought. Many of the ships held large cargoes of oil and aviation fuel and these pollutants leaked from the submerged hulks in significant quantities right up to the 1970's and 1980's. Although the rate of leakage tailed off in the 1980's, several of the wrecks continue to leak smaller amounts of oil and fuel to the surface to this day – sometimes causing skin burns to locals and visiting divers. Nowadays the leakage seems to have greatly diminished but there can still be on occasion a noticeable smell of gasoline, and a kaleidoscopic sheen on the surface of the water, above some of the wrecks as a rotted 55-gallon Avgas fuel drum from WWII finally releases its contents.

The Japanese had unsuspectingly moored their ships in waters that were mostly deeper than their wartime salvage diving capability. The ships and their cargoes could not be recovered - and were consequently completely lost to the Japanese war effort.

After the war, the wrecks were never deemed worthy of commercial salvage – even though they still carried their valuable non-ferrous props, engines and condensers along with their war cargoes. The ships still lay in deep water for salvage diving, and Truk itself of course is situated in a very remote location that made the costs of commercial salvage uneconomical. Thus, most of the wrecks were simply left intact on the bottom of the lagoon, slowly rusting - untouched by Man. Nature took control, slowly covering the wrecks in an explosion of life with a myriad of corals and sea creatures – the wrecks had become artificial reefs.

In 1969, the legendary French oceanographer Jacques Cousteau mounted an expedition to Truk. Many of the ship's locations and identities were unknown at this time - but armed with old charts and taking advantage of local knowledge from Trukese islanders, they began to locate and identify some of the wrecks. The resulting mesmeric yet haunting television documentary *Lagoon of Lost Ships* was an instant hit around the world and is still available today. Such was the power of Cousteau's name and the potency of the moving images he broadcast that the diving world's attention focused on the wrecks lying silently at the bottom of the Truk lagoon.

Divers started to visit Truk in increasing numbers and in 1976 National Geographic carried a 40-page feature on Truk by Al Giddings. A local Chuukese, Kimiuo Aisek, who had been a young man on the island during Operation HAILSTONE, opened the first dive shop in Truk in 1973 and went on to rediscover a large number of the lost ships in the lagoon. But even so, at that point only a fraction of the ships sunk had been rediscovered. Kimiuo became a deeply revered and preeminent figure in Truk diving for many years. That first dive shop in Truk has gone on to become the beautifully located 54-room Blue Lagoon Resort.

Klaus Lindemann, whose name would become synonymous with Truk diving, joined Kimiuo later in the 1970's and together over several years from 1980 onwards they conducted extensive searches. In their first season they found 16 new wrecks - and subsequently went on to locate even more. Collating much historical and first-hand information, Klaus Lindemann published the first edition of his definitive book *Hailstorm Over Truk Lagoon* in 1982 - with an updated second edition published in 1991.

The other great name in literature about Truk's wartime legacy is that of Dan E. Bailey who published his thoroughly researched book *WWII Wrecks of the Kwajalein and Truk Lagoons* in 1989. I made my first visit to Truk Lagoon in 1990 and it was the brand new, must have, book to take home as a souvenir at that time. Then, as more information became available, he published the definitive historical guide to Truk, *World War II Wrecks of the Truk Lagoon* in 2000. Throughout my writing career I have referenced many books on a range of shipwrecks and historical events, but it is safe to say that I have never seen a book so well researched with so much original first-hand detective work. My book does not seek to challenge that authoritative book in respect of the historical narrative – my book seeks to focus more on the diving side of Truk - and I would like to think that the two books complement each other in giving a full story about Truk's wartime legacy.

Over the last 40 years or so, aided by such influential characters as Cousteau, Giddings, Aisek, Lindemann and Bailey, Truk has gone on to become the most celebrated wreck diving location in the world. But even today, despite the countless tens of thousands of dives made in the lagoon, some ships known to have been sunk at Truk have not been located. Others are known to have been present in Truk at the time of the raids but to have been sunk outside the lagoon in water far too deep for today's scuba divers. Their exploration will be left to the divers and underwater explorers of the future. This book is a guide to the shipwrecks likely to be dived today – and is not a historical listing of all the casualties of Operation HAILSTONE. I would refer the curious reader for more information to the other fine books listed above.

Whilst all the major shipwrecks are now well known, every now and then, another smaller shipwreck or airplane wreck, lost since 1944, is discovered in the lagoon. The 400-ton auxiliary transport *Sapporo Maru* was discovered in the early 2000's, whilst an as yet unidentified 300-tonne IJN fleet tug was discovered off Weno in 2018. An unidentified Bonito-style fishing boat (a fishing boat rigged for line fishing of bonito (tuna) in place of nets) has been located as well as a small harbour gun boat.

As diving technology has progressed, divers have been able to dive deeper and longer – and wrecks that could perhaps be seen and bounced with air diving technology have now become usefully diveable. Today's technical divers, using rebreathers and mixed gases, are able to visit wrecks at Chuuk in depths impractical for air divers – and stay down much longer, with shorter decompression times. By way of example, the destroyer IJN *Oite* lies in about 65 metres, the cargo ship *Katsuragisan Maru* lies in 70 metres with 62 metres to the deck - and the *Reiyo Maru* lies in 65 metres with 53 metres down to the deck. These wrecks are too deep to safely and usefully dive on air - but are a lovely depth for a technical diver, who despite the depth, can safely spend lengthy bottom times on the wrecks before an admittedly lengthy decompression ascent. Some of the wrecks are so big that even after a deep exploration dive, the shallowest parts rise up to such a modest depth that most of your decompression penalty incurred on the deeper part of the dive can be burnt off exploring the shallower parts as you ascend.

Diving in Truk lagoon holds something for everyone. Far removed from the deep wrecks suitable for today's technical divers, there are shipwrecks and aircraft wrecks that you only need a snorkel to explore. There are wrecks in shallow depths teeming with sea life that are ideal for novice divers to explore.

For wreck enthusiasts the number and condition of the wrecks are unparalled. The main wrecks are well documented and will fill a lifetime's diving – however there are other less well-known shipwrecks and parts of ships scattered across the lagoon. Some such as the Special Sub Chasers, and *Tachikaze* have never been located - or if located in the past, their location has slipped from consciousness.

A couple of weeks before Operation HAILSTONE, the Minekaze-class destroyer *Tachikaze* had accidently run aground on the southwest fringing reef of Kuop, the large atoll to the south of the Truk lagoon. It was still there when Task Force 58 (TF58) planes attacked on 17 February 1944. *Tachikaze* took several bomb hits that caused her to slide off the reef into deeper water. I don't know the exact depth of water - but whilst she was perhaps too deep to dive in the past, it would be now worth devoting some time to searching for her remains – as today's technical divers might be able to reach her. I've pencilled that in for the future.

The requisitioned cargo ship *Tachi Maru* was bombed and sunk by TF 58 aircraft whilst at anchor to the north west of Fefan island. The heavily damaged ship was located and dived in the early 1980's but I'm not aware of it being dived nowadays or of any guides who know of its whereabouts. The Auxiliary Subchaser *Cha 46* was sunk by B-24 bombers east of Weno in April 1944 and to the best of my knowledge has never been found. Truk thus still has many secrets to give up, sunken ships that remain lying silently on the bottom of the lagoon awaiting eventual rediscovery. There is a *Kaiten*, a one-man Japanese suicide submarine halfway out to the barrier reef from the east of the Fourth Fleet Anchorage. It is so small that it is seldom dived.

Other places in the Truk lagoon were used as dumping grounds for suddenly redundant hardware and aircraft after the Japanese surrendered. There has not been enough space in this book to detail those. Likewise, the large tanker *Tonan Maru No 3* was salvaged and removed in the 1950's - but significant sections of her were left behind. They are really only for the enthusiast or the academic and again have been omitted from this book.

The question of human remains is a very real issue at Truk. When I first dived Truk in 1990, I, like most, dived using a single AL80 scuba tank and visited the easily accessible parts of the most popular wrecks. Covered in beautiful corals and teeming with exotic fish life, they were stunning, simply beautiful - and fully occupied my trip. Wreck penetration on a single tank has never been advisable, and few dived doubles or carried stage tanks then. Closed Circuit Rebreathers didn't hit the sport diving market in force until the mid 1990's – and thus, few ventured far inside the wrecks. I didn't see any human remains in situ during those early visits.

As diving at Truk became more popular, official Japanese divers came to Truk in the 1980's and 1990's and removed all easily accessible Japanese human remains for religious cremation ashore. Nevertheless, the more I dived Truk, as I went further into the wrecks – I began to come upon human remains in places that the Japanese divers had been unable to reach. The Truk lagoon is a battlefield that has been left largely as it ended - and the scale of the human loss at Truk in just the two days of Operation HAILSTONE is overwhelming. If you venture deep into the wrecks, you may well come upon human remains. Please treat these remains with dignity – they are people, and still have sons, daughters, and grandchildren alive. Please do not touch, move or disturb the remains in any way. I have deliberately not included any images of human remains in this book out of respect for the fallen.

The wrecks are classified as underwater museums and divers, and the people of Chuuk, are strictly forbidden from removing any artifacts from the wrecks. Please respect this so that these sights are left for future generations of divers to marvel at.

Fair winds and following seas

Rod Macdonald

Author's Note: This book is about the shipwreck legacy of Operation HAILSTONE at the bottom of the lagoon at what was at the time, called Truk. Truk was officially renamed as Chuuk in 1990 - and the islands of Moen and Dublon were renamed Weno and Tonoas. Tonoas was Dublon's original name until 1814 when Manuel Dublon landed there and humbly renamed it after himself. But as all the shipping references and action reports date from 1944 and refer to the names in usage at that time, I have kept the old nomenclature.

I have used the metric system for modern day details such as depths for diving purposes - but for wartime references I have used the imperial system then in use. I felt it would be insensitive and artificial to convert everything into a metric system that wasn't being used at the time.

EXPLANATORY NOTES

U.S. Plane General Abbreviations

'V' prefix denotes 'heavier-than-air'
'F' prefix denotes fighter
'SB' prefix denotes scout bomber
'T' prefix denotes torpedo plane
Designation ending: 'C' = aircraft manufactured by Curtiss Aeroplane & Motor Co.
                    'D' = aircraft manufactured by Douglas Aircraft Co.
                    'F' = Grumman Aircraft Engineering Corp.
                    'M' = aircraft manufactured by General Motors

U.S. Plane Designations

B-17   US Army Air Force (USAAF) four-engine bomber, the Boeing Flying Fortress
B-24   USAAF four-engine bomber, Consolidated or Ford Liberator
B-25   USAAF two-engine bomber, the North American Mitchell
B-29   USAAF four-engine bomber, the Boeing Super-Fortress
F4U   Navy single-engine fighter, the Chance-Vought Corsair
F6F   Navy single-engine fighter, the Grumman Hellcat
PBY   Navy two-engine long range maritime reconnaissance flying boat - the Consolidated Catalina
PB4Y   Navy-Marine four-engine bomber - the Consolidated or Ford Liberator
SBD   Navy single-engine Scout Bomber Douglas – the Douglas Dauntless
SB2C   Navy single-engine scout dive bomber- the Curtiss Helldiver
TBD   Navy single-engine torpedo bomber – the Douglas Devastator
TBF   Navy single-engine torpedo bomber – the Grumman Avenger
TBM   Navy single-engine torpedo bomber – the General Motors Avenger

Allied & Japanese Aircraft Reporting Code Names - Designations

Betty	Mitsubishi G4M/G4M3	Navy Type 1 Attack Bomber
Dave	Nakajima E8N	Navy Type 95 Reconnaissance Seaplane
Emily	Kawanishi H8K	Navy Type 2 Flying Boat

Hamp	Mitsubishi A6M3	Navy Type O (Zero variant) Carrier Fighter
Jake	Aichi E13A	Navy Type O Reconnaissance Seaplane
Jill	Nakajima B6N	Navy Carrier Attack Bomber
Judy	Yokosuka D4Y	Navy Carrier Bomber Suisei
Mavis	Kawanishi H6K	Navy Type 97 Flying Boat
Nate	Nakajima Ki-27	Army Type 97 Fighter
Nell	Mitsubishi G3M	Navy Type 96 Medium Attack Bomber
Pete	Mitsubishi F1M	Navy Type O Observation Seaplane
Rufe	Nakajima A6M2	Navy Type 2 Fighter Seaplane
Sam	Mitsubishi A7M *Reppū*	Navy fighter
Tojo	Nakajima Ki-44	Army Type 2 Single-seat fighter
Tony	Kawasaki Ki-61	Army Type 3 Fighter
Val	Aichi D3A	Navy Type 99 Carrier Bomber
Zeke	Mitsubishi A6M	Navy Type O (Zero) Carrier Fighter Reisen

U.S Naval Squadron/Unit Designations

BatDiv	Battleship Division
CarDiv	Carrier Division
CruDiv	Cruiser Division
DesDiv	Destroyer Division
DesRon	Destroyer Squadron
ServRon	Service Squadron
TF	Task Force
TG	Task Group: a subunit of a Task Force
TU	Task Unit: a subunit of a Task Group
VB	Dive Bomber
VF	Fighter
VB(F)	Fighter Bomber
VF(N)	Night Fighter
VT	Torpedo Plane
VTB	Torpedo Bomber

The number following the initials VB, VF, VB(F), VF(N), VT and VTB initially referred to the assigned carrier from which the Air Group was operating, such as CV-6, CV-7 etc. Later in the war Air Group numbers were randomly assigned, to prevent the enemy ascertaining individual carrier deployment.

U.S Ship Type Designations & Acronyms List

AGC	Amphibious Command Ship
AK	Cargo Ship
AM	Minesweeper

AP	Transport
AO	Fuel Oil Tanker
BB	Battleship
CA	Heavy Cruiser
CC	Battlecruiser
CH	Submarine Chaser
CHa	Auxiliary Submarine Chaser
CL	Light Cruiser
CV	Aircraft Carrier (heavier than air planes)
CVE	Aircraft Carrier Escort
CVL	Light Aircraft Carrier
DD	Destroyer
DUKW	Amphibious trucks (*Ducks*)
LCT	Landing Craft, Tank
LCVP	Landing Craft, Vehicle, Personnel
LST	Landing Ship, Tank
LVT	Landing Vehicle, Tracked
SS	Submarine
TB	Torpedo Boat

The number following the initials BB, CA, CL, CVL, DD and SS refers to the assigned vessel number and class.

U.S. Japanese Merchant Ship Recognition Coding

The Restricted wartime Division of Naval Intelligence document *Japanese Merchant Ships - Recognition Manual* (ONI 208-J) (revised 1944) (and now de-classified) established a standard method of enemy merchant ship identification, providing identification codes for all known Japanese merchant ships of over 500 gross tons.

The first identification step divided enemy vessels into four main groups of ship type based solely on the position of engines and type of superstructure. Each of the four main ship types was then subdivided into a number of variants based on features such as how many funnels there were, the type of bow (e.g., plumb or raked) and the type of stern (e.g., cruiser stern or counter stern). The four basic ship types are:

1. Passenger type (Variant No's 1-12)
2. Cargo type with composite superstructure (No's 13-28)
3. Cargo type with split superstructure (No's 29-44)
4. Ships with engines aft (No's 45-65)

Once the basic ship type and variant had been determined and an initial number allocated, a code for the ship under observation would then be formulated in three more stages that looked at the number and location of masts, funnels and kingposts. Thus, if the ship was a Type 24 Cargo Vessel with a composite superstructure, then looking at the ship from the port side, from the bow aft the silhouette showed a foremast, funnel, kingpost and mainmast then the sequence would be M-F-K-M, and the final code description of the vessel would be 24 MFKM. If the ship was e.g., a Type 3 Passenger Vessel, and looking at the ship from the port side, from the bow aft the silhouette showed a foremast, then two funnels and a mainmast, the code would be 3 MFFM.

The Recognition Manual lists performance details such as length, beam, speed and range along with photos, outline drawings and the code worked out as above of all the individual Japanese merchant ships of more than 500grt known to the Division of Naval Intelligence at the time. Each ship was then allocated a Potential Naval Value, allowing e.g., a U.S. submarine commander observing an enemy ship, to work out the code and then identify the actual ship, or certainly the class of ship, along with its characteristics from the Recognition Manual. The Potential Naval Value allowed the sub skipper to work out if the ship should be attacked, or, if there was a convoy with many targets, which one was the most important to go after.

Naming Convention of Japanese Navy ships

By WWII, the Imperial Japanese Navy had a standardised convention for naming their warships. There were many classes, but for the type of vessel referred to in this book, the conventions were as follows:

Battleships were named after places in Japan or names of Japan. For example, *Yamato* refers to the Yamato Period of ancient Japan from 250-710 CE and *Nagato* is a province in southwest Honshū.

Aircraft carriers were named after birds or mythical creatures – e.g., *Hiryū* is a flying dragon

Battlecruisers & heavy cruisers were named after mountains - e.g. *Takao* is a mountain near Kyoto.

Cruisers were named after rivers or shrine – e.g. *Tone* is a river in the Kanto region

Destroyers were named after oceanic or meteorological phenomena or plants -e.g. *Ōite* means *Fair (or Favourable) Wind*

In 1937, in efforts to overcome social unrest and develop a new Japan, the militaristic Japanese government issued the *Kokutai no Hongi*, a document setting out cardinal principles for the new Japan. At this time, the Japanese government adopted what was known as the 'Romanji' system of spelling the Latin version of Japanese ship's names, and this spelling was used in Lloyd's Register for merchant ships from 1938/9 until 1949/50.

WWII era Japanese warships were commonly named in *kanji*, the Japanese adaption for Chinese characters. Romanization of Japanese ship names into English (Romanji) was done only to aid non-Japanese speakers - and Romanized warship names carry no legal or official validity in the Imperial Japanese Navy. In this way, the correct name for the IJN destroyer sunk near North Pass during Operation Hailstone is 追風 This kanji name broadly translates as *Fair (or Favourable) Wind* – and so, the correct kanji name is Romanized to its Romanji equivalent, *Oite*. That's how the wreck is known to westerners diving at Truk today - but that Romanized name has no real significance or validity.

To complicate matters further, there are *three* systems of Romanization available, but most English printed documentation uses the Hepburn system - where the pronunciation of the kanji is close to what is perceived by English speakers. The Romanization of kanji ship names is fraught with difficulty for westerners - but the result for us is that it is common to see the Romanized names of Japanese ships spelt in several different ways. There is no *correct* way of spelling Japanese kanji ship names in English – all are incorrect, the true name is in kanji.

The wartime established methods for transliteration of Japanese words into English spelling were the Hepburn and the Kokutai official Japanese system. The Hepburn system was the most nearly phonetic rendering of spoken Japanese and was employed by the United States Navy, except for Japanese merchant ships for which Kokutai was used.

Hepburn or Phonetic: Fu, Shi, Sh, Chi, Tsu, Ch, Ji, Ju

Kokutai (official):　　Hu, Si,　Sy,　Ti,　Tu,　Ty, Zi, Zyu

After the war it was found that the 'Romanji' system had been discarded in favour of the original spellings. The significance of the wartime *Kokutai* diminished and in Autumn 1945 circulation of the *Kokutai no Hongi* was forbidden.

To avoid confusion, the original Romanized spelling at the date of construction of the ship is used in this book, with other 'Romanji' versions set out where appropriate.

Where a Japanese merchant ship was registered with a Romanized English version name at Lloyds, I have used the registered spelling.

A number of navy's around the world use a prefix before the names of their warships. For example, the British Royal Navy places the prefix HMS (His/Her Majesty's Ship) before the names of their warships. The United States Navy likewise places the prefix USS (United States Ship) before the names of their warships. Some western authors extend this practice, when referring to WW2-era Japanese warships, and use the prefix IJN (Imperial Japanese Navy) and HIJMS (His Imperial Japanese Majesty's Ship). But this is an entirely western practice and had no official equivalent or place in the WW2-era Japanese Navy.

Requisitioned Civilian ships. Most Japanese civilian ships of the era had the suffix *Maru*, which means 'circle'.

As with all nations in all large-scale maritime conflict situations, the IJA and IJN requisitioned a large number of civilian merchant ships for war use.

a. Merchant ships requisitioned by the IJN were called *Tokusetsu Unsosen Zatsuyosen* (Converted Auxiliary Transports)

b. Merchant ships requisitioned by the IJN but not enlisted were operated by a civilian crew with often a Navy Reserve captain. They were called *Ippan Choyosen* (General Requisitioned Ships). The *Ko* category had an IJN Captain whilst the *Otsu* category did not.

c. Merchant ships requisitioned and armed as Auxiliary Cruisers (such as *Aikoku Maru*) were called *Tokusetsu Junyokan*

d. Merchant ships requisitioned by the Imperial Japanese Army were called *Rikugun Yusosen* (IJA Transports)

Miscellaneous

AA	Anti-Aircraft
AP	Armour Piercing
ASDIC	Anti-Submarine Detection Investigation Committee
ASP	Anti-Submarine Patrol
ASW	Anti-Submarine Warfare
Avgas	Aviation gasoline
BL	Breach Loading
Cal	calibre
-cal	length of gun barrel from breach to muzzle in calibres. Eg, 16"/50-cal, where the length of the barrel is 50 x the internal barrel diameter of 16-inches.
CAP	Combat Air Patrol
CIC	Combat Information Centre – the nerve centre of the ship where information from radars and sounding was plotted, evaluated and sent to the bridge.
CINC	Commander-in-Chief
CINCLANTFLT	Commander in Chief U.S. Atlantic Fleet
CINCPAC	Commander-in-Chief Pacific
CINCPACFLT	Commander-in-Chief U.S. Pacific Fleet
CINPOA	Commander in Chief Pacific Ocean Areas
COMINCH	Commander-in-Chief, United States Fleet
CNO	Chief of Naval Operations
DC	Depth charge
DEMS	Defensively Equipped Merchant Ship.
DP	Dual Purpose – naval gun able to hit surface and AA targets
DWT	Dead Weight tonnage
F	Full load – the Deep load displacement at its greatest allowable draft full of ammunition, stores and fuel.
GP	General Purpose
GRT	Gross Registered Tonnage
HA	High Angle gun
Higgins boat	LCVP
ihp	indicated horse-power
LA	Low Angle

N	Normal displacement with all outfit, 2/3 supply of stores, ammunition etc on board.
nhp	nominal horse-power
nm	Nautical Mile, 1nm = 2025 yards
oa	overall
pdr	pounder
pp	Between perpendiculars
QF	Quick Firing
RAS	Replenishment-at-Sea
RDF	Radio Direction Finder
S	Standard displacement, also known as 'Washington displacement' per the Washington Naval treaty of 1922. The displacement of a ship, fully manned, engined, equipped, including all armament, ammunition, provisions, fresh water etc but without fuel or reserve boiler feed water on board.
SAP	Semi-Armour Piercing
shp	Shaft horse-power
TBS	High frequency short range radio used for tactical manoeuvering in a naval formation
UDT	Underwater Demolition Team
wl	waterline

PART 1

WAR

CHAPTER 1

PRELUDE TO WAR IN THE PACIFIC
A little bit of background

To understand a wreck properly, I've always felt you need to know the background, the history, the chain of events that led to the wreck lying on the bottom where it is. So, by way of setting the scene for your amazing diving in Truk lagoon, here's a bit of background as to why Japan possessed this distant atoll – and why it was so important to the Pacific war.

At the dawn of the 20th century, Japan, an island country with limited natural resources of its own, was determined to become a modern, industrial nation – but she was heavily dependent on imported raw materials.

During the First World War of 1914-18, implementing the Anglo-Japanese Alliance of 1902, Japan entered the war against Germany. Japan saw the opportunity to expand her power and influence in the Pacific, allowing Britain to maintain only a small squadron in the Pacific to deal with the limited German naval presence. Japan declared war on Germany on 23 August 1914. Although publicly maintaining that she was honouring her commitments under the 1902 Anglo-Japanese alliance, in reality, Japan was moving to protect her Pacific freight and passenger shipping routes and saw the war as being an opportunity to acquire advanced naval bases in the South Pacific. Japan joined Britain in attacking the German held colony of Tsingtao on the coast of China whilst the Imperial Japanese Navy (IJN) moved to eliminate German naval power in the Pacific by pursuing and destroying the German East Asiatic Squadron of six major warships, which were dispersed at various colonies in the Pacific on routine peacetime missions. The six German cruisers were outnumbered and outgunned in the Pacific – with no secure harbour and unable to safely reach Germany. Rounding Cape Horn, on the Tierra del Fuego archipelago of southern Chile, the German squadron broke into the Atlantic, intent on forcing a way north towards home. The Squadron was however caught and decimated by a British battlecruiser force on 8 December 1914 at the Battle of the Falkland Islands.

By October 1914, with the German East Asiatic Squadron gone from the Pacific, the IJN had seized German possessions in the Mariana, Caroline, Marshall and Palauan island groups and seized German possessions in China.

At the end of WWI, the victorious Allies established the League of Nations under the Versailles Treaty of 28 June 1919 - and the ex-German colonies in the Pacific were divided amongst the victors under the League's South Pacific Mandate. Japan was granted a South Pacific Class C Mandate to administrate the former German Pacific Islands, north of the equator. Japan now controlled hundreds of ex-German island territories, including the extensive Caroline Islands archipelago, situated to the north of New Guinea, which has the Federated States of Micronesia (including Chuuk) at its eastern end and Palau and Yap to its west. The Marshall Islands, situated at the north east of the Carolines, and including atolls such as Kwajalein, Bikini and Majuro all fell under Japanese administration as did the Northern Mariana Islands. (America retained control of Guam at the southern end of the Marianas chain of islands).

All the territories mandated to Japan would be administered under Japanese law as its own territory. Japan established a new unified command based at Truk and the IJN set up naval districts at Palau, Yap, Saipan, Truk, Ponape and Jaluit. The Governors appointed for these territories were mostly admirals or vice-admirals – and the IJN immediately began issuing laws, promoting Japanese enterprises, instigating public works programs and beginning a policy of educating the indigenous population to the Japanese way of life. Japanese cultural institutions such as schools, shrines and temples were constructed.

There were provisions built into the League of Nations Mandate that prohibited Japan from establishing military or naval bases and from erecting fortifications on the islands it would administer. But however, when no open-door trade policy was provided for, Japan soon established a trade monopoly that allowed her to effectively seal off the islands from the outside world. Japan would not allow any foreign ships to enter the waters of its newly occupied territories – the ban extending to the ships of her erstwhile Allies in World War I.

America was deeply alarmed at the League of Nations policy on Japan and strongly opposed Japanese administration of the islands – insisting on military neutrality. Congress refused to ratify the Versailles treaty - the United States would not be part of the League of Nations.

The Nippon Yusen Kaisha shipping line (N.Y.K.) was given a government contract to provide a steamship service between the Japanese home islands and the main ports in the South Seas, which would facilitate the import to the Japanese home islands of vast quantities of natural resources that were vital to Japan's aims to expand in the Pacific.

Two main shipping routes were established - one western and one eastern. Ships would carry cargoes of building materials, machinery, coal and foodstuffs out to the South Seas islands from Japan for use in developing their island infrastructures. On the return leg, the same ships would carry natural resources back to Japan such as the aluminium ore known as bauxite, which was the world's main source of aluminium, vital for aircraft manufacture. Vast quantities of lignite were shipped back - a combustible brown sedimentary rock known as the lowest form of coal. Mined phosphate minerals were also shipped to Japan for use in agriculture and industry along with other local products such as shell products, fish, copra (the dried meat or kernel of the coconut used to extract coconut oil), coconut oil, starch and pineapple.

The political situation in 1930's Japan - Manchuria

The Great Depression from 1929 onwards, and the subsequent collapse in world trade, hit Japan's export-oriented economy hard. The depressed western economies placed barriers on Japanese trade to protect their own colonial markets. Many Japanese believed that the international peace established by the League of Nations favoured the western nations that controlled the world's resources. The economic crisis led the Japanese military to become increasingly convinced that Japan needed guaranteed access to new markets, and raw materials, on the Asian mainland. Japan's population had more than doubled and demand was high for food, coal and materials.

On the military side of things, during the negotiations towards the London Naval Conference Treaty in 1930, the Prime Minister of Japan, Osachi Hamaguchi, tried - and failed - to secure a better ratio of battleships for Japan viz a viz Great Britain and the USA. His failure, and subsequent settlement of the Conference Treaty, led the Japanese public to feel that he had sold out Japanese national security - prompting a surge of Japanese nationalism. On 14 November 1930, Hamaguchi was shot by a member of an ultra-nationalist group in Tokyo Station. He was hospitalised for several months until he returned to office on 10 March 1931. He resigned a month later.

With Hamaguchi's firm rule no longer at the helm, a growing militarism took hold in Japanese politics. When Japan's vital economic position in her Manchuria territories on mainland northeast Asia was threatened by China, on 18 September 1931, officers of the Kwantung army (the Japanese forces in Manchuria) took matters into their own hands. Without advising their Commander-in-Chief, or the Tokyo civilian government, the Japanese officers staged a bombing incident on a railway they were guarding near the town of Mukden.

The Kwantung army claimed that local Chinese forces were responsible and launched a military campaign, occupying several major Manchurian cities and surrounding areas. The military established a puppet state, which the Tokyo civilian government was forced to rubber stamp after the event.

Aggrieved Chinese leaders appealed to the League of Nations - of which China was a member - for a peaceful solution. The League of Nations began an investigation into the war in Manchuria, but whilst this was still ongoing, a *coup d'état* was staged in Japan on 15 May 1932 in which 11 IJN officers assassinated Prime Minister Tsuyoshi - and brought the civilian government to its knees. The military now gained control of the country - and unchecked by a civilian administration, massive increases in Japanese military spending began.

On 24 Feb 1933, when the League of Nations Assembly in Geneva called upon Japan to withdraw her troops and restore Manchuria to Chinese sovereignty, the Japanese delegation, dramatically walked out of the Assembly hall. That year, with Japan no longer part of the League of Nations and bound by the Mandate prohibitions against the establishment of military bases, as Japanese militarism grew stronger, the IJN began preliminary surveys of their mandated South Seas islands for potential naval and air bases. In 1936, more detailed surveys followed to establish locations for airfields, anchorages, communications, fuel and ammunition storage facilities and defensive emplacements. The Caroline Islands were identified as the first line of defence in the event of war with America in the Pacific.

In 1937, following on from the previous surveys, the IJN began a clandestine militarisation of her Pacific holdings - constructing fortifications, establishing naval ports and constructing airfields. Japan viewed her island airfields scattered throughout the Pacific as unsinkable aircraft carriers that provided a network web of mutual air support. A major airfield construction program started in Palau 1939 to allow long-range offensive air missions against U.S. and British holdings in the Pacific.

Kwajalein Atoll, in the Marshall Islands, more than 2,200 nautical miles out into the Pacific east of Palau, was developed into an air base, which would support the attack on Pearl Harbor (which lay some 2,500 nautical miles further north east towards America). Palau would be used to support the campaign to take the Philippines whilst Truk, in Micronesia, more than 1,100 nautical miles out into the central Pacific to the east of Palau, would be used as a forward base for the amphibious landings on Tarawa, Makin and Rabaul.

Japan's lack of oil was a critical vulnerability. Japan had an industrial economy, and a large navy and merchant marine, but yet imported 90% of her oil and much of her iron primarily from the United States. Ironically, it was American trade and exports throughout the 1930's, which had largely underpinned Japan's war industries and expansionism. Japan relied on America for about one third of its general imports from cotton to oil – and more than 70% of its scrap iron, which was used to make munitions and ships. Japan relied on America for more than 90% of its copper - used to make detonators and shell casings. With America as the likely main foe in any military expansion, this critical vulnerability in oil resources led Japan to eye the oil rich Dutch East Indies (now Indonesia) and French Indochina (now Vietnam, Laos and Cambodia), with special interest.

Japan had long coveted South-East Asia, where since the latter part of the 19th century, France had controlled a group of colonial territories in Southeast Asia, known collectively as French Indochina – comprising modern day Vietnam, Cambodia, Laos and parts of Thailand. In addition, Spain had ceded the Philippines, Puerto Rico and Guam to the USA after the Spanish American War of 1898. Britain and the Netherlands had large important colonial holdings. If French Indochina and the American, British and Dutch territories could be seized, Japan would control the eastern regions of China, Vietnam, Cambodia, Laos, the resource rich Philippines, Malaya, Singapore and the Dutch East Indies. Japan wanted to be self-sufficient in resources of oil, petroleum, iron, rubber, nickel, tin, bauxite, rice and much more.

Japan launched a full-scale invasion of China in 1937, which quickly led to a souring of relations with the USA, which had substantial commercial interests in China. Japanese troops soon began the systematic massacre of an estimated 300,000 civilian residents of Nanking (now Nanjing) in what became known as the Rape of Nanking. Then, on 12 December 1937, American public opinion turned sharply against Japan when Japanese aircraft attacked an American oil tanker convoy as it was being escorted up the Chinese Yangtze River by the U.S. gunboat *Panay*. Newsreel cameramen were aboard and filmed part of the attack, and after they reached shore, they filmed the *Panay* as it sank in the middle of the river - and as Japanese aircraft fired on survivors in small boats. Two months later the U.S. consul in Nanking was attacked and American property looted.

On 26 July 1939, after continued attacks by the Japanese military on American citizens and the encroachment on American interests in China, the United States withdrew from the U.S.-Japan Treaty of Commerce and Navigation, which regulated trade between the two countries. On 1 September 1939, Germany invaded Poland, beginning World War II.

Two months later, in November 1939, as Japan made ready for a Pacific war, the IJN Fourth Fleet was organised to protect her Pacific island territories and those that she intended to seize. The belligerent IJA General Hideki Tōjō was appointed Minster of War in July 1940.

During 1940, Japan's military leaders deliberated how to win a Pacific war against the USA and its Allies. The Army wanted to push into Southeast Asia and the Netherlands East Indies – and seize the Philippines. With the fall of France to Nazi Germany in 1940, the French hold on Indochina was weak. With Great Britain fighting Nazi Germany in Europe, her ability to defend her colonial possessions such as Singapore and Hong Kong was also weakened. When Dutch troops in Holland surrendered to German forces on 14 May 1940, it was clear that Holland would not be able to put up much of a fight to protect her Asian territories such as the Dutch East Indies with its abundant resources such as rubber and oil.

In early 1940, when Japan began to fortify her Marshall Island territories between Hawaii and the Philippines, the move threatened American shipping and commerce. Up until May 1940, the U.S. Navy had its Battle Fleet HQ at Los Angeles Harbor on the USA west coast. But faced with the Japanese threat, President Franklin D. Roosevelt ordered the United States Pacific Fleet to move its main base west to Pearl Harbor in the Hawaiian Islands, hoping that the forward deployment of the fleet to Pearl would act as a deterrent to Japanese aggression against American, British and Dutch colonial possessions in East Asia. It was a risky move – as it placed the U.S. Pacific Fleet within striking distance of Japan's navy. Japan began to formulate plans for a knock-out strike against the US Pacific Fleet at Pearl Harbor.

Throughout the 1930's, Japan had been building closer relations with Nazi Germany – which was now at the peak of its power. With France, Britain and Holland all weakened by the war in Europe, the moment seemed ideal for Japan to form an alliance with the Nazis. Japan invaded French Indochina on 22 September 1940 and then on 27 September 1940 entered the Tripartite Pact with Germany and Italy, in which the three nations agreed to aid each other if one of their number was attacked by a power not involved in a current conflict. Membership of the Pact for Japan ensured that Germany recognised that East Asia was a Japanese sphere of influence. Germany and Italy intended to establish a New Order in Europe - Japan would do likewise in East Asia. Germany hoped that Japan would restrain America whilst she dealt a final knockout blow to Britain. Conversely, the Pact allowed Japan to consider the possibility of a simultaneous war with America and Britain more seriously.

The Japanese attack on French Indochina, coupled with the ongoing brutal war with China, the Tripartite Pact with Germany and Italy and an obvious increasing militarism, led America to begin a series of legislative measures and sanctions intended to restrain Japan economically.

The U.S. government had already passed the Export Control Act on 26 July 1940, which authorised the licensing or prohibition of the export of essential defence materials including iron, steel, oil, aircraft, parts, chemicals, minerals and munitions. Beefing this up, on 16 October 1940, less than a month after the Japanese invasion of Indochina, in a move clearly aimed at Japan, an American embargo was placed on all exports of aircraft, parts, machine tools, scrap iron and steel to destinations other than Britain and the nations of the western hemisphere. The Panama Canal was closed to Japanese shipping. America did not however cut off Japan's oil at this stage – aware that an oil embargo would likely lead directly to war, and an oil-starved Japan moving to seize the oil fields of the Dutch East Indies. These export controls however caused Japan to eye even more closely the resource rich French, British, Dutch and American possessions – and finally free herself from her dependency on the west.

On 13 April 1941, Japan signed a non-aggression Neutrality Pact with her old enemy, the Soviet Union. With the Russian threat in the north removed, Japan could now shift her focus to the south seas. The same month, under German and Japanese pressure, the Vichy government in France allowed Japan the use of air and naval bases in south Indochina. Japan was now directly threatening British interests in Malaya, Singapore, Burma, northern Borneo and Brunei.

On 22 June 1941, Germany invaded the Soviet Union, with who, despite the recently signed Neutrality Pact, Japan had a long history of conflict. But with Russia now concentrating on fighting off the Nazis, Japan was free to consider a more aggressive policy in South-East Asia.

At the Imperial Conference in Tokyo on 2 July 1941, despite USA pressure, Japan resolved to continue its war in China, to await developments with Russia and to prepare for an expansion into South-East Asia.

On 14 July 1941, the French authorities in Indochina were given a set of Japanese demands. With little room to manoeuvre, the demands were accepted on 23 July - and on 24 July 1941, the first of some 140,000 Japanese troops destined for the invasion of the Dutch East Indies moved into southern French Indochina. Japanese warships were stationed at coastal ports and air force units were stationed at key airfields around Saigon.

Once the Japanese had established themselves in southern Indochina, they were closer than ever to Singapore, the Philippines and Dutch East Indies. Without firing a shot, the Japanese had secured bases only 450 miles from Malaya and 700 miles (less than the length of Britain) from Singapore. These British possessions were now well within range of Japanese bombers and Japan soon had over 400 land-based aircraft stationed in Indochina and 280 carrier-based aircraft available in addition.

Responding to the Japanese occupation, the U.S. froze or seized all Japanese assets on 26 July 1941 – only a special licence from the U.S. government could release Japanese assets to pay for American exports, including, most critically oil. By early August 1941, the previous year's export controls had thus been increased to a full embargo - preventing the export to Japan of the oil and other materials that had been fuelling the Japanese war machine for years.

Commercial relations between America and Japan were now at an end. Britain and Holland followed the American lead, by imposing their own trade embargoes on Japan from their colonies in Southeast Asia – Japan was now isolated from the west and cut off from her sources of vital raw materials, including 90% of its vital oil supply. Fearing such a move, Japan had already stockpiled 54 million barrels of oil – but that was estimated to last just 18 months. Japan either had to back down and give up its war in China - or secure its own supplies.

The oil embargo was particularly damaging to Japan. Oil was Japan's most crucial import – and from the Army's perspective, a secure fuel supply was essential for its warplanes, tanks and trucks. The Navy also needed vast amounts of oil for its warships and planes. The complete oil embargo had effectively reduced Japan's options to either seizing Southeast Asia before her own 18-month stockpile was depleted – or giving in to U.S. demands that she must withdraw her forces from the Asian mainland of China, Korea and Manchuria before oil supplies to Japan would resume.

Unwilling to give up her war in China, Japan's militaristic leaders determined that she must secure her own supplies of oil, coal, iron, bauxite, tin and rubber. She had to free herself from her dependency on western imports - and the pressure the western powers were applying with their economic sanctions. The solution was to send the Navy south and seize the oil fields in the Dutch East Indies, the Philippines and British possessions.

At the Imperial Japanese Conference of 6 September 1941, in the presence of the Emperor, it was decided to complete war preparations by the end of October. On 14 October 1941, the Japanese prime minister Prince Fumimaro Konoe attempted to persuade the Army Minister, General Hideki Tōjō, to stand down from war and agree to US demands for military withdrawal from China and Indochina. Tōjō was a belligerent advocate of war with the USA – he bluntly told the Japanese Cabinet that widespread troop withdrawals in China were not acceptable to the military and that hundreds of thousands of troops were already being moved south. On 16 October 1941, the Japanese prime minister Prince Fumimaro Konoe, who had presided over the Japanese invasion of China in 1937, resigned with his Cabinet, unwilling to launch another war.

On 17 October 1941, the day after the government resigned, Army Minister, General Hideki Tōjō, was appointed Prime Minister of Japan by Emperor Hirohito – Tōjō would also continue as War Minister. Essentially the army had now become dictator to Japan – and Tōjō, the army representative, was now Prime Minister.

Both the Army and Navy wanted war for their own reasons. The IJN was concerned about the diminishing oil reserves - and the IJA believed that American aid to China would increase and undermine its position there. Japan determined to pursue diplomatic negotiations with the Allies to try to end the embargo – but only until midnight 30 November. When that date passed, at a Japanese Imperial Conference on 1 December 1941, with no end to the embargo agreed, Prime Minister General Tōjō advised that war was necessary to preserve the Japanese Empire - and war was finally sanctioned against the "United States, England and Holland". Orders were sent out to military commanders that hostilities would commence on 8 December (7 December east of the International Date Line).

By striking powerfully and expanding rapidly, Japan's war planners hoped to quickly build an empire so large that the western powers would not be able to countenance the cost of retaking it. Japan also hoped that in Europe, her Axis partners, Germany and Italy, would prevail over the Soviets and Britain - and that this global strategic situation would allow Japan to negotiate a peace deal with an isolated United States. The Japanese plan however depended to a large degree upon Germany winning in Europe. It was a gamble where they didn't hold all the cards.

Japanese military planners had formulated five separate simultaneous operations to take place on the outbreak of war on 7 December 1941 (8 December in Asia/West Pacific time zones), against key strategic targets vital to her campaign.

1. Six Japanese fast carriers would sail eastwards to destroy the U.S. Pacific Fleet now based at Pearl Harbor, Hawaii, refueling en route from oilers.

2. Strikes would launch against the American Clark and Iba airfields in the Philippines, a precursor to a full amphibious invasion of the Philippines.

3. The strategically important islands of Guam (at the south of the Marianas chain of islands) and Wake, 1,500 miles east of Guam in Micronesia, would be seized along with Tarawa and Makin in the Gilbert Islands. Midway atoll, between Hawaii and Japan, and second in importance to Pearl Harbor for the protection of the U.S. west coast, would in time be seized. These operations would allow the establishment of airfields and a defensive perimeter through the Marshalls and Gilberts to New Guinea and the Solomons.

4. British Hong Kong would be assaulted along with attacks on British and American warships at Shanghai. Operations against British positions in Burma and Borneo would soon begin.

5. Landings in Siam (Thailand) and Malaya would be followed by a thrust south toward the great British naval base of Singapore. From Singapore, the Combined Fleet could operate to meet any threat to the perimeter - allied to the Japanese bases already established at Rabaul in the Bismarck Archipelago or Truk in the eastern Carolines.

The plan was breath-taking in its audacity.

In advance of the date for war, the six Japanese carriers *Akagi, Kaga, Sōryū, Hiryū, Shōkaku*, and *Zuikaku* departed Japan on 26 November 1941 and crossed the Pacific in great secrecy. Early on the morning of 7 December 1941, they successfully arrived undetected at their holding position, approximately 200 miles north of Oahu island, Hawaii. The six carriers of the *Kidō Butai* carried a total of some 360 aircraft for two waves of the planned attack. The attack achieved complete surprise, and all 8 US battleships present were sunk or damaged. However, none of the American fleet carriers deployed in the Pacific had been present or damaged and the vast fuel storage facilities for the U.S. Pacific Fleet had surprisingly not been damaged. Hawaii would remain a powerful U.S. naval base; a submarine and intelligence base which was later instrumental in Japan's defeat. Of the eight American battleships damaged or sunk, all but the *Arizona* were later raised, with 6 being repaired and returned to service. Rather than crippling American naval power in the Pacific for long enough to allow Japan to secure her position, the raid had left Hawaii - and American naval power in the Pacific – to fight another day. Japan declared war on the United States later in the day and a few days later on 11 December, Germany and Italy also both declared war on the United States.

Japan's 2nd offensive

The first strikes of the Japanese offensive on 7 December 1941 and the days that followed had been stunningly successful - and yet had cost the Japanese only relatively light casualties. The apparent weakness of American and British military power had in Japanese eyes been demonstrated. Japan had achieved its initial strategic goals – and as a result, Japan began a second expansion, commencing in January 1942 with the seizure of Tulagi in the Solomon Islands - and Port Moresby on the southern tip of Papua New Guinea. Success in these operations would give Japan mastery of the air above the vital Coral Sea – which lies between north east Australia and the bounding island groups of New Caledonia and Vanuatu to the east, and the Solomon Islands and Papua New Guinea to the north. Gaining control of these strategically important bases would prevent an Allied build-up of forces in Australia and would secure Japan's southern flank.

If those assaults were successful, then in a second phase to this operation, the Combined Fleet would cross the Pacific to annihilate the remains of the U.S. Pacific Fleet at Pearl Harbor - and capture Midway Island and the western Aleutian Islands. Japanese military commanders felt that with the U.S. Pacific Fleet crippled at Pearl Harbor, these new Japanese conquests could be made impregnable. From Midway, Japanese air power could threaten Pearl Harbor and the west coast cities of America themselves. It was hoped that, tiring of a futile war in the Pacific, and war against Germany and Italy to the east, the United States would negotiate a peace that would leave Japan as masters of the Pacific.

But Japanese commanders failed to understand that their plans to carve out a Pacific empire depended on having an adequate sea supply system to support the distant perimeter - and on having the naval and air power required to protect long lines of communication and shipping supply. Japan's merchant tonnage was in fact insufficient and too inefficiently organised to meet these sea supply requirements. She did not have the industrial capacity or manpower necessary to build the large numbers of additional merchant ships that would be required to service and supply the distant perimeter. It was a fatal flaw – the obsessive aggressive focus on winning the *decisive battle* had blinded Japan to the need to supply her distant holdings and to protect her sea routes. This failing would cost her the war.

Japanese expansion was halted in 1942 by two famous battles - fought entirely by aircraft carriers in 1942. The Battle of the Coral Sea, off northeast Australia, took place between 4-8 May 1942 and arose as a result of Japan's planned occupation on 7 May 1942 of Port Moresby, the last Allied stronghold in New Guinea. The Battle of the Coral Sea was particularly

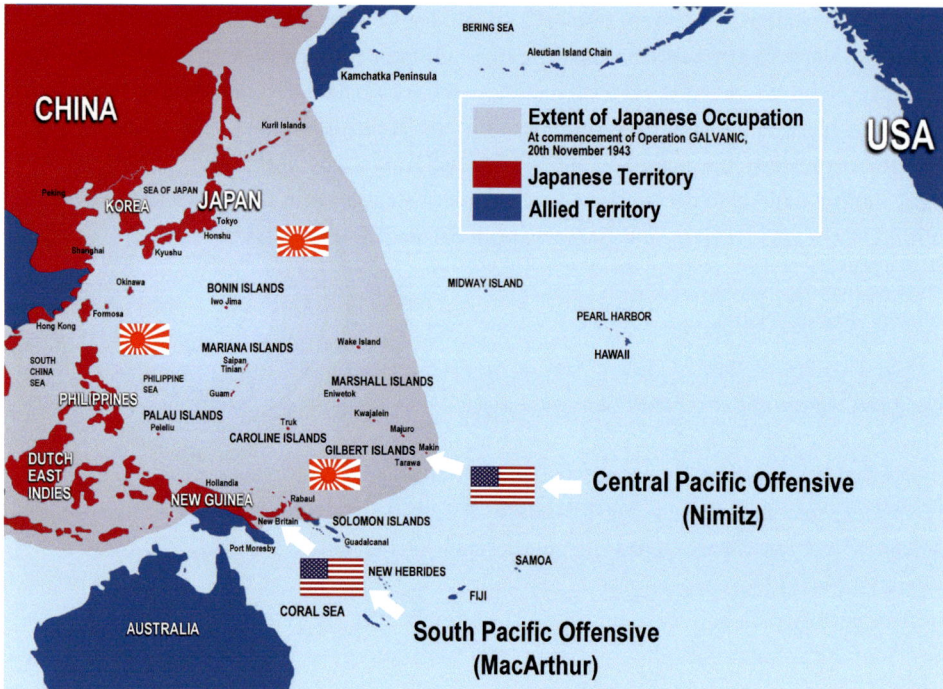

Chart of the Pacific showing extent of Japanese occupation by November 1943, prior to commencement of the Allied Operation GALVANIC offensive to retake the Gilbert and Marshall Islands. (Author)

significant in naval history as it was the first action in which aircraft carriers engaged each other directly. It was also the first battle in which the ships of the two opposing sides neither sighted each other directly, nor fired on each other. The fleet carrier USS *Lexington* was sunk as was the light carrier IJN *Shōhō*. IJN *Shōkaku* was heavily damaged, as was USS *Yorktown*. There were heavy losses of Japanese aircraft with *Zuikaku* losing more than half of her aircraft. With only four operational fleet carriers at the time, the U.S. had just lost 25% of its carrier strength.

The second pivotal battle of 1942, the Battle of Midway, was fought between 4-7 June 1942 (just some four weeks after the Battle of the Coral Sea) and was one of the most decisive battles in naval history - a complicated battle in which the Imperial Japanese Navy suffered crippling losses of the four fleet carriers, *Akagi, Kaga, Sōryū* and *Hiryū* (all part of the 6-carrier *Kidō Butai* force that had attacked Pearl Harbor six months earlier) and the heavy cruiser *Mikuma*. On the American side, the battle-scarred *Yorktown* (CV-5) would be sunk - as well as the destroyer *Hammann* (DD-412).

The cumulative effect of the Battles of the Coral Sea and Midway fatally degraded Japan's ability to undertake major offensives and paved the way for the Allied Operation WATCHTOWER landings on Guadalcanal from 7 August 1942 to 9 February 1943 - and for the bitter Solomon Islands campaign, which would later converge with the New Guinea campaign. WATCHTOWER marked the turning point of the war, when the Allies, on the back foot since the Pearl Harbor raid on 7 December 1941, were finally able to begin to move from defending against the Japanese onslaught - to an offensive campaign of their own.

The Pacific war would be a carrier war – and long-range, fast carrier Task Forces would be crucial to American plans. The newly created American fast carrier of 1943, the 27,100-ton (S) Essex-class carrier surpassed every other 'flattop' that had preceded it, such as the Yorktown-class.

The new Essex-class carriers were 820 feet long, post to post, and carried an air group of 90-100 aircraft, made up of three squadrons – 36 fighters, 36 scout/dive bombers and 18 torpedo planes. The new *Essex*-class could make 33 knots and had a range of 20,000 nautical miles at 15 knots. They would be the spearhead that won the war in the Pacific.[1]

---

1 For more information on the Pacific War, the strike on Pearl Harbor and the fast carriers of Task Force 58, check my books *Task Force 58 -the US Navy's Fast Carrier Strike Force That Won the War in the Pacific* and *Pearl Harbor's Revenge – How the Devastated US Battleships Returned to War*

CHAPTER 2

Operation HAILSTONE

17-18 February 1944

Japan's raw materials passed by sea from her South Seas holdings to Japan through a natural restriction, the area of sea between Luzon in the Philippines, Taiwan (then Formosa) and mainland China, an area which during WWII became known as the Luzon bottleneck. In a two-pronged move northwest towards the common objective of corking this bottleneck, General Douglas MacArthur's Southwest Pacific Force and Admiral Chester Nimitz's Central Pacific Force would each drive westwards separately. Once the Formosa-Luzon-China area was secure, an indirect blockade of Japan could begin.

If all went to plan, with the bottleneck corked and Japan's supply routes cut off, a major landing in this area would take place around the spring of 1945. (The exact landing place would be determined later as the operation advanced – it would turn out to be Luzon in the Philippines).

To be able to establish forward land-based air bases that would be capable of supporting U.S. operations across the Central Pacific, towards the Philippines and Japan, U.S. strategists determined to take the strategic islands of the Mariana Islands archipelago, principally Saipan and Guam, with landings to begin around 1 October 1944. If a foothold was successfully established on the Marianas, B-29 bombing strikes on Japan itself would commence from there by the end of 1944.

The nearest islands capable of providing land-based airfields to support the seizure of the Marianas were the Japanese held Marshall Islands, which host many names that are iconic of the Pacific War – such as Kwajalein, Bikini and the capital Majuro. The Marshalls however were cut off from direct communications with the U.S. naval base at Pearl Harbor in Hawaii by a Japanese garrison and air base on the small island of Betio on the western side of Tarawa Atoll in the Gilbert Islands. Thus, to be able to seize the strategically important Mariana Islands, the Allied advance westwards towards Japan had to begin far to the east with the seizure of the Gilbert Islands and then the Marshall Islands.

In late 1943, successful but costly landings took place at Tarawa and Makin in the Gilberts under the overall command of Vice Admiral Raymond Spruance (Commander Central Pacific Force). Such was the command of the air that followed, that Admiral Chester Nimitz, the Commander in Chief of the U.S. Pacific Fleet (CINCPAC) and of the Pacific Ocean Areas (CINCPOA), had the confidence to bypass all the Marshall Islands except Kwajalein, Majuro and Eniwetok atolls - leap frogging lesser islands to get at the larger ones. Operation FLINTLOCK, which began on 31 January 1944 and continued until 4 February 1944, saw the invasion of Kwajalein and the seizure of Majuro Atoll, which holds a fine strategic anchorage. The next phase to the operation would be Operation CATCHPOLE - the capture of Eniwetok Atoll (today known as Enewetak) and other islands commencing on 17 February 1944. To avoid enemy planes and warships from Truk interfering with the Eniwetok operation, Truk would be attacked simultaneously in a 2-day fast carrier raid codenamed Operation HAILSTONE.

Task Force 58 is formed

For these forthcoming operations, 12 fast carriers were brought together as the new fast carrier strike force, called Task Force 58, which was formed on 6 January 1944. Rear Admiral Marc 'Pete' Mitscher was assigned command of TF 58, hoisting his flag aboard the new *Essex*-class fast carrier *Yorktown* (CV-10).

Task Force 58 comprised a core of twelve fast 33-knot carriers (surrounded by a screen of battleships, cruisers and destroyers) that could provide direct air support to ground units and short- and long-range bombing and reconnaissance operations. Task Force 58 would become the main striking force of the United States Navy from January 1944 through to the end of the Pacific war in August 1945 and was composed of a number of smaller Task Groups, each of which was commanded by a rear admiral and typically focused around 3-4 fast carriers and their support screen of screen of cruisers, destroyers - and modern fast battleships. Supporting the fast carrier Task Force 58 were fleet oilers, ammunition ships and refrigeration and dry stores ships. In all, as the war progressed, there were often more than a hundred ships in Task Force 58, carrying more than one hundred thousand men afloat.

The immense striking power of Task Force 58 is legendary – by 1945, TF 58 had grown to comprise 17 fast carriers that could launch some 1,000 combat aircraft in under an hour. These aircraft carried out many famous operations as TF 58 swept north west from the Solomon Islands, through the Gilbert Islands, the Marshall Islands, neutralising the island fortress of Truk and then Palau in the Western Caroline Islands. The fast carriers supported the Mariana Islands operations such as at Saipan and Guam, fighting legendary air battles in the Philippine Sea as Japan rolled the dice for an all-out decisive battle to win the war. Task Force 58 aircraft supported the invasion of the Philippines and corked the Luzon bottleneck - before moving northwards to attack Iwo Jima and Okinawa. Finally, TF 58 strikes began against the Japanese home islands themselves - as, unknown to most, the Pacific war drew towards its nuclear finale in August 1945.

When the fast carrier strike force operated as part of Admiral Spruance's Fifth Fleet, it was designated Task Force 58. When, after rotation of command, it was subsequently led by Admiral Halsey as part of the Third Fleet, the carrier force was designated Task Force 38. The ships remained the same.

Onshore planning for upcoming operations was completed when each admiral and his staff rotated out of active command of the fast carrier Task Force. By allowing significant periods of time for shore-based planning, this allowed the Navy to perform at a higher operational tempo, while initially fooling the Japanese into believing that there were in fact two fleets and that the U.S. was able to deploy greater naval assets than were actually available.

Task Force 58 would go on to take part in all the U.S. Navy's Pacific battles in the last two years of the war and usually consisted of four task groups that could operate independently or combine for major operations as required. Each task group would remain distinct - but operate in close proximity to the other groups to provide the task force with maximum striking power and protection.

The overall command of the Task Force 58 lay with Rear Admiral Marc Mitscher, who deployed the Task Force, designated missions and gave instructions to the task group commanders, who in turn passed on those orders to the ship's captains and to the air-group commanders. Above Mitscher was the fleet commander, either Spruance or Halsey, who directed the fleet in accordance with the area strategy that came from Nimitz's HQ at Pearl. Only rarely did Spruance or Halsey assume tactical command – both accepting that Mitscher was supreme in operation of the fast carrier task force. Similarly, Mitscher also seldom interfered with his task group commanders once he had given them their orders.

The ships of each Task Group sailed in a circle formation centered on the carriers - with another concentric ring of alternating battleships and cruisers that provided tremendous AA fire. Outside would be a circular screen of destroyers, usually a squadron that would carry out Anti-Submarine Warfare (ASW) sweeps and provide AA cover. The support ships sailed in relatively close proximity so that their AA guns could be added to those aboard the carriers to provide a dense AA screen against enemy aircraft that tried to close the Task Group.

The fast carrier task groups of Task Force 58 would become the major naval striking force in the Pacific, providing strategic air support for operations in the Gilbert, Marshall, and Mariana Islands, whilst targeting areas of Japanese logistical and force build-up behind the front line of combat.

In early 1944, Rear Admiral Mitscher, as Commander Task Force 58 (CTF 58), had operational control of 12 carriers, (including the two new light carriers, *Langley* (CVL-27) and *Cabot* (CVL-28)) and a screen of battleships, heavy cruisers, light cruisers and 27 destroyers. If a surface big gun contact offered, Rear Admiral Willis. A. 'Ching' Lee, the Commander Task Force 54 (ComBatPac) would extract his six new fast battleships and their escorts from the TF 58 screen to form line of battle.

In early 1944 fast carrier operations such as at Truk, the twelve carriers of Task Force 58 carried 650 combat planes and were divided into four smaller Task Groups - each built around three aircraft carriers and their support vessels.

Task Force 58 composition

1. **Task Group 58.1** - Rear Admiral J.W. Reeves, Jr (ComCarDiv 4)
   - *a.* *Enterprise* (CV-6)   Air Group 10
   - *b.* *Yorktown* (CV-10)   Air Group 5
   - *c.* *Belleau Wood* (CVL-24) (light carrier)   Air Group 24

4. **Task Group 58.2** - Rear Admiral A. E. Montgomery (ComCarDiv 12)
   - *a.* *Essex* (CV-9)   Air Group 9
   - *b.* *Intrepid* (CV-11)   Air Group 6
   - *c.* *Cabot* (CVL-28) (light carrier)   Air Group 31

4. **Task Group 58.3** - Rear Admiral F.C. Sherman (Com CarDiv 1)
   - *a.* *Bunker Hill* (CV-17)   Air Group 17
   - *b.* *Monterey* (CVL-26) (light carrier)   Air Group 30
   - *c.* *Cowpens* (CVL-25) (light carrier)   Air Group 25

4. **Task Group 58.4** - Rear Admiral S.P Ginder (ComCarDiv 11)
   - *a.* *Saratoga* (CV-3)   Air Group 12
   - *b.* *Princeton* (CVL-23) (light carrier)   Air Group 23
   - *c.* *Langley* (CVL-27) (light carrier)   Air Group 32

The invasion of Eniwetok Atoll

Operation CATCHPOLE - 17 February 1944

Enewetak Atoll (present name) is a large almost circular coral atoll, 50 nautical miles in circumference and 23 miles in diameter that comprises some 40 islands surrounding a deep lagoon. It is situated to the northwest of Kwajalein Atoll and approximately 190 nautical miles west of Bikini Atoll. Enewetak Atoll's narrow strips of coral have a total land area of just over 2 square miles, and none are more than 5 metres above sea level. During World War II it was known as Eniwetok, its name being changed in 1974 to Enewetak.

Japan had constructed an airfield on Engebi Island, at the northern end of Eniwetok Atoll, in late 1942. The airfield was used for refuelling aircraft travelling between Truk, to its west, and other islands to the east. The Allied invasion of Eniwetok Atoll would thus provide Allied forces with an airfield and a large lagoon harbour that could be used to support the forthcoming campaign to take the Mariana Islands, more than 1,000 nautical miles to the west, towards the Philippines.

There was however one major complication for any assault on Eniwetok - that would have to be dealt with first. Any Allied shipping in the vicinity of Eniwetok, and any Allied troops on the beaches, would come within range of aircraft based at the greatest Japanese naval and air base in the Central Pacific – Truk, which lay almost 800 nautical miles west south west of Eniwetok. Spruance proposed a fast carrier raid to strike Truk, simultaneous with the Eniwetok invasion. The Truk raid was codenamed Operation HAILSTONE.

Unknown to the Allies, Japanese aircraft losses by this point of the war were at a critically high level, following the ill-fated deployment of carrier aircraft to defend Rabaul. Although several Japanese carriers had been lost to enemy action, there were still Japanese fleet carriers available - but those heavy losses of experienced pilots and their planes had made them ineffective. Japanese commanders now considered the remaining air cover as inadequate to support Combined Fleet operations at sea. There was no alternative but for the Combined Fleet to hole up in the perceived safety of the Truk fortress – virtually immobilised.

Truk

Truk Atoll lies to the west of Enewetak Atoll and the other Marshall Islands – and just over 1,100 nautical miles east of Palau. The 140 miles of barrier coral reefs around the Truk lagoon protect some 245 islands and islets within. Truk had become the Combined Fleet's main forward naval base from 1942-1944. (The Japanese Combined Fleet had been formed during the 1904-5 Russo-Japanese War and comprised a unified command for the three separate fleets of the Imperial Japanese Navy. The 1st Fleet had been the main battleship fleet, the 2nd Fleet was a fast, mobile cruiser fleet and the 3rd Fleet a reserve fleet of obsolete vessels. By WWII the Combined Fleet had become synonymous with the Imperial Japanese Navy and consisted of battleships, aircraft carriers, cruisers and all the ancillary craft that made up the main fighting strength).

The two new 27.5-knot fast superbattleships, *Yamato* and *Musashi,* each sporting nine of the largest naval guns ever fitted to a battleship, the 46cm Type 94 naval gun (18.1-inch), regularly graced Truk's waters. Battleships, new and old, aircraft carriers, cruisers, destroyers, tankers and submarines, along with countless minor vessels such as tugs, gunboats, minesweepers and landing craft, all thronged the Truk lagoon.

In addition to the front-line battle fleet, a large number of auxiliary transport ships, often converted requisitioned civilian passenger/cargo vessels, worked as tenders for the fleet and its submarines, carrying naval shells, ammunition, torpedoes, stores, spares - and everything else needed to keep a battle fleet in operation.

Other auxiliary transport vessels, usually freighters and cargo vessels, either requisitioned or purpose built under the mass *standard ship* building program, arrived continuously. As Truk became threatened with attack, during early 1944 the deep cargo holds of these large transport vessels held munitions, tanks, trucks, land artillery, beach mines and the like – all destined to be offloaded to fortify Truk's land defences and to resupply troops billeted there. Other transports arrived carrying troops to stiffen Truk's defences. Landing craft were heavily used to ferry the war cargoes from the auxiliaries to the shore. Convoys of escorted transport ships holding similar cargoes, stopped over at Truk to refuel, replenish and regroup, before heading off in convoy for other outlying Japanese island garrisons.

The Japanese fortified Truk with a number of Coastal Defence guns. Coastal Defence guns are classified as either *close defence guns* or *counter-bombardment guns.* Counter-bombardment guns were usually large calibre naval guns with a high elevation, designed to destroy any enemy capital ships that might stand off, 10 miles or more away, and bombard from a distance. Close defence guns were smaller calibre, 6-inches or less, with lower elevation mountings so the barells could be depressed to target enemy vessels much closer.

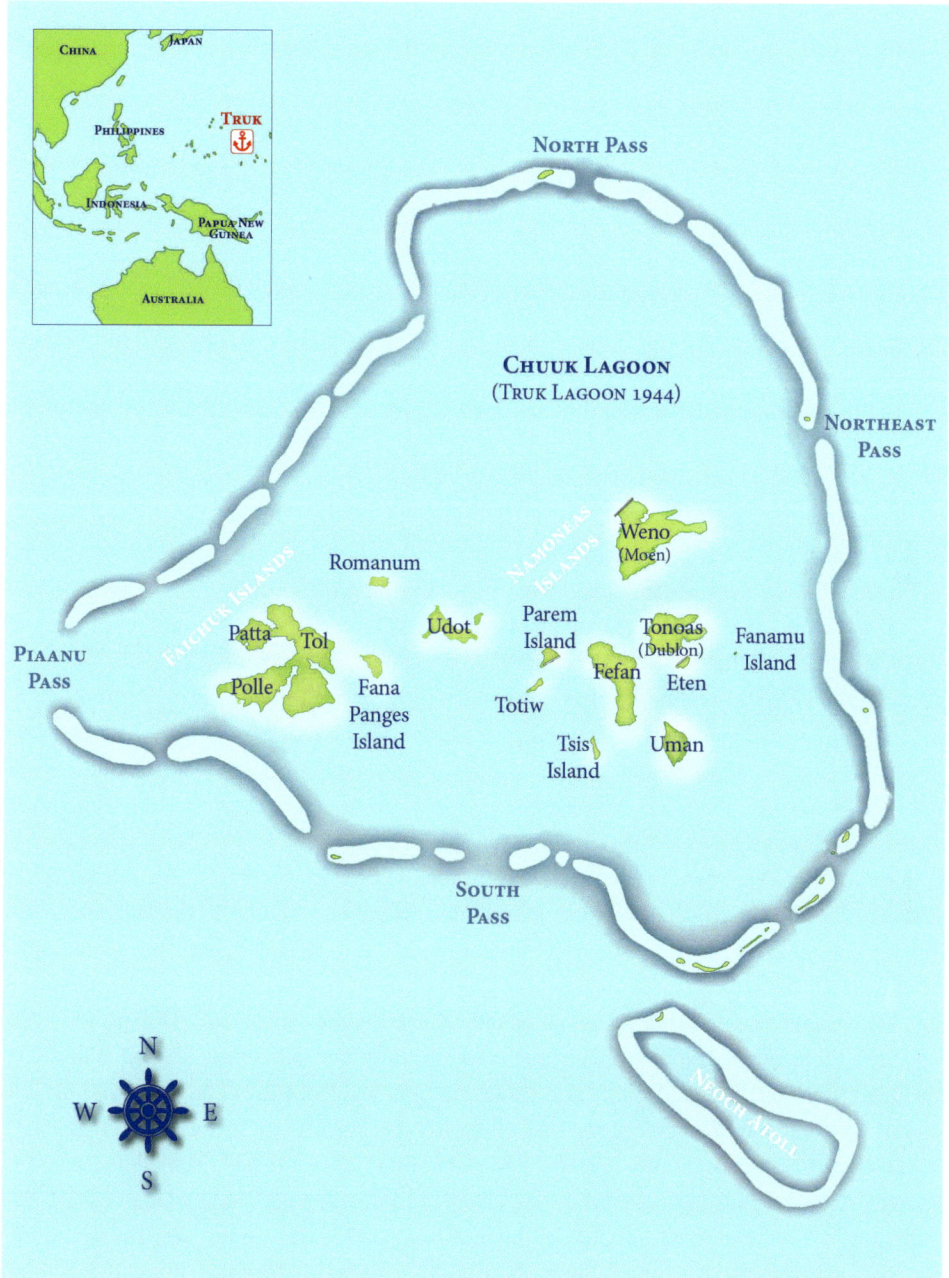

Chart of Chuuk Atoll and its location in the Pacific (Author)

The Japanese positioned their 20cm (8-inch) counter-bombardment guns on strategically important peaks, hillsides and promontories so that they could deal with any enemy warships attempting to penetrate into the lagoon through the five navigable Passes. The counter-bombardment guns were often old naval guns set in their turrets, salvaged from decommissioned warships. These 20cm (8-inch) guns formed the main battery of Japan's heavy cruisers in the inter-war years leading up to WWII. They had a range of 25,000-30,000 yards – some 14 -17 miles.

On the main island of Moen (now Weno) with its wartime large airfield, a battery of four 20cm (8-inch) guns mounted in heavy cruiser turrets were set in open pit emplacements near the lighthouse – covering North Pass. Three 15cm (6-inch) naval guns were set in tunnelled out cave complexes high on a hill overlooking the airfield.

On the southmost large island in the lagoon, Uman Island, three 15cm (6-inch) guns in turrets were set high on the mountain top on its southeast side. These guns covered the approach into the lagoon via South Pass. Similar gun emplacements, AA gun emplacements and other fortifications were dug in throughout the other islands in the lagoon - and possible beach landing sites were made into killing zones with mortar emplacements for short range engagements, beach mines, pill boxes and fortified firing positions.

In addition to these defences, the many islands of Truk harboured a number of airfields and seaplane bases that bristled with hundreds of fighters, dive bombers, torpedo and high-altitude bombers and reconnaissance float planes. The large island of Moen accommodated Moen No 1 Airfield at its north western tip - and Moen No 2 Airfield and the Moen Seaplane Base at its south western corner. The next largest island, Dublon (now Tonoas), to the south of Moen, held the Dublon Seaplane Base. There was another airfield on Param Island and an airfield under construction during 1944 on Mesegon Island.

The primary Japanese fighter airfield used for the defence of Truk was located on Eten (Etten) Island to the south of Dublon Island. Eten Island was known to the Japanese as the Takeshima Air Base and accommodated the 21st, 22nd, 25th, 26th Air Flotillas and the *Kōkū Sentai* carrier division.

Eten Island was originally a small island with a higher central hill. During 1941, the Japanese used forced labour to begin the creation of an aircraft carrier shaped island - an unsinkable aircraft carrier. Rubble and stone was quarried from the central hill and used to create a carrier shaped rubble stone seawall with a pier measuring 95 feet by 30 feet with a boom rigged crane. Once the carrier shaped island had been formed, infilled and levelled, a single runway running the length of the island, and measuring 3,440 feet long by 270 feet wide, was created and surfaced with 1.5-inch of concrete for all weather use. The island HQ was situated to the south east of the runway along with repair facilities, living quarters for 1,200 personnel, power plant, radio and the air traffic control tower. 40 fighter and 7 larger bomber revetments were set alongside the runway, along the remaining hillside.

Although aware of Truk's strategic location, the Allies knew very little about enemy operations there. But they knew of its excellent natural defences – Truk became known as the "Gibraltar of the Pacific." The Japanese fortification of Truk before the war had been carried out in the utmost secrecy - with no foreigners allowed anywhere near the islands. The Allies believed that there was a large Japanese air base holding as many as 300 aircraft - but little else was known. The journalist Elmont Waite, who would travel with Task Force 58 for the subsequent Palau strike, writing in his article *He Opened the Airway to Tokyo* in the Saturday Evening Post of 2 December 1944, quotes Rear Admiral Marc Mitscher, the Commander of Task Force 58 (CTF 58) as saying to him: 'All I knew about Truk was what I'd read in the National Geographic, and the writer had been mistaken about some things.'

As the Allies advanced, and successfully seized the Tarawa and Makin atolls in the Gilbert Islands on 20-23 November 1943, Truk became vulnerable to attack. Faced with the threat of imminent invasion, an advance party of 300 IJA officers and men of the 52nd Division arrived in Truk that month to assess the position - quickly concluding that Truk was poorly equipped to defend against an amphibious invasion.

As a result, a first echelon of IJA troops arrived on 4 January 1944, and believing that Truk may be next in line to be assaulted, possibly around 21 February 1944, the Japanese began actively building up Truk's defences. Beach defences of reinforced concrete pill boxes and blockhouses were established at the shoreline, supplemented by mine fields. Numerous AA gun positions were established - and eventually there would be over eighty 25mm and 12cm AA guns in emplacements, along with many lighter AA weapons.

Three of the five navigable Passes into the 140-mile circumference barrier reef of the Truk lagoon were mined. The remaining two navigable passes, one to the North and one to the South, were protected by Coastal Defence Guns.

Following the Battle of Kwajalein (31 January – 3 February 1944), as Truk now became vulnerable to attack, Admiral Mineichi Koga, Commander-in-Chief of the Combined Fleet, who had based himself in Truk, began dispersing units of the Combined Fleet westwards, away from the Allied advance to

The dual mount Type 96 25mm autocannon was widely used throughout the IJN on both ships and land installations.

safety. Second Fleet warships were sent west towards Palau, which was still at this point out of range of Allied land-based and carrier aircraft. Palau became the Second Fleet HQ.

The battleships *Nagato* and *Fūso* and escort destroyers left Truk west bound for Palau on 1 February 1944 - and the super battleship *Yamato* along with other battleships, cruisers and destroyers left on 3 February 1944. Admiral Koga remained at Truk aboard his flagship, the battleship *Musashi*.

In early February 1944, a second echelon of IJA troops arrived at Truk and *kaiten* manned suicide torpedo bases were established on the outer islands. Daihatsu landing craft were converted into torpedo boats. More heavy naval coastal defence guns were set in caves

Japanese *Kaiten* human torpedo on a launching cart at Dublon, 19 November 1945. This has a very large conning tower, apparently strapped atop a torpedo. This appears to be a non-standard *Kaiten* and may be a locally produced version. (National Archives 80-G-276351)

USAAF Consolidated B-24M Liberator. Naval B-24s were redesignated PB4Y-1, meaning the 4th Patrol Bomber designed by Consolidated Aircraft (National Archives)

on strategic island peaks and promontories. Anti-submarine netting was placed around docks and key anchorages.

By mid-February 1944, Truk was now heavily fortified with a military infrastructure of roads, trenches, bunkers, caves, five airstrips, seaplane bases, a torpedo boat station, submarine repair centres, a communications centre and a radar station. The Japanese garrison now consisted of almost 17,000 IJA troops in addition to the IJN personnel.

Pushed back in the Gilberts in November 1943 and then at the Marshall Islands of Kwajalein and Majuro in late January 1944, much of the IJN Combined Fleet had gathered in their perceived stronghold of Truk - amidst the intense work ashore to fortify Truk's defences.

4 February 1944 - Photographic overflight

On the evening of 3 February 1944, two U.S. Marine, long range, Consolidated PB4Y-1 Liberator photo-reconnaissance planes rose into the air from their Stirling Island airfield in the Solomon Islands, for a 2,000-mile round trip to overfly Truk and photograph Japanese shipping and land fortifications. The PB4Y-1 reconnaissance aircraft had four Pratt & Whitney radial engines that gave them a top speed of 300mph – fast for such a big aircraft and almost as fast as the Japanese Mitsubishi A6M Zero fighter. The PB4Y-1 had a service ceiling of 21,000 feet – and in addition to speed, the Navy PB4Y-1 Liberator was well armed, bristling with six gun turrets, each holding twin M2 Browning 0.50-calibre machine guns. Armour plating protected the pilots.

After their long flight, the two Navy PB4Y's arrived undetected over Truk early the next morning, 4 February 1944. Scattered cloud cover partially obscured some of the shipping below - but through gaps in the cloud they were still able to take a number of photographs from a height of 20,000 feet. The U.S. aircraft were spotted and the Japanese AA battery on Dublon Island opened up - and was soon followed by other shore batteries and some naval AA guns. The super battleship *Musashi*, at anchor below, opened up with her AA batteries.

Caught napping, with no patrolling fighters in the air, the Japanese scrambled two or three fast and agile land-based A6M Zero fighters and a similar number of Nakajima A6M2-N Rufe (Zero variant) floatplane fighters. Japanese pilots rushed to their aircraft as ground crew prepared them for flight – but it would take time to get airborne and rise up to 20,000 feet to attack the fast U.S. aircraft. The Zero's had a ceiling of more than 30,000 feet and a top speed, slightly faster than the PB4Y's, of 328mph.

After spending more than 20 unopposed minutes, overflying and photographing shipping in the lagoon and land fortifications,

The Marine aviators who made the first reconnaissance mission over the Japanese Naval Base at Truk on 4 February 1944 with their PB4Y-1 patrol bombers. This photo is probably taken at Bougainville soon after their return from their 2,000-mile combat mission (National Archives 80-G-208975)

the two U.S. aircraft turned unscathed to head back to their distant Solomon Islands airbase at full speed – knowing that Japanese fighters would be coming after them. Although one Rufe seaplane almost caught up, the Navy PB4Y's were able to outdistance the Japanese fighters and disappear to return the precious film for analysis.

The U.S. reconnaissance overflight was enough to convince Admiral Koga that an attack by the Americans was now imminent and that his remaining Combined Fleet battleships, aircraft carriers, cruisers, submarines and ancillary craft were in danger. Koga believed that the Americans, now converging on Truk from the Gilberts and Marshalls, would next attack the Philippines, Guam and Saipan, all well to the west of Truk. He knew that Nimitz could not bypass Truk without attacking: Nimitz could not leave Truk to his rear, from where air attacks from behind the Allied front could be launched, for its submarines to put to sea, for its warships to attack Allied shipping.

On the day of the Truk overflight, 4 February 1944, a group of battleships, cruisers and escorts departed Truk, westbound for Palau. The carriers of First Air Fleet were sent to the great harbour of Singapore, seized from the British in February 1942 – and much further to the west.

On 10 February 1944, Admiral Koga left Truk bound for Japan aboard his flagship *Musashi,* with four carriers, escort cruisers and destroyers and several fleet supply ships. Koga also ordered part of the IJN Fourth Fleet underway, from its anchorage to the east of Dublon Island. But not all of the ship's captains had yet been given their sailing orders and many warships lingered in the Fourth Fleet Anchorage - such as the light cruisers *Naka*, *Agano* and *Katori*, the large auxiliary transports *Aikoku Maru* and *Kiyosumi Maru*, the submarine

tenders *Rio de Janeiro Maru* and *Heian Maru* together with an assortment of tankers and other auxiliary transport vessels.

The ex-civilian merchant ships, requisitioned and militarised for use as transport ships, could not leave with their holds and decks still crowded with tanks, trucks, tankers, beach mines, land artillery, vital aircraft and spare parts, shells for the big land guns and for warships, together with light weapons, machine guns, rifles and massed amounts of small arms ammunition - all earmarked to be offloaded to Truk in preparation for the anticipated U.S. amphibious assault.

There was a frantic rush to move fuel from tankers to the shore-based installations and to finish the general re-supplying of the Truk base to allow transport vessels to depart. The destroyers *Fumizuki, Tachikaze, Maikaze, Oite* and *Nowake* came and went as they escorted convoys to Palau, Rabaul and other distant garrisons. For other less fortunate ships, damaged by attacks elsewhere in the Pacific and immobilised in Truk's Repair Anchorage, there could be no escape – they were not fit to leave for the open sea.

When the U.S. aerial reconnaissance photographs were safely returned and analysed, they revealed the land fortifications of the Japanese stronghold in astounding detail and permitted the drawing up of a well-coordinated plan of attack. Suddenly, from not knowing what shipping was at Truk before the overflight, it now became instantly clear that nearly all of the Combined Fleet had been there.

Aerial reconnaissance photo of Japanese facilities at Truk taken by a Marine Corps PB4Y-1 patrol bomber on 4 February 1944. Dublon Island is at bottom left, and Fefan Island is in lower right. In centre is the artificial aircraft carrier shaped Eten Island Air Base. Two aircraft carriers are visible at right and several warships and many merchant vessels are clustered in the Fourth Fleet Anchorage to left, where today the wrecks of many famous ships such as *Aikoku Maru, Rio de Janeiro Maru* and *San Francisco Maru* are found. (National Archives 80-G-208972)

Task Force 58 fast carrier USS ESSEX (CV-9) underway with 24 SBD scout bombers parked aft, 11 F6F fighters parked in the after part of midships area and 18 TBF/TBM torpedo planes parked amidships (National Archives 80-G-68097). (National Archives 80-G-68097)

The *Musashi* was clearly identified along with two aircraft carriers, 20 destroyers, 10 cruisers, 12 submarines and more than 50 other surface vessels. U.S. High Command immediately advanced plans to attack shipping in the anchorage – the original plan had been for an attack on 15 April 1944.

Vice Admiral Raymond Spruance, Commander Central Pacific Force, would be in overall command of Operation HAILSTONE from his flagship, the TG 50.2 battleship *New Jersey*. Rear Admiral Marc Mitscher, as Commander of the Fast Carrier Force, had operational control of the 12 TF 58 carriers. Of the assembled might of Task Force 58, the three TG 58.4 carriers *Saratoga*, *Princeton* and *Langley* were tasked to cover the Eniwetok landings, whilst the nine other TF 58 carriers would strike Truk. The Truk strike force comprised TG 58.1 (*Enterprise*, *Yorktown* and *Belleau Wood*), TG 58.2 (*Essex*, *Intrepid* and *Cabot*) and TG 58.3 (*Bunker Hill*, *Cowpens* and *Monterey*). In total, more than 500 combat aircraft would be carried to strike Truk.

On 11 and 13 February, planes from the three TG 58.4 carriers worked over the Eniwetok atoll islets - destroying most of the atoll's defences. The naval bombardment of Eniwetok would begin on 17 February 1944, the same day as the nine carriers of TG's 58.1, 58.2 and 58.3 would begin their 2-day air attack on Truk: their mission, to destroy the Japanese air capability and ensure that no Japanese aircraft interfered with the Eniwetok amphibious landings.

The 22nd Marine Regiment would land on Engebi Island at Eniwetok atoll the following day, 18 February, by when the air and naval ability of Truk would be heavily degraded by the first day's strikes of Operation HAILSTONE.

From an American perspective, it was possible that as the Truk and Eniwetok strikes took place, the IJN Combined Fleet might sortie from Truk and offer battle. If so, Task Group 50.9 under Vice Admiral W. A. 'Ching' Lee, (ComBatPac), would form a Battle Line of the six fast battleships, *Iowa*, *New Jersey*, *Massachusetts*, *Alabama*, *South Dakota* and *North Carolina* with six heavy cruisers, four light cruisers and 29 destroyers of the screen. The two other fast battleships would support TG 58.4 at Eniwetok.

As the TF 58 air strikes went in against Truk, a surface big gun force, Task Unit 50.9.1 would detach from TG 58.3 under Spruance's direct command. Comprising the two fast battleships *Iowa* and *New Jersey*, the cruisers *New Orleans* and *Minneapolis* and the destroyers *Bradford*, *Izard*, *Charrette* and *Burns*, TU 50.9.1 would make a counter-clockwise sweep around the Truk atoll to catch and destroy any enemy vessels attempting to leave the lagoon.

Ten Task Force 17 lifeguard submarines were sent to patrol the waters outside Truk with orders to remain submerged until the attack. The submarines would then surface as required to rescue any U.S. aviators downed outside the lagoon. The submarines *Tang*, *Sunfish* and *Skate* were tasked to operate south and south west of Truk whilst *Sea Raven* and *Darter* would be stationed to the north. *Aspro*, *Burrfish*, *Dace* and *Gato* would cover the remaining exits from the lagoon. American aviators downed inside the lagoon would be rescued by Kingfisher floatplanes and flown out to the submarines.

On 10 February 1944, the U.S. submarine *Permit* reported that two Japanese heavy ships, believed to be the battleships *Nagato* and *Fusō*, had left Truk. The Americans however were unaware that by now, the majority of the IJN warships had left the lagoon, leaving only a few light cruisers and destroyers for escort duties along with almost 50 naval auxiliaries, tenders, cargo vessels, oilers and tankers. Most of the vessels at anchor in Truk were lightly armed merchantmen.

Task Force 58 sortied from Majuro on 12-13 February for the first independent carrier strike of that size of the war – the 9-carrier force bound for Truk some 1100nm distant, was much more powerful than the Japanese 6-carrier force that had raided Pearl Harbor at the very beginning of the war. Commander Phil Torrey, skipper of Air Group 9 on *Essex*, is quoted by Oliver O. Jensen in his book *Carrier War* (New York, 1945, p 97) as saying: "They didn't tell us where we were going until we were well on the way. They announced our destination over the loudspeaker. It was Truk. My first instinct was to jump overboard."

On 14 February 1944, Task Force 58 refuelled from ServRon 10 oilers, 640 miles northeast of Truk. The ServRon 10 oilers then returned to Kwajalein to take on oil from tankers in readiness for a post-strike refuelling rendezvous, a procedure that would become standard.

Every day, unaware of the approach of the undetected American fast carrier task force, more Japanese transport ships arrived from Japan, some destined for other Japanese island strongholds. Such was the pace of the war that supply ships, setting off from Japan to reinforce distant outposts, reached Truk en route - only to learn that the Allies had overrun their final destinations.

On the morning of 15 February, the Japanese Fleet Monitoring Unit intercepted a radio message from a U.S. carrier pilot to the carrier *Essex*. The Japanese now knew that at least one carrier was somewhere out there in the vast expanses of the Pacific. An American attack

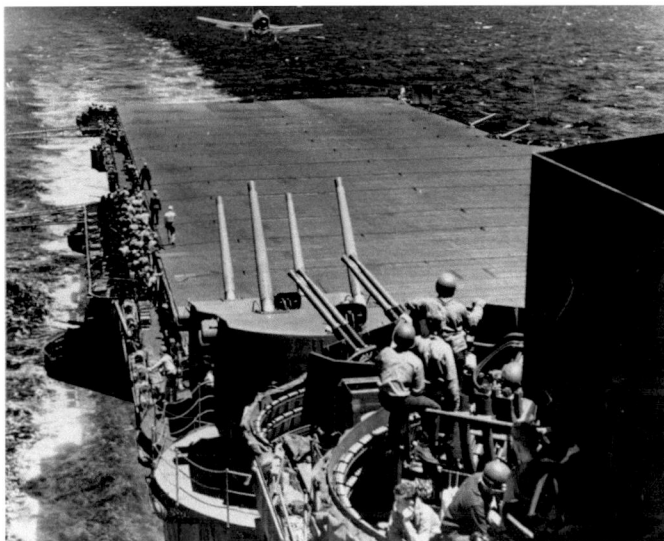

A study in fast carrier operations. An F6F-3 Hellcat fighter lands aboard a fast carrier (USS LEXINGTON (CV-16) during the Marianas Turkey Shoot on 19 June 1944), covered by 40mm guns in the foreground and 20mm guns in the gun gallery along the starboard side of the flight deck. (National Archives 80-G-236955)

was therefore now suspected - and a number of Japanese aircraft were deployed in a search pattern around Truk. The Americans however already knew the Japanese search patterns, from previously intercepted radio transmissions, and took precautions to avoid known search areas.

Just after midday the same day, 15 February, during refuelling operations, CAP Hellcat fighters from the light carrier *Belleau Wood* shot down a single long-range Japanese twin-engine Mitsubishi G4M reconnaissance bomber (Allied Reporting name *Betty*) 40 miles due west of the Task Force. It was one of four Betty's conducting routine search missions that day – and it was splashed before it sighted the Task Force. The Betty was shot down so quickly that its crew didn't have time to transmit a warning radio message back to Truk.

However, when the Betty bomber subsequently failed to return from patrol, at 0230 on 16 February, Vice Admiral Koboyashi, commander of the Fourth Fleet at Truk, ordered the Truk defences to their highest state of alert. At first light at 0500, five Japanese Betty bomber reconnaissance aircraft took off from Moen airfield for a special search. They did not spot any American ships or planes during their patrol and so, at 0900, the alarm status was reduced to a regular alarm. After 12 hours, when no attack had come and there was still no sign of the enemy, the alarm was cancelled. Japanese forces were stood down and returned to a state of normal preparedness.

The ten U.S. submarines took up their assigned positions as the 53 warships of TF 58, battleships, cruisers, destroyers and fast carriers, closed on Truk completely undetected. The surface units arrived on station in darkness 94 miles north east of Truk on the evening of 16 February 1944.

Each of the nine carriers supported an Air Group which comprised two sections of fighters, dive-bombers and torpedo-bombers that would alternate combat duties to minimise aircrew fatigue. At the beginning of the war, the air group squadrons took the

CV number of the particular carrier they were assigned to. Thus eg, *Hornet* (CV-8) carried VF-8 fighter squadrons, VB-8 dive bomber squadrons and VT-8 torpedo plane squadrons. By 1944 however, squadron numbers were being randomly assigned to carriers to avoid the enemy detecting a particular carrier's deployment from the squadron numbers of the planes it carried. Thus, *Enterprise* (CV-6) was carrying Air Group 10 and fielded its Hellcats as Fighting Squadron 10 (VF-10), its dive-bombers as Bombing Squadron 10 (VB-10) and torpedo-bombers as Torpedo Squadron 10 (VT-10), although the torpedo planes mostly carried bombs during the strikes and fighters also carried bombs. The dive bombers were mostly Douglas SBD Dauntlesses except for *Bunker Hill*, which had the only squadron of Curtiss SB2C Helldivers.

Operation HAILSTONE was scheduled to commence before dawn the following day, 17 February 1944 – designated DOG-DAY-MINUS-ONE.

Over the two days of the planned raid, thirty waves of attacking aircraft would continuously bomb and strafe any shipping they encountered and destroy shore facilities.

17 February 1944

DOG-DAY-MINUS-ONE

a. 0600 - Initial fighter sweep by 72 F6F Hellcats

American commanders knew that they had to gain air superiority before committing to bombing and torpedo attacks on the shipping and land installations of Truk. Rear Admiral Mitscher, the commander of the Fast Carrier Strike Force, came up with the idea of an initial all-fighter sweep designed to clear the air of Japanese fighters and give the bombers a clear approach to target. A sweep gave the fighters great latitude to attack targets of opportunity – as opposed to a strike, which was an attack against pre-briefed specific targets. It was a great improvement on the previous inflexible tactic of having the fighters escort the bombers all the way in.

Grumman F6F Hellcat fighters from the four light carriers, *Belleau Wood, Cabot, Monterey* and *Cowpens*, would provide combat air patrols (CAP) above the Task Force, at the holding position 90 miles outside the lagoon - to deal with any Japanese counter attack that may materialise and to act as a reserve force should the need arise.

Just over one hour before dawn on 17 February 1944, between 0440 and 0454 (local time), the first 12 VF-10 Grumman F6F Hellcats of a combined fighter force of 72 F6F Hellcats, began to take off from the Task Group 58.1 carrier *Enterprise*. Their launch was timed so that they would arrive over Truk at 0600 - sunrise was at 0609, sunset would come at 1804. Similar squadrons of Hellcats prepared to take off from the other carriers.

The 12 VF-5 Hellcats roaring off the flight deck of *Yorktown* in the pre-dawn half-light would join the 12 *Enterprise* Hellcats for a low altitude sweep at 6,000 to 8,000 feet. The 12 VF-9 Hellcats lifting into the air from *Essex* would carry out an intermediate sweep at 10,000 -15,000 feet, along with the 12 VF-6 Hellcats from *Intrepid*. The 24 VF-17 Hellcats from *Bunker Hill* would provide high altitude cover at 25,000 feet.

Once airborne, the groups of 12 Hellcat fighters flew low and fast towards Truk from a northerly direction at about 1,000 feet above sea level - to avoid Japanese radar. Once they

Grumman F6F-3 Hellcat fighters landing on USS ENTERPRISE (CV-6) after strikes on Truk, 17-18 February 1944. Flight deck crew are folding plane's wings and guiding them towards the parking area. (National Archives 80-G-59314)

were about 15 minutes flying time from Truk, the flights of Hellcats started to rise up to their assigned patrol altitudes at designated rendezvous points. TG 58.1 – 15 miles north of North Pass; TG 58.2, 15 miles northeast of North Pass and TG 58.3, 15 miles east of North Pass.

At 0520, Japanese radar based in Truk detected the approach of a large formation of aircraft and the Truk commander, Vice Admiral Kobayashi, ordered the highest state of alarm. An initial Japanese analysis of the radar reflections however concluded that a large land-based bomber formation was approaching Truk - it wasn't believed that such a large force could be solely carrier-based fighter aircraft.

After about 46 minutes of flight, at about 0600, the first of the 72 Hellcats, swept into the skies above the lagoon at 8,000 feet - above the two northerly sea passages into the lagoon, North Pass and Northeast Pass. They made an unchallenged circular run around nearly the whole lagoon before encountering any enemy fighters. Once alerted however, Japanese fighters scrambled and made to rise into the air, striving to quickly gain enough altitude to attack the successive groups of Hellcats that were now arriving over Truk.

As well as dealing with enemy fighters, the Hellcats were tasked to strafe Japanese airfields to destroy enemy aircraft on the ground before they could get into the air - and to render the airstrips unserviceable. Japanese air strength had to be sufficiently degraded to allow the slower more vulnerable dive-bombers and torpedo-bombers that would soon follow on, to do their job.

The large airfield at the north end of the largest and most northerly island, Moen (now Weno) was strafed. From there, Hellcats swept south to strafe the seaplane base at the southern end of Moen before moving on to Dublon (now Tonoas), the next largest island just to the south, to strafe the seaplane base. Other Hellcats vectored further south to strafe the airfields on the smaller islands of Eten and Param.

Although Japanese radar had detected the approaching formation about half an hour before the first aircraft reached the coral barrier reef of the lagoon, there were problems with Japanese command and communications. As a result, Eten Island airfield only learned of the incoming U.S. strike some ten minutes before Hellcat strafing fire from 0.50-inch M2 Browning machine guns and 20mm cannon swept the runway - and the mass of stationary, parked up fighters. The first target, the larger Moen Island airfield received no warning at all of the attack – the first they knew of the raid was when Hellcats swept over the runway destroying Japanese aircraft parked up on the ground.

Having been stood down from highest alert the day before, when the highest alert was initi-ated again at 0530, most Japanese pilots were in town or in bed - some on different islands from their planes. Japanese aircrew scrambled to get to their aircraft and get airborne as fast as possi-ble – whilst all the time, Hellcats were strafing their parked-up Zeros and Nakajima Ki-44 *Tojo* fighters – as well as hitting Nakajima A6M2 *Rufe* seaplane fighters afloat at the seaplane bases.

Desperate to save as many aircraft as possible, Japanese officers ordered aircraft me-chanics and technicians to take off and head north. On Eten Island airstrip, absent pilots arriving by boat from other islands were beaten by their 2nd Commanding Officer. As the local Trukese population on the islands realised the expected attack was now happening, many of them fled to caves in the hills.

On the aircraft carrier shaped Eten Island airfield, there was a congestion of planes that had been offloaded from supply ships - many of which had not yet been assembled. As the Hellcats swept overhead on their strafing runs, they found Zekes, Betty bombers and Nakajima Ki-44 Tojo fighters lined up wingtip-to-wingtip – easy prey. Many Japanese aircraft started their motors and attempted to take off – but they were shot up as they taxied along the

Eten Island airfield burning at left, as seen from an INTREPID (CV-11) plane on the first day of Operation HAILSTONE, 17 February 1944. Dublon Island and town is in the middle background, with several merchant ships offshore in the 4th Fleet Anchorage. The large tanker *Fujisan Maru* is moored to the fuel pier in left centre and is riding high at the bow. (National Archives 80-G-215153)

The artificially constructed Japanese aircraft carrier shaped Eten Island Airfield photographed from a USS YORKTOWN (CV-10) plane on the first day of Operation HAILSTONE, 17 February 1944. There are a large number of Japanese planes on the field and numerous bomb craters. Dublon Island is in the background, at top. (National Archives 80-G-216891)

runway - or shot down as they laboured into the sky shortly after taking off, crashing into the water just off the end of the runway.

Japanese land-based AA emplacements opened up on the attacking American aircraft, throwing up a thick hail of flak. Long, seemingly slowly moving trails of flak followed the fighters through the skies. Lieutenant John Sullivan from Fighting 9 Air Group on *Essex* recalled in The Fast Carriers by Clark G. Reynolds (New York 1968, p137) : "Our first sight of Truk was a black curtain of A.A. They held it until we got over the target, but they weren't too sharp. We surprised them. Their ships were at anchor, dead in the water, and that made them duck soup. It was wonderful!' Lieutenant Marvin Franger: "Right over the center of Truk all hell broke loose. God Damn! That was the worst scared I ever was."

The carrier planes strafed and destroyed some 150 Japanese aircraft parked up on Truk's various air strips – leaving more than 100 undamaged. Despite these losses on the ground, some 80 -100 Japanese fighters finally gained enough altitude to take on the Hellcats – and the sky was soon filled with swirling fighters as dogfights broke out in what would become one of the greatest all fighter aerial battles of WWII.

Such was the superiority, by this stage of the war, of U.S. pilots and planes that some 50 Zeros were shot down for the loss of four Hellcats. Lieutenant Eugene A. Valencia shot down three Japanese planes: 'These Grummans are beautiful planes. If they could cook, I'd marry one.' In the article *Air Group Nine Comes Home* in Life magazine of 1 May 1944, Herb Houck is quoted: 'It was our superior pilots and superior tactics that gave us victory over the Japs.'

In the early days of the war, the Mitsubishi A6M Zero fighter (Allied reporting name Zeke) had been untouchable by most other aircraft and superior to the early U.S. fighters. It had long range and was more manoeuvrable with a rate of climb three times more rapid than any U.S. plane in theatre at the time. But the Zero had a crucial design weakness in that it was fitted with little protective armour - when hit, it would burst into flames and burn fiercely. The Model 22 was an improvement on the early Model 11 that had escorted the bombers to hit Pearl, but by this stage of the war, Japan had lost so many aircraft and so many of her seasoned pilots (who had little chance of survival if their plane got hit) that her inexperienced pilots were now markedly at a disadvantage compared to the seasoned U.S. pilots in their well-protected Hellcats. The Zero was by now simply outclassed by the F6F Hellcat. In the subsequent *Yorktown* Action Report, it was noted: 'The Hellcats performed well, and outclimbed, outturned and outdove the Japanese planes which only seemed to have an edge at slower speeds.'

The 12 battle-hardened Hellcats from the *Enterprise* were covering the lowest altitude layer at 8,000 feet where it was expected the heaviest enemy opposition would be. They encountered about 47 airborne enemy aircraft and shot down 16 with the loss of one Hellcat. *Yorktown* planes in wild and turbulent dogfights, shot down eleven bogies. *Essex* Hellcats made five strafing runs on the Moen seaplane base where about 25 planes were parked on the ramp and in shallow water, claiming 10-12 Rufe's destroyed before they could take off. They then moved on to strafe Param airfield where some 12 Kates and Bettys were shot up. The division from *Essex* at higher altitude was attacked by Japanese fighters coming out of the sun from above and a 45-minute long dogfight ensued. *Intrepid* Hellcats shot down 17 Japanese aircraft aloft and claimed 43 destroyed on the ground.

At the highest altitude 20-25,000 feet, *Bunker Hill* Hellcats watched the cloud tops – looking for Japanese fighters that had run out of the combat zone at lower levels and were climbing out of sight of the dogfight until they reached high altitude - from where they would dive down out of the sun onto the Hellcats deployed at lower levels.

As a great fighter battle now took place in the skies above Truk, combat reports being fed back from the fighters and observer planes to their carriers revealed however that the Japanese warships the two Liberator reconnaissance aircraft had spotted 12 days before were nowhere to be seen. The main elements of the Imperial Japanese Navy, the battleships, battlecruisers and carriers and most of the other heavy warships had escaped the trap and vanished. There were still, however, some 50 armed merchantmen as well as a number of IJN light cruisers and destroyers below.

With Truk now under heavy attack, the Operation CATCHPOLE assault on Eniwetok could take place simultaneously without fear of Japanese interference from Truk.

b. The torpedo and bombing strikes begin

Immediately following the launch of Hellcats for the initial fighter sweep, Douglas SBD Dauntless dive-bombers (and Curtiss SB2C dive-bombers on *Bunker Hill*), Grumman TBF Avenger torpedo-bombers along with Hellcat fighter escorts were spotted on the flight decks. They were armed and fuelled, ready to take off to attack shipping and designated land targets - each strike being assigned areas and targets identified by aerial reconnaissance aircraft.

In all, six waves of dive- and torpedo-bomber aircraft would lift off from the carriers, the planes forming up aloft for six coordinated group strikes spread throughout the day, designated A, B, C, D, E and F. A prefix number was assigned according to individual Task Groups. Thus, strikes by TG 58.1 carriers *Enterprise* and *Yorktown* were designated 1A, 1B, 1C-1F etc. Strikes by TG 58.2 carriers *Essex* and *Intrepid* were designated 2A, 2B, 2C- 2F and for TG 58.3 *Bunker Hill* strikes were designated 3A-3F.

Japanese shipping under attack in the 4th Fleet Anchorage, Truk, as seen from
a USS INTREPID (CV-11) plane on the first day of Operation HAILSTONE,
17 February 1944. Dublon Island is at left with Moen Island in the background.
Four ships appear to have been hit by this time. *Aikoku Maru* has already
sunk and *Nippo Maru* is absent – either sunk or moved elsewhere.

Vessels present - left to right:

   a. Foreship of an unknown ship,

   b. IJN ammunition ship *Soya*, steaming west – undamaged.

   c. *Seiko Maru* is undamaged half obscured by smoke.

   d. *Momokawa Maru* is half obscured by smoke.

   e. *Hokuyo Maru* in centre is undamaged.

   f. *San Francisco Maru* (top) is on fire amidships, her smokestack is gone.

   g. *Hoki Maru* (below) is smoking – and has the white ring
     of a near miss bomb off her starboard quarter.

   h. *Nagano Maru* is listing to port.

   i. *Shotan Maru* (centre right) points to bottom right.

   j. *Reiyo Maru* is damaged, burning with a long trail of smoke from right to left of shot.

   k. Unknown ship of approx. 2,000-tons with near miss off starboard quarter.

   l. IJN *Akitsushima,* flying boat tender (top right) is damaged and trailing
     a long plume of white smoke. She was repaired and escaped the
     lagoon at dawn of the 2nd day of the raid, 18 February 1944.

(National Archives 80-G-215151)

Strike 1A, 2A and 3A aircraft were launched so that they would arrive to operate over Truk between 0615-0700. Strike 1B, 2B and 3B aircraft launched with a time over target assigned for between 0815 – 0900. Strikes 1C, 2C and 3C had a time at target of 1015 – 1100.

Task Group 58.1 planes (*Enterprise* and *Yorktown*) were assigned to attack targets in the Combined Fleet Anchorage south of Moen. TG 58.2 planes (*Essex* and *Intrepid*) were to hit targets south of Eten Island in the Sixth Fleet Anchorage. TG 58.3 *Bunker Hill* planes would hit shipping in the Fourth Fleet Anchorage, east of Dublon.

With the Hellcats now establishing air superiority, Strike 1A, 2A and 3A torpedo and dive-bombers were soon attacking Japanese shipping in their designated target anchorages. U.S. planes hit shipping to the east and west of Dublon, where some 15 Japanese transport ships had been spotted - whilst others attacked shipping in the Eten anchorage to the south, where another 15 ships were seen. On the land, airfields, barracks, ammunition and fuel supplies were attacked. In these early raids, the U.S. pilots were careful not to hit the large land-based fuel tanks - they would be left until later in the day to avoid black smoke obscuring the selection of targets.

At about 0620, *Yorktown* Strike 1A aircraft arrived over the Combined Fleet Anchorage, west of Moen Island and north of Fefan Island. Although there were many ships below, none of the expected heavy warships and carriers were present. Target priority was thus given to submarines, oil tankers, fleet auxiliaries and destroyers and to ships in the Repair Anchorage.

Yorktown Dauntless SBD dive-bombers pushed over for their dives from a height of 11,000 feet – they would release their 1,000-lb bombs at 1,000-2,500 feet above the target vessel. As the SBD's screamed down at their targets, AA fire from the target ships below rose to meet them - in addition to incoming AA fire from shore batteries on Fefan, Ulalu and Param Islands.

A number of famous present day Truk shipwrecks – such as the *Hoyo Maru*, *Kiyosumi Maru*, *Heian Maru* and *Kensyo Maru* were attacked here in the Repair Anchorage. The IJN Repair Ship *Akashi* and the IJN Auxiliary Repair Ship *Urakami Maru*, both anchored close to Dublon, were attacked – although both would survive HAILSTONE and escape to Palau, where they would be sunk 6 weeks later in Operation DESECRATE 1. The large 19,209grt former whale oil factory ship *Tonan Maru No3.*, anchored further to the north was attacked – although she would survive the day, she would be sunk the following day. Many of the ships in the Repair Anchorage were reported by the first Group Strike aircraft to be starting to hastily get underway following the dawn Hellcat fighter sweep.

Douglas SBD Dauntless dive bomber – note the perforated air brakes on the aft edge of the wings (National Archives)

Back on the carriers, some 100 miles distant, Strike 1B Hellcats escorting SBD Dauntlesses and TBF

32

An F6F Hellcat fighter is ready for launch aboard a fast carrier during operations in 1944. The battleship NORTH CAROLINA and two other battleships in the distance provide cover. (National Archives 80-G-236892)

Avengers launched just after 0700, from *Enterprise* and *Yorktown* for the second combined group strike of the day, their time over target assigned for 0815-0900. The inbound strike aircraft were tasked to target enemy warships - with priority to battleships, then carriers, heavy cruisers and light cruisers. As they sped towards Truk, two Japanese cruisers were spotted and attacked 20-30 miles northwest of North Pass. They were left damaged and smoking. Another group of warships was spotted and attacked about 10 miles northwest of North Pass.

The light cruiser *Naka* had been spotted and attacked off Dublon between 0615 -0700 during the first Strike 2A by *Essex* planes. She was spotted again by *Bunker Hill* Strike 3C planes (time at target 1015-1100) making a high-speed 25-knot run away from the atoll, some 25 miles southwest of Piannu Pass at the west of Truk atoll. The *Naka* was attacked again by TBF Avengers and SB2C Helldivers and hit by one or two torpedoes. By the time the attack broke off, the cruiser was down by the head with her No 1 main battery turret awash. She was left for dead – but was subsequently found to be still afloat later that afternoon at 1445 by *Cowpens* planes. The cruiser was trailing a slick of oil as she made her way slowly at about 6-knots towards South Pass. She was attacked and sunk.

Japanese cruiser KATORI under attack during Operation HAILSTONE, 17 February 1944. (National Archives 80-G-215147)

At 0430 earlier that day, the Japanese cruiser *Katori*, the two destroyers *Nowaki* and *Maikaze* and the minesweeping trawler *Shonan Maru No 15*, escorting the 7,398-ton armed merchant cruiser *Akagi Maru*, had departed from the Truk lagoon via North Pass. The flotilla was spotted and attacked some 15-20 miles northeast of North Pass by *Yorktown*, *Intrepid*, *Bunker Hill* and *Cowpens* aircraft. *Akagi Maru*, which had embarked many Japanese personnel and civilians, was sunk and *Katori* was strafed and hit by a torpedo, which did minor damage. (Several hours later, the big guns of the detached Task Force 50.9 would finish her off).

Once over the lagoon, the *Yorktown* Strike 1B fighters of the second group strike claimed a further 11 aircraft kills including a Zero hit on take-off that cartwheeled into a row of parked bombers, destroying three. The F6F Hellcats destroyed three Kawanishi H6K *Mavis* flying-boats and two Kawanishi H8K *Emily* flying-boats on the ramps of the Dublon seaplane base.

Almost simultaneously, Strike 2B aircraft from *Essex* were attacking enemy shipping in the Dublon and Eten anchorages. *Essex* Hellcats claimed 21 Japanese planes shot down with another probable, before attacking Param airfield and the seaplane base at the south end of Moen. Hellcat pilots claimed 15 aircraft destroyed on the ground at Param and 12 floatplanes destroyed at the Moen seaplane base - for the loss of one U.S. aircraft. Strike 2B aircraft from *Intrepid* pressed home their attacks along with Strike 3B aircraft from *Bunker Hill*.

As the first waves of group strikes swept over the lagoon it was established that Japanese AA fire was not radar controlled and was not particularly effective - being reduced to barrage fire. Unknown to the Americans, the crew of the 6-inch gun on Dublon had been told to expect an attack on 21 February and had dismantled it for cleaning - so it remained silent throughout the attack. The Japanese officer in charge of this installation was subsequently executed.

Down at sea level, it was a scene of carnage on the Japanese ships – one they had only limited AA weaponry to defend against. Some ships were still crammed full of their cargoes of munitions - and when they were hit, violent secondary explosions of embarked munitions almost vapourised large sections of the ship. One of the largest vessels below in the Fourth Fleet Anchorage, east of Dublon Island, was *Aikoku Maru*, a requisitioned fast and spacious 492-foot long 10,500grt, twin-screw former passenger & cargo liner, whose forward holds were filled with a cargo of munitions: mines, bombs and other high explosives - along with shells for her defensive gun near her bow. In addition to her crew, more than seven hundred troops were being carried in her cabins and Third-Class passenger rooms, and in makeshift billets in her aft holds.

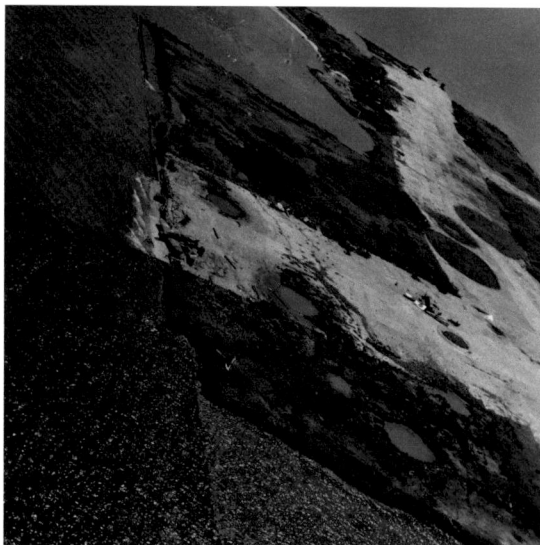

Wrecked Japanese Navy aircraft on the seaplane ramp of a heavily bombed Truk airfield. This photo taken 26 August 1945 between the cease fire and the surrender on 2 September 1945. (National Archives 80-G-490381)

During the first Strike 1B, *Intrepid* SBD Dauntless dive-bombers and TBF Avenger torpedo-bombers planes armed with bombs attacked

Aikoku Maru, scoring four 500-lb bomb hits that started a fire which spread quickly. During the next attack, Strike 2B at about 0830, she was again attacked and struck in the vicinity of Hold No. 1, which housed her cargo of munitions. Moments later, there was a catastrophic secondary explosion that scattered debris and parts of the ship all around the epicentre of the blast. The forward section of the ship, from just in front of the smokestack to the bow had been almost vapourised. The remaining aft section of the ship sank like a stone within two minutes taking almost 1,000 troops and crew to the bottom – there was only one survivor.

The successive group strikes continued throughout the day and one by one the exposed Japanese ships were sunk. The 7,624grt auxiliary transport *Amagisan Maru* was attacked during Strike 3D by five VB-17 *Bunker Hill* Curtiss SB2C Helldivers and four VT-17 TBF Avenger torpedo-bombers. The dive bombers pushed over for their dives from high above – coordinating as trained with the torpedo bombers, which attacked low and slow, the combination splitting Japanese AA fire.

The SB2C Helldivers scored a direct hit with a 1,000-lb bomb near the starboard side of the fantail, whilst the TBF's attacked from her starboard quarter. An action photograph taken by a U.S. aircraft, shows one torpedo porpoising after entering the water - whilst another runs straight and true for the starboard side just forward of the bridge superstructure. The torpedo hit and detonated, sending an expanding pillar of smoke and debris more than a hundred feet into the air. *Amagisan Maru* was carrying a cargo of aviation gasoline (Avgas) in drums in her holds - and the Avgas in the foredeck Hold No 2 ignited. As the plume of white smoke from the torpedo explosion dissipated, a large column of dense black smoke from the burning fuel started to billow up from the ship. Meanwhile, another torpedo sped towards her stern. Within 15 minutes of the attack, she was burning fiercely and sinking by the bow.

The 4,776grt naval auxiliary *Sankisan Maru* was anchored near *Amagisan Maru* – and she was attacked next. Unbeknown to the American pilots, her aft holds were filled with

'Dynamic State'. The motion of its props causes an aura to form around this F6F Hellcat on USS YORKTOWN (CV-10) in November 1943. Rotating with the blades, the halo moves aft. (National Archives 80-G-204747)

munitions - and when she took a direct hit aft, a massive secondary explosion completely destroyed the aft section from the bridge to the stern. Sections of ship were flung over the lagoon and her now severed prop, rudder and sternpost fell to the seabed below - the rest of the aft portion of the ship was gone.

The 6,938grt aircraft transport vessel *Fujikawa Maru* had arrived at Truk a few weeks earlier with a cargo of disassembled B6N Jill bombers, A6M Zero aircraft bodies, spare wings, blades and spare parts in her holds. She had anchored in the Fourth Fleet Anchorage, south of Eten Island - and a few days before DOG-DAY-MINUS-ONE, crew started carefully unloading her disassembled B6N Jill bombers to Eten airfield, where the planes would be assembled by technicians.

By the morning of 17 February, *Fujikawa Maru* had offloaded 30 of the disassembled Jill aircraft from her holds – but many others still remained stowed aboard, waiting their turn. Complete aircraft fuselages, detached wings and engines crowded her cavernous holds - all ready for delivery ashore and assembly.

Task Force 58 planners had identified the aircraft carrier shaped Eten Island airfield as one of the primary targets for attack. Anchored closeby, *Fujikawa Maru* was thus right in the thick of the action on the first day of the operation - as the initial waves of TF 58 aircraft bombed and strafed the airfield just after dawn. Her AA gunners had a busy day throwing up what resistance they could.

Strike 3E aircraft launched from *Bunker Hill* between 1310 to 1330 and as they arrived over Truk, and swept in towards Eten Island airfield, *Fujikawa Maru* herself was attacked at 1430.

One torpedo struck the large stationary transport ship just abaft the amidships superstructure on the starboard side, blasting a triangular shaped hole through her thin shell plating into her innards. She started to flood and, still at anchor, began to settle slowly by the stern – allowing her crew sufficient time to abandon ship. *Fujikawa Maru* would remain afloat through the night and into the next morning when she would be targeted again and sunk.

The 7,113-grt passenger/cargo motor vessel MV *Hauraki*, built in Scotland during 1921, had been seized in 1942 in the Indian Ocean by the two Japanese merchant cruisers *Aikoku Maru* and *Hokoku Maru*, following which she was renamed *Hoki Maru* and put to work for Japan.

Hoki Maru was anchored southeast of Eten Island, carrying in her aft holds a cargo of ammunition along with tractors, trucks cars, diggers and steam rollers for road and airfield construction work. Her forward holds were however ominously packed with aviation fuel in 55-gallon drums.

During the second group strike between 0815-0900 *Hoki Maru* was attacked and hit by bombs from Strike 2B *Essex* planes that started fires aboard amidships. During successive strikes, she was attacked again around midday by Strike 1D *Yorktown* dive bombers and Strike 3D *Bunker Hill* TBF Avengers. She was hit again - and left ablaze and smoking heavily. Her crew managed to fight the fires and she remained afloat throughout the night.

As dawn broke the next day, *Hoki Maru* was still afloat – she was quickly attacked by three Strike 3B *Bunker Hill* SB2C Helldivers carrying 1,000-lb bombs. *Hoki Maru* was hit twice, one hit causing a massive secondary explosion in the forward section of the ship as her cargo of Avgas in 55-gallon drums ignited. Both sides of her hull in front of the bridge superstructure were blown out – and the ship disappeared from sight in a plume of smoke. The damage to the fore part of the ship was catastrophic – and she sank so quickly that by the time the smoke had cleared, she was on the bottom of the lagoon.

The carnage continued throughout the day. The Hellcats had achieved complete air superiority and effectively suppressed AA fire coming from gun emplacements ashore. The dive bombers and torpedo bombers could attack Japanese ships, receiving only limited AA fire in response.

At 0927, the two battleships *New Jersey* and *Iowa,* along with the cruisers *Minneapolis* and *New Orleans* and the destroyers *Burns* and *Bradford,* detached from Task Group 58.3 and operating as TU 50.9.1, proceeded to make the scheduled counter-clockwise sweep around the barrier reef of the lagoon - to intercept any Japanese vessels trying to escape. The Task Unit was under the direct command of Vice Admiral Spruance himself in *New Jersey* – he had spent the early years of his naval career in the big gun era.

During this sweep, some forty miles outside the lagoon, the 5,890-ton Japanese light cruiser *Katori* was spotted – on fire and listing from earlier air attacks - but still under way and screened by her two destroyer escorts *Maikaze* and *Nowaki* and the minesweeping trawler *Shonan Maru No 15*. In Spruance's last *hurra* as a battleship commander, TU 50.9.1 engaged the Japanese squadron. The U.S. destroyers closed and fired six salvoes of torpedoes at *Katori* - but all missed. *Katori* replied with her own torpedoes - which also missed.

The battleship *Iowa* then closed *Katori* and fired 59 16-inch shells and 129 5-inch shells at the stricken light cruiser - quickly straddling her. After being under attack for just 13 minutes, *Katori* sank stern first. The destroyer *Maikaze* was engaged by the cruisers *Minneapolis* and *New Orleans* and was quickly sunk with all hands. The destroyer *Nowaki* was the only ship of the convoy to escape being sunk - the action had been commanded by Spruance with deadly precision. TU 50.9.1 would rendezvous with TG 58.3 at 0750 the following morning.

The last strike of DOG-DAY-MINUS-ONE, launched from *Enterprise* between 1510-1520, was Strike 1F, targeting aircraft and installations at Moen airfield. The last Strike 3F from *Bunker Hill*, operating with *Cowpens*, was launched around 1520 tasked with degrading Eten Island airfield to render it unserviceable during the night – when the Task Force was potentially vulnerable to a night torpedo attack. Quarter-ton bombs with time delay fuzes of 2-6 hours were dropped on the airfield. (Days later, as other time delay bombs dropped on Param Island airfield were collected by Japanese ground staff, they started to explode – the huge explosions being heard and felt on the neighbouring islands of Dublon and Moen).

Although the major warships of the IJN Combined Fleet were no longer present, and even though TF 58 had achieved total air superiority, nevertheless, due to suspected minefields, shore batteries and the threat of kamikaze suicide units, TF 58 remained well away from Truk during the night - in open water, protected by their own night CAP from the carriers *Belleau Wood, Cabot* and *Monterey*.

The Japanese reported 70 aircraft shot down and 96 destroyed on the ground during the first day of the raid with many more damaged. The heavily bombed airfields had been

Left: Vought OS2U 'Kingfisher' floatplane from USS NORTH CAROLINA off Truk with nine aviators on board, awaiting rescue by the submarine USS TANG (SS-306), 1 May 1944. The plane had landed inside Truk lagoon to recover downed airmen. Unable to take off with such a load, it then taxied out to TANG, which was serving as a lifeguard submarine during the follow up fast carrier strikes on Truk of 29 April – 1 May 1944. (National Archives 80-G-227991)

Right: Vought OS2U-3 Kingfisher floatplane is recovered aboard USS BALTIMORE (CA-68) after rescuing Lieut. (Junior Grade) George M. Blair from Truk lagoon, 18 February 1944. His radioman ARMC Reuben F. Hickman, is on the wing, preparing to attach the plane for hoisting aboard. Blair's F6F Hellcat of Fighting Squadron Nine from USS ESSEX (CV-9) had been shot down during the dawn fighter sweep over Truk. (National Archives 80 G 218123)

rendered useless to the extent that not one Japanese plane would rise to meet the American attackers the following day. Twelve large Japanese ships were believed sunk with eight others reported as heavily damaged.

That night, a six-plane strike of Nakajima B5N Kate torpedo bombers closed on Task Group 58.2. One of the torpedo bombers eluded a *Yorktown* night fighter and successfully torpedoed the carrier *Intrepid*, 15 feet below the waterline near the stern, causing flooding of adjoining compartments and jamming her rudder. *Intrepid* was out of the war for the time being – and had to retire to Pearl for temporary repairs before heading on to Hunters Point Naval Shipyard in San Francisco for permanent repairs that took until June 1945 to be completed.

18 February 1944

DOG-DAY

a. Night radar-guided raid

Just after 0200, during the darkness of the early hours of DOG-DAY, 18 February 1944, the first ever radar-guided night attack in aviation history was made by 12 *Enterprise* Torpedo 10

TBF's - against Japanese shipping in the Truk lagoon. As *Enterprise* steamed into the wind, 100 nautical miles north east of Truk, the 12 TBF's, armed with 500-lb bombs, roared off the flight deck catapults. In the pitch darkness of a tropical night that was lit only by a quarter moon, the 12 TBF's vectored to Truk at an altitude of 500-ft on a compass bearing. Truk was detected on the aircraft radar screens when the group was 20 miles away.

The 12 TBF's split into two groups as they approached Truk - which were detected as they crossed the reef and entered the air space above the lagoon. Japanese AA fire opened up – but despite this, eight Japanese ships would be destroyed and five damaged. Just after 0300, the *Enterprise* TBF's hit the 11,616 grt submarine tender *Heian Maru* with two bombs in the vicinity of her engine room, starting a fire that quickly got out of control. The fire moved forward and reached the bridge and soon was threatening Hold No 2, which held a cargo of Type 95 torpedoes. About 10 minutes later, around 0312, the *Enterprise* TBF torpedo-bombers scored near miss bomb hits off the starboard bow and another fire was started. The ship began to settle into the water – and about two hours later at 0500, the ship's captain gave the order to abandon ship. Most of the crew would reach the shore safely - but 17 had been killed and many wounded.

The large oiler *Sinkoku Maru*, damaged at anchor the day before in the Combined Fleet anchorage north of Fefan Island, took a near miss from a 500-lb delayed fuze bomb on her port side towards the stern. The force of the explosion blew in her shell plating over a roughly circular area of about 25 feet in diameter – parting the joints of hull plates in the centre and opening a gaping hole directly into her cavernous engine room. Water flooded unchecked into this massive space, which rises up several deck levels, and she began to settle by the stern.

In all, some 60,000 tons of Japanese shipping would be sent to the bottom of the lagoon as a result of the night TBF radar attack - for the loss of one TBF Avenger and several others damaged. This raid accounted for almost 1/3 of all 200,000 tons of shipping sunk during the 2-day operation.

As the 11 surviving TBF's broke off their attack and vectored back towards *Enterprise*, they spotted groups of the 57 Hellcats now inbound to Truk for an initial fighter sweep.

The 11 TBF's arrived back over *Enterprise* at 0555, just as the sun was coming up. Splitting into groups of four, in echelon starboard, one by one they followed each other down onto the flight deck.

b. Initial fighter sweep

Just over an hour earlier, an initial fighter sweep of 57 Hellcats launched from *Enterprise*, *Yorktown*, *Essex* and *Bunker Hill* - timed to arrive over the Truk just before dawn. Their mission was to seek out and destroy any remaining Japanese airborne opposition and destroy any enemy aircraft found on the ground.

Following the previous day's strikes, the few remaining serviceable Japanese fighters were unable to use their runways, which were pockmarked with bomb craters from the last attacks of the previous evening. Not one Japanese fighter rose to meet the U.S. air groups - although as the Hellcats swept over the lagoon, intense and accurate shore-based AA fire was encountered. The sky however belonged almost exclusively to the Hellcats.

Enterprise Hellcats made further strafing runs against Moen, Eten and Param Island airfields before turning to strafe shipping targets. *Yorktown* Hellcats strafed Moen No 1 airfield, shooting up parked up planes without encountering any Japanese fighters over the target.

c. Torpedo and bombing raids

As with the raids of the previous day, successive flights of dive-bombers and torpedo-bombers, escorted by Hellcats, rose into the sky from the carriers throughout the day, with the first Strikes 1A, 2A and 3A taking place between 0615 – 0700. *Enterprise* SBD Dauntless dive-bombers attacked the auxiliary transport *Shotan Maru* and the large oiler *Fujisan Maru,* underway between Moen and Dublon. *Shotan Maru* was hit and set on fire - and sank as she tried to beach. One bomb hit *Fujisan Maru* at the stern near her depth charge storeroom, damaging her engine room, starting fires - and sending her to the bottom.

Two Japanese ships, *Seiko Maru* and *Hokuyo Maru*, being bombed during Operation HAILSTONE – seen from USS INTREPID plane. Several small vessels are clustered close inshore to Dublon Island is in the background. The wing of the U.S. plane projects into shot at bottom left. (National Archives 80-G-221244)

Yorktown planes hit Eten airfield, making ten strafing runs and destroying aircraft on the ground. The Hellcats then attacked other targets of opportunity - merchant shipping, pillboxes, destroyers and minesweepers along with the Moen seaplane base. *Cabot* and *Essex* planes attacked shipping at the Eten anchorage whilst *Bunker Hill* planes attacked targets around Uman Island.

The submarine tender *Heian Maru* had been damaged the day before - and hit again during the night attack by *Enterprise* TBFs. She however remained stubbornly afloat – so was attacked again during Strike 1A by *Yorktown* TBF Avenger torpedo bombers. Then a little later at about 0930, she was attacked again during Strike 3B by TBF Avenger torpedo-bombers from *Bunker Hill.* She was hit by a torpedo, on the port side amidships, and flooding caused her to list progressively to port. By midday, the ship was smoking heavily, with the superstructure engulfed in flames as she settled deeper into the water. She finally disappeared beneath the surface later that afternoon.

Meanwhile, the oiler *Sinkoku Maru,* hit in her engine room on the port side aft during the *Enterprise* night attack, had settled progressively by the stern until she finally came to rest upright on the bottom of the lagoon in about 40 metres of water.

The 6,438grt auxiliary transport *Yamagiri Maru* was attacked in the Repair Anchorage, north of Fefan Island by *Bunker Hill* SB2C Helldivers with 500-lb and 1,000-lb bombs. One bomb went straight into Hold No 3 - whilst another hit the top of the bridge superstructure just forward of the smokestack. Fires took hold - and a plume of smoke rose up for hundreds of feet, followed by a series of secondary explosions as munitions and fuel ignited and blew out the bottom of the hull.

The 370-feet long, 4,739grt Type 1B Standard passenger cargo vessel *Hanagawa Maru*, was spotted way out west, at anchor near the fueling dock about 500 yards off the south eastern shore of Tol Island. The U.S. air crews mistakenly identified her as a large 12,000-ton oiler. Four Strike 3A torpedo-bombers from *Bunker Hill* and *Cowpens*, flying in column, began attack runs from the south on her starboard beam.

The first torpedo was a direct hit on the stationary *Hanagawa Maru*, between her bow and bridge superstructure - the explosion causing a large burst of flame as her cargo of aviation fuel in her foredeck holds ignited. Black fuel oil smoke billowed upwards - she had been dealt a mortal blow.

The stricken ship started to go quickly down by the head – and within 3-4 minutes, *Hanagawa Maru* had sunk from sight leaving only a burning slick on the surface. Burning debris floated ashore and reportedly started a fire in a mangrove swamp, which spread to some local buildings and a church.

One of the few IJN warships sunk was the Kamikaze-class destroyer *Oite*. On 15 February 1944, *Oite* had left Truk with *Subchaser No 28,* escorting the light cruiser *Agano* for Japan via Saipan. The American submarine *Skate* detected the vessels en route approximately 160 nautical miles northwest of Truk and at sundown, fired four torpedoes at *Agano* from a distance of 2,400 yards – scoring three hits. The damage to the lightly armoured cruiser from the three torpedo hits was substantial – she caught fire and started to slowly sink. *Oite* searched for the submarine fruitlessly - and *Skate* was able to escape undetected.

Oite stayed with the stricken *Agano* throughout the night, receiving the transfer of *Agano*'s fuel and more than 500 of her officers and men. *Oite* was then ordered to return to Truk with the survivors - ignorant of the imminent HAILSTONE raid.

During the fighter sweep early on 18 February, *Bunker Hill* Hellcats spotted *Oite* entering the lagoon through North Pass. During Strike 3B, she was attacked and strafed by Hellcats from *Bunker Hill*

VT17 torpedo planes from USS BUNKER HILL (CV-17) attacking an IJN destroyer, believed to be *Oite*, on 18 February 1944. The destroyer was completing a series of evasive turns at flank speed, her bow is to left and she is making smoke. A slick of oil can be seen at bottom. It appears that the destroyer has already broken in two pieces from the large explosion seen just above. (National Archives 80-G-218544)

41

and *Monterey* - her Captain was killed in his bridge and fires broke out abaft the smokestack. Captain Matsuda Takatomo of the *Agano* assumed command of the ship.

Five *Bunker Hill* torpedo-bombers then joined the attack. The new skipper of *Oite* threw his charge about in a desperate attempt to avoid the bombs and torpedoes of the U.S. aircraft – but whilst making a high-speed evasive turn to starboard, *Oite* was hit by a single aerial torpedo abaft the bridge. The effect of the torpedo on such a relatively small, lightly protected ship was catastrophic. Travelling at flank speed, she broke her back, the bow section slewing round to starboard as the aft section, with her engines and screws still turning, drove onwards. Both sections sank almost immediately. 172 of the *Oite's* crew and 522 crew rescued from *Agano* were killed, most of the *Agano* survivors being trapped below decks as she went down. There were only some 20 survivors in total.

The 5,831grt IJA transport *San Francisco Maru* was packed full of a war cargo of anti-invasion beach mines, munitions, army trucks, bulldozers, petrol tankers, fuel, ammunition, aircraft bombs, aircraft engines, Long Lance torpedoes and carried a deck cargo of Type 95 HA-GO light tanks. *San Francisco Maru* was hit by a number of 500-lb bombs, one destroying Hold No 5 and another blowing out the side of Hold No 4. She was dragged under by the stern into deep water with all her valuable war supplies.

By the time U.S. aircraft had completed these last strikes of the day and were returning to their carriers, a further 27 Japanese ships had been damaged or sunk.

In all, over the two days of the assault, according to U.S. figures, between 250-275 Japanese aircraft had been destroyed, the seaplane base at Moen had been put out of action, 90% of the atoll's fuel supply had been set on fire and all the other airfields and installations were damaged to differing extents. 45 Japanese ships had been sunk – over 220,000 tons of shipping – a two-day record for the entire war.

Task Force 58 now retired from the area, leaving behind only the lifeguard submarines to rescue any downed U.S. aviators in the water. The U.S. had lost 17 aircraft to enemy action with the loss of 26 crewmen – whilst the carrier *Intrepid* had been torpedoed.

As TF 58 withdrew, hundreds of bloated bodies of Japanese dead began to wash up on the shores of the Truk islands - along with empty oil drums and the debris of the ships' passing. Japanese dead were recovered and buried in mass graves on Dublon.

Rear Admiral Michio Sumikawa, Chief of Staff of the Fourth Fleet, reported that there had been 365 aircraft on Truk at the time of the attack and that 235 aircraft had been destroyed. In addition to the huge amount of valuable shipping sent to the bottom of the lagoon, military bases, infrastructure and airfields had all been extensively damaged.

The two days of the Operation HAILSTONE raids had achieved all their objectives. Japanese air power had been virtually obliterated, airstrips had been left unusable and land fortifications were largely smashed. Truk was left as an impotent, demolished enemy base.

The Japanese still believed however that an amphibious invasion might take place and so, despite the hammering Truk had taken, the reinforcing and fortification of Truk would continue – and by the end of March 1944, over 30,000 troops had been stationed there. By mid-April 1944, all construction work on the land defences was complete and those radar units that had been inoperative during HAILSTONE were now in service. For future Allied raids, advance warning was given, and valuable equipment could be got under cover and fighters scrambled into the air. Truk was however simply bypassed by the Allies - and the beleaguered Japanese defenders were left isolated and cut off.

Any possible resurgence of Japanese air strength at Truk however would still require to be neutralised. The Allies had to ensure that the Japanese in Truk were prevented from getting aircraft airborne to bomb Allied shipping and attack the Allied forces massing in the increasing number of U.S.-held territories such as Eniwetok and the Solomon Islands (to the south) for the drive north west across the Pacific towards the ultimate goal, Japan itself.

The loss of the Gilberts and Marshall Islands forced the Japanese to draw back to a new defensive perimeter, the *Absolute National Defence Zone*, which included the Marianas and Palau. Urgent heavy fortifications were set in place for an anticipated American assault – the Japanese knew that if captured, the airfields on these islands would put American land-based bombers within range of Tokyo itself.

After the Truk raid, Task Force 58 split up - but most of the carriers remained deep inside Japanese waters. *Enterprise* along with the anti-aircraft cruiser *San Diego* and 4 destroyers headed east to Majuro, bombing by-passed Jaluit on the way on 21 February 1944. *Cabot* and the damaged *Intrepid* had already departed.

Just four weeks later, Task Force 58 would reform in full strength for a copycat 2-day raid, Operation DESECRATE 1, on the Japanese staging and shipping hub of Palau, some 1,000 miles west of Truk, on 30 & 31 March 1944.

Admiral Nimitz ordered a second carrier raid on Truk to be made by Task Force 58 on 29-30 April 1944. This second carrier raid, although essential, would accomplish far less than the first Operation HAILSTONE raid. With many of the Japanese shipping routes now closed due to Allied victories in the Pacific, Truk was right in the front line and was now deemed too unsafe by Japan for use as a major harbour. Fewer ships were thus present in Truk during the April 1944 raid - and only three small ships were sunk, including the 1,000-ton auxiliary transport *Hino Maru No 2* and the 400-ton auxiliary transport *Sapporo Maru*, which was damaged by bombs and sank on 4 May. Other smaller tugs, harbour vessels, barges were sunk, in addition to the submarine *I-174*.

Five SBD's from a fast carrier peel off for a strafing attack on a Japanese radio station on Ulalu Island, Truk Atoll in the strike of 29-30 April 1944. (National Archives 80-G-45463)

Left: Ships of the U.S. Pacific Fleet anchored at Majuro, 25 April 1944, shortly before leaving to attack Truk in the follow up raid to Operation HAILSTONE. USS ENTERPRISE (CV-6) is at right, with four Essex-class carriers beyond. Battleships at left include IOWA (BB-61) and NEW JERSEY (BB-62) (National Archives 80-G-225251)

Right: Smoke billows up from the Dublon seaplane base during the follow up fast carrier strikes of 29-30 April 1944. (National Archives)

During the raids of 29/30 April 1944, the Americans claimed 60 aircraft destroyed on the ground with a further 63 shot down in dogfights over Truk during some 2,200 sorties. They lost 35 of their own planes – more than in Operation HAILSTONE – as a result of improved Japanese air defences and radar warning. The runways on Eten, Moen and Param Islands were again left unserviceable – denying the Japanese from using their remaining aircraft to target Allied shipping, shore installations and troops on other islands.

d. Aftermath

Immediately following the second carrier raids of 29/30 April 1944, on 1 May 1944 the IJN 4th Base Force HQ on Truk demobilised - and later that month, 71 aircraft (including 59 fighters) were moved from Truk to Guam and Yap. Largely neutralised as a naval base, and now with its air power denuded, the importance of Truk to the Japanese war effort had been greatly diminished. Truk was gradually cut off from Japan.

Seven American aviators, who had been shot down over Truk and plucked from the water by Japanese vessels, were taken ashore on Dublon Island where other captured American service personnel, transferred from other Pacific theatres, were being held.

Whilst most of the U.S. POW's would subsequently be shipped to Japan for internment in prison or forced labour camps, four of the American aviators shot down during Operation HAILSTONE itself, were tied up and beaten. Resisting interrogation, two of the captured American aviators were led out from the hospital where they were being held. Their hands were tied behind their backs, they were shirtless and blindfolded - with rags gagging their mouths. The two bound aviators were led towards the hill behind the hospital by armed Japanese guards – all the time being struck and clubbed with rifle butts.

A short distance up the hill, the two aviators were knocked to the ground and beaten up. They were then tied on the ground to stakes. One guard placed a stick of dynamite between the two aviators as the rest of the Japanese guards ran away. The Japanese guard then lit the fuse on the dynamite and fled. The subsequent explosion blew the legs off both Americans. Lt Shinji Sakagami returned to the scene, and finding the two U.S. aviators mortally wounded but still alive, he strangled them to death with his bare hands. (At the subsequent war crimes trials, he would be found guilty of their murder. He was executed by hanging in 1947).

About a week later, two other U.S. aviators downed during HAILSTONE were brought out of their confinement. Again, they were shirtless, gagged and blindfolded with their hands tied behind their backs. They were marched up the hill to the same vicinity as the previous week's murders. This time a spot was chosen between two large coconut trees and a long metal bar was wedged across the gap between the branches of the two trees. The two Americans were tied by their hands to the bar - hanging suspended above the ground with their feet unable to reach the ground to support them.

The Japanese officer in charge of the party ordered his men to line up in two columns of 6 men and to fix bayonets. On command, the first Japanese soldier of each column ran forward and bayoneted one of the U.S. airmen. The second soldier in line then rushed forward to repeat the brutal assault - followed by each subsequent soldier in turn. A witness later reported that it took until the 4th soldier in each column for the aviators' screams to die away.

Once all 12 had practised their bayonet drill, the dead aviators were cut down and beheaded. Two holes were dug, and the two dead men were rolled into their shallow graves.

———————

Truk had been brutally cut off from the rest of the Japanese empire and was now left to survive largely on its own meagre resources – which were really only suitable for feeding its own small native population. Although some re-supply shipping did arrive at Truk in the months following the raids, no more significant supplies from Japan would arrive.

Truk had been cut off with almost 50,000 people on its islands – made up of some 38,355 Japanese army and naval personnel, 9,100 Trukese and 970 other nationalities. The sparse natural resources of the atoll could never feed this many people. And so, isolated and cut off, Truk began to starve.

After August 1944 the situation got markedly worse. Allied gains across the Pacific had pushed Japanese forces further back towards Japan and cut off remaining supply routes. No re-supply ships at all were able to get through from Japan - and only a few submarines were able to visit. A Japanese flying boat did manage to get through with a small amount of supplies once a month - but it made little dent in the hunger of those marooned on Truk, who continued to starve.

Every inch of usable ground was turned over to agriculture for sweet potatoes, which could be eaten with bananas, coconut and breadfruit, supplemented by the decreasing amount of fish that could be taken out of the lagoon. Rats were everywhere and when caught were eaten. Bugs and worms ravaged the sweet potato crop on which the garrison largely depended - and all the Japanese troops suffered from malnutrition.

The major thrust of the American advance was ever westwards towards the Marianas, the Philippines - and then north towards the home islands of the Japanese empire. Although a ground force would never assault Truk, land-based B-24 bomber attacks continued through to October 1944. These continued bombings, following on from the Fast Carrier strike of 29/30 April 1944, left Truk with less than a dozen serviceable aircraft

Starved Japanese troops on Truk surrender to General R. Blake USMC. (National Archives)

In June 1945, a British carrier task force centered on the carrier HMS *Implacable,* escorted by cruisers and destroyers, made further attacks on Truk.

Less than a year would pass from the Operation HAILSTONE raids of 17/18 February 1944, before American B-24 and B-29 bombers lifted off in February 1945 from captured airfields on the Mariana Islands of Saipan and Tinian for the first of many bombing raids against the city of Tokyo itself. In the first raid alone, 88,000 people are estimated to have died with 41,000 injured.

On 8 May 1945 Germany surrendered. Japan was now left alone, but steadfastly refused to surrender. On 6 August 1945, the American Boeing B-29 Super fortress bomber *Enola Gay* left Tinian in the Marianas to drop the first nuclear bomb *Little Boy* on Hiroshima. 70,000 to 80,000 people were killed – some 30% of the population - with 19,700 injured and 170,000 rendered homeless.

On 9 August 1945, a second nuclear bomb, *Fat Man*, was dropped from the B-29 bomber *Bockscar* on the city of Nagasaki, a secondary target, with similar devastating effect. The original target was the city of Kokura but on the day of the attack it was obscured by cloud - the third target would probably have been Tokyo itself. But six days after the second A-bomb was dropped on Nagasaki, a cease-fire was arranged for 15 August 1945.

Once the cease-fire was in effect, the destroyer *Stack* (DD-406) and destroyer escort *Osmus* (DE-701) arrived at Truk on 30 August carrying Navy and Marine Corps officers for a preliminary conference with the Japanese military authorities regarding the surrender of Truk. The squadron hove to outside the lagoon and Japanese representatives came out and boarded the destroyer to be informed of the requirements for surrender.

Vice Admiral George D. Murray, Commander Mariana Islands, would accept the surrender of the Carolines. Murray's flagship, the veteran cruiser *Portland* (CA-33) subsequently arrived at Truk and on 2 September, Japanese surrender party boats came alongside. Murray then accepted the surrender of all Japanese islands controlled by the Truk Headquarters.

When American forces accepted the surrender of Truk, initially all appeared in order. Three months of routine war crimes investigations revealed no leads on any possible atrocities. But the truth will always out – and locals, initially cowed into silence by earlier

Japanese delegation comes aboard USS PORTLAND (CA-33). 2 September 1945, to surrender the Truk base. The Japanese officers present, left to right are: Lt Gen Shunzaburo Mugikura, Commanding General, 31st Army; Vice Admiral Chuichi Hara, Commander, 4th Fleet; Rear Admiral Aritaka Aihara, head of the Eastern Branch of the South Seas Government, and Lt Kenzo Yoshida, Aide to LtG. Mugikura (carrying bundle). (NH 62798 courtesy of the U.S. Naval History & Heritage Command)

threats of violence from the Japanese, began to tell their story once they felt secure in the U.S. conquest. Reports of war crimes by numerous Japanese personnel started to come to light - involving ten Americans, twelve Nauruans, five Australians, one British, one French, one Swiss, four Trukese and thirteen white victims whose nationality could not be established.

After the war crimes investigations had been completed, 137 Japanese service personnel were tried for war crimes. 129 were convicted of crimes such as murder, torture, medical experimentation, cannibalism, command and neglect of duty. Although these barbaric atrocities were found to have been committed during their command, the highest Japanese officers such as Vice Admiral Chuichi Hara and Vice Admiral Masashi Kobayashi were only convicted of the lesser crime of Failure to Control and were given jail sentences. Others such as Captain Masaharu Tanaka and Lcdt. Yoshinuma Danzaki were convicted of killing 7 prisoners of war on Dublon by beating, beheading and stabbing. Lt Shinji Sakagami was convicted of strangling the two U.S. aviators to death with his bare hands. Surgeon Captain Hiroshi Iwanami and eighteen other Japanese were convicted of performing illegal medical experiments on prisoners of war. They had murdered six prisoners by injecting streptococcus bacteria into their veins, causing blood poisoning and by placing tourniquets on the arms and legs of others for periods of up to seven hours, resulting in death by shock. Captain Iwanami was found to have dissected and mutilated the bodies, cutting off their heads and boiling the flesh off to use the skulls as medical specimens. Surgeon Commander Chisato Ueno and eight others were convicted of the murder of one American prisoner by chloroforming him and dissecting him alive on an operating table before carrying him outside, beheading him and rolling him into a shallow grave.

Two gallows were erected on Truk for the simultaneous execution of those condemned to death. The executions were poignantly carried out on 17 February 1948 – exactly four years to the day since the Operation HAILSTONE raid on Truk began.

⚓ THE SHIPWRECKS OF TRUK LAGOON ⚓

1	Aikoku Maru	15	Inter-Island Supply vessel	29	San Francisco Maru
2	Amagisan Maru	16	Katsuragisan Maru	30	Sankisan Maru
3	Fujikawa Maru	17	Kensho Maru	31	Sapporo Maru
4	Fujisan Maru	18	Kikukawa Maru	32	Seiko Maru
5	Fumizuki	19	Kiyosumi Maru	33	Shinkoku Maru
6	Futagami	20	The Lighter	34	Shotan Maru
7	Gosei Maru	21	Momokawa Maru	35	Taiho Maru
8	Hanakawa Maru	22	Nagano Maru	36	Unkai Maru No 6
9	Heian Maru	23	Nippo Maru	37	Yamagiri Maru
10	Hino Maru	24	IJN Oite	38	Yubae Maru
11	Hoki Maru	25	Ojima	39	Unidentified 300-ton
12	Hokuyo Maru	26	Patrol Boat No 32 Susuki		IJN tug
13	Hoyo Maru	27	Reiyo Maru		
14	I-169	28	Rio De Janeiro Maru		

⚓ JAPANESE AIRCRAFT WRECKS OF TRUK LAGOON ⚓

a	BETTY Bomber	b	EMILY Flying boat
c	JILL torpedo-bomber & MYRT	d	JUDY dive-bomber
e	ZEKE (ZERO) fighters		

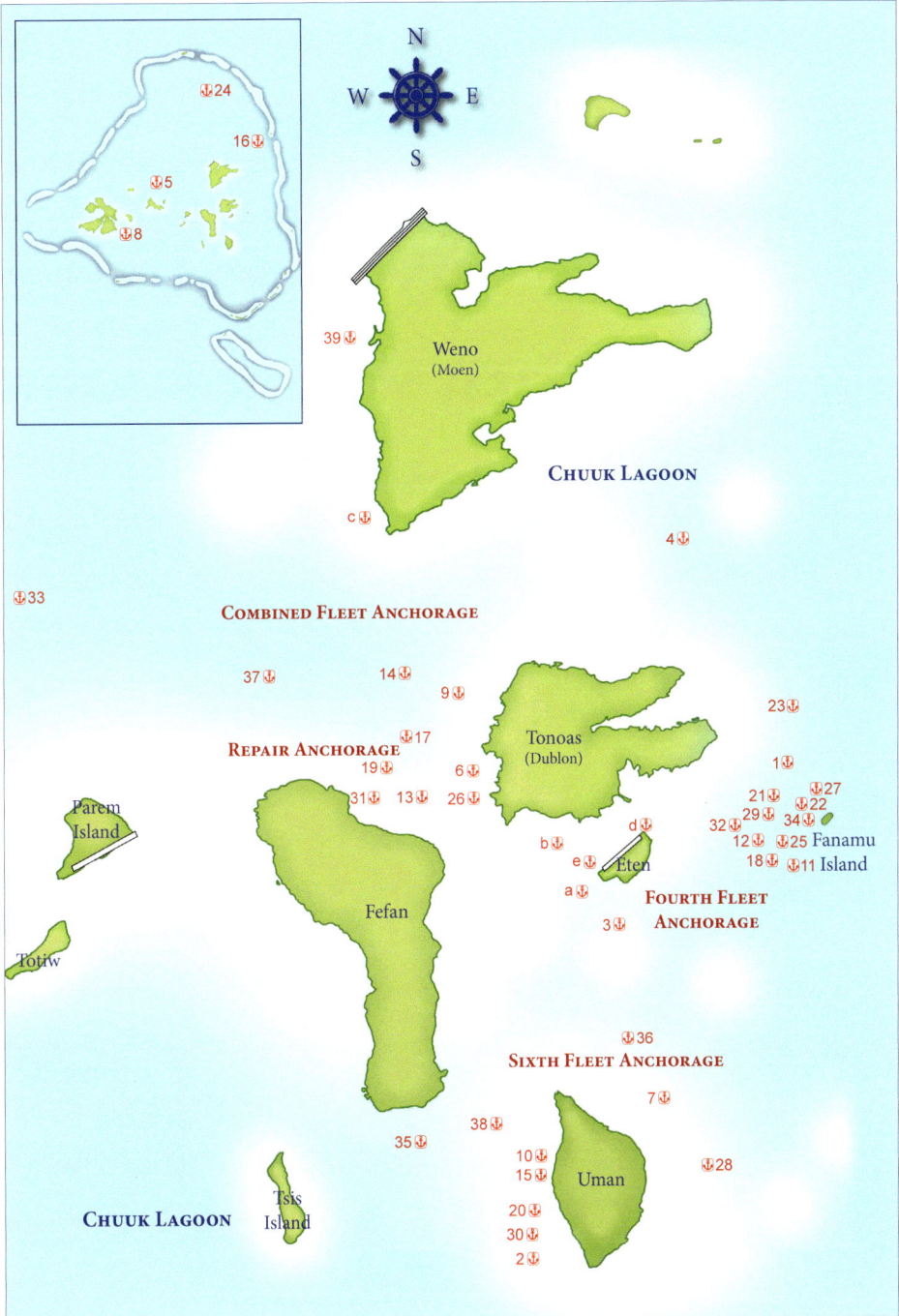

Chart showing location of present-day shipwrecks in the Truk lagoon (Author)

PART 2

THE SHIPWRECKS OF TRUK LAGOON

1. *Aikoku Maru*
Passenger-cargo liner (1940)
IJN *Tokusetsu-junyokan* - Armed Merchant Cruiser (1941)
IJN Special Transport (1943)
U.S. Recognition Code: 24 MFM

Fourth Fleet Anchorage

Tonnage:	10,500grt
Dimensions:	492.1ft; beam of 66.3ft; draught of 40.7ft.
Launched:	25 April 1940
Sunk:	17 February 1944
Cause of loss:	Catastrophic secondary explosion of embarked munitions following bombing by TF 58 aircraft during Operation HAILSTONE
Wreck location:	Fourth Fleet Anchorage east of Tonoas
Depth to seabed:	65 metres.
Least depth:	40 metres to top of superstructure

Aikoku Maru was laid down on 29 December 1938 at the Tama Zosensho K.K. Shipyard in Tamano. She was a fast and spacious twin-screw passenger & cargo ship with a cruiser stern destined for the Osaka Syosen K.K. (Osaka Mercantile Steamship Co. Ltd) service from Japan to South America. She was named and launched for fitting out afloat on 25 April 1940.

The 10,437grt passenger-cargo liner *Aikoku Maru* pre-war. Launched in 1940 she was requisitioned by the IJN as an armed merchant cruiser, before being re-rated as a transport ship.

Fitting out of such a substantial ship took some – and she was completed 16 months later on 31 August 1941. The following day, 1 September 1941, she was requisitioned by the IJN - just three months before war in the Pacific broke out on 7 December 1941. She would never serve as an ocean liner as intended.

Her builders, Tama Zosensho K.K, (the Tama Ship Building Co. Ltd.) began life as part of the Mitsui Engineering & Shipbuilding Company, which had been established in 1917 as the Shipbuilding Division of Mitsui & Co., whose first shipyard was established in Tamano in the Okayama Prefecture of southern Japan. In 1937 that shipyard became a separate legal entity from Mitsui & Co. and was named the Tama Shipyard. Just over a year later *Aikoku Maru* was laid down.

Aikoku Maru was constructed with a raked bow, a raised foc'sle and three foredeck cargo holds. Hold No's 1 & 2 were set in the well deck - with a large mast house between them from which a goalpost pair of kingposts rose with a foremast set in the middle of the cross-bracing bridge of the kingposts. Hold No 3 was contained within the extended section of superstructure projecting forward from the base of the bridge superstructure. On its leading forward bulkhead, a second goalpost pair of kingposts was situated - with an intricate cross braced bridge, a feature unique to Japanese ships of the era - and a topmast.

Rising four decks above Hold No 3 was the composite superstructure, which had the navigating bridge and pilot house at the highest levels. Immediately abaft the bridge stood the squat banded smokestack, with the engine room deep in the bowels of the ship below. In the spaces around and abaft the engine casing lay multiple decks of spacious cabins that could accommodate up to 400 passengers in comfort.

The aft part of the ship largely mirrored the layout of the foredeck with the hatch for Hold No 4 being situated at shelter deck level in the extended section of superstructure projecting aft. A goalpost pair of kingposts was set immediately abaft Hold No 4.

Holds 5 & 6 were deep, cavernous spaces that dropped to the very bottom of the ship, their hatches being separated by a masthouse that ran the full 66 feet of her beam. A mainmast rose from the middle of the bridge between the two kingposts.

A substantial poop island was set at the stern, designed to support in wartime a 5-6-inch deck gun on top, to deal with surface threats such as a submarine closing on the surface. Docking bridges ran out to either side of the poop island - and another ran to the very stern. An auxiliary steering position with helm and telegraph was situated on the centerline here where the three docking bridges met.

The great ship was powered by two 24-cylinder Mitsui Burmeister & Wain 2-stroke diesel engines manufactured under licence by the Tama Ship Building Co. Ltd. These engines developed 2490 NHP and drove her twin screws to give her a speed of 21 knots, fast for the day and allowing her to easily able to outrun most merchant ships of the era. It was this design speed and cargo carrying ability that would allow her to be converted if required for the Combined Fleet as an Auxiliary Cruiser or fast transport - at a time when most merchant vessels had a service speed of 10-12 knots. She would be able to use her great speed to catch and destroy enemy shipping, in the same way that German Armed Merchant Cruisers had had such success in the other theatres. She carried a crew of around 130.

Japan had been making preparations for war for some time prior to her construction and although she was ostensibly a luxury ocean passenger ship, the military had had a say in her design with a view to using her as a troop transport if, as appeared likely, Japan went to war. The vessel was built with large government subsidies that had been available since 1936 to encourage the production of large, high-speed transports and tankers that could quickly be converted to military uses.

During construction, *Aikoku Maru* was fitted with reinforced decks to support heavy deck guns - and thus, on 5 September 1941, just days after being requisitioned and, whilst she was still at Tamano, work began at Mitsui Engineering to convert her to a *Tokusetsu-junyokan*, the IJN designation for their Armed Merchant Cruisers.

Four single-mount 41st Year Type 15cm/50 main guns were fitted. These guns had a 152mm (5.9-inch) bore and could fire six 100-lb shells per minute to a distance of about 20,000 metres, more than 11 miles.

Two 8cm/40 3rd Year Type Dual Purpose (DP) naval guns were also fitted. These DP guns were a direct copy of the British QF 12-pounder 12cwt naval gun and fired a 3-inch (76mm) shell. They had a rate of fire of up to 20 rounds per minute with an effective firing range of 5,400 metres and a maximum range of 10,800 metres – almost 7 miles.

Two twin Type 93 13.2mm heavy machine guns with periscopic sights were fitted. Each was in theory able to fire 450 rounds per minute – but the magazine only held 30 rounds and reloading made a rate of 250 rounds per minute practical. The Type 93 had been designed in 1933 and had an effective range against aircraft of 1,000 metres and a maximum range of 2,000 metres. It was found that this machine gun was inadequate against modern fast aircraft.

Two twin 533mm (21-inch) torpedo tubes were installed along with heavy duty booms for loading and recovering her Type 94 Kawanishi E7K2 twin-float reconnaissance seaplane (Allied reporting codename *Alf*) which was carried on top of the hatches for Hold No 5 on the aft portion of the ship. A second E7K2 was carried as a spare. One 1100mm and one 900mm searchlights were installed, one fore and one aft of the funnel on the Boat Deck along with two range finders on the bridge.

In all, 14 merchant ships were converted and armed in this fashion for the role of Armed Merchant Cruiser. *Aikoku Maru's* sister ships, *Gokoku Maru* and *Hokoku Maru*, built for Osaka Shosen K.K. at the same time, were also requisitioned in 1941 and converted.

On 15 October 1941, the 24th Squadron (Raider) was established under the command of Rear Admiral Takeda Moriji and assigned to the Combined Fleet. *Aikoku Maru* was assigned to Cruiser Division 24 (CruDiv 24) along with her sister *Hokoku Maru* and *Kiyosumi Maru*. On 31 October, *Aikoku Maru* put to sea from Tamano for Iwakuni, from where on 24 November she and *Hokoku Maru* departed to take up a standby position at Jaluit Atoll in the Marshall Islands, preparatory to the planned opening of hostilities on 7 December 1941.

As war in the Pacific erupted with the surprise attack on Pearl Harbor, *Aikoku Maru* and *Hokoku Maru,* now with false markings, headed southeast from their standby position and on 12 December 1941, about 600 miles north west of Easter Island, the two ships encountered the 6,210grt American merchant ship SS *Vincent*, en route from Brisbane to New York via the Panama Canal with a cargo of rice.

Just after 1900, *Hokoku Maru* fired eight shells at the American freighter and set her on fire. The *Vincent's* crew took to three lifeboats and once they were clear a single torpedo was then fired at *Vincent* that sent her to the bottom. *Hokoku Maru* subsequently picked up all nine officers and 27 of the *Vincent's* crew from the lifeboats. (After two months aboard the *Hokoku Maru*, the *Vincent's* crew would be put ashore at Oita Bay in Japan on 13 February 1942. Two would die in a POW camp but the others would survive the war).

On 31 December 1941, the Kawanishi E7K2 Alf reconnaissance seaplane from *Aikoku Maru* was scouting out ahead of the cruisers when it spotted the unarmed 3,275grt American freighter SS *Malama* cruising past Tubuai Island in the Society Islands - south of the Cook Islands. This steamer was owned by the Matson Navigation Co. of San Francisco and had originally sailed from Honolulu on 12 December 1941 in convoy with five other merchant ships, escorted by two destroyers, that were carrying military equipment and supplies destined for Manila in the Philippines. The convoy had however dispersed and *Malama* had proceeded alone.

The small Alf floatplane, emblazoned with the marking Z-1, circled the *Malama* several times before disappearing to the east. The same Alf returned later, circled the *Malama* again before disappearing to the west. The Alf however never subsequently returned to *Aikoku Maru* and despite a search for it, no trace was found.

Just after 0900 on 2 January 1942, a second Alf floatplane from *Aikoku Maru*, marked Z-11, approached the *Malama* and signaled that she should stop. The Alf floatplane then disappeared to the northwest. The skipper of *Malama* immediately had a radio message sent to Radio Raratonga to advise that his ship had been stopped - and then, fearing seizure of his valuable war supplies, had his crew prepare rapid scuttling charges.

Five hours later, just after 1400, the Alf floatplane Z-11 returned - now armed with bombs. It fired warning shots and signalled for the crew to abandon ship. Two lifeboats were lowered, and the crew abandoned ship taking sextants, charts and a chronometer in each boat. All the ship's important secret codes and papers were thrown over the side in weighted bags.

After all hands were safely off the ship, the prepared scuttling charges went off. The floatplane made several threatening passes over the lifeboats but then turned to bomb the *Malama*. Four direct hits were scored – one of which set off some oxygen cylinders in Hold No 3, starting a fire that would hasten her demise.

At about 1530, *Aikoku Maru* and *Hokoku Maru* closed on the two lifeboats that were filled with the *Malama's* crew. 33 crew and five U.S. Air Corps Specialists were taken aboard *Aikoku* where the American ship's officers had to endure several days of intense questioning - the Japanese suspected the *Malama* had shot down the first Alf floatplane that had failed to return.

The patrol of the two Armed Merchant Cruisers ended on 20 January - and the two ships then moved through the Gilbert Islands, removing their false markings before arriving at Truk on 4 February 1942. From Truk, the two raiders were sent back to Oita Bay, Japan where the crew of the *Malama* were offloaded from *Aikoku Maru* and the crew of the *Vincent* offloaded from *Hokoku Maru* – in total some 76 POW's.

From Oita Bay the two raiders moved to the Kure Naval Shipyard where they began a refit and an armament modernisation programme. The four older 41st Year Type 15cm/50 guns were removed and eight 3rd Year Type 14cm/50 cal (5.5-inch) low angle guns were added. The designation '3rd Year Type' refers to the type of breach block, which was designed in 1914, the 3rd year of reign of Emperor Taishō and used in a number of Japanese naval guns.

One 3rd Year Type 14cm gun was set on an elevated circular platform on the fo'c'sle deck at the bow and another on a similar platform on the stern poop deckhouse – the remaining

14cm guns were set one either side of the forward Holds 2 & 3, and one either side of the aft Holds.

On 10 March 1942, now converted for submarine resupply duties, *Aikoku Maru* and her sister *Hokoku Maru* were attached to Vice Admiral Komatsu Teruhisa's Sixth Fleet (Submarines), tasked with the dual role of replenishing submarines at sea with torpedoes, stores and fuel as well as raiding Allied commerce vessels. They were painted with the distinctive slanted black & white camouflage lines designed to break up sharp angles in much the same way that dazzle painting had been used to great effect during WWI. The two *Marus* would operate with the new 8th Submarine Squadron, SubRon 8. On 16 April 1942, in this new role, the two *Marus* were sent to the Indian Ocean via Singapore, Penang and Malaya to support the 8th Submarine Squadron submarines *I-10, I-16, I-18, I-20* and *I-30*.

The Japanese Army had landed several months previously in December 1941 in northern Malaya and Siam (modern day Thailand). The IJA troops had driven south through the Malayan jungle, forcing British & Commonwealth troops to retreat to Singapore Island. On 14 February 1942 the great British fortress of Singapore fell, and some 90,000 Allied troops were captured in what was Britain's greatest military defeat. The Japanese troops marched into Singapore and took over – and her navy soon followed to the strategically positioned fine natural harbour. *Aikoku Maru* would temporarily use Singapore as a base for her submarine support and raiding operations.

On 9 May 1942, *Aikoku Maru* and *Hokoku Maru,* operating together, captured the 7,987grt Royal Dutch Shell tanker SS *Genota,* which had been requisitioned for war use by Britain - and also sank another vessel. (A prize crew and 30 naval troops were put aboard *Genota* and she was sailed back to Singapore, where she was subsequently renamed IJN *Ose* on 20 July 1942 and converted to serve as a fleet oiler). On 5 June 1942 in the early morning *Aikoku Maru* shelled and sunk the 6,757grt British merchant ship *Elysia,* which was carrying Allied troops.

The Japanese armed merchant cruiser *Aikoku Maru* at Seletar, Singapore, 26 June 1942, wearing light grey and black camouflage designed by Lieutenant Commander Fukui. Copied from *U.S. Naval Technical Mission to Japan* target report X-32, *Camouflage of Japanese ships and naval installations*, December 1945, p 14. (NH 79967 courtesy of the U.S. Naval History & Heritage Command)

On 12 July 1942, while operating from Singapore, between Fremantle in Western Australia and Colombo in Ceylon (Sri Lanka) the two raiders captured the 7,113grt New Zealand Union Steamship Co., merchant ship SS *Hauraki,* which was en route from Fremantle via Colombo for Egypt with war supplies. A Japanese prize crew was again put aboard - and the vessel's deck crew were locked below. The ship's engine room crew, under Japanese guard, had to remain at their stations and run the ship's machinery to take her back to Japan. During the voyage back, the engine crew managed to ditch most of the spare parts over the side and cause much trouble for the Japanese - at great peril to themselves. Once back in Japan, *Hauraki* was renamed *Hoki Maru* and assigned to the Imperial Japanese Navy. She would later be sunk in Truk along with *Aikoku Maru* during the Operation HAILSTONE raids of 17 & 18 February 1944. During the summer of 1942, *Aikoku Maru's* two Alf floatplanes were exchanged for two long range Aichi E-13A seaplanes, Allied reporting name *Jake*.

Aikoku Maru was then despatched to Singapore – arriving at the former British Seletar Naval Base at Singapore on 10 August 1942. Here a reserve aircraft was taken aboard, and her torpedo supply for submarines was increased to 70. Two Type 96 twin mount 25mm AA auto cannons were also fitted.

In September 1942, *Aikoku Maru* was attached to the Southwest Area Fleet to ferry the IJA 38th Infantry Division from Singapore to Rabaul as part of the reinforcement of Guadalcanal. Her dazzle camouflage was replaced by a new experimental design painted in three colours; black, dark grey and light grey at this time. In October, once her troop transport mission was completed, she was reactivated as a commerce raider and moved to the Indian Ocean via the Sunda Strait - again operating with the *Hokoku Maru*.

On 11 November 1942, south west of the Cocos Islands, the two raiders attacked the 6,341grt Royal Dutch Shell tanker MV *Ondina*, en route from Fremantle to Diego Garcia. The tanker was escorted by the small 733-ton Royal Indian Navy corvette HMIS *Bengal* (J243), which was armed only with a single 4-inch Quick Firing (QF) Mark XIX gun. This was the standard British Commonwealth naval AA and Dual Purpose (DP) gun of the time and fired a 35-lb HE or SAP shell with a maximum range of 18,500 metres.

Outnumbered, and vastly outgunned, the *Bengal* fought back against the two merchant cruisers. To protect the valuable tanker, *Bengal* closed the range and opened fire with her 4-inch gun at the closer of the two raiders, *Hokoku Maru* - just as the larger cruiser herself opened fire. DEMS Gunners aboard *Ondina* also opened up with their 4-inch gun. *Aikoku Maru* was about six miles distant at this time and closing at speed.

Hokoku Maru was a big ship – and a big target. Accurate gunners on both *Bengal* and *Ondina* successfully hit her – and the perils of converting a thin-skinned merchant ship into a commerce raider were immediately exposed. The 35-lb rounds from a QF 4-inch gun would be largely impotent against an armoured warship – but they easily penetrated *Hokoku Maru's* thin 1-inch thick shell plating. One round hit her starboard torpedo tube – detonating a loaded torpedo. A fire started immediately - and had soon spread out of control and reached the after magazine, triggering a series of explosions as munitions cooked off. The sides of *Hokoku Maru* were blown out and she sunk quickly by the stern.

As *Hokoku* exploded and sunk, *Aikoku Maru* managed to score a hit on *Bengal* that disabled her. The *Ondina* could make 12 knots – and her skipper, not aware of *Aikoku's* great speed, possibly believed that she could perhaps outrun the raider. He disengaged and made to leave the scene as quickly as possible. But *Aikoku Maru* was much faster and couldn't be shaken off, and her gunners scored six hits on *Ondina* that disabled her and set the tanker on fire. *Aikoku Maru* then fired two torpedoes at the beleaguered tanker - but both missed.

Aboard *Ondina,* with their ammunition now expended and the vessel on fire and disabled, the crew took to the lifeboats – only to be machine gunned by *Aikoku Maru* gunners.

Aikoku Maru picked up 278 of the *Hokoku Maru*'s crew - and then fired a last torpedo at the burning *Ondina*. Believing that she was now sinking, *Aikoku Maru* left the scene, leaving the *Ondina*'s surviving crew behind, adrift in their lifeboats.

The heavily damaged *Ondina* however did not sink – tankers are heavily compartmentalized and could take a number of hits and remain afloat. Once the two Japanese raiders had disappeared, *Ondina*'s crew reboarded the ship and, after making temporary repairs, were able to get her under way and limp back to Fremantle, Australia.

In December 1942, *Aikoku Maru* was reassigned back to the IJN 8th Fleet, primarily as a military transport – and her now redundant Aichi E-13A Jake scout planes were disembarked. Beginning on 19 December 1942, she participated in Operation C - the reinforcement of New Guinea, and she was put to work carrying troops, vehicles and arms - making several return trips to Japan.

On 10 July 1943, the patrolling American submarine *Halibut* (SS-232) spotted *Aikoku Maru* some 170 miles north of Truk and attacked, firing six torpedoes. One torpedo struck her - causing flooding in her aft Hold No 6 and in her propeller shaft alleys - and instantly killing 21 of her crew. *Aikoku Maru* was however able to limp on to Truk for repair, arriving there the following day.

Aikoku Maru was soon back on convoy duty - before a return to Kure, Japan, in September 1943 for the installation of two 15cm guns and four twin mount Type 96 25mm AA machine cannons. One of her holds was converted to be able to carry a supply of submarine torpedoes – and the works had been completed by 31 December 1943.

Aikoku Maru now bristled with four twin mount Type 96 25mm AA cannons set atop her superstructure. Two were set high up on the Boat Deck, one either side of the searchlight platform (abaft the smokestack) and the other two set a deck level higher, one either side of the bridge.

The Type 96 25mm auto cannon was the standard IJN medium AA weapon – and it was one of their most effective AA guns, with a rate of fire of between 200 and 260 rounds per minute. But it was most effective only at close ranges of fewer than 1,000 metres with fire at aircraft at a height of more than 1,000 metres, and beyond a range of 2,000 metres, being completely ineffective.

The 25mm Type 96 was hampered by slow training and slow elevation speeds, excessive vibration and muzzle flash. The sights were found to be ineffective against high-speed targets – a critical problem that would be badly exposed as the new fast breeds of American aircraft appeared to wreak havoc. Worse, ammunition was fed from a 15-round fixed magazine, so that the gun had to cease firing every time the magazine had to be changed. The Type 96 was vastly inferior to the 40mm Bofors used by U.S. vessels which could put out a sustained rate of fire with a constant fire top fed ammunition clip design.

Once the works were completed, *Aikoku Maru* was moved to Yokosuka, Japan, where she embarked 629 Naval Guard Unit troops, detached from the Kwantung Army in Manchuria. She also loaded 1,200 mines, dynamite, artillery shells, food and construction materials bound for Brown Island in the Marshall Islands. She then formed up at Tateyama, Japan, in a convoy bound for Truk with the submarine depot ship *Yasukuni Maru* and the *Akagi Maru*. The convoy departed Tateyama for Truk on 25 January 1944, escorted by the two destroyers *Michishio* and *Shiratsuyu* and the minelayer *Nasami*.

On 31 January 1944 however, whilst en route for Truk, the Allied Operation FLINTLOCK began – the invasion of the Marshall Islands. The U.S. 4th Marine Division and the Army's 7th Infantry Division landed at Kwajalein and Majuro Atolls. As these landings were going in, the American submarine *Trigger* (SS-237) attacked the *Aikoku Maru* convoy, 300 miles north west of Truk. Although the minelayer *Nasami* was sunk, *Aikoku Maru* escaped unscathed and entered the Truk lagoon safely on 1 February 1944. She soon departed, with her troops and supplies for Brown Island, as scheduled - but was forced to abandon the mission because of enemy air activity in support of Operation FLINTLOCK.

Aikoku Maru returned to Truk from her aborted supply run to Brown Island, entering the lagoon late in the afternoon of 16 February 1944 and anchoring in the Fourth Fleet Anchorage, to the east of Dublon Island. She immediately began loading ammunition, preparatory to departing for Rabaul - her 629 Naval Guard Unit troops bound for Brown Island were crammed inside her superstructure accommodation and in makeshift billets in her aft holds.

On the first morning of Operation HAILSTONE, 17 February 1944, as the TF 58 carriers held station about 90 miles northeast of Truk, after the 72 Hellcats of the initial fighter sweep had roared over Truk at dawn, just after 0600, the first group strike of the day began, with the planes from Strikes 1A, 2A and 3A arriving over Truk between 0615-0700.

Just after 0700, the planes of Strike 2B launched from *Intrepid* and *Essex* for the second group bombing strike of the day, allocated a time at target over Truk between 0815-0900. 12 SBD Dauntless dive-bombers and nine TBF Avenger torpedo bombers, escorted by 12 Hellcat fighters roared off *Essex's* flight deck into the wind. Shortly after, 12 SBD Dauntlesses

Japanese merchant ships in the 4th Fleet anchorage south east of Dublon under attack early on the first day of Operation HAILSTONE, 17 February 1944. The large ship in the foreground is A*ikoku Maru*. The ship in the left foreground smoking in her foredeck holds appears to be *Nagano Maru*. Above her, *Reiyo Maru* is smoking from bomb hits amidships. Both ships later sunk. (National Archive 80-G-216903)

armed with 1,000-lb bombs and eight TBF Avengers carrying bombs rose from *Intrepid*'s flight deck with their escort of 12 Hellcats.

The inbound Strike 1B planes spotted a large ship, very much like an ocean liner, anchored about 2 miles east of Dublon – it was *Aikoku Maru*. The US planes swept in for their attack - and the great ship was soon hit by four 500-lb bombs, one of which exploded in the officers' wardroom galley and started a fire that spread quickly.

At about 0825, a Strike 2B TBF Avenger hit *Aikoku Maru* with a bomb in Hold No 1 in her foreship, where the magazines for her forward gun were housed along with her cargo of mines, munitions, bombs and other high explosives.

Moments later, there was a catastrophic massive secondary explosion – the force of which can be seen in the attack photo taken from an *Intrepid* aircraft. A huge pillar of smoke rises up from where *Aikoku Maru* had been just moments before. Debris, parts of the ship and its cargo are scattered all around the epicentre of the blast with a few particularly large white splashes indicating where large sections of the ship had been thrown. The foreship, from just in front of the funnel was almost vapourised, its pieces being dispersed and spread out for some distance around her position. Where her hull was ripped apart, parts of the remaining shell plating under her bridge were curled backwards under her hull.

The explosion was so sudden, so great and so unexpected that an *Intrepid* TBF Avenger, which was over the ship having bombed it, was caught in the blast - crashing into the stricken ship near the bridge area and being destroyed. Another Japanese eye witness recounted that the plane was hit by AA fire and crashed into the foreship and it has been speculated that this may be what set off the final massive munition's explosion. The truth of what really happened is now lost in the mists of time - as there was only one survivor from the crew and billeted troops. The forward section of the wreck was obliterated from the surface of the lagoon and there is no physical evidence left to analyse.

The vast former passenger cargo ship *Aikoku Maru* had originally been built to carry 400 fare paying passengers - so her cabins and Third-Class passenger rooms had been utilised as accommodation for her embarked troops bound for Brown Island. In addition, between the

On 17 February 1944, the first day of the fast carrier raid, Operation HAILSTONE, the cargo of munitions carried in the foredeck holds of the 10,437grt auxiliary transport ship *Aikoku Maru* explodes after a bombing attack. Pieces of the ship are scattered over a vast distance. The pilot and crew of the aircraft are presumed lost, when their plane was caught in the massive secondary explosion. Dublon Island is at right and Eten Island Airfield is in the middle distance. Facilities on both are afire. (National Archives 80-G-215155)

upper Tween Decks space of Hold 4, the Japanese had built special living quarters to house more troops. Troops crammed her below deck spaces at the time of the explosion and all bar one was killed in an instant. Japanese sources report that a total of 945 troops and crew were lost.

In 1984, the remains of about 400 service personnel were recovered from the wreck by official Japanese divers and cremated ashore before their ashes were returned to Japan.

The wreck today

Today only the aft half of the *Aikoku Maru* lies intact on the seabed. There is little trace of the bow section from the bridge forward – fragments of it being dispersed in a wide semi-circle forward from the stern section. The ship was lightly constructed, with simple 1-inch steel shell plating over her web frames and stringers. The outward force of the expanding blast would simply have blown away and effortlessly disintegrated the shell plating, as it separated web frames and stringers. Everything would then be thrown outwards in isolated clumps for some distance.

There has been some speculation of late that the bow section is actually underneath the stern section. But that simply can't be the case. This was a big 150-metre long ship, that was heavily loaded and sitting deep in about 60-65 metres of water. With a recorded draft per Lloyds of 41-feet, some 13 metres, her keel would only have been about 40 metres above the seabed. The missing front half of the ship, some 70-80 metres long, was about twice the length of the depth of water under her keel. The explosion blew outwards, disintegrating the hull - and although there are some sections of the keel curled underneath the ship where the plating was severed, it is nothing more than you would expect with a catastrophic explosion like this.

The stern section today sits on a relatively even keel in 60-65 metres of water - however she was such a big ship that the least depth over the highest part of the wreck at the collapsed smokestack on the Boat Deck is between 40- 45 metres. In the good underwater visibility here, the seabed far below is usually visible from the boat deck. All the starboard side cargo booms that run from the two goalpost pairs of kingposts are swung over to the starboard side of the ship – implying that the stern section must have listed to starboard as it quickly sank.

The wreck is cut almost cleanly straight across just forward of the smokestack and distressed sections of deck plating, girders and spars forward of the smokestack point almost directly down to the seabed – revealing how this part of the ship was lifted up violently by the explosion. As this is the shallowest part of the wreck, it is near here that a fixed marker buoy to the surface is usually set by local dive charters - allowing divers to start in the shallowest part and choose where to venture and to what depth. The seabed is usually visible 25 metres below.

The smokestack has now collapsed aft, leaving the circular remnants of its base from which one large internal exhaust pipe points almost directly upwards whilst another lies at an oblique angle beneath it. The covered walkway visible in black & white archive photographs that led along either side of the boat deck here has collapsed and disintegrated. A small section of the starboard side of the bridge superstructure has survived.

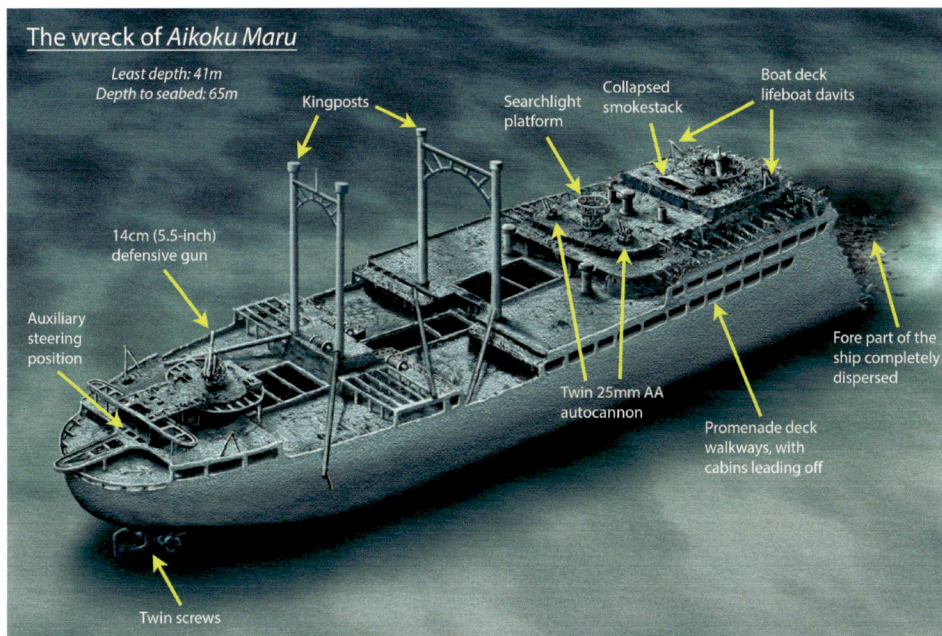

The wreck of *Aikoku Maru*

Least depth: 41m
Depth to seabed: 65m

Kingposts

Searchlight platform

Collapsed smokestack

Boat deck lifeboat davits

14cm (5.5-inch) defensive gun

Auxiliary steering position

Twin 25mm AA autocannon

Fore part of the ship completely dispersed

Promenade deck walkways, with cabins leading off

Twin screws

Artist's impression of the stern section of *Aikoku Maru* resting upright in 65 metres of water with a least depth to her Boat Deck of just over 40 metres. The forward section was completely destroyed by a massive secondary explosion of embarked munitions.

On either side of the boat deck, the triangular lifeboat davits can be seen. A few feet abaft the collapsed smokestack is the small, pitched roof of the engine room with its characteristic skylights. The uppermost engine room compartments and workshops are at a depth of about 50 metres, whilst the bottom deck of the cavernous engine room is at seabed level of 65 metres.

Below the boat deck, a large galley with ovens, china, sinks, bottles and hot water containers can be found – the Mess is located just forward with skeletal table frames lying about. The partitions dividing compartments, spaces and cabins have long ago rotted away to leave large open spaces. Electric cabling has fallen from rotted fixtures and now hangs down from ceilings.

Moving aft on the Boat Deck, past the collapsed smokestack, the stumps of forced draft ventilator funnels are dotted around before, near the aftmost edge of the deck, a large, tall searchlight platform mount stands on the centre line. On either side of the searchlight platform is set a dual mount Type 96 25mm AA cannon – the starboard side gun being particularly photogenic, pointing upwards as though still firing at attacking U.S. planes.

The aft end of the boat deck, with the searchlight platform and AA guns, has now collapsed downwards such that the bulkhead beneath has lost almost all of its height. The expanse of the Promenade Deck below projects outwards - almost to above the forward edge of the hatch for Hold No 4, which is set another deck level below on the shelter deck.

Dropping over the after end of the Promenade Deck, down to the Shelter Deck, the hatch for Hold No 4 is located. Hold No 4 is formed within the extended section of the main central superstructure (that held the bridge forward, and the engine rooms and passenger cabins). The Shelter Deck is a deck level higher than the weather deck, in which the hatches for Holds No's 5 & 6 are set.

Moving underneath the cover of the overhanging Promenade Deck above, an athwartships bulkhead is found which is dotted with open doors and portholes. At either side of this bulkhead, covered walkways lead forward along either side of the superstructure.

A single hatch cover beam bisects Hold 4, which is dark, very deep and brooding. Cargo handling to this hold was carried out from a goalpost pair of kingposts situated on the aftmost side of this hatch. The goalpost kingposts still stand tall - with a horizontal connecting bridge at the highest point and a second curved bracing spar just slightly lower.

Special living quarters to house embarked troops had been constructed in the tween deck space of this hold. At the time of her sinking she was carrying 629 Naval Guard Unit troops bound for Brown Island, many of whom were housed in this Hold and in the cabins of the main superstructure.

When the wreck was located during Jacques Cousteau's expedition to Truk in 1969, divers penetrated into these living quarters and footage of hundreds of skeletons lying in the silt in these quarters was obtained and broadcast in the resultant documentary, *Lagoon of Lost Ships*. In the early 1980's there were still a large number of human remains here, amongst the remnants of bunks and blankets. The force of the massive explosion would most likely have killed these soldiers instantly and the bent and buckled bulkheads and structural beams in this area demonstrate the extreme force of the explosion. The unfortunate troops crowded into the cramped quarters so close to such a devastating explosion had no chance of survival and were killed en masse and taken down with the ship. As the days and weeks following the sinking passed, their bodies would have gassed up and floated up to be trapped against the roofs of the rooms in which they died. Gradually, the flesh would have been eaten away and the bones would eventually have fallen gently to rest on the floors in the grisly scene that confronted the Cousteau divers.

In July 1984, with local government cooperation, a delegation from Japan arrived to collect and cremate the remains of the dead – the Japanese Shinto religion believes that the souls of men who perished in battle live in limbo and only by recovering their remains and performing a religious ceremony can their souls be set free. The remains of approximately 400 men were recovered by Japanese divers from the Tween Decks and aft areas of *Aikoku Maru*. The remains were ritually cremated on Truk and the ashes taken back to Tokyo to be scattered at sea following ceremonies at the Tomb of Unknown Soldier at the Japanese National Cemetery for War Dead. There are still however many human remains in the deep, dark recesses of this wreck and respect should be given if encountered. They should not be touched, moved or interfered with in any way.

Moving further aft across the shelter deck, past the hatch for Hold 4, divers arrive at the drop down to the well deck – which is at a depth of just over 50 metres. Here the large rectangular hatch for Hold No 5 can be seen – presumably this is the hold set up to handle torpedoes during the ship's conversion for submarine resupply duties in 1942. The hold is a vast dark, cavernous void - and the two cargo booms from the goalpost pair of kingposts adjacent to Hold No 4 have fallen across it to starboard. These heavy-duty booms were used for handling her scout seaplanes when she was acting as an armed merchant cruiser.

At the after edge of hatch No 5, another pair of goalpost kingposts rise tall, with a horizontal bridge connecting the posts and a section of mainmast rising from the middle. The kingposts run down and through a masthouse that runs athwartships, from one side of the hull to the other. At either forward side of this masthouse, a rectangular section of the masthouse projects forward to hatch No 5 – and each forward projecting section of masthouse has a sturdy cargo winch set on it for working the derrick systems of the aftmost kingposts.

Moving further aft towards the stern from the masthouse, the narrow rectangular hatch for Hold No 6 is found. The port cargo boom is still held fore and aft in its cradle, whilst the starboard boom has swung to starboard as the ship sank (like the lifeboat davits) and now projects over the gunwale. A hatch cover beam bisects the hatch athwartships and sections of the hatchcover itself to fore and aft of the hold are still in place. At the front end of the hatch, a small trapdoor is open, which would have allowed access down to the fixed internal ladder rungs that ran up the bulkhead beneath.

Near the very stern at a depth of about 50 metres, a flight of steps runs up from the well deck, on either side of Hold No 6, to the top of the poop island deckhouse. On top of the poop island is an impressive 3rd Year Type 14cm/50 cal (5.5-inch) low angle deck

At the very stern of *Aikoku Maru*, a docking bridge extends to either side and over the stern, with an auxiliary steering position in the centre. The defensive 14cm (5.5-inch) gun is swung to port. The rudder and twin screws can be seen below the fantail.

Looking from astern forward to the fantail of *Aikoku Maru* with docking bridge and 14cm gun visible above (Courtesy of Ewan Rowell)

The 14cm gun sits on its platform on top of the poop island and is swung to port. The goalpost kingposts situated between Hold No's 5&6 can be seen forward in the distance (Courtesy of Ewan Rowell)

Twin exhausts of the collapsed smokestack (Author)

The 14cm (5.5-inch) defensive gun atop the *Aikoku Maru* poop island. (Courtesy Ewan Rowell)

Dual mount Type 96 25mm AA autocannon on the Boat Deck of *Aikoku Maru*. (Courtesy Ewan Rowell)

gun, set on an elevated circular platform mount. Much of the platform has rotted away to reveal the structural beams and girders and the circular compartment that held the training gear. The mount is integral to, and projects for half its diameter from, the poop island deckhouse. This dual-purpose gun had a rate of fire of about six shells per minute and had an effective maximum ceiling against aircraft of 27,000 feet. The gun is still partially elevated to port – frozen forever in time as it fired on the attacking American aircraft.

At the very stern, the auxiliary steering position is set on the centre line of the docking bridge, which runs athwartships, level with the top of the poop island deckhouse. The docking bridge wings project out to the port and starboard gunwales whilst the aft section of docking bridge projects dead astern well out over the centre of the rounded fantail of the stern.

The auxiliary steering position on the docking bridge holds an auxiliary helm directly above the steering gear and rudder – if the ability to steer the ship from the command bridge was lost, the ship could be manually steered from this auxiliary position. Although the wooden helm and spokes have long since rotted away, the circular reinforcing band to which the spokes were screwed is now resting over the main body of the helm.

A single kedge anchor capstan is set on the centre line under the aft section of the docking bridge. At either side of the fantail a square box recessed into the bulwark rail contains a dropping mine: a depth charge for use against submarines.

Looking out over the stern of the vessel the rudder and the twin screws, one either side, can be seen far below half buried in the seabed. The white sand of the seabed is scattered here and there with sections of ship, tossed here by the catastrophic explosion in the foreship.

2. *Amagisan Maru*
Passenger Cargo vessel (1933)
Tokusetsu Unsosen Zatsuyosen Converted Auxiliary Transport (1941)
U.S. Recognition Code: 23A MKFKM

Sixth Fleet Anchorage

Tonnage:	7,624grt
Dimensions:	454ft long; beam of 60ft; draught of 37ft.
Launched:	6 November 1933
Sunk:	17 February 1944
Cause of loss:	Bombed and torpedoed by TF 58 aircraft during Operation HAILSTONE
Wreck location:	Sixth Fleet Anchorage, southwest of Uman Island
Depth to seabed:	Bow 40 metres. Stern 60 metres.
Least depth:	31 metres to foredeck starboard rail

The 7,624grt, passenger cargo ship *Amagisan Maru* was laid down on 22 February 1932 at the Mitsui Bussan Kaisha Ltd shipyard in Tama, a city in the western portion of the Tokyo metropolis. Mitsui Bussan Kaisha were the shipbuilding division of Mitsui & Co. She was constructed with two decks, a cruiser stern and eight watertight bulkheads.

On 6 November 1933, the ship under construction was named *Amagisan Maru* and launched for fitting out afloat. Her single propeller was driven by Burmeister & Wain 2-stroke 6-cylinder diesel engines manufactured under licence by Mitsui Bussan Kaisha. These modern diesels developed 1,230 NHP and gave her a relatively quick service speed

The 7,600grt auxiliary transport ship *Amagisan Maru* (from ONI Manual). Some ONI manuals identify this ship as her sister ship *Azumasan Maru*). (NH 95298 Courtesy of Naval History & Heritage Command). She was launched in 1933 and requisitioned by the IJN as an auxiliary transport ship in 1941.

of 15 knots, a top speed of 18.5 knots and an operating radius of 33,000 nautical miles at 16 knots. She carried a crew of 48 and had accommodation for a modest number of passengers.

Amagisan Maru was a big workhorse of a ship constructed with a modest composite amidships superstructure that housed the bridge, passenger and officer accommodation with the large banded smokestack abaft, and the engine room below.

Forward of the composite superstructure were three cargo holds, with the hatches for Hold No's 1&2 in the well deck and the hatch for Hold No 3 in the extended shelter deck section of superstructure in front of the bridge.

A goalpost pair of kingposts rose from a masthouse on the well deck between the hatches for Hold No's 1 & 2. A topmast extended upwards from the middle of the cross braced bridge.

A second wider goalpost pair of kingposts rose from the leading edge of the shelter deck superstructure. Winches were dotted around the bases of the kingposts to work the heavy-duty cargo derricks.

Abaft the composite superstructure was a similar extended section of the composite superstructure housing the hatch for Hold No 4 at shelter deck level. Mirroring the layout of the foredeck cargo holds, a goalpost kingpost with winches and cargo booms was set at the aftmost bulkhead of the shelter deck.

Further aft, the shelter deck dropped down to the well deck where Hold No's 5 & 6 were located – separated by a small deckhouse from which the 4th goalpost pair of kingposts rose up, for cargo handling. As with the foremast, the mainmast rose up from the middle of the bridge between the aftmost goalpost pair of kingposts.

At the very stern, the poop island deckhouse held the steering gear below with an auxiliary steering position above on a docking bridge that extended athwartships to either side of the ship and also extended out over the fantail to the stern, much like the set up on *Aikoku Maru* in the preceding chapter. She was equipped to carry oil cargo above 50°F in her deep tank.

Amagisan Maru was finally completed and registered to Mitsui Bussan K.K.in the port of Kobe on 26 December 1933 - and having been built for the Japan to New York run, two days later she departed on her maiden voyage to New York.

On 27 January 1934, *Amagisan Maru* was assigned to Mitsui Bussan's commercial run from Yokohama, in Tokyo Bay, to New York and she served on this route without incident for several years until the clouds of war darkened the blue skies of the Pacific.

On 28 September 1941, in the immediate run up to the outbreak of the Pacific war (on 7 December 1941), *Amagisan Maru* was requisitioned for war service by the Imperial Japanese Navy and just a week later, on 5 October 1941, she was registered in the IJN as a *Tokusetsu Unsosen Zatsuyosen* – a Converted Auxiliary Transport and attached to the Maizuru Naval District Work on the west coast.

In the run up to and during the Pacific war, the IJN enlisted large numbers of Japan's merchant fleet for war service. Freighters, liners and passenger cargo ships were all converted for military use and became *Tokusetsu Unsosen Zatsuyosen*. In all some 223 merchant ships were requisitioned into the IJN as *Zatsuyosen* - whilst a number of ships of other categories were re-rated as *Zatsuyosen*. Where civilian ships were requisitioned by the Navy but not formally enlisted, they were called *Ippan Choyosen* – General Requisitioned Ships. *Ippan*

Choyosen kept their civilian crew but often had a Navy Reserve Captain. Where civilian ships were requestioned into the Imperial Japanese Army, they were called *Rikugun Yusosen* – IJA Transports. Merchant ships requisitioned and armed as Auxiliary Cruisers, such as *Aikoku Maru* were called *Tokusetsu Junyokan.*

Work to convert her for war service began the following day, 29 September 1941, at Maizuru shipyard - and was completed by 13 November 1941. She was then assigned to the 11th Air Fleet, Supply Unit and moved to Taiwan (Formosa) where she embarked troops for the forthcoming operation for the invasion of Davao and Mindanao in the Philippines. On 1 December 1941, her ropes were cast off and she transferred to a muster point at the naval stronghold of Palau – arriving there on 5 December, just a few days before the surprise raid on Pearl Harbor.

Amagisan Maru departed Palau on 17 December 1941 with the Davao Occupation Convoy, and after completion of her tasking, she departed Davao on 8 January, in time to participate in Operation H - the Invasion of Celebes in the Dutch East Indies. She received light damage from a near miss by Dutch aircraft on 11 January 1942.

On 14 February 1942, off Davao, she was hit in her stern by a torpedo from the American submarine *Swordfish* (SS-193). Although she was taking on water, she was able to limp to Pujada Bay on the east side of Davao where she underwent emergency repairs that took until the end of June 1942 to be completed. She then returned to Tama in Japan where she entered drydock on 28 July 1942 for full repair works that took until February 1943.

After undocking, she returned to service – being heavily involved until October 1943 in resupply voyages from Japan and Singapore to garrisons such as Rabaul, Truk, Palau and Saipan.

On 8 October 1943, about 100 nautical miles south-south east of Truk she was hit in No 6 Hold by a torpedo from the submarine USS *Gato* (SS-212). But luck was with her, the Mark 14 torpedo turned out to be a dud and only light damage was received. She was able to continue and complete her voyage to Truk before heading to Singapore for further passages to Java, Luzon, Ambon and Balikpapan.

Just two weeks before Operation HAILSTONE, on 3 February 1944, *Amagisan Maru* set out in convoy for Truk from the important Japanese refineries in Balikpapan on the east coast of Borneo. She was carrying 733 Air Force personnel whilst her holds were filled with aviation gasoline in 55-gallon drums. At the time, some 60% of all Japanese aviation fuel came from Balikpapan along with about half of the lubricating oils used by the Japanese military. The auxiliary oilers *Fujisan Maru* and *Sinkoku Maru* sailed with the same convoy, which was escorted by the destroyers *Shigure* and *Harusame*.

After a week at sea, on 10 February 1944, the important resupply convoy arrived at the Ulithi Atoll anchorage in the Caroline Islands - almost midway between Palau and Guam. Her crew may well have learned there of the U.S. photographic reconnaissance overflight of Truk on 4 February - but they were certainly unaware of the clandestine approach to Truk of Task Force 58 and of the danger into which the convoy was now sailing. The convoy departed Ulithi for Truk the next day on 11 February 1944.

The convoy arrived safely at Truk on 14 February (just three days before HAILSTONE) and *Amagisan Maru* anchored in the Sixth Fleet Anchorage south west of Uman Island. She transferred her 733 Air Force personnel to the auxiliary transport *Koshin Maru* whilst her crew busied themselves transferring her 55-gallon drums of aviation fuel to the auxiliary transport. Little did her skipper know that out in the vast expanses of the Pacific, Task Force 58 was steaming directly towards Truk, the nine aircraft carriers fully combat ready with F6F Hellcat fighters, dive bombers and torpedo bombers. His ship's date with destiny was unknowingly approaching.

Three days after anchoring south west of Uman, on 17 February 1944, the first morning of Operation HAILSTONE strikes, aircraft from Task Group 58.3 carrier *Bunker Hill* were tasked to attack shipping found in the anchorage between Fefan and Uman Islands. At 7,620grt, *Amagisan Maru* was the largest ship present and a valuable target.

Strike 3D launched from *Bunker Hill* between 1115-1145, the planes being allocated a time over Truk from 1215 – 1300. 12 SBC2 Helldivers armed with 1,000-lb bombs with

On the first day of Operation HAILSTONE, 17 February 1944, a Mark XIII aerial torpedo hits the starboard side of *Amagisan Maru* forward of the bridge. Looking at the torpedo wake bottom left, this torpedo went deep when it entered the water - and when it went deeper than its depth setting of 10-feet, the rudder caused it to power ascend. Before it levelled off, the torpedo porpoised out of the water a couple of times - but on the last jump out of the water, the torpedo veered off to the right slightly – running a perfect course to hit the ship forward of the bridge. A number of near miss bomb impacts on the water can be seen around the stern. The ship top left is the *Yubae Maru*. (National Archives 80-G-217624)

contact and short delay fuzes roared off the flight deck into the wind with 10 TBF Avengers, each of which was carrying a single torpedo. 12 F6F Hellcat fighters would provide escort. The TG 58.3 planes would overlap over Truk with the planes of Task Groups 58.1 and TG 58.2 and in all, there would be some 34 planes in the group strike. (*Bunker Hill* was the only carrier with SB2C Helldivers – the other carriers deployed Douglas SBD Dauntless dive bombers).

The *Bunker Hill* Strike 3D planes climbed to 12,000-ft as they approached Truk inbound and then swept over the atoll's barrier reef, close to Northeast Pass. By 1250, five *Bunker Hill* SB2C Helldivers from Bombing 17 had selected their first target and commenced their attack on a large ship estimated to be 10,000-tons and 500-ft in length - it was *Amagisan Maru*. One Helldiver scored a direct hit with a 1,000-lb bomb at the stern.

The dives by the SB2C Helldivers were followed by an aerial torpedo attack on *Amagisan Maru* by four Torpedo 17 TBF Avengers from her starboard quarter. The action photograph above taken by U.S. aircraft shows the ship targeted by several torpedoes. One hit the starboard side just forward of the bridge. The torpedo detonated, the large explosion sent an expanding pillar of smoke and debris more than a hundred feet into the air.

Amagisan Maru was still carrying large quantities of her cargo of aviation gasoline in 55-gallon drums in her holds. As the torpedo hit forward of the bridge, the explosion ignited the fuel in Hold No 2. As the plume of white smoke and spray from the torpedo explosion dissipated, a large column of dense black smoke from the burning fuel started to billow up from the ship. The *Bunker Hill* planes had already moved on to attack their next target, *Sankisan Maru*.

Within 15 minutes of the attack the ship was burning fiercely and sinking by the bow. She disappeared into the depths shortly thereafter, with the loss of three crew.

The wreck today

Today the wreck of the 7,624grt *Amagisan Maru* is one of the largest in the Truk lagoon. She rests on her port beam ends at a 45-degree angle on the underwater slope that leads to Uman Island. Her bows are in shallower water of about 42 metres of water and her stern further down the slope in deeper water of about 60 metres. The depth to her shallower starboard bulwark and starboard bridge superstructure is about 31 - 35 metres.

At her bow, the vessel's name is welded in large Roman letters on the hull - with the corresponding Kanji characters above. The port anchor chain is run out from its hawse at the raked bow and disappears along the seabed into the distance. The starboard anchor is not run out but hangs loosely from its hawse, partly draped over the stem.

On top of the elevated fo'c'sle deck just back from the stem, her two anchor chains rise out of their hawse pipes and run to the large intricate anchor windlass, which is flanked either side by pairs of mooring bitts.

Immediately abaft the anchor windlass, a circular gun platform stands about 4 feet above the deck with a Type 41 8cm (3-inch) naval gun set on it - pointing dead ahead out over the stem, and not elevated. The aft portion of the gun platform extends aft above the hatch for Hold No 1.

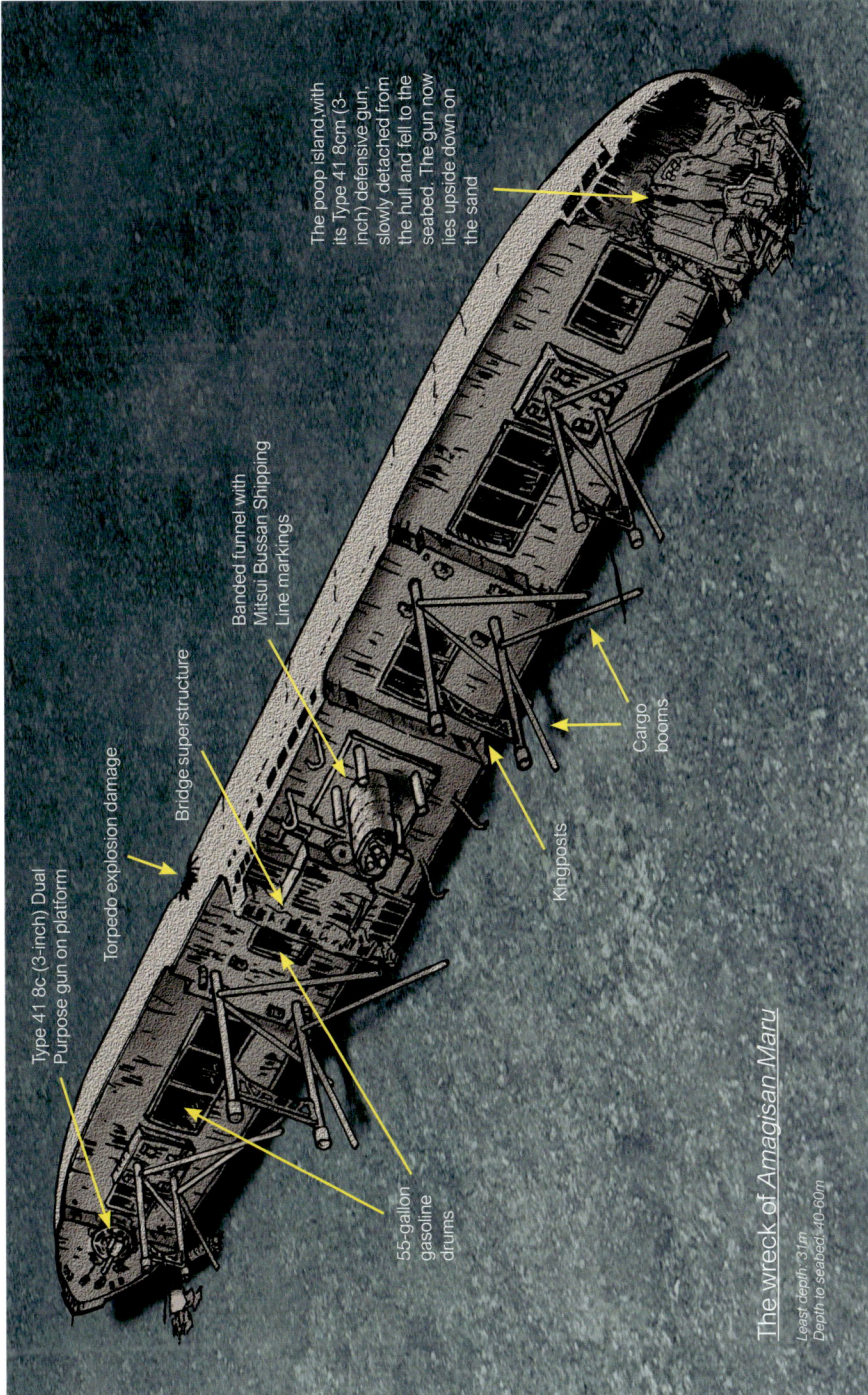

The poop island, with its Type 41 8cm (3-inch) defensive gun, slowly detached from the hull and fell to the seabed. The gun now lies upside down on the sand

Banded funnel with Mitsui Bussan Shipping Line markings

Bridge superstructure

Torpedo explosion damage

Type 41 8c (3-inch) Dual Purpose gun on platform

55-gallon gasoline drums

Kingposts

Cargo booms

The wreck of Amagisan Maru

Least depth: 31m
Depth to seabed: 40-60m

Artist's impression of the 7,600grt *Amagisan Maru*, which today lies on her port beam ends in 40-60 metres and is one of the largest in the lagoon.

Moving aft, there is a single deck drop from the fo'c'sle deck to the well deck, with two doors opening forward through the bulkhead into the fo'c'sle spaces. The hatches for Holds 1 & 2 in the well deck are separated by a masthouse - from which a goalpost pair of kingposts rise for cargo handling, with fixed ladder rungs running up each to a walkway between the kingposts, high up atop the cross bracing of the kingpost bridge. The foremast itself extends upwards, now at a 45° angle, from the bridge that connects the tops of the two kingposts.

Sturdy cargo winches are positioned on top of the masthouse, two forward and two abaft the kingposts. The cargo booms, that ran out forward and aft from the base of each kingpost, have swung over to port with the heel of the ship. They now extend out over the lower port side of the wreck and angle downwards to rest their ends on the seabed. A tanker truck, which would have been deck cargo, has fallen from the deck and now lies off the wreck on the seabed opposite the forward hold. One of the cargo handling booms rests on top of it. Hold No 1 still has all its hatch cover beams in place.

Moving aft, past the masthouse between Hold's 1 & 2, you arrive at the hatch for Hold No 2. All bar one of the hatch cover beams for this hold at the main deck have been removed for offloading cargo – or blown away by the explosion. Most of the lower tween deck beams are still in place, but several are dislodged and out of place.

Moving deep into Hold No 2 and passing through the tween deck hatch beams, hundreds of 55-gallon fuel drums begin to appear, along with aircraft wings (in the tween deck), propellers, aerial bombs, general spares and wooden planking. A 10-12 foot long minesweeping paravane, nose down, is suspended by its tail fins on the port side of the hatch coaming.

Continuing aft, the hatch for Hold No 3 is set a deck level higher on the shelter deck of the extended section of superstructure, immediately in front of the bridge. At the front of this shelter deck is a second goalpost pair of cross braced kingposts with winches and booms for cargo handling - the booms are again swung down to port. All the hatch cover beams for this hold are missing – no doubt blown away in the torpedo explosion.

Looking into this dark brooding hold from above, on the starboard side down far down below the original waterline, light blue daylight streams in through the hole in the starboard side shell plating made by the torpedo strike that set-in motion the chain of events that sent her to the bottom.

The torpedo hole is easily large enough to swim through into open water outside the ship - and evidence of the power of the explosion can be seen all around. Looking at the torpedo hole from outside, it is almost 10 metres in diameter with the surrounding shell plating blown inwards to make a concave depression in the hull that runs from virtually her keel halfway up the side of the ship. At the aft end of this hold, in the tween deck, a large damaged staff car can be found - along with more 55-gallon fuel drums, bicycles and wooden planking.

The composite bridge superstructure rises up for three further deck levels above the shelter deck extended section of superstructure. The wooden decking that once covered the roof of this superstructure has been burnt away in the wartime fires, to leave the metal skeleton of the structure open and exposed. The bridge superstructure extends to either side of the ship and has a walkway around its front with large rectangular openings, the steel frontage being dotted with portholes. On top of this superstructure stands the much smaller

Right: The banded smokestack of *Amagisan Maru* (Author)

Below: A diver enters the *Amagisan Maru* through the torpedo hole in the keel just forward of the bridge. (Author)

pilot house, which has a single large front facing rectangular window and an open doorway on the starboard side. The mess and radio room, which still holds two large radio sets, are located one deck level below the bridge. The galley at the rear of the superstructure has a large stove and is crammed with pots and pans.

Moving aft from the pilot house on the boat deck, atop the main superstructure and amidst a forest of forced draft ventilators, the large smokestack still rises up, banded by three large encircling rings – the markings of the Mitsui Bussan shipping line. Just in front of the smokestack is an empty AA gun platform – the gun itself has fallen from its mount to lie on the seabed to port. To either side of the boat deck lifeboat davits stand empty.

Abaft the smokestack, the engine room roof has a row of four skylights either side of the centre line, with forced draft ventilators dotted around it. At the aft end of the Boat Deck you are at a depth of about 40 metres. The superstructure here drops further down to shelter deck level where the hatch for Hold No 4 is set on an extended section of superstructure - that mirrors the set up in front of the bridge. A goalpost pair of kingposts, with an intricately cross braced bridge, stands at the aftmost edge of the shelter deck. The hatch cover beams for Hold No 4 are still in place.

Moving further aft your depth is now increasing steadily. The aft section of the ship here is a mirror image of the forward section with Hold No 4 set on the extended shelter deck of the main superstructure with its own goalpost pair of kingposts and cargo winches. Its cargo handling booms have also swung down to port on their mounts. Fixed steps lead down to the well deck on either side of the ship.

With the wreck lying on a slope with the bow up the hill in shallower water, as divers move aft from the shelter deck at Hold No 4 down to the well deck that houses Holds 5 & 6, the water gets markedly deeper. The hatch cover beams for Hold No 5 had been removed prior to the attack for offloading cargo – they are all neatly stacked on the deck on the starboard side of the hatch.

A mast house, from which the aftmost goalpost pair of kingposts rise up amidst a forest of forced draft ventilators, separates Hold No's 5&6 and has heavy duty cargo winches set fore and aft of the kingposts. Once again, the cargo handling booms have swung down to port towards the seabed.

At the very stern, abaft Hold No 6, there is a poop island, which holds the steering gear below deck. Set on top of this superstructure is an elevated circular gun platform with the same Type 41 8cm (3-inch) gun as at the bow. The aft part of the ship and the poop island was quite heavily damaged by bombing during the attack. Plating, spars and guardrails are deformed or bent out of shape. Although the defensive gun had remained on its circular platform atop the poop island since the war, in about 2013, gravity began to triumph over the decaying and weakened structure of the ship here. The uppermost starboard side of the deck finally detached from the starboard side hull of the ship and the whole poop island with gun on top began to peel away, taking the deck with it, the whole structure sagging progressively to the seabed. By 2020, the gun was lying upside down on the sand, largely obscured by the collapsed poop island.

Moving out over the starboard side of the ship, degaussing cables are still fixed in position running the whole length of the hull. Magnetic mines detect the increase in magnetic field when the steel of a passing ship concentrates the Earth's magnetic field above it – triggering them to explode. German magnetic mines had caused major shipping losses for Britain during the early days of WWII. To counter this, British Admiralty scientists developed systems that induced a small "N-pole up" magnetic field in ships - so that the net magnetic field was the same as the background. The Germans used the *Gauss* as the unit of the strength of the magnetic field in their mine trigger mechanism and hence the Admiralty scientists started to call the magnetic mines counter measure process *degaussing*. The Japanese adopted this invention and degaussing cables are seen on many of the Japanese ship in the Truk lagoon.

The fantail sweeps down towards the single screw and rudder at seabed level.

3. *Eisen No 761*
300-tonne IJN *Zatsueki-sen* Harbour Tug

West of Tonoas

Displacement:	300-tonne (N)
Dimensions:	121ft 5" (oa); beam of 23-ft; draught of 8-ft 1"
Launched:	1936-44
Sunk:	August 1945-1947
Cause of loss:	Surrendered to Allies at war's end – believed scuttled post war
Wreck location:	200 yards west of Tonoas
Depth to seabed:	16 metres.

Artist's impression of the 300-ton IJN tug *Eisen No 761*.

At the beginning of the Pacific war, Japan already had a large fleet of seagoing tugs – and this was soon greatly increased by the seizure of Allied Far-Eastern utility vessels. The Japanese classified their tugs in five broad categories, namely:

i.   EISEN (tugboats)
ii. EIRYO (tug, 'travel')
iii. EIKA (tug, 'cargo')
iv. EIKO (tug, 'alternate')
v.   EISAI (tug, 'ice breaker')

The Japanese developed a fleet of harbour tugs of varying tonnages from 400-tonne, to 300-tonne, 250-tonne, 150-tonne wooden tugs down to 100-tonne and small 20-tonne harbour tugs and lighters. But broadly, all Japanese tugs fall into the following range of characteristics:

TONNAGE: Average, 100-230 (gross); maximum, 450 (gross)
LENGTH:　Average, 75-110-ft; maximum 150-ft
SPEED:　　9-11 knots (average maximum)
DRIVE:　　Usually reciprocating engines. Newer vessels had diesel engines.

The IJN also developed a number of classes of fleet salvage and repair tugs, from larger sea-going 800-tonne Tategami-class fleet tugs, such as the present day Truk wreck *Ojima* (lost whilst assisting *Kikukawa Maru*) to the slightly smaller 600-tonne Hashima-class tug *Futagami* sunk after war's end off Dublon.

Eisen No 761 is one of some fifteen 300-tonne tugs built by an array of shipbuilders such as Fujinagata Ship Building Co. of Osaka, Hitachi of Kanagawa, Mitsubishi at Shimonoseki and Ujina at Hiroshima. There were minor builder's variations between the tugs constructed. Records and service history of these small vessels are incomplete.

The 300-tonne tugs were twin screw vessels, giving great manoeuvrability – and they were powered by two sets of vertical triple expansion engines that developed 800ihp, steam being provided by two boilers. They could make about 12 knots and were fitted with salvage pumps. They were unarmed.

At the end of the war there was a detailed study of Truk's defences that resulted in a voluminous document by the United States Pacific Fleet & Pacific Ocean Areas entitled *Field Survey of Japanese Defenses on Truk* (CINCPAC-CINCPOA Bulletin NO. 3-46 dated 15 March 1946). In this document, *Eisen No 761* and *Futagami* were listed as being located at Truk at the end of the war and surrendering to U.S. forces in August 1945. Both these vessels had been assigned to the Japanese naval base on Dublon during the war – and at war's end appear to have been sunk or scuttled just off the west side of Dublon, there is no damage to either.

The Wreck Today

Today the wreck of this 300-tonne harbour tug sits upright in just 16 metres of water only some 200 yards off the west side of Tonoas (Dublon) – there are some rusting landing craft nearby on the shore.

As with *Futagami* nearby, being so close to Tonoas, the visibility on this wreck is usually poor – a silty 5-10 metres. It is covered in a fine layer of silt that is easily stirred up. As a result, with so many other amazing wrecks to dive as the second dive of the day, the tug is only very infrequently dived.

The wheelhouse still holds the rudder stand with integral compass. On either side of the helm stands a small engine telegraph (one for either engine). The white porcelain faceplates of the telegraphs have black kanji engine command lettering.

At the back of the wheelhouse, there are two doorways, the port side opens to a small galley with wok stove whilst the starboard side door contains the head (toilet).

The engine room is tight to enter – but can with difficulty be accessed through an engine room roof skylight abaft the bridge, where the two triple expansion engines are located, the walls lined with pipes and gauges.

At the stern, both props are still in place.

4. *Eisen (unknown)*
Unidentified 300-tonne IJN *Zatsueki-sen*
Harbour Tug & floating electricity generator

West of Weno

Displacement:	300-tonne (N)
Dimensions:	94-ft 4" (oa); beam of 23-ft; draught of 8-ft 1".
Launched:	1936-1944
Sunk:	August 1945-1947 (assumed)
Cause of loss:	Believed surrendered to Allies at end of war and scuttled
Wreck location:	west of Weno
Depth to seabed:	30 metres.

A number of *Zatsueki-sen* Harbour tugs and floating electricity generators were built to order by Kawasaki in Kobe between 1936 and 1944 - and requisitioned by the Imperial Japanese Navy. They were small powerful vessels with one screw driven by two diesel engines that developed 700 SHP and gave a service speed of 12 knots. These tugs were unarmed and were fitted with one 400kw AC and one 130kw DC diesel generators and HP compressors.

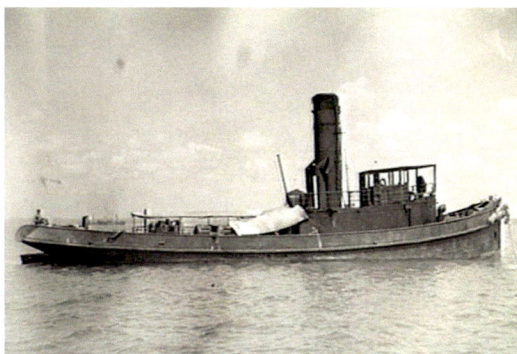

IJN harbour tug

An anchor windlass sat on the foredeck with a hatch nearby allowing access to storage compartments below in the forward part of the ship.

A tall deckhouse on two levels held the wheelhouse at its highest level - with smokestack and engine machinery spaces immediately abaft. The deckhouse stepped down behind the smokestack to the Boat Deck where engine room roof skylights were located. Abaft them, a large fixed tow hook was situated.

On the after deck, a heavy-duty tow windlass was situated on the centre line, with a thick curved steel stanchion (guide) that ran from one side of the ship to the other immediately aft of it. The wire from the tow hook passed underneath this guide to the stern of the ship – the guide was designed to stop the tow wire under tension from moving too far forward up the side of the tug and thus endangering it with a capsize. A strong samson post for securing tow ropes, and for mooring, was set on the centre line of the deck at the very stern.

Other than the tugs *Futagami* and *Eisen No 761*, no other fleet tugs are listed in United States Pacific Fleet & Pacific Ocean Areas *Field Survey of Japanese Defenses on Truk* (CINCPAC-CINCPOA Bulletin NO. 3-46 dated 15 March 1946). It is known however that two tugs of the 4th Naval Construction & Repair Department at Truk were assigned to Moen Island.

This IJN fleet tug is one of the most recent finds in the lagoon, being only recently located by Truk Stop Dive Center & Hotel in about 2018 - and they kindly took me on one of the first dives on it.

On this dive, we entered the tight engine room and captured on video the Maker's Plate on the switching panel. At the time of this book going to print, the tug's identity is still however unknown. Rather rudimentarily, I used a phone app to translate the old kanji script on the corroded maker's plate, which confirms that the maker is Kawasaki. A number is given on the plate, but the first numeral is corroded over but looks like a 3, followed clearly by '945'. This may be simply the maker's plate for the switching panel - or perhaps intriguingly it gives an ID of Eisen No 3945. I will check when I get back to Chuuk, as at the time of writing, I haven't yet been back to Chuuk since it was closed off to diver visitors in March 2020 as a result of the Covid crisis, and only reopening in late 2022.

Beneath the marking set out above, is another stamp – and after some kanji text, there is a space for 2 numbers: the first number is illegible, but the 2nd is '3'. After a short space there is another stamped section with '40' on it. So, the whole thing looks like:

3945
?3 40

If this tug hasn't been identified by my next visit, then I suspect that I will be heading into the engine room to have a better look around!

The wreck today

The wreck of this 300-tonne harbour tug lies not far offshore from the west side of Moen, north of the pier for Truk Stop Hotel & Dive Center. It sits perfectly upright in about 30 metres of water and is quite well settled into the silty seabed, which rises up to just 1-2 metres short of engulfing the stern. Being so close to Moen, the visibility has been a bit misty, or silty, on the days I have dived it – but still in the order of 10-15 metres or so. The wreck itself is layered with fine silt that is easily disturbed.

The vessel looks like your classic idea of a tug: short, squat and powerful. The bow is intact and strong, and a sturdy anchor windlass sits on the foredeck. Neither the anchors nor any chain from the anchor windlass are present – perhaps being easy to remove, and valuable, it was taken off before she was scuttled. There is no sign of any wartime damage on the hull that might have sunk her.

Abaft the anchor windlass, a hatch, open today, allowed access to storage spaces below deck. A coil of steel warp lies beside it. The tall wheelhouse then rises up two deck levels,

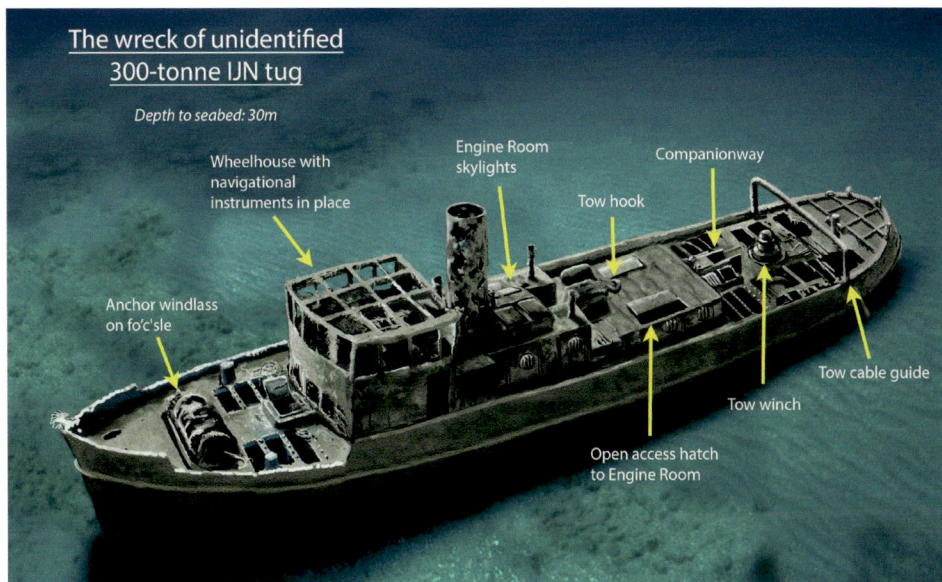

The wreck of unidentified 300-tonne IJN tug

Depth to seabed: 30m

Wheelhouse with navigational instruments in place

Engine Room skylights

Companionway

Tow hook

Anchor windlass on fo'c'sle

Tow cable guide

Tow winch

Open access hatch to Engine Room

Artist's impression of an unidentified 300-tonne IJN tug and floating electricity generator, sitting upright in about 30 metres of water west of Weno.

with three rotted rectangular openings at the lowest frontage and large rectangular windows ringing along the front and sides of the highest deck level, the navigating bridge. The window glass is long gone.

The wooden decking of the wheelhouse roof has rotted away to leave the lattice work of its structural frames and stringers exposed. Doors at either side of the rear bulkhead of the wheelhouse allow access – and across the port doorway lies what appears to be a searchlight or machine gun stand, that has fallen through the roof from above. Inside the wheelhouse, the telemotor still stands, with rudder direction indicator and the remnants of wooden spokes emanating in places from it. Nearby, the engine order telegraph and compass binnacle stand.

Between the smokestack and the aft bridge bulkhead, an access hatchway is open with the hatch flung back against the smokestack. The heavily corroded smokestack still stands upright with four engine room roof skylights in the closed position immediately abaft.

Moving aft, the deckhouse drops down to a single storey rectangular superstructure above the engine room, on the port side of which is an open access hatch through which a diver can fit with care on a single tank. It is a tight squeeze with a twin set and virtually impossible on a rebreather. A heavy-duty, hydraulicly dampened tow hook is located immediately beside the open port hatch, on the centre line.

Entering the engine room, it is possible to move over a grated catwalk and then descend down a stairwell between two large air blowers - down into the engine room proper. Here you can move along inside the ship between her two long diesel engines. Where the engines end, you arrive at an athwartships bulkhead which is literally covered in large switches and gauges

On the after deck of the 300-tonne salvage tug, a companionway staircase leads below (Author)

The robust stern of the 300-tonne tug is well settled into the silt. The guide stanchion for the tow wire runs across the beam of the ship with the tow windlass beneath in the middle, just forward. (Author)

for her role as floating electricity generator, able to supply electrical power to other ships that perhaps had no power of their own but required eg., light, or power for welding operations. To one side of the bulkhead is the corroded aluminium makers plate referred to above.

At the after end of this superstructure, the quarter deck has an open companionway access and a large heavy duty tow winch with the side-to-side guide stanchion just aft. The very stern is well settled into the silt and the rudder and prop are deeply buried.

5. *Fujikawa Maru*

Passenger/cargo vessel (1938)

Kokuki-Umpansen - Armed Aircraft Transport (1940)

IJN Auxiliary transport (1944)

U.S. Recognition Code: MKFKM

Fourth Fleet Anchorage

Tonnage:	6,800-grt
Dimensions:	436.4ft long; beam of 58.5ft; draught of 32.8ft.
Launched:	15 April 1938
Sunk:	17 February 1944
Cause of loss:	Torpedoed by TF 58 aircraft during Operation HAILSTONE
Wreck location:	Fourth Fleet Anchorage south of Eten Island
Depth to seabed:	Bow 30 metres. Stern 35 metres
Least depth:	10 metres to top of superstructure

The 6,800grt transport vessel *Fujikawa Maru* is perhaps the most famous and most dived shipwreck in the Truk lagoon. She is a big ship, sitting on her keel in relatively shallow clear water with her holds still part filled with wartime cargo.

Fujikawa Maru was designed as an 8-deck passenger-cargo vessel and was laid down on 20 October 1937 at the Mitsubishi Heavy Industries (Mitsubishi Jukogyo K.K.)

The 6,800grt passenger-cargo ship *Fujikawa Maru*, launched in 1938 and requisitioned by the IJN in 1940.

shipyard in Nagasaki for Toyo Kaiun K.K. Some six months later, she was named and launched on 15 April 1938 - and within two months of her launch, fitting out had been completed on 1 July 1938. The new ship was fitted with a single screw and her 2-stroke 6-cylinder diesel engines gave her a service speed of about 13 knots. She had six cavernous holds and carried a crew of 162.

The brand new *Fujikawa Maru* was registered in Tokyo and placed in service with her new owners, Toyo Kaiun K.K. on the Japan to North America run. After just a few months service she was chartered to Mitsui Bussan K.K. on routes to South America and India, carrying passengers both ways as well as taking raw silk, cotton, jute and flax back to Japan.

On 9 December 1940 (almost exactly one year before the attack on Pearl Harbor), *Fujikawa Maru* was one of 10 similar sized merchant ships requisitioned by the Imperial Japanese Navy as *Kokuki-Umpansen* – armed aircraft transports. She was moved to the port of Kobe where Kawasaki Heavy Industries began work on 18 December 1940 to convert her for her new role transporting disassembled and crated aircraft, spares and air personnel. Degaussing cables were fitted around the outside of her hull underneath the guard rail, to counter her magnetic signature, which might detonate any magnetic mines she passed close to.

Fujikawa Maru was armed at her bow and stern with old British 6-inch guns, salvaged from obsolete decommissioned cruisers of the Russo-Sino War of 1904-5. A bronze plate on the bow gun on the wreck today still clearly bears the legend specifying the gun as being a 6-inch, Breach Loading (BL) gun manufactured at Elswick Ordnance Co (EOC), in Britain in 1899.

EOC

6 In,. B.L.

No 12469

1899

The Elswick Ordnance works was a major British industrial maritime company based at Elswick, Newcastle upon Tyne that included shipyards for construction of both commercial ships and warships. The company sold guns and ships to many other countries, including Japan - who had defeated Russia in 1905 using Elswick made guns on Elswick built warships.

Kawasaki Heavy Industries had completed the conversion works by 20 January 1941 and on 21 March 1941, the newly converted aircraft transport *Fujikawa Maru* left Japan for the central east China coast where she served as part of the 12th Seaplane Tender Division until the latter part of the year, when she was sent to Saigon in Indochina. There, on 8 December 1941 at the outbreak of war in the Pacific, she was assigned to the 22nd Naval Air Flotilla of the 11th Air Fleet for Operation E – the Invasion of Malaya.

On 23 December 1941, *Fujikawa Maru* moved south from Indochina to Kota Bharu, one of the Malayan invasion beaches where Japanese troops had landed a few weeks earlier on 8 December. RAF Kota Bahru was a Royal Air Force airfield that was the first to be occupied by Japanese troops in December 1941, so it is likely she was carrying airfield materials and possibly crated aircraft for offloading to the captured British airfield and assembly. She arrived at Kota Bahru on 27 December 1941 and after offloading was complete, she returned to Camranh Bay, Indochina from where she departed on 30 January 1942 with 22nd Naval Air Flotilla personnel and construction materials bound for Kuching, Borneo.

Throughout 1942 she was heavily involved ferrying personnel, aircraft and spares around Japanese holdings in Indochina, Borneo, Saigon, Bangkok, Palau, Truk and Rabaul - returning to Japan on many occasions to collect more vital aircraft and spares.

From December 1942 until August 1943, she was reassigned directly to the 11th Air Fleet and was busy delivering aircraft, stores and spares to Japan's scattered island bases such as Kwajalein, Jaluit and Taroa in the Marshalls, Tarawa in the Gilberts, and Truk and Nauru in Micronesia, returning often to Japan to pick up more aircraft cargo and aviation gasoline. On 10 June 1943 she was attacked by the submarine USS *Flying Fish* (SS-229), south southeast of the Bonin Islands. The American submarine fired three torpedoes at *Fujikawa Maru,* but the attack was unsuccessful.

On 11 September 1943, she departed Kwajalein in convoy with the cargo ships *Chihaya Maru* and *Katori Maru* and the 15,450-ton fleet oiler *Shiretoko,* escorted by the subchaser *CH-31,* the auxiliary subchaser *Cha-46* and a patrol boat. In the early hours of 12 September 1943, *Fujikawa Maru* was hit by a torpedo from the American submarine *Permit* (SS-178) north east of Truk, whilst the valuable oiler *Shiretoko* was hit twice. The light cruiser *Naka* was despatched from Truk to assist the stricken ships. Despite significant damage, *Fujikawa Maru* was able to limp to Truk for repair before returning safely to Kwajalein on 15 September 1943.

On 4 December 1943, American naval aircraft from the Task Force 50 fleet carriers *Yorktown* and *Lexington* and the light carrier *Independence* attacked Kwajalein and Wotje Atolls. *Fujikawa Maru* was damaged, as were the light cruisers *Nagara* and *Isuzu* – and many transport ships were sunk or damaged in the attack.

On 24 December 1943, the damaged *Fujikawa Maru* departed Kwajalein under tow by *Mikage Maru No 18,* in an escorted convoy. The flotilla arrived at Truk on 31 December where *Fujikawa Maru* was anchored in the Repair Anchorage near to the IJN Repair Ship *Akashi.* On 1 January 1944, on completion of the repairs, *Fujikawa Maru* was re-rated as an auxiliary transport and reassigned to the Navy Supply Force, attached to the Maizuru Naval Station.

In early February 1944, *Fujikawa Maru* arrived once again at Truk, this time her holds were filled with a cargo of disassembled Nakajima B6N torpedo bombers (Allied reporting name Jill), single seat A6M Zero aircraft bodies, spare wings, blades, engine aircraft cowlings, radial aircraft engines, aircraft wheels, engine manifolds and other spare parts, along with aviation gasoline in 55-gallon drums and 3-inch artillery shells, AA ammunition and aircraft bombs. She anchored in the Fourth Fleet Anchorage south of the small airfield of Eten Island - to the south of Dublon Island in anticipation of offloading her aircraft there.

Two days before DOG-DAY-MINUS-ONE, around 14 February, as the 9 carriers of Task Force 58, screened by 6 battleships, 10 cruisers and 28 destroyers were closing on Truk, crew on *Fujikawa Maru* started carefully unloading her disassembled B6N Jill bombers to Eten airfield, where technicians would assemble them. The B6N Jill carried a crew of three, pilot, navigator/bombardier and radio operator/gunner and was the standard IJN carrier torpedo bomber for anti-ship operations.

A number of disassembled aircraft had already been offloaded to Eten airfield from two other aircraft transports in the preceding days and airfield mechanics and technicians ashore were busily trying to assemble the aircraft as soon as they were offloaded. The reconstructed aircraft however were not yet operational and were closely parked on Eten airfield apron.

By the morning of 17 February, *Fujikawa Maru* had offloaded about thirty disassembled B6N Jill bombers from her holds – but many others still remained aboard waiting their turn to be offloaded. Complete aircraft fuselages, detached wings and engines crowded her holds - all ready for delivery ashore and assembly.

American Task Force 58 planners had identified the aircraft carrier shaped Eten Island airfield as one of the primary targets for Operation HAILSTONE. Anchored closeby, *Fujikawa Maru* was thus right in the thick of the action on the first day of the raids, 17 February, as the initial waves of U.S. aircraft bombed and strafed the airfield just after dawn.

Later in the day, Strike 3E launched after 1300 from the Task Group 58.3 carriers *Bunker Hill* and *Monterey*. Approximately one hour later, the Strike 3E aircraft were over Truk and sweeping towards Eten airfield to begin their attack. At 1430, *Fujikawa Maru* was targeted and with her antiquated 6-inch bow and stern guns and poor AA defences, she was virtually defenceless. Two TBF Avenger torpedo bombers came in low and slow, escorted by Hellcats who strafed to suppress shipborne AA fire.

Of the two aerial torpedoes launched, one torpedo failed to run true. It missed the ship and ran onto the nearby shelving reef, where it failed to explode. The second torpedo however struck *Fujikawa Maru* just abaft the amidships composite superstructure on the starboard side, tearing a triangular shaped hole in her shell plating in the vicinity of her engine compartments before exploding. With her hull blasted open to the sea, water poured into her cavernous engine room compartments. Still at anchor, she started to list to starboard and settle slowly by the stern – giving time for her crew to abandon ship safely. There were no casualties.

Fujikawa Maru sank to the bottom of the lagoon – with many of her aircraft and spare parts still inside her. She came to rest on an even keel with the topmost 15-25 feet of her two masts sticking out of the water. Sometime after the war, the uppermost parts of the masts were removed to reduce the danger to shipping.

The Wreck today

Today the wreck of *Fujikawa Maru* sits upright on her keel with a slight list to starboard – on a gentle underwater slope, south of Eten Island. Her bow is in 30 metres whilst her stern rests in 35 metres.

A quick glance at the archive images of Eten Island might suggest to you that it looks very much like the outline of an aircraft carrier. Eten was in fact originally a small island with a higher central hill. During 1941, the Japanese used forced labour to begin the creation of an aircraft carrier shaped island - to create an unsinkable aircraft carrier. Rubble and stone was quarried from the central hill and used to create a carrier shaped rubble stone seawall with a docking pier measuring 95 feet by 30 feet, which had a boom rigged crane.

Once the carrier shaped island had been formed, infilled and levelled, a single runway running the length of the island, and measuring 3,440 feet long by 270 feet wide, was created and surfaced with 1.5-inch of concrete for all weather use. The island HQ was situated to the south east of the runway along with repair facilities, living quarters for 1,200 personnel, power plant, radio and the air traffic control tower. 40 fighter revetments and 7 larger bomber revetments were set alongside the runway, along the remaining hillside.

Japan had many island airfields scattered on atolls throughout her South Seas holdings from which land-based aircraft operated in an interlocking grid like system, each able to support and reinforce others. But as the Allies drove westward, bypassing or neutralizing

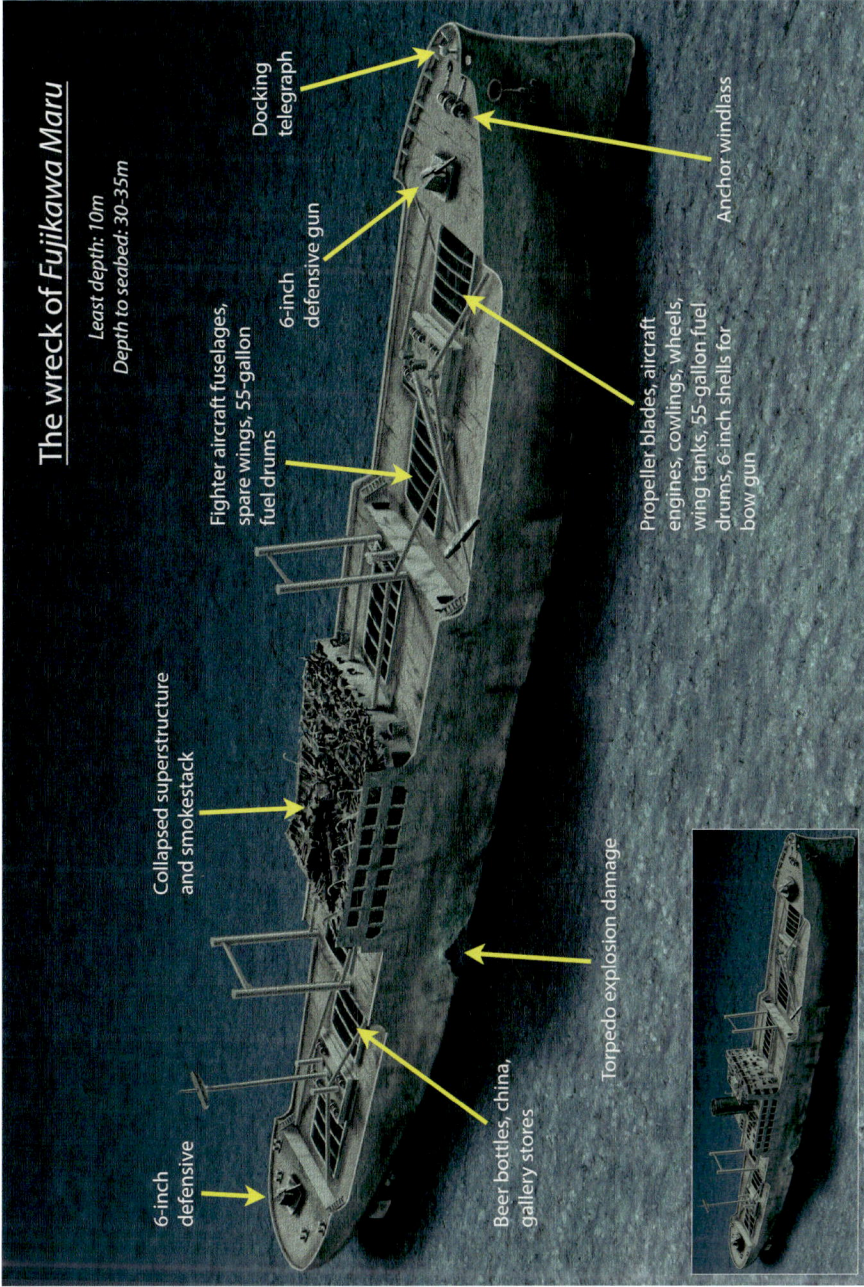

The wreck of Fujikawa Maru

Least depth: 10m
Depth to seabed: 30–35m

Docking telegraph

Anchor windlass

Fighter aircraft fuselages, spare wings, 55-gallon fuel drums

6-inch defensive gun

Propeller blades, aircraft engines, cowlings, wheels, wing tanks, 55-gallon fuel drums, 6-inch shells for bow gun

Collapsed superstructure and smokestack

6-inch defensive

Beer bottles, china, gallery stores

Torpedo explosion damage

Artist's impression of the wreck of *Fujikawa Maru*, sitting upright in 35 metres of water south west of Eten Island.

Inset: The wreck of *Fujikawa Maru* prior to the collapse of her upper bridge and smokestack in about 2013.

The bow of *Fujikawa Maru* with the docking telegraph near the prow and the 6-inch bow gun aft. (Courtesy Ewan Rowell)

The 6-inch B.L gun with splinter shield sits atop the fo'c'sle, and is swung out to starboard (Courtesy Ewan Rowell)

The docking telegraph at the bow of *Fujikawa Maru* (Author)

these airfields, the problem with having unsinkable island aircraft carriers became clear. They could not move and were left to the rear.

With a beam of almost 60 feet, the 437-feet long wreck of *Fujikawa Maru*, feels like a massive ship when you dive it. Her six cavernous holds are large open spaces that drop down through several deck levels – they are still filled with much of her war cargo - aircraft fuselages, engines, wings, ammunition and stacks of 55-gallon fuel drums. She is a fascinating wreck dive for all levels of divers – from novice scuba divers who can visit her shallowest bridge superstructure in just over 10 metres, to technical divers who can make long penetrations and lengthy dives. She is very much a standout, favourite dive with visiting divers.

Bow docking telegraph of
Fujikawa Maru with commands
in English. (Author)

Fujikawa Maru was a three-island vessel - that is, she had a raised fo'c'sle at the bow, a tall central composite superstructure holding the bridge, with the smokestack directly abaft. Her engine room compartments were situated below, flanked on either side of the fireproof engine room casing with passenger accommodation. At the stern was her poop island, which held her steering gear below.

On the fo'c'sle at the bow, her 6-inch BL (Breach Loading) gun, cannibalised from an old cruiser from the WWI era, still sits pointing slightly upwards and trained to starboard, frozen in time at the moment of her demise during Operation HAILSTONE in February 1944. The gun's bronze maker's plate is still clearly stamped with the gun details and the date of manufacture, 1899. It is one of the must-see features of this wreck. Nearby, coral covered boxes of ready use ammunition sit behind the gun. The gun may well have been firing as she was attacked - but an antique single shot 50-year old 6-inch gun would have been of little use against the fast, modern American aircraft.

Forward of the bow gun platform on the fo'c'sle deck sits a large anchor windlass from which her two anchor chains run out to their hawse pipes, one on either side of the hull. She was anchored with her port anchor when she was attacked - and the chain drops down to the seabed from its hawse pipe - and then runs out along the seabed. Her starboard anchor hangs limply from its hawse pipe.

Just forward of the anchor windlass, right up at the very bow, a docking telegraph stands upright, firmly bolted to the deck on the centreline of the ship. The skipper on the bridge could direct anchor handling operations by using a bridge telegraph to send anchor handling commands to this bow telegraph - such as instructing crew to drop or weigh anchor. The bridge DOCKING commands on the telegraph face are in English, such as ANCHOR – and the pointer is set at MAKE FAST. The metal face of the telegraph is stamped:

MANUFACTURED BY

OSAKA NUNOTANI SEISAKUSHO

HYOGOKEN JAPAN

Spent (fired) 6-inch shell casings for the bow gun are scattered around the fo'c'sle deck – evidence that the bow gun was firing during the attack. The steel fo'c'sle deck and equipment

The machine room, deep inside the Fujikawa Maru (Author)

being in relatively shallow water are heavily covered in abundant coral heads – except for the deck around the brass docking telegraph, which is completely clean. Corals hate the taste of copper and brass and there is a perimeter, distasteful to coral, around where the telegraph is bolted to the deck, past which the corals won't encroach.

Two aft facing entrances are set in the athwartships fo'c'sle bulkhead below that give access from the well deck into the fo'c'sle compartments. Inside, the original dividing walls that separated the fo'c'sle into separate rooms, such as the lamp room, crew spaces etc., have all rotted away to leave one common space, which is strewn with warps of steel cable, 55-gallon fuel drums - and a spare propeller blade, propped upright against a wall.

The foremast, which rose up from the mast house between the hatches for Hold No's 1 & 2, lies fallen to the starboard side of the deck. Heavy-duty cargo booms extend out from short kingposts, on either side of the foremast, and are swung over to starboard – evidence that she listed to starboard, the side she was torpedoed, as she sank. The masthouse is a large open space strewn with objects – and can be entered in a number of places.

Hold No 1 still has its hatch cover beams in place. This hold can be entered by dropping in between the hatch cover beams to the tween deck, which is the deck immediately below the weather deck. Divers can then drop through the tween deck hatch cover beams to reach the bottom of the hold below. Here can be found heavy machine guns and ammunition for aircraft, 55-gallon fuel drums, radial aircraft engines, aircraft wheels, wings, propellers and manifolds, stacks of spare propeller blades, rounded sleek aircraft engine cowlings and wing tanks. A number of 6-inch shells for the bow gun are stored

Detail of the forward section of *Fujikawa Maru*

vertically here - and closeby are smaller 3-inch shells and AA ammunition. Possibly the most famous outboard motor in the Pacific has been placed on top of a large square tank – you'll understand what I mean when you see it! It was there in 1990 when I first visited this wreck. The sides of the hold show the web frames, which sweep together towards the bow itself.

Hold No 1 connects to Hold No 2 at tween deck level and Hold No 2 also has its hatch cover beams in place at both deck levels. The tween deck holds some more 55-gallon fuel drums and aircraft wing tanks. Dropping through the hatch cover beams of the tween deck level to the bottom of the hold reveals four single seat aircraft fuselages, spare wings and more 55-gallon fuel drums.

Exiting Hold No 2, and moving aft towards the bridge, two fixed sets of steps, one either side of the well deck, lead up to the shelter deck of the extended section of superstructure in front of the bridge. The hatch for Hold No 3 is located here and still has its hatch cover beams in situ.

A goalpost pair of kingposts are set on the forward leading edge of the shelter deck for cargo handling. Large heavy-duty cargo booms run aft from the base of either kingpost to cradles on the front of the bridge superstructure. Dotted around the shelter deck hatch are forced draft ventilators, designed to force fresh air down to the below deck spaces as the ship moves, particularly important for spaces such as the engine room.

The central composite superstructure originally rose up for several deck levels with large rectangular windows and an open navigating bridge at the top. In previous years, the top levels of the bridge superstructure were intact, and the smokestack stood tall. No sooner had the 1st edition of this book been published in 2014, when the upper levels and the smokestack collapsed violently. A rumour went around that this was caused by local dynamite fishing. Whereas previously you could easily enter the navigating bridge and drop down to the deck level below which held the radio room, officer's quarters and pharmacy, the whole upper area today is a collapsed mess.

A diver enters the ship through the triangular torpedo impact hole in the starboard beam. (Courtesy Ewan Rowell)

Entering the back of the lower bridge superstructure on the port side through an open doorway, divers can swim carefully over a large pile of hundreds of sake and beer bottles into the large open space of the tween deck of Hold No 4 - on the aft section of the ship on an extended section of superstructure that mirrors the set-up of the foreship. Most of the Japanese ships at Truk have large quantities of beer and sake bottles in them, navy and army personnel each getting 1-2 a day to ease the rigours of shipboard life in the tropical climate. The centre of Hold No 4 is open and divers can drop down to the

Detail of the aft section of *Fujikawa Maru*

bottom of the hold, which is largely empty – but where the triangular burst in the starboard shell plating, now at seabed level, caused by the entry of the torpedo can be seen. The ship's hull plates are torn open and bent inwards by the torpedo impact.

Adjacent to Hold No 4 at tween deck level, a hatch with a fixed ladder leads down to the engine room, which takes up the lower aft portion of the superstructure. Inside the cavernous engine room, the large 6-cylinder diesel engine can be found - running fore and aft on the centre line of the vessel. Along the port side of the engine room is a well-equipped workshop with a spares area, an air compressor located in the forward section and a workbench with its drawers pulled open and vice clamps. Wall shelves at the forward end hold spares such as cage lamps, fan blades and light bulbs.

A stairway on the starboard side leads down to the lower engine room spaces where more spares are mounted on the walls along with many control gauges - each with a small bronze plaque with a kanji inscription beneath it. Narrow catwalk gratings lead through the lower engine room spaces in amongst intricate machinery and pipework.

Either side of the composite superstructure, passenger cabins flank the fireproof engine casing and lead off promenade deck walkways that allowed passage fore and aft along either side of the superstructure. Doorways allow access from the promenade deck walkway into the passenger accommodation, each outboard cabin having its own porthole. On the port side, the crew heads can be found with deep white tiled baths and a row of white wash hand basins, visible from the walkway through an open doorway and large square windows.

Mirroring the layout of the forepart of the ship, the extended section of shelter deck superstructure housing Hold No 4 has a goalpost pair of kingposts and derricks for cargo handling.

Moving further aft there is a drop down from the shelter deck to the aft well deck where the hatches for Hold No's 5 & 6 are set. The mainmast rose up from a mast house in between the hatches but has been shortened to reduce the danger to shipping - the topmost part now lies fallen to starboard.

The rudder and prop of *Fujikawa Maru* (Courtesy Ewan Rowell)

Hold No's 5& 6 are largely empty - the hatch cover beams are not in place and the cargo has been removed. The port and starboard sides of Hold 5 still however hold galley stores, beer bottles, china, mess kits, pots and pans.

Along the starboard side of the hull is a large, long docking strake, the docking strake on the port side is much shorter and is only 3-4 metres long.

At the very stern, as at the bow, an antiquated British-made 6-inch BL defensive gun is set on its firing platform on top of the poop island deckhouse, with its barrel pointed out slightly towards starboard, like the bow gun. This is perhaps physical evidence of the direction of the last attack before her eventual sinking – like the torpedo damage. Shells for the 6-inch gun are stored beneath.

Directly underneath the aft gun platform, the stern castle holds the steering gear and auxiliary steering equipment with a copper compass binnacle with deviation balls. The rudder stand is nearby, the wheel now rotted away and missing. If the ability to navigate the ship from the bridge was lost, then it was possible to navigate the ship from here at the stern. Chains could be shackled in for direct manual turning of the rudder directly below.

In similar fashion to the bow, where a docking telegraph stands near the stem, here at the very stern there are two deck mounted docking telegraphs.

6. *Fujisan Maru*
Merchant tanker (1931)
Yusosen - Converted Merchant Transport (Oil Supply) (1941)
U.S. Recognition Code: MKMF

Fourth Fleet Anchorage

Tonnage:	9,517-grt
Dimensions:	493.4-ft long; beam of 65-ft; draught of 37-ft.
Launched:	31 May 1931
Sunk:	18 February 1944
Cause of loss:	Bombed by TF 58 aircraft during Operation HAILSTONE
Wreck location:	Fourth Fleet Anchorage between Weno and Tonoas
Depth to seabed:	58 metres – bow.
	50+ metres - stern
Least Depth:	38 metres to bridge superstructure.

The 9,517grt merchant tanker *Fujisan Maru* was launched in 1931, and requisitioned by the IJN in 1941.

The merchant tanker *Fujisan Maru* was laid down on 28 August 1930 by shipbuilders Harima Shipbuilding & Engineering Co. Ltd in Harima, in the south of Honshū, Japan, for the tanker fleet of Iino Shoji Kisen Kaisha of Fuchu. She was named and launched for fitting out less than a year later on 31 May 1931. She was completed three months later on 27 August 1931.

This large vessel was powered by a 2-stoke 7-cylinder diesel engine that developed 1,857 NHP and allowed her single screw to give her an impressive service speed of 16 knots when laden with a cargo of up to 12,000 tons of fuel. Unladen, she could make 19 knots – fast for the day.

The background to her construction springs from a decision in 1929 by the Imperial Japanese Navy that IJN warships would fuel only with heavy oil. The IJN wanted large high-speed oilers – because the existing Notoro-class and Ondo-class oilers could only make 12 knots. Being that slow, they were unable to operate with the new breeds of fast IJN fleet carriers such as the 32-knot *Akagi* commissioned in 1927 and the 28-knot *Kaga,* commissioned in November 1929.

Although in the fragile peace of the early 1930's, the new ships would be constructed ostensibly as merchant tankers, the IJN paid a grant towards their construction. The grant enabled the builders to meet IJN design requirements on speed, cargo carrying ability etc. that would give the new tankers the size and performance needed to operate with the fleet as oilers in time of war.

Whereas merchant tankers load oil cargo at one port and transport it to another port for offloading, *oilers* are simply tankers which are equipped to replenish other vessels at sea - with tall Replenishment-At-Sea (RAS) masts or tripods, high pressure pumps, booms and fuel hoses capable of reaching another ship steaming parallel nearby.

Two marine transportation companies would construct the new merchant tankers in a succession of evolutionary classes that began in 1931 with the 9,849-ton *Teiyō Maru*, which could make 17.5-knots, and the 9,517-ton 19-knot *Fujisan Maru*. The IJN was satisfied with these two initial ships and went on to order the first two production Tōa Maru-class tankers, which launched from the Kawasaki Dockyard in Kobe in 1934.

The second production model Tatekawa-class tankers were built to the same basic hull design as the Tōa Maru-class - but had individual design differences, such as the removal of dry cargo holds on some. The famous Truk shipwreck *Sinkoku Maru* is one of this class. The Tatekawa-class was followed by the Nisshō Maru-class, the Kuroshio-class and the Akatsuki-class. In all, 17 such tankers would be built to IJN design requirements during the 1930's, all capable of conversion to oilers.

The tankers of the early part of the 20th century were of relatively simple construction – being basically a long steel box subdivided into a series of compartments and spaces. The forward spaces were designed to carry water and dry cargo such as oil in drums. The after spaces held water, bunker fuel, cargo pumps and the ship's engines. Between these two end spaces, the rest of the tanker was divided on a gridiron plan into cargo compartments or tanks. This extensive subdivision, with sometimes as many as 33 compartments, gave tankers exceptional strength and stability. The war years showed that tankers could stay afloat despite several breaches of the hull beneath the water line.

In hot weather, the oil cargo in a tanker expands and in cold weather it contracts. If the ship's tanks were completely sealed this expansion and contraction of the cargo would create a vacuum and allow dangerous internal pressures to build up. To let the cargo breathe, small pipes ran from the top of each tank to the ship's masts – running up to flameproof venting outlets safely high above the deck and any possible causes of ignition. At the bottom of the cargo tanks, a system of heating coils was installed through which steam was passed if heavy grade oil was being carried which required heating to make it viscous enough to be pumped.

Each cargo tank could be filled and emptied independently of the others so that different types of oil could be loaded into separate tanks and discharged without being cross contaminated. Numerous valves linked each cargo tank to a system of pipelines inside the ship that led to the ship's pumps. Another set of pipelines led up from the pumps on to the tanker's deck where they were conveniently located for connecting to shore pipelines for loading and discharging.

Pumps are the beating heart of a tanker. Pumps bring on the oil, pumps force it off and pumps bring ballast aboard. The pumps are controlled by old fashioned circular spin valves in a Control Room, where the pumpman was in charge of balancing the ship when it carried oil and maintaining the same balance with water filling drained tanks.

The Pump Control Room was housed deep inside the ship with a vertical stairwell leading up to a small deckhouse on the weather deck. There could be several control rooms, one for the foreship usually set on the foredeck just in front of the bridge superstructure, and another for the aft ship tanks. The 'pumpman' had to control the flow of oil from the pump room, and then physically ascend the staircase, often several decks, to then carefully measure tank depths from topside. The ship's pumps were primarily used for pumping the cargo out of the ship to shore storage tanks - and for pumping ballast water in or out of the ship. Shore pumps were used for pumping the cargo aboard from the land.

The deck of a tanker was a continuous weather deck only penetrated by small raised cargo hatches, one for each tank, which were fitted with watertight steel lids – and kept dogged down and sealed when the ship was loaded.

Rising above the weather deck were three superstructures – the fo'c'sle, the bridge superstructure just forward of amidships, and the poop island or stern deckhouse.

The fo'c'sle spaces were used to store ship's equipment, such as the chain locker, the lamp room etc. The amidships superstructure held the command bridge, chart room, radio room, storerooms and officer's accommodation. The stern deckhouse held the rest of the ship's company, the mess room, galley, refrigerated space and the steering gear with the quadrant that turned the rudder. The ship's machinery, boilers, engine, condensers, pumps etc. would be situated at the stern so that the prop shaft, which ran aft from the crank shaft at the engine, did not have to pass through tanks etc. as it would if the engine was situated amidships.

A fully laden tanker would lie deep in the water and in rough seas, the weather deck was continuously swept by seas. The tanker would thus become a three-island ship with only its three superstructures visible from any distance. To allow crew to pass in safety from each of the three islands when decks could be awash, an elevated catwalk walkway called a *flying bridge* ran from the fo'c'sle to the bridge - and then aft to the poop island, connecting all three superstructures.

After joining Iino Shoji's tanker fleet on completion of her construction, *Fujisan Maru* set off on her maiden voyage a month later in September 1931 transporting heavy oil from Sakhalin to Tokuyama in Japan. She then went to work transporting crude oil on Iino Shoji's North America to Japan oil transport service, making eight voyages to America to collect oil cargo, four for the Imperial Japanese Navy. With only scarce raw materials and natural resources of her own, Japan desperately needed oil and in the 1930's largely depended on American exports of oil and iron. Throughout the 1930's, *Fujisan Maru* made on average 8-10 regular passages each year to America to collect oil – mostly destined for the Imperial Japanese Navy.

On 22 November 1941, just a few weeks before the famous attack on Pearl Harbor, the IJN requisitioned *Fujisan Maru* as a Converted Merchant Transport (Oil Supply). Work to convert her for war began on 2 December 1941, just days before Pearl Harbor. Two 120-mm (4.7-inch) High Angle (HA) guns were fitted, one at the bow and one at the stern along with two 25mm AA auto cannons, depth charge rails and a passive sonar hydrophone.

Fujisan Maru was soon in operation, as she replenished submarines involved in Operation Z, the *Kidō Butai* fast carrier attack on Pearl Harbor. She then returned to Kure in Japan, where her conversion work was completed on 24 December 1941.

On 5 February 1942 she departed Kure bound for Palau with a cargo of oil. Once there she refueled submarines *I-1, I-2* and *I-3*, before returning to Kure. In March 1942, she was attached to the Sixth Fleet (Submarines), tasked with supplying bunker oil.

In May 1942, the Japanese prepared to launch their complicated Operation MI, in which some 350 warships of all types, and more than 1,000 aircraft, would be deployed in an attempt to lure the three remaining U.S. carriers in the Pacific into a trap off Midway - where the Japanese intended to annihilate them.

The Midway invasion plan called for landings by the Imperial Japanese Army far to the north on the Aleutian Islands, the long arc of islands that stretches out from Alaska, on the western U.S. coast, towards Japan. The Aleutian Islands of Attu and Kiska would be invaded and seized, the invasion ships and troops being supported by a powerful Japanese Northern Area Force of heavy warships, carriers and destroyers, which would be fuelled by the oilers *Fujisan Maru* and *Nissan Maru*.

Although the Japanese landings on Attu and Kiska were successful, as history bears witness, U.S. analysts had broken some of the Japanese codes and were able to establish the date and approximate time of the main attack on Midway. Instead of languishing far to the rear in Pearl Harbor, the three remaining U.S. carriers moved in advance to a holding position just to the north east of Midway, and comprehensively defeated the far stronger Japanese force in the Battle of Midway from 4-7 June 1942 in which the four Japanese carriers, *Akagi, Kaga, Sōryū* and *Hiryū* (all part of the *Kidō Butai* six-carrier force that had attacked Pearl Harbor six months earlier) were sunk.

Whilst still in the Aleutians, on 3 July 1942, American B-24 Liberator and B-17 Flying Fortress bombers carried out a bombing raid on Agattu Island harbour where *Fujisan Maru* was at anchor. She escaped unscathed - but departed the Aleutians the same day. She arrived at Ominato in northern Honshū on 13 July 1942.

With landings by US forces on Guadalcanal and Tulagi in the Solomon Islands chain beginning on 7 August 1942, on 20 August 1942, *Fujisan Maru* was reassigned to the IJN Combined Fleet and departed Japan for Rabaul on 25 August 1942, escorted by the destroyer *Hatsuharu*. From Rabaul she was able to refuel warships involved in Operation KS, the reinforcement of Guadalcanal in September 1942.

On 10 December 1942, *Fujisan Maru* and *Toa Maru* were attacked at Shortland Island in the Solomon Islands to the east of Papua New Guinea, by eleven American B-17 bombers, escorted by fighters. A bomb from one B-17 hit her aft - and set her on fire. The fires were contained and then extinguished, and she was able to transfer her cargo of oil in the Shortlands to the oiler *Toa Maru* - before moving to Rabaul for temporary repair. She thereafter returned to Yokohama, Japan in January 1943 to be dry-docked for permanent repair.

Repairs completed, she returned to service 28 March 1943 - and was soon fully employed collecting oil at Balikpapan and delivering it throughout the summer to Palembang, Takao, Singapore and Manila. From July 1943 she carried oil to fuel warships in more advanced garrisons at Palau, Truk, Jaluit, Kwajalein and Saipan.

On 29 December 1943, *Fujisan Maru*, along with the oilers *Akebono Maru* and *Sinkoku Maru* and escorts, set off from Balikpapan via Palau for Truk. The convoy arrived at Palau on 4 January 1944 - and departed the following day for Truk escorted by the destroyers *Uzuki* and *Tachikaze*. On 10 January 1944, the convoy entered the Truk lagoon and *Fujisan Maru* transferred some 1,500 tons of fuel the same day to the heavy cruiser *Tone*.

Fujisan Maru departed Truk on 13 January 1944 to load oil at Tarakan, Borneo and from there moved to Balikpapan before setting off once again with precious fuel for the IJN warships that were now effectively holed up at Truk. She arrived at Truk on 16 January 1944 and began transferring her oil. On 19 January 1944, she departed Truk once again in an escorted convoy with the oiler *Sinkoku Maru* - bound for the refineries at Tarakan, Borneo before moving on to Balikpapan.

Fujisan Maru departed Balikpapan on 3 February 1944 for Truk in convoy with *Sinkoku Maru*, and the requisitioned Converted Auxiliary Transport ship *Amagisan Maru*, which was carrying aviation gasoline in hundreds of 55-gallon drums in her holds. The convoy was escorted by the destroyers *Shigure*, *Harusame* and *Oite* and put in at Ulithi Atoll en route to offload some fuel before departing Ulithi on 11 February 1944 for Truk.

The convoy passed through the Truk atoll barrier reef and entered the lagoon on 14 February 1944. *Fujisan Maru* moored just off the fuel pier on the south shore of Dublon Island where offloading of her precious cargo of heavy oil immediately began.

Just two days later, on 16 February 1944, Task Force 58 completed its long clandestine approach and arrived on station, 90 miles off Truk, in preparation for the commencement of Operation HAILSTONE, before dawn the next morning.

The requisitioned tanker *Fujisan Maru* was moored at the Dublon fuel dock as Operation HAILSTONE began on 17 February 1944. She is empty and trimmed up at the bow. (National Archives)

By dawn on the morning of 17 February, *Fujisan Maru* had completed offloading her cargo, and was weighing anchor and beginning to get under way just as Strike 2B aircraft from *Intrepid* swept in to attack the Dublon seaplane base and Eten Island airfield installations. *Fujisan Maru* recovered her anchor and then working up speed, made for North Pass out of the lagoon. It was almost 20 miles distant - but at her top unladen speed of 19 knots she would be there in just over an hour.

Just as *Fujisan Maru* started to move through North Pass, Strike 3B dive-bombers from the carrier *Bunker Hill* attacked her – and she was struck by a single 1,000-lb bomb, which caused a fire to break out. Despite the vulnerability of her predicament at this time, luck was with her - as the tasking for all the U.S. Strike Groups was to attack the more important IJN warships grouped northwest of North Pass. The U.S. aircraft did not press home their attack on *Fujisan Maru*.

Seeing the concentration of U.S. aircraft attacking the Japanese warships ahead, and damaged and on fire, *Fujisan Maru* came about and headed back towards the perceived safety of the land-based AA gun batteries on the main Truk islands in the centre of the lagoon. These would offer her some protection in addition to her own meagre AA defences – she had survived DOG-DAY-MINUS-ONE.

As dawn broke on the following morning, DOG-DAY, 18 February 1944, Hellcat fighters once again arrived over Truk at dawn for an initial fighter sweep. Shortly after the Hellcats had launched from their carriers and were on their way, 12 SBD dive bombers with 8 Hellcat fighter escorts launched around 0500 from TG 58.1 carrier *Enterprise* for the first bombing attack of the day, Strike 1A. The *Enterprise* planes had been allocated a time over target between 0615 – 0700, but the flight arrived over the lagoon before it was light enough to attack and had to circle for 10 minutes. The *Enterprise* SBD's spotted *Fujisan Maru* underway - heading to the east through the channel between Moen and Dublon Islands, at the north of the Fourth Fleet Anchorage.

A division of *Enterprise* Hellcats and dive bombers attacked the valuable oiler, which was a priority target - and dropped three 1,000-lb armour-piercing bombs, targeting her engine machinery aft. Two were near misses – one either side - but one struck her in the vicinity of her stern depth charge storeroom, beside her engine room. The force of this massive explosion ripped open a section of her hull almost 20 metres in width - bending the steel plating of the boat deck upwards at right angles and at the same time removing about 25 metres of hull. The explosion ignited her bunker fuel in her aft fuel tank and a fire quickly started – a column of black fuel oil smoke billowed high into the air. Her engine room had been devastated and put out of action.

The two near miss bombs had exploded one beside her starboard quarter and the other beside her port quarter. Even though they missed, the force of the explosions transmitting through incompressible water would have caused much further damage to her hull, inboard machinery and pipework. The shock of these three massive explosions caused havoc throughout the whole ship and triggered her port anchor to break free from its bow stopper and run out unchecked to the seabed. *Fujisan Maru* lost headway and slewed to a stop.

Heavily damaged, the oiler began to list to port and sink, going down by her ravaged stern. By 1100, all hope of saving her had been lost and the order to abandon ship was given. Meanwhile, the second division of Hellcats and SBD dive bombers from *Enterprise* Air Group 10 was attacking and sinking the auxiliary transport *Shotan Maru* west of Fanamu, just to the south. *Fujisan Maru* and *Shotan Maru* were the only sizeable ships located by the American aircraft in the harbour at this time.

As the stern of *Fujisan Maru* went steadily under, some of the fires were extinguished and the black smoke of burning fuel became clouded with white steam as sea water made contact with red hot hull plates. Fuel oil bubbled up from her wrecked aft bunkers and started to form a slick on the surface.

As her aft spaces filled with water, their dead weight dragged her stern further under until it eventually came to rest on the bottom. Her undamaged buoyant forward spaces held her bow aloft, her bow rising up into the air as her stern went under. *Fujisan Maru* is reported to have hung upright with her bows pointing skyward for almost an hour before she finally went under.

The wreck today

Today the 490-ft long structurally intact wreck of the tanker *Fujisan Maru* rests upright with a 45° list to port. She rests on a gently sloping bottom, her bows pointing to the north in deeper water of about 58 metres – her stern sitting in just over 50 metres. The very tip of her bow is at about 45 metres, whilst the least depth down to the top of her bridge superstructure is about 38 metres. This wreck is therefore a deep dive where divers will inevitably be at general depths of 45-50 metres, with the possibility to go much deeper – *Fujisan Maru* is not a dive to be lightly undertaken. If you go to the bottom of the engine room, you will be in depths of about 60 metres. For any serious exploration, she has to be treated as a full-scale technical dive.

At the very bow, on the fo'c'sle deck, a docking telegraph for anchor handling commands is still bolted upright to the deck at a depth of about 45 metres. Chains would run from this telegraph (below deck) to the bridge telegraph and allow the captain to give commands to the anchor crew to let go the anchor, or make fast.

Immediately abaft the stem, at a depth of about 45 metres, a sturdy anchor windlass sits on deck with both chains run out through their hawse pipes. The port anchor and chain, which had broken free from its bow stopper during the ferocious attack, is run out to the seabed and wraps under the hull bottom – she was still moving forward when this happened. The starboard anchor also jarred during the attack has dropped a few metres to hang loosely from its hawse.

Immediately abaft the anchor windlass is the bow gun platform, the 120mm (4.7-inch) HA gun itself is missing – and the mount on which it was situated, and turned, appears to be sheared off, possibly during the attack or sinking.

Moving aft from the fo'c'sle deck down to the weather deck, a spare anchor can be found in a stowage cradle beside an entrance door into the fo'c'sle spaces. On the well deck, a number of raised hatches for the forward oil tanks are dotted here and there. This area clearly shows the ravages of the attack.

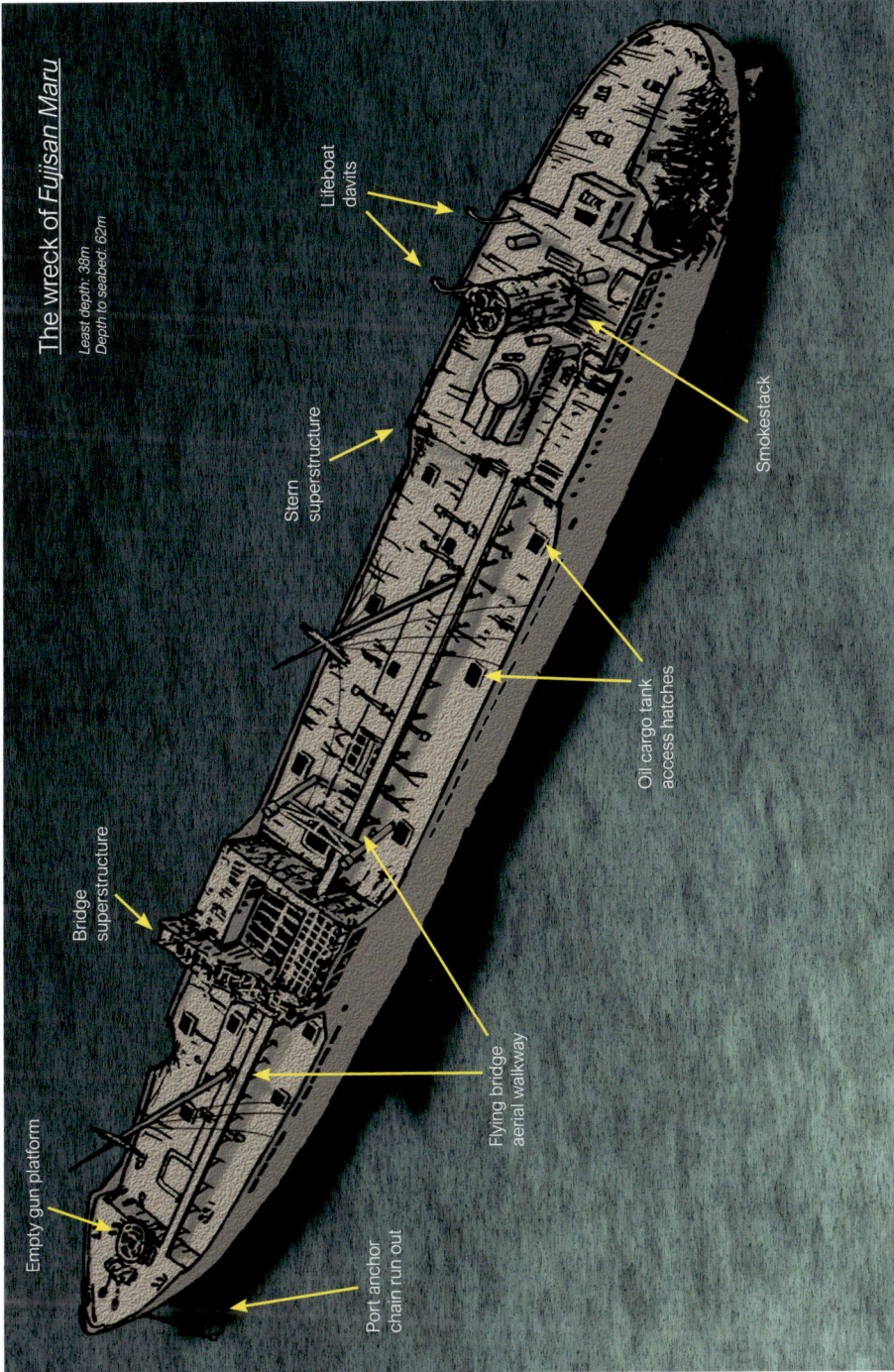

The wreck of *Fujisan Maru*

Least depth: 38m
Depth to seabed: 62m

Lifeboat davits

Smokestack

Stern superstructure

Oil cargo tank access hatches

Bridge superstructure

Flying bridge aerial walkway

Empty gun platform

Port anchor chain run out

Artist's impression of the wreck of the tanker *Fujisan Maru*, which today sits upright with a list to port in 62 metres.

A few metres above the weather deck, the flying bridge walkway (that connects all three island superstructures) is set on the port side of the vessel, now at about 49 metres. This flying bridge is not situated on the centre line of the ship, as on many other tankers and oilers. It was details such as the position of the flying bridge that allowed U.S. aviators to identify the class of tanker below them. In this forward part of the ship, the flying bridge and its supports are distressed and at awkward angles. Sections of the deck itself are deformed and sag inwards, a result of her empty foredeck tanks compressing due to increasing water pressure as she sank.

The foremast still stands and reaches up to about 30 metres from the surface. The cargo booms, goosenecked to the foremast, have swung to point down to port as she sank. Two minesweeping paravanes lie nearby on the starboard side of the foredeck.

On the starboard side of the hull between the bridge superstructure and fo'c'sle there are two large sections of shell plating, each 20-30 metres wide, that are deformed and indented from near miss bomb explosions. There is further similar deformation of shell plating on the port side of her hull in the vicinity of her cargo tanks, empty at the time of the attack.

The bridge superstructure is set forward of amidships and shows evidence of being swept by fire before she sank. The wooden decking above has largely rotted away to expose the structural beams and girders of the superstructure and it is possible to drop in between the beams into the bridge below. Here the telegraph lies fallen, its pointer still in the FULL AHEAD position, as it was when she was attacked whilst under way.

At a depth of about 53 metres, on the forward frontage of the bridge superstructure at weather deck level, two open doorways allow access into the lower decks of the superstructure, which formerly held accommodation compartments. The internal dividing walls of cabins are all now rotted away to leave a large common space that is filled with scattered stoves, china, sake dishes, bottles, wash hand basins and toilets.

In this bridge superstructure area can be found a number of white glazed 4-gallon water filter bodies, which are similar to modern water dispensers with a small tap at the bottom to draw water. The white, ceramic water filter bodies stand out in the uniform brown of the silt layering these compartments. The ceramic bodies are stamped as manufactured by Seto & Co in Yokohama. Seto, located close to Nagoya, is one of the Nihon Rokkoyo, the six old kilns of medieval Japan – and Seto was the only one to glaze its pottery during the medieval period from 1158-1333. Seto was ideal for production of pottery and ceramics as the soil around the city contains good quality porcelain clay and silica and dense forests nearby provided abundant firewood for fuel.

Shafts of bright blue light stream into the bridge superstructure from above, through the structural girders and beams of the deckhouse, whilst in the distance, light streams in through open doorways in the aft bulkhead of the superstructure – which allow exit points to the long wide expanse of the aft weather deck. A searchlight platform complete with signalling light has fallen from the top of this superstructure to now lie on the seabed below, at about 59 metres. The iris blades of the signal light are in the closed position.

At a depth of about 45 metres, divers moving aft now face a long swim over the weather deck, from the bridge superstructure to the poop island. On the way, divers will pass a number of raised oil tank hatches, the pump house, a goalpost pair of kingposts and the

Looking aft towards the boiler room deckhouse of *Fujisan Maru*. The short starboard kingpost with cargo boom swung to port is visible. (Author)

Ascending the downline above the bridge of *Fujisan Maru*. The wooden decking of the roof is gone, to now reveal the structural framework. (Courtesy Pete Mesley)

upright mainmast - before arriving at the after superstructure, which holds the engine room and associated machinery. On the port side of the deck, the flying bridge runs, about 8-feet above the deck, all the way from the bridge superstructure to the poop island. It is in much better condition that the foredeck section.

As divers finally arrive at the poop island, they can rise up one deck level to the shelter deck. On either side here, there are long rectangular open hatches allowing easy access below deck. Moving further aft there is a smaller deckhouse, with an open doorway on the higher starboard side. This small deckhouse is flanked on either side by a single kingpost, the boom from the higher starboard kingpost has swung round to port as the ship settled, to rest its end on the deckhouse.

An unusual circular deckhouse, like a sheared off smokestack (although that's not what it is) rises several metres above the top of this deckhouse, with the cylindrical shafts of several large forced draft ventilators standing around it.

A diver hangs motionless beside the large screw and rudder of *Fujisan Maru* (Courtesy Pete Mesley)

Moving further aft, on the centre line of the ship, just beside the smokestack at about 45 metres, are set a row of ventilation skylights, each with three round portholes in them, the glass now gone.

The tall smokestack has a fixed ladder running up its front edge. The lifeboat davits either side of the smokestack are still swung inboard.

There are a number of ways for adventurous suitably trained divers to get into the engine room here through open doors and hatches. It is a large cavernous space, where the shallowest sections are at about 42-45 metres. The large circular bolted cylinder tops of her 7-cylinder diesel engine can be spotted, with catwalks criss crossing around and above them. The metalwork here is distressed and jumbled in places, as well as being blackened by wartime fires. Fuel pump controls and spares panels can be seen, and through an open doorway the machine shop can be entered which has a number of large fixtures and fixed work benches with lathes and vices.

On the lower port side of the weather deck near the mainmast, the force of the explosion can be seen - with deck plates bent upwards at almost 90° and about 20 metres of the ship's hull missing. A lot of the poop island superstructure here is destroyed or badly mangled and any wooden decking has been completely burnt away by the intense fire. There are only a few parts of the stern gun platform remaining, the 120mm HA gun itself, like the bow gun, is missing.

On the starboard side of the hull towards the stern there is a large indentation in the hull caused by the force of one of the near miss bombs stoving in her hull plating.

Underneath the fantail, the large 4-bladed propeller sits with its lower blade partially buried in the seabed at about 50 metres with the rudder intact immediately behind it.

7. *Fumizuki*
Mutsuki-class 1ˢᵗ-class *Destroyer No 29* (1926)
Renamed 文月 (*Fumizuki)* - 1 August 1928

Combined Fleet Anchorage

Displacement:	1,315-tons (light). 1,772 tons (N). 1,913-tons after reconstruction
Dimensions:	338-ft 9" long (wl); beam of 30-ft; draught of 9-ft 8"
Launched:	16 February 1926
Sunk:	18 February 1944
Cause of loss:	Bombed by TF 58 aircraft during Operation HAILSTONE
Name translation 文月:	*Seventh Month of Lunar Calendar (July)*
Wreck location:	Combined Fleet Anchorage, west of Weno, north of Udot Island
Depth to seabed:	38 metres
Least Depth:	30 metres.

———————————

The Mutsuki-class destroyer IJN *Fumizuki* (No 29). This photo was taken before her alterations in 1942 - when her four older 12cm (4.7-inch) main battery guns were replaced with two more modern 12cm guns, No 1 at the bow and No 4 at the stern. Her amidships No 2 and No 3 guns were not replaced.

In 1898, Japan began construction of 23 turtle-back destroyers under the Ten-Year Naval Expansion Programme – most of which would be built in Britain at Yarrow and at Thornycroft. The programme also provided for the construction of 16 1ˢᵗ-class torpedo boats and a sizeable number of smaller 2ⁿᵈ & 3ʳᵈ Class boats.

Despite the IJN interest in torpedo boats and destroyers, by the beginning of WWI, the IJN still had too few destroyers, despite having concentrated since the Russo-Sino War of 1904-5 on building destroyers in Japan that were based on a British design. The IJN destroyers carried heavier armament than their British or German counterparts and were now subdivided into three grades of destroyers: (i) the large *1st Class* or ocean-going type of over 1,000 tons, (ii) the *2nd Class* type of 600-1,000 tons and (iii) the smaller *3rd Class* type of under 600 tons, although no more 3rd Class boats were built after 1909.

During WWI, the torpedo boat and the larger torpedo boat destroyer, had played a vital role, such that the ships collectively came to be known simply as 'destroyers'. The torpedo boat and torpedo boat destroyer were a very potent weapon of the German High Seas Fleet during WWI, being able to attack at speed and disable British warships.

By the end of WWI, with the earlier demise of the 3rd Class destroyer, Japanese destroyer construction had evolved into two main types: (a) the **1st Class destroyer** of some 1,300 tons (such as the Truk wrecks of *Fumizuki* and *Oite)*, fitted with 3 or 4 12cm (4.7-in) main battery guns and six 21-in torpedo tubes, and (b) the **2nd Class destroyer**, a smaller vessel of some 850 tons (such as the Truk wreck *Patrol Boat No 34* (ex-*Susuki*)), which were fitted with three 12cm guns and six torpedo tubes.

Japan had been allied to Britain during WWI, and at war's end Japan had received five German destroyers by way of war reparations. From 1919 onwards Japan embarked on constructing a series of destroyers – all built in Japan. Japan essentially reverse engineered the German destroyer design and then sought to improve on the design to produce a new type of 1st-class destroyer – the Minekaze-class.

Japan wanted a destroyer that was *larger* and *faster* than the German WWI destroyers – a ship that would be able to operate in the rough waters of the Pacific in any future conflict with America. With this in mind, during the development process, Japanese naval architects moved the bridge further aft and placed a well deck in front of it. A high fo'c'sle was designed, which was lengthened and given a turtle back that would reduce the impact of heavy seas on the bridge. The new 1st class Minekaze-class destroyers were fitted with geared turbines that replaced the direct drive turbines of earlier classes and gave a maximum speed of 39 knots. Only two further classes of 2nd Class destroyers were built – the 21 ships of the Momi-class and the 8 ships of the Wakatake-class.

The first fifteen Minekaze-class destroyers were ordered in the 1917-20 building programs and the first units began to enter service in 1920. At first, these destroyers would be given simple identifying numbers - but after 1928 they were assigned individual names.

The second batch of Minekaze-class units was ordered in 1921-22, but because of slight differences in design, they were designated as a new class, the Kamikaze-class.

Twelve more 1st class destroyers were ordered under the Japanese 1923 Fleet Program. These units would be slightly larger than their Minekaze-class and Kamikaze-class predecessors, such as *Oite*. The new units were designated as the Mutsuki-class - and included *Destroyer No 29*, which would be renamed *Fumizuki* on 1 August 1928. In all, 36 1st class destroyers were completed to the basic *Minekaze* design and until the advent of the Special Type destroyers in 1929 these ships formed the core of the Japanese destroyer force.

Destroyer No 29 was laid down by Fujinagata Zosen in Osaka on 20 October 1924. Her hull was launched for fitting out afloat on 16 February 1926 and the completed ship was commissioned into the IJN as *Destroyer No 29* on 3 July 1926.

The Mutsuki-class destroyers were broadly similar to the preceding *Minekaze*-class and Kamikaze-class destroyers - however as a direct result of the Washington Naval Treaty of 1922, a number of new features were introduced due to the IJN focus on heavy torpedo armament.

The Washington Naval Treaty of 1922, also known as the Five-Power Treaty, was ratified by the major nations that had won WWI - and was designed to prevent an arms race and curb Japanese expansion, by limiting naval construction. This arms control treaty pegged Britain's Royal Navy at roughly the same size as the US Navy and placed stringent restrictions on the building of new capital ships: battlecruisers, battleships and latterly aircraft carriers. The 1922 Treaty allowed Britain and the USA a tonnage equivalent to 15 capital ships whereas Japan was only allowed nine capital ships and France and Italy, five capital ships each.

Whilst Japan had been forced to accept a naval inferiority in respect of capital ships, the Treaty did not restrict the numbers or design of lighter ships such as cruisers, destroyers and submarines – and simply limited their maximum displacement to 10,000 tons.

With Japan's military aims shackled by the Treaty, Japan moved to redress the balance by arming these lighter types of ship as heavily as possible – a strategic move implemented immediately with the 12 new Mutsuki-class destroyers, which began launching in 1925. For the first time, a Japanese destroyer was now fitted with six 24-inch torpedo tubes in two triple launchers, in place of the three twin 21-inch launchers of earlier classes.

The forward triple 24-inch torpedo tube launcher was set abaft the foc'sle on the well deck, immediately in front of the bridge superstructure. The bridge superstructure itself was set forward of amidships and housed the conning tower at the front with the navigating bridge one deck higher - with two optical range finders set on top. The foremast with crosstree was located at the aft bulkhead of the bridge. Two raked smokestacks rose up from her boiler rooms abaft the bridge superstructure. A long flat expanse of weather deck abaft the smokestacks accommodated the second triple 24-inch torpedo tube launcher. Ten torpedoes were carried to allow for reloads.

The destroyer was now a powerful offensive weapon that was being maximized as a night-combat torpedo platform.

To improve seaworthiness, the new Mutsuki-class destroyers featured an elongated, narrow, 'S' shape bow, with a more prominent flare. This gave the ship a greater overall length and increased displacement. The same engine machinery was installed as in the preceding Kamikaze-class, whose destroyers had a creditable speed of just over 37 knots. Propulsion was delivered by 4 Kampon boilers, two Parsons geared turbines that developed 38,500 SHP - and two shafts. However, with these design alterations, the full-load speed for the Mutsuki-class destroyers would turn out to be a disappointingly reduced 33 knots at best. The class carried 420 gallons of fuel oil that provided a range of 4,000 nautical miles at 14 knots. They carried a crew of 150.

The Mutsuki-class destroyers were initially fitted with the same four 12cm/45-cal (4.7-inch) 3rd Year Type Dual Purpose (DP) single-mount naval guns as on the Kamikaze-class. This older design of gun was manually loaded and fired a 45-lb HE shell that required a separate bagged charge. This made gun operation cumbersome and susceptible to water damage on decks that were being swept by heavy seas. One 12cm gun was installed on the raised foc'sle deck at the bow, one on the centre-line abaft the bridge superstructure between the two smokestacks, and two were set on the centre line, one fore and one aft of her mainmast towards the stern. Two single 7.7mm machine guns were fitted for AA protection - placed abreast the bridge.

Finally, the quarter deck of the new Mutsuki-class units abaft the masthouse was given over to anti-submarine, minesweeping and mine laying gear. Two roll off rails ran off one either side of the fantail. Two Type 81 depth charge projectors were fitted, the depth charges being racked abaft the masthouse. By 1941-2, the class carried 16 mines and 18 depth charges as standard.

Following the naming convention set out in the Explanatory Notes, xxii, above, on 1 August 1928, *Destroyer No 29* was renamed *Fumizuki*, which means *Seventh Month of Lunar Calendar:* July.

Japanese naval leaders knew Japan would be at a disadvantage in numbers of capital ships in any Pacific conflict with the United States. They were also aware of the 1924 American *Plan Orange* for dealing with a Pacific clash with Japan. *Plan Orange* called for the U.S. Pacific Fleet to advance west across the Pacific to relieve the Philippines, if seized by Japan as was likely.

At some point in such a Pacific war, IJN naval doctrine envisaged that a *decisive battle* would require to be fought with the U.S. fleet. With fewer capital ships as a result of the naval treaties, Japan looked for a way to reduce her numerical disadvantage in capital ships before such a battle. If the playing field could not be levelled, the inferior Japanese battle line would quickly be smashed by the might of the American capital ships.

Torpedo tactics and night combat were seen as one way to reduce American naval numbers as the U.S. Fleet made its way across the Pacific to the Philippines. Japanese destroyer squadrons would attack en masse at night – and redress the balance of power by sinking American capital ships.

Japan thus set in motion plans to implement this new strategic line of thinking - and to create the weapons it needed to implement the tactic. Japan went to great lengths to develop new ship-killer torpedoes that could be launched from submarines, ships and torpedo aircraft. The result was that Japanese torpedoes showed a steady progression of improvements throughout the 1920's and 1930's - culminating in the famous wonder weapon, the *ship launched* Type 93 Long Lance torpedo that entered service in of 1933.

Most torpedoes of the era used compressed air as the oxidizer, with a long internal air cylinder charged to about 2,500-3000psi – the same pressure as today's conventional scuba cylinders. Compressed air however is 79% inert nitrogen, and this unspent nitrogen left a noticeable bubble trail. The Type 93 ship launched Long Lance torpedo (the development of which ran parallel with development of the Type 95 submarine-launched model) ingeniously used *compressed oxygen* as the fuel oxidizer in place of compressed air.

Since air contains only 21% oxygen, pure 100% oxygen provides five times as much oxidizer in the same tank volume - and this greatly increased torpedo range. The absence of inert 79% nitrogen resulted in significantly fewer exhaust bubbles as the combustion product was only carbon dioxide (CO_2) and water vapour. With CO_2 being significantly soluble in water, the resulting exhaust gas mixture greatly reduced tell-tale bubbles in its track. Compressed oxygen is however dangerous to handle - but IJN engineers found that by starting the torpedo's engine with compressed air, then gradually switching to oxygen they were able to overcome the often-lethal explosions, which had hampered it's use before. To conceal the use of dangerous pure oxygen from the ship's crew, the Japanese called the oxygen tank the *secondary air tank*.

The Type 93 Long Lance torpedo had a maximum range of about 25 miles at 38 knots and it carried a large 1,080-lb high explosive warhead. Its long range, high speed, heavy warhead and lack of a giveaway bubble trail, marked it as a quantum leap forward in torpedo development - and it was far ahead of any Allied torpedo of the time. The U.S. Navy's standard surface launched torpedo of WWII, the Mark 15 had a maximum range of 7.4 nautical miles at 26 knots or just three nautical miles at 45 knots and it carried a smaller 827-lb warhead.

In 1935/36, after many ships were damaged by a typhoon, *Fumizuki* and five of her 11 sisters had sea going improvements carried out that involved a redesigned and strengthened bridge and raked smokestacks. With torpedo crews being exposed to decks being swept by water in poor seas, and also being exposed to enemy fire on an open deck, the triple torpedo tube launchers had protective watertight shields fitted around them, to essentially make a protected torpedo room that crew would operate in. The torpedoes could now be deployed in all weather conditions.

Launching of the Long Lance torpedoes was from six 61cm (24-inch) 8th Year Type torpedo tubes in two triple deck mounts. One triple launching mount was fitted in the well deck, forward of the bridge – a position that would prove to be impractical in combat in a heavy sea when the area was swept by water. The other triple mount was fitted aft, forward of the mainmast deckhouse and abaft the second smokestack.

The Long Lance torpedo carried a 490kg (1,080lb) warhead, at a time when British anti-torpedo side protection systems on capital ships were designed to withstand torpedoes with a warhead of up to 340kg (750-lbs) of TNT. American torpedo defence systems in the South Dakota- and Iowa-class battleships were designed to absorb torpedo hits with warheads up to 317kg (700-lbs), the Navy's guesstimate of the warhead on Japanese 1930's torpedoes. The new Japanese Long Lance torpedoes had the potential to penetrate capital ship side protection systems.

During WWII, in an effort to provide increased AA ability for convoy escort duties, *Fumizuki* underwent a second refit in 1943 that reduced her surface warfare capability but increased her AA ability - so that she could operate as a fast transport. At this time, her *four* existing older 12cm (4.7-inch) 3rd Year Type guns (based on an 1895 design) were removed and replaced with *two* modern 12cm/50-cal 11th Year Type naval guns, one forward and one aft. For the first time, these guns were provided with a 3mm splinter shield, which also protected crew from the weather. Her older No 2 gun (between the smokestacks) and No 3 gun (forward of the mainmast) were not replaced.

The new 11th Year Type guns had a quicker rate of fire than those they replaced of about 5-6 rounds per minute. The new guns had an elevation of +10° to +55° and could traverse 360°. They had a range of 16,000 metres at 33° and were equally suited to firing at a low angle against surface craft, as they were elevating to hit more distant targets, although with a maximum elevation of +55°, they could not really be classed as Dual-Purpose guns. The 11th Year Type naval gun had a horizontal sliding-block breach and fired separate loading *cased* charges and projectiles. The cased charge was easier to load than the previous 3rd Year Type bagged charge and wasn't as susceptible to water on wet decks.

To increase her AA capability, the two old single 7.7mm single machine-guns abreast the bridge were removed and replaced by five Type 93 13mm AA machine guns. These 13mm AA machine guns had a practical rate of fire of 250 rounds per minute and a range at 50° of about 6,500 metres - and had an effective range against aircraft of about 1,000-2,000 metres.

In addition, 20 25mm Type 96 AA auto cannons in 10 dual mounts were installed. The Type 96 fired a 25mm HE shell, and had an effective rate of fire of about 110 rounds per minute and an effective firing range of about 4 miles at 45°. Firing range against aircraft was roughly 3-5 km (10,000 – 18,000 feet).

The aft mine sweeping and mine laying gear was completely removed and replaced by an increase to four depth charge throwers. She could now carry 36 depth charges in place of her original 18 – and these were deployed via tracks and winches to the four throwers and to the roll off rails.

At the beginning of the Pacific war, no Japanese destroyers were equipped with radar, it would be mid-1943 before some destroyers began to be fitted with the No. 22 radar.

The cumulative effect of these changes increased *Fumizuki*'s displacement to 1,913-tons - and reduced her speed to 34 knots.

The IJN Third Fleet had originally been created in 1903 - but had been disbanded and reconstituted on a number of occasions as required, most lately being disbanded in November 1939. On 10 April 1941, as Japan prepared for her Pacific war, the Third Fleet was once again reconstituted for the specific task of invading the Philippine Islands - and designated the 'Southern Expeditionary Fleet'. The 1st Class destroyer *Fumizuki* was assigned to DesDiv 22, which formed part of Destroyer Flotilla 5 of the Third Fleet based in Takao, Formosa (modern day Taiwan).

Operation M - the invasion of the Philippines - was scheduled to begin on 7 December 1941. And so, in preparation, at the end of November 1941, Desron 5 (incorporating DesDiv 22 with *Fumizuki)* was sent to the major IJN naval base at the port of Mako in the Pescadores Islands in the Taiwan Strait, just a few hundred miles north of the Philippines.

Virtually simultaneous with the Pearl Harbor raid on 7 December 1941, Operation M, the invasion of the Philippines, began. Desdiv 22 with *Fumizuki* departed Mako, heading 200 miles south in support of the invasion force bound for Aparri at the northern tip of the large northern Philippine island of Luzon. Then, on 22 December 1941, Desdiv 22 screened the main invasion force bound for Lingayen Gulf, on the northwest side of Luzon. Lingayen was strategically important to the Japanese as it was a gateway to the central plains of Luzon that would allow Japanese troops to press south to seize Manila, the capital of the Philippines, towards the south of Luzon. Japanese landing forces swiftly overran most of Luzon.

The following month, January 1942, Desdiv 22 was deployed to escort troop convoys staging from Formosa for Operation E, the invasion of Malaya. In February 1942, Desdiv22 was deployed for Operation J, the invasion of Java and the Dutch East Indies.

From March 1942, Desron 5 was re-assigned to the Southwest Area Fleet, escorting troop convoys from Singapore to Penang and Rangoon. *Fumizuki* returned to Sasebo Naval

Arsenal in July 1942 where she was drydocked to allow the fitting of improved underwater sound detection gear.

The work on *Fumizuki* was completed by the end of August 1942 when she began convoy escort duties. However, just a few weeks later, on 16 September 1942, she was heavily damaged in a collision with the transport ship *Kachidoki Maru* in the Taiwan Strait. *Fumizuki* returned to Mako for emergency repairs before heading to Sasebo where she was dry docked for permanent repair.

One year into the Pacific war, Desdiv 22 was deactivated on 10 December 1942 - and *Fumizuki* was assigned to the 1st Surface Escort Division. In late January 1943, with two other destroyers, she escorted the seaplane tender *Kamikawa Maru* from Sasebo via Truk and Rabaul to Shortland Island in the Solomon's. *Fumizuki* remained based at Rabaul throughout February 1943 to cover Operation KE, the troop evacuations from Guadalcanal - supporting three evacuation runs from Guadalcanal.

Fumizuki participated in the *Tokyo Express*, the Allied name for the relief operation for Japanese forces around New Guinea and the Solomon Islands - conceived to thwart Allied daytime air superiority. The Tokyo Express operation involved the use of fast warships, mainly destroyers, and latterly submarines, to deliver personnel, supplies and equipment to outlying garrisons. The ships would offload their supplies and then return to base, all within the darkness of a single night so that Allied aircraft would not detect them. At the end of February 1943 Desdiv 22 was reactivated and attached to Desron 3 of the Eighth Fleet.

Whilst operating around Papua New Guinea, *Fumizuki* was damaged by strafing attacks at Finschhafen in March 1943 and at Kavieng in April. In May 1943 she returned to Yokosuka Naval Arsenal in Japan (escorting the present day Truk wreck, the submarine tender *Heian Maru*), where she was docked for repairs and maintenance. It was at this time that the modernisation of her main battery, the installation of the 10 dual-mount 25mm AA auto cannons and the removal of the aft triple torpedo tube launcher (referred to above) took place.

Fumizuki departed Yokosuka on 20 August 1943, escorting convoys via Sasebo to Saipan, Truk and Rabaul. She went on to make many more Tokyo Express runs, evacuating troops from Kolombangara and Vella Lavella Islands in the Solomon's and landing troops at Buka, Bougainville and other areas of New Guinea.

On 2 November 1943, whilst at Rabaul, *Fumizuki* was strafed and damaged in an air attack. Six of her crew were killed and four injured – but she was soon back on transport runs to Bougainville, Rabaul, New Guinea and Truk.

On the night of 4 January 1944, she suffered damage in an air raid near Kavieng, New Guinea, which resulted in some flooding. But again, she was soon back in action on troop transport runs.

On 31 January 1944, whilst in Rabaul she received serious damage from land -based B-24 bombers. Although damaged, she was still able to escort a lumbering convoy from Rabaul to Truk, where she could be repaired. She was further damaged en route, taking some light damage from strafing.

When the convoy arrived at Truk on the evening of 6 February 1944, the damaged *Fumizuki* was anchored temporarily in the Combined Fleet Anchorage before being assigned a

IJN *Fumizuki* under attack at Kavieng on 4 January 1944, a month before Operation HAILSTONE (National Archives 80-G-208609)

berth near the IJN fleet repair ship *Akashi* in the Repair Anchorage just to the north of Fefen Island and to the north west of Dublon Island. Close to her were the *Kensyo Maru, Hoyo Maru, Kiyosumi Maru* and *Tonan Maru 3*, all being worked on as a result of torpedo or bomb damage.

Mechanics and technicians from *Akashi* soon had *Fumizuki's* turbines and boilers stripped down for repair, whilst repairs were started to the damage to her hull.

As the first air raids of Operation HAILSTONE swept across the lagoon at dawn on the morning of 17 February 1944, *Fumizuki* was sitting helplessly at anchor with both her turbines out of action. The U.S. aircraft however at first largely initially ignored her, pressing home attacks on other higher priority targets whilst AA gunners on *Fumizuki*, which now bristled with 10 dual-mount 25mm autocannon and five 13mm machine guns, fired at U.S. aircraft where they could, to defend the other shipping in the anchorage.

During the early waves of U.S. attacks, repair crew on *Fumizuki* started to frantically reassemble the ship's machinery to allow her to manoeuvre - and soon had one of her two turbines back online. *Fumizuki* worked up a head of steam, weighed anchor and began to move out into the open waters west of Moen Island, where she would have room to make evasive manoeuvres – albeit that she was handicapped by having only one of her turbines working. But even so, it was far harder for the U.S. aircraft to hit a moving target than a stationery one. She now had a limited ability to turn away from aerial torpedoes as she brought her formidable AA weaponry to bear on any attacker.

Fumizuki started to take evasive action as best she could with her one operating turbine. She made erratic and severe turns to both port and starboard as she headed south west towards the centre of the lagoon. But just before 1000, she was attacked and took a near miss bomb hit that holed her on the port side of her hull in the vicinity of her aft engine room. Water flooding into the engine room soon had put her one working turbine out of action. *Fumizuki* slewed to a stop and started to settle slowly by the stern. She was once again unable to navigate – and her starboard anchor was dropped to prevent her drifting onto nearby scattered sand spits and small islands. At this point, she was in no danger of sinking, and below decks, her crew fought to contain the flooding in her engine room.

Between 1415-1500, Strike 1E TBF aircraft from *Enterprise* attacked the stranded *Fumizuki*, dropping four 500-lb bombs. U.S. aircrew reported two direct hits and one possible hit that started fires aboard her. A near miss bomb on her starboard side stove in her hull plating and caused a vertical fissure that accelerated the rate of water flooding her innards.

When the first day's air raids ended, with the planes of the last Strikes 1F, 2F and 3F departing the Truk skies just before 1700 to head back to their carriers and land before dusk, *Fumizuki* remained at anchor and unable to navigate.

When night fell, *Fumizuki* was still afloat – but as the hours of darkness went by, her position worsened. By 2030 she had taken on an 8° list to port and water was now washing over her main deck. She was now in imminent danger of sinking.

The destroyer *Matsukaze* approached the stricken *Fumizuki* and attempted to take the destroyer in tow to save her by beaching. But, with *Fumizuki* badly flooded, she was now heavy in the water and the tow was unsuccessful. The target ship *Hakachi* also approached and along with *Matsukaze* rescued surviving crew from *Fumizuki*. 29 of her crew had been killed in the attacks.

At about 2040, the patrol boat *Kokko* approached *Fumizuki* and reported on arrival that the stricken destroyer was on the verge of sinking. An attempt was made to take *Fumizuki* in tow to the Naval Station at Dublon but with *Fumizuki* in such a precarious state, the tow was eventually abandoned at about midnight and *Fumizuki* was abandoned to her fate.

As the rescue vessel was making its way back to Dublon, the night radar attack by *Enterprise* TBF aircraft took place. The tug was bombed but escaped unscathed.

At about 0530, in the half light of nautical dawn on 18 February 1944, those aboard the tug saw the bow of *Fumizuki* rise high into the sky as she went down by the stern.

The wreck today

Today the wreck of the destroyer *Fumizuki* lies isolated from the main collection of wrecks in Truk lagoon, a number of miles west of Weno Island (Moen) in an open location with no protection from the larger islands. An uncovered sand spit lies a few hundred yards to the north with large chunks of exposed dead coral atop it.

The main section of the wreck, from the stern to the foredeck torpedo launcher sits on its keel with a 20° list to port in about 38 metres of water. There is a least depth over the deck and remaining superstructures of about 30-33 metres.

The fore part of the ship, from the torpedo launcher to the stem was upright and undamaged when I used to dive this wreck in the 90's and early 2000's. When after an absence of several years I went back to the wreck in 2013 to review my information for the 1st edition of this book, I was disappointed to find that the fore part of the ship now lies on its port beam ends. It is as though a large anchor has been dragged through the fragile wreck from the starboard side, rolling the upright bow section onto its port side, in a fashion similar to *Oite*. Degaussing cables running along the side of the ship are now suspended tightly in free water, as they run from the upright hull of the ship to the collapsed bow.

At the bow, the starboard anchor chain runs out from its now near vertical windlass to its hawse pipe. The port anchor chain is broken and drapes over a deck valve below the starboard chain and then hangs down to the seabed, ending short of its hawse pipe, which is empty of chain and anchor.

The No 1. forward 12cm/50-cal 11th Year Type gun with splinter shield formerly sat on a small platform atop the fo'c'sle – the gun now lies on its port side on the sand with the barrel facing forward. Unopened steel banded boxes of ready use shells are scattered around its base, they would have been stacked behind the gun on the platform. The area immediately abaft the bow gun is heavily smashed up.

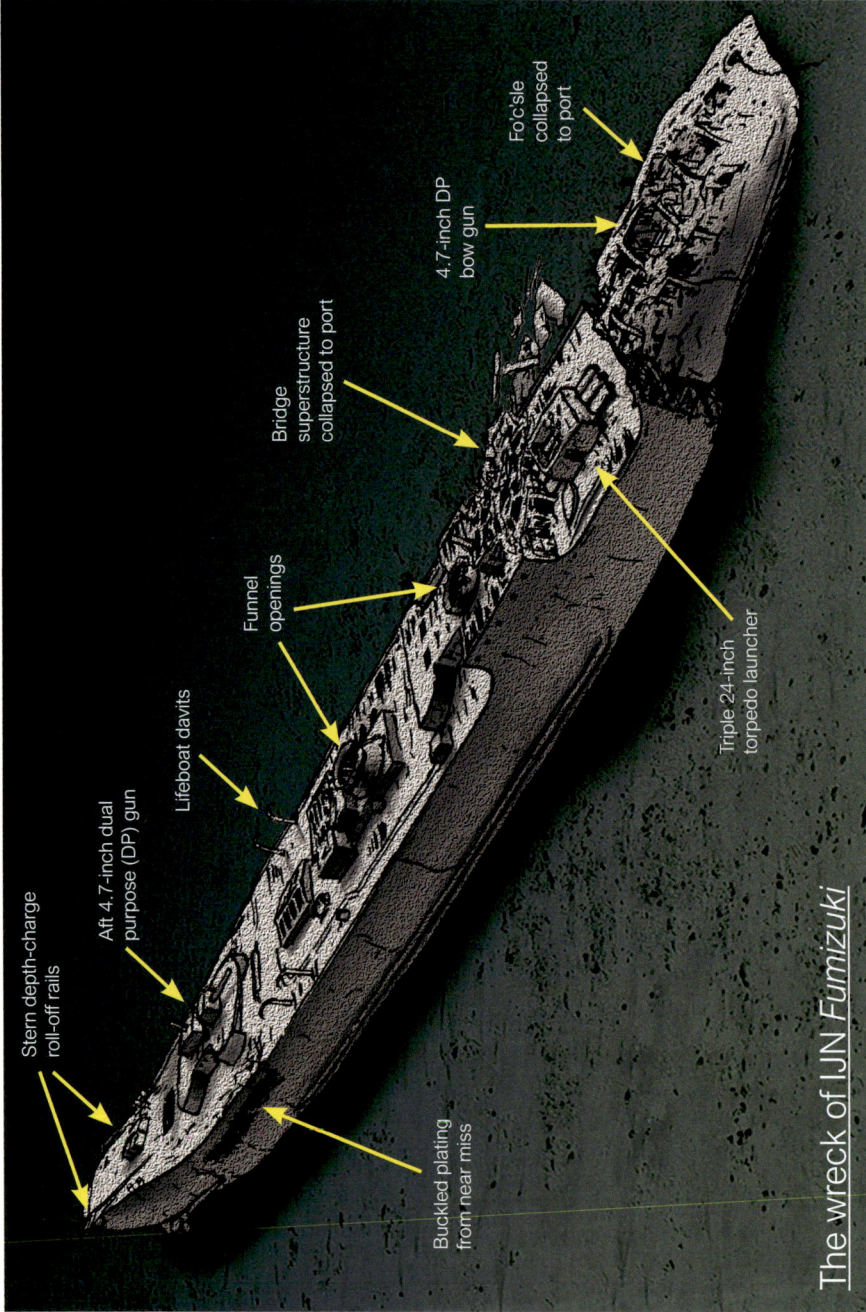

The wreck of IJN *Fumizuki*

Fo'c'sle collapsed to port

4.7-inch DP bow gun

Bridge superstructure collapsed to port

Funnel openings

Lifeboat davits

Aft 4.7-inch dual purpose (DP) gun

Stern depth-charge roll-off rails

Buckled plating from near miss

Triple 24-inch torpedo launcher

Artist's impression of the wreck of the destroyer IJN *Fumizuki*, which today lies upright in 38 metres. Her bow has been dragged over onto its port side in recent times.

The hull of the ship reforms at the triple Long Lance torpedo launcher, situated in the well deck just in front of the bridge superstructure. The severed remains of the torpedo tubes partly project from the control room into free water.

In 1935/6, to protect torpedo crews being exposed to decks being swept by seawater in poor seas, and exposed to enemy fire on deck, these triple torpedo tube launchers were fitted with protective watertight shields, creating a protected torpedo room where crew could operate in all weather conditions. The whole control room and integral torpedo tubes would swivel to port or starboard to fire as desired. The torpedo control room on *Fumizuki* is one of the highlights of diving this wreck. There is a door into the torpedo control room on the starboard side - the room is only partially covered by a roof.

The forward bulkhead of the control room is intact, so if you approach the control room, swim round to the back edge of the control room and you will find it is open and easy to then enter. Moving inside the control room, the three torpedo tubes can be seen at deck level, with a large circular turn valve beside them and the remains of a metal seat. The forward wall of this room is covered with control and junction boxes, switch panels and voice pipes.

The torpedo control room was situated immediately in front of the bridge superstructure. On leaving the torpedo control room and continuing aft, you will find that the bridge superstructure collapsed to port many years ago - and its debris now lies upside down on the seabed. The base compartments of the superstructure are now exposed.

Prior to the collapse of the bridge, the two ship's telegraphs stood side by side along with many gauges. The pointer on the port telegraph was fixed at 12 o'clock – at the STOP position in Japanese kanji lettering. Presumably this was the engine that had not yet been reassembled and started as she moved away from her Dublon anchorage. The starboard telegraph was at 3 o'clock – HALF AHEAD. Voice tubes led down to the engine room - where human remains of the 29 crew were found. The surviving crew abandoned ship to the rescue destroyers, so it would appear that these remains were victims of the initial air attacks.

Although the wound that caused her demise was a near miss on the port side near here, that area is now on the sand and not accessible. However, on the exposed starboard side of the hull here there is a long concave depression from the effect of a near miss bomb that popped rivets and allowed a vertical fissure to open up.

The two raked smokestacks abaft the bridge have collapsed, their deck openings remain visible. In between where they stood is an empty 12cm gun platform from where her original older No 2. 12cm gun was removed during reconstruction.

The aft portion of the superstructure is the most intact, with doorways and windows, the glass long gone. Abaft the aftmost smokestack, at shelter deck level, there is a searchlight platform before a drop down to a long expanse of open weather deck, which has hatches dotted here and there. The seabed is only a few metres beneath the port guard rail here. The after triple Long Lance torpedo launcher was originally set here – but was removed during her second reconstruction in 1943. The large empty circular mount remains visible on the deck, spanning almost the whole deck athwartships. Narrow gauge rail tracks for the carriages used to move the heavy 30-foot Long Lance torpedoes are still evident. Empty lifeboat davits bear silent witness to the evacuation of the ship, some are swung out, others in the stowed position.

Further aft, the masthouse rises up for one deck level, the mainmast collapsed long ago. Just in front of the base of the mainmast and facing forward in the original No 3. gun position, is the second 12cm gun with its splinter shield heavily covered in coral. Abaft the mainmast, at shelter deck level, can be found the mounts for some of her 25mm AA autocannon.

Abaft the mainmast deckhouse is a loading crane used for handling depth charges and moving them from the Ready Use rack to the two Depth-Charge Throwers, situated immediately aft. On the outboard side of the Ready Use rack are pairs of rails, one pair on each side of the deck. Each set of rails leads aft and projects out over the cruiser stern - from where depth charges could be rolled out over the stern.

A large area of buckled in plating from a near miss is evident near the stern on the starboard side and there is a split in the hull. The whole aft section is noticeably bent upwards and the deck buckled.

The fantail is clear of the sand and the rudder is intact. The lower port side propeller is buried in the seabed whilst the higher 3-bladed starboard side propeller is visible. Just forward of the prop is the A-bracket prop shaft support bearing with the free section of starboard shaft running to its stern tube, where it enters the ship.

8. *Futagami*
Hashima-class *Kyunan-sen ken Eisen*
Fleet Salvage Tug (1939)

West of Tonoas

Displacement:	600-tons (S)
	625-tons (N)
Dimensions:	143-ft 8" long (oa); beam of 28-ft 10"; draught of 10-ft 2"
Launched:	6 February 1939
Sunk:	August 1945-1947
Cause of loss:	Surrendered to Allies at end of war. Believed scuttled
Wreck location:	West of Tonoas
Depth to seabed:	Bow - 30 metres.
	Stern 18 metres
Least Depth:	Stern – 10 metres.

The 600-tonne Hashima-class salvage tug *Futagami* was built by the Harima Sanbashi shipbuilding company in Aioi in the southern part of Japan, being laid down on 21 October 1938 and launched for fitting out on 6 February 1939. She was completed on 30 April 1939 and registered to the Kure Port Captain.

Artist's impression of the large 625-ton IJN Salvage Tug *Futagami*

Futagami was fitted with two Kampon water tube boilers to provide steam to two vertical triple expansion engines. These developed 2,200 iHP (indicated horsepower) and drove her two shafts to give a speed of about 14.5 knots. She was a tough powerful tug, and her twin screws gave her exceptional mobility.

For AA protection she was fitted with two 25mm auto cannons, whilst for salvage duties she carried two 2-tonne and one 5-tonne salvage derricks along with dewatering salvage pumps. She also carried depth charges.

On 1 April 1943, *Futagami* was assigned to the 4th Base Force Harbour Master's Office at Fefan Island at Truk. One year later, on 4 April 1944, northwest of Dublon Island, the submarine *I-169* was victualing on the surface at anchor when at about 0900, a warning was issued of an imminent American B-24 bombing raid. The watch officer ordered *I-169* to dive immediately – she would lie on the bottom until the raid was over.

However, in the rush to dive, the main induction valve was not secured, and the submarine's aft compartments began to flood. The crew of *I-169* frantically closed off hatches inside the submarine to seal off the flooded area as they made a desperate attempt to resurface. But the submarine sank to the bottom of the lagoon and came to rest upright on the seabed in almost 40 metres of water.

Once the air raid alert was ended, when the submarine failed to resurface and couldn't be contacted, a diver was brought in and sent down to the submarine. An induction valve on the after part of the conning tower was found to be a few inches open. The diver was able to establish that some crew were still alive, by tapping with his hammer. He received responses from crew at four of the five hatches, with no response coming from the control room beneath the conning tower.

The following day, the salvage tug *Futagami* and a repair ship with a 30-tonne crane, arrived on scene above the stricken submarine. An attempt would be made to hoist the bow to the surface and let the crew out. But as the attempted lift took place in the afternoon, the flooded submarine proved too heavy and the crane's cable broke.

As time passed, the tapping by trapped crew diminished and was eventually only heard coming from the aft compartment. Air hoses were lowered, and holes drilled into the ballast tanks to try and provide positive buoyancy and float the submarine to the surface. But it proved impossible to signal to the crew that they should open the air valves to ballast the tanks. By midnight, all tapping had petered out - all the beleaguered crew had died in the submarine.

Being a small target of little value, *Futagami* survived Operation HAILSTONE raid and the other raids that followed, although she was damaged on 18 September 1944 in Puluwat atoll, west of Truk, by American B-25 Mitchell bombers.

When the war ended with Japan's surrender in August 1945, *Futagami* was present at Truk and in serviceable condition. At the end of the war there was a detailed study of Truk's defences that resulted in a document by the United States Pacific Fleet & Pacific Ocean Areas entitled *Field Survey of Japanese Defenses on Truk* (CINCPAC-CINCPOA Bulletin NO. 3-46 dated 15 March 1946). In this document, *Eisen No 761* and *Futagami* were both listed as being located at Truk at the end of the war and surrendering to U.S. forces in August 1945. Both these vessels appear to have been sunk or scuttled after the war just off the west side of Dublon, there is no damage to either, in similar fashion to the unidentified IJN tug west of Weno.

The wreck today

Today the salvage tug *Futagami* sits on her keel with a 45° list to port on a sloping bottom at the mouth of Dublon River in murky water – her bows pointing out to sea. Although I personally like diving salvage tugs, with so many other larger world class wrecks in the lagoon, in stunning visibility, *Futagami* is only infrequently dived.

Futagami sits on the underwater slope with her bow in deeper water of just over 30 metres. Her stern is in shallower water of about 18 metres.

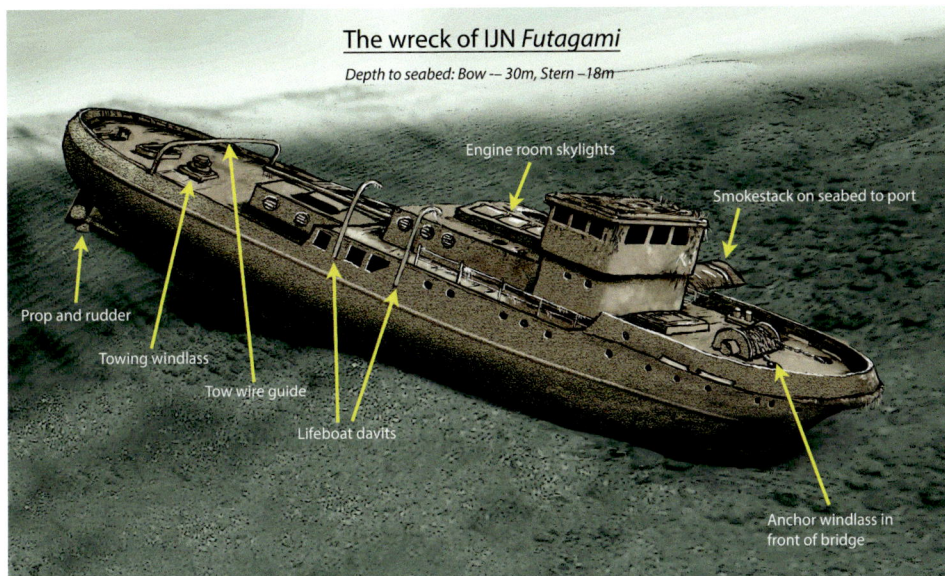

The wreck of IJN *Futagami*

Depth to seabed: Bow -- 30m, Stern –18m

Engine room skylights

Smokestack on seabed to port

Prop and rudder

Towing windlass

Tow wire guide

Lifeboat davits

Anchor windlass in front of bridge

Artist's impression of the IJN Salvage Tug *Futagami*, which rests on a gentle slope with her bow in deeper water of about 30 metres.

On her foredeck, anchor chains lead from her windlass to a hawse pipe on either side. A small hatch in front of the wheelhouse superstructure leads to storage and crew's quarters.

The wheelhouse rises up for 2 deck levels. On the upper level, three large rectangular windows face forward - with others on either side. There are two engine order telegraphs bolted to the wheelhouse deck, one either side of the helm telemotor. The wooden spokes of the helm itself have rotted away.

Abaft the wheelhouse, there is a drop down to the Boat Deck where the base of her smokestack can be seen – the smokestack itself has collapsed to lie on the seabed to port nearby. Empty lifeboat davits are set either side of the smokestack on the Boat Deck.

Immediately abaft the smokestack is the small pitched engine room roof with ventilation skylights. There are hatches either side and it is possible to get down into the engine compartment through an open hatch on the starboard side – but care needs to be taken as it is tight for a diver down in the engine room. A grated steel walkway leads aft between the two powerful engines and there are two repeaters for the bridge telegraphs set underneath a panel of gauges.

The 5-tonne derrick lies across the aft hold hatch in its stowed position. Stowed in the hold are salvage dewatering pipes for pumping water out of a flooded vessel and a towline lies on the deck with a large tow hook behind.

The after deck has a large capstan adjacent to a wire guide that runs athwartships from one side of the deck to the other to stop the tow wire going over the side amidships.

At her shallowest stern section, the rudder and her two three bladed screws are visible.

9. *Gosei Maru*
Standard Coastal cargo freighter (1937)
IJN *Ippan Choyosen* Auxiliary transport ship (1941)
IJA *Rikugun Yusosen* Transport (1943)
U.S. Recognition Code: 46 MKMF

Sixth Fleet Anchorage

Tonnage:	1,931grt
Dimensions:	271.6-ft long; beam of 40-ft; draught of 20.3-ft
Launched:	6 February 1939
Sunk:	18 February 1944
Cause of loss:	Torpedoed by TF 58 aircraft during Operation HAILSTONE
Wreck location:	Sixth Fleet Anchorage, northeast of Uman Island
Depth to seabed:	Bow - 35 metres. Stern 10 metres
Least Depth:	Stern – 3 metres.

The small 1,931grt engines aft coastal freighter *Gosei Maru* was launched in 1939.

The shipbuilders Tsurumi Seitetsu Zosen K.K. began construction of the medium sized coastal cargo ship *Gosei Maru* in Yokohama in 1937. She was one of a class of such freighters that were mass produced to a standard design prior to the outbreak of war in much the same way as Great Britain had used mass produced *standard ships* during WWI and the USA would produce *Liberty* ships to a standard design during WWII.

She was constructed with one deck, and her engine and machinery were set aft below the poop island at the stern of the ship. She was navigated from a slender bridge superstructure set forward of amidships, towards the bow.

Cargo holds consumed basically the full length of the ship from her machinery compartments aft at the poop island, extending beneath the bridge superstructure to the bow. She was fitted with a steam engine manufactured by Tsurumi Seitetsu Zosen K.K. that drove her single screw to push her along at a service speed of 10 knots and a maximum speed of 13 knots. She had an operating radius of 6,800 nautical miles at 11 knots.

At the bow, her raised fo'c'sle held the anchor windlass. Her foremast rose from the fo'c'sle bulkhead and was fitted with cargo handling booms and associated winches.

Dropping down to the well deck, forward of the bridge, a large cargo hatch gave access to her foredeck Hold No 1, which dropped down to the bottom of the ship and extended beneath the bridge superstructure.

The slender bridge superstructure rose up three deck levels with a pilot house on top. Immediately abaft the bridge was a goalpost pair of kingposts with cargo booms to work her large rectangular main hold between the bridge superstructure and her larger stern deckhouse.

The mainmast rose up from the leading edge of the poop island with cargo booms and associated winches to work the main hold. Her tall coal burner's smokestack rose up from the stern superstructure, on top of which the ship's lifeboats swung in davits on the Boat Deck. Cabins at shelter deck level, each with a porthole, ringed around the poop island, flanking the engine casing. The boiler room and engine room were situated below - and at the stern, her steering gear was housed directly above the rudder.

Gosei Maru was launched 6 February 1939 and fitted out afloat before being registered in Tokyo and entering service with Koun Kisen K.K. under the managership of the well-established Yamashita Kisen K.K. (formed in 1901).

Less than two years later, at the outbreak of war, *Gosei Maru* was assigned as a supply ship for the Sixth Fleet – the submarine fleet – and during 1942 transported torpedoes and depth charges around Japan.

During 1943, she operated as an IJA *Rikugun Yusosen* transport ship used in a variety of transport roles ferrying military personnel and supplies such as food, torpedoes, steel, crated fighters, aircraft spares, bombs and shells between the Marianas, Caroline's and Marshall Islands and the Palaus. In this role she made many voyages from Japan out to forward bases such as Rabaul and Truk.

On 2 November 1943, she was lying at Rabaul when 75 American B-25 Mitchell medium bombers escorted by 70 Lockheed P-38 Lighting fighters raided airfields and shipping. *Gosei Maru* was one of the many ships damaged in the attack but was soon repaired.

On 2 December 1943, *Gosei Maru* was able to depart Rabaul for Truk in an escorted convoy – arriving at Truk on 5 December 1943. She thereafter returned to Yokosuka in Japan to collect further supplies for another voyage to the beleaguered outposts of Truk and Rabaul.

Gosei Maru departed Yokosuka on 9 January 1944 in a convoy bound for Truk and Rabaul. The convoy was escorted by the auxiliary netlayer *Kogi Maru* and the modern 255-ft long escort vessel *Fukue,* which was armed with three 12cm (4.7-inch) main guns, four 25mm AA autocannon and carried 36 depth charges. The holds of *Gosei Maru* were crowded with 10 crated Mitsubishi A6M Type O Zero fighters and some 180 belly tanks for Zeros, bombers and reconnaissance planes, which extended the aircraft's range. She also carried aerial bombs, 250 tons of shells, provisions, landing barges and coal.

Travelling at 9.5 knots, the convoy stopped over at Chichi Jima for a couple of days before pushing on to Truk, where the convoy arrived on 24 January 1944. Six days later, on 30 January, *Gosei Maru* departed Truk in convoy for Rabaul, where she arrived on 4 February 1944.

Just three days later, on 7 February 1944, she departed Rabaul for Truk, carrying torpedoes for the Sixth Fleet submarines as well as depth charges. She arrived in the Truk lagoon for what would be the last time on 12 February 1944 and anchored up about 200 yards offshore from Uman Island, the southmost of the main group of islands used as the Sixth Fleet Anchorage.

As the Operation HAILSTONE air raids exploded across the skies of Truk just five days later at dawn on 17 February, *Gosei Maru* was still anchored close to Uman Island and was one of a group of four cargo ships off Uman attacked by TF 58 aircraft. She however survived the day's attacks.

The following day, 18 February 1944, Strike 3C aircraft from *Monterey* and *Bunker Hill* raided shipping off Uman between 1015 - 1100. As they swept in from the south east, they found that the largest of four cargo ships off the east shore of Uman, *Unkai Maru No 6*, had already been attacked and was on fire and smoking heavily.

The U.S. pilots turned their attention to the unfortunate *Gosei Maru*, the TBF torpedo bombers manoeuvering into position for their attack runs. The first two TBF's attacked and dropped their torpedoes - but got erratic runs. One torpedo passed forward of *Gosei Maru's* bow and sped off into the distance. The other ran through all four cargo ships narrowly missing three of them.

The second pair of *Monterey* TBF's then attacked – and a torpedo from one hit *Gosei Maru* – just forward of her superstructure on the starboard side adjacent to Hold No 1, blasting a large hole open to the sea. It is believed that the ship was light, with her holds by this time largely empty, as American aviators reported that the ship was riding high before their attack. *Light* cargo ships were known to sink quickly, often within just a few minutes, as the large holds became vast spaces that could take on an enormous volume of water. If holds were full with a cargo, such as timber, then only a fraction of the volume of water could get in - and the timber cargo would give some buoyancy.

Mortally wounded, *Gosei Maru* listed to port, rolled over and rapidly sunk.

The wreck today

Today, the wreck of *Gosei Maru* lies on her port beam ends on a sloping seabed with her bows in deeper water of about 35 metres and her uppermost stern sitting in just 10 metres of water. The deeper bow rests on the flat seabed at the bottom of the slope whilst the stern of the wreck, with her rudder and 4-bladed propeller, projects up over the top of the sandy reef flat. The uppermost starboard rail rises to just a few metres short of the surface and this is where you start the dive, from where you will see the ship below you from the surface. You can then follow the wreck down the slope to the atmospheric bow in 35 metres - before rising back slowly up the wreck, decompressing gently as you go. The gentle depth makes this wreck ideal as a second dive of the day.

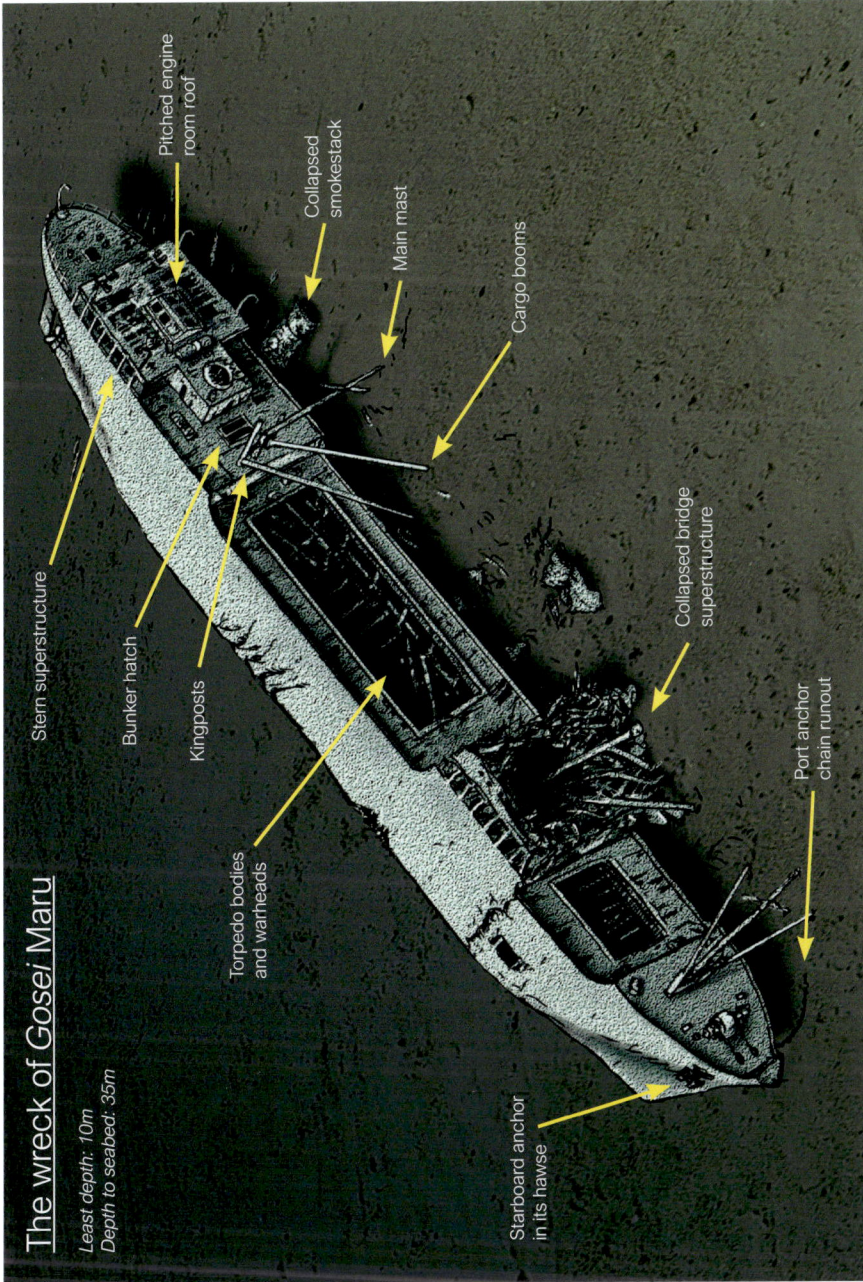

The wreck of *Gosei Maru*

Least depth: 10m
Depth to seabed: 35m

Stern superstructure

Bunker hatch

Kingposts

Torpedo bodies
and warheads

Starboard anchor
in its hawse

Pitched engine
room roof

Collapsed
smokestack

Main mast

Cargo booms

Collapsed bridge
superstructure

Port anchor
chain runout

Artist's impression of the wreck of *Gosei Maru*, which lies on a gentle slope with her stern in just 10 metres and her bow is in 35 metres.

At the bow, on the now almost vertical fo'c'sle deck, sits the anchor windlass, from which both chains run out to their hawse pipes. The port anchor chain is run out along the seabed from its hawse – curving away into the distance out of sight along the white sand. The starboard anchor is still held snug in its hawse. The lower section of the stem, beneath the starboard anchor, shows violent deformation whilst the adjacent shell plating shows compression damage from a near miss bomb.

The foremast, which rose up from the aft bulkhead of the fo'c'sle deck has snapped a few metres above the deck, and the upper section now angles downwards to rest on the port arm of its crosstree. The cargo booms, goosenecked to short kingposts either side of the foremast, also run downwards to rest their ends on the seabed. Heavy duty winches for cargo handling are set at the mast foot.

Moving aft and beginning to rise up the wreck, the large open hatch for Hold No 1 appears, forward of the bridge superstructure. At the bottom of the hull here, almost underneath the bridge, there is a large hole in the keel, some 5 metres across, where a torpedo has hit, just forward of the bridge superstructure. The edge of the hole in the shell plating is curved smoothly inwards - and it is easy to swim in and out of the ship here. Light from outside the ship floods into the hold through this hole – and the hole seems so far down towards the keel of the ship that I suspect she must have already been listing when this torpedo struck.

The bridge superstructure shows much evidence of damage caused by the torpedo strike to the hull nearby. Structural beams and framing have been mangled and distorted with some plates being blown away. Over time, the weakened superstructure has collapsed downwards and forwards towards the seabed taking the goalpost pair of kingposts, immediately abaft, with it.

Aft of the bridge superstructure, the well deck between the bridge and poop island is essentially one large rectangular cargo hold, which has no hatch cover beams in place. The forward section of this hold contains dozens of torpedo bodies that have tumbled to the lower port side of the hold. Each torpedo body has two counter rotating propellers. The warheads are not connected to the bodies but are stored separately. Most of these torpedo bodies are relatively intact although several have corroded away to reveal the inner propulsion machinery and smaller internal propellant tanks of the torpedo.

The aftmost section of this hold, just forward of the stern deckhouse, has large sections of hull plating lying over it, obscuring access. A final small hold near the machinery spaces held her bunker coal.

The mainmast has a fixed ladder running up it – and is situated at the leading edge of the stern deckhouse. It now angles downwards, like the foremast, to rest its port crosstree arm on the seabed. Two heavy-duty cargo booms run out from short kingposts either side of its base to rest their ends on the seabed. The tall smokestack that marks her as a coal burning ship has collapsed to the seabed where it lies near the wreck.

The poop island deckhouse remains fairly intact, although the wooden decking has rotted away to reveal the latticework of her structure. The engine room is situated at the very stern and has a pitched roof with skylights on top of the deckhouse, which are open and allow access. Access is also possible from the cargo hold and the bunker hold - or via the funnel opening. Inside the engine room, the triple expansion steam engine is ringed with catwalks, gauges and valves.

On top of the stern deckhouse on the boat deck, pairs of empty lifeboat davits are situated on either side of the deck. Those on the starboard side are still in the swung-in position - as the ship quickly rolled to port, these boats would not have got away. The davits on the port side are in the swung-out position. Forced draft mushroom ventilators are dotted around with two small kingposts with fixed ladders running up them. In places on the starboard side of the hull here there are entry wounds through the shell plating from strafing by U.S. planes.

A swim round the fantail reveals the photogenic rudder and large 4-bladed propeller.

10. *Hanagawa Maru*
Wartime Standard Merchant Type 1B cargo ship (1943)
U.S. Recognition Code: MKFM

Tol Island

Tonnage:	4,739grt
Dimensions:	367.5-ft long; beam of 52-ft; draught of 30-ft approx.
Launched:	31 August 1943
Sunk:	18 February 1944
Cause of loss:	Torpedoed by TF 58 aircraft during Operation HAILSTONE
Wreck location:	Tol Island, western lagoon
Depth to seabed:	25-30 metres
Least depth:	15 metres - bridge
Other name:	*Hanakawa Maru*

The passenger cargo vessel *Hanagawa Maru* was built during 1942 and 1943 for Kawasaki Kisen K.K. at the Kawasaki Dockyard in Kobe. She was built as one sixteen similar *standard ships* – built to a standard design and specification. More commonly known today as *Hanakawa Maru*, she was a three island, well deck vessel, with a raised fo'c'sle at the bow, two foredeck cargo holds, a split

The 4,667grt *Bingo Maru* – sister ship to *Hanagawa Maru*

superstructure amidships, two holds in the aft well deck and a poop island superstructure at the stern.

A small hold for bunker coal split the tall bridge superstructure from the superstructure that housed the boiler room and engine room and which had a limited number of passenger cabins along either side of the fireproof engine casing. A coal-fired reciprocating engine drove her single screw to achieve a modest service speed of 11 knots.

During the 1930's, Japanese ships were built to modern fast designs. However, with her sea-lanes enormously extended soon after the outbreak of the Pacific war, and with the successful degradation of her existing shipping stock by U.S. submarines, Japan realised that she had to radically boost ship production - and so began work on new modern standard ship designs in 1942. But with approximately two years required to design and begin building new types of standard ship, construction of the newer designs of standard ships would only start in early 1944. In the interim, to boost her supply fleet to service her far-flung Pacific garrisons, from 1941 onwards, Japan started a program of mass standard ship production using older, tried and tested, pre-war designs. Between December 1941 and July 1944 some 125 standard ships were built to a number of different designs.

The Japanese adopted the Wartime Standard Merchant Type 1B cargo ship design in 1943, constructing 16 Type 1B's in 1943 and 1944. The Type 1B's had five deck hold hatches and used coal-fired steam turbine engines that were housed amidships. They had a single shaft and double bottoms.

The hull of the Type 1 B cargo ship *Hanagawa Maru* was launched in Kobe on 31 August 1943 and after fitting out afloat she entered service with the IJN on 25 October 1943. She would only have a short service career of four months before Operation HAILSTONE consigned her to the bottom of the Truk lagoon for eternity.

Just five days after joining the IJN, she departed Mutsure in Japan on 30 October 1943, bound for Takao, Formosa in a large supply convoy consisting of two tankers and fourteen merchant ships escorted by Patrol Boat PB-2 (ex Minekaze-class destroyer *Nadakaze* (1918)) and the auxiliary gunboat *Kazan Maru*. The convoy arrived at Takao on 4 November 1943.

On 25 January 1944, *Hanagawa Maru* departed Yokosuka, Japan, in convoy No. 3125 bound for Truk. With her were the present day Truk wreck *Reiyo Maru* and the 3,560-ton Zatsuyosen *Tamashima Maru*. The convoy was escorted by the IJN Shimushu-class *kaibokan* escort vessel *Hirado* and the sub chaser CH-52.

On 30 January 1944, five days into the passage, the convoy was attacked by the American submarine *Spearfish* (SS-190). Although *Hanagawa Maru* escaped injury, *Spearfish* hit *Tamashima Maru* with a torpedo that detonated her cargo of ammunition. The resulting explosion was catastrophic, and the ship sunk almost immediately.

Hirado drove off *Spearfish* by dropping 46 depth charges, allowing the rest of the convoy to proceed, and eventually enter the Truk lagoon on 7 February 1944. Two days later, on 9 February 1944, *Hanagawa Maru* departed Truk with *Reiyo Maru* for Saipan - again in a convoy escorted by the IJN escort vessel *Hirado*.

After a quick turnaround in Saipan, *Hanagawa Maru* was soon back in Truk with a cargo of aviation fuel and fuel oil in 55-gallon drums packing her holds. She moved to the fueling dock on Tol Island, on the western periphery of the main group of Truk islands, unknowingly immediately before the opening of Operation HAILSTONE on 17 February 1944.

As the first waves of TF 58 planes swept over Truk, U.S. aviators spotted *Hanagawa Maru* at anchor about 500 yards off the south eastern shore of Tol Island. The ship was mistakenly identified by *Bunker Hill* aircrew as a 12,000-ton oiler and so was not attacked on the first day of the HAILSTONE raid, possibly to avoid clouds of burning black fuel oil obscuring target selection.

On the second day of the operation, DOG-DAY, 18 February 1944, as waves of TF 58 aircraft once again swept across the lagoon, unchallenged by any Japanese fighters, *Hanagawa Maru* was still anchored with her stern towards Tol Island near the fueling dock.

13 SB2C Helldivers armed with one 1,000-lb bomb or two 500-lb bombs, and eight TBF Avenger torpedo-bombers carrying a single torpedo set to run at 6-ft, launched from *Bunker Hill* between 0515 and 0530 for Strike 3A. Escorted by 4 Hellcat fighters, the flight reached North Pass and then followed the west side of the atoll reef to the south before the SB2Cs began diving at shipping off Uman - hitting several freighters, including *Sankisan Maru*. The TBF Avengers had followed the SB2C's south as they arrived over the lagoon, but when the SB2C's turned east to attack shipping off Uman, the TBF's turned north towards the south side of Tol where they spotted what had been reported the day before as a large oiler or tanker near Tol. The flight leader broke off for a two-plane attack, making a broadside run from the south as the rest of the TBF's watched events unfold.

The *Bunker Hill* TBF Avenger dropped its torpedo, set for a running depth of 6-feet, and scored a direct hit on the starboard side of the stationary *Hanagawa Maru*, between her bow and bridge superstructure. This first torpedo explosion caused a large burst of flame as her cargo of aviation fuel in her foredeck holds ignited, blowing away the hatch cover beams, which went flying into the air along with 55-gallon drums of Avgas.

It was immediately clear that she had been dealt a mortal blow – and she began to settle quickly by the bow, a slick of burning fuel spreading outwards towards the shore. Black fuel oil smoke started to immediately billow upwards from the forward section of the stricken ship. The damage was so severe that within 3-4 minutes *Hanagawa Maru* had sunk from sight leaving only a burning slick on the surface. Burning debris floated ashore and reportedly started a fire in a mangrove swamp, which spread to some local buildings and a church.

The wreck today

Today the wreck of the passenger/cargo vessel *Hanagawa Maru* rests upright on her keel in about 25-35 metres of water. The wreck lies some several hundred yards from shore, near the southeast end of Tol Island – where she had been at anchor. The shallowest parts of the wreck and the masts can be seen from the surface as the dive boat arrives on scene.

Tol is one of the small group of islands well to the west of the main central islands of the atoll, Weno and Tonoas, and it is a transfer by fast boat to the site of more than an hour. This distance, when there are so many classic wrecks much closer, means that the wreck is dived relatively infrequently.

When she sank in 1944, she had a full cargo of aviation fuel and fuel oil in 55-gallon drums in her holds and as a result of corrosion, this dangerous cargo, largely unnoticeable to a diver's eyes, has leaked to the surface since. For a long time, the wreck was more or less off limits for diving and was avoided by locals and visiting divers alike. Divers reported painful skin burns that left scars in addition to damaging kit.

There was still a strong general smell of fuel in the 1980's above the wreck but over more recent years these problems have been dissipating. Throughout the 1990's small droplets of fuel still meandered slowly to the surface – but on occasion, even today, if the cargo has been disturbed, or more corroded drums have finally succumbed to corrosion and released their contents, the strong smell of fuel still greets divers as they arrive topside. Divers today take great care in the cargo holds to avoid disturbing any fuel drums or dislodging sediment,

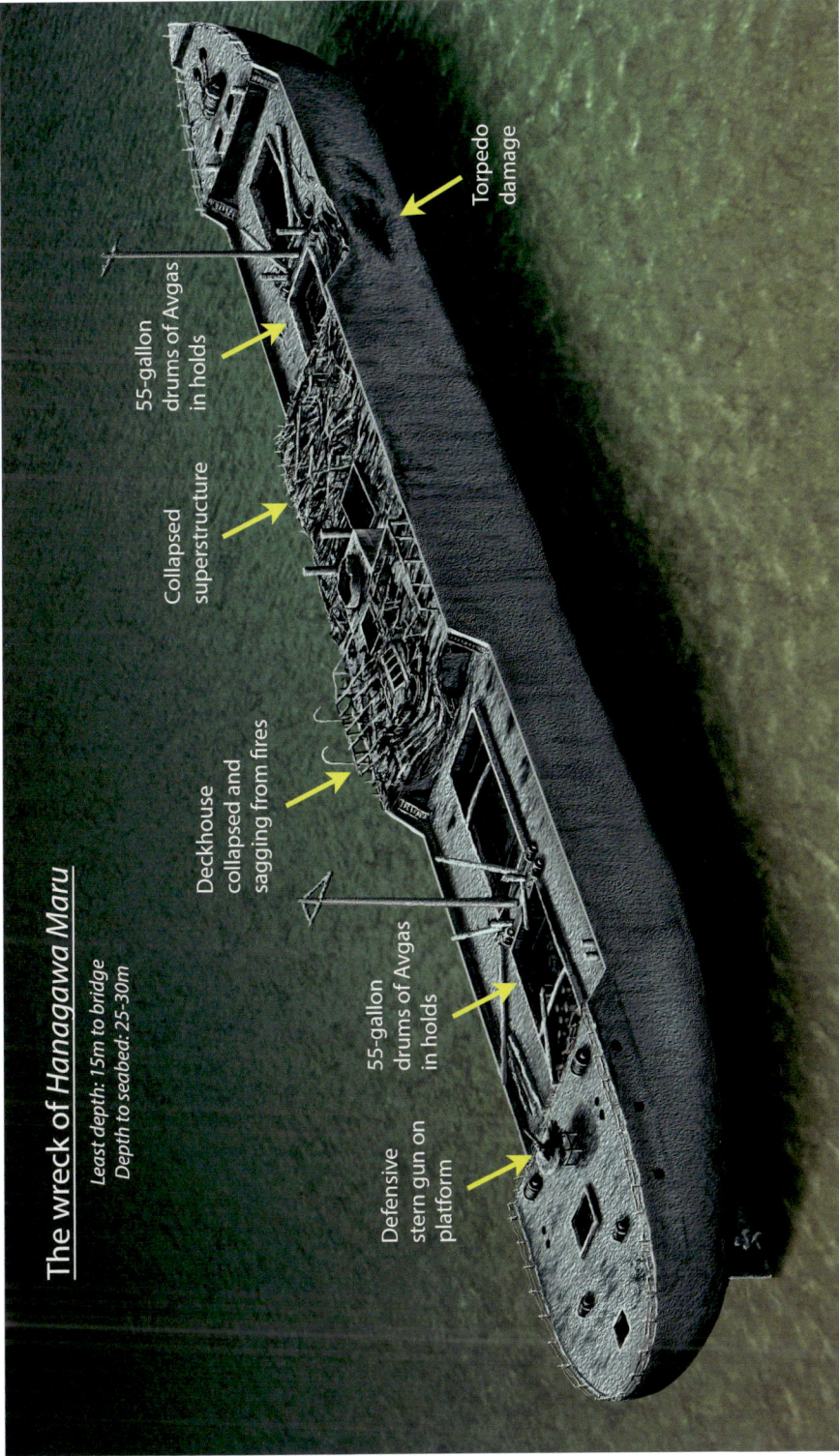

The wreck of *Hanagawa Maru*

Least depth: 15m to bridge
Depth to seabed: 25-30m

Torpedo damage

55-gallon drums of Avgas in holds

Collapsed superstructure

Deckhouse collapsed and sagging from fires

55-gallon drums of Avgas in holds

Defensive stern gun on platform

Artist's impression of the wreck of *Hanagawa Maru*, lying in 25–30 metres of water in a remote location but still holding much of her cargo of AvGas in 55-gallon drums.

which is impregnated with fuel, by careless finning. I have seen a diver's skin quickly blister up back in the dive boat after a dive where he had unknowingly swum through some leaking invisible fuel cargo. The skin blisters, the blister goes brown and then quite rapidly goes black.

Down on the wreck, at the bow, there is a twin anchor windlass sat on the fo'c'sle deck - with the starboard anchor still run out to the seabed under tension (she had been at anchor when she was sunk). The guardrail around the fo'c'sle deck is still evident, heavily covered with coral. A fixed set of steps on either side of the fo'c'sle bulkhead leads down to the well deck. Beside each set of steps is an open doorway into the fo'c'sle spaces. The starboard door lies fallen against the stairway steps.

The internal dividing walls of the fo'c'sle spaces have largely rotted away to leave one large common space where there are coiled warps of mooring cables stowed in between the spurling pipes, which led the anchor chains up from the anchor locker below, to the windlass above on the fo'c'sle deck.

The large rectangular hatch for Hold No 1 is found on the well deck. There are no hatch cover beams in place, they were blown away during the explosion. The hold is full right up to the underside of the prominent tween deck with 55-gallon fuel drums - some still holding their contents. The cargo booms from the foremast, which when stowed extended over this Hold, are also missing, no doubt blown away.

The foremast, with its crosstree, is still upright and rises up to a depth of about 6 metres. Cargo winches and forced draught ventilators are dotted around its base.

On the starboard side of Hold No 2, can be seen the fatal damage from the torpedo explosion and the secondary explosion as the fuel cargo ignited. There is a gaping 25-foot-wide hole fringed by torn and jagged metal, that runs from the keel almost to the weather deck. The tween deck has been severed and blown out of shape on the starboard side and the hatch cover beams are also missing. Cement bags and more 55-gallon fuel drums lie scattered about inside the hold whilst others have tumbled outside to the seabed.

Moving aft from Hold No 2, the frontage of the bridge superstructure rises up before you. On either side of the well deck, fixed steps lead up to walkways at shelter deck level along the side of the superstructure - and tall forced draft ventilators still stand just inboard. Despite the collapse of the upper bridge levels, doors open into the passenger/crew accommodation low down on either side of the superstructure. The galley with its stoves and ovens, plates and bottles can be found at the aft end of this superstructure and bottles, pans and crockery have been taken out and placed on top of the collapsed bridge.

Only the lowest molded steel level of the bridge superstructure is still present. Whilst it is fairly intact on the starboard side, this level of the superstructure seems to be angled backwards and is collapsing on the port side from the devastating effect of the large blast in Hold No 2.

The 3-4 deck levels above this bottom level of superstructure, which would have been constructed of thin steel plating and wood on a steel skeletal frame, have collapsed down and concertinaed. The superstructure has been weakened by the fierce explosion, just in front in Hold No 2 and by fire. Hanging in the water just above the collapsed bridge at a depth of about 15 metres, the top is uneven to the eye, with distressed rotted roofing. You can see the deck levels squished down one on top of the other, the normally robust girders and stringers of the structure are weakened and out of line.

Abaft the collapsed bridge superstructure is the small coaling hatch for the bunker hold in the gap between the two sections of the split superstructure. Cargo winches are set on the deck aft of the hatch and a cargo derrick lies across the hatch.

A quadruple kingpost structure with ventilators was set abaft this hatch and immediately in front of the single-story engine casing and passenger accommodation superstructure. Only the two outer kingposts were still standing on my last visit in 2018 and the cross member connecting all four kingposts is no longer there.

Continuing to move aft, the upper levels of the split superstructure above the boiler and engine rooms have collapsed. The smokestack has also collapsed, but aft of its rim can be found the pitched roof and skylights of the engine room - with more forced draught ventilators dotted around. Outboard, lifeboat davits are swung inboard. Such was the speed she sank that the crew never had the opportunity to swing the boats out.

The aft section of this deckhouse has sagged and collapsed, almost to well deck level, again it would appear that the structural beams of its skeleton have been weakened by fire. But despite this, the engine room can be entered. It is a large space criss crossed by catwalks, the walls adorned with gauges and valves. The collapse above is evident with flat sections of plating strewn all over the place on top of the engine and catwalks. This area is very fragile nowadays and I wouldn't advise doing much penetration here.

The aft portion of the ship is in much better condition, with large rectangular hatches for Hold No's 4 & 5 set in the well-deck, at a depth of about 28 metres. Each hatch has a solitary cover beam across its middle. The tween decks are intact.

The mainmast rises up from a small masthouse on the deck between the two holds and has a short kingpost either side. The two cargo booms running forward from the kingposts over Hold No 4 are swung to port indicating the list of the ship as it sank. The two booms running aft over Hold No 5 are also swung to port, with the starboard boom being sheared off and having lost about half its length.

There are hundreds of 55-gallon fuel drums in both levels of both holds, with more in Hold No 5 than Hold No 4. Many appear still intact - and holding their contents. I can't stress how fragile these are, please do not go into the holds and disturb the drums in any way. On one dive, a diver, who had not gone into the holds, surfaced as normal at the end of the dive. Although he was unaware that he had swum into an invisible cloud of aviation fuel, his neck quickly blistered, the burn going brown then black. Give these holds a wide berth.

At the very bottom of the aft holds, the prop shaft tunnel can be seen running aft on the centre line with several hatch cover beams fallen across it.

Approaching the poop island, a stairway leads up from the well deck to the poop deck on either side. Two open doors into its dark innards, which are lit by blue light streaming in through the portholes that ring around the poop island. The floor inside is strewn with bottles and coiled warps of cables.

Pressing aft through the poop island, an open doorway leads into the aftmost space, which houses the steering gear and quadrant and has a deck access hatch above to the

Above: Crockery is stamped
TOYO TOKI KAISHA, now part
of Noritake Co Ltd in Nagoya.

Left: Inside the poop island at the
stern, the steering gear (Author)

auxiliary steering position. At the aftmost side of the steering quadrant there is a large wheel which was used for manual rudder steering by crew. The vertical rod that rises from the steering gear to the auxiliary steering position above can also be seen.

On the poop deck above at the stern, is set a semi-circular gun platform with a 12 cm/12 short naval gun (4.7-inch) of the type commonly installed as a defensive gun on Japanese WWII merchant ships of less than 5,000-tons. The gun fired fixed QF rounds, where the shell was attached to the propellant cartridge like a rifle bullet. The 12cm short gun had a rate of fire of 8 rounds per minute and a horizontal maximum firing range of just over 3 miles. The gun could elevate to give an effective AA range of 2,800 metres (9,200ft) at +75° but the rate of elevation and traverse was found to be too slow for effective AA use against the new breeds of fast U.S. aircraft. The gun could be used for any surface contact and for anti-submarine defence.

The 12cm short naval gun on *Hanagawa Maru* is elevated upwards towards the sky – frozen in action at the moment of the attack.

The auxiliary steering position at the stern has a fallen engine order telegraph and in the rooms beneath are artillery shells for the 12cm gun and depth charges for the stern roll off boxes.

The four-bladed propeller can be seen at a depth of about 30 metres.

11. *Heian Maru*
Passenger Cargo liner (1930)
IJN *Tokusetsu Sensui-Bokan* Auxiliary Submarine Tender (1941)
Combined Fleet Anchorage
U.S. Recognition Code: 12 MFKMK

Combined Fleet Anchorage

Tonnage:	11,616grt
Dimensions:	511.6-ft long; beam of 66-ft; draught of 41-ft
Launched:	16 April 1930
Sunk:	18 February 1944
Cause of loss:	Bombed and torpedoed by TF 58 aircraft during Operation HAILSTONE
Wreck location:	Combined Fleet anchorage, west of Tonoas
Depth to seabed:	35 metres
Least depth:	12 metres

The 11,616grt passenger-cargo liner *Heian Maru* was laid down in Osaka on 19 June 1929 by the shipbuilders Osaka Iron Works Ltd for Nippon Yusen Kabushiki Kaisha Line, otherwise known as the NYK Line, one of the largest shipping companies in the world.

In the late 1920's NYK began a major shipbuilding program aimed at expanding its international passenger service - and eight passenger liners were built. Three of the passenger liners, *Hikawa Maru*, *Hie Maru* and *Heian Maru* were built specifically for the NYK's North Pacific passenger/cargo service between Yokohama (Japan) and Seattle in Canada. The luxurious design of the ships was based on the traditional British liner with lounge, reading room, writing room, dining salon and décor throughout following the theme.

A sizeable ocean-going vessel, she was powered by two 8-cylinder 4-stroke Burmesister & Wain diesel engines that drove her two propellers to give a service speed of 15 knots and a range of 18,700 nautical miles at 15 knots. She was fitted out for

The 11,616grt IJN Submarine tender *Heian Maru* was launched in 1930 and requisitioned by the IJN in 1941.

carrying oil in 3 deep tanks aft and had three decks, with a 4th deck in Hold No 3. She was fitted with nine watertight bulkheads and could carry 330 passengers in luxury.

On 16 April 1930, 11 months after being laid down, the ship was named after the Heian Shrine, a Shinto Shrine in Kyoto, and launched for fitting out afloat. She was completed on 24 November 1930 and almost a month later embarked on her maiden crossing from Hong Kong to Seattle on 18 December 1930. When she arrived in Seattle in January 1931, she had set a new transpacific speed record for Nippon Yusen Kaisha ships and had also impressed Seattle shippers engaged in the Oriental trade. Following the positive press on her arrival, the ship was opened up to the public and nearly 15,000 people toured the vessel, with hundreds more being turned away.

Heian Maru initially entered NYK's regular passenger/cargo service from Hong Kong, via Shanghai, to Japanese ports such as Kobe and Yokohama and then on to Victoria in Canada and to Seattle. In 1935 she worked on the Osaka to Seattle route via Vancouver, Nagoya, Shimidzu and Yokohama.

In July 1941, as tensions between the USA and Japan rose, President Franklin D. Roosevelt ordered the freezing of Japanese assets in America whilst *Heian Maru* was en route to Seattle with a cargo of raw silk and many Jewish refugees from war torn Europe. The ship had to stop about 150 miles off Cape Flattery and spend two days sitting there whilst officials worked out a guarantee that the ship would not be seized when it entered American waters to offload its cargo of raw silk. All passengers disembarked in Seattle and there was outrage when 144 Japanese passengers, preparing to board for the return voyage to Yokohama, were strip-searched by U.S. officials. *Heian Maru* sailed for the last time, in ballast, from Seattle on 4 August 1941, arriving in Yokohama on 16 August 1941.

On 3 October 1941, just two months before Japan began her Pacific war with the surprise raid on Pearl Harbor, the IJN requisitioned *Heian Maru* and her sister ship *Hie Maru* as Heian Maru-class auxiliary submarine depot ships.

Two weeks later, on 15 October 1941, *Heian Maru* was attached to the Yokosuka Naval District and conversion works started at Mitsubishi Heavy Industries shipyard in Kobe. She was fitted with four 15cm/45 (6-inch) 41st Year Type single mount BL deck guns, which fired separately loaded bagged charges and projectiles. The guns offered a rate of fire of about five rounds per minute and a maximum range of about nine miles.

Two dual mount Type 93 13-mm machine guns were also fitted at this time, along with one 1100mm diameter searchlight, one 900mm diameter searchlight and a 3.5 metre rangefinder. Degaussing cables were fitted around her hull to counter her magnetic signature and give protection against magnetic mines.

Two months after the conversion works started, war erupted in the Pacific with the surprise strike on Pearl Harbor on 7 December 1941. Three weeks after the Pearl raid, the conversion works were completed on 30 December 1941.

Heian Maru was initially assigned as a submarine depot ship to the 1st Submarine Squadron (SubRon 1) of the three Submarine Squadrons of the Sixth Fleet (Submarines) based at Kwajalein in the Marshall Islands. The following day, 31 December 1941, she departed Kure for Kwajalein – arriving there to take up her duties on 8 January 1942.

On 1 February 1942, whilst still at Kwajalein, she saw her first action during air raids launched against Kwajalein and Wotje by Vice Admiral William F. Halsey from the Task Force 8 carrier USS *Enterprise* (CV-6). Douglas SBD Dauntless dive-bombers of VB-6 and VS-6, along with VT-6 Douglas TBD Devastator torpedo-bombers sunk a transport ship and damaged the submarine depot ship *Yasukuni Maru*, along with several other ships and the light cruiser *Katori*, which was the flagship of the Commander of Sixth Fleet (Submarines) Vice Admiral Shimizu Mitsumi. On 9 February 1942, *Heian Maru* was despatched from Kwajalein to Kure in Japan.

During the latter part of 1942, and the early part of 1943, after the IJN Combined Fleet had moved its main base to Truk, *Heian Maru* made several trips from Japan to Truk and Rabaul, carrying troops and vehicles as well as supplying torpedoes, provisions, spares and crew transfers for Sixth Fleet (Submarines) based there.

Rabaul is situated at the northern end of the island of New Britain, some 370 nautical miles north east of New Guinea and at the north western end of the chain of Solomon Islands that leads to Bougainville island. At the time, Rabaul was the main Japanese base for the Solomon Islands and New Guinea campaigns. Known as the Pearl Harbor of the South Pacific, Rabaul was defended by thousands of troops, more than 350 AA gun installations and five airfields.

Whilst in Rabaul, the Allied operation to isolate Rabaul gained momentum, and on 1 January 1943, USAAF B-17 Flying Fortress and B-24 Liberator bombers attacked shipping in Simpson Harbor. *Heian Maru* escaped unscathed, whilst her AA gunners fired some 8,000 13.2mm rounds in response.

On 3 January 1943, another American attack took place against shipping at Rabaul just after dawn - this time with six B-17 bombers and six B-24 bombers flying from Espiritu Santo. Several USAAF bombers targeted *Heian Maru*, scoring a number of near misses on her port side. Hits were scored on about 10 Japanese ships, one broke in two and six others were left burning. AA gunners on *Heian Maru* fired off more than 7,000 rounds at the American bombers during this attack, in which two B-17's were shot down.

In May 1943, the Imperial General HQ decided to evacuate their garrison troops at Kiska Islands in the Aleutian chain of islands, which lie south of the Bering Sea, spanning the North Atlantic between the Kamchatka Peninsula and Alaska. They had been seized by Japan the previous year in June 1942 at the time of the failed Midway invasion.

As part of the Kiska evacuation, codenamed Operation KE, on 27 May 1943, *Heian Maru* departed Yokosuka for Paramushiro, and throughout June and July 1943, the ship served as Rear Admiral Koda's HQ during the evacuation of the Kiska garrison. The operation was completed on 28 July 1943, when *Heian Maru* returned to Yokosuka.

On 5 September 1943, *Heian Maru* was attached directly to the Combined Fleet and sent to Shanghai. She arrived there on 19 September and hastily embarked 1,900 troops of the 17th Infantry Division, 240 vehicles, supplies and a cargo of torpedoes.

The following day, 20 September 1943, she departed Shanghai bound for Truk and Rabaul in a transportation convoy of several *Maru*'s escorted by three destroyers and a flying boat tender.

The convoy arrived at Truk, where by now most of the Combined Fleet was holed up, on 2 October 1943. *Heian Maru* unloaded her torpedoes before the convoy departed that evening for Rabaul, arriving there on 5 October 1943. After offloading the remainder of her cargo there, the convoy set off for the return passage, via Truk. *Heian Maru* arrived back at Yokosuka on 21 October 1943.

Between 23 October and 7 November 1943, *Heian Maru* was refitted at Yokosuka. Her four older 15cm (6-inch) 41st Year Type deck guns were removed and replaced by two more modern 12cm (4.7-inch) 11th Year Type naval guns. These guns fired separately loaded cased charges and projectiles, the cased charges being easier to load and not so susceptible to water damage on wet decks as bagged charges. In addition, two twin mount Type 96 25mm AA auto cannons and two twin Type 93 13.2mm machine guns were added, along with sonar.

On 7 November 1943, with her refitting works completed, she departed Yokosuka in a convoy bound for Truk. En route, early on the morning of 19 November, the American submarine *Dace* (SS-247) attacked the convoy. *Heian Maru* was targeted – but the torpedo missed. The Japanese *kaibōkan* escort vessel *Oki* attacked *Dace* with depth charges, and *Heian Maru* dropped one of her stern mounted depth charges. *Dace* was forced to withdraw, undamaged, and the convoy arrived safely at Truk on 23 November 1943. Here, for the next months up until the HAILSTONE raid on 17/18 February 1944, *Heian Maru* was flagship for SubRon 1, tending to submarines operating from Truk, transferring torpedoes, water, fuel and stores.

On 17 February 1944, the first morning of Operation HAILSTONE, the dazzle painted *Heian Maru* was anchored off Dublon Island opposite the Naval Station and the submarine-servicing base. The cargo ship *Urakami Maru* (now a Palau wreck) was anchored about 250 yards away whilst the brilliant all-white hospital ship *Tenno Maru* (later *Hikawa Maru No 2*) was at anchor about 6-700 yards to the northwest.

Just before dawn, an air raid alarm was given and the SubRon 1 flagship *Heian Maru*, which was carrying Vice Admiral Takeo Takagi and his Sixth Fleet staff, weighed anchor and got under way, steering a zigzag course north of Dublon.

At 0630, just after dawn, Strike 1A SBD dive-bombers from *Yorktown* attacked shipping in this area and scored hits on three ships anchored west of Dublon. *Heian Maru* was later strafed by Strike 1C *Enterprise* Hellcats around 1015 whilst her own gunners returned AA fire. A fire was started aboard *Heian Maru* and as it began to spread, firefighting efforts began.

After an interlude of a few hours, just after 1300, the burning ship was attacked by a single SB2C Helldiver dive-bomber from *Bunker Hill*. Two 500-lb bombs were near misses astern, but the shock of the explosion, transmitting though incompressible water, damaged one of her propeller shafts, allowing water to enter the ship and flood the aft Hold No. 6. Her crew countered by pumping fuel to her bow tanks and were able to correct her trim.

After sunset brought some respite from the marauding U.S. aircraft, the ship returned to Dublon, mooring at the pier to allow Vice Admiral Takagi and his staff to disembark. Some of the ship's dangerous cargo of submarine launched Type 95 oxygen propelled torpedoes were also offloaded.

Just after 0100, in the early hours of the next morning, 18th February, the *Enterprise* night attack by radar equipped TBF's began - and *Heian Maru* made to get under way again. The searchlights of the hospital ship *Tenno Maru*, anchored nearby, were switched on, illuminating the large red crosses on her white hull. Warning rockets and flares were fired - and Japanese AA guns ashore opened up whilst a large searchlight on Moen Island lit up the skies.

Just after 0300, *Heian Maru* was hit by two bombs in the vicinity of her engine room on the port side, starting a fire that quickly got out of control. The fire moved forward and reached the bridge and soon was threatening the foredeck Hold No 2, which held her remaining cargo of Type 95 torpedoes. About 10 minutes later, around 0312, the *Enterprise* TBF torpedo-bombers scored near miss bomb hits off the starboard bow.

As a result of the damage, *Heian Maru* settled increasingly deeper into the water- such that about two hours after the first two hits, at 0500, the ship's captain had to give the order to abandon ship. Most of the crew would reach the shore safely - but 17 had been killed and many wounded.

Four hours later, at about 0930, Strike 3B TBF Avenger torpedo-bombers from *Bunker Hill* put in a further attack on *Heian Maru*, which was still on fire. For this second strike of the day, 23 planes launched from *Bunker Hill*. Four F6F Hellcats escorted 9 TBF Avengers carrying torpedoes and 10 SB2C Helldivers, five of which were loaded with 2 x500-lb bombs whilst the other five were carrying a single 1,000-lb bomb.

The Strike 3B planes arrived over Truk at about 10,000-feet. Two SB2C Helldivers attacked a large 8,000-ton ship off the southeast tip of Dublon, their bombs causing a large explosion that sent the ship quickly to the bottom stern first. Two more SB2Cs attacked another ship in the same area again causing a large explosion. West of Fefan, the *Yamagiri Maru* was attacked by four more *Bunker Hill* SB2C planes, hit by two bombs and sunk.

Meanwhile, the TBF Avengers carrying torpedoes, joined with the F6F Hellcats which were attacking a destroyer manoeuvering at flank speed up towards North Pass, it was *Oite*. Strafing by Hellcats set *Oite* on fire, but as *Oite* completed almost a full circle by way of a S-turn, five of the TBF Avengers made a coordinated attack in which *Oite* was hit by a torpedo just abaft the bridge as it completed its starboard turn. The destroyer broke its back, splitting into two pieces and sinking.

The remaining TBF Avengers attacked two ships west of Dublon, sinking *Kensyo Maru* and attacking the damaged *Heian Maru,* which had been abandoned and was still smoking from the earlier attack - and sitting helplessly at anchor. *Heian Maru* was hit by a torpedo, on the port side amidships, that caused her to list progressively to port.

By midday, the ship was burning heavily, with the superstructure engulfed in flames as she settled deeper into the water. She finally disappeared beneath the surface later that afternoon, coming to rest on her port beam ends in 35 metres of water.

The wreck today

Today the *Heian Maru* is the largest diveable wreck in the lagoon – located to the north west of Tonoas Island (Dublon). Its uppermost parts can

A pre-war postcard of the NYK Liner *Heian Maru*

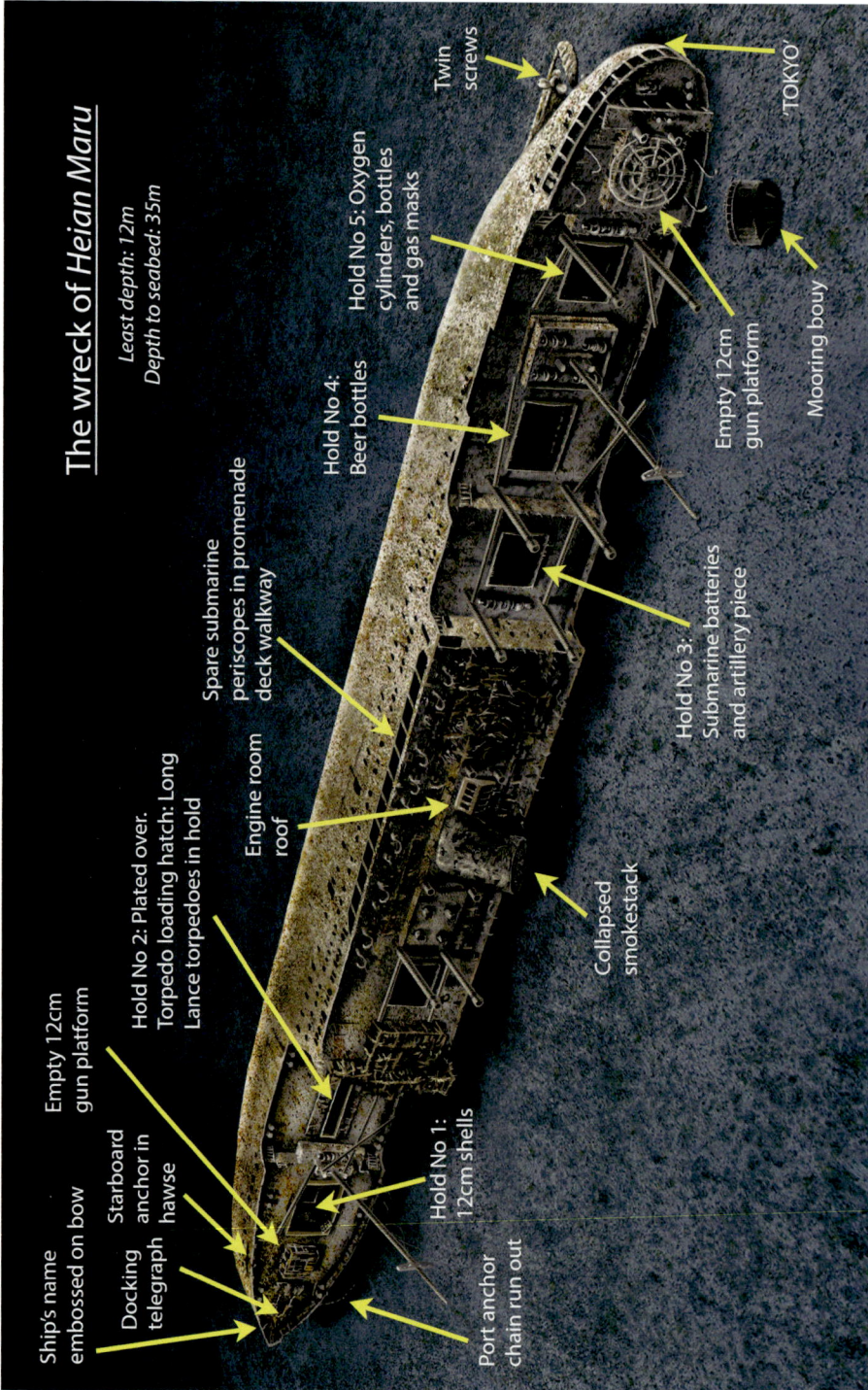

The wreck of *Heian Maru*

Least depth: 12m
Depth to seabed: 35m

Twin screws

'TOKYO'

Hold No 5: Oxygen cylinders, bottles and gas masks

Hold No 4: Beer bottles

Empty 12cm gun platform

Mooring bouy

Spare submarine periscopes in promenade deck walkway

Engine room roof

Hold No 3: Submarine batteries and artillery piece

Collapsed smokestack

Hold No 2: Plated over. Torpedo loading hatch: Long Lance torpedoes in hold

Empty 12cm gun platform

Starboard anchor in hawse

Docking telegraph

Ship's name embossed on bow

Hold No 1: 12cm shells

Port anchor chain run out

Artist's impression of the 11,616grt IJN Sixth Fleet submarine tender *Heian Maru* – the largest diveable wreck in the lagoon today.

often be seen from the surface. She lies on her port side on a gently sloping bottom with her bow in about 35 metres and her stern slightly shallower. With a beam of more than 20 metres, the least depth down to the shallowest parts of superstructure amidships is about 12 metres.

With the wreck lying on its port beam ends, her decks are now almost vertical. At the bow, on the uppermost starboard side shell plating, the embossed non-ferrous lettering of her name *Heian Maru* rises 1- 2-inches off the hull plates – the individual letters being about two feet tall. The kanji characters for her name are set directly above.

On the foc'sle deck, at the very tip of the bow, a docking telegraph for anchor handling commands to deck crew can be found. Nearby is the large bandstand platform for the bow gun– the platform however is empty as the 12cm (4.7-inch) 11th Year Type gun is believed to have been blown away during the attack. No one knows – and the gun has not been found elsewhere on the seabed (at the time of printing). Spent shell casings lie on the seabed directly below the platform – evidence that the gun was in action just before she sank.

The port anchor chain runs out from a large anchor windlass, which sits on deck just forward of the gun platform. The chain disappears through the port hawse pipe and then runs aft along the seabed. The starboard anchor is still held snug in its hawse.

The foredeck has two holds, both of which have been modified for the ship's wartime role as an auxiliary submarine tender. Entering the small square hatch for Hold No 1, immediately abaft the bow gun platform, there are stowed 12cm shells for the bow gun and a torpedo body. The steel shell warheads are well corroded.

The foremast projects out horizontally between the foredeck cargo hatches – with standing rigging hanging down from its crosstree.

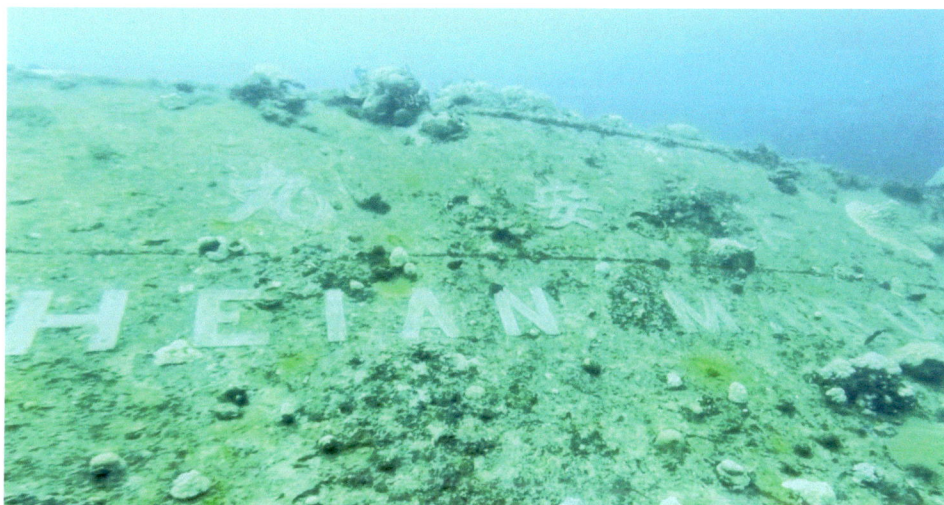

The kanji characters of the ship's name stand above the 2-foot high letters of the ship's Romanized name (Author)

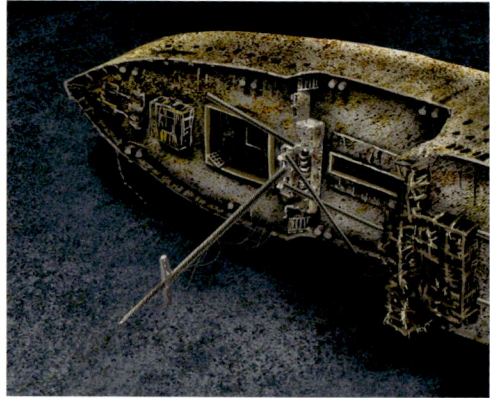

Right: The bow section of Heian Maru – note the slender torpedo loading hatch to Hold No 2.

Below: A diver enters Hold No 2 through the slender torpedo loading hatch (Author)

Much of the original hatch for Hold No 2, directly in front of the bridge superstructure, has been plated over during her conversion to auxiliary submarine tender. There is now a narrow 5-foot wide, 30-ft long rectangular slit hatch for loading torpedoes.

Moving through the slit hatch into the cavernous Hold No 2, the uppermost tween deck is largely empty. There is another identical 5-ft wide, 30-ft long rectangular hatch in the tween deck that leads horizontally to the bottom of the ship. Here there are about ten jumbled 30-foot Long Lance torpedo bodies, which have tumbled from their stowed position as the ship capsized to port. Some torpedoes stand vertically against the ship's bottom, whilst others lie flat, fallen against the lower port side of the hull. Each torpedo has twin counter-rotating propellers.

At the opposite (forward) end of the torpedoes from the twin props, you will see a curved end, like part of a sphere. This is not the warhead - which were stowed separately and would be bolted on to the body here. This is the end of the pressure vessel that held the compressed propellant gas. The steel of some of the bodies has rotted through to reveal the inner workings of the torpedo.

Left: 12cm (4.7-inch) naval artillery shells with corroded steel warheads in the foredeck holds of *Heian Maru* (Courtesy Ewan Rowell)

Lower left: 30-ft Type 95 Long Lance torpedoes stand nose down inside Hold No 2. Each has two counter rotating propellers (Courtesy Ewan Rowell)

Nearby are winch apparatus, pulleys and chains - used for handling the torpedoes. A doorway leads from Hold No 2 forward into Hold No 1. Most of the steel in this area is blackened by wartime fires.

The large rectangular frontage of the bridge superstructure rises up for several deck levels abaft the hatch for Hold No 2. The frontage of the superstructure is largely intact - although most bridge fittings and sections of plating inside have collapsed and fallen to the bottom. Burnt and charred decking, here and there, bears silent witness to the fire that engulfed the bridge. The entire topmost wooden open navigation bridge is missing – consumed by the fires. At the aft side of the superstructure, the radio room still has three radio racks in it.

On the starboard side of the hull, along the shelter deck, a row of cabin portholes dots the shell plating of the superstructure. Some of the glass in these portholes shows evidence of melting and bubbling from the intensity of the fire.

One deck higher, at promenade deck level, a now horizontal walkway extends the whole length of the large liner's superstructure. Leading off this walkway are many passenger cabins flanking the smokestack and engine casing. At the time of her sinking, the Japanese had used this long, elegant promenade deck walkway to store spare 15-metre-long submarine periscopes. There appear to be four larger night periscopes with a large head providing the highest usable light-gathering power. Two low profile attack periscopes are also present, slender with a tapered upper section and smaller head designed to leave a small wake and minimize any water disturbance that could betray a submarine's presence. At the lower end of the periscopes can be found the classic fold up handles and eyepieces, which would have been used by the submarine's skipper in action. Other periscopes can be found nearby and further inside the wreck.

The large composite superstructure shows evidence of bomb damage around the engine room, where an explosion took place during the last torpedo attack. The engine room can be entered in a number of ways – it is a large space but is jammed with engine room fittings and fixtures. Finding a way through it is tight and with the ship lying on its beam ends, confusing. Penetration into the engine room is only for suitably qualified divers with a local guide.

Above: Slim low profile attack periscopes designed to produce minimum wake visible to an enemy surface vessel. (Courtesy Ewan Rowell)

Left: Four spare submarine periscopes are stored on the starboard promenade deck walkway. (Courtesy Ewan Rowell)

Left: The aft quarter of *Heian Maru* with empty gun platform and the large mooring buoy dragged down from the surface as she sank. A buoy this large was likely a communications buoy with a direct phone line to shore.

Right: A diver approaches the large communications mooring buoy that lies on the seabed near the stern of *Heian Maru* (Author)

Entering the innards of the ship via a large square deck hatch abaft the superstructure, divers enter a dark world. No light reaches in here – and all steel bulkheads and fixtures are heavily blackened by wartime fires. Moving horizontally, you are now moving down through three deck levels towards the bowels of the ship – intact brass and glass cage lamps still hang from thick electric cables.

Pressing on further, deep into the ship, some compartments contain a number of jumbled steel bed frames, possibly the hospital ward. Piles of silt covered crockery and rice dishes lie here and there in places.

Deeper into the ship, and you can enter the engine room where the two 8-cylinder Burmeister & Wain diesel engines can be found, ringed by gratings, gauges, pipes and valves and the bridge telegraph repeaters. Elsewhere the engine control panels can be found, gauges still gleaming white in diver lights.

Eventually it is time to rise up and leave the darkness of the engine room spaces, moving shallower and rising up towards the starboard side of the ship, where open doors lead onto the promenade deck walkway along the side of the ship, close to the four night periscopes. The large smokestack lies fallen downwards with its top edge resting on the seabed.

At the aftmost end of the central superstructure, on the extended section of superstructure at shelter deck level, is the hatch for Hold No. 3, which has a kingpost pair set aft for cargo handling. Hold No 3 contains submarine batteries and a large artillery piece at its forward end. Another field gun lies spilled onto the sandy seabed about 10 feet away and slightly forward.

Hold 4 at weather deck level contains timber, wooden cases/crates and many beer bottles. The mainmast projects horizontally from a masthouse on the deck in between Hold No's 4 &

Right: The high starboard side propeller of *Heian Maru*,
now above the rudder (Courtesy Ewan Rowell)

5. Abaft the mainmast, Hold No 5 contains banks of oxygen cylinders, wooden cases, bottles and gas masks.

The poop island superstructure contains crew accommodation spaces whilst a hatch in the deck at the very stern allows access to the steering gear compartment. Here at the auxiliary steering position a telegraph lies fallen from its deck mount.

On top the poop island deckhouse is the large skeletal framework of the bandstand platform for the aft 12cm (4.7-inch) 11th Year Type gun. As with the bow gun platform, the 12cm naval gun itself here is also missing.

Nearby on the seabed lies the 15-foot wide steel mooring buoy - dragged down as the ship sank. Two chains and a thick old electrical cable, no doubt with telephone cable, lead from the buoy to shore.

Moving around and under the fantail of the ship, two large propellers flank the rudder and are very photogenic – the shallower starboard side propeller is in 20-25 metres.

'TOKYO' is embossed in large brass letters around her fantail.

12. *Hino Maru No 2*
Cargo ship (1935)
IJN auxiliary netlayer (1941)
IJN auxiliary gunboat (1942)
IJN *Zatsuyosen* auxiliary transport (1943)
U.S. Recognition Code: MFM

Sixth Fleet Anchorage

Tonnage:	1,000-grt
Dimensions:	200.1-ft long; beam of 35.1-ft; draught of 17.1-ft
Launched:	16 September 1935
Sunk:	29-30 April 1944
Cause of loss:	Strafed and bombed by TF 58 aircraft during follow up raid 29/30 April 1944
Wreck location:	Sixth Fleet Anchorage, 150m west of Uman Island
Depth to seabed:	Bow - 9 metres. Stern 21 metres
Least Depth:	Bow – 3 metres.

———————

The single-screw, coastal motor ship *Hino Maru No 2.* was built by Mitsubishi Jukogyo K.K. (Mitsubishi Heavy Industries) in the port of Kobe, near Osaka, towards the south of Japan. She was laid down on 16 May 1935 and launched and named on 16 September 1935. Her fitting out afloat was completed on 14 December 1935 and she was registered in Kobe to the Nippon Shokuen K.K. shipping line.

The 1,000 grt motor ship *Hino Maru* No 2.

The ship was constructed with a cruiser stern and two holds forward and two holds aft of a composite central superstructure. Propulsion was delivered by 4-stroke 6-cylinder oil engines manufactured by her builders Mitsubishi Jukogyo K.K. that powered her single screw to give the ship a modest service speed of 10 knots.

The national flag of Japan is a white rectangular flag with a large red circle, representing the sun, in the centre. The flag is commonly known as *Hinomaru* – the 'circle of the sun'. The sun emblem Hinomaru flag differed from the 16-ray Rising Sun flag that was used from 1870 until the end of WWII (and which was subsequently re-adopted in 1954 and is still in use today by Japan's military). The Nippon Shokuen K.K. shipping line named all their ships *Hino Maru* and allocated an individual number.

After six years of civilian service, on 11 November 1941, just weeks before Pearl Harbor, *Hino Maru No. 2* became one of more than 100 civilian merchant vessels requisitioned by the IJN and converted and armed during WWII to serve as gunboats.

Hino Maru No.2 was moved to the Nagasaki Shipyard of Mitsubishi Heavy Industries K.K., where with war one week away, she was registered in the IJN on 1 December 1941 as an auxiliary netlayer attached to the Sasebo Naval District and her conversion works began.

A naval deck gun was installed on a platform on her foc'sle at the bow, whilst an anti-submarine warfare (ASW) hydrophone was fitted to her keel. Roll-off depth charge racks and depth charge throwers were fitted at her stern.

On 10 December 1941, just three days after the Japanese raid on Pearl Harbor on 7 December 1941, *Hino Maru No 2* was assigned for defence duties to the Mako Guard District, Base Defence Unit in the Pescadores Islands in the Taiwan Strait. Her conversion works as an auxiliary netlayer were completed by Mitsubishi Heavy Industries K.K. at the Nagasaki Shipyard on 25 December 1941 and she was assigned to defend the waters around Mako.

Hino Maru No 2 departed the Nagasaki Shipyard on 9 January 1942 and moved to take up her duties at Mako, arriving there on 10 January 1942. She began operating regularly between Mako and Formosa (now Taiwan) and laid a protective net at Mako on 23 February 1942.

On 20 March 1942, she was removed from the Mako Sea Defence Force and Mako Guard District and registered the same day as an auxiliary gunboat to the Sasebo Naval District. She was assigned to the Fifth Fleet in the 2nd Picket Boat Division.

In May 1942, now five months into the Pacific war, *Hino Maru No 2* was assigned to Operation AO, the invasion of the Aleutian Islands of Kiska and Attu, an operation that would run simultaneously with Operation MI, the Japanese attempt to seize Midway that triggered the catastrophic Battle of Midway, far to the south.

As Operation AO began, the Japanese No. 3 Special Landing Party and 500 marines went ashore at Kiska on 6 June 1942, capturing the sole inhabitants of the island, being a small U.S. Navy weather detachment of ten men, a lieutenant and a dog. The Japanese proceed to reinforce and fortify their new Aleutian outpost.

Hino Maru No 2 arrived at Paramushiro in the Aleutians on 31 May 1942 and then moved to Kiska on 10 June 1942, where she would remain for some time. At the end of July 1942, *Hino Maru No 2*, with the minelayers *Ishizaki* and *Ukishima*, laid a protective net at Kiska Harbor.

On 5 August 1942, *Hino Maru No.2* and *Hyuga Maru* towed the damaged 6,940grt auxiliary transport ship *Kano Maru* to Kiska and *Hino Maru No.2* transferred her crew ashore. The damaged *Kano Maru* would later serve as an artificial harbour off the shoreline for landing craft. *Hino Maru No 2* departed Kiska on 15 August and arrived at Yokosuka in Japan on 28 August 1942, when she was fitted with a new ASW hydrophone.

Hino Maru No. 2 was engaged carrying out picket duties until November 1942 when she was transferred to the Fifth Fleet, 22nd Squadron. On 1 February 1943, she was attached to the Yokosuka Guard District and began operating from Yokosuka ferrying cargo, food, fuel, water and personnel. She carried out patrol and picket duties, receiving a new camouflage paint scheme in early April 1943. In June 1943 she was assigned as flagship of the auxiliary gunboats assigned to patrol the Paramushiro Strait North exit, a post she held until 30 September 1943.

On 1 October 1943, *Hino Maru No 2* was registered as an auxiliary transport (Otsu category with no IJN captain) and attached to the Yokosuka Naval District, with Yokosuka as her home port. Her conversion work by Mitsubishi Heavy Industries K.K. began at their Yokohama Shipyard on 1 October 1943.

Following completion of the conversion works on 12 November 1943, the auxiliary transport *Hino Maru No 2* carried out several transport passages from Japanese ports to South Korea before entering drydock in Asano on 3 January 1944 for repairs that took until 30 January 1944 to be completed, when she was undocked.

On 11 February 1944, only a week before Operation HAILSTONE, she left Tateyama, Japan bound for Truk via Chichi-Jima and Iwo Jima in the Bonins and Saipan in the Marianas. She was in Chichi-Jima when Operation HAILSTONE unfolded over Truk on 17/18 February 1944 - and so is not a casualty of that 2-day raid.

Hino Maru No 2 departed Chichi-Jima on 29 February 1944 and after calling at Iwo Jima and Saipan, arrived at Truk safely on 21 March 1944 - no doubt to a scene of devastation from the Operation HAILSTONE raid two weeks earlier.

She departed Truk a few days later on 24 March 1944 for passages to Mortlock in the Central Carolines, Chichi-Jima and Iwo Jima, before returning to Truk in April, where she was assigned to the 4th Base Force.

The TF 58 follow-up fast carrier raid to Operation HAILSTONE took place on Truk on 29/30 April 1944. On 30 April, *Hino Maru No 2* was attacked several times by U.S. carrier aircraft and was hit by one bomb, rocketed and strafed by *Bunker Hill* and *Cabot* (CVL-28) aircraft. Fires were started and near miss bombs burst some of her plates - she started to list.

With his ship smoking heavily, flooding and listing, the Captain ran her to the shore and beached, bow to shore, stern afloat in deeper water. The ship however was ravaged by the fire and became a burnt-out hulk. Badly damaged, *Hino Maru No 2* sank a few days later on 4 May 1944.

The wreck today

Today the wreck of the *Hino Maru No 2* rests on her keel just 150 metres from the west shore of Uman Island on a sloping bottom that rises towards the shore. Her stern is in deeper water of 21 metres and her bows in much shallower water of 9 metres. She has a 10° list to starboard

For many years her correct identity was unknown - and she was known locally simply known as the *Gun High* wreck due to the photogenic bow gun pointing dead ahead, mounted on a square platform at her highest part - just a few feet beneath the surface. The area around the gun platform has now collapsed - and the gun mount has fallen so that the barrel now points downwards. The ship makes an interesting snorkel in between dives.

The foremast, originally situated between the hatches for Hold No's 1 & 2, now lies out to starboard. Along the starboard side of the hull, near the top of the foremast, are the frame of a 4-wheel railroad car and the remains of another small wooden vessel.

The composite bridge superstructure and funnel are totally destroyed, and the ship's hull is torn, ragged and broken open - holding much of the debris of her destruction. All her internal bulkheads are gone - and the hull seems just like one big open space. The ship's diesel engines lie on the seabed about 20 yards away.

Towards the stern are the two hatches to the after deck holds and a large split in the hull on the starboard side. The port side of the hull has collapsed inwards to lie on the ship's bottom. The mainmast lies over the wreck on starboard side.

The stern is a tangled mess of bent metal amidst which can be found the propeller and the rudder lying on the seabed.

13. *Hoki Maru (ex-Hauraki)*
Passenger-cargo motor vessel (1921)
IJN *Zatsuyosen* Auxiliary transport (1943)
U.S. Recognition Code: 32 KMKFKMK

Fourth Fleet Anchorage

Tonnage:	7,113 grt
Dimensions:	450.3-ft long; beam of 58.2-ft; draught of 31.4-ft
Launched:	28 November 1921
Sunk:	18 February 1944
Cause of loss:	Catastrophic explosion following fires and bombing by TF 58 aircraft during Operation HAILSTONE
Wreck location:	Fourth Fleet Anchorage - east of Eten Island
Depth to seabed:	45-50 metres
Least Depth:	Superstructure – 25 metres

The 7,113-grt passenger/cargo motor vessel *Hauraki* was built in Scotland during 1921 by the well-known shipbuilders, William Denny & Brothers in Dumbarton (Yard No 1039). She has the distinction of being the only Japanese war prize sunk in the Truk lagoon.

William Denny & Brothers were a respected Scottish shipbuilding company, with roots going back to about 1811. Amongst many famous ships built by Denny, in 1869 they completed the famous clipper *Cutty Sark* (now preserved at Greenwich, London) after the

Left: The 7,113grt passenger-cargo vessel and IJN requisitioned auxiliary transport *Hoki Maru* (ex Hauraki)

Right: Starboard view of *Hoki Maru*

147

contracted builders Scott & Linton went insolvent. (*Cutty Sark* takes its name from the famous poem by Robert Burns *Tam O'Shanter*. A *sark* in old Scots means a shirt or night gown, whilst *cutty* means short. So the name *Cutty Sark* simply refers to the short nightie worn by one of the main characters in the poem. When I was growing up in Fraserburgh, a fishing town on the north east coast of Scotland, the old fisher folk still all referred to their shirts as sarks). The Denny yard was situated near the junction of the River Clyde and the River Leven, the yard itself being on the Leven.

Hauraki was named and launched for fitting out afloat on 28 November 1921. The hull was subsequently towed along the Clyde to Whiteinch for the installation of her engines at Barclay, Curle & Co. Ltd – her sea trials were run in early 1922.

On 17 March 1922, the completed *Hauraki* was delivered to the Union Steam Ship Company of New Zealand at a cost of £317,600. She was the Union SS Co's first motor ship and was the first motor ship in New Zealand waters. She was registered in London on 13 May 1922.

The *Hauraki* was constructed with two steel decks and a shelter deck and had accommodation for 12 passengers. Her two screws were driven by two modern, 8-cylinder, 4-stroke diesel engines built by the North British Diesel Engine Works Ltd of Glasgow - at a time when many ships were still being fitted with triple expansion steam engines.

Hauraki was the first ship William Denny & Brothers had designed for the new diesel mode of propulsion that was starting to replace coal powered steam engines. Diesel oil was a far easier fuel to handle compared to much bulkier coal for steam engines - it was easier and quicker to fuel and gave far greater range and reliability. It also greatly reduced the number of crew previously required to be employed in the stoke hold to feed steam boilers with coal. The new diesel engines gave her a service speed of 12 ½ knots. She carried a crew of 56.

Her maiden voyage in 1922 was from the River Clyde in Scotland to San Francisco with a cargo of coal and from there she crossed the Pacific to Wellington, New Zealand. Her regular runs in the years that followed were Trans-Pacific cargo trade, mostly between Sydney, Melbourne, Fiji, San Francisco and Vancouver - but she also made runs to Europe.

In 1940, after almost 20 years plying the seas delivering passengers and cargoes, as war erupted across Europe, *Hauraki* was one of many vessels requisitioned by the British Ministry of War Transport and placed under the command of the Australian Captain Albert William Creese. Crewed mainly by New Zealanders and Australians, the *Hauraki* was now in the Merchant Navy and served initially carrying badly needed war cargoes on the North America route during the dark days of the Battle of the Atlantic.

In February 1942 she was assigned to a new route from Sydney via Colombo (Sri Lanka), Aden, Port Said (Egypt) to Haifa (in present day Israel). On 9 June 1942, she departed Sydney for Colombo. After calling at Melbourne, the ship had to make an unscheduled stop at Fremantle, near Perth, Western Australia, for some repair work to be carried out following storm damage in the Great Australian Bight. It must have been quite something of a storm as heavy seas had wrecked some of her lifeboats and damaged her engine room skylights. Water had got into the engine room, forcing her engines to be stopped.

Repairs duly completed, *Hauraki* was able to depart Fremantle on 4 July 1942, travelling alone with war supplies for Allied troops in Palestine. On 12 July 1942, she was sighted in the Indian Ocean by the two Japanese armed merchant cruisers *Aikoku Maru* and *Hokoku Maru*.

That night, at about 2200, the two Japanese merchant cruisers came up either side of her astern - and then fired two warning shots across her bow, forcing her to stop. Below decks, her crew started to prepare scuttling charges, however in a blaze of floodlights, armed Japanese troops quickly boarded her and stopped the scuttling at gunpoint. The captured crew of 56 was one of the largest groups of New Zealand personnel to fall into Japanese hands during WWII.

Two hours later, the ship was under way again, this time with a prize crew from *Hokoku Maru* aboard. The ship's original civilian crew were however forced to sail the ship under armed guard via Penang to the former British fortress of Singapore, which had fallen to the Japanese in February 1942. The Japanese had quickly started using Singapore's great natural harbour and the former British naval base there – and the two Japanese merchant cruisers were operating from Singapore at this time.

The *Hauraki* arrived at Penang in July 1942, where the IJN prize crew disembarked and returned to *Hokoku Maru* and other *Hauraki* non-essential personnel, classified as civilians and not military combatants, were then interned for the duration at Changi Gaol in Singapore (where the author's grandfather was also interned during the war).

The *Hauraki* was renamed *Hoki Maru* in September 1942, and the ship was assigned to Mitsui Kisen K.K. But as the Japanese did not understand the, by now, vintage diesel engines properly, 23 of the *Hauraki*'s civilian engineers and other essential crew were forced to sail the war prize via Saigon (also in the possession of the Japanese), to Moji, in the Fukuoka Prefecture of Japan.

Legend has it that en route, at great risk to themselves, the civilian crew dropped as many pieces of machinery and spare parts over the side as opportunity permitted, to thwart the Japanese. The engine plans along with spare parts for generators and fluke pumps all went overboard and some 60-70 tons of fuel was surreptitiously pumped out. By the time the vessel was on the final leg of the voyage it was very short of fuel.

En route Japan, *Hoki Maru* arrived at Saigon on 27 November 1942, departing Saigon on 5 December 1942 and arriving at Moji on 16 December 1942. There, on 31 December 1942, *Hoki Maru* was registered in the IJN as a *Zatsuyosen* auxiliary transport (Otsu) category – the class of transport vessel that did not have a supervising IJN Captain aboard. She was then attached to the Yokosuka Naval District, on the northwest side of the entrance to Tokyo Bay.

On 1 June 1943, conversion works began at the Asano Dock K.K. shipyard in nearby Yokohama to re-fit her as a *Zatsuyosen* auxiliary transport. The seaport of Yokohama, on the northwest entrance to Tokyo Bay was an important base for the IJN and merchant fleets.

The refit works were difficult, her engines were by then old with many parts deemed to be worn out. She made one trial coastal voyage - and now satisfied with the engines, the original Union Steam Ship Co civilian engineers were removed and dispersed as forced labour around the POW camps that the Japanese had attached to various war industries.

Some of the crew were sent to the Mitsubishi Dockyard at Yokohama. Several had died before liberation came in 1945.

The conversion works were completed on 30 October 1943 and she was put to her war duties. But on 18 November 1943, after just 6 weeks of carrying war cargoes, she was involved in a collision with the tanker IJA *Nanei Maru* whilst in convoy from Sasebo for Takao and Batavia. Further repairs were required before she was fit for a passage to Dalian in northern China in December 1943.

On 10 January 1944, she formed up in an escorted convoy of tankers and other transports at Nagoya in the Inland Sea on the Pacific coast of the central home island of Honshū . The convoy headed to Yokosuka in Tokyo Bay, arriving there on 13 January.

On 20 January 1944, *Hoki Maru* left Yokosuka with a cargo of coal, aviation fuel in 55-gallon drums, bombs, ammunition, tractors, four Isuzu Type 94 trucks, cars, diggers, bulldozers, steam rollers and personnel in a convoy bound for Truk that included the auxiliary transport *Kowa Maru* and the IJA transports *San Francisco Maru* and *Unkai Maru No 6* – both the latter being well known Truk wrecks today. The convoy was escorted by the IJN *kaibōkan* escort vessels *Oki* and *Manju* – the *kaibōkans* were the equivalent of Allied destroyer escorts and frigates.

The convoy departed Tokyo Bay on 21 January 1944, but such was the attrition of Japanese shipping by American submarines at this stage of the war, that the very next day, the kaibōkan *Manju* detected a US submarine and attacked, dropping some 20 depth charges. The next day, 23 January 1944, *Manju* was in action again against renewed approaches by US submarines - and as tracking of the convoy by US submarines continued, the convoy altered course to seek refuge at the powerful Japanese naval bases at Saipan, in the north of the Mariana Island chain.

The diverted convoy arrived at Saipan on 29 January 1944, and harboured there for two days before departing for Truk on 31 January 1944. The submarine war against Japanese shipping was certainly hotting up, as the following day, *Manju* detected another US submarine and attacked with gunfire and depth charges.

On 3 February 1944, *Manju* detected another suspected US submarine and was again forced to drop depth charges. It was no doubt with great relief that the convoy passed through the protection of Truk's barrier reef into the lagoon on 4 February 1944.

Dawn on 17 February 1944 found *Hoki Maru* anchored southeast of the small aircraft carrier shaped Eten Island. She was spotted by the first waves of aircraft and between 0815 – 0900 was attacked by Strike 2B TBF Avenger torpedo bombers of VT-9 from the carrier *Essex*. She was damaged by bomb hits and fires started aboard amidships.

Around midday she was bombed by Strike 1D Avenger TBF torpedo bombers from *Yorktown* and then about an hour later was possibly torpedoed by *Bunker Hill* VT-17 aircraft. As the group air strikes of the first day ended, U.S. pilots reported her to be totally ablaze and smoking heavily.

After a difficult night fighting the fires, dawn of the following morning, 18 February 1944, revealed *Hoki Maru* to be still afloat. She was soon attacked again - by three SB2C Helldivers from *Bunker Hill* during Strike 3B between 0815 – 0900. One SB2C Helldiver scored a hit with a 1,000-lb bomb in the forward section of the ship – the bomb causing a massive secondary explosion as her cargo of 55-gallon drums of aviation gasoline in her foredeck holds ignited. The sides of the forward part of the ship were completely blown out and the ship disappeared in a plume of smoke.

By the time the smoke cleared the ship had gone to the bottom.

The Wreck today

The wreck of the war prize *Hoki Maru* is one of several ships in the lagoon that still reveal the true force and brutality of Operation HAILSTONE. For like *Aikoku Maru, Taiho Maru* and *Sankisan Maru*, half of *Hoki Maru* is intact – whilst the other half has been devastated by a secondary explosion. But the secondary explosions of munitions on *Aikoku Maru* and *Sankisan Maru* have left a markedly different legacy to the secondary explosion of aviation gasoline in hundreds of 55-gallon drums stored in the two foredeck holds of *Hoki Maru*.

The complete length of both sides of the forepart of *Hoki Maru* have been blown outwards and downwards by the expanding force of the explosion. Both sides of the ship are still there and recognisable for what they were - but are now splayed out and flattened over towards the seabed. The catastrophic secondary detonation of the munitions in the bow section of *Aikoku Maru* and the stern section of *Sankisan Maru* completely dispersed those parts of the ships – complete sections of ship being virtually vapourised by the explosion of munitions. Those

The wreck of *Hoki Maru*

Least depth: Superstructure - 25m
Depth to seabed: 45-50m

Fo'c'sle
Hold No.1
Pitched engine room roof
Trucks, rolls of steel mesh, steamrollers, bulldozers, and 55-gallon fuel drums
Docking bridge
Sides of ship blown out, scattered 55-gallon fuel drums
Twin screws

Artist's impression of the MV *Hauraki*, built in 1921/2 in Scotland for the Union Steam Ship Company of New Zealand. She became a war prize in 1942 when she was captured by the Japanese raiders *Aikoku Maru* and *Hokoku Maru*. She was renamed *Hoki Maru* and served as an auxiliary transport ship in the IJN. Following a dive-bombing attack during Operation HAILSTONE a massive secondary explosion of embarked 55-gallon drums of aviation gasoline destroyed her forward section.

Detail of the forward section of *Hoki Maru*.

secondary explosions were of a greater scale and ferocity, and very different in nature to the explosion of the Avgas carried in *Hoki Maru*.

The wreck of *Hoki Maru* rests upright on the bottom in 45-50 metres of water to the east of Eten Island where she had been anchored when the attacks went in. The wreck usually has a fixed buoyed attached to it around the shallower aft part of the superstructure at about 25 metres.

The stern section abaft the smokestack is virtually complete – and the aft holds contain all the really interesting artefacts that you will want to see.

The bow section is still largely present but has been almost completely flattened by the catastrophic explosion that blew the fore part of the ship apart. The resulting explosion ripped the decks from the ship and blew them away. Internal bulkheads were vapourised and the hull plates with web frames still attached were blown outwards on both sides and now lie almost flat on the seabed on either side of the ship. As you descend to the wreck and arrive at the higher parts of the superstructure, if you look forward there is a sheer drop of some 20 metres down to the exposed innards of the bottom of the ship at seabed level. It is as though the forward superstructure and forward section of the ship has been cleaved across and virtually removed.

At the very bow, the sturdy fo'c'sle is largely intact - although the aft portion of the fo'c'sle deck collapses downwards to where the well deck structure of the forward holds has disappeared. On the fo'c'sle deck at about 40 metres, the anchor windlass still sits in position with the port chain run out to its hawse. The ship sunk vertically so quickly, at anchor, that the chain off the seabed simply appears to have piled up – before running off along the seabed into the distance.

Abaft the fo'c'sle there is a drop down to the now exposed flattened innards of the ship, which is a mass of sand-filled debris. The ship's double bottom appears to have contained the blast and is intact, but the more lightly constructed shell plating of the hull did not - and blew outwards. The rectangular footing edges of Holds 1 & 2 can still be made out along with one of two kingposts, that stood on the foredeck beside the fo'c'sle bulkhead, lying athwartships. The foremast, which rose in between the hatches for Hold No's 1 & 2 on the foredeck is lying in the sand about 100 yards in front of the ship, flung there by the force of the massive explosion almost directly underneath it.

As divers move aft from the bow over the remains of Hold No 2, the huge mass of the structurally intact aft section of the ship looms ahead - rising up almost vertically from the bottom at 45 metres to about 25 metres at the shallowest parts. There is a scene of general devastation here with huge sections of athwartships bulkheads, shell plating, decking and sections of ship torn apart and flung backwards over the superstructure behind.

Looking from the forward port side of the ship across Hold No 2 towards the starboard side, just in front of the destroyed amidships superstructure, parts of which are seen to right of shot. The bow is off to left of shot. The web frames of the inner side of the starboard shell plating are clearly visible. (Author)

The slender bridge superstructure, situated forward of amidships, has been partly obliterated and pushed backwards– some of its bulkhead plating being flung back over the hatch for Hold No 3, that split the superstructure between the bridge and engine room.

The wreck resumes a ship shape as divers pass Hold No 3 to the superstructure that held the boiler and engine rooms below and passenger cabins either side of the engine casing. The boiler and engine room superstructure is heavily damaged – however here, divers will easily be able to recognise the ship for what it was – and then it starts to get really interesting. It is possible to enter the engine room in a few places.

Dropping down onto the intact after well deck at about 35 metres, the hatch for Hold No 4 appears, partly obscured by a section of shell plating flung here from the forepart of the ship and by a fallen kingpost. Dropping down into the hold, the tween deck hatch beams are still in place. The upper parts of this hold seem jumbled as the blast here has damaged the port side of the hull, weakening it and causing the weather deck to collapse downwards at the front of the hold, to almost rest on the tween deck. This hold contains a variety of aircraft parts and rotary aircraft propellers along with bombs, depth charges, 55-gallon fuel drums, beer bottles and mines.

Moving aft from Hold No 4, the mainmast with its crosstree still stands in place, rising out of a masthouse to less than 15 metres short of the surface. Cargo winches are dotted around the top of the masthouse and the fore and aft cargo booms are swung over to rest on the port side of the ship.

Moving further aft past the masthouse, the hatch for Hold No 5 appears, with all of its hatch cover beams still in place. This aftmost hold is the main focus of interest on this wreck – for

Left: Detail of the aft section of Hoki Maru.

Right: Trucks and rolls of steel mesh for airfield construction in Hold No 5 of Hoki Maru. (Courtesy of Pete Mesley)

Looking aft over Hold No 5 towards the stern (Author)

in here, in depths of 35- 45 metres, are intact road building vehicles, bulldozers, steamrollers, tractors, Japanese trucks, construction equipment and more 55-gallon fuel drums.

Approaching the very stern of the ship, two kingposts still stand just forward of the stern deckhouse, which holds the steering gear.

The rounded fantail of the stern shows evidence of bomb damage and there is a hole on her starboard side into Hold 5.

Her twin screws and banded rudder at about 50 metres are a magnificent sight.

14. *Hokuyo Maru*
Passenger-cargo vessel (1936)
IJA *Rikugun Yusosen* Transport ship (1936)
IJN *Hokuyo Maru*-class *Zatsuyosen* Auxiliary Transport (1941)
U.S. Recognition code: 37 MFM

Fourth Fleet Anchorage

Tonnage:	4,217 grt
Dimensions:	357-ft long; beam of 49.2-ft; draught of 28.9-ft
Launched:	November 1936
Sunk:	17 February 1944
Cause of loss:	Bombed and torpedoed by TF 58 aircraft during Operation HAILSTONE
Wreck location:	Fourth Fleet Anchorage - east of Eten Island
Depth to seabed:	60 metres (stern)
Least Depth:	Bridge superstructure – 46 metres. Well deck - 53 metres

---

The 4,217-grt passenger-cargo vessel *Hokuyo Maru* was laid down by Uraga Dock Co. Ltd, in November 1935 in Uraga, Yokosuka, part of the slender peninsula that projects out to form the western side of the entrance of Tokyo Bay. The ship was completed in June 1936 and delivered to her new owners, the Kita Nippon Kisen K.K. shipping line and registered in Kobe.

Built as a well-deck steamer, she had two decks and a cruiser stern. *Hokuyo Maru* was originally designed for voyages between North Korea, Hokkaido (on the northmost of the

The 4,217grt passenger cargo ship *Hokuyo Maru* was requisitioned by the IJA in the 1930's for the war with China. She was then requisitioned in 1941 by the IJN as an auxiliary transport ship.

main Japanese islands) and the other outlying north Japanese islands where ice floes in winter were common. Her bow was consequently specially strengthened during construction.

A raised fo'c'sle at the bow held her anchor windlass and steps led down from the fo'c'sle deck to the foredeck in which the hatches for Holds No's 1&2 were set. In between these hatches was set the foremast with cargo winches dotted around its base and two cargo handling booms extending forward over Hold No 1, and two aft over Hold No 2. The superstructure between bridge and boiler and engine rooms aft, was split by the hatch for her bunker Hold No.3.

A number of passenger cabins ran down either side of the superstructure above the engine room, flanking the fireproof engine casing. The ship's lifeboat were swung on davits on the boat deck above.

Abaft this long low superstructure, the ship dropped down to the aft well deck, where the hatches for Hold No's 4&5 were separated by the mainmast with its winches and cargo handling derricks. A poop island at the stern housed the steering gear, above the rudder.

Although diesel engines were becoming more common at the time of her construction, *Hokuyo Maru* was fitted with an older style coal fired 4-cylinder triple expansion steam engine geared to a low-pressure steam turbine manufactured by the Uraga Dock Co Ltd. Consequently, a tall narrow smokestack was fitted, common to coal burners - and all the archive photographs of her show clouds of black smoke billowing from her smokestack. Diesel engines gave great advantages in economy, range and ease of fueling compared to coal powered vessels. Her old-fashioned engine however powered a single screw that gave her a creditable service speed of 14 knots and a maximum speed of just over 16 knots. She could carry 470 tons of bunker coal in Hold No 3 that gave her an operating radius of 6,000 nautical miles at 13 knots.

Her short peacetime career from completion in 1936 was abruptly interrupted when she was requisitioned by the IJA for service as a transport ship for the invasion of China in 1937. Then in October 1941, just before the Pacific war began, she was requisitioned by the IJN as a general transport along with the other ship in her class *Hokusho Maru*.

On 8 March 1943, she set off from Kobusaki for Tokyo in a large convoy of merchant ships under naval escort. En route, the convoy was attacked by the American submarine *Permit* (SS-178), which successfully torpedoed and sunk the merchant ship *Hisajima Maru*, which was carrying a cargo of 3,850 tons of coal. *Hokuyo Maru* was able to rescue survivors from the water – returning to Hokkaido to offload them, whilst the rest of the convoy retreated to Yamada Port.

In July 1943, *Hokuyo Maru* was sent to Takao to collect a cargo. Once laden, she departed Takao on 27 July 1943 in a supply convoy bound for Hainan Island, just to the north of Vietnam in the South China Sea. Hainan Island was an important Japanese military and naval base, and had been pivotal in the conquest of Malaya, Singapore and the Philippines. After offloading her cargo there, *Hokuyo Maru* returned to Otaru, in northern Japan near Sapporo, and once resupplied, departed Otaru on 29 August 1943 for Ominato and Tennei (near Tokyo) before returning again to Otaru.

Hokuyo Maru was then sent to Singapore - and from there she moved to Palembang in Sumatra and then to Formosa (Taiwan). On 20 September 1943, she sailed in an escorted convoy of tankers and merchant ships from Takao for Moji (in Japan) that was attacked in darkness the following night at about 2100 in the East China Sea by the surfaced submarine USS *Trigger* (SS-237). A torpedo from *Trigger* hit the lead ship *Shiriya*, which was carrying aviation gasoline. Much like would happen to *Hoki Maru* later at Truk, the torpedo explosion set off a catastrophic secondary explosion of the Avgas cargo that sunk the ship in minutes. A second ship, the freighter *Argun Maru* was also hit amidships – she broke her back and sank quickly. *Trigger* then torpedoed and sunk the auxiliary oiler *Shoyo Maru,* which was carrying 3,000 tons of crude oil.

In October 1943, the IJN planned to send five Type B midget submarines, which would be towed by merchant ships, from Japan to the important Japanese naval and air base of Rabaul in New Britain - via Truk and Palau. On 9 October 1943, *Hokuyo Maru* departed Yokosuka in convoy, each ship towing a midget submarine. The convoy safely arrived at Truk on 20 October 1943 and very quickly, on 23 October 1943, *Hokuyo Maru* departed Truk for Rabaul, towing her midget submarine, and escorted by the sub chaser *CH-33.* The group arrived safely at Rabaul on 28 October 1943.

Hokuyo Maru was still in Rabaul when a few days later on 2 November 1943, 75 American B-25 Mitchell medium bombers escorted by 70 Lockheed P-38 Lighting fighters raided airfields and shipping. *Hokuyo Maru* and a number of other ships, including the present day Truk wreck *Gosei Maru*, were damaged.

Hokuyo Maru was repaired at Rabaul by the Repair Ship IJN *Akashi* (a present-day Palau wreck) and was soon back in service. She departed Rabaul on Xmas Day 1943 for Truk in convoy with *Kimishima Maru* and an escort, the convoy arriving in Truk on 30 December 1943.

In mid-February 1944, *Hokuyo Maru* was anchored with her port anchor in the Truk lagoon in the Fourth Fleet Anchorage to the east of the small aircraft carrier shaped Eten Island and south east of the much larger Dublon Island. She was positioned between the present-day wrecks of *Seiko Maru* and *San Francisco Maru.*

On the first day of the Operation HAILSTONE air raids, 17 February 1944, Strike 2B planes from TG 58.2 carrier *Essex* began launching at 0711 for the second group bombing attack of the day, with a time at target assigned for 0830-0845

12 SBD Dauntless dive bombers roared off the *Essex* flight deck into the wind, along with nine TBF Avenger torpedo bombers and an escort of 12 F6F Hellcat fighters – the strike was tasked to hit shipping south and west of Dublon.

On the inbound flight, the Hellcats had a number of dogfights with multiple Japanese A6M Zero and Hamp fighters before the flight arrived over the lagoon, when Param airfield was strafed. Some 14 Japanese fighters had been destroyed in the air by this inbound flight.

The SBD's first attacked a destroyer anchored west of Dublon, which exploded at the bow. A transport ship tied up alongside the destroyer was also hit and a fire started. Northeast of Fefan Island, an oiler was attacked - although the bombs missed.

The TBF Avengers were repeatedly attacked by Japanese fighters – who had to be fought off by the Hellcats. But despite this attention, at about 0825, the *Essex* TBF Avengers attacked the large cargo liner *Aikoku Maru* – which detonated in a massive secondary explosion of embarked munitions in the foredeck holds.

The next ship to be attacked was the second from the east in the Fourth Fleet Anchorage, *Hokuyo Maru*. The US pilots scored two 500-lb bomb hits on the aft part of the ship on the port side, that heavily damaged the aft quarter and poop island. Although a fire broke out, she was in no danger of sinking. Meanwhile the U.S. strike planes were already attacking other ships in the Fourth Fleet anchorage including the famous present day Truk wrecks of *San Francisco Maru*, *Seiko Maru* and *Nippo Maru*.

Hokuyo Maru is the ship on the right being bombed during Operation HAILSTONE – seen from USS INTREPID plane. The ship to left is *Seiko Maru*. (National Archives 80-G-221244)

Later that day, 15 SB2C Helldivers, carrying 1,000-lb bombs, 6 TBF Avengers carrying torpedoes and 12 Hellcat fighter escorts launched from *Bunker Hill* between 1310 and 1330 for Strike 3E, the fifth group strike of the day. The *Bunker Hill* planes had an assigned time at target of 1415 – 1500.

Strike 1E planes from *Enterprise* and *Yorktown* were also allocated a time at target of 1415-1430 whilst Strike 2E planes from *Essex* and *Intrepid* had a time at target assigned of 1430-1445. The strike by *Bunker Hill* planes would leave six Japanese ships badly damaged.

As the flight arrived over Truk, *Unkai Maru No 6* was bombed by Helldivers south of Dublon. Then, southwest of Eten Island, *Fujikawa Maru* was hit by a torpedo on her starboard side and *San Francisco Maru* in the Fourth Fleet anchorage was hit aft.

The damaged *Hokuyo Maru* was still anchored south east of Dublon in the Fourth Fleet anchorage. She was again attacked during this Strike 3E by *Bunker Hill* TBF Avenger torpedo-bombers. Two aerial torpedoes were launched, one missed - but the other struck her almost dead centre on the starboard side in the vicinity of her boiler room and engine room. There appears to have been a secondary explosion from her boiler as tons of seawater rushed into the boiler room and made contact with it. She was left with two large holes in her starboard side - and with her hull so badly holed she sank to the bottom of the lagoon.

The wreck today

Today the 357ft long *Hokuyo Maru* rests on her keel in about 60 metres of water at her stern - and is one of the deeper dives in the lagoon. She is largely intact with both her masts still upright to the crosstrees at a depth of about 42 metres - with encrusted rigging hanging down from the crosstrees. The least depth to her shallowest parts at the top of her superstructure is about 46 metres. It is a deep 53 metres down to the well deck of the ship.

On top of her raised fo'c'sle at the bow, at about 49-50 metres, an anchor windlass has both chains running out to their hawse pipes on either side of the ship. The port anchor is run out to the seabed, whilst the starboard anchor is still held snug in its hawse.

Moving aft and dropping down from the fo'c'sle deck to the well deck at 53 metres, a spare anchor is bolted to the bulkhead of the fo'c'sle. Two doors, one to port and one to starboard, lead forward into the fo'c'sle spaces. On the starboard side inside the fo'c'sle is the Lamp Room, which holds several copper and brass navigation lanterns.

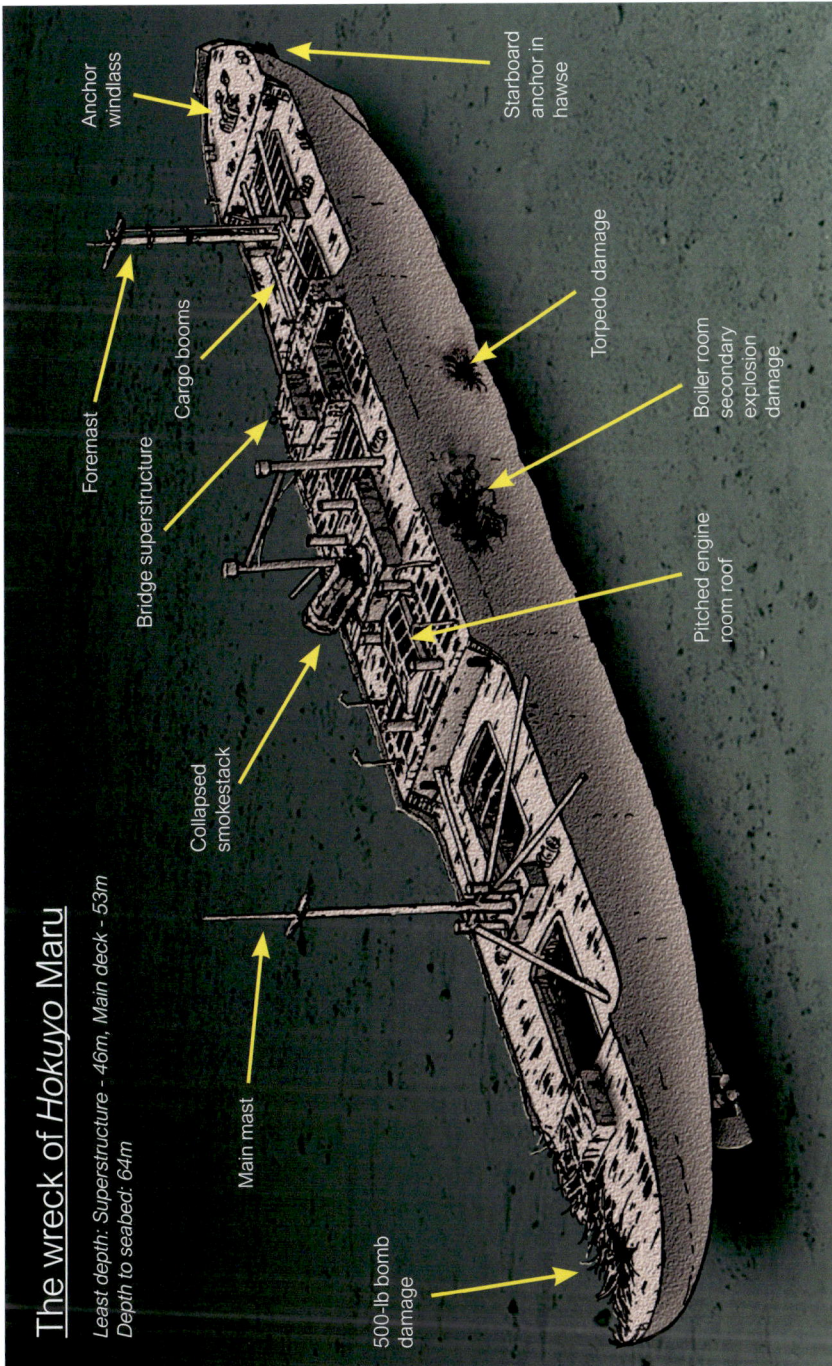

The wreck of *Hokuyo Maru*

Least depth: Superstructure - 46m, Main deck - 53m
Depth to seabed: 64m

Anchor windlass

Starboard anchor in hawse

Foremast

Cargo booms

Torpedo damage

Bridge superstructure

Boiler room secondary explosion damage

Collapsed smokestack

Pitched engine room roof

Main mast

500-lb bomb damage

Artist's impression of the 4,217grt IJN auxiliary transport ship *Hokuyo Maru*, which sits upright in 64 metres of water in the 4th Fleet Anchorage. The torpedo hole on her starboard side is visible along with a second hole from a boiler explosion as she sank.

The hatches for Hold No's 1 & 2 on the foredeck are at a depth of about 53 metres. Both still have with their hatch cover beams in place - with the foremast, with its crosstree, rising from a masthouse in between. Two cargo handling booms run forward from short kingposts either side of the foremast across the hatch for Hold No.1, whilst two booms run aft across the hatch for Hold No. 2. There is little by way of cargo in Hold's 1 & 2.

The bridge superstructure rises up abaft Hold No.2, with a walkway around its frontage a few decks up at a depth of about 48 metres. Fixed steps rise from the well deck at 53 metres on either side of the bridge frontage to walkways that run along the side of the superstructure at shelter deck level.

At the bottom of the frontage of the bridge superstructure, on either side of the foredeck at about 53 metres, open doorways lead from the foredeck into the superstructure. Divers can move inside the superstructure and head aft inside, through rotted compartments, to the tween deck of Hold No 3 and then on to the engine room. Divers can leave the wreck via a large horizontal tear in the shell plating of the hull on the port side at a depth of about 55 metres.

The topmost navigating bridge, now at a depth of about 46 metres, was made of wood panels on a metal frame. The wood is completely gone as a result of the intense wartime fires - leaving two engine order telegraphs and the helm telemotor, with rudder direction indicator, standing bolted to the steel deck - but exposed in free open water. The brass circular helm ring, to which the spokes of the helm were screwed, can also be found here – the wooden

Left: Looking aft from the bridge of *Hokuyo Maru* over the skylights of the pitched engine room roof with forced draft ventilators standing upright. Lifeboat davits stand outboard of the Boat Deck. (Courtesy Pete Mesley)

Lower: The bridge of *Hokuyo Maru* - looking from the port side towards the starboard bridge wing. The front of the bridge is to left and the hatch cover beams and cargo booms of Hold No 2 are just visible far below (left). With the upper wooden bridge structure now gone, the ship's compass stands exposed in free water in the foreground with an engine order telegraph further to starboard. The helm stands on the centre line to right of shot. (Courtesy Pete Mesley) spokes of the helm have rotted or been burnt away to leave only the circular non-ferrous ring. Although the wooden deck planking is almost completely gone, here and there small sections of the wooden decking are evident where planks were fixed to the metal framework of the superstructure.

Abaft the navigating bridge, the split superstructure drops down towards the hatch for Hold No. 3, with a coaling shute nearby and forced draft ventilators and kingposts set abaft. Aft of this hatch is the collapsed smokestack with its distinctive Kita Nippon markings on its side.

Abaft the collapsed smokestack, at about 48 metres is the pitched roof of the engine room, which has a couple of the skylights closed - although most are open. Two forced draft ventilators stand at the aft end of the pitched roof - and on either side of the deck, there are exposed deck support beams. The empty lifeboat davits are still swung in – such was the speed she sank that the crew did not have time to swing them out and lower the boats.

The engine room itself can be accessed in a number of ways, through doorways fore and aft into the bridge superstructure or through the engine room skylights. The engine room is a large space but is cluttered with many rotted fallen spars and pieces of ship, scattered around in the violence of her sinking or succumbing to the ravages of her long immersion. At the top of the engine cylinders, your depth will be about 55 metres with the potential to go deeper to the lower levels – but I would caution against that due to the multiplicity of very fragile rotted fitments above you.

Below the gunwale on the starboard side of the superstructure there are two large holes in the shell plating of the hull. The lower is just above the seabed and is about 20 feet in diameter – this is where the torpedo from *Bunker Hill* aircraft is believed to have hit later in the day during Strike 3E – the plating is blown inwards.

The higher hole opens directly into the boiler room. The plates here have been blown outwards as from an internal explosion, common in sinking ships when cold water contacted hot boilers.

Moving aft and dropping down to the well deck, the hatches for Hold No's 4&5 are found at about 53 metres with the mainmast with its crosstree rising from a masthouse standing in between. Two cargo booms would have led forward from the mainmast kingposts across the hatch for Hold No. 4 whilst two more led aft from the mainmast across Hold. No 5. These cargo booms have been deflected by the bomb blast or the sinking process and most now lie swung over to starboard.

The port side of the deck at Hold No. 4 is buckled and has sagged – the shell plating of the hull is detached and falling outwards. The damage on the port side extends all the way aft from here to the stern and is the result of the hits by 500-lb bombs from *Essex* TBF Avenger aircraft early in the day. The hatch cover beams have all been blown away although a few of the lower hatch beams are still in place.

The poop island is severely damaged and blown upwards by the effects of a bomb hit. On the port side, all structural frames, bulkheads and plating are destroyed.

The rudder disappears into the sandy seabed in the amidships position at about 60 metres, and the propeller is half buried to the shaft.

15. *Hoyo Maru*
Merchant Tanker (1936)
Converted Merchant Transport (Oil Supply) (1940)
Hoyo Maru-class *Yusosen* Auxiliary Oiler (1941)
U.S. Recognition Code: 54 MKMKFK

Repair Anchorage

Tonnage:	8,692 grt
Dimensions:	474-ft long; beam of 61-ft; draught of 37.5-ft
Launched:	29 August 1936
Sunk:	17 February 1944
Cause of loss:	Bombed by TF 58 aircraft during Operation HAILSTONE
Wreck location:	Repair Anchorage, north of Fefan.
Depth to seabed:	Bow – 15 metres
	Stern - 30 metres
Least Depth:	Bow – 3 metres

The 8,691-grt merchant tanker *Hoyo Maru* was laid down on 15 October 1935 at Mitsubishi Jukogyo K.K. in Yokohama for Nippon Shosen K.K. of Tokyo, (Nippon Tanker K.K.). She was launched for fitting out afloat on 29 August 1936.

Hoyo Maru was completed on 5 November 1936 and delivered to her new Tokyo owners. Her only sister ship in the Hoyo Maru-class was the *Kaizyo Maru No. 2*, which would be sunk near Truk by an American submarine in March 1942.

Hoyo Maru was constructed with a main weather deck and a second deck clear of the cargo tanks, below. She was built with a cruiser stern and her machinery, in common with

The 8,692grt merchant tanker *Hoyo Maru* was launched in 1936 and requisitioned by the IJN as an auxiliary oiler in 1941. This is her sister ship *Kaizyo Maru No. 2*.

The IJN auxiliary oiler *Hoyo Maru* was bombed during Operation HAILSTONE. Mortally wounded she capsized on the surface as she sank and came to rest with her foreship aground in shallower water with her screw and rudder projecting above the surface over deeper water. The damaged ship eventually broke her back and the stern settled into deeper water.

virtually all tankers and oilers of the era, was housed aft. She was fitted with 2-stroke 6-cylinder diesel engines manufactured by her builders Mitsubishi Jukogyo K.K., which powered a single screw to give a fast service speed of 16 knots and a maximum speed of 19.5 knots. She had a radius of 19,000 miles at 16 knots and could carry 95,000 barrels of oil – a barrel being 42 U.S. gallons.

On only her second voyage, in January 1937, she ran aground in the Ariake Sea, an inland sea that opens to the East China Sea, west of off Kyushu, the southmost main island of Japan. Although her hull was seriously damaged, she was successfully refloated and taken to the Asano Shipyard in the Kanagawa Prefecture for repair.

After three years of civilian service with her original owners she was transferred on 15 April 1940 to a new tanker firm called Nitto Kogyo Kisen, which had only been founded in 1937. Nitto Kogyo Kisen would grow to quickly become the largest of all Japanese deep-sea tanker firms, controlling 62,000-tons of shipping by the outbreak of the Pacific war in 1941.

Aware of the importance of being able to replenish the fleet at sea in any war, the IJN requisitioned *Hoyo Maru* on 25 December 1940 for use as a Converted Merchant Transport (Oil Supply). *Hoyo Maru* was attached to the Kure Naval District and as part of her conversion works to an oiler, a refueling tripod kingpost was added on the port side just abaft the smokestack towards the stern.

On 20 February 1941, when notwithstanding Japan's war with China, America was still supplying oil to Japan, *Hoyo Maru* departed Kobe on a return journey to San Francisco. Further voyages were undertaken to Hainan Island off China and to the Dutch East Indies (modern day Indonesia), the north American coast and mainland Japan.

On 28 July 1941, in preparation for an invasion of the Dutch East Indies, some 140,000 Japanese troops began to arrive in southern French Indochina. Japanese warships were stationed at coastal ports and air force units were stationed around Saigon. The Japanese were now were closer than ever to Singapore, the Philippines and the Dutch East Indies.

To be able to replenish the fleet at sea in any conflict, the IJN would requisition 77 merchant ships from their civilian owners for conversion to *Yusosen* auxiliary oilers. By late 1941 however, just before the Pearl Harbor attack, Japan had only 49 merchant tankers and the IJN had 9 fleet oilers in service.

In late August 1941, just over three months before the Pearl Harbor raid, work began to convert *Hoyo Maru* to a *Yusosen* auxiliary oiler. She was fitted with two 80mm (3.15-inch) guns, one at her bow and one at her stern. The conversion work was completed on 11 October 1941 – she was rerated as a Converted Merchant Transport (Oil Supply) and attached to the Fourth Fleet, which was based at Truk atoll.

On 21 November 1941, just three weeks before the Pearl Harbor raid, the converted auxiliary oiler *Hoyo Maru* departed Yokosuka bound for Truk to join the Fourth Fleet. With hostilities not yet commenced, she arrived there safely on 3 December 1941, just a few days before the Pearl Harbor raid.

Departing Truk on 13 December 1941, a week after war began, *Hoyo Maru* sailed to the Japanese outpost at Kwajalein atoll from where she made supply voyages around the atoll and west to Lamotrek atoll in the central Caroline Islands. During late December 1941, in anticipation of the Operation R Invasions of Rabaul (on New Britain Island) and Kavieng to its north (on New Ireland Island), *Hoyo Maru* departed Kwajalein on a passage back to Japan, arriving at Yokosuka on 13 January 1942.

Just one week later, she departed Yokosuka on 21 January 1942, escorted by the auxiliary gunboat *Kasagi Maru* to refuel naval units taking part in the invasions of Rabaul and Kavieng. When the invasion forces swiftly overcame light Australian opposition and occupied Rabaul and Kavieng, *Hoyo Maru* was released and headed back to Truk, arriving there on 28 January 1942.

Hoyo Maru left Truk on 5 February 1942 and after calling at Kavieng she reached Rabaul on 8 February 1942 where she refueled IJN units. Whilst there, she was damaged in a US carrier raid by Douglas SBD Dauntless dive-bombers and Douglas TBD Devastator torpedo-bombers launched from Task Force 8. During the raid a Japanese transport ship was sunk and the light cruiser *Katori*, the oiler *Toa Maru*, the submarine *I-23*, the submarine depot ship *Yasukuni Maru* and several other ships were all damaged.

After repair, *Hoyo Maru* returned to Truk in late February 1942, where she refueled the carrier *Shōhō* before departing Truk for Yokosuka, Japan, arriving there on 7 March 1942. Refueled and revictualled, just a week later on 14 March 1942, she departed Yokosuka in a return convoy to Truk – arriving there safely on 22 March 1942.

On 28 March 1942, *Hoyo Maru* departed Truk in convoy for Rabaul - and whilst on passage she was attacked on 31 March 1942 by a surfaced American submarine. Using her defensive 80mm (3.15-inch) bow and stern guns, on the oiler's more stable gun platforms, she was able to fight off the submarine and use her speed to escape unharmed. She reached Rabaul safely - where she refueled several cruisers before moving north to Kavieng.

In May 1942 she was involved in Operation MO – the Invasion of Tulagi and Port Moresby in Papua New Guinea, which triggered the famous Battle of the Coral Sea. She subsequently carried out further RAS duties for a number of months around Truk, Rabaul and Bougainville before returning to Japan in July 1942 for repair.

From August 1942 onwards, she carried out refueling passages from Japan to the Marshall Islands, Truk, Singapore and Palau before she was damaged by a mine off the Northern Marianas on 19 December 1942. She was sent to Truk for repair and remained there until March 1943.

In April 1943 she was damaged in a bombing attack and had to return to Japan for repairs in Osaka by Hitachi Zosen. Returning to service on 14 July 1943, *Hoyo Maru* departed Kure the following day for Mutsure and then Moji, where she formed up in an escorted convoy with three other oilers, army and navy transports and several other supply ships bound for Formosa, and then onwards south to Singapore. After carrying crude oil for refining at Balikpapan, she left Balikpapan under escort for Truk on 23 September 1943 with a cargo of oil – arriving at Truk on 4 October, where she quickly refueled the light cruiser *Naka*.

On 17 October 1943 the Japanese intercepted U.S. radio traffic, which led them to believe that the U.S. was planning another raid on Wake Island. Admiral Koga sortied a powerful Japanese fleet from Truk, which included the battleships *Yamato, Musashi, Nagato, Fusō, Kongo* and *Haruna*, the fleet carriers *Shōkaku, Zuikaku* and *Zuihō*, along with supporting cruisers and destroyers. The fleet arrived at Brown Atoll, Eniwetok on 19 October 1943.

On 21 October, *Hoyo Maru* along with the destroyer escort *Amatsukaze,* departed Truk for Eniwetok to oil the fleet units. The fleet however made no contact with American naval forces and the Japanese Fleet returned to Truk on 26/27 October 1943.

On 5 November 1943, *Hoyo Maru* departed Truk in an escorted convoy bound for Palembang, Sumatra and Singapore. Early in the morning of 6 November 1943, at 0100, near Orolup Island, west of Truk, the American submarine *Haddock* (SS-231) attacked the convoy in darkness, on the surface. During this radar guided attack, six torpedoes were fired from 3,000 yards at *Hoyo Maru* and a second tanker, *Genyo Maru*. The submarine then swung around and as it evaded the destroyer *Yakaze* fired four torpedoes from her stern tubes at *Yakaze* from about 3,145 yards. As *Yakaze* made evasive turns, it collided with the tanker *Genyo Maru*, damaging the destroyer's bow.

After withdrawing to reload the torpedo tubes, about an hour later *Haddock* made a second attack on the convoy firing her last four torpedoes, two at each of the two valuable oilers. One torpedo hit *Hoyo Maru* at the stern, damaging her engine and starting a fire. Water flooded into her aft engine compartments and she began to settle by the stern. The crew was ordered to abandon ship – leaving only a skeleton crew of about 12 aboard. Some 90 crew were picked up by the destroyer *Yakaze*.

As daylight came, *Hoyo Maru,* with her engines disabled, was drifting powerless and settling by the stern. The destroyer *Yakaze*, having split its bow plating when it collided with *Genyo Maru* and having taken on water could herself, only make 6 knots. *Yakaze* stood by the stricken *Hoyo Maru* – although she was unable to approach because of the fires aboard. At 1130, the light cruiser *Nagara* arrived on scene and reported that *Hoyo Maru* was still burning heavily, abandoned and down by the stern.

By 1710, the fires aboard *Hoyo Maru* had finally been extinguished and she was taken in tow for repair at Truk. *Nagara* managed to set up her bilge pumps to start pumping out the after section of *Hoyo Maru*.

Four days later, on 10 November 1943, the slow tow of the stricken *Hoyo Maru* arrived at Truk. Once inside the lagoon, her valuable fuel cargo was discharged, and she was anchored for repair 400 yards north east of Fefan and west of Dublon Island in the Repair Anchorage - alongside the repair ship *Akashi* and other damaged vessels such as *Kensyo Maru, Tonan Maru 3* and *Kiyosumi Maru*.

On 7 February 1944, whilst still under repair, *Hoyo Maru* was formally assigned to the Fourth Fleet's Inner South Seas Force. 10 days later, as the initial fighter sweep of Hellcats swept over Truk at dawn on 17 February 1944 to begin Operation HAILSTONE, valuable oilers and tankers were not hit in the first strikes for fear of clouds of black smoke from burning tankers obscuring other targets. However, later in the afternoon between 1415 and 1500, while still at anchor in the Repair Anchorage between Dublon and Fefan Islands, *Hoyo Maru* was attacked in strength by Strike 1E SBD Dauntless dive-bombers from *Enterprise* and *Yorktown*.

The largely defenceless oiler was hit by a 1,000-lb GP bomb abaft the bridge, on her starboard side, just aft of amidships, causing extensive structural damage. A second 1,000-lb bomb hit her forward of her poop island near her previously damaged stern that set her fuel bunkers on fire. She also took a near miss or a hit on her port side.

Hoyo Maru had been mortally wounded. As water flooded into her cavernous aft machinery spaces, her stern settled into the water and she took on a heavy list, before eventually capsizing. U.S. post-strike photos show the ship capsized with part of her keel and her screw projecting above the surface of the water.

During the follow up American Task Force 58 fast carrier strikes two months later on 29-30 April 1944, she was observed to be in the same capsized position, with her screw and aft section of keel still proud of the water.

The ship had been moored above an underwater slope that ran up to a reef flat. Structurally damaged by bombing just abaft the bridge, in the years that followed the weakened ship broke her back and the stern section settled down into deeper water, coming to rest on the underwater slope – stern deep. The capsized forward section settled onto shallower seabed, the two sections coming to rest on the seabed still partially connected - but a few metres apart at the keel.

The Wreck today

Today the wreck of *Hoyo Maru* rests upside down in two loosely connected sections between the islands of Fefan and Tonoas (Dublon) on a sloping seabed that runs from a depth of about 15 metres at the bow down to around 30 metres at the stern.

The stern of *Hoyo Maru* is about 400 metres from the island of Fefan to the west - whilst her bow points east towards the island of Tonoas. The hull is split athwartships, just aft of amidships – with the two sections being about 6-7 metres apart.

With only about 4 metres of water above the upturned forward section of the keel, the ship from the split in the hull to the bow is easily visible from the surface. Once you descend however you will find that the ship is in an area of somewhat murky 10-20 metres average underwater visibility, common for the wrecks that lie just off the major islands.

The upturned, almost flat, 60-ft wide keel of the bow section rises up imperceptibly from the split towards the stem where the sides of the ship sweep together towards the bow. Bathed in sunlight, the upturned keel is now almost completely covered in a vibrant coral garden.

The rear section of the ship drops away from the split into deeper water of just over 30 metres at the fantail. The whole ship is now underwater – unlike the wartime U.S. pilot reports of the propeller and part of the keel being visible above the surface. With the bow section on shallower flat seabed, the stern of the ship must have been projecting out into deeper water.

Artist's impression of the wreck of the auxiliary oiler *Hoyo Maru*.

At some point after the war, gravity won its battle over the ship's structure, which was already weakened by the wartime 1,000-lb bomb hits and the stresses of the difficult capsize. The ship broke her back and the stern section settled into deeper water.

Local dive boats usually anchor beside the split between the two sections – although there is little point in entering the ship here as you just move into oil storage spaces.

The wreck rests on an uneven seabed that allows divers underneath the upturned weather deck, which is in places held off the ground. In other places the edge of the deck is hard down on the sand. The stern superstructure keeps the weather deck in front of it off the seabed.

Moving aft from the hull split, the top of the inverted poop island is hard down on the sand, with the smokestack being rammed into the seabed. There is a large space in front of the superstructure, where the weather deck and flying bridge (which runs forwards towards the bridge superstructure are held a few metres off the seabed for some distance.

On the port side of the hull aft is a large hole in her plating, likely the torpedo hit from the American submarine *Haddock* on 6 November 1943 that disabled her engines and caused her to be taken to Truk for repair. There is another smaller hole further aft, which is likely a bomb hit suffered during Operation HAILSTONE.

Divers can enter the wreck through the torpedo hole, which is about 7 metres in diameter, and move directly into the engine room and machinery spaces originally underneath the poop island. Tankers invariably had their engines and machinery at the stern, to free the majority of the hull space for oil cargo tanks. If the engine machinery were situated amidships then this would involve having a prop shaft tunnel running aft inside the ship to where the shaft exits the ship to the prop itself. You often see a prop shaft tunnel running aft from an amidships engine to the prop at the bottom of aft holds on a 3-island freighter. It's not a problem to stack dry cargo around it in a hold - but it is a problem for oil tanks, which would have to be contoured around it with much valuable oil cargo space being lost.

Entering the engine room through the torpedo hole, the inverted diesel engine cylinders can be located, fallen from their mounts amongst debris on the bottom. A large geared flywheel can be spotted at the rear of the engine with part of the prop shaft visible. Catwalks lead here and there amidst a mass of pipework, machinery and a large fire blackened control panel covered in switches, gauges and white ceramic insulators – which is top left as you enter.

Wherever I have dived in the Pacific, when you see the wrecks of tankers and oilers, they almost invariably have been hit in the stern at the engine spaces. I recollect talking to an old submariner who said that when attacking, you always aimed for the engine room to disable the ship. For example, the *Sinkoku Maru* here at Truk has a large hole in her port side engine room - and the two *Shiretoko*-class oilers *Iro* and *Sata* at Palau both have taken hits at the stern. The aerial torpedo stern hits are not random chance - but clinical precision strikes by U.S. aviators.

With tankers being so heavily compartmentalized, with sometimes more than 30 individual oil tanks or compartments, a tanker could take one or more hits in amongst her tanks - but remain afloat. However, if a hit was scored on the vast cathedral like machinery spaces at the stern, when these filled with water, a tanker could be pulled under by the stern. Even if it didn't sink, with the engine wrecked, an important tanker or oiler would be immobilised, and out of the war for a very long time. Japan's war effort depended on an ability to bring vital oil to her army and to her warships, which were scattered widely across her Pacific garrisons. Hit a tanker at her engine areas and she was out of the war for months – or permanently.

Only suitably qualified divers should explore deep into these aft areas, with a local guide – it is quite silty inside the wreck, and once you penetrate any distance inside, it is pitch black and you are reliant on your torch.

Portholes ring around the fantail and allow shafts of blue light from outside to weakly light up some of the internal spaces. It is possible to go far into the ship and pass through a number of fire blackened deck levels, scattered with all sorts of debris, including 55-gallon drums of aviation fuel from dry cargo spaces that have rotted over time and fallen from above. Large sections of rotted bulkhead plating have fallen here and there – and there is much fragile material and fitments suspended above you. A number of divers have perished inside this wreck such that for a time, local Chuukese guides thought the ship was haunted. Take extreme care if you go inside.

Moving back outside the wreck and around the fantail at the very stern, the large 4-bladed propeller and rudder are still in place, heavily covered in corals.

Turning the dive here to move shallower, you can now begin to move forward to the bow section. As you rise and reach the break in the hull, it is possible to peek into the forward oil tank. Heating coils are fixed at the bottom of the tank (now above you) – steam was passed through these coils to gently heat heavy oil to make it viscous enough to be pumped out of the tanks to the shore.

Continuing to move forward into shallower water, on the port side, it is possible to duck under the overhanging weather deck, which is clear of the sandy seabed in places, and swim forward for some distance. When you pop back out, you are approaching the bow itself and will see the anchor chain run out along the seabed. About 10 metres from the stem on the port side there is another bomb hole.

As you arrive at the near vertical stem, the seabed has risen from about 30 metres at the stern to 15 metres here. You can rise up the stem towards the keel and then head back to the dive boat at the amidships split, whilst doing your 6-metre safety stop.

16. *I-169*
Kaidai Type 6A 1st class submarine – I-69 (1934)
(renumbered I-169 – May 1942)

Combined Fleet Anchorage

Displacement:	1,400 tons standard surfaced; 1,785 tons deep load; 2,440 tons submerged
Dimensions:	336ft 7-in long (wl); beam of 26-ft 11-in; draught of 15-ft
Launched:	15 February 1934 (as I-69)
Sunk:	4 April 1944
Cause of loss:	Crash dived with induction valve open during air raid and flooded
Wreck location:	Combined Fleet Anchorage, west of Tonoas Island
Depth to seabed:	Bow – 36 metres
	Stern - 43 metres
Least Depth:	33 metres

———————————

The first Japanese *Kaidai* Type 1 experimental 1st Class or cruiser-type submarine was laid down under the 1919 Programme and was based on the large British submarines. *Kai* means 'gun' whilst *Dai* means 'large'. They had a diving depth of about 200-feet. In all, the *Kaidai* series of large submarine-cruisers would be in production for more than 20 years, from 1921-1943.

The Type 2 boats were the next evolution of the *Kaidai* submarine, following on under the 1920 Programme. The Type 3 & Type 4 boats were ordered under the 1923-1928 Fleet Law whilst the Type 5 boats were ordered under the 1927-31 Fleet Law.

Artist's impression of the large *Kaidai* Type 6A submarine I-169. When warned of an imminent air attack on 4 April 1944, the submarine was dived without the main induction valve being secured. The submarine flooded but some of her crew survived in sealed off compartments. Despite frantic salvage efforts over the coming days, all attempts to raise the submarine failed and the crew were lost.

The eight Kaidai Type 6 boats, such as I-69, were improved Type 5 boats, ordered under the First Replenishment Law 1931. These new submarines were of an improved design with a stronger pressure hull and a new double-acting 2-stroke diesel motor.

I-69 was one of an initial group of six of the new Type 6A large cruiser submarines. Two more improved Type 6B boats would follow 3-4 years later under the 1934 Fleet Law and carried stronger armament. The stronger pressure hull gave the first two Type 6A boats, I-68 and her sister I-69, a diving depth of 230 feet - whilst the four later boats in the class, I-70, I-71, I-72 and I-73 had a diving depth of 250-feet.

I-69 was laid down on 22 December 1931 at the Mitsubishi shipbuilding yard in Kobe, just to the west of Osaka – who also built I-72. I-69 was launched into Osaka Bay on 15 February 1934 for fitting out afloat. She was completed in the autumn of the following year on 28 September 1935, when she was attached to the Kure Naval District.

Submarines at this time used diesel engines to run on the surface and switched to electric engines to run underwater as required. Submerged, with greater drag and running on electric motors, submarines were much slower than when running surfaced on diesels. I-69 was fitted with two 9,000hp Kampon 2-stroke diesel engines that drove her two screws to give her a surfaced speed of 23 knots. She carried 341 tons of diesel fuel that gave her an operating radius of 14,000nm at 10 knots.

Whilst submerged and running on her two electric motors she could make 8.2 knots with an operating radius of 65nm at 3 knots. She carried a complement of 60-84 crew.

I-69 was fitted with six 21-inch torpedo tubes, four in the bow and two in the stern and carried 14 torpedoes. She was also fitted with a 10cm (3.9-inch) high angle (HA) deck gun mounted in front of the conning tower and a single 13mm AA machine gun mounted aft of conning tower.

The submarines I-68 to I-70 were refitted in 1938 with improvements to machinery. I-68 would go on to distinguish herself in the Battle of Midway on 6/7 June 1942, during which the carrier *Yorktown* was attacked by Japanese carrier aircraft. She was bombed and then hit and disabled by two Type 91 aerial torpedoes. Listing heavily, *Yorktown* had to be abandoned and was taken under tow. The destroyer *Hammann* (DD-412) came alongside the stricken carrier to provide salvage pumps and power to reduce the flooding.

I-68 (by then renumbered I-168) approached the disabled carrier undetected and around noon on 6 June 1942, fired a salvo of four torpedoes, one of which hit *Hammann*, breaking her back and splitting her in half. *Hamman* sank quickly in about four minutes. Two of the other torpedoes hit *Yorktown*, fatally wounding her and leading to her subsequent capsize and loss. The war would catch up however with I-68 the following year on 27 July 1943, when she disappeared without trace, believed torpedoed by *Scamp* (SS-277) off the Bismarck Islands between New Ireland and New Hanover.

In early November 1941, just a month prior to the outbreak of hostilities, I-69 was assigned to the Advanced Expeditionary Force of the Sixth Fleet based in Kwajalein in the Marshall Islands. She departed from Saeki, beside Hiroshima (to the south of Japan) on 11 November

1941 bound for Kwajalein along with her sister *Kaidai* boats I-68, I-70, I-71, I-72 and I-73.

In preparation for the historic attack on Pearl Harbor scheduled for 7 December 1941, I-69 departed Kwajalein on 23 November 1941 to close Hawaii, where she was to lay off the entrance to Pearl Harbor to rescue the crews of five midget submarines that were to penetrate Pearl's harbor defences and attack U.S. warships.

Once I-69 and I-69 were a few days into the voyage, on 26 November 1941, Admiral Chūichi Nagumo, Commander in Chief of the First Air Fleet, sortied his powerful *Kidō Butai* striking force of the 6-carriers *Akagi, Kaga, Sōryū, Hiryū, Shōkaku, Zuikaku* and escorts from the Kurile Islands, the chain of islands that stretch from the north of Japan to the Kamchatka Peninsula. In complete secrecy, the *Kidō Butai* striking force, carrying some 400-strike aircraft moved to a point in the Pacific, a few hundred miles north west of Hawaii.

As I-69 moved to her assigned position, on 2 December 1941, the famous Wabun Code signal "*Niitakayama nobore* (Climb Mount Niitaka) *1208*" arrived on Nagumo's flagship from Admiral Isoroku Yamamoto, Commander in Chief of the IJN Combined Fleet. On receiving the coded signal, Admiral Nagumo opened a set of top-secret documents that had been prepared and given to him before departure. These confirmed that Japan would be going to war with the United States, Britain and Holland - and gave the date for the opening of hostilities as 8 December 1941, Japan time (7 December 1941 in the United States).

On the morning of the attack, I-69, her sister I-68 and seven other submarines took position south of Oahu, off the entrance to Pearl Harbor. Five Type A midget submarines were launched from the decks of other mother submarines outside the entrance to Pearl Harbor to take part in the 2-pronged attack of U.S. warships from air and from underwater. I-68 and I-69 were to rescue any midget submarine crews who escaped from the attack, and to attack any U.S. ships that might steam out of Pearl Harbor as the attack began. They would also rescue any downed air crew.

As I-68 and I-69 lay off the entrance to Pearl Harbor, officers and deck crew witnessed explosions and columns of fire in the harbor as the two waves of Japanese aircraft attacked, beginning just before 0800 on Sunday 7 December 1941.

Later that night, whilst on the surface attempting to recharge her batteries and air supply, she was spotted by American destroyers and forced to dive with her batteries not fully charged. After moving on her electric motors to Barber's Point, at the very southwest tip of Oahu, I-69 located an American destroyer, fired a torpedo but missed. In response, I-69 was unsuccessfully depth charged.

The two submarines I-68 and I-69 waited until the following day, 8 December for any of the five midget submarines to return from the strike for the rendezvous. But none of the midget submarine crews would return from the U.S. naval stronghold - all five were lost in the attack.

The following day, 9 December 1941, I-69 was still patrolling around Hawaii searching for any shot down air crews. She unsuccessfully attacked a cargo ship, south of Oahu – the attack resulting in more depth charging.

That same day, off Barber's Point at the southwest tip of Oahu, I-69 became entangled in anti-submarine nets. The captain of I-69 struggled for hours, without success, to break his submarine free of the nets - by moving forward and backwards and flooding and blowing ballast tanks.

During the darkness of the night of 9/10 December, I-69 again struggled, and failed, to break free of the nets – being forced to lie on the bottom throughout the following day for fear of detection. As the submarine lay on the bottom waiting for the next night's darkness to resume her attempts to break free, carbon dioxide built up to a dangerous level and the crew came close to starting to suffocate.

The following night however, she successfully broke free of her entanglement, damaging her periscope in the process. She had been submerged for about 39 hours and so with little hope of spotting or rescuing downed aircrew, she turned to head back to her base at Kwajalein - arriving there on 27 December 1941.

On 12 January 1942, fully repaired and replenished, I-69 left Kwajalein for her second war patrol - to reconnoitre Midway Island for the forthcoming Japanese invasion, Operation MI.

I-69 arrived off Midway on 21 January 1942, and around dusk on 8 February, she bombarded Sand Island, Midway from about 1,000 yards offshore with her 10 cm (3.9-inch) deck gun, targeting the radio station. In response, the U.S. coast defence battery on Sand Island opened up with their 5-inch weapons, forcing I-69 to submerge after three rounds were fired.

I-69 continued to patrol around Midway the following day 9 February 1942 and through the night into 10 February. Once again, around dusk on 10 February 1942, I-69 surfaced about 1,000 yards offshore for a second attempt to shell the radio station on Sand Island. This time she was spotted by two U.S. Marines F2A-3 Brewster Buffalo fighters, based on the Midway airfield that were patrolling overhead. I-69 got off two rounds at the radio station before the Buffaloes swooped in to attack.

The Buffaloes bombed the surfaced submarine, scoring two near misses and carrying out strafing runs. Lightly damaged, I-69 submerged and headed back to her Kwajalein base.

I-69 subsequently carried out her 3rd and 4th combat patrols from Kwajalein towards Rabaul and Wake Island before returning to Kwajalein on 9 May 1942.

On 20 May 1942, shortly before the Battle of Midway, I-69 was renumbered as I-169 and assigned to SubRon 3, which sortied from Kwajalein for the Midway invasion. I-169 took up position along the American reinforcement route from Hawaii.

The Battle of Midway was contested between 4-7 June 1942 – and was a disaster for Japan who had four fleet carriers and a heavy cruiser sunk. The battle effectively ended Japan's ability to expand her empire further.

After the disastrous carrier losses of the Battle of Midway, I-169 returned to her base at Kwajalein - before resuming combat patrols in the New Caledonia and New Hebrides areas. Later that same year she took part in the invasion of Guadalcanal before returning to Sasebo in Japan in September 1942 for overhaul.

The early 1930's design of Kaidai Type 6A attack submarine had by 1942 become outdated by the rapid advances in Allied anti-submarine warfare (ASW) technology. Thus, I-169 was modified to allow her great size to be utilised as an underwater transport to carry supplies to frontline outposts such as Truk. (After the fall of Saipan in June 1944 this would be the only way Truk could be supplied). Once the works were completed I-169 moved to Truk with SubRon 3 to take part in the Guadalcanal campaign.

In January 1943, I-169 was sent with several other submarines to Kiska in the Aleutian Islands on a return supply mission. Then on 15 February 1943, I-169 along with I-171 departed Kure once again for Kiska, carrying a Type A midget submarine, its torpedoes, 125 tons of supplies and IJA troops.

I-169 was assigned to the Fifth Fleet for the duration of the Aleutian campaign - and saw service supplying isolated Japanese island garrisons and patrolling off the Aleutians and Kuriles until August 1943 when she was sent back to Kure in Japan for another overhaul.

Overhaul completed, I-169 sortied from Kure on 25 September 1943 for Truk - from where she patrolled between Hawaii and the Marshall Islands before forming part of a picket line off Tarawa, as the 200-ship strong American invasion fleet opened Operation GALVANIC, the invasion of the Gilbert Islands, with the seizure of Tarawa and Makin on 20 November 1943.

Submarine operations from Kwajalein Atoll had become unsafe by December 1943, and Sixth Fleet (Submarines) transferred to Truk. Operating from Truk, I-169 received torpedoes from the submarine tender *Heian Maru* (a well-known Truk wreck today) on several occasions throughout December and January 1944.

On 31 January 1944, I-169 departed Truk on a supply mission to Buka and Buin Islands, more than 1,000 nautical miles to the south. By a quirk of fate, she was therefore absent from Truk when the Operation HAILSTONE strikes took place on 17/18 February 1944.

I-169 returned to Truk on 11 March 1944, three weeks after Operation HAILSTONE. After a brief supply mission, at the beginning of April 1944, I-169 was back in Truk replenishing between patrols in the Combined Fleet Anchorage, northwest of Dublon Island.

At about 0900 (local) on 4 April 1944, an alert was issued of an American air raid by PB4Y Liberator bombers. The watch officer on I-169 ordered her to dive immediately to avoid the first wave of inbound bombers - but the main induction valve had not been secured. The main induction valve is part of the ventilation system that allows air to be drawn into the boat by suction blowers through the main and auxiliary induction line to purge and fill the submarine with fresh air. The main induction usually ran outside the pressure hull with a vertical standpipe that extends up to the top of the periscope shears and has at the top the outboard valves through which fresh air is drawn. If the main induction valve is left open as a submarine submerges, the ventilation system will flood.

As a result of the main induction being left open, as I-169 submerged, her aft compartments began to rapidly flood – and despite a desperate attempt to surface, she sank to the bottom of the lagoon. As the submarine came to rest on the seabed in 35-40 metres of water, the trapped crew managed to seal off the flooded areas.

Once the bombing raid was over, when I-169 didn't surface, an attempt was made to contact the submarine. When no reply was received, it became clear that the submarine was in distress. A vessel equipped for diving operations was sent to the scene and a diver was sent down to the submarine to try to establish contact with any surviving crew by tapping on the hull. The control room, beneath the conning tower, was found to be completely flooded with no response there, however the diver received responses to his hammering from compartments around the other 4 of the 5 hatches (excluding the control room). It appeared that the crew had been able to close the watertight doors inside the submarine and seal off the flooded control room.

The following day, 5 April, a repair ship with a 30-ton crane and the tug *Futagami* (a present day Truk wreck) arrived on scene to attempt to lift the bow to the surface and let the crew escape. Attempts to rescue the stranded submariners got under way as divers attached lifting cables to the submarine - but at about 1530 as the lift began, the deadweight of the flooded submarine proved too heavy - and the cables broke. By this time, divers were reporting that the tapping noises were only coming from one compartment aft.

Holes were drilled into the submarine's ballast tanks and air hoses inserted to blow the tanks - but the divers were unable to communicate to those alive that they should open the air valves to the ballast tanks. By midnight, all responses from inside the submarine had stopped – the surviving crew had suffocated or drowned.

Japanese hardhat divers spent 6 weeks unsuccessfully attempting to raise the submarine – in the process recovering 32 bodies from the forward compartments.

By May 1944 there was an imminent threat of a U.S. land invasion of Truk - and so to prevent their submarine technology falling into U.S. hands, I-169 was depth charged with the bow and conning tower being heavily damaged.

Divers relocated I-169 in 1971 and human remains were found inside at this time. Some remains were lying on top of the two diesel engines, as though crew members had climbed onto the engines to get above rising water or to get the last air in the compartment.

When a documentary film using the footage of human remains was shown in Japan, there was quite a public outcry that led to funds being raised that financed an expedition in 1973 employing Fukuda Salvage Co Ltd from Japan with a diver support vessel and 6 commercial divers. The human remains were duly recovered and subsequently cremated in a religious Shinto ceremony. The bell was recovered and put on display at the Yasukuni Shrine in Tokyo.

The Japanese commercial divers then attempted to weld the hatches shut to prevent recreational divers entering the submarine - however divers soon began to enter the submarine through the engine room hatch and in 1974, two divers were killed, one trapped inside the engine room whilst the other died after running out of air attempting to rescue him and was forced to surface.

The Wreck today

Today the wreck of large *Kaidai* Type 6A cruiser submarine I-169 sits upright on a gently sloping bottom with her bow in about 36 metres and her stern deeper in 43 metres. She is a big vessel – the intact sections of her hull rising up some 7 meters from the seabed. She lists over to port.

The bow has been largely demolished by the wartime depth charging and in places only the bottom of the hull can be made out. Her four bow torpedo tubes are visible in amongst the general wreckage and debris. A section of the foreship reforms around the circular forward escape hatch into the pressure hull.

The wreck of IJN *I-169*

Least depth: 30m
Depth to seabed: Bow 35m, Stern 43m

Bow damaged by Japanese depth-charging

Conning tower demolished by Japanese depth-charging

Hatch to pressure hull

Stern torpedo tubes

Starboard prop shaft

Artist's impression of the wreck of the submarine I-169, sitting upright on the bottom of the lagoon. Her fore part and conning tower were heavily damaged by Japanese wartime depth charging to prevent the military technology being acquired by the Allies. The aft part of the submarine is intact.

Moving aft along the wreck, the foreship resumes a scene of destruction around the conning tower, which has been knocked over by the depth charging and taken a severed section of the top of the pressure hull with it. The conning tower now lies almost flat on its port side on the sandy seabed on the port side of the wreck. The conning tower access hatches are visible as are the low-profile attack periscope and larger night periscope – now extending downwards and disappearing into the sandy seabed. The 10cm (3.9-inch) deck gun, which would have been mounted in front of the conning tower, lies in the wreckage.

A long section of the aft part of the submarine from the conning tower area to the stern is largely intact – and swimming aft along it, you get a feel for the true size of this cruiser submarine. The raised superstructure deck above the pressure hull and free flooding area, was constructed of a steel framework with a wooden deck – to avoid the effects of the blistering heat in the tropics, and freezing cold elsewhere, on a steel deck. The wooden deck planks have all rotted away to leave the skeletal framework exposed. Thick degaussing cables run around the whole length of the hull, draped over the damaged bow sections.

Towards the stern, the circular after deck escape hatch is open - and still able to move on its hinges. This hatch gives access below to a second hatch into the pressure hull itself, to the engine room and aft quarters. The hatch is a tight squeeze for a diver wearing anything but a single tank or side mount rig - but once inside, it is possible to move forward and pass through a circular hatch into the engine compartment and continue forward between the two diesel engines. The walls are lined with pipes, valves and gauges - whilst cage lights with their glass still intact line the roof.

Moving further forward inside the submarine, a second circular hatchway is found, likely to the damaged control room. The hatch is only half open and the area beyond is crowded and cluttered with scattered metal work and debris, likely from the wartime depth charging of the conning tower area.

Back outside the pressure hull, on deck, a tripod jackstaff, a few metres tall, originally stood just aft of this after deck hatch towards the stern – you can usually see an IJN ensign flying from it in archive photographs of the I-class boats afloat.

It is a long swim aft along the hull from the demolished conning tower before the raised deck framework finally ends as the hull tapers towards the almost pointed stern. Here at the very stern, the doors for both torpedo tubes are open.

Both propellers are still present, held in their support bearing A-frames. The free sections of shaft run forward until they enter the hull through shaft tubes.

The white sandy seabed around the submarine is strewn with bits and pieces of submarine, scattered during the depth charging. Air hoses and cables used in the rescue attempts during the war, to blow her ballast tanks, still lie along the sides of the hull between conning tower and stern.

17. *Inter-Island Supply Vessel*

Sixth Fleet Anchorage

Tonnage:	130 tons (est.)
Dimensions:	95ft long (est.); beam of 18ft (est.)
Sunk:	29-30 April 1944 (assumed)
Cause of loss:	Strafed by TF 58 aircraft during follow up raid
Wreck location:	Sixth Fleet Anchorage, west of Uman Island
Depth to seabed:	25 metres

———————————

The wreck of a small coastal auxiliary vessel, perhaps a requisitioned ex-fishing boat used as a picket boat or auxiliary sub chaser for supplying troops stationed on Truk's islands, lies not far from *Hino Maru No 2* in about 25 metres of water to the west of Uman Island.

There were a number of smaller craft such as this present west of Uman Island when the follow up Task Force 58 carrier raid on Truk took place on 29-30 April 1944. These vessels were strafed and bombed and although there is no specific information recorded about the circumstances of this vessel sinking, it is believed to have been sunk at that time. There is a projectile penetration hole in the starboard side of her hull in front of the wheelhouse, likely the fatal strafing damage that sunk her.

The vessel is about 100 feet in length with a narrow beam of about 20 feet, the same dimensions as many auxiliary subchasers, and sits upright on her keel with her bows pointing towards Uman.

The vessel has a raked bow and a heavily encrusted raised fo'c'sle, with an anchor windlass atop. There are two hatches in the forward well deck that give access to the single forward hold, originally likely a fish hold.

The wheelhouse amidships rises up two deck levels and is still largely intact with square windows ringing around it and an aft facing doorway on the port side. Inside stands an encrusted helm stand and rudder direction indicator pedestal.

Abaft the wheelhouse, the deckhouse extends over the engine room below. There are a few deck hatches to the engine room – and the funnel is now missing.

At the very stern, a small deck house served as crew quarters and galley. An aft facing open doorway at the aftmost bulkhead of the deckhouse allows access into what would have been the galley, crew accommodation spaces and mess.

18. *Katsuragisan Maru*
Cargo ship (1925)
IJA *Rikugun Yusosen* Transport (1941)
IJN *Ippan Choyosen* General Requisitioned Ship (1943)
U.S. Recognition Code: 38 MFM

Northeast Pass

Tonnage:	2,427 grt
Dimensions:	284.5ft long; beam of 42-ft; draught of 23.2ft
Launched:	29 December 1924
Sunk:	7 January 1944
Cause of loss:	Entered friendly minefield at Northeast Pass and hit IJN mine
Wreck location:	Northeast Pass
Depth to seabed:	70 metres
Least Depth:	55 metres - superstructure
	62 metres - deck

The 2,427grt cargo ship *Katsuragisan Maru*, was laid down on 20 June 1925 at the Mitsui Bussan Kaisha Ltd. shipyard in Tama, Tokyo. One of four sister ships, the others were *Kachaosan Maru, Kasagisan Maru* and *Kasugasan Maru*. All four Mitsui Bussan Kaisha sister ships had two decks, a plumb stem and a counter stern.

The 3-island steamer *Katsuragisan Maru* was fitted with a coal-fired 3-cylinder triple expansion steam engine and a single screw that gave her a service speed of 10 knots and a maximum speed of 12.5 knots. She had an operating radius of 4,800 nautical miles at 10 knots.

The 2,427grt cargo ship *Katsuragisan Maru* was one of four identical ships completed to the *Kachosen Maru* (shown) design in 1925 for Mitsui Bussan K.K. She was requisitioned by the IJA as a transport ship in 1941, and then requisitioned by the IJN in 1943. She ran into a Japanese minefield and hit a friendly mine as she entered the Truk lagoon via Northeast Pass, which had, unknown to her captain, been closed off and mined by Japan.

179

The *Katsuragisan Maru* had been built for Mitsui Bussan Kaisha just before the company acquired the rights to diesel engines from Burmeister & Wain in 1926. She had just missed out in the great change in marine propulsion and was thus fitted with a traditional reciprocating triple expansion steam engine. Her service speed of 10 knots was standard for the older ships of the day, but slow in comparison to the new breed of ships fitted with diesel engines that would follow.

Katsuragisan Maru was constructed as a well deck steamer with a raised fo'c'sle, two foredeck holds in the well deck before a composite superstructure amidships that had a tall narrow bridge superstructure forward and the engine casing superstructure and smokestack aft. Two more holds were set in the after well deck before the poop island, which held the steering gear below.

In July 1937, at the time of the Japanese invasion of China, *Katsuragisan Maru* was requisitioned by the Imperial Japanese Army (IJA) as a transport vessel. She was released back to Mitsui Bussan Kaisha the following year in April 1938.

At the outbreak of war in the Pacific in December 1941, *Katsuragisan Maru* was again requisitioned by the IJA (along with her sister ship *Kachaosan Maru*) and converted for use as an *Rikugun* Auxiliary Transport. An 8 cm (3-inch) Type 41 dual purpose (DP) naval gun, a design dating from before WWI, was mounted on a circular gun platform on top of the poop island at the stern.

Her two other sister ships, *Kasagisan Maru* and *Kasugasan Maru,* were at the same time requisitioned by the IJN as auxiliary transports. Of the four sister ships, only *Kasugasan Maru* survived the war – being broken up for scrap in 1965. *Kasagisan Maru* was sunk by U.S. carrier aircraft on 25 November 1944 in Lingayen Bay in the Philippines whilst *Kachaosan Maru* was sunk by U.S. carrier aircraft six months later on 23 March 1945 off the Ryuko Islands.

Once the conversion works were completed, *Katsuragisan Maru* embarked on her duties as an IJA transport – initially carrying cargoes around the Japanese home islands. On 11 June 1942, she departed the east coast port of Yokohama, in Tokyo Bay, in a northbound convoy of IJA transports and merchant ships. Then, on 25 June 1942, she departed Tokyo Bay for Ominato, on the west coast of Honshū, in a convoy that was escorted by the destroyer *Okikaze*. On 9 April 1943 she departed Kobe, in southern Japan, in a convoy of IJA transports, merchant ships and tankers with a minesweeper as escort, bound for Yokosuka in Tokyo Bay.

In 1943, *Katsuragisan Maru* was released back from the IJA to her civilian owners Mitsui Bussan – but it was to be a brief interlude, as towards the end of that year on 17 December 1943, she was requisitioned once again for war service, this time by the IJN as an *Ippan Choyosen*, a General Requisitioned Ship that kept its civilian crew but often had a naval officer as Captain.

Three days later, on 20 December 1943, *Katsuragisan Maru* departed Tokyo for Truk, carrying rolls of steel mesh matting, military trucks and general cargo. She called at Yokosuka and harboured there for a few days before heading south for Truk on Xmas Day 1943 in convoy with *Matsutan Maru* (which is the present day Truk wreck known as *Shotan Maru*) and escorted by the kaibōkan *Hirado*.

The convoy arrived safely at Truk and just before dawn on 7 January 1944 and *Katsuragisan Maru* made to enter the Truk lagoon through **Northeast Pass**.

There are only a handful of passes or channels through the 140-mile circumference of the coral barrier reef that rings around the Truk lagoon that are suitable for navigation by larger vessels. As part of their fortifications for the defence of Truk, on the outbreak of hostilities, the Japanese had closed off and mined all shipping channels into the lagoon, leaving open only **North Pass** and **South Pass**. They were the only channels open for navigation and were heavily defended.

Northeast Pass, which *Katsuragisan Maru* was about to navigate had been the main shipping channel prior to the war. But it was now closed off and heavily mined to prevent any Allied incursion into the lagoon by submarine or surface craft.

Katsuragisan Maru steamed unwittingly into Northeast Pass - and in the half light of dawn at about 0515, she struck one of the defensive mines in the Pass. The explosion appears to have been on the starboard side just abaft the amidships superstructure. Five of her crew were killed and she sank quickly into 70 metres of water coming to rest upright on the bottom of the lagoon. Her momentum and possibly the tide had carried her about half a mile into the lagoon, inside the barrier reef.

The inadvertent and calamitous loss of such a valuable ship and its war cargo on the doorstep of one of their own bases triggered an enquiry, which concluded that IJN convoy escort vessels were not being sufficiently informed about the location of minefields and areas restricted to navigation. The enquiry determined that all new captains and masters navigating the area for the first time should be made aware of the location of the minefields and that up-to-date charts should be available. Notifications were sent out to the Commanders of the naval bases such as Saipan and Rabaul (from where ships were likely to come to Truk) as well as to the Fleet Commanders of the Combined Fleet and the China Area Fleet, stressing that the only channels into the Truk lagoon open to navigation were North and South Pass; and advising that the sea area within the lagoon was dangerous for navigation for four kilometres in from the inner edge of the reef - except for those in possession of details of the mine fields.

Lost to history after the war, the wreck of *Katsuragisan Maru* had not been located by 1989, and was thus not included when the famous pioneering Truk author Klaus Lindemann published his groundbreaking book *Hailstorm Over Truk Lagoon*. Klaus however was aware of the sinking and had a good idea where the wreck would be. Working with a side scan sonar expert Peter Fox and a Canadian TV production company during a pioneering expedition they found the wreck using side scan sonar.

The subsequent TV documentary produced in 1994 was entitled 'The Legacy of Truk Lagoon' and marked the 50th anniversary of Operation HAILSTONE. The documentary was available on YouTube at the time of going to print - and includes many eyewitness reports from both U.S. and Japanese combatants and from local Chuukese who witnessed the raid, such as the legendary founder of Truk diving Kimiuo Aisek. If you are interested in the history of Chuuk diving then I recommend this documentary to you – particularly, wearing my diver's hat, to witness the excitement of finding a long lost Truk shipwreck and seeing the first dives on it by Klaus Lindemann, who despite the great depth bounce dives it on a single AL80 cylinder of air.

The Wreck today

Today the wreck of *Katsuragisan Maru* is the deepest wreck in the lagoon, sitting upright on her keel on a gently sloping bottom in 70 metres of water. With a depth to her weather deck of 62 metres and a least depth to her superstructure and fo'c'sle deck of about 55 metres, she is a wreck for technical divers only. Located out at the barrier reef that surrounds the lagoon, so far away from the main islands of the atoll, she is blessed with some of the best underwater visibility to be found on any of the Japanese wrecks and is frequently visited by sharks.

An anchor windlass sits on the foc'sle deck close to the plumb stem of her bow. Two chains run out from their spurling pipes below deck to the windlass - and from there to hawse pipes either side of the deck. As the ship was underway and making way at the time she hit the mine, both anchors are still held snug in their hawse pipes. Two aft facing doors in the foc'sle bulkhead lead from the well deck into the foc'sle spaces. Portholes dot the bulkhead between the doors and a set of fixed steps at either side of the weather deck that lead up to the foc'sle deck. Some of the shell plating is falling away from the hull on the starboard side of the bow.

The hatch for Hold No 1 is set close to the foc'sle at a depth of about 62-64 metres. The hatch has a high raised coaming, and the cover beams are still in place. The hold contains tyres, gas masks and canisters - and rolled up steel mesh matting for use in airfield construction.

The foremast, which rose up from a masthouse in between the hatches for Hold No's 1 & 2, has fallen forward and slightly diagonally to port across the hatch for Hold No 1 and now rests with its crosstree on the foc'sle. Cargo winches are dotted around its base. Hold No 2 has a single hatch cover beam *in situ* and contains spare propeller blades, spare tyres, tracks, electrical equipment and rolls of hawser cable.

The superstructure amidships is quite chaotic. A serious fire appears to have broken out following the mine explosion in the aft starboard part of the ship – and this has ravaged the bridge, consuming all wooden structures and decking and weakening steel beams and girders such that the whole upper works of the bridge superstructure has largely collapsed and is now quite flat.

The crew accommodation cabins outboard and either side of the engine casing have also been degraded, exposing the triple expansion steam engine itself. The galley was situated at the aft end of this superstructure to starboard and scattered china can be found here.

On the aft well deck, the hatches for the two aft Hold No's 3 & 4 are located at a depth of about 64 metres. The mainmast would have stood between them but has now broken and fallen forward to lie diagonally to port across the foremost hatch for Hold No 3, its triangular crosstree resting on the port side of the deck.

The aftmost Hold No 4 contains about half a dozen military trucks and an officer's car parked up in lines. The starboard side of the hull adjacent the Holds shows heavy structural damage from the mine explosion. The hull plating is bent over inwards from the contact and the hull and main deck has collapsed down almost splitting the ship in two. The force of the

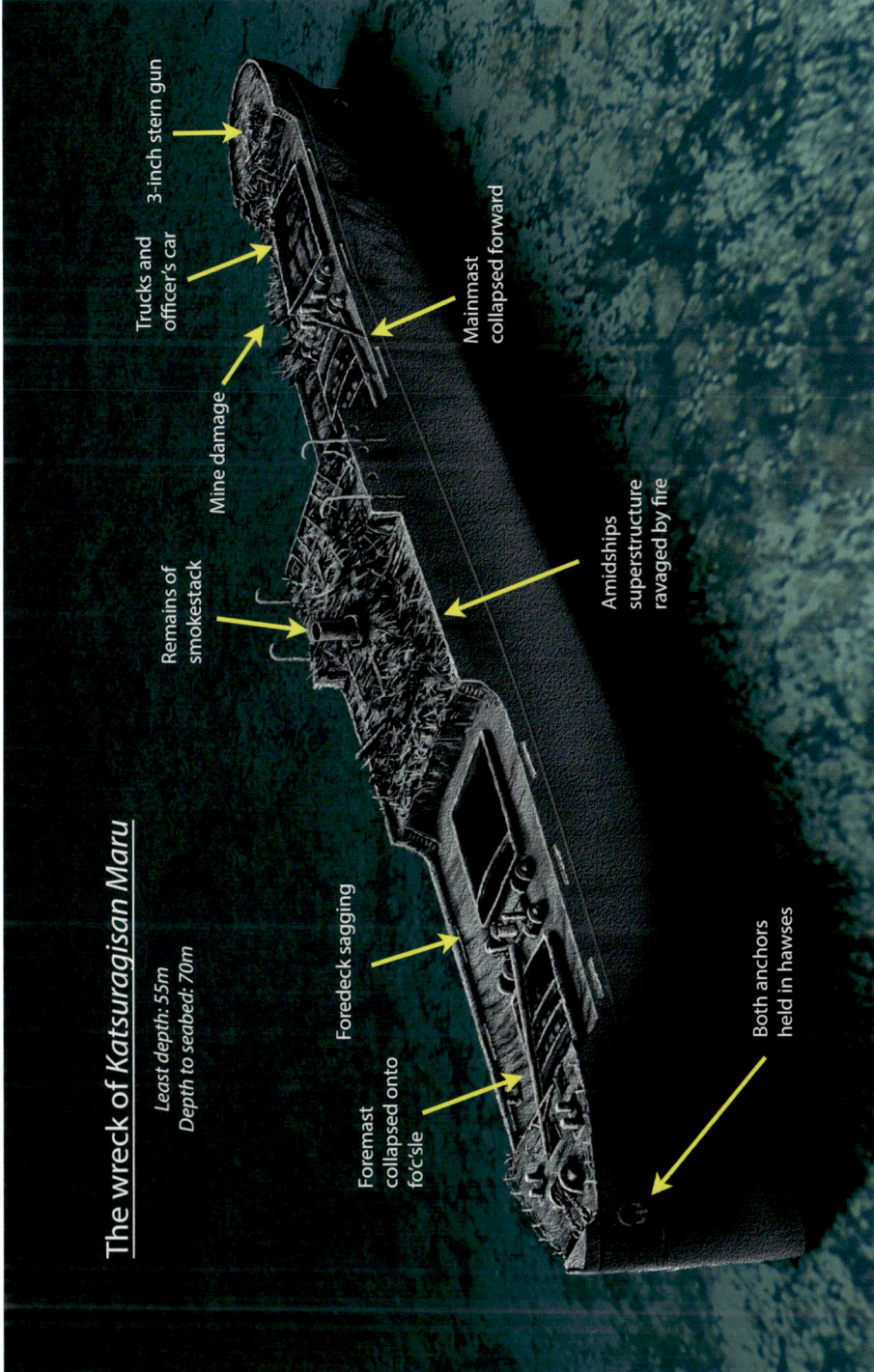

The wreck of *Katsuragisan Maru*

Least depth: 55m
Depth to seabed: 70m

3-inch stern gun

Trucks and officer's car

Mainmast collapsed forward

Mine damage

Remains of smokestack

Amidships superstructure ravaged by fire

Foredeck sagging

Foremast collapsed onto fo'c'sle

Both anchors held in hawses

Artist's impression of *Katsuragisan Maru*, the deepest wreck in the lagoon in 70 metres.

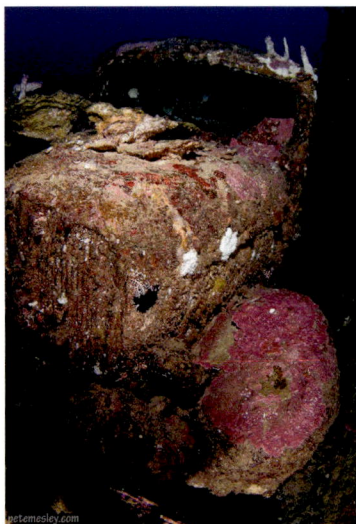

Staff car in the aft Hold of the deep wreck *Katsuragisan Maru*. (Courtesy Pete Mesley)

explosion blew the hatch cover beams into the air and they have fallen to lie scattered amongst the trucks. The end of one hatch cover beam has gone straight through the windscreen of one truck as it has fallen down into the hold.

At the very stern, the 8 cm (3-inch) Type 41 defensive gun, still with its splinter shield, sits on its small circular mount on top of the stern deckhouse – the barrel points slightly to port. The steering gear is housed in the spaces below.

———————

Finally, a word of caution from personal experience on this wreck.

When the tide is flooding into the lagoon through Northeast Pass, a tidal eddy is created inside the lagoon, such that a free-drifting diver, hanging on a Delayed Surface Marker Buoy (DSMB) to ascend, will eventually begin to drift out to the side of the original direction of tidal flow. The eddy will drift the diver eventually into a complete 180° change of direction - such that the diver will then be drifting seemingly against the tidal flow - back out towards the barrier reef in the opposite direction to the tide.

We almost lost a diver once who decided without warning to do a free hanging ascent under a DSMB - rather than coming up the shotline as normal from the wreck. I wasn't diving this particular day due to an ear infection but was topside in the boat. My buddies, who'd been on the dive, told me that arriving back at the bottom of the shotline as usual, although slack water had now passed and a current was running, he just swam off down current and disappeared into the blue to do a free ascent under a DSMB.

You can read the whole story in my book *Deeper into the Darkness* – but in essence, over the course of a 1-hour deco hang, the tidal flow took him very quickly away from the wreck, and our dive boat, drifting him in towards the centre of the lagoon, towards Weno. He then entered the eddy - and began to be swept around to one side, to the east, and then started being drifted back towards our dive boat. Hanging below his DSMB, he drifted back past our dive boat - a few hundred metres away – before continuing on, heading back out towards the barrier reef.

He was almost aground on the reef, and almost completely out of sight, when he finally surfaced with his deco completed.

Whatever else you do on this wreck, make sure you come back to the shotline to ascend and don't drift off out into the blue – the nearest U.S. Coastguard Sector Search & Rescue service that covers Chuuk is I believe some 650 miles away in Guam. They won't be coming quickly to go find you!

19. *Kensyo Maru*
Passenger-cargo vessel (1938)
IJN *Ippan Choyosen* General Requisitioned Ship (1940)
IJN Zatsuyosen – *Otsu* category - Auxiliary Transport (1941)
U.S. Recognition Code: 23A MKFM

Repair Anchorage

Tonnage:	4,862 grt
Dimensions:	384.4ft long; beam of 52.5 ft; draught of 30.3ft
Launched:	30 June 1938
Sunk:	18 February 1944
Cause of loss:	Bombed and torpedoed by TF 58 aircraft during Operation HAILSTONE
Wreck location:	Repair Anchorage, west of Tonoas Island (Dublon)
Depth to seabed:	36-40 metres
Least Depth:	12 metres – smokestack
Other name:	*Kensho Maru*

The passenger-cargo ship *Kensyo Maru* was laid down at the Tama Zosensho K.K shipyard (Tama Shipbuilding Co Ltd) on 28 February 1938 as Ship No 44843. The city of Tama is situated in the western portion of the Tokyo metropolis, with the River Tama opening into Tokyo Bay.

Kensyo Maru was constructed with two decks and a cruiser stern. She had a raised fo'c'sle and two foredeck holds, split by a section of weather deck on which stood a masthouse and a goalpost pair of kingposts. The foremast rose from the bridge that connected the tops of the two kingposts.

The passenger cargo ship *Kensyo Maru* was launched in 1938 and requisitioned by the IJN as a transport ship in 1940. She was bombed and sunk by TF 58 aircraft during Operation HAILSTONE.

The hatch for Hold No 3 was set at shelter deck level in the extended section of superstructure in front of the bridge superstructure. Another goalpost pair of kingposts was set here with derricks to work cargoes.

The composite superstructure held the navigating bridge at its forward highest levels with the boiler room, smokestack and engine rooms immediately abaft. Promenade deck walkways ran down either side of the superstructure with cabins opening off them.

The aft well deck held Holds 4 & 5 with a masthouse and a goalpost pair of kingposts in between, before the poop island at the very stern of the ship.

The ship was fitted with 6-cylinder 2-stroke diesel engines that drove a single screw and gave a service speed of 15 knots and a maximum speed of 17 knots. She had an estimated operating radius of 21,600 nautical miles at 15 knots.

The hull was launched for fitting out and the ship named *Kensyo Maru* on 30 June 1938. Completed quickly by 30 August 1938, the ship was registered to Inui Kisen K.K., in Kobe. *Kensyo Maru* was subsequently chartered by Mitsui, and by Kawasaki Kisen Kaisha (the 'K' Line).

After two years' service, in the run up to war, *Kensyo Maru* was requisitioned by the IJN on 14 September 1940 as an *Ippan Choyosen* general requisitioned transport. She was attached to the Yokosuka Naval District, working out of Tokyo Bay transporting military personnel, livestock, food and supplies. On 15 October 1941, she was rerated as a *Zatsuyosen* Auxiliary transport – *Otsu* category, with a civilian crew and no military captain.

The following day, 16 October, she set off from Yokosuka for Truk, arriving there on 2 December 1941, less than a week before the surprise attack on Pearl Harbor. She departed for Kwajalein the next day, 3 December 1941, and as the Pearl Harbor raid was unfolding on 7 December 1941, she was on her approach to Kwajalein. After a quick turnaround, she was soon on her way back to Japan, arriving at Yokosuka on 27 December 1941.

During the first half of 1942 *Kensyo Maru* made a number of supply voyages to Truk, Rabaul, Saipan, Wake, Kwajalein and Taroa – returning to Yokosuka with war resources before re-loading with more outbound stores and supplies.

In late June 1942, she was docked at the Mitsui Engineering & Shipbuilding yard for maintenance and repair and at this time a Type 41 8 cm (3-inch) bow gun was installed on a circular gun platform on top of the fo'c'sle and part of the chain locker was modified for ammunition storage. A 5-man gun crew was added to the ship's crew. She was undocked a month later at the end of July 1942 and resumed her duties carrying supplies to the Caroline Islands, the Marianas and to the Marshall and Gilbert Islands garrisons, making frequent returns back to Japan for resupply.

On 1 March 1943, she stranded off Omaezaki in the Shizuoka Prefecture of Japan. The ship was refloated the following day and on 12 March she was moved to Yokohama where she was drydocked for extensive repairs to the damage. At this time, she was also modified by the removal of the timber hatch covers on Hold 3, which were replaced with steel. The tween deck space was plated over, and the area thus created just in front of the bridge was converted to a small hospital with sick bay and X-ray room. Extra medical staff were added to her crew - and during succeeding years, after taking outbound supplies to distant island garrisons, she would carry wounded personnel on the return leg back to Japan.

On 13 November 1943, *Kensyo Maru* departed Yokosuka in a large convoy escorted by the destroyer *Ikazuchi* and the kaibōkan *Hirado* that arrived at Truk on 23 November 1943. On 14 December, she departed Truk with *Shoei Maru* for Kwajalein, escorted by the subchaser *CH-29*.

The small escorted 2-ship convoy arrived safely at Kwajalein on 19 December 1943– but their arrival coincided with a major air attack on the atoll, in which *Shoei Maru* was hit and heavily damaged. She would sink the following day.

Kensyo Maru may have escaped that attack, but the very next day, 20 December 1943, she was heavily damaged in another airstrike by 16 American Consolidated B-24 Liberator bombers. One bomb struck her on the aft part of the ship, starting a fire and partially flooding the engine room. The ship had been left unnavigable and so was taken in tow by the auxiliary transport *Yoshida Maru* and run aground before she could sink. The fire was finally put out after 3 hours.

Kensyo Maru subsequently underwent temporary repairs - before on 3 January 1944, she was towed by *Yoshida Maru* to the north end of Kwajalein Atoll. Here, on 29 January 1944, the requisitioned transport *Momokawa Maru* (a present day Truk wreck) took her in tow for repair at Truk.

The tow arrived safely at Truk and entered the lagoon on 4 February 1944. *Kensyo Maru* was towed to the Repair Anchorage, to the west of Dublon Island, and anchored near the Repair ship IJN *Akashi,* the damaged destroyer *Fumizuki* and the transports *Tonan Maru No 3, Kiyosumi Maru* and *Hoyo Maru.* She would have temporary repairs made to her here, sufficient to allow her to return to Japan for permanent repair. She would however never leave the Truk lagoon.

On 17 February 1944, as the first waves of U.S. aircraft from Task Force 58 swept across the skies of Truk, *Kensyo Maru* was still at anchor and unable to navigate close to the Repair Ship *Akashi* in the Repair Anchorage, west of Dublon and north of Fefen.

Following the launch of the F6F Hellcats for the dawn initial fighter sweep, the TG 58.1 carriers *Yorktown* and *Enterprise* had begun launching their Strike 1A planes at 0500. SBD Dauntlesses and TBF Avengers roared off the flight decks into the wind, to rendezvous with their escort Hellcat fighters and head for Truk. The first Strike 1A aircraft from TG 58.1 *Yorktown* and *Enterprise* had a scheduled time at target over the lagoon between 0615 and 0630.

Meanwhile, Strike 2A planes from TG 58.2 carriers *Essex* and *Intrepid* launched with a time at target over Truk assigned for between 0630-0645, the division being tasked to hit shipping in the Fourth Fleet Anchorage.

To complete the 1st group strike of the day, Strike 3A planes from the TG 58.3 carriers *Bunker Hill* and *Cowpens* would follow in between 0645-0700 as the two bombing attacks from TG 58.1 and TG 58.2 were in their final stages.

As the Strike 1A planes of TG 58.1 arrived over Truk, the SBD Dauntlesses and TBF Avenger pilots selected their targets - their dives and attack runs would be covered by Hellcats for protection against Japanese airborne fighters. The Strike 1A *Enterprise* planes initially attacked the seaplane tender *Akitsushima,* a destroyer and an oiler, before the TBF's, which were armed with fragmentation and incendiary clusters, headed to Moen airfield to knock out as many Japanese planes as they could on the ground.

Yorktown Strike 1A planes had been tasked to attack Japanese shipping north east of Fefan at the Combined Fleet Anchorage and the Repair Anchorage, and south west of Dublon at the Sixth Fleet Anchorage. The *Yorktown* SBD's dived on the *Akashi*, *Kiyosumi Maru* and *Kensyo Maru,* whilst the TBF Avengers were initially hampered by thick cloud cover and had to circle until they had better visibility and could select their own targets.

At 0815, about one hour after the first Strikes 1A, 2A and 3A had been completed, the planes of the second group strike began to arrive over the lagoon. The *Enterprise* and *Yorktown* Strike 1B planes arrived first, followed shortly after around 0830 by Strike 2B planes from *Essex* and *Intrepid* and then by Strike 3B planes from *Bunker Hill* and *Cowpens.*

Essex Strike 2B comprised 12 Hellcats, 9 TBF Avengers and 12 SBD Dauntless dive bombers and had launched around 0710, tasked with hitting shipping south and west of Dublon. *Essex* SBD dive-bombers attacked three ships west of Dublon, the first being the Repair Ship *Akashi*, before *Kensyo Maru* and *Kiyosumi Maru* were attacked.

The *Essex* SBDs pushed over for their dives on the anchored and immobile *Kensyo Maru*. A 1,000-lb bomb struck her amidships, setting her on fire and killing six of her crew. She was however able to remain afloat.

The following day, 18 February 1944, as dawn lit up the lagoon, *Kensyo Maru* was still afloat. Task Force 58 now had unchallenged air superiority – and *Kensyo Maru* was again attacked by aircraft from *Enterprise*, *Monterey* and *Bunker Hill*. With the ship unable to navigate or adequately defend itself, the crew took to the lifeboats and rowed ashore to Dublon Island - from where they would witness the destruction of their ship.

The last effective strike of the TF 58 raid was Strike 3B from TG 58.3 *Bunker Hill*. 23 planes launched, comprising 10 Helldivers, 9 Avengers and four Hellcat fighters. Five of the Helldivers were armed with two 500-lb bombs, whilst the other five carried a 1,000-lb bomb. The TBF's were carrying aerial torpedoes.

The *Bunker Hill* Strike 3B planes were over the lagoon between 0815-0900. The Helldivers attacked a damaged 450-ft long ship off the southeast tip of Dublon, hitting it amidships with a 1,000-lb bomb that caused a large explosion that sunk the ship quickly. The Helldivers then hit another 400-ft ship, which exploded in a large secondary detonation of munitions. Once the smoke cleared, the ship had disappeared.

The *Bunker Hill* Helldivers then attacked the *Yamagiri Maru*, west of Fefan and scoring hits with a 1,000-lb bomb and a 500-lb bomb. *Yamagiri Maru* rolled to port and sunk. The only Helldiver left with any bombs was meantime pushing over for a dive on an oiler south of Eten.

Whilst the *Bunker Hill* Helldivers were busy, the *Bunker Hill* TBF Avengers went to the assistance of the Hellcats who were strafing the destroyer *Oite,* which had entered the lagoon through North Pass (carrying more than 500 rescued sailors from the *Agano*) and was running south at flank speed.

As that attack began, the destroyer *Oite* began a series of evasive manoeuvres. Five TBFs responded and made a coordinated attack, one of their torpedoes catching the unfortunate

Oite as she was making a turn to starboard at flank speed. The explosion was devastating: the destroyer broke its back abaft the bridge. The two sections of the destroyer jackknifed and sank quickly with great loss of life.

The remaining four *Bunker Hill* TBF Avengers attacked two targets off Dublon. Two torpedoes hit the *Heian Maru*, sending her to the bottom. The TBF's then turned their attention towards the second smaller target – time was up for the damaged and immobile *Kensyo Maru*. She was hit by an aerial torpedo – it was the coup de grace.

With their weapons now spent, the *Bunker Hill* planes turned to head back to their carrier, leaving *Kensyo Maru* in her death throes. She was observed to take on a list to port - but was still afloat as the TG 58.3 planes departed Truk air space. None of the U.S. aviators witnessed *Kensyo Maru* finally slip beneath the water. But still at anchor, she sank to the bottom of the lagoon, coming to rest upright in 35 metres.

During a hydrographic survey in 1968/9, the survey ship USS *Tanner* (AGS-15), herself a veteran of the Pacific War, found and plotted the wreck's location. The 1969 Cousteau Expedition found and dived *Kensyo Maru* using the USS *Tanner* survey for reference.

The wreck was rediscovered for sport divers in 1980, by Klaus Lindemann, the author of *Hailstorm over Truk Lagoon,* and his wife Mary Lindemann, on their way to dive the *Kiyosumi Maru* close by.

The Wreck Today

Today the wreck of *Kensyo Maru* sits largely intact and upright with a slight list to port on a gently sloping bottom - her bow sits in 36 metres and her stern in slightly deeper water of 40 metres. She is perhaps most famous for her intact, cavernous and easily accessible Engine Room – one of the iconic 'musts' for diving in Truk. She is also a relatively easy wreck to visit with a least depth to the intact smokestack of 12 metres - and to the boat deck with the engine room skylights at about 20 metres. Sitting in a sheltered, benign sea area, she remains in very good condition.

On the fo'c'sle deck at a depth of about 20 metres, at the bow, two chains run out from the anchor windlass, each to a hawse pipe on either side of the deck. The starboard anchor is run out along the seabed whilst the port anchor is held snug in its hawse pipe.

Just abaft the anchor windlass, the prominent Type 41 8 cm (3-inch) DP gun, heavily covered in corals, sits on its circular elevated platform with the barrel pointing to starboard. Three boxes of ready use shells sit behind the gun on the platform.

With her engine disabled and being at anchor for repair, *Kensyo Maru* wasn't carrying any great amount of cargo in her holds at the time she was sunk. Her two foredeck holds are empty and have their hatch cover beams still neatly in place, both on the weather deck and at tween deck level.

Kensyo Maru bow detail

The wreck of *Kenyso Maru*

Least depth: 12m
Depth to seabed: 40m

Kingposts

Bridge superstructure

Engine room skylights

Smokestack

Type 41 8cm (3-inch) bow gun

Lifeboat davits

Cargo boom

Port anchor in hawse

Artist's impression of the largely intact wreck of the IJN transport *Kensyo Maru*, sitting upright in 35-40 metres of water. Her cavernous and easily accessible Engine Room is one of the jewels of Truk Lagoon diving, the pitched Engine Room roof skylights are seen between the smokestack and the bridge.

Kensyo Maru amidships composite superstructure detail

A goalpost pair of kingposts rise from a deck masthouse in between the two-foredeck cargo holds. The two kingposts are connected horizontally at the top by a bridge with intricate cross bracing, a feature to the best of my knowledge unique to Japanese merchant ships of this era. A topmast extends upwards from the span that bridges the gap. A cargo handling boom runs forward from the base of each of the kingposts over the hatch for Hold No 1 – they are displaced to port from the sinking. Another two booms run aft over the hatch for Hold No 2, again displaced to port. Fixed steps lead up from the well deck to the shelter deck on either side of the bulkhead.

Hold No 3 is built into the higher shelter deck extended section of superstructure just in front of the bridge - and also has its hatch cover beams in place. A goalpost pair of kingposts stand at the leading bulkhead of this superstructure with cargo winches dotted around its base. Cargo handling booms run aft from the kingposts across the hatch for Hold No 3. The boom ends would have rested on cradles on the front of the main superstructure, but the booms are again displaced to port as a result of the sinking. Inside Hold 3, at the aft end of the tween deck, a passageway leads towards the engine room.

The main bridge superstructure is situated abaft Hold No 3. *Kensyo Maru* has a single composite superstructure, which houses both the bridge and the machinery spaces for her engine. Immediately abaft the bridge, on either side of the engine casing and smokestack, rows of cabins on two deck levels with a covered promenade deck walkway run down each side of the superstructure.

The highest part of this superstructure is the navigation bridge, which can be entered through the bare steel beams of the roof, at a depth of just over 15 metres. The engine order telegraph and telemotor for the helm still stand in place along with the compass binnacle. One deck level down is the radio room and chart room, where two large racks of radio equipment remain in situ. The next level down was the officer's mess and here beer and sake bottles and crockery can be found scattered about.

The crew's mess and the galley are located on the starboard side at the rear of this composite superstructure. The galley still holds a cooking range with ovens and stoves – on which nowadays bottles, crockery and cooking implements have been placed. A steel shelf above has a stack of several blue uniforms or fire blankets. The floor of the galley, in common with many of the ships in the lagoon, is composed of small nonslip mosaic tiles.

The jewel of the *Kensyo Maru* is however the massive 30-40 foot high engine room – perhaps the finest and most easily accessible in the lagoon with multiple entry and exit points.

The most common and convenient method to get into the engine room after a descent from the surface is through the open engine room ventilation skylight hatches, which are found at a depth of about 20 metres on the boat deck between the aft of the highest bridge deck and the upright smokestack, which still has distinctive banding. Drop in through these skylights and you enter the topmost parts of a cavernous space, at the highest part of the engine room. The engine room can also be accessed from the Hold No. 3 tween deck passage and also from the rooms either side of the engine casing.

Once in the engine room, a catwalk passes athwartships high up at a depth of about 23 metres - from one side of the ship to the other. Doorways at either side lead off into the bowels of the ship and a grated steel staircase leads down to the upper engine room deck.

The 6-cylinder diesel engine manufactured by her builders, the Tama Shipbuilding Co., sits fore and aft on the centre line of the vessel, three cylinders ahead of the athwartships catwalk and three cylinders aft. Catwalks ring around the cylinders, the tops of which are at about 26 metres. The Tama Shipyard had entered a technical licensing agreement in 1926 with Burmeister & Wain A/S of Denmark for the rights to manufacture these engines to the advanced B&W designs and specification.

By descending down a stairwell on the port side, access is possible to the lower engine room spaces, which are in about 28-30 metres of water. The walls of the lower deck level are lined with switches, gauges, fuse boxes panels, command bridge repeaters and a spares panel that takes up almost a complete wall. The spares panel neatly holds a wide variety of spare nuts and bolts that range in size all the way up to large cylinder-head nuts and bolts. The vibration of the engine cylinders when in operation made it not unusual to need to replace them. Spare piston rings, spare valves, bolts and gears are all neatly racked in place.

At a depth of about 30 metres, a distinctive brass control panel 4 feet wide by 3 feet high still has the easily legible embossed legend on it.

TAMA DOCKYARD LTD, JAPAN
DIESEL ENGINE NO 164, 1938

There are six glass oil flow inspection panels beneath, one for each of the 6-cylinders. At top, there are two larger glass inspection panels, one for each of the two main bearings that hold the crankshaft in place and allow it to rotate – they must be kept lubricated. One bearing is Ahead on the crankshaft and one Astern, the relevant bearings being indicated by arrows in the centre of the panel and the words AHEAD and ASTERN.

In the heads, glazed white urinals and sinks gleam in diver's torches – the sinks are stamped with a circular blue motif with a lion on top and the legend TOYOHASHI JAPAN around it. In the middle are the initials 'TS', presumably for 'Tama Shipyard'.

It is easy to spend a long time exploring this beautiful and fascinating engine room – but eventually, exiting through the engine room skylights, the exploration can continue to the aft portion of the ship. Whilst on some Japanese *Maru*'s, there is an extended section of shelter deck mirroring the extended superstructure on the foreship, on this type of *Maru* there is no after extended section of superstructure. The superstructure simply ends with a drop down to the after well deck, which accommodates the hatches for Hold No's 4 & 5. In between these hatches is a masthouse from which a goalpost pair of kingposts rises with a cross-braced bridge in between them at the top. A topmast rises from the centre of the bridge. Two cargo handling booms run forward from the kingposts over Hold No 4 – and two more run aft over Hold No 5, all again are swung over to port.

Left: Brass oil flow control and inspection panel inside the *Kensyo Maru* engine room. (Courtesy Ewan Rowell)

Right: Close detail of oil flow inspection panel. There are six glass oil flow inspection panels at the bottom, one for each of the 6-cylinders of the engine. At top, there are two larger glass inspection panels, one for each of the two main bearings that hold the crankshaft in place and allow it to rotate. One bearing is Ahead on the crankshaft and one Astern, the relevant bearings being indicated by arrows in the centre of the panel. (Courtesy Mike Boring)

Above: Paul Haynes hangs in front of a switching panel. (Courtesy Ewan Rowell)

Left: A diver hangs midwater above the engine cylinder tops, in front of an athwartships catwalk. The roof skylights can be seen above. (Courtesy Ewan Rowell)

Left: Deep inside the *Kensyo Maru* engine room, a wall panel neatly holds engine spares, gears, piston rings, cylinder head bolts and nuts. (Courtesy Ewan Rowell)

Right: Nuwa Paul hangs motionless in the *Kensyo Maru* Radio Room

Hold No 4 is largely empty, barring a salvage pump and hoses, which are stowed in the tween deck on the starboard side forward. These were possibly being used whilst she was being repaired, A number of hatch cover beams can be found at the very bottom of the hold amongst 55-gallon drums and other cargo.

Left: Finning along the superstructure of *Kensyo Maru* at shelter deck level and about to descend a stair well. Portholes hang open at right of shot, as they were for ventilation when the ship was sunk. (Courtesy Ewan Rowell)

Lower left: The *Kensyo Maru* galley – mosaic nonslip floor tiles, pans and bottles on the cooking range and coarse blue uniforms or fire blankets on the shelf above. (Courtesy Ewan Rowell)

Hold No. 5 holds cast iron pipe sections, valves, acetylene/oxygen welding tanks, likely being used in repair work - as well as a supply of beer bottles, a common feature on many Truk wrecks.

At the stern there is a raised poop island with a winch set on top. On the port quarter some bomb damage is evident to the hull.

The propeller and rudder remain *in situ*.

20. *Kikukawa Maru*
Passenger-cargo vessel (1937)
IJA *Rikugun Yusosen* Army transport (1937)
IJN *Ippan Choyosen* general requisitioned transport (1941)
U.S. Recognition Code: 23A MKFM

Fourth Fleet Anchorage

Tonnage:	3,833 grt
Dimensions:	354.7-ft long; beam of 50 ft; draught of 27.5-ft
Launched:	16 December 1936
Sunk:	7 October 1943
Cause of loss:	Fire and explosion at anchor
Wreck location:	Fourth Fleet Anchorage, east of Eten Island
Depth to seabed:	37 metres
Least Depth:	20 metres – port side keel
Other name:	*Kikugawa Maru*

Kirikawa Maru, sister to the 3,833grt requisitioned IJN transport ship *Kikukawa Maru*, sunk in a catastrophic explosion following a fire whilst lading on 7 October 1943. The unfortunate salvage tug *Ojima* was tied alongside her whilst firefighting, she was cleaved in two and her pieces flung some distance by the force of the explosion.

The wreck of the 3,833grt passenger-cargo ship *Kikukawa Maru* is not a legacy of Operation HAILSTONE – but of a tragic accident that took place on 7 October 1943, four months before the planes of Task Force 58 swept across the Truk lagoon.

Kikukawa Maru was built by the Kawasaki Dockyard Co in Kobe as Ship No 42941 for Kawasaki Kisen Kaisha of Kobe. She was laid down on the 22 August 1936 and launched for fitting out and named on 16 December 1936. Constructed with 2 decks and a cruiser stern, she was fitted with two modern double reduction geared steam turbines manufactured by the Kawasaki Dockyard. Her single screw gave her a service speed of 12-14 knots and a maximum cruising speed of 14-16 knots. She carried 1,000 tons of bunker coal that gave an estimated operating radius of 10,000 nautical miles at 12 knots.

According to the now de-classified wartime document *Japanese Merchant Ships* prepared by the Office of the Chief of Naval Operations O.N.I. 208-J (Revised), *Kikukawa Maru* was built as a classic three-island vessel with a raised fo'c'sle at the bow and two holds set in the forward well deck with a foremast with crosstree rising from a masthouse between the two hatches. The hatch for Hold No 3 was set in the shelter deck of the extended section of superstructure just forward of the bridge. A goalpost pair of kingposts was set at the forward edge of the shelter deck, equipped with cargo handling derricks.

The amidships superstructure incorporated the command bridge and abaft this super-structure were the hatches for Hold No's 4 & 5, separated by a section of weather deck, from which the mainmast rose. At the very stern, the poop island held the steering gear below.

Japanese Merchant Ships also classifies her as being of the same style as the present-day classic 3-island wrecks of *Momokawa Maru* and *Nippo Maru,* both of which have their engine amidships in composite superstructures. She is also listed as being of the same style of construction as *Kirikawa Maru*, pictured above. I am not aware of any verified photos of *Kikukawa Maru* herself.

Interestingly, every single one of the Lloyds entries for *Kikukawa Maru* however states that she was fitted with her *machinery aft*, that is, with her engine room spaces at the stern like a tanker. This is pretty fundamental - how can it be?

This may in fact be an example of how as tensions heightened between the USA, Britain and Japan, to conceal the true nature of its shipbuilding program, from about 1934-35 Japan banned Lloyds agents. Lloyds agents were prevented from getting access to official sources and were reliant on gleaning information from builder's yards. Accordingly, some of their entries are best guesses - and occasionally inaccurate. But it is a fundamental error, one which is carried through quite a number of Lloyds entries.

Whilst researching shipwrecks, over the years I have seen a number of instances of this sort of inaccuracy, albeit on more minor aspects. For example, whilst writing *Dive Palau – the Shipwrecks*, during my research into the famous unidentified Palauan shipwreck known simply as the 'Helmet Wreck', I was able to establish her likely identity as the netlayer *Nissho Maru No 5*. However, the Lloyds entry for *Nissho Maru No 5* lists the machinery as being, rather vaguely, simply *oil engines*. The usual details of those engines, such as the number of cylinders, the NHP (Nominal Horsepower) and the manufacturer etc. are not listed as you would expect. In reality, and contrary to what the Lloyd's Register entry states, *Nissho Maru No 5* is fitted with a traditional triple expansion steam engine. But that discrepancy is rather minor, compared to getting the complete layout of the ship wrong as is possibly the case with *Kikukawa Maru*, even taking into account that Lloyds agents had been banned a couple of years before her construction.

The ship was named and launched for fitting out afloat on 16 December 1936, a speedy construction from laying down in August 1936. Fitting out was completed on 10 April 1937 and she was delivered to her new owners, Kawasaki Kisen K.K. and placed on their K-Line eastern Osaka route.

On 7 July 1937 however, just two months after her launch, Japan launched a full-scale invasion of her old enemy, China. The Second Sino-Japanese War had begun. As Japan sought to ferry large numbers of troops and war materials to China, fast, spacious modern ships like *Kikukawa Maru* were urgently required as troop transports. Thus, in August 1937, just four months after her launch, and a few weeks into the invasion, the Imperial Japanese Army requisitioned her for use as a *Rikugun Yusosen* army transport.

The IJA transport *Kikukawa Maru* was quickly put to work and within a few weeks had embarked the 3rd company of the IJA 5th tank battalion. *Kikukawa Maru* departed Moji, at the north of the southmost Japanese home island of Kyushu on 28 August 1937, moving northeast along the coast of the main home island of Honshū to Ujina, in Hiroshima Bay. There she formed up with other ships that had embarked the 1st and 2nd companies of the IJA 5th tank battalion, along with the ammunition train and HQ facilities – the convoy bound for Shanghai.

The heavily laden convoy arrived at Shanghai on 2 September 1937 and after offloading the IJA 5th tank battalion troops and equipment, *Kikukawa Maru* returned to Japan. There she embarked more troops and equipment for a further run to Shanghai - arriving there on 12 November 1937.

With the fall of Shanghai on 26 November 1937, Chinese troops retreated over 300 kilometres inland along the Yangtze River to Nanjing - in the face of Japanese flanking manoeuvres. *Kikukawa Maru* was no longer required and the following month, in December 1937, she was released back to her civilian owners.

Four years later, on 27 March 1941, in the run up to the Pacific war, *Kikukawa Maru* was again requisitioned – this time by the IJN for use as a Shunko Maru-class *Zatsuyosen* Auxiliary Transport with the other ships in this class being *Hunko Maru, Kirikawa Maru, Matsukawa Maru, Momokawa Maru* and *Hiyoshi Maru*. All the ships of this class were completed between 1936 and 1941 for a number of shipping companies, with *Kirikawa, Hiyoshi* and *Kikukawa Maru's* being requisitioned by the IJN whilst *Shunko, Matsukawa* and *Momokawa Maru* were requisitioned by the IJA to serve as Army transports. All the ships in this class would be sunk during WWII.

The months following her requisition saw her operating in Korean waters, in the South China Sea and then around Japan and across to China. On 15 October 1941, she was registered as an *Ippan Choyosen – Otsu* category auxiliary transport, with a civilian crew and no IJN captain. She was attached to the Sasebo Naval District and began to operate around French Indochina, Formosa, Pescadores, Hainan Island and the Hong Kong and Chosen areas. In June 1942 she was fitted with an 8cm/40 3rd Year Type 41 deck gun for defence. The Type 41 gun was widely used as a coastal defence gun and AA gun and was often deployed aboard IJN warships and armed merchant ships.

On 9 July 1942, *Kikukawa Maru* was assigned to the defence operations surrounding the Aleutian Islands in the north Pacific, which had recently been seized simultaneously with the unsuccessful invasion of Midway. After embarking 250 troops and their equipment, and escorted by the destroyer *Kagero*, she departed Yokosuka in Japan. After stopping at Kushiro, the flotilla arrived at the Aleutian island of Kiska on 19 July 1942 and began disembarkation of troops and their equipment. On 31 July 1942, *Kikukawa Maru* was detailed to tow the damaged auxiliary transport *Kano Maru,* successfully recovering the damaged vessel to Kiska on 2 August.

Kikukawa Maru departed Kiska on 6 August 1942 - but two days into her passage, on 8 August 1942, she was attacked by a U.S. submarine. Although she was hit by a torpedo, it was a dud that caused no damage, something that was quite common with U.S. submarine-launched Mark 14 torpedoes at this point of the war.

Towards the latter part of 1942 and into 1943, *Kikukawa Maru* was busy carrying supplies, ammunition, fuel, coal and general cargo from Japan out to Truk, Palau Saipan, Kwajalein and Rabaul.

Her final voyage was in a large convoy of IJN and IJA transport ships, an auxiliary oiler and a repair ship that was escorted by the kaibōkan's *Oki* and *Fukue*. The convoy set off for Truk from Yokosuka, Japan, on 21 September 1943, and was joined by a minesweeper en route the following day.

As the convoy pressed south and closed the great Japanese stronghold of Saipan, some ships joined the convoy whilst others left for their final ports of call. The convoy eventually reached Truk on 1 October 1943 and once inside the lagoon, *Kikukawa Maru* anchored in the Fourth Fleet Anchorage, east of Eten Island.

A week later, on 7 October 1943, the crew of *Kikukawa Maru* completed the day's loading of aircraft parts and ammunition at about 1800. But about an hour later, a fire started in the aft section of the ship - where *Kikukawa Maru* was carrying a dangerous cargo that included 55-gallon drums of aviation gasoline - and munitions. The situation rapidly became extremely precarious – and whilst fire and rescue parties were sent from the shore to assist, all ships anchored nearby were ordered to leave their berths as a result of the volatile cargo.

The large 812-ton salvage tug *Ojima* arrived on scene to assist the burning vessel and tied up alongside the stricken ship. Firefighting efforts began as pumps were put aboard two landing craft and two 150-ton and 300-ton rescue ships. By about 2230 however, after 3-4 hours of firefighting, the flames reached and ignited the volatile cargo in Hold No 4 towards the stern of the ship. There was a sudden massive explosion of the embarked Avgas and munitions that was heard throughout the islands in the lagoon. Trees were defoliated ashore on Dublon and Eten Islands and windows shattered.

The aft portion of the ship and most of the amidships superstructure was devastated in an instant - and sections of ship's hull, plating and frames were dispersed over a large area. Although this was an accident, the result was much like the secondary munitions explosions that almost vapourised one half of *Aikoku Maru* and *Sankisan Maru* during Operation HAILSTONE.

The intact forward section of *Kikukawa Maru*, still at anchor, rolled over to starboard and quickly sank, landing almost upside down on an underwater slope - with the starboard crosstree of its foremast resting on the seabed.

The force of the explosion was so great that the unfortunate 800-ton tug *Ojima*, tied up alongside, was cut into two sections that were flung away from the ship. The two pieces of *Ojima* then sank almost immediately, coming to rest on the seabed 80-100 yards apart and some 500 yards from the wreck of *Kikukawa Maru*.

The wreck was rediscovered in about 1980 and identified by her name, which is welded in Kanji and Roman letters on the bow.

The Wreck Today

The remains of the forward section of the *Kikukawa Maru*, from just forward of the bridge to the bow, today lie almost upside-down and resting on her starboard rail. The wreck lies almost parallel with and across a sloping sandy bottom in 37 metres of water. The sandy slope shelves off quite steeply into the depths beyond the wreck. The higher port side of her keel is reached at about 20 metres. It is possible to go under the higher overhanging port gunwale and into the foredeck cargo holds.

At the bow, both her anchor chains are run out and have crossed as the ship rolled over to starboard and sank. The name of the vessel is still welded onto the bow in Roman and Kanji lettering but is well covered in growth. Inside the fo'c'sle, at a depth of about 35 metres, the Lamp Room still holds a number of copper and brass navigation lanterns.

The foremast runs out from a masthouse between the hatches for Hold No's 1 & 2 and the starboard stanchion of its crosstree is jammed into the seabed.

Divers descending to the upturned keel, can drop down the higher port beam of the ship to arrive at the port gunwale, where the well deck returns back under the upturned ship. Moving under the overhanging deck gives access to the three foredeck holds.

Hold No 1 is largely empty but does contain some 55-gallon fuel drums along with scattered china and bottles. There are also some heavy pieces of machinery here, such as a wheeled compressor and wheeled pump, which may be some of the firefighting equipment deployed at the time of the explosion.

Hold No. 2 contains more 55-gallon fuel oil drums, which tumbled to starboard as the ship sunk and now lie jumbled up in the tween deck and on the seabed below in a heap. There

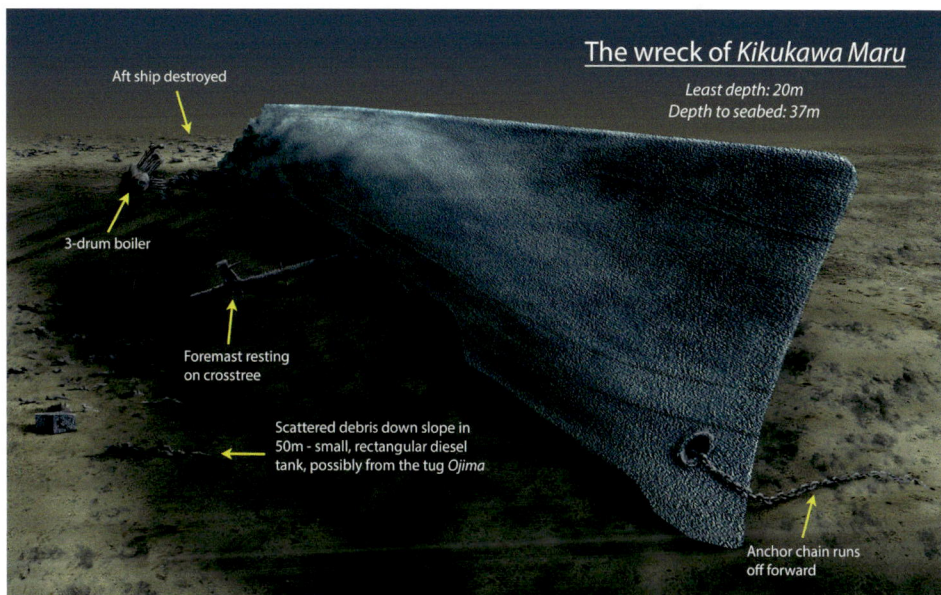

The wreck of *Kikukawa Maru*

Least depth: 20m
Depth to seabed: 37m

Aft ship destroyed

3-drum boiler

Foremast resting on crosstree

Scattered debris down slope in 50m - small, rectangular diesel tank, possibly from the tug *Ojima*

Anchor chain runs off forward

Artist's impression of the bow section of the wreck of *Kikukawa Maru*.

are also quite a number of aircraft propeller blades, cables, wheels, aircraft nose fairings, radial engines and a fuselage - all lying randomly strewn about where they fell in the confusion of the explosion and capsize. There are also some seaplane floats and aircraft drop tanks.

Hold No. 3 contains a large amount of bunker coal for her engine, which is relevant to the discussion about her machinery. The large goalpost pair of kingposts set forward of Hold No 3 has been destroyed and sections of it are strewn across the seabed.

Whilst the aft bulkhead of Hold No 3 is recognisable, the nearby shell plating of the hull shows a deep compression mark followed by a number of S-shaped ripples. Abaft this area, the amidships superstructure is well disintegrated and now unrecognizable. The bridge, engine casing, smokestack and Boat Deck have been completely destroyed and their remains are strewn about the seabed; there is no sign of the engine - although the boiler is reported to be lying on the seabed some 400-500ft off the foreship.

The structure of the aft portion of the ship has been devastated – with bulkheads, web frames, decking and cross beams all blown away in the massive explosion. In amongst the dispersed remains of the ship here are remnants of the cargo from the aft holds, scattered hatchcover beams, sections of kingposts and cargo booms. The mainmast is reported to lie some distance away.

A section of the propeller shaft and the propeller itself lie amid the debris.

21. *Kiyosumi Maru*
Passenger-cargo vessel (1934)
IJN *Tokusetsu Junyokan* armed merchant cruiser (1941)
IJN *Ippan Choyosen* transport ship (1943)
U.S. Recognition Code: 15 MKFKM

Repair Anchorage

Tonnage:	6,984grt (civilian)
	8,614 grt (IJN)
Dimensions:	453.7-ft long; beam of 61-ft; draught of 31.1ft
Launched:	30 June 1934
Sunk:	17 February 1944
Cause of loss:	Bombed by TF 58 aircraft during Operation HAILSTONE
Wreck location:	Repair Anchorage – 500 yards north of Fefan Island
Depth to seabed:	35 metres
Least Depth:	12 metres - uppermost starboard hull
Other name:	*Kiyozumi Maru*

The large passenger-cargo ship *Kiyosumi Maru* was laid down on 30 May 1933 at the Kawasaki Dockyard in Kobe for the Tokyo based Kokusai Kisen Kaisha. She was launched and named on 30 June 1934 and after fitting out afloat she was completed on 5 October 1934 and registered in Tokyo.

Kokusai Kisen Kaisha christened all of its motor ships with names beginning with the letter "K". *Kiyosumi Maru* was named after a famous shrine in Kyushu – and the Kokusai Kisen K. K. steam ships were often given names of countries or cities. Kokusai Kisen Kaisha ran passenger and cargo services from the Orient to New York - and cargo only services to Hamburg and Australia, Bombay, Africa, Formosa and to many European ports.

The 6,984grt passenger cargo ship *Kiyosumi Maru* was launched in 1934. She was requisitioned as an IJN armed merchant cruiser in 1941 and then re-rated as an IJN transport ship in 1943.

Kiyosumi Maru was constructed with two decks and a cruiser stern. Her cavernous holds had a 3rd tween deck, except for the aftmost hold. Her single screw was driven by a 2-stroke

Left: The passenger cargo ship *Kiyosumi Maru* entering New York harbour at speed in about 1936.

Right: Overhead aspect of *Kiyosumi Maru* (NH 111562 Courtesy of Naval History & Heritage Command)

7-cylinder Mitsubishi–Sulzer diesel engine manufactured by Mitsubishi Zosen Kaisha Ltd in Nagasaki that gave her a fast service speed of 16 knots - and a maximum speed of 19 knots. She had a service radius of 34,000 nautical miles at 16 knots. She was also equipped to carry cargo oil above 150°F in deep tanks.

Following her completion on 5 October 1934 and delivery to her new owners Kokusai Kisen K. K., *Kiyosumi Maru* spent the first seven years of her service career chartered to the Nippon Yusen K.K. shipping line (NYK). She ran three times a year on their route from the large city port of Kobe in Osaka Bay (on the southern side of the main island of Honshū) to New York, stopping at several ports of call such as Singapore, Manila and Los Angeles before passing through the Panama Canal and heading north to New York. She came off charter to NYK in 1938 but continued on the same route.

Her civilian career ended on 5 September 1941, when Rear Admiral Okamura Masao was appointed as her Commanding Officer, simultaneously assuming command of the armed merchant cruiser *Aikoku Maru* (a present day Truk wreck). She was formally requisitioned by the IJN on 1 November 1941. With her size and creditable speed, *Kiyosumi Maru* was assigned to the Combined Fleet to operate as an armed merchant cruiser along with the 24th Raider Squadron armed merchant cruisers *Aikoku Maru* and *Hokoku Maru* in the Java Sea/Indian Ocean area, where German and Italian armed merchant cruisers already operated.

Kiyosumi Maru arrived at Osaka on 1 December 1941 (a week before the Pearl Harbor attack), for conversion to an armed merchant cruiser. She was registered in the Kure Naval District.

At Osaka, *Kiyosumi Maru* was fitted with eight powerful 14cm/50 cal 3rd Year Type low angle (LA) naval guns in single mounts. One 14cm LA gun was installed on a platform at the bow, one on either side of the foredeck Hold No 2 and another two set one either side of Hold No 3. Another two 14cm LA guns were set one either side of the aft holds and finally a stern gun was mounted on a platform on top of the poop island deckhouse. She was also fitted with two 13.5mm AA guns and two 533mm (21-inch) torpedo tubes, set one mount either side of Hold No 5. She was equipped to carry a single Type 94 Kawanishi E7K2 reconnaissance floatplane – Allied Reporting codename *Alf*.

The conversion works were speedily completed by 18 December 1941, less than a fortnight after the outbreak of war following the Pearl Harbor raid on 7 December 1941. The conversion works and additions had increased her tonnage from 6,984-tons to 8,614-tons in her military configuration.

On 29 March 1942, just a few months after her completion, the 24th Cruiser Squadron was disbanded - and the following month, in April 1942, she was assigned to the Southwestern Area Fleet. On 9 May 1942, she berthed at the Kure Naval Arsenal in Japan and began loading heavy equipment and the amphibious troops of the Kure No.5 Special Landing Force, for transport to Guam.

Once loaded, she formed up in an escorted convoy that departed Kure for Guam on 15 May 1942. The convoy arrived in Guam on 18 May and shortly afterwards, *Kiyosumi Maru* departed for Saipan to join the oilers and transport ships of the Midway Invasion Force Transport Group on 28 May 1942. 248 planes of Vice-Admiral Chūichi Nagumo's 1st Carrier Striking Force, (the four carriers *Akagi, Kaga, Hiryū* and *Sōryū*) would carry out initial air strikes against Midway, intended to destroy U.S. defences and aircraft on the Atoll.

In addition to the four fleet carriers, five battleships, four heavy cruisers, two light cruisers and two light carriers would support the invasion - the U.S. Fleet had no operational battleships left in the Pacific after the attack on Pearl Harbor.

However, ……. unknown to Japan, American cryptographers had already broken the main Japanese naval code and deciphered some details of the plan. The U.S. Navy planned its own ambush – and the three carriers *Enterprise, Hornet* and *Yorktown* were deployed in advance of their invasion of Midway, taking up a holding position to the north east of Midway at Point Luck.

At about 0900 on 3 June, an American Consolidated PBY Catalina flying boat from Midway spotted the Japanese Occupation Force approximately 500 nautical miles to the west southwest of Midway and the alarm was broadcast for American forces defending the atoll. Nine Boeing B-17 Flying Fortress four-engine bombers took off from Midway at 1230 for the first air attack. At about 1700, they found the Transport Group, of which *Kiyosumi Maru* was part, carrying 5,000 IJA invasion troops. As the Japanese destroyers opened up with their AA guns, the B-17 Flying Fortresses released their payloads – but no serious damage was done. It is extremely difficult to hit a moving ship from altitude.

The Midway Occupation Force convoy was subsequently attacked by Consolidated PBY Catalina flying boats carrying torpedoes – and during the attack, *Kiyosumi Maru* was strafed whilst the oiler *Akebono Maru* was hit in the bow.

The subsequent legendary Battle of Midway would be a disaster for the Japanese and turn the tide of the war. The four IJN fleet carriers *Akagi, Kaga, Sōryū* and *Hiryū* would be sunk for the loss of the American carrier *Yorktown* (CV-5) and the destroyer *Hammann* (DD-412)). Admiral Yamamoto, aboard his flagship, the super battleship *Yamato,* ordered the invasion cancelled on 5 June. The Transport Group returned to Guam and between 13-16 June the 5,000 IJA invasion troops and their equipment were disembarked.

Following the disastrous Midway operation, *Kiyosumi Maru* was assigned to operate in the Penang-to-Singapore area - before carrying troops and materials to Rabaul for the reinforcement of Guadalcanal. In September 1942, she was sent to Panay where she loaded IJA troops and equipment for the Rabaul landings that began on 6 October 1942.

In December 1942, she carried assault troops and Airfield Construction Battalions from Singapore to Rabaul for the reinforcement of New Guinea - before proceeding to Wewak carrying more troops.

By January 1943, she was in Tsingtao in China, embarking troops of the 41st Army Division along with vehicles and general cargo destined for the reinforcement of New Guinea. She proceeded to Palau and from there she moved to Wewak on 26 February and disembarked her army forces before heading back to Kobe via Formosa (Taiwan).

During 1943, she underwent a partial reconversion from armed merchant cruiser to transport vessel and although her eight 14cm/50-cal 3rd Year Type deck guns were removed at this time, much of the associated fitments and gun mounts and platforms, AA guns, range finders for main naval guns were left in situ.

In September 1943, *Kiyosumi Maru* formed up in a large escorted convoy in Shanghai that was destined for Truk and Rabaul and was carrying 5,940 infantry troops, a Tank Regiment, a Division Communication Station and 650 vehicles and supplies. *Kiyosumi* embarked 1,300 infantry of the IJA 17th Division, 170 vehicles, munitions and supplies.

The convoy arrived in Truk on 2 October – the lagoon being dominated by almost the entire IJN Combined Fleet lying at anchor. The massive superbattleships *Yamato* and *Musashi* were present along with many other capital ships, carriers, cruisers, destroyers and submarines, all clustered in the anchorages around the central islands of the Truk lagoon.

Kiyosumi Maru then departed for Rabaul - where on 5 October she disembarked her 1,300 IJA 17th Division troops, vehicles and supplies. She then returned to Truk and went on to Shanghai where she embarked 1,342 troops of the IJA 17th Division along with field artillery, Engineer Regiment personnel and their equipment. She then formed up in a convoy bound for Kavieng, on the northern side of Papua New Guinea, via Truk. The convoy arrived at Truk on 28 October 1943, despite attacks from American submarines.

On 1 November 1943, *Kiyosumi Maru* departed Truk heading south for the next leg of the passage to Kavieng, on the northern side of Papua New Guinea with her embarked IJA troops and their equipment. The light cruisers *Isuzu* and *Naka* escorted the convoy.

On 3 November 1943, 19 American B-24 Liberator bombers attacked the convoy 60 miles north of Kavieng. The *Naka* suffered a near miss and *Kiyosumi Maru* herself was damaged. When her engine room flooded and she was rendered unable to navigate, she was taken in tow by the light cruiser *Isuzu* for Kavieng.

The following day, the destroyer *Minazuki* departed Kavieng to assist the tow of *Kiyosumi Maru* - the destroyer *Isokaze* and light cruiser *Yubari* also were called to assist. In a delicate and coordinated movement, the *Yubari* removed 196 men and three field guns from *Kiyosumi Maru* whilst *Isuzu*, *Naka*, *Minazuki* and *Isokaze* removed the remaining troops and field guns. The troops were landed at Rabaul where *Kiyosumi Maru's* cargo of ammunition and supplies was also offloaded. The light cruiser *Isuzu* then took her in tow to Kavieng for repair.

Whilst still at Kavieng, she was attacked on 25 December 1943 by aircraft from the U.S. Task Force 58 carriers *Bunker Hill* and *Monterey*. Although set on fire, she was only been lightly damaged and after temporary repairs, she set off for Truk on 30 December 1943 for permanent repair work - escorted by the destroyer *Yukaze* and the minesweeper W-22. The following day however, the small group was spotted by the American submarine *Balao* (SS-285), which started tracking the group on the surface. On 1 January 1944, south west of Truk, *Balao* fired six bow torpedoes at *Kiyosumi Maru* – three of which hit her, flooding her forward holds and disabling her.

The destroyer *Naka* was called out from Truk on 1 January to assist, and when she arrived, she took the stricken *Kiyosumi Maru* in tow for repair at Truk. As the tow to Truk began, the destroyer *Tanikaze* left Truk on 2 January, to assist the *Naka* - and the light cruiser *Oyodo*, the destroyer *Akizuki* and a minesweeper also arrived on scene to provide an escort for the valuable ship. As the tow neared Truk on 4 January 1944, the light cruiser *Oyodo* and the destroyer *Akizuki* were detached to head back to Truk.

The light cruiser *Naka* and the destroyer *Tanikaze* arrived at Truk with *Kiyosumi Maru* in tow on 8 January - *Kiyosumi Maru* was towed to the Repair Anchorage where urgent repair work on her started immediately.

On 17 February 1944, just over a month later, when the Operation HAILSTONE raids began with the dawn Hellcat fighter sweep, *Kiyosumi Maru* was still anchored in the Repair Anchorage - just north of Fefan Island and west of Dublon Island.

Following the dawn initial fighter sweep, the first Strike 1A aircraft from TG 58.1 *Yorktown* and *Enterprise* arrived over the lagoon between 0615 and 0630. The *Yorktown* planes had been tasked to attack Japanese shipping north east of Fefan at the Combined Fleet Anchorage and the Repair Anchorage, and south west of Dublon at the Sixth Fleet Anchorage. The *Yorktown* and *Enterprise* SBD Dauntless and TBF Avenger pilots selected their targets - their dives and attack runs would be covered by Hellcats for protection against Japanese airborne fighters. *Yorktown* SBD's attacked the *Akashi*, *Kiyosumi Maru* and *Kensyo Maru*. Although *Kensyo Maru* was hit by a 1,000-lb bomb, *Kiyosumi Maru* escaped serious damage.

During the second group strike between 0815 – 0900, *Kiyosumi Maru* was again attacked by Strike 1B SBD Dauntless dive-bombers from *Yorktown*. At about 0900, the SBD dive bombers scored a direct hit in the foredeck Hold No 2. The bomb dropped right into the hold and the explosion blew out the bottom of the ship and started a fire. The hold flooded - but the damage was contained, and she was able to remain afloat.

Around 1302, launching began aboard *Yorktown* for Strike 1E, the fifth group bombing strike of the day. 13 SBD Dauntless dive-bombers, 6 TBF Avengers torpedo-bombers and 12 escort Hellcats roared off the *Yorktown* flight deck into the wind – and by 1415, the flight was arriving over Truk, to a scene of devastation below. The escort Hellcats had a short engagement with Japanese fighters, in which they shot down three - before going on to strafe Eten airfield, an oiler, two freighters and a destroyer.

The Strike 1E *Yorktown* TBF Avengers meanwhile attacked the damaged *Kiyosumi Maru* north of Fefan and then *Yamagiri Maru*, northwest of Fefan. Several SBD's attacked *Yamagiri*

Maru, and a transport at anchor east of Eten, before attacking a tanker northwest of Fefan – *Sinkoku Maru.*

Then, at about 1330, Strike 1E SBD dive bombers from *Enterprise* attacked the beleaguered *Kiyosumi Maru.* The SBD's scored hits with bombs amidships, on either side of the bridge - killing 43 of her crew including Captain Maki.

With Hold No 2 already flooded due to the bomb hit at 0900, and after further near misses had caused even more damage, the cumulative effect of these hits and the original torpedo damage to her foreship, proved too much. *Kiyosumi Maru* took on a list to port and sank where she lay at anchor into 35 metres of water - coming to rest on her port beam ends.

The Wreck Today

Today the substantial wreck of the *Kiyosumi Maru* rests on her port side in 35 metres of water in the Repair Anchorage about 600 yards off the north shore of Fefan Island. She is one of the stars of Truk lagoon wreck diving and such a big ship, lying in such a modest depth, allows divers long exploration dives for only minimal decompression obligations. The least depth down to her upmost starboard side of her massive hull is about 12 metres. The wreck is bathed in sunlight and the starboard hull has consequently turned into a beautiful coral garden.

For more than 40 years fuel oil leaked from the wreck – gaining her the local name of the Oil Slick Wreck. Hold No 2 still contains a number of 55-gallon fuel drums – but most of these lost their contents long ago and are now empty. The slick dissipated during the 1990's and the writer has seen no evidence of any significant amounts of oil escaping the wreck in this century.

The tide, and the location of the wreck between Dublon and Fefan Islands, seems to produce slightly misty or cloudy underwater visibility. Swimming around outside the wreck, the water seems not as clear as the deeper wrecks in the Fourth Fleet Anchorage. But inside the wreck, the water is crystal clear – make no mistake this is a stunning wreck to dive.

At the bow, on the fo'c'sle deck at a depth of about 27 metres, stands the partial skeletal framework of a bare circular gun platform - left after her conversion in 1943 from an armed merchant cruiser to transport vessel and the removal of her 14cm guns. Moving onto the upmost starboard side of the hull here towards the bow, the embossed letters of the ship's name can just be made out - largely obscured by heavy coral. The starboard anchor chain runs out from the anchor windlass to its hawse pipe before draping over the stem to the seabed.

Moving aft to the well deck, the uppermost and now horizontal, starboard door in the fo'c'sle bulkhead allows divers to enter the fo'c'sle spaces. Moving about 10- 15 feet inside, divers can look upwards and into the Lamp Room (frequently to be found on the starboard side of a ship's fo'c'sle). Here, at a depth of about 25 metres, quite a number of copper and bronze navigation lanterns are still stacked neatly in place on with red (port), green (starboard) steaming lanterns and all-round white steaming/anchor lanterns to be found.

Continuing to move aft from the bow, the hatch cover beams for Hold No 1 remain in place both at the weather deck and also inside the hold at tween deck level. The hold is largely empty - her cargo had been offloaded prior to repair work starting. Here and there however quite a number of 55-gallon oil drums, that gave her the old nickname the *Oil Slick Wreck,* can still be found. Cargo handling booms from the foremast run across the hatch.

The wreck of *Kiyosumi Maru*

Least depth: 12m
Depth to seabed: 35m

Empty 5.9-inch gun platform

Entry to starboard lamp room

Bottom of Hold No.2 blown out by bomb hit

Pitched engine room roof

Twin torpedo launchers on swivel mounts

Bridge superstructure damaged by 1,000lb bomb hit

55-gallon fuel drums and propellor blades

Empty 5.9-inch gun platform

Artist's impression of the large wreck of *Kiyosumi Maru*, which today rests on her port beam ends in 35 metres of water.

The hatch cover beams for Hold No 2 are missing – she took a direct bomb hit in this hold from a *Yorktown* SBD Dauntless dive-bomber that blew out the bottom of the hold. The expanding force of the explosion likely blew the hatch cover beams off and also set fire to the 55-gallon drums of fuel here. The hold today is thus also largely empty.

The most striking feature in Hold No 2 is however the gaping hole in her keel where the bottom of the hold has been blown out by the bomb – it is easy to swim out of the hole to open water on the keel side of the ship. There is a second large hole some 30 feet in diameter, slightly further back on the starboard side of the ship where the plating is blown inwards. Set on the deck, one on either side of this hold and Hold No 3, are empty single mounts for her 14cm/50 LA guns, removed in 1943.

The foremast with its crosstree still juts out horizontally from a masthouse set on the well deck in between the hatches for Hold No's 1 & 2. Cargo handling winches are set around its base.

The hatch for Hold No 3 still has its cover beams in place and appears to have been plated over in part. At its forward edge, the goalpost pair of kingposts with intricate cross bracing still stand in place.

The large amidships composite superstructure appears to retain some of its basic shape when seen from the foredeck - but moving past the bridge frontage, it is clear that it is only the lower sections and just part of the front of the higher bridge levels that remain intact. Behind the front facade, the tremendous force of the 1,000-lb bomb explosions can be seen - the superstructure from the front of the bridge to just forward of the smokestack has been destroyed, torn apart and devastated. In recent years, with its structural integrity destroyed, much has collapsed to the seabed. In the debris at about 30 metres can be found the bridge navigational instruments, an engine order telegraph and a rudder direction indicator pedestal.

The large smokestack survived the force of the explosions and is still *in situ*, angled downwards at 45° to rest its upper end on the seabed. Normally made of thin steel, in exposed water, smokestacks rust away very quickly – they are largely absent on most WWII-era wrecks. The sheltered waters of the Repair Anchorage however have helped preserve the ship in remarkably good condition and it is possible to make out the "A" insignia of the original commercial owners Kokusai Kisen Kaisha on the funnel. Lifeboat davits hang empty nearby on the uppermost side of the Boat Deck. Open ventilation skylight hatches either side of the stack lead down into the engine room.

It is possible for suitably trained divers to swim aft from Hold No 2 at tween deck level (under the weather deck) on the high starboard side of the ship and pass through a rotted steel bulkhead into Hold No 3. Divers can then enter the engine room, where the large round tops of her 7-cylinder Mitsubishi-Sulzer diesel engine can be found and the once vertical exhaust trunking for her smokestack. Thick electric cables run up walls and along roofs to intact brass cage lights still in situ.

With care it is possible to move past the engine and head laterally deeper into the wreck, towards the bottom of the ship. This area is tight, confused and layered with silt that is stirred up by poor finning technique. The still water in here is however crystal clear and reveals that decks, walls and bulkheads are all heavily blackened by fire damage. Fixed ladders and staircases, once running vertically now lead off horizontally.

The machinery associated with the 7-clylinder diesel engine is complicated and extensive – walls are covered in switches, control panels, gauges and valves. As you explore in this area, deep in the bowels of the ship, every now and then a chink of blue light from outside penetrates down though the damaged superstructure, through gaps and companionway openings, to help you reorientate yourself amidst all the twists and turns.

Moving aft from the composite superstructure, the hatch for Hold No 4 (set in the after weather deck) still has its hatch cover beams in place - both on the weather deck and below at the tween deck level. But as with the foredeck holds, with all her troops and cargo offloaded, it is now empty.

Between the aft Hold No's 4 & 5, a goalpost pair of kingposts jut out horizontally. Cargo booms are goosenecked to each kingpost and their ends drop down to rest on the seabed. Hold No 5 has torpedo tube launchers on swivel deck mounts either side.

The mainmast still projects out horizontally from a small masthouse between the hatches for Hold No's 5 & 6 - its cargo handling booms are still present, their ends have also dropped from their cradles to now rest on the seabed. These holds contain many 55-gallon fuel drums along with spare propeller blades.

The poop island deckhouse holds the auxiliary steering flat with the steering gear and quadrant. The empty circular platform for the 14cm/50-cal stern gun is still present on top.

Moving around the fantail of the stern the large rudder and single screw are still in place - dominating divers with their very size.

22. *The Lighter*

Sixth Fleet Anchorage

Tonnage:	300 tons (est)
Dimensions:	125ft long (est); beam of 24ft (est)
Sunk:	29-30 April 1944 (assumed)
Cause of loss:	Strafing by TF 58 aircraft during follow up raid (assumed)
Wreck location:	Sixth Fleet Anchorage, west of Uman Island
Depth to seabed:	25-30 metres
Least Depth:	20 metres

A small water tanker, or lighter, estimated to be around 300-tons lies just a few hundred metres from the west shore of Uman Island not far from the wreck of the coastal freighter *Hino Maru No 2*. The lighter is believed to be one of three water lighters that were stationed at Truk to supply ships and troops on outlying islands of the atoll with fresh water.

There is little historical record to be found regarding this small vessel. She is believed to be a casualty of strafing by Task Force 58 air groups during the follow up fast carrier raid on Truk on 29-30 April 1944.

The vessel sits on her keel with a slight list to port on a gently sloping bottom. Her bows point away from the west coast of Uman Island and consequently the stern sits in shallower water - the bows being 3-4 metres deeper.

The main deck is a single flush weather deck that was ringed with guard rails – there is no raised foc'sle. At the bow, there is a small anchor crane used for anchor handling and also to take hoses associated with water supply operations. A spare anchor lies on deck nearby.

An anchor windlass sits near the bow with triangular supports mounted fore and aft that were likely used to support hoses during water transfer operations. Just abaft the windlass on the foredeck, the skeleton of a small deckhouse stands above a small access hatch below.

The amidships superstructure held the wheelhouse at its leading frontage, once enclosed by wood or canvas on a steel structure of support rods. The walls and roof of the wheelhouse however are long gone and now the telegraph and helm stand exposed in free water but blanketed in heavy coral.

Abaft the wheelhouse was the pump room deckhouse - which had four water lines available, connecting through small hatches to four pipe terminals covered with steel plates and embossed with the Japanese numerals 1- 4. The pumps are mounted on deck.

The weather deck abaft the pumping station here is slightly elevated and the water tanks are believed to be situated beneath.

The lighter's diesel engine machinery was housed below deck at the stern and access is possible to see the diesel engine and fitments. The engine room skylights are closed. On top of the after deckhouse there are sheared off forced draft ventilators towards the front.

The 10-foot high smokestack still stands upright - and abaft it, towards the fantail of the stern, is another higher deckhouse with entrances at either side and companionways leading below. On top of this deckhouse is a cylindrical tank on its side beside the remnants of a davit. You see a similar arrangement with a cylindrical tank beside refueling tripods on fleet oilers – an engineer acquaintance told me that it was possible that the tank accommodated a high-pressure pump.

A spare propeller sits on the port side of the deck near the stern.

23. *Momokawa Maru*
Passenger-cargo vessel (1941)
IJA *Rikugun Yusosen* Transport (1942)
IJN *Ippan Choyosen* - General Requisitioned Ship (1943)
U.S. Recognition Code: 23A MKFM

Fourth Fleet Anchorage

Tonnage:	3,829 grt
Dimensions:	354 ft long; beam of 50ft; draught of 23 ft
Launched:	17 August 1940
Sunk:	18 February 1944
Cause of loss:	Bombed by TF 58 aircraft during Operation HAILSTONE
Wreck location:	Fourth Fleet Anchorage, east of Dublon Island
Depth to seabed:	42 metres
Least Depth:	27 metres – bridge superstructure
Other name:	*Momogawa Maru*

The 3,829grt passenger cargo ship *Momokawa Maru* was launched in 1940. She was requisitioned first by the IJA in 1942 and then by the IJN in 1943.

The 3,829grt cargo-passenger vessel *Momokawa Maru* was built by the Kawasaki Dockyard Co Ltd in Kobe for Kawasaki Kisen K.K. – the 'K' Line. She was named and launched for fitting out afloat on 17 August 1940 and subsequently completed on 31 March 1941.

Momokawa Maru was built as a classic three-island vessel with a raised fo'c'sle, a composite superstructure amidships, which held the bridge with the machinery spaces abaft and below. The smokestack was situated immediately abaft the bridge with lifeboats swinging in davits either side and engine room skylights nearby. Steps led up from the forward well deck to a walkway along either side of the superstructure at shelter deck level. Passenger cabins were situated off this walkway along either side of the engine casing. A small poop island deckhouse at the stern held the steering gear and crew accommodation. The bulk of the ship, forward and aft of the amidships superstructure, was given over to cargo holds.

Momokawa Maru was the same basic design and specifications as the other present day Truk wrecks of *Nippo Maru* and *Kikukawa Maru*, as well as *Kirikawa Maru, Matukawa Maru, Toei Maru* and *Toho Maru*. She displayed a noticeably raked stem, a cruiser stern and had five cargo holds. Three holds were set forward of the composite bridge superstructure with the hatch for Hold No 3 set in the shelter deck extended section of superstructure immediately in front of the bridge. The foremast was positioned between the hatches for Hold No's 1&2 and a goalpost pair of kingposts was situated at the leading edge of the extended section of superstructure that housed Hold No 3, forward of the bridge.

There were two after well deck holds, with no section of extended superstructure, as in front of the bridge. The mainmast was set between the two aft well deck Hold No's 4 & 5.

Momokawa Maru was fitted with a single screw driven by steam turbines that gave her a service speed of 12-14 knots and a maximum speed of 16 knots. She was fueled by coal and consequently had a tall narrow smokestack designed to get the resultant black smoke as high away from the aft deck as possible. She had a radius of some 10,000 miles at 12 knots.

After her completion in March 1941, just nine months before the Pearl Harbor raid, she was put to work in her peacetime role as a timber transporter, carrying timber from Siberia to Japan. Because she would encounter ice floes on this route, her bow and stern were structurally strengthened and the hatches for her holds were lengthened to accommodate loading of long tree trunks.

In November 1941, as war loomed, after just eight months of civilian life she was requisitioned by the Imperial Japanese Army as an IJA *Rikugun Yusosen*– a merchant ship converted for military use as a Transport. She was fitted with one 8cm/40 cal deck gun, one 7.7mm machine gun and carried five rifles.

In June 1943, after some 18 months of Army service, *Momokawa Maru* was released by the IJA to her civilian owners - but then immediately requisitioned by the IJN as an *Ippan Choyosen*, a General Requisitioned Ship manned by a civilian crew but often with a Navy Reserve captain.

Momokawa Maru was converted to a Shunko Maru-class *Zatsuyosen* Auxiliary Transport, with the other ships in this particular class being *Hunko Maru, Kirikawa Maru, Matsukawa Maru, Kikukawa Maru* and *Hiyoshi Maru* – all completed between 1936 and 1941 for a number of shipping companies. Of this class, *Kirikawa, Hiyoshi* and *Kikukawa Maru's* were requisitioned by the IJN whilst *Shunko Maru, Matsukawa Maru* and *Momokawa Maru* were requisitioned by the IJA. All the ships in this class would be sunk during WWII.

In her new role, on 24 June 1943, *Momokawa Maru* departed Yokosuka with concrete for the fortification of Tarawa in the Gilbert Islands. Japan was already on the back foot by this stage of the war and the Gilberts were the likely focus of forthcoming Allied amphibious landings. After delivering her cargo to Tarawa, she headed west towards Truk, arriving there on 12 July 1943. She left Truk on 10 August to return to Yokosuka in a convoy, escorted by the IJN kaibōkan *Fukue*, which arrived at Yokosuka on 18 August 1943. Within a few days, *Momokawa Maru* departed Yokosuka for Kirun in Formosa (Taiwan) - before heading outbound once again to Truk.

Momokawa Maru departed Truk on 23 September 1943 bound for Kwajalein in a convoy escorted by the subchaser CH-29. The convoy arrived at Kwajalein Atoll on 28 September

1943, and whilst there, *Momokawa Maru* was tasked to tow the large damaged 14,050-ton oiler *Shiretoko,* torpedoed by USS *Permit* (SS-178), from Kwajalein back to Sasebo in southern Japan for repair. On 13 November, west of the Marianas, *Shiretoko* was torpedoed, during the tow, by the American submarine *Scorpion* (SS-278). The damaged oiler had a higher naval value than the transport ship towing her. The torpedo hit caused the oiler to settle by the stern – but remain towable. The tow successfully arrived at Sasebo Naval Base on 23 November 1943. (*Shiretoko* was a sister oiler of the two famous present day Palauan shipwrecks, *Iro* and *Sata*).

On 3 December 1943, *Momokawa Maru* departed Yokosuka with a cargo of fuel in drums, calling at Nagasaki to collect military stores and bunker coal before heading on to Tokuyama, in Tokyo Bay and then to Yokosuka.

On 19 December 1943, she departed Yokosuka in a convoy bound for Kwajalein via Saipan and Truk with a cargo of aviation fuel, coal, landing barges, 50 depth charges, sampans and automobiles. The convoy arrived at Saipan on Xmas Day 1943, departing two days later, on 27 December 1943, in a convoy that arrived Truk on 31 December. She then departed Truk for Kwajalein carrying fuel oil in drums and a number of landing barges.

Another famous Truk shipwreck, the transport *Kensyo Maru* had been bombed and badly damaged at Kwajalein on 20 December 1943 by American B-24 Liberator bombers. One bomb had hit the aft part of the ship and she was left unnavigable and partially flooded. *Kensyo Maru* had been towed to the north part of Kwajalein atoll and run aground before she could sink. Emergency repairs were carried out to make her watertight.

On 28 January 1944, *Momokawa Maru* took the still unnavigable *Kensyo Maru* in tow and departed Kwajalein along with *Katori Maru* in a convoy bound for Truk, where *Kensyo Maru* would have permanent repairs carried out in the Repair Anchorage. The convoy arrived safely at Truk on 4 February 1944, with *Kensyo Maru* still under tow by *Momokawa Maru*.

Two weeks later, at dawn on 17 February 1944, on the first day of Operation HAILSTONE, *Momokawa Maru* was anchored in the Fourth Fleet Anchorage, east of Dublon Island. She and the other ships in the anchorage were attacked by aircraft from the American carriers *Bunker Hill*, *Essex* and *Yorktown*. *Momokawa Maru* received some light damage but remained afloat.

The following morning, 18 February 1944, 23 planes roared off the *Bunker Hill* flight deck into the wind for Strike 3B, the second bombing strike of the day following on after the initial dawn fighter sweep by Hellcats. Strike 3B would be the last effective strike of the raid.

Of the ten Strike 3B Curtiss SB2C Helldivers launching, five were carrying two 500-lb bombs, whilst the other five carried 1,000-lb bombs. The nine TBF Avengers were carrying anti-ship torpedoes. Four Hellcat fighters would provide escort.

The *Bunker Hill* planes arrived over the southern end of the Truk lagoon around 0815 at a height of about 10,000-feet. The SB2C Helldivers first attacked a large ship, estimated by pilots at 450ft long, off the southeast tip of Dublon. The Helldivers scored a hit with a 1,000-lb bomb aft that caused a large explosion and started fires. The unfortunate target below the Helldivers was in fact the *Momokawa Maru*, and the 1,000-lb bomb had hit her in the vicinity of her aft Hold No 5.

Water flooded into her through her damaged shell plating - and as her aft holds filled with water, she started to settle steadily by the stern. The fierce fires started by the bomb burned for some time. By the time the U.S. aircraft broke off their attack, only her bow was left above the water, her stern was already resting on the seabed.

Momokawa Maru finally sank from sight, rolling to port as she disappeared below. She settled on the bottom of the lagoon on her port beam ends in just over 40 metres of water.

The wreck was located by the Cousteau expedition in 1969.

The Wreck today

The wreck of the *Momokawa Maru* is one of my favourite in the Truk lagoon – but a wreck that is almost underrated and doesn't get as much attention as the more well-known wrecks. But she is a beautiful, virtually intact, ship lying in a perfect depth, that has lots to see, from her bridge with telegraphs and telemotor still in situ - to an easily accessed engine room. The ship's bell was found in 1982 in the large pile of debris and sediment on the seabed underneath the bridge superstructure, and her name is welded onto her bow in kanji and Roman letters.

Momokawa Maru lies on her port side on a gently sloping bottom in 42 metres of water, between the wrecks of *Aikoku Maru* and *San Francisco Maru*. She rests approximately ½ mile offshore east of Tonoas Island in the Fourth Fleet Anchorage, with Fanamu Island to the south east. The least depth down to the higher starboard side of the bridge superstructure is about 27 metres. Just 5-10 metres away from her now vertical deck, the seabed slopes away dramatically into the depths.

At the bow, the fo'c'sle deck is screened by a raised bulwark. The anchor windlass sits atop the fo'c'sle with its chains emerging from their spurling pipes and chain lockers, just aft. The two anchor chains run out from the windlass to hawse pipes on either side of the deck near the bow. The port chain is run out to the seabed and runs around the bow to the keel side of the ship. The starboard anchor is held snug in its hawse pipe. There is no bow gun or platform on the fo'c'sle deck. Two aft facing doors in the fo'c'sle bulkhead allow entry into the fo'c'sle spaces.

The foremast, with its distinctive crosstree, projects out horizontally between the foredeck hatches for Hold No's 1 & 2. The standing rigging which braced the crosstree to the hull hangs loosely, now covered in thick sea life. The jumbo boom, which would have been stowed upright against it, has fallen to rest at an angle of 45° with its top end on the seabed.

The hatches for the cargo holds have a raised coaming. Several hatch cover beams for Hold No 1 are still in place, with a few beams missing. The beams at tween deck level are still in place.

The cargo in these foredeck holds tumbled to port as she heeled over and sank – but inside the hold are aircraft parts, tail sections, tyres, fuel drums, bombs, radial engines, wings, propeller blades and wing and belly fuel tanks. It appears that a complete aircraft is stowed here in sections - its parts spread between both holds. The aircraft lies facing aft with the tail and rear fuselage in No 1 Hold and the nose section and forward fuselage in No 2 Hold. The aircraft's detached wings, engines and tail parts, originally all stowed nearby are now all scattered below.

Most of the hatch cover beams for Hold No 2 remain in place - the hold contains a number of trucks and 55-gallon AvGas drums. Cargo booms run fore and aft from short kingposts either side of the foremast, the boom ends have fallen down to port to rest on the seabed.

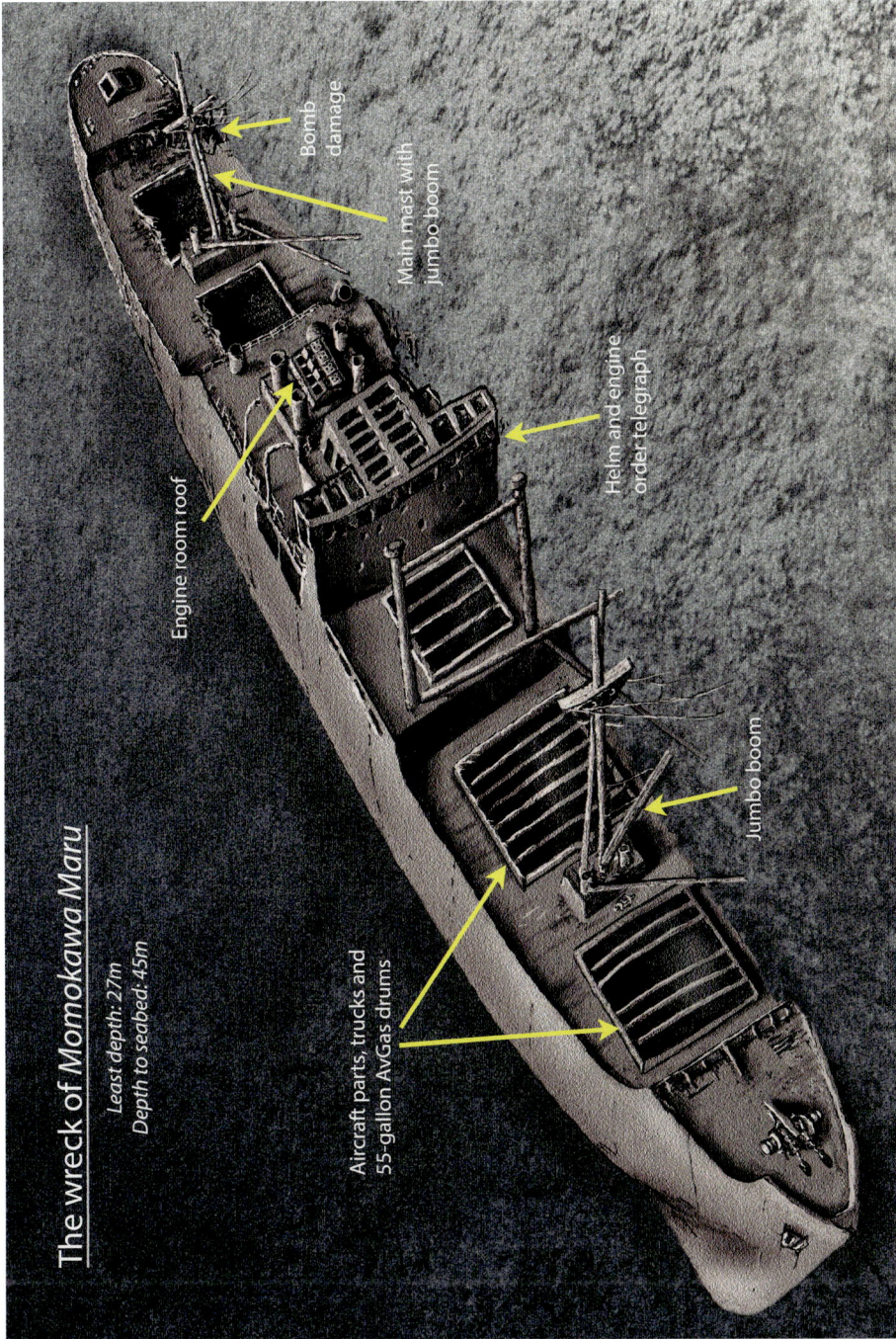

The wreck of *Momokawa Maru*

Least depth: 27m
Depth to seabed: 45m

Bomb damage

Main mast with jumbo boom

Helm and engine order telegraph

Engine room roof

Jumbo boom

Aircraft parts, trucks and 55-gallon AvGas drums

Artist's impression of the largely intact wreck of *Momokawa Maru* resting on her beam ends in 45 metres.

As you move aft, the forward well deck, that accommodates the hatches for Holds 1&2, rises up one deck level to the extended shelter deck section of the amidships superstructure, immediately in front of the bridge superstructure. At the leading edge of the extended section of superstructure, a goalpost pair of kingposts still stand, their cargo booms swung round to rest their ends on the seabed below. This extended superstructure accommodates the hatch for Hold No 3, which holds bunker coal for the ship's engine, as well as more 55-gallon fuel drums.

Abaft Hold No 3, the front of the composite superstructure juts out, now horizontally. The navigation bridge at its highest level can be entered through the exposed beams of the roof or through its large rectangular windows. Inside, the ship's twin engine order telegraph still stands, with voice tubes fixed to the forward bulkhead nearby that were used for communicating with the captain when in his quarters and with the boiler and engine rooms.

The telemotor for the helm and the rudder direction indicator are bolted to the deck of the bridge – the wooden spokes of the helm itself have disintegrated over the years. Seen from outside, the original wood planking of the roof of this deckhouse is all gone, leaving just the structural beams and girders. There is a pronounced slender bridge wing at either side, used in docking manoeuvres. Many crockery pieces still bearing the logo of the shipping line have been pulled out of the silt lining the aft spaces of the superstructure and placed on the higher starboard side.

Immediately abaft the bridge, in this composite superstructure, stands the remains of the smokestack. Made of lighter steel, it has rotted away over the years and the topmost part has now fallen to the seabed below. Dotted around its base are several forced draft ventilators, designed to scoop up air as the ship moved and funnel it down to the spaces below.

Abaft the smokestack is the pitched roof of the engine room, easily identified by its rows of skylights, each with three small portholes in it. These are mostly open, as they were for

Momokawa Maru – rudder and screw (Author)

ventilation at the time the ship sank. It is possible to access the cavernous innards of the engine room below, where the steam engine is surrounded by catwalks, gauges, wall panels and staircases.

Abaft the smokestack on the Boat Deck, two pairs of empty lifeboat davits are situated on the higher starboard side of the ship. The aft pair is swung outward while the forward pair remain in their stowed swung-in position.

Continuing to move aft from the boat deck, you now leave the composite superstructure and move to the after well deck, where the hatches for Hold No's 4 & 5 are visible with the mainmast with its crosstree set in between them - still projecting horizontally outwards. A tall jumbo boom for heavy lifts is stowed in place tight against the mainmast. Cargo booms run out fore and aft from short king posts set either side of the mainmast, their ends resting on the seabed below.

All the hatch cover beams for Hold No's 4 & 5 are missing. Hold No 4 is largely empty whilst in Hold No 5 there are just a few scattered 55-gallon gasoline drums and aircraft wings lying around along with about 25 3-4-ft long artillery shell casings, which lie jumbled about in the lower tween decks space.

There is much evidence of wartime damage around Hold No 5, where the fatal 1,000-lb bomb hit went in. The bulkhead to Hold 4 has been blown out – whilst at the aft bulkhead of Hold No 5, the forward part of the poop island is damaged - as is the aft part of the hatch coaming. There is a 10-foot-wide tear in the starboard side of the hull and a section of hull bulges outwards. The bomb hit here this is what likely blew off the hatch cover beams in Hold No 5. At the very stern there is a substantial ripple in the poop deck from the effects of the bomb hit.

Two field artillery guns were formerly set either side of the poop deck on carriage mounts, with the wheels removed. There is little trace of them easily visible today but the mount for the lower gun is still on the wreck, although the gun itself has fallen to lie on the seabed beneath. Boxes of ready use shells for the guns – once stowed at the base of the guns, have fallen to the seabed.

On top of the poop island there is a central raised skylight with a pitched roof. The hatch or glass is long gone and now allows access below into the steering flat where the steering gear is located.

The fantail is still intact, tapering to a narrow cruiser stern. Her rudder lies almost flat on the seabed with her single 4-bladed screw still in place.

24. *Nagano Maru*
Passenger-Cargo vessel (1917)
IJA *Rikugun Yusosen* transport (1937)
IJN & IJA Auxiliary transport (1941)
U.S. Recognition Code: 24 MFM

Fourth Fleet Anchorage

Tonnage:	3,824 grt
Dimensions:	345-ft long; beam of 50-ft; draught of 29-ft
Launched:	25 April 1917
Sunk:	17 February 1944
Cause of loss:	Bombed by TF 58 aircraft during Operation HAILSTONE
Wreck location:	Fourth Fleet Anchorage, east of Dublon Island
Depth to seabed:	62 metres
Least Depth:	47 metres – bridge superstructure & fo'c'sle
	50+ metres – weather deck average

The 3,824grt *Nagano Maru* was laid down on 12 October 1916 as a classic three-island passenger cargo vessel with composite superstructure amidships, by Mitsubishi Dockyard in Nagasaki for the famous Tokyo based shipping line Nippon Yusen Kisen Kaisha (NYK).

The 3,824grt passenger cargo ship *Nagano Maru* was launched in 1917. This old ship was requisitioned by both IJA and IJN in 1941and sunk during Operation HAILSTONE in 1944.

During the first half of the 20th century, the majority of Japanese ships, tankers and liners sailed under the NYK flag. From 1924 onwards, all new NYK cargo ships were motor ships – however the *Nagano Maru* was constructed before that change, and so was fitted with the older traditional coal driven 3-cylinder triple expansion engine.

Nagano Maru was constructed with two decks, a raised fo'c'sle at the bow, and a poop island at the stern that held the steering gear below. The foredeck and after deck, flanking either side of the composite superstructure each held two large cargo holds. The composite superstructure held the navigating bridge and officer accommodation - with the boiler

218

The plumb stem of *Nagano Maru* – iconic of the era she was built.

and engine rooms abaft and below. Passenger cabins lined along either side of the engine casing to port and starboard. The tall smokestack of a coal burning vessel rose up immediately abaft the bridge.

Nagano Maru was fitted with a single screw, which gave her a service speed of 10 knots and a maximum speed of 13.5 knots. She had an operating radius of 11,000 nautical miles.

The steamer *Nagano Maru* was named and launched for fitting out afloat on 25 April 1917. The ship was completed by 21 May 1917, when she was delivered to her new civilian owners, NYK, and began a long sea career.

Nagano Maru was already a 20-year-old ship when, on 12 September 1937, she was requisitioned by the Imperial Japanese Army and converted to a troop transport to carry troops to China for the 2nd Sino Japanese War, the full-scale invasion of China by Japan triggered by the Marco Polo Bridge Incident on 7 July 1937. She was released back to the NYK Line on 12 December 1937.

In the run up to war in the Pacific, she was briefly requisitioned by the IJN on 16 June 1941 but released three months later on 10 September 1941. She was requisitioned once again by the IJA the following month in October 1941, just two months before the Pearl Harbor raid, for service as a *Rikugun Yusosen*, an armed IJA transport. She was fitted with two deck guns and several AA machine guns on her Boat Deck.

WWII would be devastating for the NYK Line, whose fine ships were heavily utilised as military transport and hospital ships for both the IJA and IJN. So comprehensive was Japan's defeat, that only 37 NYK ships would survive the war. Although at war's end, the Allies confiscated all surviving NYK vessels and equipment by way of reparations, by the 1950's, NYK ships were again starting to be seen around the world. As the demand for passenger services diminished in the 1960's, the NYK line expanded its commercial cargo operations and today, the NYK Line is one of the largest shipping companies in the world.

Four months into the war, the IJA transport vessel *Nagano Maru* departed Lingayen (north Luzon) on 5 April 1942, carrying troops in a large escorted convoy for the invasion of Cebu, in the central Visayas group of the Philippines. The convoy arrived at Cebu on 10 April and the troops aboard *Nagano Maru* were disembarked. On 15 April 1942, whilst still at Cebu, she was damaged by bombs during an Allied air attack. Despite this, she was still able to depart Cebu on 26 April 1942 in a southbound escorted convoy for the invasion of Mindanao, the second largest island in the Philippines after Luzon. Mindanao was secured on 9 May 1942 and *Nagano Maru* moved to Mako and then returned to the port of Mutsure in Japan.

After participating in a number of convoys during 1943 to distant Japanese holdings such as Rabaul, Palau and New Guinea, on 2 September 1943, *Nagano Maru* arrived in convoy at Wewak, which was home to the largest Japanese airbase in mainland New Guinea and was being repeatedly bombed by Australian and American forces. After anchoring offshore on her arrival on 2 September 1943, she was lightly damaged during an attack by some 30 Allied B-25 Mitchell medium bombers, escorted by P-38 Lightning fighters. Several ships of the convoy were sunk and others damaged. The convoy departed the same day – but *Nagano Maru* remained behind.

Two days later, on 4 September 1943, *Nagano Maru* was again bombed, and this time was rendered unnavigable. The oiler *Kyoei Maru No.2* took her in tow for 200 miles north west along the New Guinea coast to Hollandia (now Jayapura) for repair. A month after her arrival at Hollandia she was able to depart Hollandia in a small convoy for Palau on 7 October 1943.

By the beginning of January 1944, *Nagano Maru* was in Truk. She made a short return run with supplies southeast to Satawan Atoll in the south of the Mortlock Islands of present-day Micronesia. In early February 1944, she set off south east again from Truk with supplies bound for another island airfield garrison at Morotok (today called the Nomoi Islands), located about 160 nautical miles southeast of Truk and to the northwest of the Mortlock Islands. Once her supplies were off-loaded, she returned to Truk and anchored in the Fourth Fleet Anchorage to the east of Dublon Island.

At dawn on the morning of 17 February 1944, lookouts aboard *Nagano Maru* spotted the Hellcats of the initial fighter sweep and AA gunners aboard *Nagano Maru* engaged the Hellcats with their AA machine guns. *Nagano Maru* was strafed in the first group strike by torpedo planes from *Essex* and then subsequently hit by two 500-lb bombs with several near misses.

The bomb hits started fires in Hold No's 1 & 3, whilst the near misses had sprung leaks in her shell plating. On fire, she began to settle into the water. By about 0900, the position was so severe that her crew were forced to abandon her as the fires ran out of control. By noon she was gone.

The wreck was located by the Cousteau expedition in 1969.

The Wreck today

Today the wreck of the *Nagano Maru* lies in the centre of the Fourth Fleet Anchorage east of Dublon Island. The wreck sits upright on her keel with a slight list of about 20° to port in about 62 metres of water on a gentle underwater slope. The least depth to top of bridge and fo'c'sle deck is 47 metres with the well deck at over 50 metres – so this wreck is right at the very limit of air diving and is a wreck more suited to today's technical divers.

The wreck leaked a slick of oil from 1944 onwards – and although the rate of escape of fuel diminished in the 1990's, from time to time there is still a noticeable smell of fuel above the wreck. The bell was recovered some time ago confirming the identity of this wreck - it is believed to be on display in Hawaii.

At the bow, the impressive plumb stem, iconic of the era of her construction, drops vertically down to the seabed far below. On the fo'c'sle deck, her two anchor chains run out from the chain locker far below via spurling pipes to the anchor windlass - before disappearing out through hawse pipes on either side of the deck. The starboard anchor was run out at the time of sinking and a pile of anchor chain rests on the seabed beneath the hawse pipe.

The fo'c'sle deck gun platform has toppled over so that the gun itself lies on the fo'c'sle deck covered in coral. Fixed steps lead down from the fo'c'sle deck to the well deck where open

The wreck of *Nagano Maru*
Least depth: 47m (bridge)
Depth to seabed: 62m

Lifeboat davits swung out
Poop deckhouse
Engine Room roof skylights
Collapsed smokestack
Anchor windlass
Three large cooking cauldrons
Mainmast fallen to port
Toppled bow gun
Jumbo boom
Foremast fallen to port

Artist's impression of the wreck of *Nagano Maru*, which was hit by two 500-lb bombs by SBDs during Operation HAILSTONE that started fierce fires. Holed and swept by fire she sank and settled upright on the bottom of the lagoon in about 62 metres of water.

doors in the fo'c'sle bulkhead lead into the fo'c'sle spaces. Shell casings fired during the attack are scattered around, whilst rotted guard rails ring around the fo'c'sle deck.

On the well deck, the open hatch for Hold No 1 is found, where a fierce fire had raged during the attack. Several of the hatch cover beams remain, but most are missing. The silty hold contains many 55-gallon fuel drums standing on their ends – and larger torpedo bodies laid horizontally.

The foremast was located in between the hatches for Hold's 1 & 2 and has short king posts one on either side. The foremast has broken off six feet from its base and now lies directly to port extending out over the bulwark. A jumbo cargo boom used for heavy lifts, and perhaps originally secured upright to the foremast, has also fallen to lie out over the port side.

Descending into Hold No 2 through the hatch cover beams, in the tween deck space at a depth of about 57 metres, up against port side of the ship in the aft part of the hold, is a Nissan flatbed truck in good condition. The bodywork and most windows are in place. A tracked bulldozer sits nearby. A second truck, a trailer and a diesel roller can also be found at the bottom of this hold in about 62 metres of water.

On the starboard side of the weather deck, a deck cargo of trucks can also be found. Steps lead up from the weather deck to the shelter deck where walkways run down either side of the composite superstructure to the aft part of the ship.

The bridge superstructure has a least depth of about 45 metres to its top. The wooden topmost structures, the bridge wings etc, are all largely gone, and all wood decking of the bridge has rotted or been burnt away to reveal the lattice work of the steel structure. Some of the structural horizontal steel beams have sagged – perhaps evidence of the heat of the fire here.

On top of the bridge superstructure, an engine order telegraph lies fallen on its side and now in free open water. It is held by its chains that link to the repeater in the engine room. The telemotor with rudder direction indicator pedestal lies on its side in the deck below - fallen through the floor of the bridge from above. The wooden spokes of the helm have rotted or been burnt away - and the circular bronze helm band, to which the spokes (located in their notches on the central axle of the helm) were screwed, lies nearby.

In between the navigation bridge and engine room sections of this composite superstructure, a hatch opens down into a small bunker hold for coal; there is a small superimposed deckhouse nearby. Forced draft mushroom ventilators are dotted about – designed to draw air down to the engine room as the vessel was under way.

A narrow deckhouse, above the boiler room, connects the back of the bridge superstructure to the engine room superstructure, which opens out to the full beam of the ship and had the boat deck on top with lifeboats swung in davits. Covered walkways run down either side of this composite superstructure, fore and aft. All wooden decking is gone now to reveal the skeletal structure.

At a depth of about 48 metres, the tall narrow smokestack, characteristic of coal burning ships, has fallen over to port immediately forward of the pitched roof of the engine room, and now is angled almost vertically down the port side of the amidships deckhouse.

Further aft, the aftmost skylight on the starboard side of the engine room roof is open and allows access down into the cavernous engine room, which drops down through several deck levels. The cylinder tops of the triple expansion steam engine, at a general depth of about 55 metres, dominate the space - they are surrounded by catwalk gratings. Dropping down further through stairwells to the deck below you will be in about 60 metres or more. The large crank-shaft can be located here at the bottom of this space, connected to the prop shaft that runs aft and then through its prop shaft tunnel at the bottom of Holds 3 & 4 to the propeller at the stern. The engine room walls are covered in pipework and gauges - with repeaters linked by chains to the engine order bridge telegraphs. All the metal work in here is heavily blackened by fire.

Passenger cabins ran along either side of the superstructure, at a depth of about 55 metres. Situated on either side of the fireproof engine casing, in wartime they would have likely served as officer's cabins, with the crew bunking in the more uncomfortable fo'c'sle and poop island. The fire however has consumed the roofing and internal walls of these rooms to reveal the latticework of the structure and leave a single large open void filled with individual cabin sinks, light switches, cabling and portholes.

Continuing to move aft and exiting the composite superstructure, you move onto the after well deck, at a depth of about 50 metres. Here are the hatches for Holds 3 & 4 - separated by the mainmast, which, like the foremast, has also fallen to port. The severed main mast is flanked by a short kingpost on either side and has cargo winches situated two forward and two aft at its base.

The hatch cover beams for Hold No 3 are all missing, bar one – a few of them lie haphazardly about in the bottom of the hold. One 500-lb bomb hit near here and started a

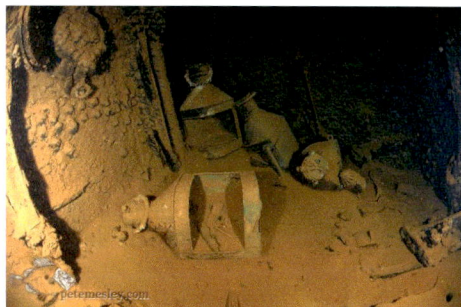

Left: Nissan truck in Hold No 2 of *Nagano Maru* (Courtesy Pete Mesley)

Right: *Nagano Maru* Lamp Room. (Courtesy Pete Mesley)

fierce fire – the blast perhaps displacing them and allowing them to tumble down. Although the hold is largely empty, there are two large spare propeller blades secured to the forward bulkhead of the tween deck. Back up on the port side of the weather deck there are three large circular vessels, that look like cooking vats, neatly lined up fore and aft.

Hold No 4 has several hatch cover beams still in place – and contains a large number of 55-gallon fuel drums, both at the bottom of the hold, at a depth of about 60 metres, and in the tween deck above. These were likely full when the ship sunk - as they did not float out of the hold, and they have retained their shape and not been crushed if empty by the pressure change from the surface.

From time to time, small droplets of oil escape from these drums and rise to the surface, no doubt being the reason for the old oil slick and smell of oil above the wreck. There are many shell casings strewn about the weather deck here – and in the tween deck space there are more loose shells and wooden boxes, each holding four 6-inch shells, whilst other wooden boxes hold clips of small arms ammunition.

The poop island deckhouse at the stern holds an auxiliary steering platform on top of it with a rudder direction indicator and helm, which stands almost directly above the rudder. Just abaft the rudder stand is a steering engine with port/starboard steering chains leading to a steering quadrant geared to the engine for direct turning of the rudder below.

25. *Nippo Maru*
Passenger-cargo vessel (1936)
IJN *Tokusetsu Unsosen Kyusuisen* water transport and auxiliary distilling ship (1941)
U.S. Recognition Code: 23A MKFM

Fourth Fleet Anchorage

Tonnage:	3,764 grt
Dimensions:	353.6-ft long; beam of 50-ft; draught of 27.9-ft
Launched:	16 September 1936
Sunk:	18 February 1944
Cause of loss:	Bombed by TF 58 aircraft during Operation HAILSTONE
Wreck location:	Fourth Fleet Anchorage, east of Tonoas Island
Depth to seabed:	45-50 metres
Least Depth:	24 metres – bridge superstructure

The 3,764 grt passenger cargo vessel *Nippo Maru* was laid down on 14 April 1936 by the Kawasaki Dockyard Co. Ltd in Kobe for the Kobe based Okazaki Honten Steamship Co (who named all their ships with the letter "N"). She was a similar design to the *Momokawa*, *Kikukawa, Kirikawa, Matukawa, Toei* and *Toho Maru's* – the first two of which were also sunk at Truk.

Nippo Maru was a classic 3-island steamship with a raised fo'c'sle, two holds in her forward well deck and a third foredeck hold situated in the extended section of the main superstructure in front of the bridge. Her composite superstructure held the bridge forward with her smokestack immediately abaft, above her boiler room and the engine room and machinery spaces. Passenger cabins ran along either side of the engine casing, opening onto a covered walkway outboard that ran the full length of the superstructure. Her after well deck held two further holds before the poop island, which held her steering gear below. She carried a cruiser stern.

Nippo Maru was fitted with two coal-fired double reduction steam

The 3,764grt passenger cargo ship *Nippo Maru* was launched in 1936. She was requisitioned by the IJN in 1944 as a water transport and auxiliary distilling ship. She was bombed and sunk during Operation HAILSTONE in 1944.

turbines, manufactured by the Kawasaki Dockyard, that were geared to a single shaft. This arrangement gave her a service speed of 12-14 knots and a maximum speed of 14-16 knots. She could carry 1,000 tons of coal in her bunkers - giving a range of about 10,000 miles at 12 knots.

After being named and launched for fitting out afloat on 16 September 1936, she was completed on 10 November 1936 and delivered to her new owners. She was registered at Kobe and was initially chartered to Osaka Shosen K.K. (OSK) in December 1936. In 1938, with the 2nd Sino Japanese war raging following the Japanese invasion of China, she was requisitioned by the IJA as a *Rikugun Yusosen* army transport. She was released back to her owners the following year in 1939.

On 24 August 1941, just a few months before the surprise raid on Pearl Harbor, she was requisitioned by the IJN and fitted out in Nagasaki as a *Tokusetsu Unsosen Kyusuisen* auxiliary water tanker *Otsu* category. As with *Ippan Choyosen* General Requisitioned Ships, there were two categories of *Kyusuisen*: 'Ko' which had an IJN Captain aboard and 'Otsu' which had no naval captain. *Nippo Maru* would be one of nine such *Kyusuisen* requisitioned by the IJN between 1937 and 1945 to transport fresh water.

Nippo Maru was registered to the Sasebo Naval District - and her conversion works at Nagasaki took just two months, being quickly completed by 31 October 1941, when she was attached to the Mako Guard District.

With the outbreak of war in the Pacific on 7 December 1941, *Nippo Maru* began making frequent short runs from Mako to Takao and Kirun, in Taiwan. Six months later, she was attached on 15 May 1942 to the Fourth Fleet based at Truk. Now that she would be operating in a forward area, she was fitted with a single Type 92 7.7mm machine gun and five Type 38 Ariska rifles were boarded. These bolt action IJA service rifles fired a 6.5mm round but had proved to be underpowered, with a number of serious shortcomings such as bursting charges, common misfires and jams that had led to a further generation of rifles being introduced to the IJA in 1939.

Towards the end of May 1942, *Nippo Maru* departed Mako for Truk. She loaded fresh water en route in Palau and arrived at Truk in the first week of June 1942. At about this time she was scheduled to be fitted with an 8cm/40-cal deck gun on a bandstand platform atop her foc'sle.

During the remainder of 1942 and 1943 she was engaged resupplying far flung Japanese forward garrisons such as Truk, Saipan, Ponape and Kwajalein. Vessels requiring fresh water or water for boilers would come alongside her for replenishment. Whilst at Truk, on 25 December 1942 she undertook a salvage operation with the submarine rescue ship *Mie Maru* to refloat the submarine I-33, which had accidentally sunk there on 26 September 1942. I-33 had been tied up alongside the 6th Fleet Repair Ship *Urakami Maru* (a present-day Palau wreck) with her stern moored to a wharf on Dublon. Whilst attempting repairs to a torpedo tube, by raising her bow, the submarine's buoyancy was fatally compromised. She flooded, snapped the hawser to the wharf - and sank within two minutes with the loss of 33 crew. *Mie Maru* and *Nippo Maru* successfully refloated I-33 on 29 December 1942 – and just over two months later, on 2 March 1943, *Nippo Maru* departed Truk under escort for Japan towing

I-33. The tow reached Saeki, Japan safely on 18 March 1943 where repair works started on I-33 at the Kure Naval Arsenal. The repair work was completed on 1 June 1944, and on 13 June 1943, I-33 began a series of dives for her acceptance trials, during which she would again sink: this time with the loss of 102 crew.

Nippo Maru once again returned to Truk, from where she made several passages to Ponape and Kwajalein in convoys carrying troops throughout the latter part of 1943.

On 24 January 1944, *Nippo Maru* set off from Truk in a convoy bound for Eniwetok Atoll in the Marshall Islands, carrying Navy Construction Unit personnel and civilian workers. The convoy, which was escorted by the destroyer *Suzukaze* and subchaser CH-33, was attacked two days later by the American submarine *Skipjack* (SS-184), which fired four torpedoes. Two torpedoes hit the destroyer *Suzukaze*, which sank quickly. The subchaser CH-33 began a search for the American submarine - and as *Skipjack* was forced to take evasive manoeuvres, *Nippo Maru* and the other convoy vessels cleared the area. *Skipjack* however didn't give up the fight and after avoiding CH-33, she tracked the convoy for two more days before successfully torpedoing the large IJN transport *Okitsu Maru*, which sank with the loss of 169 Navy Construction Unit personnel and several crew.

On 10 February 1944, just a week before the Operation HAILSTONE raids, *Nippo Maru* arrived at Truk with war supplies in a convoy from Ponape. In *Nippo Maru*'s Hold No 1 were stacked hemispherical anti-invasion beach mines, boxes of ammunition and field kitchen supplies. Hold No 2 held hundreds of shells and her large rectangular metal water tanks at the bottom. Up on her foredeck she carried a deck cargo of Type 95 Ha-Go light tanks and trucks.

A deck cargo of howitzer type field guns and larger artillery barrels were secured on her after well deck. The pedestal mounts, and recoil breaches for these artillery pieces were stowed in Hold No 5 alongside large squat circular base foundations - to which the pedestal for the artillery weapons would be mounted. These circular base foundations would be embedded in steel reinforced-concrete, in pits, as a secure base for the gun mounts. In amongst all this heavy-duty weaponry were the smaller essentials for the combat soldier such as bottles, gas masks and mess kits,

A week after arriving at Truk, on the first day of Operation HAILSTONE, 17 February 1944, *Nippo Maru* was anchored with her port anchor at the north of the Fourth Fleet Anchorage, east of Dublon Island as the initial fighter sweep Hellcats swept in over the lagoon. Strike 1A from TG 58.1 *Enterprise* and *Yorktown*, Strike 2A from TG 58.2 *Essex* and *Intrepid* and Strike 3A from TG 58.3 *Bunker Hill* would follow for the first bombing strikes of the day.

Aboard *Essex*, 35 planes launched in about 20 minutes beginning at 0514. Ten Hellcats, nine TBF Avengers and 17 SBD Dauntless dive bombers carrying 500-lb or 1,000-lb bombs roared off the flight deck into the wind - with a time at target assigned for 0630-0645 (local).

As the *Essex* flight arrived over Truk, little enemy fighter activity was encountered – the initial fighter sweep had cleared the skies in the area of operation allocated. The bombers went to work attacking ships in the Fourth Fleet anchorage east of Eten Island, where many transport ships were clustered. The TBF's attacked *Nippo Maru* and at about 0700 scored three hits with 500-lb bombs in the mid and aft sections of the ship, causing much damage and starting fires. One bomb was a direct hit in the bunker coal hold. The *Essex* planes departed the scene without observing if *Nippo Maru* had sunk.

Some two hours later, as the planes of Strike 2B attacked *Aikoku Maru*, which had been anchored just to the south of *Nippo Maru*, *Nippo Maru* was not present. Whilst in the past it had been assumed that *Nippo Maru* had simply sunk quickly before *Aikoku Maru* was attacked, research narrated in www.Combinedfleet.com suggests that she attempted to proceed to the harbour but later that day at 1800 was ordered to return to her anchorage - that might explain why she was not present when *Aikoku Maru* was attacked. It is narrated in combinedfleet.com that *Nippo Maru* received another hit in her engine that night (presumably during the night radar guided attack on ships in the Fourth Fleet anchorage) and that she sank at 0310 with no casualties.

As she sank into the waters of the lagoon, she landed partly on the shelving edge of an underwater sand bank. Her massive weight caused the slope to yield before her - and she slid down the slope for a short distance, her keel carving out a large V in the seabed of the underwater hill.

The slope soon bottomed out and there she came to rest on her keel, with a list to port and her bow skewed slightly upwards at the stem. The sand and debris she had dislodged during her passage down the side of the sand bank, followed on down the hill behind her and partly engulfed her port quarter.

The Wreck today

Today the wreck of the passenger cargo vessel *Nippo Maru* lies upright in 45-50 metres of water with a pronounced list to port. The least depth to the wreck is 24 metres to the top of the bridge superstructure, which is where the surface buoy and downline is usually attached. Divers can explore the deeper sections of the wreck first, perhaps dropping deeper into the holds to examine her cargo, before returning to the shallower bridge superstructure to gently ascend and burn off part of any decompression obligation exploring the photogenic bridge superstructure.

At the bow, the base of the stem sits off the seabed – this is a result of the manner in which she came to rest after slithering down the underwater slope. The port anchor is run out to the seabed whilst the starboard anchor is held tight in its hawse. Both chains run back to the anchor windlass on the fo'c'sle deck - from which they descend through their spurling pipes down to the chain locker deep below the fo'c'sle. Immediately behind the windlass is the circular skeletal framework of the forward 8cm gun platform – the gun itself is now missing. Rotted guardrails ring around the top of the fo'c'sle deck – all now heavily encrusted with coral.

Moving aft from the fo'c'sle deck, there is a drop down to the well deck and the foredeck cargo holds. Open doors in the fo'c'sle bulkhead lead into the spaces where crew formerly were billeted.

Hold No 1 has only one hatch cover beam left in place along with a big H-beam seemingly thrown there to now straddle the coaming, athwartships. On the port side of the deck, the skeleton of a truck, easily recognisable from its tyres, frame and transmission, lies half over the side of the wreck. It has been dislodged and then swept away from its storage position

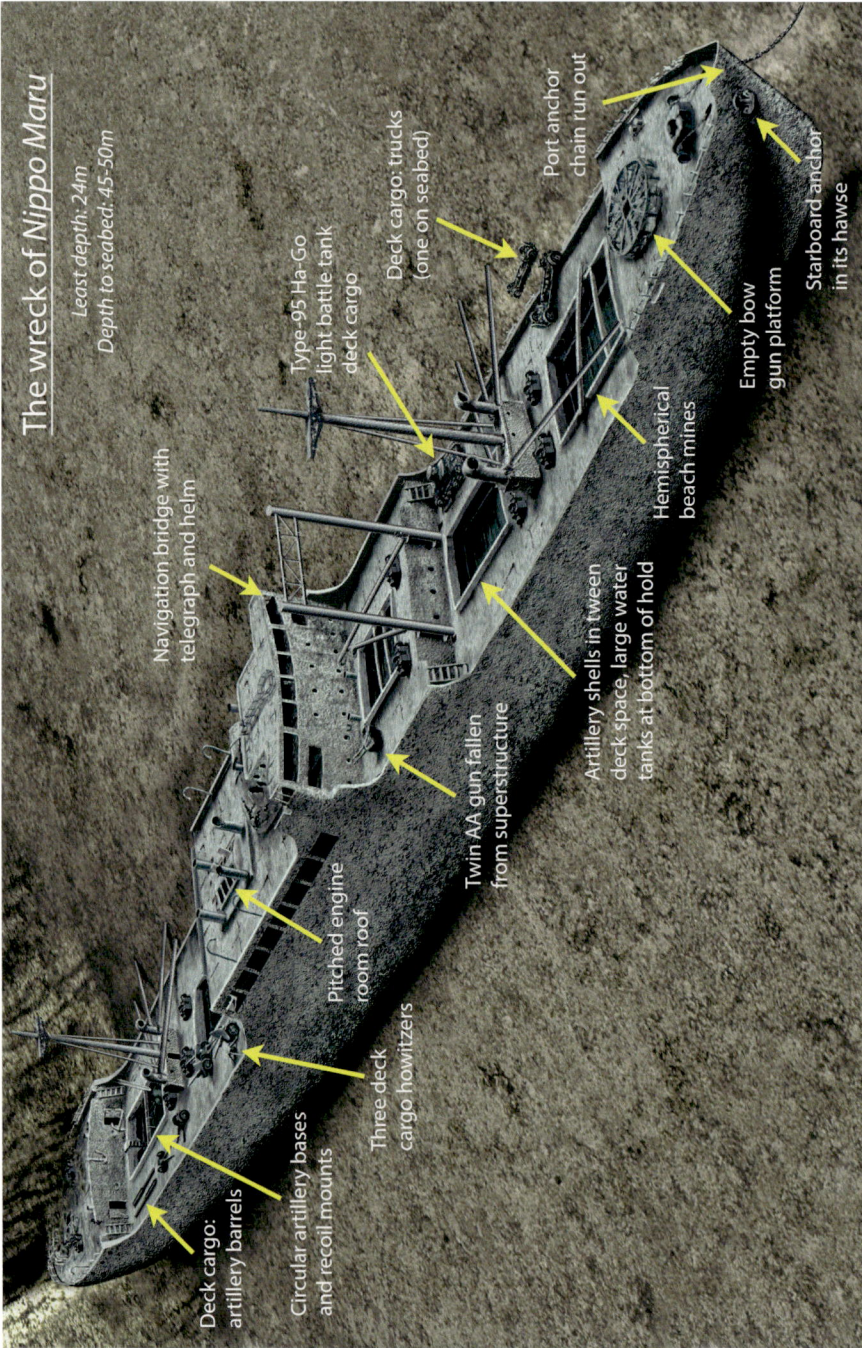

The wreck of Nippo Maru

Least depth: 24m
Depth to seabed: 45-50m

Navigation bridge with telegraph and helm

Type 95 Ha-Go light battle tank deck cargo

Deck cargo: trucks (one on seabed)

Port anchor chain run out

Starboard anchor in its hawse

Empty bow gun platform

Hemispherical beach mines

Artillery shells in tween deck space, large water tanks at bottom of hold

Twin AA gun fallen from superstructure

Pitched engine room roof

Three deck cargo howitzers

Circular artillery bases and recoil mounts

Deck cargo: artillery barrels

Artist's impression of the wreck of the *Nippo Maru*, which today rests upright in 45-50 metres of water and still has her deck cargo of howitzers adjacent her aft Holds and a Type 95 Ha-Go light tank on the port side forward of the bridge superstructure.

The wreck of *Nippo Maru* has a slight list to port. Her port chain is run out whilst the starboard anchor is held in its hawse. (Courtesy Ewan Rowell)

Looking into the command bridge of *Nippo Maru* from the starboard side – the bow of the ship is off to the right of shot. Helm telemotor, with engine order telegraph beside and forward of it. (Courtesy Ewan Rowell)

Looking forward inside the bridge of *Nippo Maru*. The helm telemotor is in centre with an engine order telegraph to right. The glass of the rectangular windows is long gone. The goalpost kingposts are visible in the distance. (Courtesy Ewan Rowell)

as the ship sank. Another similar truck lies on the seabed to port nearby - presumably these trucks were stowed as deck cargo one either side of Hold No 1 before the ship went down.

In between the hatches for Hold No's 1 & 2 there is a small masthouse with cargo handling winches set fore and aft on either side. The foremast rises from the mast house and still has its inverted crosstree in place. Forced draft mushroom ventilators stand either side of the foremast. Standing rigging, heavily encrusted with coral, runs up from the mast house to meet the foremast at the crosstree.

Two cargo booms ran from short kingposts at the base of the foremast, forward over Hold No 1 - whilst two other booms ran aft across Hold No 2. All bar the forward starboard boom, have swung over to port as the ship listed on the surface and dropped towards the seabed below.

Dropping into Hold 1, divers will find boxes of ammunition, mess kits and field kitchen supplies and a single hatch cover beam fallen to the bottom. There are also a number of hemispherical Type JE Anti-boat land mines – each with two handles welded on top. These anti-boat land mines were destined to be deployed on beaches thought likely to be assaulted

Nippo Maru bow detail – the Type 95 Ha-Go tank can be seen as deck cargo on the port side adjacent Hold No 2. A truck can be seen half over the port gunwale at Hold No 1 and another truck rests on the seabed. The starboard anchor is held in its hawse whilst the port anchor is run out.

by the Allies - and are the same mines as found in Hold No 1 of the deeper *San Francisco Maru*. The all-welded mine was about 2-feet in diameter and about 1-foot in height and had an explosive charge of about 46.5-lbs of TNT.

The IJA had ample time to construct strong defensive installations on islands likely to be invaded and used Type JE anti-boat and anti-vehicle double-horn hemisphere mines as seen in this hold in great numbers on likely invasion beaches. They were not deployed inland in mine fields.

The detonators of these anti-boat mines consisted of two lead-alloy horns, each containing a vial of acid. When either horn is bent or crushed, the acid vial is broken. The acid then contacts battery plates and generates a current which detonates the mine. Boxes of detonators lie at the bottom of Hold No 1. Do not interfere with them in any manner as they are still dangerous.

The Japanese used this type of hemispherical anti-boat mine in several ways. Usually, the mines were set in the sand so that they would detonate when pressure was put upon trip wires connected to the detonating horns. At the Battle of Tarawa, which began with amphibious landings on 20 November 1943, these mines were encountered deployed in shallow water offshore between posts and anti-boat obstacles. Trip wires were strung from the horns to the top of each adjoining obstacle.

During the subsequent amphibious landing on Tinian Island on 24 July 1944, just a few months after Operation HAILSTONE, hemisphere mines were found buried on the beach between the high and low water marks where they would be a hazard to LVT's and Higgins landing boats beaching at high tide. These mines would also take their toll of landing troops wading ashore from boats at low tide, as several would be connected by trip wires strung between the horns, allowing them to serve as anti-personnel as well as anti-vehicle mines.

A large number of these hemisphere mines have been lifted over the years from several Truk wrecks by local divers, who have successfully extracted the TNT explosive for use in dynamite fishing. Hold No 1 is now largely empty, but at the bottom are artillery shells for the 8cm bow gun and 55-gallon drums of AvGas.

The tween deck space of Hold No 2 still contains a large number of artillery shells. The bottom level of the Hold is dominated by at least four large rectangular water tanks – relics of the ship's role as auxiliary water transport. The tanks are about 7-metres long by 3-metres wide and look as though they were half filled when the ship sank - as they show evidence of hydrostatic compression.

On the port side of the well deck, in front of the shelter deck bulkhead, sits a single Japanese Type 95 Ha-Go light tank. These small manoeuvrable tanks were used for infantry support and being lightly armed and armoured were not designed to fight other tanks. The main weakness of the tank was its 12mm face hardened armour, which was only good against 7.7mm small arms rounds. This had been adequate in the Sino-Japanese war in the 1930's but the tanks were outdated by the Pacific war when their vulnerabilities would be exposed – they could be taken out by a bazooka or tank round.

The Type 95 Ha Go performed well in in the invasion of Malaya where the wet jungle terrain was little obstacle and Type 95's were important in the eventual Fall of Singapore.

Paul Haynes hangs beside the deck cargo Type 95 Ha-Go tank on the port side adjacent Hold No 2 (Courtesy Ewan Rowell)

However, by late 1942, the Type 95's were coming up against Allied tanks and it was discovered that its main weapon, the Type 98 37mm (1.45") gun could not penetrate the armour of Allied medium tanks. The Type 95 Ha Go also had an air cooled 110hp diesel engine, the air intakes for which on the back of the tank were also susceptible to a determined attack by an infantryman with a grenade.

The Type 95 carried a crew of three men; a commander/gunner, a gunner who was also the driver and a hull gunner/mechanic. Only the commander was seated – he was housed in the cramped, hand-operated turret and so was responsible for loading, aiming and firing the main gun. The barrel of Type 98 37mm main gun was removable for transport and replacement, and two types of shell, both high-explosive and armour piercing, were carried. Secondary armament consisted of two 7.7mm Type 97 light machine guns, one mounted in the hull and the other in the turret. There are similar Type 95 Ha Go tanks being carried as deck cargo on the foredeck of the *San Francisco Maru*.

The Type 98 37mm gun barrel on the Type 95 Ha Go deck cargo tank on this wreck is not apparent - and was most likely removed and stowed for transit inside the tank, which is now well sealed over by encrusting coral. This particular tank had been suggested as a Type 97 - however the Type 95 has four road wheels (and two bogie wheels) inside the track, as with the tank on this wreck, whereas the larger Type 97 medium tank had six road wheels and two bogie wheels.

Moving aft, the forward well deck rises up to the extended section of shelter deck superstructure in front of the bridge superstructure – where the hatch for Hold No 3 is located. A goalpost pair of kingposts is set on the leading edge of this extended superstructure - with a horizontal bracing bridge connecting the two kingposts tops. The port cargo boom runs back from the kingpost to sit in its cradle on the front of the bridge superstructure. The starboard boom has come out of its cradle, with the roll of the ship to port, and now lies diagonally across the hatch for Hold No 3.

The tween deck spaces of Hold No's 2 & 3 are connected - and four 4-foot long bronze rangefinders sit amidst bottles, mess kits, gas masks and other smaller cargo items. On the starboard side of the hatch for Hold No 3, a twin 7.7mm machine gun (MG) mount lies on its side - likely fallen from atop the bridge superstructure. The two barrels point aft towards the front of the bridge. Two such twin 7.7mm AA MG's were originally mounted on top of the bridge superstructure - the other 7.7mm MG gun lies on the seabed upside down with its barrels buried in the sand off the port side of the ship.

Nippo Maru aft ship detail – deck cargo howitzers adjacent Hold No 3. Artillery barells on starboard side adjacent Hold No 4. The underwater hill has engulfed the port quarter.

The bridge superstructure rises up three deck levels above the extended superstructure shelter deck. The bottom level of the frontage is studded with a row of portholes – all still with the glass in place. The middle deck level, just above, also has a row of portholes in the middle with, at either side, large rectangular openings to walkways that lead aft to the boat deck, abaft the bridge. The top deck level of this superstructure has large rectangular windows along its full frontage, through which it is possible to enter the command bridge – which still has its original teak deck planking visible, even after all these years submerged. Here in the bridge, a twin-handle engine order telegraph still stands *in situ* bolted to the floor with the telemotor for the helm just behind it. The main central room of the bridge tapers on either side to narrow wings that have doors opening aft.

On top of the bridge superstructure a guardrail gangway allowed officers and men to move forward into a larger circular railed enclosure, which perhaps would have been used for a small arms weapons, a searchlight or simply for observation. The starboard side green lensed copper and brass navigation lantern is still in place.

Moving further aft on top of the composite superstructure, the Boat Deck has its empty lifeboat davits in the swung in position at either side. This could be seen as evidence that the ship sank quickly with the crew not having time to swing out and lower the lifeboats as the ship sank. There were however no casualties from her sinking - so perhaps the lifeboats here were destroyed in the various fires that were started and hence not launched. The crew could have abandoned ship in another way, by using other boats or by another vessel coming along side to take them off.

The tall smokestack in the centre of the Boat Deck has collapsed to port, the direction of the ship's list. Immediately abaft the crumpled remains of the smokestack is the pitched engine room roof, with its ventilation skylights open. Forced draft mushroom ventilators are studded around the pitched roof.

Deck cargo of howitzers on starboard side of Hold No 3, the amidships composite superstructure is in the distance (Courtesy Ewan Rowell)

Enclosed walkways run down either side of the composite amidships superstructure, off which passenger cabins are set, flanking the engine casing. Each cabin has its own porthole and white sink.

The composite superstructure ends with a drop down to the after well deck where the hatches for Hold No's 4 & 5 are set. On the starboard side of the hatch for Hold No 4 can be found three Type 90 75mm howitzer field guns, which still have their tyres and splinter shields in place - two rest very close together and are iconic images of Truk Lagoon. This 75mm field gun was built in two versions, one with wooden wheels suitable to be pulled behind horses – and the version present on this wreck, which has solid rubber tyres and a stronger suspension suitable to be towed behind motor vehicles. These adaptable field guns could fire a variety of shells, from high explosive (HE) contact shells, to high-speed armour piercing (AP) shells suitable for use against armoured vehicles - as well as shrapnel, incendiary, smoke or illumination shells.

The mainmast still has its inverted crosstree in place and rises out of a small mast house with cargo winches set fore and aft and forced draft mushroom ventilators on top. The four cargo handling booms, which run from its base (originally two forward and two aft), have all swung round to port and their ends have fallen down to the seabed.

Hold No 4 bears witness to one of the 500-lb bombs that sank the ship. The port side of the hull has been opened to the sea beneath the waterline with an approximately 3m diameter

The author heading forward from the poop island over Hold No 4. (Courtesy Ewan Rowell)

Nuwa Paul above the aftmost hold, with circular artillery foundation
mounts and recoil sections beneath. (Courtesy Ewan Rowell)

hole in the shell plating. Water would have rushed inside here and started to roll her over to port. Given this significant wound, I wonder whether this is the hit in the engine room (just forward) reported to have happened during the night of 17/18 February.

Hold No 4 appears largely empty but at tween deck level on the port side is a large pile of hundreds of sake and beer bottles. This cargo has shifted and tumbled to port as she sank. As with Hold No 2, there are a number of large rectangular water tanks sitting fore and aft at the bottom of this hold, some snugly part covered by the tween deck. The tanks are about 7-metres long by 3-metres wide and it is noticeable that there is a space in the middle of the hold on the centre line. The remaining tanks look as though they were half filled when the ship sank - as they show evidence of hydrostatic compression. The late Klaus Lindemann in his authoritative book *Hailstorm over Truk Lagoon* (Pacific Press Publications (1989), p 220, records that one of the tanks floated off the sinking ship and beached slightly south of the reef marker east of Dublon.

Hold No 5 contains at least six large circular artillery foundation mounts, which appear to be sitting at about tween deck level on top of more large water tanks at the bottom of the hold. These circular bases would have been set into steel reinforced concrete in a gun pit and the pedestal on which the gun turned would then be installed in the centre aperture. Recoil sections and breaches for the guns also lie strewn about in the hold - and up on the starboard side can be found a deck cargo of the large artillery barrels themselves.

The poop island is ringed with portholes, most still with their glass in place. On the poop deck there is an anchor windlass, auxiliary steering gear and coiled hawsers. The circular skeletal framework of the empty aft gun platform is half buried in the mass of sand that has cascaded down the underwater slope to engulf the port quarter of the ship.

If you look astern from the fantail on the starboard side, you will see the white sandy slope of the seabed rising up - with the large V in it, carved out by her hull as she slid down the slope.

It is clear that with the large water tanks carried in Hold No's 2, 4 and possibly Hold No 5, that this *Tokusetsu Unsosen Kyusuisen* auxiliary water tanker vessel could carry a substantial amount of water.

26. *Oite*
Kamikaze-class 1st-class *Destroyer No 11* (1924)
Renamed 追風 *(Oite)* - 1 August 1928

North Pass

Displacement:	1,400-tons (N)
	1,720-tons (F)
Dimensions:	336-ft 6" long (oa); beam of 30-ft; draught of 9-ft 7"
Launched:	27 November 1924
Sunk:	18 February 1944
Cause of loss:	Bombed and torpedoed by TF 58 aircraft during Operation HAILSTONE
Name translation of 追風 *(Oite):*	*Fair* or *Favourable Wind*
Wreck location:	Towards North Pass
Depth to seabed:	62 metres
Least Depth:	56 metres

After WWI, Japan developed a new breed of 1st-class destroyer that was a hybrid of traditional British and German designs, the Minekaze-class. To be able to operate in the rough waters of the Pacific, Japanese naval architects altered the British/German design by moving the bridge further aft and placing a well deck in front of it. A high fo'c'sle was designed into the new Minekaze-class, which by being lengthened and given a turtle back, reduced the impact of heavy seas on the bridge. The new Minekaze-class was fitted with geared turbines that replaced the direct drive turbines of earlier

The 1,720-tons (F) Kamikaze-class destroyer *Oite* was launched as Destroyer No 11 in 1924 and carries her identifying '11' amidships. She was assigned as flagship of Destroyer Division 29 (DesDiv 29) and carries her DesDiv identification '29' towards her bow. She is seen here around 1927 in her original configuration with four 12cm (4.7-inch) guns set one on the fo'c'sle, one between her smokestacks and two set one on either side of the mainmast aft.

classes and gave the Minekaze-class destroyers a maximum speed of 39 knots. In all, 36 1st-class destroyers would be completed to the *Minekaze* basic design and until the advent of the Special Type destroyers in 1929 these ships formed the core of the Japanese destroyer force.

The first 15 Minekaze-class destroyers were ordered in the 1917-20 building programs, with the first beginning to enter service in 1920. The second group of nine Minekaze-class destroyers (including *Oite*) was ordered in 1921-22 - and due to improvements and slight differences in design, this second group were eventually designated as a new class of destroyer – the Kamikaze-class – even though the new ships were virtually identical to the last three ships of the first group of the Minekaze-class.

The bridge structure of the Kamikaze-class units was modified from the Minekaze-class with the installation (for the first time in IJN destroyers) of an armoured, fixed steel covering in place of the previous canvas screen. This extra weight, and a larger beam and draught, increased the vessel's displacement and improved sea handling and stability – but reduced the top speed by 2 knots.

Destroyer 11 (*Oite)* was one of this second group of nine destroyers; the order for the last two was subsequently cancelled. Laid down on 16 March 1923 by the Uraga Dock Co Ltd of Tokyo, the hull was launched a year and a half later on 27 November 1924. After fitting out afloat No 11 was completed almost a year later on 30 October 1925.

The Kamikaze-class were twin screw, their two propeller shafts being driven by Parsons geared turbines that were powered by 4 Kampon boilers. They could make 37 knots – fast even by today's standards 100 years later.

Following the naming convention (cf Explanatory Notes) that destroyers were named after oceanic or meteorological phenomena or plants, on 1 August 1928, Destroyer No 11 was renamed 追風, The Romanized equivalent is *Oite*, which means *Fair* or *Favourable Wind* in Japanese – as in *fair wind and a following sea*. She had a range of 3,600 nautical miles at 14 knots and carried a crew of 148.

When she was first built, *Oite*, as with all the Minekaze-class destroyers, was fitted with four 12cm (4.7-inch) DP naval guns in single mounts. One was set on the fo'c'sle, two on the centre-line amidships and one abaft the mainmast. She was also fitted with three twin 21-inch torpedo tube launchers – one twin mount situated in the well deck in front of the bridge and the other two twin mounts set one behind the other on the centerline abaft the aftmost smokestack. She carried two 7.7mm machine guns mounted one either side of the bridge.

By WWII, some fifteen years after *Oite* had been commissioned, the Minekaze-class and Kamikaze -class destroyers were considered old second-line units - more useful as destroyer transports and escorts, rather than front line warships. At the time of construction in 1923/24, the threat to a warship of air attack had been negligible – and her original design was almost completely devoid of any anti-aircraft weaponry with only the two single 7.7mm machine guns for AA defence.

By the onset of WWII however, the threat of air attack had been fully realised and was a major concern for the IJN. Accordingly, in 1941-42, a programme of modernisation of the Kamikaze-class units weapons suites began. *Oite's* four older 12cm (4.7-inch) DP main guns made way for three modern 12cm/45-caliber 11th Year Type naval guns set one on the raised fo'c'sle at the bow, one in the amidships Q position between the smokestacks and the third situated aft on a deckhouse just in front of the mainmast. The 11th Year Type naval gun differed from the earlier 3rd Year Type as it had a horizontal sliding-block breech and fired separate loading cased charges and projectiles - the earliest versions of the older 3rd Year Type had fired a projectile with a separately loaded bagged charge that made gun operations susceptible to water damage on wet decks. The new 12cm naval guns fitted could fire 5-6 20kg (45-lb) projectiles per minute with a range of 16,000 metres. The gun could elevate to +55° and depress to -10°, but with this maximum elevation of 55° it could not function as a true DP gun.

During this 1941/2 modernisation, in addition to the No 4 gun being removed, the after twin torpedo launcher (of three) was also removed to make room for increased AA and ASW weaponry. She now carried two twin 21-inch torpedo launchers – one in the well deck forward of the bridge and the other abaft the aftmost smokestack.

Being now an older unit, her torpedo capability was not upgraded to the 24-inch *Long Lance* torpedo - such as carried by *Fumizuki*, which had two sets of triple 24-inch torpedo launchers. (For a discussion on the development of the *Long Lance* torpedo, cf *Fumizuki*). She carried 18 depth charges that were deployed on two roll-off rail tracks (one either side of the stern) and four Type 81 depth charge projectors.

With her role now being more as destroyer transport or convoy escort vessel, rather than a front-line warship, her AA and ASW weaponry was beefed up. She now bristled with ten Type 96 25mm AA cannons in addition to her two original 7.7mm machine guns. The Type 96 25mm auto cannon was the standard IJN medium AA weapon of WWII with a rate of fire of between 200 and 260 rounds per minute. But it was most effective only at close ranges of less than 1,000 metres with fire at aircraft at a height of more than 1,000 metres, and beyond a range of 2,000 metres, being completely ineffective.

The 25mm Type 96 was a poor weapon in comparison to its Allied counterparts – being hampered by slow training and slow elevation speeds, excessive vibration and muzzle flash. The sights were found to be ineffective against high-speed targets – a critical problem that would be badly exposed as the new fast breeds of American aircraft appeared. Worse, ammunition was fed from a 15-round fixed magazine so that the gun had to cease firing every time the magazine had to be changed. The Type 96 was vastly inferior to the 40mm Bofors used by U.S. vessels which could put out a sustained rate of fire with a constant fire top fed ammunition clip design.

During the first years of WWII, Japanese depth charges were rather light, and they were usually fuzed too shallow by IJN crews who were unaware that the modern American submarines could dive to 300 feet or more. The standard Japanese Type 95 depth charge at the start of WWII carried a 220-lb (100kg) explosive charge. Its fuze had a water inlet that detonated the charge when a certain pressure of water had entered – and there were just two depth settings, 100 feet (30 metres) and 200 feet (60 metres). The deeper setting was well above the diving depth capability of an American submarine. This shallow setting of depth charge fuzes allowed many American submarines to survive depth charging by running deep, as seen in so many post war movies.

The Japanese in fact only discovered that U.S. submarines could dive deeper than they believed from a chance public remark by a U.S. Congressman. Armed with this unfortunate intelligence leak they increased the explosive charge to 324-lb (147kg) and added an additional 300 feet (90 metre) depth setting. The Japanese loaded depth charges on almost every ship that could carry them and made heavy use of depth charge throwers – the typical load on a fleet destroyer such as *Oite* was increased from 18 to 30 depth charges.

Oite was assigned as flagship to the four Kamikaze-class destroyers that made up Destroyer Division 29 (DesDiv 29) of the Fourth Fleet, based at Truk. The four DesDiv 29 units *Oite* and her sisters *Hayate, Asanagi* and *Yunagi* formed part of Destroyer Squadron 6 (DesRon 6), which comprised several DesDiv's to give DesRon 6 a total strength of 12 destroyers.

In the run up to Japan's entry into WWII, in late November 1941, just over one week before the Pearl Harbor raid, DesDiv 29 advanced from Truk to Kwajalein. On 8 December 1941, *Oite* sortied from Kwajalein with the Wake Island invasion force, steaming some 700 miles north to Wake for the invasion scheduled for 11 December 1941. Simultaneous with the Pearl Harbor raid on 7 December, 36 Mitsubishi G3M medium bombers flying from air bases in the Marshall Islands bombed Wake, followed up by another raid the following day designed to degrade U.S. military defences on Wake in preparation for Japanese troop landings.

As the invasion armada approached Wake on 11 December, the U.S. Marine gunners manning their six 5-inch (127mm) coast-defence guns held their fire until the armada had moved well within range. When the lead destroyers had closed to 4,000 yards, the Marines opened up with their 5-inch guns.

Oite was lightly damaged by near misses from accurate U.S. fire, whilst her sister *Hayate* received at least two direct hits to her magazines. She exploded, broke in two and sank within two minutes with the loss of nearly all her crew. The destroyer *Kisaragi* was also sunk with almost all hands when a Wildcat fighter scored a bomb hit on her stern where her depth charges were stationed. USM gunners also claimed to have hit the light cruiser *Yubari*. With two destroyers sunk, the invasion flotilla withdrew without attempting landings, in the first Japanese failure of the war.

A 2nd successful attempt was made to seize Wake on 23 December 1941. Due to the failure of the first attempt, this time a more powerful naval armada took part, including two fleet carriers, two Cruiser Divisions and a large number of destroyer escorts, amongst which was *Oite*, carrying an advance landing party. After a preliminary bombardment, Japanese troops began landing at 0235 and after fighting that lasted through the night, Wake was finally surrendered to the Japanese at midday.

In January 1942, *Oite* was involved in the Operation R invasion of Rabaul, New Britain and then Operation SR, the invasion of Lae/Salamua in March 1942. *Oite* returned to Sasebo Naval Base in April for repairs – and on completion she escorted a convoy from Sasebo to Truk.

Oite was then assigned as part of the Operation MO escort group for the invasion of Port Moresby in New Guinea, the operation which triggered the famous Battle of the Coral Sea on 7/8 May 1942. When that operation was subsequently cancelled, she was reassigned to the Solomon Islands, where she patrolled from Rabaul.

Operating initially out of Rabaul and then from Truk for the rest of 1942 and into 1943, *Oite* was heavily involved in transport and convoy escort duties between garrison islands such as Kwajalein, Rabaul, Saipan and Guadalcanal. On 21 September 1943 whilst escorting a convoy from Truk to Japan she was hit by an American torpedo, which turned out to be a dud and only caused minor damage.

On 15 February 1944, *Oite* left Truk with *Subchaser No 28* escorting the light cruiser *Agano* for Japan via Saipan. The submarine USS *Skate* (SS-305) detected the naval vessels en route approximately 160 nautical miles northwest of Truk. At sundown, *Skate* fired four torpedoes at *Agano* from a distance of 2,400 yards – scoring three hits out of the four. The lightly armoured cruiser caught fire and started to slowly sink. *Oite* searched for the submarine – but *Skate* was able to escape undetected.

Oite stayed with the stricken *Agano* throughout the night, receiving the transfer of *Agano*'s fuel and 461 officers and men (107 officers and men from *Agano* had been lost in the attack). *Oite* was then ordered to return to Truk with the survivors, ignorant of the looming Operation HAILSTONE raid.

During the initial fighter sweep early on the second day of the raids, 18 February 1944, at 0655 *Bunker Hill* planes reported that a destroyer (*Oite*) was approaching North Pass through the lagoon's barrier reef.

Oite cleared through North Pass just after 0700 - and continued to make her high-speed dash south to Dublon. The *Bunker Hill* F6F Hellcats engaged her, and as they strafed the speeding destroyer, they killed her captain Lt. Cdr Uono in his bridge and caused fires to break out abaft the smokestack. The rescued Captain Matsuda Takatomo of *Agano* assumed command of *Oite*.

A photo taken from an INTREPID (CV-11) plane and reported as showing the Minekaze-class destroyer *Akikaze* manoeuvering at flank speed whilst under air attack off Truk during Operation HAILSTONE. Note her wake and another wake above, indicating that she is following the passage of another destroyer. There are strafing splashes in the water at her bow and her wake has her deck awash amidships. A TBF is overhead. This may in fact be *Oite*, as the Minekaze-class and Kamikaze-class were virtually identical, and the destroyer shown is being strafed – whilst *Akikaze* survived Operation HAILSTONE without damage. (National Archives 80-G-216899)

A division of five *Bunker Hill* TBF Avenger torpedo-bombers then began to circle *Oite*, which was by now trailing a slick of oil from the Hellcat's strafing. The Avengers formed a circle for a coordinated attack from all directions that would give *Oite* little chance. They began their attack from the stern.

As the attack began the *Oite's* stand-in captain began to take evasive manoeuvres. At flank speed he made a short high-speed turn to starboard at about 30-knots, followed by a feint to port - and then began a full turn to starboard. *Oite* completed almost a full 180° circular turn to come back and approach its own wake, in what we would almost call today in modern powerboating a Williamson Turn.

This manoeuvre however was the standard IJN anti-torpedo manoeuvre – and had been expected by the US aviators. As they saw *Oite's* starboard turn, they dropped their torpedoes – and *Oite* was hit by a single torpedo abaft the bridge.

The effect of the torpedo on such a relatively small, lightly protected ship was catastrophic. As her undamaged engines drove her forward to starboard at flank speed, she broke her back amidships in the vicinity of her aftmost smokestack.

As her engines drove the stern section forward turning to starboard, it began to fill with water and drive down into the water, simultaneously pushing the loosely attached bow section forward. The two sections of the ship jack-knifed, the tip of the bow slewed round until it almost pointed aft, level with the stern. The two sections of ship were torn completely apart. The stern section disappeared in clouds of white and black smoke – and sunk quickly.

The foc'sle, of the now free bow section, rose up until it pointed almost vertically into the air, hanging upright, close to the oil slick that marked her original southbound wake.

The weight of the upright bow section dragged it down into the water, compressing the air inside as it submerged. Finally, it too disappeared under the water and fell to the seabed below, capsizing as it went.

172 of *Oite's* crew, and 522 of the crew rescued from the *Agano,* were killed in this contact. Of those aboard, only about 20 survived the attack. Japanese government divers visited the wreck in the 1990's, cutting a large hole into the stern section to remove many of the human remains of her crew and the crew of the *Agano* for cremation.

The Wreck today

The wreck of *Oite* was rediscovered in 1986 and is now one of the most remote of the wrecks in the Truk lagoon – requiring a pleasant boat journey of an hour or more north from Weno. With the seabed at about 62 metres and the wreck only rising a few metres off the bottom, *Oite* is also one of the deeper wreck dives in the lagoon.

The wreck of this destroyer lies on a beautiful white sandy seabed. The warship is split into two sections that are arranged on the seabed in a large inverted 'V' shape, where the tips of the bow and the stern form the bottom two ends of the inverted 'V'. The bow and stern are level but about 30 metres apart. The top of the inverted 'V' is where the ship split - and the two amidships parts lie much closer, only some 10 metres apart.

It is recorded that as she sank, the bow rose up on the surface to point skywards. The forward section of *Oite* capsized as it went under and now lies completely upside down on

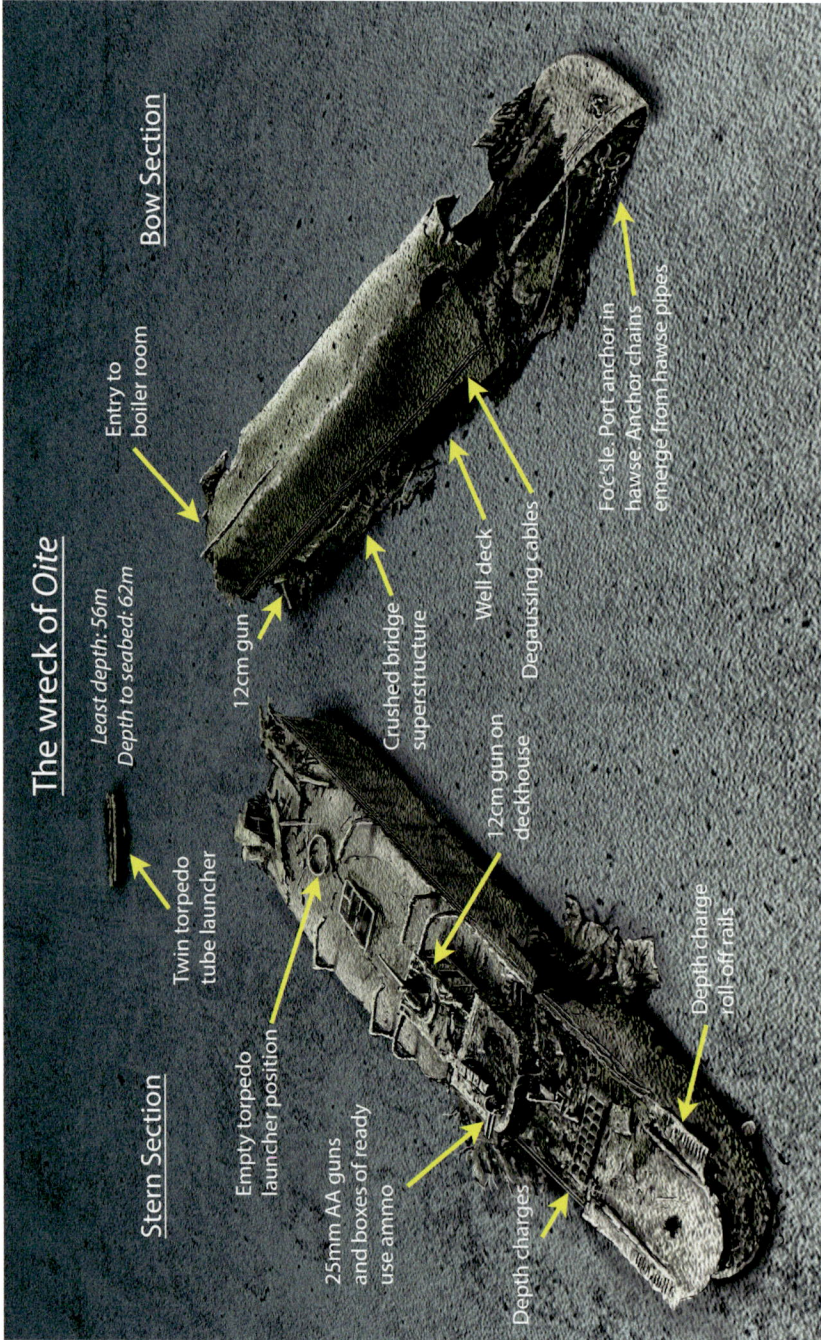

The wreck of Oite

Least depth: 56m
Depth to seabed: 62m

Bow Section

Entry to boiler room

12cm gun

Crushed bridge superstructure

Well deck

Degaussing cables

Fo'c'sle. Port anchor in hawse. Anchor chains emerge from hawse pipes

Stern Section

Twin torpedo tube launcher

Empty torpedo launcher position

25mm AA guns and boxes of ready use ammo

Depth charges

12cm gun on deckhouse

Depth charge roll-off rails

The destroyer Oite was hit by an aerial torpedo from a TBF whilst turning to starboard at flank speed. She broke her back and jack knifed into two sections. The stern section disappeared in clouds of white smoke and sunk, whilst the foc'sle of the bow section rose up until it pointed almost vertically - before sinking into the depths of the lagoon with great loss of life.

the seabed. The stern section however sits upright on its keel, with a slight list. The deck of the aft section is reached at about 57 metres. Degaussing cables run around both sections.

Of late, there has been a fixed downline attached at the fantail at the very stern of the ship. The buoy on the downline, as is the common practice in Truk with all the wrecks, is at a depth of 6 metres - to allow other vessels to pass safely over it. This does however make finding it out here towards the barrier reef something of an art form for boats without GPS.

On the occasions I have dived this wreck, as we descended, once the two parts become visible on the white seabed far below, we left the stern downline and crossed over, still descending in free water, to the bow section. After exploring the bow section aft to amidships, you arrive at the gap between the two sections – with just a twin 21-inch torpedo tube launcher visible lying in isolation in between on the seabed, about 20 metres out into the blue.

Crossing over to the stern section amidships, you can continue the exploration – moving aft along the ship to eventually arrive back at the downline to ascend. Given the significant depths to the wreck and seabed, *Oite* is a wreck firmly in the realm of the technical diver using trimix. Despite the depth, you do see divers on it using standard compressed air, with nitrox for decompression – but at that depth, on air, no matter how good the visibility is, divers will be suffering heavily from nitrogen narcosis. You will certainly be tweaking the dragon's tail if you dive this on air.

If you follow the dive plan I've suggested, by going down the stern shot and crossing over to the bow section, you will first arrive at the very tip of the bow, which has been dragged over onto its starboard side. The tip of the fo'c'sle is almost detached from the inverted main bow section – as though something like a modern large anchor has been dragged through the wreck: it is very reminiscent of the relatively recent damage to the bow of the destroyer *Fumizuki*.

Both anchor chains rise up via spurling pipes to their hawse pipes, with the uppermost port anchor visible. As the ship was in action when it was sunk, the anchor is held snug in its hawse pipe on top of the bow section. At the very tip of the stem, hanging a few metres off the seabed your depth will be around 57 metres.

The tip of the bow lies on its starboard side. The two anchor hawse pipes have anchor chains running through them. Degaussing cables run loosely aft. (Author)

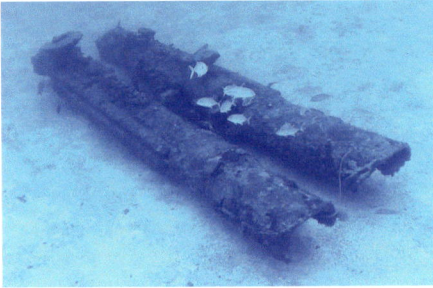

Lying out on clean white sand between the two sections of ship is the twin 21-inch torpedo launcher. (Author)

Moving aft from the stem, what would have been the forward part of the upturned fo'c'sle deck is very broken up – but it is possible to make out the underside of the No 1. main battery 12cm (4.7-in) 11th Year Type gun mount.

Immediately abaft the damaged fo'c'sle area, the ship assumes its inverted form as you move aft. The fo'c'sle reforms its shape around the upturned well deck.

Moving aft along the port side of the wreck, almost at seabed level, the upturned well deck gives way to the bridge superstructure. The uppermost levels of the bridge have been crushed onto the seabed, but the (original) lower levels with openings, doors and portholes can clearly be made out. It is possible to enter the wreck here in a number of places although the corridors in this small destroyer are quite tight for a bulky technical diver. Abaft the bridge superstructure, the barrel of the No 2 12cm main gun, which was situated between the two smokestacks, juts out to port at almost 90°. Degaussing cables run along the whole length of this section.

Immediately abaft the No 2 12cm gun, the ship is cleaved in two – the ends of the hull are torn and curled back from the huge stresses of her brutal demise. Moving round the torn edge to face forward into the innards of the hull, there is a large space, formerly the boiler rooms, into which it is easy to swim. The bottom of this space is filled with a mass of destroyed steam pipes and general debris, whilst further forward her four Kampon boilers can be made out, with large circular steam valves dotted around.

Retreating out of the hull, about 20 metres out into the blue you will see one of her two twin 21-inch torpedo tube launchers lying on the sand, along with a depth charge that is almost completely buried in the sand beside it. This twin 21-inch torpedo launcher must

Left: Looking aft from the break over an empty 21-inch torpedo launcher mount. Lifeboat davits line either side of the hull forward of the main mast deckhouse. (Author)

Right: Dual mount 25mm AA autocannons beside several closed and open ready use ammo boxes. (Author)

have sprung from its mount (likely the one abaft the aftmost smokestack) as the ship broke in two. You are at your maximum depth here on the sand of about 62 metres.

Turning around, you will see the dark outlines of both sections of ship visible in the distance. Finning over to the stern section you can rise up onto the weather deck and begin to move aft towards the downline. The first thing you will notice is the empty circular mount for the aftmost 21-inch torpedo launcher - from where the tubes you have just inspected out in the blue likely fell.

The aft weather deck is now largely empty – and on either side, the lifeboat davits are understandably in the swung in position. Given the speed at which she sank there was no time for the crew to swing out the davits and launch the boats.

Moving further aft along the empty weather deck between the davits, the outline of the deckhouse from which the mainmast rose emerges from the haze. The mast has in front of it the No 3 main battery 12 cm gun, its barrel pointing dead ahead, the splinter shield disintegrated. Boxes of ready use shells and separate loading cased charges are scattered around its base. On either side of the deckhouse below the 12cm gun, are open doors – the port side doors hold the ships heads: wc's and whb's gleam in the torch beams. Two sets of twin 25mm AA cannons, both pointing to port, are mounted atop the aft end of the deckhouse - with rectangular boxes of ready use ammunition beside them.

The port side of the ship is damaged and seems to be sagging, crumpling and losing its structure – but taught degaussing cables still span the gap where the hull would have been.

On the port side here, lying almost flat at the side of the deckhouse, is a steel doorway, or hatch, with a circular window in it from which the glass is long gone. Looking into the circular opening in the middle of the top of the door, divers confront a gruesome forest of human bones: complete skeletons, skulls crowded together.

It is a scene of great tragedy and one which made me gasp when it was first shown to me. It appears to me that as the ship sank, these unfortunate crew, perhaps from the engine room, would have run up to this door to try and escape. Perhaps the ship went down too

The cruiser stern of IJN Oite with minelaying tracks running off the deck on either side. The buoyed downline is usually secured to the deck here (Author)

The No 3 main battery 12cm/45-cal 11th Year type gun on top of the aft deckhouse points forward. (Author)

fast, or for some reason they couldn't undo the dogs on the door in time. Either way, these crew members have been drowned right here – these bones were people, terrified - facing imminent death by drowning. The scene is a brutal long forgotten time capsule, a terrifying glimpse of the tragedy of this war that spanned the globe. When I see this sort of thing, I imagine how the people I am looking at had been loved as children – parents beaming at the first words, at the first attempts to walk. I imagine them growing up, the laughter, the tears – any dad will understand where I'm coming from. I imagine how these children would have gone to school, maybe to university, the endless hours of study, the traumas, the loves, the highs and lows of life. And then the evil of war took them, trained them to fight, made them killing machines - and caused them to end their days, brutally, here in a beautiful remote atoll, specks of coral in the vast expanses of the Pacific. It is incredibly sad.

Abaft this masthouse, the quarterdeck holds the Anti-Submarine Warfare (ASW) apparatus. Two pairs of rails run to the stern from the ready-use depth charge loading stand. Depth charges could be moved along the rails to the edge of the ship and dropped over the stern as the ship moved ahead.

Immediately forward of the loading stand is a pair of coral covered depth charge throwers with centrally located tail plug, ignition device and a pair of port facing and starboard facing projector thrower tubes. A depth charge loading davit, used to lift the depth charges from the loading stand and swing them to the throwers, and to the roll off rails stands just forward of the throwers. Six depth charges are held within an athwartships loading stand, ready for use. Along the starboard side of the wreck rails used for moving torpedoes can be seen.

Underneath the cruiser stern, the rudder stands half buried in the sand with its twin screws set one either side - the free sections of each shaft run forward to its support bearing bracket before disappearing into the hull.

27. *Ojima*
Tategami-class *Kyunansen ken Eisen* Salvage & Repair Tug (1940)

Fourth Fleet Anchorage

Displacement:	812-tons (N)
	800-tons (S)
Dimensions:	175-ft 6" long (oa); beam of 31-ft 2"; draught of 11-ft 4"
Launched:	1940
Sunk:	7 October 1943
Cause of loss:	Destroyed by explosion whilst firefighting alongside *Kikukawa Maru*.
Wreck location:	Fourth Fleet Anchorage, east of Tonoas
Depth to seabed:	45 metres – bow
	50 metres - stern

The 800-tonne Tategami-class salvage & repair tug *Ojima* was launched in 1940 at the Maizuru Naval Dock Yard on the west coast of Japan. She was completed and registered in the IJN in 1941. She was one of three such tugs in the class constructed between 1936-1940 in the immediate years before war broke out, the first of which was the lead ship of the class, *Tategami*, launched in 1936. With a displacement of 800-tonnes, *Ojima* was a larger tug than the 600-tonne tug *Futagami,* off Tonoas, and considerably larger than the 300-tonne unidentified IJN tug recently found off Weno.

Artist's impression of the IJN tug *Ojima*

Ojima was a large seagoing tug with a range of approximately 1,000 miles at a service speed of 10 knots. She was constructed with two boilers that provided steam for two sets of powerful vertical triple expansion engines that developed 2,200iHP and allowed her twin screws to give her a maximum speed of 15 knots. These salvage tugs were well-equipped with three 5-tonne derricks and one larger 10-tonne derrick, winches, two powerful salvage pumps, air compressors and workshops.

During construction she was fitted with two 13.2mm AA machine guns, however these were quickly replaced during 1941 in the run up to war with two Type 96 25-mm AA cannons. She carried six depth charges.

In January and February 1942, Japan invaded and occupied the strategic township of Rabaul, which had a fine natural harbour, on the island of New Britain in the Australian Territory of New Guinea. With Rabaul pacified, the Japanese began to prepare for Operation MO, the invasion of Tulagi in the Solomon Islands chain - and Port Moresby on the southern tip of Papua New Guinea. By May 1942, *Ojima* was in Rabaul for the imminent Operation MO – the Rabaul harbour area was crowded with a formidable array of naval vessels.

Tulagi is situated directly north of Guadalcanal Island in the Solomons, across a stretch of water just over 20 miles wide that would come to be known as Ironbottom Sound. Guadalcanal and Tulagi lie at the south east end of the two roughly parallel lines of the Solomon Islands chain, which run broadly northwest to southeast. Tulagi has a fine natural anchorage, control of which would give Japan a naval anchorage and a seaplane base - and provide greater defensive depth for her major base at Rabaul.

A successful invasion of Tulagi and Port Moresby would give Japan mastery of the air above the vital Coral Sea – which lies between north east Australia and the bounding island groups of New Caledonia and Vanuatu to the east, and the Solomon Islands and Papua New Guinea to the north. Gaining control of these strategically important bases would prevent an Allied build-up of forces in Australia and would secure Japan's southern flank.

Control of the Coral Sea was vital to Japan's strategic aims. Whilst it would secure Japan's southern flank, it would also allow offensive strikes to be made against the coastal cities of Queensland, in north east Australia, which were vital Allied terminal points in the supply line between the United States, Australia and New Zealand.

On 4 May 1942, as Operation MO began, the salvage and repair tug *Ojima* departed Rabaul as part of the large Transport Force carrying the landing troops and their gear for the Port Moresby assault. Sailing with the convoy were five IJN transports, six IJA transports, the tankers *Goyo Maru* and *Hoyo Maru*, the fleet oiler *Iro* (now a famous wreck in Palau) and an escort of destroyers, minelayers and minesweepers. The powerful tug *Ojima* would give assistance to, or take in tow, any vessel that was damaged or disabled as the Transport Force sailed towards Port Moresby. She would also be useful close into the invasion beaches for dragging off any stranded lighters or landing barges.

As history records, this Japanese operation triggered an Allied response that led to the naval Battle of the Coral Sea on 4-8 May 1942. This battle is particularly significant in naval history as it was the first action in which aircraft carriers engaged each other directly. It was also the first battle in which the ships of the two opposing sides neither sighted each other directly, nor fired on each other. The Battle was a brutal confrontation in which the carrier USS *Lexington* (CV-2) and the Japanese light carrier *Shōhō* were both sunk, whilst *Shōkaku* was heavily damaged, as was *Yorktown* (CV-5).

The battle was a strategic Allied victory – for the Japanese fleet carriers, *Shōkaku* and *Zuikaku* were both damaged and as a result of the heavy losses of Japanese carrier aircraft, the Japanese invasion fleet bound for Port Moresby was recalled. With the Port Moresby invasion cancelled following the Battle of the Coral Sea, *Ojima* steamed back to Rabaul with the Attack Force.

By January 1943, *Ojima* was stationed at the Truk naval base - and on 18 January she towed the oiler *Sanyo Maru* from off Uman Island to Dublon.

The following month, *Ojima* was in Wewak, on the northern coast of New Guinea. From there she was despatched on 17 February 1943 to assist the destroyer *Harusame*, which had been torpedoed on 24 January 1943 by the American submarine *Wahoo* (SS-238). The torpedo had damaged her bow and nearly broken her back and she was already under tow by the destroyers *Amatsukaze* and *Urakaze*. *Ojima* arrived back in Truk with the tow on 23 February 1943 and *Harusame* was put alongside the Repair ship IJN *Akashi* for emergency repairs and fitting of a false bow.

On 1 October 1943, the ammunition supply ship *Kikukawa Maru* arrived in convoy at Truk and anchored in the Fourth Fleet Anchorage east of Eten Island. At about 1900 on 7 October, just an hour after crew aboard *Kikukawa Maru* had completed loading of aircraft parts and ammunition, a fire started aft in Hold No 4 - where *Kikukawa Maru* was carrying a large cargo of fuel in 55-gallon drums. The situation was extremely dangerous.

Fire and rescue parties were immediately sent from the shore and all ships anchored nearby were ordered to move berths as a result of the volatile cargo. *Ojima* was sent to assist - and after arriving on scene, tied up alongside the stricken *Kikukawa Maru*. Her crew immediately started assisting with fire-fighting – using her sea pumps to feed water to the fire-fighting teams aboard the ammunition supply ship. Landing craft and other small vessels were closeby - probably engaged bringing fire-fighters to the scene and evacuating crew.

By about 2230 however, after some 3-4 hours of firefighting, it had proved impossible to get the fires under control. The flames reached and then ignited the volatile cargo in the aft holds and there was a massive explosion that was heard throughout the islands of Truk; trees were defoliated on Dublon and Eten Islands and windows ashore shattered.

The aft section of the *Kikukawa Maru* and the superstructure amidships were completely destroyed in an instant - and sections of ship's hull, plating and frames were thrown over a large area. The ship had been cleaved in two just forward of the bridge. The intact forward section of the *Kikukawa Maru*, still at anchor, rolled over to starboard and quickly sank. There was great loss of life.

The force of the explosion was so great that it cut the unfortunate *Ojima,* still tied up alongside, into two sections, killing most of her crew in an instant. Both sections sank immediately.

The Wreck today

Today the wreck of the salvage tug *Ojima* is only infrequently dived, given its depth, the relatively small size of her two parts - and the distance they are separated by. Such was the tremendous force of the fatal explosion of *Kikukawa Maru* that *Ojima*, tied up alongside, was cleaved in two - with both parts being flung several hundred feet away from *Kikukawa Maru*.

The two sections that made up the 175-ft long tug *Ojima* now lie on the bottom of the lagoon some 50-100 metres apart - to the north east of the *Kikukawa Maru*. That a sturdy strong vessel like this big tug could be ripped into two parts – and the parts both be lobbed several hundred feet away is mind boggling.

The forward section of *Ojima* rests on its keel, listed over to port in about 45 metres of water. The wheelhouse, which was located towards the bow, has either collapsed or been blown away by the force of the explosion. A Daihatsu landing craft lies on the seabed not far from where the ship broke, its curved armour plate for coxswain protection still bearing its horizontal row of viewing slits

The shorter aft section of *Ojima* lies off the port bow in deeper water of 50 metres or more, upright but with a list to starboard. A hatch in the after deck allows views of salvage anchors and cables stowed there. Both her twin screws are in place, flanking her rudder.

A second Daihatsu landing craft lies on the seabed just off the starboard side of the stern section at the break. The two landing craft, one near either section of tug, were probably tied off to *Ojima* during the fire-fighting operations. They may have carried fire fighters out or been used for running goods and supplies out from shore. When *Kikukawa Maru* blew up they were blown away with *Ojima* – and then dragged under.

28. *Patrol Boat No 34 (ex- Susuki)*

Momi-class 2nd-class destroyer 薄 (*Susuki*) (1921)

IJN Patrol Boat (1939)

Repair Anchorage

Displacement:	As built – 1,020-tons (F)
	850-tons (N)
	After reconstruction – 1,162-tons (F): 935-tons (N)
Dimensions:	280-feet long (wl): beam of 26-feet: draft of 8-feet
Launched:	21 February 1921
Sunk:	3 July 1944
Cause of loss:	Bombed by U.S. aircraft
Name translation of 薄 (*Susuki*):	*Bell Tree*
Wreck location:	Repair Anchorage – 400 yards west of Dublon Island
Depth to seabed:	15 metres – stern
Least Depth:	3 metres – fo'c'sle
	10 metres –aft deck
Other names:	*Sutsuki*

Patrol Boat No. 34 – ex Momi-class 2nd-class destroyer *Susuki*.

Fumizuki and *Oite* were both 1st-class destroyers of about 1,700-tons (F) and 1,300-tons (N) built to the basic Minekaze-class design developed at the end of WWI. Japan also developed at this time a slightly smaller 2nd-class destroyer, the Momi-class, with a displacement of 1,020-tons (F), 850-tons (N) and 770-tons (light).

A total of 21 of these Momi-class units were built between 1919 and 1923. The first eight were built under the 1918 Construction Programme, then five more under the 1919 Programme and the last 8 under the 1920 Programme. The Momi-class were a development of the Enoki-class destroyer of 1917-1918 and are notable as being the first Japanese destroyers to be armed with 21-inch torpedo tubes.

The Momi-class 2nd-class destroyer *Susuki* was one of the second group of five to be built, under the 1919 Programme. She was laid down on 3 May 1920 at the Ishikawajima Shipyard

Starboard bow photo of Patrol Boat 28, ex IJN *Tade*, a sister Momi-class 2nd-class destroyer to *Susuki*.

in Tokyo, Japan's first modern shipbuilding facility. She was named and launched for fitting out on 21 February 1921 and completed on 25 May 1921. Her name *Susuki* uses the official Kokutai spelling of the time but she is also sometimes referred to as *Sutsuki*.

Susuki was fitted with 3 Kampon boilers that provided steam for two Parsons turbines and powered her twin screws, which had a very high pitch, to achieve a maximum speed of 36 knots. These ships were hailed at the time as being the fastest in the world - and had an operating range of 3,000 nautical miles at 15 knots.

The new Momi 2nd-class units inherited a number of features from the larger Minekaze 1st-class units, which had been based on influences from German destroyers handed over to Japan as reparations at the end of WWI. The Momi-class carried three main battery 12cm (4.7-inch) 45-cal guns, two 7.7mm machine guns, minesweeping gear and four 21-inch torpedo tubes in two twin launchers, one installed on the well deck in front of the bridge and the other abaft the aftmost of two smokestacks, and forward of the mainmast.

The 2nd-class destroyers were around 280 feet in length at the waterline with a beam of 26 feet. They were thus shorter and narrower in the beam than the 330-feet long 1st class units, which had a beam of about 30 feet. The 2nd-class destroyers had a shallow draught of just 8 feet and proved excellent for use in the shallow waters along the coast of China in support of amphibious landings during the 2nd Sino-Japanese War that began in July 1937 with the invasion of China. That same year, *Susuki* and her sisters *Fuji, Hishi, Hasu, Tsuka, Yanogi* and *Tade* had their smokestacks raised and capped.

The Momi-class destroyers may have been fast ships at the time they were built (even now some 100 years later, they would still outpace most modern dive RIB's) but by the eve of WWII, twenty years later, the *Momi*-class units were outdated, old ships of little strategic value. Their old boilers were degrading and some of the units could not make even 30-knots. Thus, in 1939, a program began to re-arm and refit them to convert them from outdated frontline warships to the vital role of patrol boat and convoy escort. The first eight of the 21 Momi-class destroyers, including *Susuki*, began a refit which lasted throughout 1940, the year before the Pacific war began. Another five Momi-class would begin a slightly different reconstruction in 1940, some retaining their 21-inch torpedo tubes.

One of their three Kampon boilers was removed, drastically reducing speed to 18 knots – but which was still sufficient to protect a slow-moving convoy and hunt down a submerged submarine. The four 21-inch torpedo tubes (in two twin mounts) were removed as was the mine sweeping gear and one of her three 12cm/45-cal main battery guns. The Momi-class vessels were then refitted for AA and ASW convoy escort duty with six 25mm cannons, 60 depth charges and depth charge racks and throwers being installed. They retained two 12cm/46-cal main battery guns.

This 1940 refit increased the normal displacement of the first 8 refitted Momi-class units from 850-tons to 935-tons - and Full Load displacement increased from 1,020-tons to

Stern view of the fast transport IJN T.1, showing a ramped aft deck and stern with two sets of rails and runners for launching and recovering Daihatsu landing craft.

1,162-tons. The re-fitted 2nd-class destroyers were then re-rated as Patrol Boats, *Susuki* being designated *Patrol Boat No 34* on 1 April 1940 (PB-34). The refit works on Patrol Boat 34 were completed by November 1940 when she embarked on several months of combined training exercises.

In 1941, Patrol Boat No's 32-39 underwent further re-fitting, with the stern being rebuilt and extended by 10 metres to allow transportation and launching of a single 46-ft long Daihatsu landing craft on the aft section of the vessel. Versatile Daihatsu landing craft were used in a number of roles such as carrying troops, tanks and materials directly to shore, and loading and offloading merchant ships.

During this refit, the aftmost smokestack was removed to make deck space and the stern was paired down with a sloping deck that extended to the waterline and then continued like a ramp or slipway underneath the water. Heavy-duty electric winches and handling gear was installed near the after gun platform with two sets of rails being welded on the after deck. After the Daihatsu landing craft had launched off the stern and deployed embarked troops and equipment to invasion beaches, the empty landing craft could return to the Patrol Boat and be winched back aboard the sloped deck.

The Patrol Boats had their forward interior spaces modified to provide accommodation and facilities for 150-250 landing troops and the number of depth charges carried was reduced to 18. The refitted Patrol Boats still carried two 12cm/45-cal main battery guns and six 25mm AA autocannon.

The refit works for Patrol Boat 34 were completed by October 1941, just over a month before the Pearl Harbor raid on 7 December 1941. After conducting exercises with her new configuration, just days before the Pearl raid, PB-34 was sent to Palau. On 8 December 1941, she departed Palau escorting the Third Fleet landing force bound for Legaspi on the island of Luzon in the Philippines. The Japanese intended to seize a number of local airstrips that could be used as forward bases by fighter aircraft to operate over the Philippines. After the landing troops went ashore on 12 December 1941 and subsequently secured their position, PB-34 returned to Palau, arriving there on 22 December 1941.

A month into the war, on 9 January 1942, PB-34 took part in the Invasion of Celebes in the Netherlands East Indies, today known as Sulawesi in Indonesia. Later that month she formed part of a powerful armada screening six troops transports carrying Special Naval Landing Forces for the Invasion of Kendari in Celebes.

On 31 January 1942, PB-34 screened 10 troop transports bound for the Invasion of Ambon Island in the Netherlands East Indies. Just days after the invasion, PB-34 was back in business with the Invasion of Makassar, Celebes on 5-10 February 1942, followed by operations at Portugese Timor. On 25 February 1942 she participated in the occupation of Surabaya, Java and then in late March 1942 took part in the seizure of Christmas Island.

After escorting transports from Kure to Guam and Saipan in May 1942, she then took part in the failed attempt to occupy Midway Atoll that led to the Battle of Midway from 4-7 June 1942. After Midway, PB-34 departed Guam for Saeki, Japan, on 26 June 1942 escorting *Zenyo Maru* and *Nankai Maru*.

The first Allied offensive campaign in the Pacific, the Operation WATCHTOWER invasion of Japanese held Guadalcanal, began on 7 August 1942. As WATCHTOWER began, PB-34 was sent to Moji, from where she would escort the fast army transports *Asakasan Maru* and *Sado Maru* to Palau, before proceeding onwards to Truk.

At Truk, she was assigned escort duties for a reinforcement convoy carrying troops and supplies in an attempt to relieve the beleaguered Japanese troops fighting on Guadalcanal to retake Henderson Field airfield, which was now held by U.S. forces.

On 19 August 1942, the Japanese reinforcement convoy arrived off Guadalcanal and Japanese troops began landings near Lunga Point, preparatory to storming Henderson Field. But when, about midnight, Japanese troops attempted to storm Henderson Field, they were cut down by defensive fire from entrenched U.S. Marines. The failed attempt was catastrophic – such that the Japanese commander, Lt Col Ichiki, committed suicide.

As the initial run of early Japanese successes of the war dried up, urgent troop reinforcements became needed to relieve outlying beleaguered garrisons. Conventional, slow merchant troop transports had proved too vulnerable to Allied air attack – and so, the legendary *Tokyo Express* relief system around New Guinea and the Solomon Islands was conceived to get around Allied air superiority. The Tokyo Express, in which PB-34 participated, involved the use of fast warships, mainly destroyers and latterly submarines, to deliver personnel and supplies to beleaguered island garrisons during the darkness of night. The ships would return to their originating base the same night so that Allied aircraft would not be able to detect them during daytime.

The following year, PB-34 was severely damaged on 6 March 1943 south of Kavieng (New Guinea) in a nighttime collision with a target ship, the old Minekaze-class destroyer *Yakaze*. The forward section of PB-34 was sheared off as it punctured the port side of *Yakaze*, flooding her boiler and engine rooms.

The stricken PB-34 was towed almost 600 nautical miles from Kavieng to Truk where she was dry docked for repairs. A makeshift rudimentary false bow of welded plates was fitted – and once these emergency repairs made her watertight, she was taken out of dry dock and put on a mooring in the Repair Anchorage, east of Fefan Island, west of Dublon. She was not used again operationally - and permanent repairs were never carried out.

PB-34 escaped significant damage during Operation HAILSTONE but was bombed, set on fire and sunk on 3 July 1944 whilst still anchored in the Repair Anchorage, just a few hundred yards to the west of Dublon.

The Wreck today

Today the wreck of the former Momi-class 2nd-class destroyer Patrol Boat No 34 sits upright on her keel with a list to port on a gently sloping seabed that is deepest at her stern, in about 15 metres of water. The least depth to her foredeck is 3 metres and it's about 10 metres to her quarter deck. She can therefore easily be explored as a snorkel in between dives or a shallow second or third dive.

The jury-rigged false bow is obvious as a crude temporary repair and has holes in it allowing access and allowing light in. The bridge superstructure is largely missing, demolished and collapsed. The base of her single remaining smokestack abaft the bridge is present along with now bare 25mm AA gun positions. The engine room can be entered through skylights but it is tight in comparison to the large cavernous engine rooms of the *Maru's*.

The long ramped aft section of deck is still discernable and has a row of racked depth charges along either beam.

At the very stern there is a centrally positioned A-frame for lifting landing craft. A heavy-duty winch for recovering the landing craft, is situated further forward on the port side.

Underneath her stern, her large rudder is flanked by her two screws, which are supported by A-frame bearings immediately forward, the free section of shaft running forward and into the hull.

29. *Reiyo Maru*
Passenger Cargo Vessel (1920)
IJA *Rikugun Yusosen* Auxiliary Transport (1941)
IJN *Ippan Choyosen* General Requisitioned Ship (1943)
U.S. Recognition Code: 38 MFM

Fourth Fleet Anchorage

Tonnage:	5,446 grt
Dimensions:	400-ft long; beam of 53.2-ft; draught of 29.4ft
Launched:	17 November 1920
Sunk:	19 February 1944
Cause of loss:	Bombed by TF 58 aircraft during Operation HAILSTONE
Wreck location:	Fourth Fleet Anchorage, east of Tonoas
Depth to seabed:	66 metres
Least Depth:	52 metres – fo'c'sle/superstructure
	56 metres – main deck

The 5,446grt passenger cargo ship *Reiyo Maru* was launched in 1920 and requisitioned by the IJA in 1941 and then by the IJN in 1943. She was bombed and sunk in the 4th Fleet Anchorage during Operation HAILSTONE

The sizeable passenger cargo vessel *Reiyo Maru* was laid down in early1920 by Asano Sanbashi Co in Tsurumi for the Tokyo based shipping line Toyo Kisen Kabushiki Kaisha (TKK – the Oriental Steamship Company). TKK operated passenger and cargo services from the Orient to New York and from Yokohama (where she was registered) to South China ports.

Reiyo Maru was built as a classic three-island passenger cargo ship - with raised fo'c'sle at the bow, an elongated split amidships superstructure and a raised poop island at the stern. Her foremast rose up from the forward well deck between the cargo hatches for Hold No's 1&2. Her bridge superstructure rose up for several deck levels and immediately abaft the command bridge was a small hatch for her bunker coal with a pair of kingposts for cargo handling set aft.

Abaft the bunker hatch stood her tall narrow smokestack - distinctive of a coal burning vessel. Immediately abaft the smokestack was the Boat Deck with lifeboats swung in davits flanking either side of the pitched engine room roof, which had skylights for ventilation. Her mainmast stood on the after well deck in between the hatches for her two aft cargo holds, No's 4 & 5.

The ship was named and launched for fitting out on 17 November 1920 and completed the following month on 27 December 1920. She was fitted with a 3-cylinder triple expansion steam engine built by the Ishikawajima Shipbuilding & Engineering Co of Tokyo that gave her a service speed of 10 knots and a maximum speed of 12 knots. She had an operating radius of 13,500 miles at 10 knots.

After 20 years of civilian service, by the time Japan was finalising her preparations for war in the Pacific, *Reiyo Maru* was already an elderly ship – but her large cargo holds would be important to the Japanese war effort. And so, on 10 October 1941, just two months before the Pearl Harbor raid, *Reiyo Maru* was requisitioned by the Imperial Japanese Army (IJA) as a *Rikugun Yusosen* Auxiliary Transport vessel. Shortly after requisition, she made a return passage from Japan to Keelung, in modern day Taiwan. In January 1942, she departed Moji, Japan, in a large convoy of more than 30 ships that was carrying elements of the 2nd Infantry Division bound for Mako in the Pescadores Islands between China and Formosa (Taiwan today). The convoy was escorted by a light cruiser and several destroyers

The following month, in early February 1942, *Reiyo Maru* was attached to the Third Fleet Southern Force and assigned to Vice Admiral Ozawa Jisaburō's Western Java Seizure Force. She assembled with 55 other troop transports in the deep-water convoy gathering point of Cam Ranh Bay in Vichy French Indochina (now modern-day Vietnam) from where the IJA 16th Army's 2nd Infantry Division would stage for the invasion of west Java. Escort light cruisers and destroyers thronged the waters offshore.

On 18 February 1942, carrying more than 1,500 IJA 2nd Infantry Division troops, *Reiyo Maru* departed Cam Ranh Bay with 14 other troop transports in an escorted invasion convoy bound for Merak, Java. The convoy arrived there on 1 March 1942 and successfully landed the invasion troops. From Merak, *Reiyo Maru* moved to Bantam Bay, Java, before departing from there on 9 March 1942 to head to Singapore, where she arrived on 16 March 1942.

A month later, with the immediate need for large numbers of troop transports now diminished, the IJA returned *Reiyo Maru* to her civilian owners on 24 April 1942. The old ship resumed her civilian duties, importing coal from Indochina to Japan, until about March 1943 - when her services were once again required for war.

In September 1943, she departed Mako in the Pescadores Islands in an escorted convoy bound for Sasebo, Japan. The following month saw her once again acting as a troop transport, departing in convoy for Zamboanga in the Philippines on 21 October 1943.

On 17 November 1943, *Reiyo Maru* was formally requisitioned by the IJN as an *Ippan Choyosen* –a General Requisitioned Ship. This meant that she was not formally enlisted into the IJN – she carried a civilian crew but was under military command, with a captain who was often Navy Reserve.

On 28 November 1943, *Reiyo Maru* departed Yokosuka, Japan, for Truk in an escorted convoy of five *Maru's* carrying supplies, military stores, landing craft and troops. En route, the following day, the convoy was detected and intercepted by the American submarine *Snapper* (SS-185), which torpedoed and sunk one of the five ships, *Kenryu Maru*.

The remaining ships of the convoy reached Truk on 12 December 1943 and after offloading her cargo, she departed Truk on 22 December 1943, homeward bound for Yokosuka in an escorted convoy. En route, the convoy was attacked on 1 January 1944 by the submarine USS *Herring* (SS-233), which torpedoed and sunk the transport *Nagoya Maru*. The remaining ships arrived at Yokosuka on 3 January 1944.

After lading, *Reiyo Maru* set off on 25 January 1944 in an escorted convoy bound for the 4th Naval Establishment Department on Truk. In the convoy was another famous present day Truk wreck, *Hanagawa Maru*.

But Japanese supply routes were stretched far across the Pacific, and Japan did not have the necessary numbers of transport ships to supply her far flung garrisons - nor did she have adequate escort vessels to counter the ever-present threat of attack by American submarines.

At this period of the war, any Japanese shipping ran a serious risk of submarine attack. Whilst Japanese convoys were escorted by destroyers, kaibōkan, subchasers and patrol boats, Japanese Anti-Submarine Warfare apparatus was much inferior to its Allied counterparts. In underwater detection, the IJN had not greatly progressed beyond the technology developed during and immediately after WWI, much of which had been acquired from Britain and Germany. The IJN had undertaken research on hydrophones in the 1920's - and in 1930 Japan imported the American MV-type hydrophone. The IJN reverse engineered the U.S. hydrophone to develop its own hydrophones – but these Japanese hydrophones had a limited detection range of only 1,000 yards throughout the entire Pacific War. The Japanese had made some progress by the time war broke out with Sound Ranging - or sonar - and some 20 IJN destroyers had been fitted with the Type 93 sonar. Development of sonar continued throughout the war but the pace of the program was slow and Japanese sets remained rudimentary. The position was not much better by early 1944 as *Reiyo Maru* set off from Yokosuka in convoy for Truk.

On 30 January 1944, east of the Marianas, the convoy was attacked by USS *Spearfish* (SS-190), which successfully twice torpedoed the ammunition ship *Tamashima Maru*. The second torpedo hit set off a sympathetic explosion of her cargo of munitions that destroyed her and quickly sent her to the bottom.

The beleaguered convoy continued on - and arrived at Truk on 7 February 1944, ignorant of the looming approach from the east by the fast carriers of Task Force 58. She departed Truk for Saipan in an escorted convoy on 9 February but by the morning of 17 February 1944, she was back in Truk, anchored in the Fourth Fleet Anchorage, east of Dublon and north of Fanamu Island. She lay about three miles north east of the artificial aircraft carrier shaped Eten Island.

Operation HAILSTONE raids began at dawn on 17 February 1944 with the undetected initial fighter sweep by 72 Hellcats wreaking havoc across the lagoon. This fighter sweep was swiftly followed by successive waves of torpedo- and dive-bombers.

At about 0514, Strike 2A, the first group strike by Task Group 58.2 planes from *Essex* and *Intrepid* launched. The *Essex* Air Group 9 launched 10 Hellcats to escort 9 TBF Avenger torpedo bombers and 17 SBD dive-bombers, with all aircraft carrying 500-lb GP bombs and 1,000-lb armour piercing bombs. The TG 58.2 planes arrived over Truk between 0630 – 0645, following in after the Strike 1A planes from *Enterprise* and *Yorktown* that were already attacking shipping in the Combined Fleet Anchorage and the Sixth Fleet Anchorage southwest of Dublon. The *Essex* and *Intrepid* planes vectored to attack Japanese shipping in the Fourth Fleet Anchorage to the east of Dublon, and to make secondary attacks on Dublon shore installations.

Just after 0630, *Essex* SBD dive-bombers attacked *Reiyo Maru*, covered by Hellcats. Two 1,000-lb bomb hits were scored in the vicinity of the bunker hold between the bridge superstructure, and the smokestack and engine room superstructure. The two large explosions left the ship ablaze amidships.

About 10 minutes later the ship was attacked again – this time by Air Group 6 SBD aircraft from *Intrepid*. A bomb burst just abaft the bridge and another was a near miss off the stern quarter.

The fire in No 3 Hold (between the bridge and smokestack) from the earlier attack, worsened and spread forward under the bridge until it reached Hold No 2 - which held a cargo of munitions. Some of the munitions stored there cooked off - resulting in a series of small explosions. There was however no catastrophic single explosion as with *Aikoku Maru* or *Sankisan Maru*.

The stricken ship is reported to have remained afloat until 19 February before succumbing to the bomb damage and to the fires, which had by then swept her from stem to stern.

The Wreck today

Today the wreck of the *Reiyo Maru* rests on an even keel in the north east sector of the Fourth Fleet Anchorage, to the east of Tonoas Island (Dublon). Sitting in 66 metres of water and with 56 metres down to the weather deck, she is the deepest known wreck in the Fourth Fleet Anchorage - and is just behind *Katsuragisan Maru* out towards North East Pass, as the deepest wreck dive in the lagoon.

The fierce fires that raged after she was hit abaft the bridge have destroyed all wooden structures, deck planking, timber wings and roofing. Many metal structures such as beams and spars have also been noticeably weakened and sagged. The middle of the foredeck, which was near the fiercest of the fires and explosions as munitions in Hold No 2 cooked off, has noticeably sagged down. The foc'sle bulkhead nearby has also noticeably sagged in the middle. The confusing scene of weakened sagging decks is reminiscent of the wreck of the *Nagisan Maru* in Palau, which was completely ravaged by fires over several days.

At the bow, the plumb stem drops off vertically into the depths – very characteristic of ships of the era of her construction. Being deeper than other wrecks, she is less covered in corals – the foc'sle deck at about 52 metres seems almost clean and bare, with its guardrail still ringing around it. A large anchor windlass sits on the foc'sle deck with both chains running out to their hawse pipes. Mushroom forced draft ventilators are dotted around - designed to bring fresh air to the foc'sle spaces below, where crew would be billeted.

The wreck of *Reiyo Maru*

Least depth: Fo'c'sle 52m
Depth to seabed: 66m

Engine room skylights open

Mainmast collapsed forward to starboard

Upper bridge levels devasted and collapsed by fire

Damage to deck and hull

Smokestack collapsed forward over hold hatch

Pile of angle iron

Sagging deck - foremast fallen forward to starboard

Anchor windlass - chains crossed halfway down stem

Above: Artist's impression of the wreck of *Reiyo Maru* (circa 2019) resting in 63 metres with a depth of 53 metres to the weather deck.

Right: The bow of *Reiyo Maru* – the wreck sits upright in 65msw. (Courtesy Pete Mesley)

The fo'c'sle deck drops down to the well deck at about 56 metres where two aft facing doors in the fo'c'sle bulkhead allow access into the fo'c'sle spaces. The fo'c'sle deck has buckled and sagged on the starboard side from the fires onboard.

Hold No's 1 & 2 appear almost empty and the foremast has broken into sections and collapsed to starboard, leaving only the base and a short kingpost on either side upright. The base section of the mast projects laterally to starboard out over the side of the ship. Cargo handling winches are set fore and aft at its base.

The hatch cover beams for Hold No 2 are missing – this was the centre of the fire and consequent munitions explosions and they were no doubt blown off. The main deck sags steeply downwards towards the centreline. A deck cargo of angle iron and iron railway tracks lie adjacent to Hold No 2 on both sides of the hatch at a depth of about 56 metres. Angle iron are lengths of sheet iron that is bent at a right angle along the centre and is commonly used for construction purposes.

The pitched engine room roof, boat deck and forced draft ventilators of *Reiyo Maru* (Courtesy Pete Mesley)

The higher levels of the bridge superstructure were completely consumed by fire and bomb hits just abaft the bridge. As a result, they have collapsed downwards, leaving only the lower moulded steel deck levels untouched.

Abaft the collapsed bridge superstructure is a small hatch for bunker coal - before the single storey superstructure that covers the boiler and engine rooms below. The smokestack, rising from the boiler room, has collapsed.

Abaft the collapsed smokestack, a small deckhouse stands in front of the pitched engine room roof, which has large mushroom type forced draft ventilators dotted around. All the engine room skylights are in the open position and allow access down into the engine room where the three cylinders of the triple expansion engine are visible, ringed by catwalks and flanked on either side with walls of switches, gauges and the repeater. I understand that there has been collapsing of this area during the Covid closure of the atoll.

As divers enter the engine room, in the open space above the cylinder tops, they will be at a depth of about 58 metres. It is possible to drop deeper between the engine and boiler (forward of it) and down staircases at either side, to the lower decks where divers will be at a depth of about 64 metres.

In the superstructure above, either side of the fireproof engine casing, would have been passenger cabins and a promenade walkway. The wooden decking of the floors and roofs of these structures has been burnt away to reveal the rooms below through a latticework of beams and frames. Some crockery can still be spotted in amongst the debris, gleaming white in torches and bearing the legend *Mino Yogyo Ltd*. Either side of the engine room roof are empty lifeboat davits, still in the swung in position.

Abaft the engine room superstructure, the depth drops down to the after well deck, which is a few metres deeper than the forward well deck. At about 60 metres the hatches for the two after deck Hold No's 4 & 5 are found, with inbetween, the A-frame for the mainmast. Like the foremast, the mainmast has also collapsed to starboard and now lies partly across Hold No 4. The deck plates around the hatch are buckled, torn and twisted as a result of the fires and there is much structural damage along the port side of the hull from near miss bombs.

Hold No 5 is largely intact although the ship does show damage to the poop island on the port quarter from a near miss bomb hit with the deck slanted to port at a pronounced angle.

As a result of the depths encountered diving this wreck, it is firmly in the realm of today's technical divers.

30. *Rio de Janeiro Maru*
Passenger cargo liner (1929)
IJN *Zatsuyosen* auxiliary transport (1940)
IJN Rio de Janeiro Maru-class Auxiliary Submarine Depot Ship (1941)
U.S. Recognition Code: 10 MFMK

Sixth Fleet Anchorage

Tonnage:	9,627 grt
Dimensions:	461.2-ft long; beam of 62-ft; draught of 39.5-ft
Launched:	19 November 1929
Sunk:	18 February 1944
Cause of loss:	Bombed by TF 58 aircraft during Operation HAILSTONE
Wreck location:	Sixth Fleet Anchorage, east of Uman Island
Depth to seabed:	35 metres
Least Depth:	15 metres – port beam of hull
Other name:	*Rio Maru*

The *Rio de Janeiro Maru* was a substantial 9,627grt passenger-cargo liner built by Mitsubishi Zosen Kaisha in Nagasaki. Her keel was laid down in May 1929 and her hull was named and launched for fitting out afloat very speedily on 19 November 1929.

Rio de Janeiro Maru was a sleek elegant 461-ft long cargo liner, and fitting out of such a large, elegant vessel took until she was completed on 15 May 1930

The 9,627grt passenger and cargo liner *Rio de Janeiro Maru* was launched in 1929. She was requisitioned by the IJN in 1940 to serve as an auxiliary submarine depot ship.

and delivered to her new owners, one of the best-known Japanese shipping companies, the Osaka Shosen Kaisha Line (O.S.K.) of Osaka. By the outbreak of WWII, the O.S.K. line was operating a fleet of 20 motor driven passenger ships including the *Rio de Janeiro's* sister ship *Buenos Aires Maru* and 26 steam passenger ships.

The *Rio's* spacious superstructure and cabins below could accommodate 1,140 passengers, whilst large cargo holds were set fore and aft of the amidships superstructure. She had a cruiser stern and propulsion was delivered by two 6-cylinder 2-stroke Mitsubishi-

Port beam shot of *Rio de Janeiro Maru*, she was bombed and sunk by TF 58 aircraft during Operation HAILSTONE

Sulzer diesel engines that drove twin screws to give a cruising speed of 15 knots and a top speed of just over 17 knots.

On 1 June 1930, *Rio de Janeiro Maru* set off on her maiden voyage from her homeport of Kobe to OSK's South American ports of call. In the coming years she would make regular voyages carrying emigrants from Japan to Brazil – usually docking at Santos, after stops at Hong Kong, Singapore, Montevideo and Buenos Aires.

The Kanji word *Maru* means 'circle' and so, in 1937, as her name suggests, she began to operate on a circular round-the-world service from Japan that included ports of call such as Hong Kong, Singapore, Colombo, Durban and Cape Town in South Africa. Crossing the Atlantic to South America, she then called at Rio de Janeiro, Santos, Montevideo and Buenos Aires, as she moved north up the east coast of South America to transit the Panama Canal to the west coast of America, where she called at Los Angeles before crossing once again to Japan.

On 4 September 1939, she was damaged in a collision with the Seaplane Tender IJN *Kagu Maru* in the North Pacific, south of the Aleutian Islands, on the final leg of a passage from west coast America to Japan. She was taken in tow by the *Kagu Maru* for Japan. The salvage tug *Seiha Maru* was despatched to the scene and many days later, arrived to take over the tow and take the *Rio de Janeiro Maru* back to Mitsubishi Jukogyo's yard at Kobe for repair.

The IJN requisitioned the *Rio* on 8 October 1940 in the run up to war, and work began at the Kure Navy Dockyard to convert her to a *Zatsuyosen* auxiliary transport ship. Two 25mm Type 96 dual-mount AA cannons were installed, along with signal equipment, and new accommodation spaces were created. The works to convert her to her military role were completed on 30 November 1940.

In February 1941, she was sent to operate off the South China coast and Formosa (modern day Taiwan) and then, the following month she was registered on 25 March 1941 as a prospective submarine tender in the Sasebo Naval District and conversion work began at the Harima Shipyard in Banshu, Hyogo.

Four 15cm/50-cal 41st Year Type naval guns were installed, one on a platform atop the fo'c'sle deck and one on a platform at the stern. These powerful naval guns had been in service aboard IJN warships since 1913 – and when in the 1930's, these guns were replaced with newer guns, the old 15cm/50-cal guns were used to arm merchant cruisers before the start of the Pacific War - so perhaps the guns present today on the *Rio Maru* (as she became to be known in the IJN) were once carried aboard an IJN battleship as secondary armament.

The 15cm/50-cal 41st Year Type naval guns newly installed on the *Rio Maru* had a 7.6 metre (25-ft) long barrel - and when you dive the wreck and see the guns for yourself you will be impressed at just how long the barrels are. A 15cm gun of 50-calibres has a barrel length of 15 x 50 = 750cm, although in actuality, the barrel of this particular type of gun is 770cm, that's 7.7 metres, or 24.6-ft. These 15cm/50-cal naval guns fired a standard 100-lb shell for a distance of 18,000 metres - over 11 miles.

During the 1941 conversion works, a range finder for the new guns was installed - and anti-magnetic de-gaussing cables were fitted around her hull to mask her magnetic signature against magnetic mines. A torpedo and depth charge hangar were constructed, along with a medical facility and motor launch loading equipment.

The conversion to a submarine tender was completed on 7 May 1941 and the tender *Rio Maru* was attached to the 5th Submarine Squadron (SubRon 5) along with the light cruiser *Yura* and the six submarines of SubDiv 28 (*I-59, I-60*), SubDiv 29 (*I-62, I-64*) and SubDiv 30 (*I-65, I-66*). Her duties were to service the six submarines by resupplying them with torpedoes, ammunition and fuel, and to carry out minor repair work and exchange crews.

On 24 November 1941, two weeks before Japan began her Pacific war with the raid on Pearl Harbor, *Yura, Rio de Janeiro Maru* and the six submarines of the 5th Submarine Squadron set off from Sasebo in Japan for Palau. En route however, the squadron was diverted to Hainan Island, China, where IJA troops were massing for the forthcoming invasion of Malaya and Siam (modern day Thailand).

On 8 December 1941, just after the attack on Pearl Harbor, SubRon 5 arrived in Cam Ranh Bay, Indochina (Vietnam) as Japanese forces began the Invasion of Malaya by making landings to the south along the beaches of peninsular Thailand and the northeastern beaches of Malaya.

On 8 January 1942, loaded with personnel and equipment of the 11th Submarine Base Unit, the *Rio* departed Cam Ranh Bay, heading south to one of the invasion beachheads at Singora, in southern peninsular Thailand. There she disembarked the 11th Submarine Base Unit before heading via Kota Bharu, on the east coast of Malaya, on to Brunei and Borneo. She then returned to Sasebo, Japan, via Penang on the west coast of Malaya.

A few months later, in May 1942, the *Rio Maru* was transferred to Kwajalein in support of the Operation MI, the invasion of Midway Atoll. She was designated as flagship of Rear Admiral Chimaki's SubRon 3 based at Kwajalein.

On 29 May 1942, north of Borneo, the *Rio* was struck by a torpedo fired by USS *Swordfish* (SS-193), a submarine notable for being the first U.S. submarine to sink a Japanese ship during WWII. A large 45-foot-wide hole in her hull was torn open in Hold No 1, which started to flood. *Swordfish* then turned her attack to the IJA transport *Tatsufuku Maru* - successfully hitting her with two torpedoes and sending her to the bottom.

The damaged Hold No 1 on the *Rio Maru* was successfully sealed and the repair ships *Kasuga Maru* and *Yamabiko Maru* then took the stricken *Rio Maru* in tow to Singapore for repair. Once there, she was dry docked in the King George V Graving Dock at the former British Seletar Naval Shipyard in the Johor Strait. Once repaired, she was released from dry dock and had returned to Sasebo by 2 July 1942.

SubRon 5 was disbanded on 10 July 1942 and the *Rio Maru* was reassigned to the Southwest Area Fleet as a submarine tender for the flagship I-8. But just two weeks later on 27 July 1942, the *Rio* was hit by a torpedo from the submarine USS *Spearfish* (SS-190) in a submerged night attack east of Cam Ranh, in the south east of modern-day Vietnam. The sub's skipper thought he had struck a fatal blow - and that she was sinking by the stern. But as damage control parties gained the upper hand, she was able to limp to Cam Ranh Bay for temporary repair, before making her way to Singapore where more permanent repairs were carried out. By October 1942, she was again taking up her duties as submarine tender with the Southwest Area Fleet.

In September 1943, the *Rio* was re-rated as a *Zatsuyosen* auxiliary transport ship and began the supply and transportation between Japan, Indochina and Formosa of military materials, personnel and Allied POW's.

On 18 January 1944, the *Rio* arrived at the Kure Naval Arsenal in Japan and loaded thousands of rounds of various calibres destined for the light cruiser *Agano*, which was under repair at Truk by the Repair Ship *Akashi*. She then moved to Yokosuka, arriving there on 29 January 1944, where she loaded a cargo of depth charges, coastal defence guns, food, mail and general supplies for transport to Truk.

On 3 February 1944, filled with war supplies, she set off from Yokosuka for Truk, escorted by the Mutsuki-class destroyer *Yuzuki*. She arrived safely at Truk eight days later on 11 February 1944 - just six days before Operation HAILSTONE.

As the Task Force 58 initial fighter sweep by the Hellcats burst over the skies above Truk at dawn on 17 February 1944, the *Rio Maru* was at anchor to the south of the Fourth Fleet Anchorage, in the Sixth Fleet Anchorage to the east of Uman Island.

In the first group strike of the day, she was hit by 1,000-lb bombs from either an *Essex* Strike 2A or *Yorktown* Strike 1A plane. The hit was observed by *Bunker Hill* Strike 3A aviators who arrived over the target slightly later than Strikes 1A and 2A and reported explosions and a subsequent fire. The *Rio Maru* was possibly hit again later in the day and left in sinking condition.

As the fires spread, some of the ammunition stored in her foredeck Hold No 1 (possibly shells for the 15cm/50-cal bow gun, stored below in the fo'c'sle) began to cook off, exploding outwards through the shell plating of her hull. The fires were so severe that they weakened the structure of her foreship. The once beautiful elegant liner *Rio de Janeiro Maru* settled progressively into the water, listing to starboard.

The coming of darkness ended U.S. air operations for the day with the closing raids, Strikes 1F, 2F and 3F. As the sudden darkness of a tropical night descended, the *Rio Maru* was still afloat but in sinking condition. She finally succumbed, unseen by U.S. eyes, early the following morning, just after midnight at about 0030. As she sunk into the waters of the lagoon, rolling to starboard, she came to rest on the seabed on her starboard beam ends. Her fo'c'sle and bow area, weakened by the intense fires, were deformed by the time she settled on the seabed.

When daylight came on 18 February, as the American F6F Hellcats flew over the lagoon at dawn for the initial fighter sweep to clear the skies for the 2nd day of the raid, there was no sign of the *Rio de Janeiro Maru*.

The Wreck today

Today the wreck of the IJN auxiliary submarine tender *Rio de Janeiro Maru* is one of the most popular in the Truk lagoon – and one that every visitor to Truk will want to dive. She is a magnificent wreck that holds something for everyone, from novice to seasoned technical diver.

The *Rio*, as she is conveniently known locally, lies some 500 yards offshore from Uman Island on her starboard side in relatively shallow water, for such a big ship, of 35 metres. Her stern points to Uman, which is located at the south east side of the central cluster of main islands in the lagoon.

With a beam of some 20 metres and lying in just 35 metres of water, her shallowest parts rise up to only 10-15 metres beneath the surface. As soon as divers enter the water, the wreck will be easily seen below, stretching for as far as the eye can see in either direction.

At 461 feet in length (some 140 metres) this is a big ship, one of the largest in the lagoon. Lying in such shallow water, divers can get long bottom times exploring this fine ship, with little decompression penalty. She is a beautiful ship – and even today more than 75 years later, it is still possible to appreciate just how elegant a ship she was. The fires that raged throughout the ship have however consumed any wooden structures and decking.

At the bow, the higher port anchor chain runs out through its hawse pipe just a few metres abaft the stem. The chain drapes over the stem before dropping down to the seabed and running off into the distance.

A few metres abaft the hawse pipe, the name of the ship is embossed on the hull plating in non-ferrous Roman lettering about 30cm (1-ft) tall and can still be easily made out. As the lettering ends, the first row of portholes of the uppermost level of the foc'sle begins above it, whilst beneath the lettering, the row of portholes of the deck level below now also begin – the lower row runs the full length of the hull to the stern. Some portholes are open, whilst many are closed with their glasses intact.

In places here near the bow, on the uppermost expanse of port side shell plating, there are holes punched through the plating, their rough edges curled upwards and outwards. These holes are the result of 15cm shells for the bow gun, stored below in the foc'sle, cooking off as the ship burned and exploding outwards through the hull.

On the now vertical foc'sle deck, the bow 15cm/50-cal 41st Year Type naval gun sits on its platform, the 7.7m (24.6-ft) long barrel angled slightly down towards the seabed. The foc'sle spaces beneath the gun, used for storing shells for the gun, housed a hydraulic system to transfer shells up to the 15cm gun.

The weather deck is buckled at the collision bulkhead and the foc'sle appears to be at a different angle to rest of the ship. The decking and bulkheads aft of the 15cm bow gun are torn and twisted, with the hatch for Hold No 1 being almost totally obscured. It is believed that fire took hold here weakening the structure of the ship and that some 15cm shells, and munitions in Hold No 1, exploded due to the heat, damaging the hull from inside. There are blown out sections of shell plating on the lower starboard side here large enough for divers to enter and exit the hold. Flooding through the starboard side here may well have contributed to her listing to starboard as she sank.

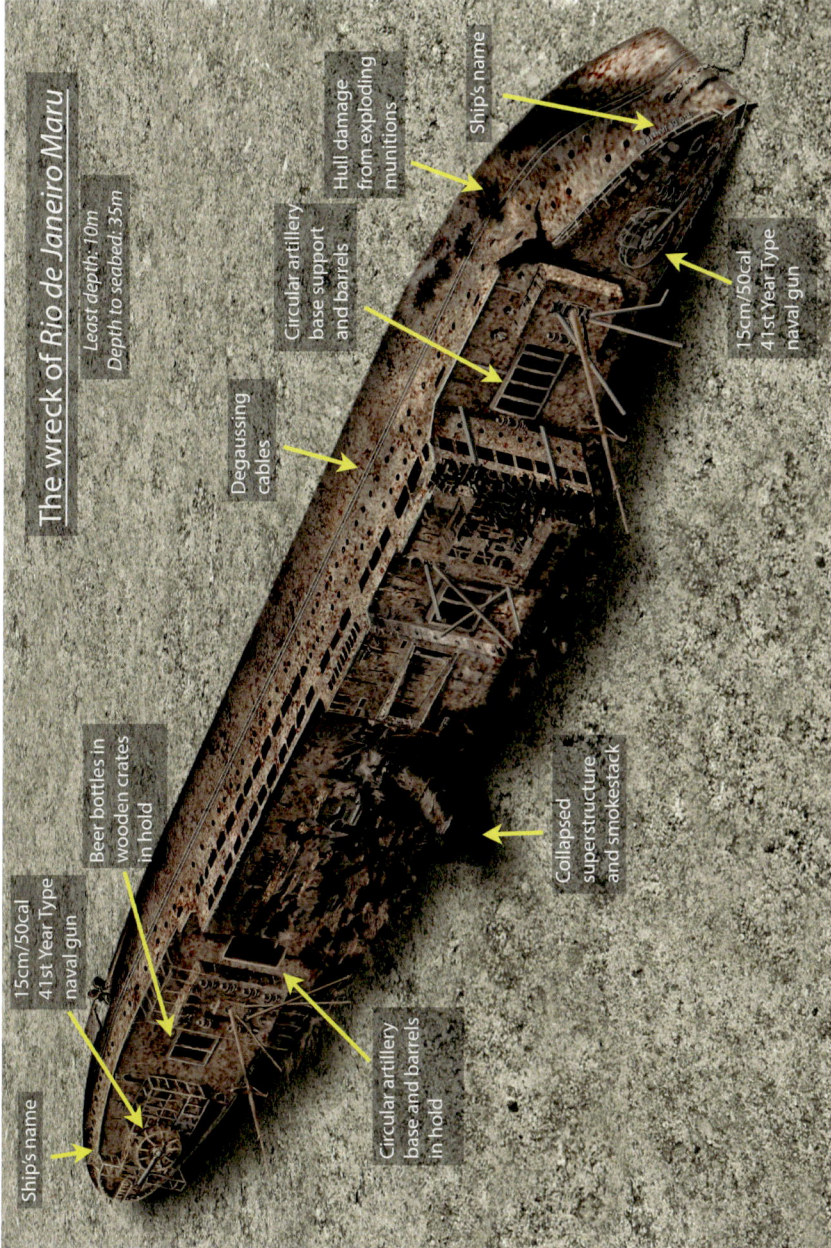

The wreck of *Rio de Janeiro Maru*

Least depth: 10m
Depth to seabed: 35m

Ship's name

Hull damage from exploding munitions

Circular artillery base support and barrels

Degaussing cables

15cm/50cal 41st Year Type naval gun

Collapsed superstructure and smokestack

Circular artillery base and barrels in hold

Beer bottles in wooden crates in hold

15cm/50cal 41st Year Type naval gun

Ship's name

Artist's impression of the large 140-metre-long wreck of *Rio de Janeiro Maru* (circa 2019), which lies on her starboard beam ends in 35 metres and is a stunning wreck to visit. Part of her superstructure and smokestack collapsed in about 2013. The mainmast aft is believed to have collapsed during the covid closure of the atoll.

With Hold No 1 flooded, and listing to starboard, she likely settled by the bow. If the bow touched the seabed first, whilst most of the ship from the bridge aft was still afloat, it is possible that the weight of the ship, resting on the fire-weakened bow structure, caused the bow to deform and leave the foreship in the condition we see today.

Moving aft from the bow, the foremast still juts out horizontally from a masthouse on the deck inbetween the hatches for Hold No's 1&2, its inverted crosstree still present. Two cargo booms ran forward and two aft from short kingposts near the base of the foremast. The booms have now swung down as the ship capsized to starboard so that their ends rest on the seabed.

Hold No 2 still has its hatch cover beams in place and contains disassembled artillery pieces destined for installation on land. Measuring the bore roughly, these appear to the writer to be 12cm/45-cal 3rd Year Type naval guns of the type used on light naval vessels during WWI and as coast defence guns during WWII. Several large circular foundation base supports can be found in the bottom level of the hold. These are some 10-12 feet in diameter and would be set in an excavated pit which would then be filled in with reinforced concrete to provide a firm base onto which the pedestal for the gun itself would then be installed. The gun would rotate on the roller bed on the top of the circular base. Nearby can be found the gun recoil springs and a number of 12cm/45-cal artillery barrels and a naval gun turret splinter shield with apertures for two barrels, evidence that these are naval guns reclaimed from an old warship. A lot of bottles and coal are also present here.

A pair of kingposts are set immediately in front of the bridge superstructure and the boom from the higher port kingpost slants down diagonally across the front of the bridge. The lower starboard boom slants downwards to rest its end on the seabed below. Rotted mushroom style forced draft ventilators are dotted at either side of the weather deck.

The bridge superstructure rises up for several decks above the weather deck and held the navigation bridge at its highest levels to the front. A small cargo hatch was situated abaft the bridge superstructure that was serviced by derricks from its own pair of kingposts on its leading edge. The engine room and machinery spaces were situated abaft and below this hatch.

In this long elegant superstructure, rows of passenger cabins lined either side of the fireproof engine casing. The lower cabins have portholes whilst the higher cabins opened off long prome-nade deck walkways that ran along the entire superstructure on either side of the ship. A number of now horizontal doorways open off these walkways, leading inboard to corridors off which the passenger cabin doors opened. The row of portholes for the lower passenger cabins, the same row that extends aft from the very bow, dots along the highest level of the hull to the stern.

Although the smokestack and upper levels of this superstructure were still relatively intact and in place at the time the 1st edition of this book was prepared in about 2013, in the years since, the smokestack has collapsed and the upper levels of the superstructure have progressively detached themselves from the port side of the hull and also collapsed downwards. It is such a pity to watch year after year as this great lady of the sea inevitably loses the fight against gravity and corrosion and collapses to the seabed. Ships are not designed to lie on their beam ends – and I am always struck just how quickly shipwrecks lying on their sides collapse, in comparison to shipwrecks sitting on their keels. The collapsing superstructure is becoming increasingly precarious and dangerous to penetrate.

For those suitably experienced and trained in wreck penetration, and with a local guide, the engine room below can still be entered with care. Divers can locate the Mitsubishi Sulzer diesel engines and now horizontal walls covered with switching panels, gauges and two engine order telegraph repeaters. Descending a now horizontal companionway beside the main switching panels leads to the lower areas of the engine room near the keel of the ship. This is a large cavernous space with tangled catwalks, pipes and spars running off in every direction.

It is easy to get confused and lost in the cavernous engine room spaces and you should not enter without a local guide. It is hard to navigate properly inside a big wreck like this when everything is 90° out of kilter – but the prominent now horizontal internal parts of the smokestack help you keep your bearings. I have spent at times an hour or so in here, exploring deep at the bottom of the ship – and on one occasion, our guide lost his bearings and had to swim off to find a way out - leaving us literally in the dark. It was a scary 10 minutes before he came back to lead us out.

An open doorway deep inside the ship opens into the starboard side of the galley. Looking into the galley from beneath you can see heavy cooking stoves and ranges hanging, seemingly precariously, in place above you. I would advise against spending too much time underneath these (!) - and would certainly advise against going into the galley and possibly disturbing anything that might fall down. The galley holds much crockery, pots and pans.

Moving aft beyond the superstructure, divers arrive at the after weather deck and the two hatches for Hold No's 4&5. These are separated by a masthouse from which the mainmast with its inverted crosstree projected out horizontally until it collapsed during covid.

Hold No 4 contains a large quantity of coal and another large circular artillery foundation base, that has tumbled out from the lowest level of the hold to lie across the tween deck. Nearby is a large 12cm/45-cal artillery barrel similar to those in Hold No 2. A bomb hit abaft the smokestack has severely damaged structural beams and hull plating on the starboard side and flooding here no doubt also contributed to her list to starboard as she sank.

Hold No 4 contains masses of beer and sake bottles. Most are now loose and piled up on the lower side of the hold, but many are still stacked (now vertically) in their original wooden crates, held in place between the keel frames.

Another 15cm/50-cal defensive naval gun, similar to the bow gun, is mounted on top of the poop island deckhouse - its 7.7m (24.6-ft) long barrel points directly aft. Shells for it can be found on the seabed directly underneath.

On the docking bridge, on the fantail directly above the rudder, is the auxiliary steering position from where the ship could be navigated should command from the bridge be lost, eg following

Detail of the stern of *Rio de Janeiro Maru* showing the large 15cm/50-cal 41st Year Type gun on its aft platform, with docking bridge adjacent. The mainmast is believed to have collapsed during the covid closure of the atoll.

Left: The name of the ship still rings around her fantail in large non-ferrous letters. (Courtesy Ewan Rowell)

Right: Promenade deck walkways run along the port side of the superstructure. Note the degaussing cables strung along the hull. (Courtesy Ewan Rowell)

Left: Switching panel deep inside the engine room of *Rio de Janeiro Maru*. (Courtesy Ewan Rowell)

Right: At the very stern of the *Rio*, a docking telegraph hangs upside down on its chains. (Courtesy Ewan Rowell)

The stern, with rudder and port prop. (Courtesy Ewan Rowell)

Catwalks surround the author as he descends into the engine room. (Courtesy Ewan Rowell)

Paul Haynes holds an officer's katana sword, present in the wreck in 2015 but now believed to be landed. (Courtesy Ewan Rowell)

a bomb hit. The engine order telegraph has fallen over and is now held suspended upside down by its chains, flush with the vertical deck. The elevated walkways of the docking bridge extend to either side of the hull, and directly to the very stern - allowing crew views of the stern for close harbour manoeuvres.

Moving around the fantail, the ship's name is easily legible in large non-ferrous letters embossed on the hull, the lettering here being much larger than the lettering at the bow.

The *Rio* was a twin-screw vessel and both screws are still present – flanking the large rudder. The large, uppermost, 4-bladed port propeller dominates the area and dwarfs any diver.

In 2013, a military *shin guntō* katana (aka samurai sword) was present on the wreck. During the pre-WWII military buildup and throughout the war, all Japanese officers were required to wear a sword. Katana swords

12cm artillery barrel in the foredeck holds. (Courtesy Ewan Rowell)

were highly treasured by families in Japanese society over a long period – and these katana swords were often passed from one generation to the next. During the war, officers were permitted to bear their family katana once it had been militarized, and an officer's rank was indicated by coloured tassels tied to a loop at the end of the hilt.

Before and during WWII, katana swords were produced on a large scale. Where officers and NCO's did not have their own katana, the Type 95 katana was released in 1935, which had machine-made blades.

The particular details of the sword found on the *Rio* are not known. Whilst it may be one of the mass-produced swords, it may alternatively have been hundreds of years old, a family heirloom handed down through the generations. It is believed that the sword has now been landed and is at work cutting mangroves on one of the outlying islands.

31. *San Francisco Maru*

Passenger-cargo vessel (1919)

IJA *Rikugun Yusosen* Auxiliary Transport (1937)

IJN *Ippan Choyosen* General Requisitioned Ship (1942)

U.S. Recognition Code: 30 MFM

Fourth Fleet Anchorage

Tonnage:	5,831-grt
Dimensions:	385.0-ft long; beam of 51.0-ft; draught of 36.0-ft
Launched:	1 March 1919
Sunk:	18 February 1944
Cause of loss:	Bombed by TF 58 aircraft during Operation HAILSTONE
Wreck location:	Fourth Fleet Anchorage, east of Tonoas
Depth to seabed:	60-63 metres
Least Depth:	45 metres - bridge
	50 metres – main deck

The 5,831grt passenger-cargo vessel *San Francisco Maru* was built in Kobe, Japan, by the Kawasaki Dockyard Co Ltd. The ship was named and launched on 1 March 1919 – a turbulent time in Europe where the hostilities of the Great War had only been halted by the Armistice five months earlier. As the *San Francisco Maru* launched down the Kawasaki Dockyard slip in Kobe, in Scapa Flow in the Orkney Islands of northern Scotland,

The 5,831grt passenger and cargo ship *San Francisco Maru* was launched in 1919 and requisitioned by the IJN in 1942.

the 74 warships of the Imperial German Navy High Seas Fleet lay at anchor, interned under British guard as a condition of the Armistice. Just three months after the *San Francisco Maru* was launched, all 74 High Seas Fleet warships would scuttle en masse on 21 June 1919. The Treaty of Versailles would be signed a week later.

San Francisco Maru was a Taifuku Maru No 1-class vessel, based on a British WWI *standard ship* design of flush-deck, split superstructure steamships. Between 1916 and 1920, the Kawasaki shipyards at Kobe built 74 standard ships of this class for Japanese and foreign clients.

By way of background about *standard ships*, during the early years of World War I, German U-boats took a heavy toll on British shipping. By the end of 1915 alone, some 1,600,000 tons of British shipping had been sunk, and hard-pressed British shipyards were unable to build enough new ships to replace the losses. The British Government turned to the neutral American shipbuilding industry for assistance. Old, ailing, American shipyards were updated and enlarged - and scores of new shipyards were set up. By March 1917, orders to U.S. yards for new British ships amounted to almost three-quarters of a million tons. These ships were mass-produced to simplified standard designs – they became known as *standard ships*, built with a standard design of hull and standard engines. In all, some 3,500 'tramp' ships were built during WWI for the Allies.

San Francisco Maru was fitted with a single screw that was driven by a traditional coal-fired 3-cylinder triple expansion steam engine manufactured by her builders, the Kawasaki Dockyard Co. This gave her a service speed of 10 knots and a maximum speed of just over 14 knots. She had a radius of 13,000 miles at 10 knots.

Cargo was carried in four main holds, two forward and two abaft the split superstructure, with a smaller bunker hold for coal set in between the bridge and engine room superstructures. The ship was built with two steel decks, with each hold being divided into an upper Tween Deck and a larger, lower main storage space.

On 1 August 1919, *San Francisco Maru* was sold to Kokusai Kisen K.K. of Yokohama, for whom she made a number of voyages in the 1920's and 1930's to Fremantle in Western Australia. Her engine was modernised to cleaner more efficient oil in 1923.

In 1937, *San Francisco Maru* was purchased by the well-known shipping line Yamashita Kisen K. K. of Kobe. When Japan invaded China that same year, 1937, beginning the bitter 2nd Sino-Japanese war, *San Francisco Maru* was requisitioned by the Imperial Japanese Army as a *Rikugun Yusosen* Auxiliary Transport.

A month after the surprise attack on Pearl Harbor on 7 December 1941, and the rapid expansion of the Japanese empire, the IJN had a pressing need for cargo shipping to transport men and supplies to her Pacific outposts and newly seized territories. On 20 January 1942, *San Francisco Maru* was released by the IJA to her civilian owners before, the very same day, being requisitioned by the IJN as an *Ippan Choyosen* General Requisitioned Ship. This category meant that she was not formally enlisted into the IJN – she carried a civilian crew but was under military command, with a captain who was often Navy Reserve.

Following her requisition in January 1942, she began carrying cargoes, troops, military hardware and supplies to Japan's front-line garrisons. On the return voyage to Japan, her holds would carry coal and other badly needed raw materials such as phosphates from Yap and bauxite ore from the Marshall Islands and Pohnpei, Truk, Yap and Palau. Bauxite is an aluminium ore that is the world's main source of aluminium, and in the 1920's and 1930's, Japan had surveyed all their mandated islands for it. Bauxite is vital in the construction of aircraft and other military hardware. It is usually easily strip-mined, being often found near the surface with little over burden.

On 28 January 1943, *San Francisco Maru* was in Palau setting off northbound for the port of Moji in Japan. Once back in Japan, she was drydocked on 21 February 1943 for repairs at

Innoshima, in the Hiroshima Prefecture of southern Honshū. After undocking on 14 March 1943, she returned to Palau in an escorted convoy in April 1943.

San Francisco departed Palau on 26 April 1943 in an escorted convoy for Wewak, New Guinea that was carrying 6,000 troops of the 41st Infantry Division along with ammunition and provisions. Four days into the voyage, on 30 April 1943, *San Francisco Maru* and the Subchaser CH-34 were detached from the convoy and sent to Kairiru Island, on the north coast of Papua New Guinea. On 1 May, she departed Kairiru Island with her escort Subchaser CH-34 and rejoined the main convoy as it returned from Wewak. She was lightly damaged during an air attack.

On 19 June 1943, *San Francisco Maru* was back in Palau, setting off northbound carrying bauxite ore in an escorted convoy for Saeki in Japan. The convoy arrived at Saeki on 28 June and within days she was heading back to Innoshima for more repair work. On 15 August 1943, she set off again in convoy for Truk.

On 5 September 1943, she departed Truk for Rabaul, New Britain, in a convoy that was escorted by a destroyer and the Sub-chasers CH-30 and CH-32. The convoy arrived at Rabaul on 10 September 1943. From Rabaul she was sent to Palau, where she departed on 20 November 1943 in an escorted convoy heading back north to Japan. A week after her arrival in Japan she entered dry dock at Innoshima once again for repair.

In January 1944, *San Francisco Maru* was berthed in Yokosuka, near Tokyo, loading military hardware, stores and munitions destined for the fortification of Truk against an anticipated land assault by the Allies. She carried a deck cargo of light Type 95 Ha-Go tanks and army trucks. Her holds were filled with staff cars, petrol tankers, bull dozers, hemispherical anti-invasion beach mines, 55-gallon fuel drums and crates of ammunition, aircraft bombs, aircraft engines and spares, Long Lance torpedoes and ordnance.

The escorted convoy of four Maru's (including the present day Truk wrecks of *Unkai Maru No 6* and *Hoki Maru*) departed Yokosuka on 20 January 1944 bound for Truk. En route, frequent and persistent attention by American submarines caused the convoy to shelter at Saipan for a few days before setting off again on 31 January 1944. The convoy was once again targeted by U.S. submarines and her escort kaibōkan's were kept busy depth charging suspected submerged targets.

The convoy arrived safely at Truk on 4 February 1944. *Unkai Maru No 6* anchored in the Sixth Fleet anchorage south of the aircraft carrier shaped Eten Island, whilst *San Francisco Maru* and *Hoki Maru* dropped anchor in the Fourth Fleet Anchorage, south east of Dublon Island amongst many other valuable requisitioned merchant ships. As Operation HAILSTONE began, these transport ships were quickly attacked by TF 58 planes in strength. Several aircraft attacked the anchored *San Francisco Maru* and she is believed to have been damaged throughout the day by aircraft from *Essex* (Strike 2A), *Yorktown* (Strike 1D) and *Bunker Hill* (Strike 3E). She was set on fire with black smoke rising amidships, but she remained afloat.

The following day, DOG-DAY, 18 February 1944, 10 SBD Dauntless dive bombers and four TBF Avengers had launched for Strike 2B from *Essex* at 0715 with 7 F6F Hellcats for protection. The flight made their way towards Truk atoll, tasked to hit shipping spotted in the Fourth Fleet Anchorage during an assigned time at target of 0830-0845. As the flight arrived over Truk, the Hellcats encountered no airborne opposition and so they swooped down on strafing runs on the Eten airfield, where they shot up Japanese planes parked up on the apron.

The SBD dive bombers bombed two transport ships, hitting one south of Eten on the port quarter and scoring a number of near misses that started fires aboard. The second victim was anchored two miles southwest of Eten and two hits were scored on the bow with three others straddling the ship.

The TBF's meanwhile bombed a freighter anchored about one mile southeast of Dublon, scoring a hit on the port quarter and a near miss off the stern. This reported target is believed to have been the *San Francisco Maru*.

A 500-lb bomb went straight through the starboard side of the hull adjacent to Hold No 5 - leaving a large gash in her side from the water line up to her gunwale. The detonation of the 500-lb bomb inside the hold devastated the whole aft section of decking, which collapsed downwards. Five crew had been killed.

The other 500-lb bomb blew a hole in the port side of Hold No 4, deforming the shell plating and bringing down the mainmast. The explosions started more fires.

With such catastrophic damage to her shell plating and hull, water flooded into her two aft holds. She was dragged under by the stern – and as the TF 58 planes of this strike departed to head back to their carriers, only a small part of the bow was showing proud of the water.

San Francisco Maru sank down into just over 60 metres of water, coming to settle on an even keel on the bottom of the lagoon.

The Wreck today

Today the wreck of the *San Francisco Maru* rests upright in 60-63 metres of clear water with a least depth to her bridge superstructure of about 45 metres and the weather deck at about 50 metres. She is filled with so much to see that she is one of the most famous wrecks in the lagoon. Being a deeper dive, if you are not dived up when you arrive on Chuuk, she is one to work up to through your trip.

The ship is still filled with most of her wartime cargo – some of which, such as her deck cargo of Type 95 Ha-Go light tanks, is particularly photogenic and one of the 'musts' for diving Truk.

The forward section of the ship is in good condition, with a lot to see that is easily accessible. The wooden structures and fitments of the upper bridge levels were consumed by the fires that raged aboard her during the attack - leaving only the skeletal framework of the spars and struts of the upper levels and bridge wings. These have largely rotted away and in recent years, the upper skeletal framework of the bridge has collapsed to leave only the steel rooms of the lower levels and the skeletal framing of the side compartments. The aft part of the ship has much to see in the cargo holds – and it is interesting to see and understand the damage that the American 500-lb bombs did here.

At the bow, her plumb stem, so characteristic of the early 20th century when she was built, drops vertically from the weather deck at 50 metres to the seabed at just over 60 metres. She

The wreck of *San Francisco Maru*

Least depth: 45m (Bridge)
Depth to seabed: 63m

Port side blown out, decking sagging due to bomb damage. Long Lance torpedoes.

Pitched engine room roof

Lifeboat davits

Two tanker trucks and a staff car in tween deck; 50lb aerial bombs, shells and aircraft engines

Type 95 Ha-Go tank

Bomb entry gash

Hemispherical beach mines, shell casings and cordite boxes

Trucks, artillery shells in boxes, hemispherical beach mines, small arms ammunition and 55-gallon fuel drums

No fo'c'sle, flush deck steamer

Type 95 Ha-Go tanks

Bow gun platform with three boxes of ready-use shells

Breakwater

Artist's impression of the wreck of *San Francisco Maru* - bombed in the stern by TF 58 aircraft and now resting in 63 metres of water in the 4th Fleet Anchorage.

Above: Detail of the bow 8cm Type 41 gun, swung to port on its platform. Three closed boxes of ready use shells are stacked on the platform behind it.

Right: Bow of *San Francisco Maru*, showing starboard anchor in its hawse and both chains running to the anchor windlass. The 8cm bow gun can be seen behind on its platform. (Courtesy Ewan Rowell)

Hemispherical beach mines stacked in the tween deck of Hold No 1. (Courtesy Ewan Rowell)

was a flush deck steamer – so there is no foc'sle – just a raised bulwark to deflect water from sweeping the deck. Sturdy anchor chains rise from the chain locker below deck via spurling pipes and lead to her anchor windlass before running forward across the foredeck near the bow and disappearing through hawse pipes at either side of the ship. The starboard anchor is still held snug in its hawse whilst the port side anchor is run out to the seabed, disappearing into the distance.

Immediately abaft the anchor windlass, and just in front of the 8cm bow gun platform, is a diagonally angled breakwater intended to deflect any water, that got over the bulwark, over the side of the ship and avoid it sweeping across the deck and endangering crew. A spare Admiralty pattern anchor, its stock neatly stowed on top, is positioned flat on deck behind the port side of the breakwater, still securely bolted to the deck.

Immediately abaft the breakwater, a Type 41 8cm/40-cal 3rd Year Type naval gun sits atop its circular bandstand platform. The gun is trained out to port - no doubt indicating the direction of the final attacks. These 8cm (3-inch) guns were a direct copy of the British QF 12-pounder naval gun of the late 1890's. They had a barrel length of 3.2 metres and could fire some fifteen 5.5kg (12-lb) shells per minute with an effective firing range of 18,000 feet, almost 4 miles. Three boxes of ready use shells sit at the rear of the firing platform.

Hold No 1 still has its hatch cover beams in place and the tween deck space is packed with hundreds of carefully stacked Type JE Anti-boat land mines – each with two grab handles welded on top. These are the same anti-boat and anti-vehicle land mines as found in the *Nippo Maru* - and were intended to be buried in large numbers on beaches thought likely to be assaulted by the Allies. Heavy artillery shells would also be buried with their fuzes exposed, both mines and shells ready to explode when they were run over. The all-welded Type JE anti-boat land mine found in this hold is about 2-feet in diameter and about 1-foot in height and had an explosive charge of 46.5-lbs of TNT. The detonators of these anti-boat mines consisted of two lead-alloy horns, each containing a vial of acid. When either horn is bent or crushed, the acid vial is broken. The acid then contacts battery plates and generates a current which detonates the mine.

In early 1944, the IJA began to reinforce Truk and set about constructing strong defensive installations. On likely invasion beaches, these anti-boat mines would be buried to horn depth between the high and low water lines, where they were a hazard to Allied amphibious LVT's and Higgins boats beaching at high tide – as well as to troops wading ashore from boats at low tide. They were not deployed inland in mine fields, although they were found emplaced in several rows in depth on some beaches, and in the area to the rear, with a trip wire between them to allow them to serve as anti-personnel weapons.

In the tween deck of Hold No 1, at the front of the hold, are a number of dropping mines (depth charges), shell casings and rectangular ribbed flash proof brass boxes, which held the powder bags of cordite that were the propellant charges for large naval guns.

The central section of Hold No 1 was until the 1990's packed to the brim with beach mines - but is now largely empty. The beach mines have been robbed out by local divers who use the TNT charge for dynamite fishing. At the very bottom of the hold however, in deep water beyond air diving range, there are still hundreds of these mines scattered about. A number of large No. 80 800-kg (1,760-lb) Land Bombs, each in its own individual wooden container are found in the lower section of this hold.

The foremast, flanked by short kingposts still stands on deck between the hatches for Hold No's 1&2 and still has its inverted crosstree in position. Winches are dotted fore and aft around its base, for operating the cargo booms; the forward two booms have been sheared off a couple of metres in front of their king posts.

Hold No 2 has its hatch cover beams in place at weather deck level, and at the tween deck below. On the starboard aft side of the weather deck, a disintegrating flatbed truck rests half on and half over the hatch – partly on top of the hatch beams. Below, two tanker trucks sit on top of the tween deck beams, parked facing forward towards the bow, with tumbled 55-gallon fuel drums scattered around. The large fuel tanks of the tanker trucks would likely have been empty during transit, being compressed and deformed by the water pressure as the ship sank. In the depths of the hold below, 50-lb aerial bombs with tailfins are stacked, alongside more shells and a radial aircraft engine.

Moving further aft, just in front of the bridge superstructure, is more deck cargo. To the starboard side, immediately to starboard of the disintegrating flatbed truck (mentioned above) are two Type 95 Ha-Go light tanks. These sit on the wide deck, the aftmost one partly resting on the gunwale and partly on top of the other, having been

Detail of the collapsed bridge superstructure showing two Type 95 Ha-Go tanks on the starboard side and a single Type 95Ha-Go tank on the port side. Two tanker trucks can be seen parked facing forward under the hatch cover beams of Hold No 2

On the starboard foredeck, two deck cargo Type 95 Ha-Go light tanks are jumbled together half over the gunwale. (Courtesy Ewan Rowell)

moved during the sinking process. The aftmost tank has its top hatch half open and both have their barrels pointing out over the starboard gunwale.

The Type 95 light tank carried a crew of three men; a commander/gunner, a gunner who was also the driver - and a hull gunner/mechanic. Only the commander was seated, in the cramped, hand-operated turret and so he was responsible for loading, aiming and firing the main gun. The barrel of the 37mm Type 98 main gun was removable for transport and replacement, and two types of shell, high-explosive (HE) and armour piercing (AP), were carried. Secondary armament consisted of two 7.7mm Type 97 light machine guns, one mounted in the hull and the other in the turret. These are the same Type 95 Ha Go tanks as the one found as deck cargo on the foredeck of the *Nippo Maru*.

On the port side in front of the bridge superstructure sits another Type 95 Ha-Go light tank, resting partly on the gunwale – its barrel pointing forward and slightly depressed. A large steamroller can be seen lying on the seabed nearby on the port side. It would have been carried as deck cargo on the port side to even the load of the two tanks on the starboard side – but it has gone over the side of the ship at some point during the sinking.

Immediately behind the Type 95 Ha-Go tanks are the remains of the bridge superstructure – now largely rotted away to reveal the structural beams and girders. The upper deck levels were largely wood on a steel frame, have been burnt away or rotted away to leave only the lowest steel bulkhead of the moulded level, which is studded with portholes. There is a small steel deckhouse on the level above –and the skeletal framework of the upper bridge wings has collapsed forward in recent years.

Detail of the Boat deck showing engine room skylights and lifeboat davits. The smokestack is collapsed leaving only the circular opening to the Boiler room.

Along either side of the bridge superstructure a covered walkway leads aft – its roofing long gone to leave just the skeleton of its framework.

The *San Francisco Maru* had a split superstructure – that is, the command bridge section of forward superstructure was split from the superstructure above the boiler and engine rooms. Inbetween the separate bridge and engine room superstructures is the small hatch for the bunker hold, originally designed for coal fuel. This hatch has a single cover beam in place at main deck level and two beams at the tween deck below. Winches are set on the deck either side of this small hatch, along with forced draft ventilators and small access hatches leading below.

Abaft the bunker hold, the boiler room deckhouse is found, from which the tall narrow smokestack has collapsed. A large section of the smokestack lies fallen on deck, now lying flush alongside the boiler room deckhouse, whilst another section lies abaft the bunker hatch.

Moving further aft, the larger engine room superstructure is found – which has the Boat Deck on top, with lifeboat davits either side. The davits are in the swung-out position, frozen in time at the moment the crew abandoned ship as it sank.

In the middle of the Boat Deck is the pitched roof of the engine room itself, with five opening skylights on either side of the pitch, each with a couple of fixed glass portholes in them. Some of the skylights are closed, whilst some are propped open and allow easy access into the engine room.

Dropping into the upper reaches of the engine room you will see, high up, a strong longitudinal beam running fore and aft, used for moving heavy engine room fitments. A suspended athwartships catwalk leads to doors on either side of this deckhouse out to the weather deck. Underneath the beam you will next see the cylinder tops of her triple expansion engine, running fore and aft, with more catwalks ringing around the engine. You can drop further down into this engine room - but be aware of your depth as you will quickly go deeper than 50 metres.

Abaft the engine room superstructure is the flat expanse of the after deck, which contains the hatches for Hold No's 4&5 with the mainmast set in between. The mainmast is broken off about 6 feet above the deck and now lies fallen astern on the port side. Deck cargo handling winches are set either side of the mast, two fore and two aft.

All the main deck hatch cover beams for Hold No 4 are missing, likely blown off during the attacks. One or two beams are present at the lower levels. There are a number of artillery shells in this hold, some in boxes, others loose, along with more hemispherical beach mines, detonators, bombs, small arms ammunition and 55-gallon fuel drums. On the port side of this hold, the shell plating is deformed and there is a gash right through the hull – the result of a bomb hit, that no doubt blew away the cover beams.

Left: The author hangs above the 8cm bow gun on its circular skeletal platform. The gun is swung to port and the boxes of ready use shells can be seen below the barrel. (Courtesy Ewan Rowell)

Lower: On the port foredeck in front of the collapsing bridge lies a single Type 95 Ha-Go light tank.

The weather deck around the hatch for the aftmost Hold No 5 is collapsed and sagging down into the hold. There is a large hole visible on starboard side, just forward of poop island deckhouse, where a bomb has gone straight through the hull before detonating inside the ship and wrecking the structure of the ship. The hold itself contains more beach mines, dozens of 30-foot Long Lance torpedo bodies - along with depth charges and a large number of 55-gallon fuel drums.

There are two small deckhouses either side of the ship towards the stern - and another amidships deckhouse at the very stern, which accommodated the docking bridge and auxiliary steering position above the steering gear. Chains run forward on either side of the aft deckhouse from deck winches, the chains would be shackled to a toothed steering quadrant for emergency direct steering of the ship if control was lost from the bridge.

On either side of the fantail, a depth charge sits in its holder, ready for dropping if an enemy submarine was detected below.

The propeller and rudder remain in place.

32. *Sankisan Maru*
Passenger-cargo vessel (1942)
IJA *Rikugun Yusosen* Auxiliary Transport (1942)
IJN *Zatsuyosen* Converted Auxiliary Transport (1943)
U.S. Recognition Code: Unknown

Sixth Fleet Anchorage

Tonnage:	4,776 grt
Dimensions:	367-ft long; beam of 52-ft; draught of 27-ft
Launched:	1942
Sunk:	18 February 1944
Cause of loss:	Bombed by TF 58 aircraft during Operation HAILSTONE
Wreck location:	Sixth Fleet Anchorage, west of Uman
Depth to seabed:	24 metres - bow
	45 metres - stern
Least Depth:	15 metres - fore deck

———————————

The 4,776-ton passenger-cargo ship *Sankisan Maru* was launched during the war in 1942 and was quickly requisitioned for war use. The Allies knew little about her.

The medium sized 4,776grt passenger-cargo vessel *Sankisan Maru* was built at the Harima Dockyard, near Osaka in Japan during 1941. She was named and launched on 29 January 1942 and after fitting out afloat entered service on 20 March 1942 with the Kaburagi Kisen Shipping Line. Her single screw was driven by a coal fired triple expansion steam engine that gave her a service speed of 12 knots. She was constructed as a three-island steamship, with two holds in her foreship and Hold No 3 set on the extended section of superstructure in front of the bridge.

She carried a composite central superstructure, and immediately abaft the bridge was the smokestack with the boiler room and engine room below. Lifeboats swung on davits on the Boat Deck either side of the smokestack. The after section of the ship contained two further cargo holds before a sterncastle, which held the steering gear.

The Allies at first knew nothing about the construction of *Sankisan Maru*. The restricted wartime US Division of Naval Intelligence document *Japanese Merchant Ships - Recognition Manual* (ONI 208-J) (revised 1944) (and now de-classified) established a standard method of enemy merchant ship identification, providing identification codes for all *known* Japanese merchant ships of over 500 gross tons.

The first step in identification divided enemy vessels into four main groups of ship type based solely on the position of engines and superstructure type. Each of the four main ship types was then subdivided into a number of variants based on features such as how many funnels there were, the type of bow (e.g., plumb or raked) and the type of stern (e.g., cruiser stern or counter stern). The four basic ship types are:

a.   Passenger type (Variant No's 1-12)

b.   Cargo type with composite superstructure (No's 13-28)

c.   Cargo type with split superstructure (No's 29-44)

d.   Ships with engines aft (No's 45-65)

Once the basic ship type and variant had been determined and an initial number allocated, a code for the ship under observation would then be formulated in three more stages that looked at the number and location of masts, funnels and kingposts.

The Recognition Manual lists performance details such as length, beam, speed and range along with photos, outline drawings and the code worked out (as above) of all the individual Japanese merchant ships of more than 500grt known to the U.S. Division of Naval Intelligence at the time. Each ship was then allocated a *Potential Naval Value*, allowing a submarine commander observing an enemy ship to work out the code and then identify the actual ship, or certainly the class of ship, along with its characteristics from the Recognition Manual. The Potential Naval Value allowed the sub skipper to work out if the ship should be attacked, or, if there was a convoy with many targets, which one was the most important to go after.

The Recognition Manual is a brilliant extensive piece of work harnessing the full might of American military intelligence at the time. But although most of the requisitioned merchant ships sunk at Truk are listed in the Recognition Manual, there is no mention of *Sankisan Maru*. Such was the secrecy surrounding Japanese ship construction as war loomed that the Allies did not know of the construction, launch or service of this sizeable ship. Constructed during the year that war in the Pacific erupted, the ship is not registered with Lloyds.

The U.S. Division of Naval Intelligence did subsequently produce a classified manual *Standard Classes of Japanese Merchant Ships* ONI 208-J (Revised) in January 1945, in which the 4,776-ton *Sankisan Maru* is named. The Allies may have been aware of her existence by then, but information about her was still vague - as she is classified as one of approximately 30 Type B Standard ships built with their machinery aft. This Office of Naval Intelligence manual, which was declassified in 1972, when dealing with the engines aft Type B standard ship does however narrate 'some of which are possibly of engines amidship construction.'

Although her existence and details may not have been fully known by the Allies during the war, in the report *Japanese Naval and Merchant Shipping Losses During World War II by All Causes* prepared after the war had ended by The Joint Army-Navy Assessment Committee in February 1947, *Sankisan Maru* is listed as sunk at Truk.

————————

After entering service in March 1942, *Sankisan Maru* was initially employed carrying cargoes of rice and foodstuffs from Thailand and Korea to Japan. But she was soon requisitioned by the IJA as a *Rikugun Yusosen* Auxiliary Transport vessel and armed with machine guns for AA defence.

On 4 June 1942, she is listed as departing Tokyo Bay in a convoy bound for Marifu, near Hiroshima, escorted by destroyer *Hatakaze*. On 5 September 1943, she departed the port of Moji, towards the southern tip of Japan in a large convoy bound for Takao in Taiwan, escorted by the 2nd Class destroyer *Sanae*. The convoy was detected, and the American submarine *Pargo* (SS-264) carried out a night surface radar attack, firing six torpedoes without any hits. The convoy arrived at the major Japanese navy base at Mako in the Pescadores Islands archipelago off the western coast of Taiwan on 11 September 1942, before departing the same day for Takao.

The following year, she was requisitioned on 7 October 1943 by the IJN, returning to the Yokosuka Naval Arsenal in Tokyo Bay – one of four principal naval shipyards operated by the IJN. On 26 October 1943, she departed Yokosuka in a convoy bound for Truk that was escorted by the kaibōkan *Fukue* and an auxiliary gunboat. Two days into the voyage, *Sankisan Maru* broke down and had to be escorted by *Fukue* to Chichi-jima, in the Ogasawara archipelago, about 150 nautical miles north of Iwo Jima. She arrived there on 30 October 1943. On 2 December 1943, *Sankisan Maru* departed Chichi-Jima along with the *Hinode Maru* to make the perilous return journey to Yokosuka, Japan, escorted by Patrol Boat PB-46.

On 31 January 1944, *Sankisan Maru* departed Yokosuka bound for Truk in a large convoy escorted by the Subchasers CH-29 and CH-64, the auxiliary Subchaser *Takunan Maru No.6* and the minesweeper *Keinan Maru*. Her holds were packed full of a cargo of war supplies, wooden cases of small arms ammunition, trucks (stowed in her holds and as deck cargo), thousands of 20mm and 25mm AA shells, hundreds of depth charges, 12cm (4.7-inch) artillery shells, munitions and ordnance. The convoy arrived at the Japanese naval base at Chichi-Jima on 3 February 1944, and after pausing there in relative safety overnight, set off the following day, 4 February, for the last leg of the voyage from Chichi-Jima to Truk. The Subchaser CH-32 was attached for protection.

The convoy entered the Truk lagoon on 13 February 1944, just four days before Operation HAILSTONE - and *Sankisan Maru* anchored off the south west shore of Uman Island in the south part of the Sixth Fleet Anchorage, just to the north of the *Amagisan Maru*.

On the first day of Operation HAILSTONE, Strike 3D aircraft from *Bunker Hill* arrived over Truk between 1215 – 1300, tasked to attack shipping found in the anchorage between Fefan and Uman Islands. The 7,620grt *Amagisan Maru* was anchored nearby at the southern end of the anchorage and was the largest ship present with the highest potential naval value.

At 1250, five *Bunker Hill* Curtiss SB2C Helldivers and four Grumman TBF Avenger torpedo bombers attacked *Amagisan Maru*.

As AA gunners and crew on *Sankisan Maru* no doubt opened fire on the American planes, the SB2C Helldiver bombers scored a direct hit on *Amagisan Maru* with a large 1,000-lb bomb – whilst TBF Avengers hit her with torpedoes, sending a pillar of smoke and debris more than a hundred feet into the air. Within 15 minutes of the attack, the ship was burning fiercely and sinking by the bow. She would disappear beneath the waves shortly thereafter.

Sankisan Maru, anchored closeby to the north of *Amagisan Maru,* was the second ship to be attacked west of Uman Island by *Bunker Hill* aircraft. Four SB2C Helldivers pushed over for their attack, one scoring a bomb hit. *Bunker Hill* planes attacked other shipping around Dublon, Fefan and Uman during the next Strikes 3E and 3F – but although they wreaked havoc, *Sankisan Maru* escaped destruction. She had survived the 1st day of the air raids.

Early the following day, 18 February 1944, *Bunker Hill* launched the first bombing strike of the day, Strike 3A, between 0515 and 0520. 13 SB2C Helldivers and 8 TBF Avengers roared off the flight deck, with four Hellcats providing escort. The Helldivers carried two 500-lb bombs or one 1,000-lb bomb, whilst the TBF Avenger torpedo bombers carried a single torpedo with running depth set at 6-feet.

The Strike 3A planes swept towards Truk - following in after the dawn initial fighter sweep. As the planes reached North Pass, they followed the western side of the barrier reef south until they were able to turn into the wind and begin their runs on ships anchored on the west side of Uman Island. The first target was a freighter anchored ½ mile west of Uman – it was *Sankisan Maru*.

The SB2C Helldivers pushed over for their dives, dropping seven bombs in all - one was a hit amidships that set the freighter ablaze. As the Helldivers completed their attack, the next 5 Helldivers were starting their attack on a cargo ship northeast of Uman.

As the strike concluded, the TF 58 planes turned to head back to their carriers, leaving *Sankisan Maru* ablaze. No Allied eyes witnessed what happened next - but at some point the fires reached the munitions being carried in the aft holds of *Sankisan Maru*. The subsequent detonation of the embarked munitions was catastrophic.

The whole aft section of the ship, from just abaft the bridge to the very stern, was blown apart and completely dispersed. Sections of the ship were flung hundreds of yards across the lagoon. All crew in the aft section of the ship were instantly killed.

The only part of the aft ship not to be dispersed was the rudder and propeller. With the ship around them obliterated, they fell straight down to the seabed, landing on the seabed upright, in isolation.

The Wreck today

Today the forward section of the wreck of the *Sankisan Maru* sits upright on a sloping bottom in 24 metres of water at the bow. The forward section sits on a sand and coral flat - and being so shallow, the wreck is bathed in sunlight. Where the aft portion of the wreck once was, from about the bridge to the stern, the seabed drops off quickly down to about 45 metres, where the prop, rudder and a small attached section of keel stand upright in isolation.

The wreck of *Sankisan Maru*
Least depth: 15m
Depth to seabed: 24m (Bow)
45m (Stern)

Rudder, propeller and section of keel

Ship dispersed abaft bridge

Jumbo boom

Deck cargo army trucks

Aircraft engines, cowlings, Isuzu trucks

Five-round 7.7mm rifle clips, 30-round machine gun clips

The stern section of *Sankisan Maru* was completely destroyed in a massive secondary explosion of embarked munitions. The ship around the rudder and stern was destroyed, and now free they fell to the seabed where they now sit in isolation.

The *Sankisan Maru* is another of the 'musts' for Truk divers. The shallow bow section holds much of interest in gentle depths that are ideal for the less experienced diver. The more experienced diver can drop down over scattered sections of ship to the bottom at 45 metres to see the prop and rudder, before returning up to the bow to burn off any decompression exploring the forepart of the ship.

The impressive bow dominates a flat, slightly shelving seabed that is covered in coral outcrops and coral covered pieces of wreckage. The port anchor is still held snug in its hawse near the stem – whilst the starboard anchor is run out. Both chains run up through their hawse pipes to an anchor windlass set on the fo'c'sle deck and now heavily encrusted in coral. The embossed name of the ship is there. It was once readable - that's how her once elusive identity was confirmed - but the letters are now well covered in coral.

Two large flat-topped upright cylindrical features stand on the fo'c'sle deck, now covered in coral. The starboard side one has been home for the last 30 years or so as an impromptu rest for a 7.7mm AA machine gun and 30-round strip-fed ammunition clips – which were there when I first dived Truk in 1990. A pair of bitts for securing mooring lines are dotted at either side of the fo'c'sle deck. Dropping down from the fo'c'sle deck to the well deck, two aft facing open doors in the fo'c'sle bulkhead allow entry into the fo'c'sle spaces.

Hold No 1 no longer has its hatch beams in place - these were no doubt blown off with the expanding force of the huge explosion. Some appear to be on the fo'c'sle deck whilst others lie around the ship on the seabed. The Hold is largely empty down to her lower web

Paul Haynes beside the bow of *Sankisan Maru*. The downline is usually tied off to the bulwark as here. (Courtesy Ewan Rowell)

Aircraft engine cowling in Hold No 2 tween deck. (Courtesy Ewan Rowell)

Radial aircraft engines in the foredeck holds. (Courtesy Ewan Rowell)

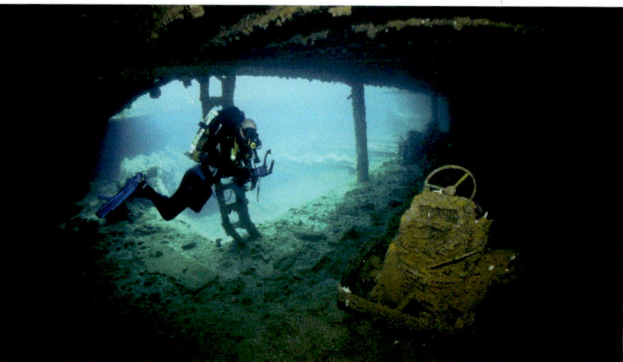

The author films a truck in the tween deck of Hold No 2. (Courtesy Ewan Rowell)

frames and beams - where there is a mass of small arms ammunition dispersed amongst the beams, some loose, others still in their wooden boxes. The wooden boxes have survived here, and not been eaten away by wood borers, due to the high copper content of the water from the ammunition. Five-round stripper clips and loose rounds of 6.5mm infantry ammunition, likely for Type 38 Ariska rifles, are mixed with loose 7.7mm rounds likely for the improved Type 99 Ariska rifle and longer 30-round strip-fed clips for air cooled 7.7mm Type 92 heavy machine guns. There are also 20mm Type 98 AA autocannon shells present.

On the port side of the weather deck abreast Hold No 1, the skeletal chassis of two deck cargo Army trucks rest upside down half over the gunwale - complete with radiators, engine, drive systems and tyres. A third truck can be found on the starboard side of the weather deck here.

In between the hatches for Hold No's 1&2, the foremast still rises up vertically towards the surface from a masthouse - and has its inverted crosstree in place. A large jumbo cargo boom for heavy lifts, goosenecked to the foremast at the bottom, is secured upright alongside the mast - giving the appearance of a twin mast. When I first dived at Truk in 1990, the top of the foremast just broke the surface, and dive boats would simply place their anchor on top of it. Divers could then follow the foremast all the way straight down from the surface to the wreck below. The top of the mast has now broken off, or been removed to reduce the danger to shipping, just above the crosstree.

The two cargo booms, that would have run forward over Hold No 1 from short kingposts on either side of the foremast, have swung out. One rests over the port gunwale and the other over the starboard gunwale.

Hold No 2 has a large section of torn metal across it at main deck level – this is a section of the aft ship that landed here after the explosion. This Hold contains radial aircraft engines, engine cowlings, wheel assemblies, exhausts and a number of 1.5-ton Isuzu trucks which are parked in the tween deck spaces on the port side - their chassis, steering wheels, gearboxes and twin sets of tyres still easily recognisable. Hold No 1 connects directly to Hold No 2 at tween deck level and it is possible to swim below decks directly from Hold No 1 to Hold No 2 right onto the trucks.

A goalpost pair of kingposts, braced at the top with a cross bridge, stand upright forward of the extended section of superstructure in front of the bridge, which has the hatch for Hold No 3 at shelter deck level. The starboard cargo boom has swung out and fallen down to rest over the starboard gunwale. The hatch cover beams for Hold No 3 are, unsurprisingly, also missing and the hold again appears largely empty. At the aft end of the hold, on the port side, the weather deck has collapsed down onto the tween deck as a result of the structure being weakened by the explosion. There is no dividing bulkhead between Hold No's 2&3 so divers can move directly between the two below deck. There is a considerable quantity of bunker coal in this hold – for the ship's engine.

Immediately abaft the hatch for Hold No 3 stood the composite superstructure - which originally rose up some five deck levels, with the command bridge at its top. But there is little left recognisable of this composite superstructure today. It has been destroyed right down to the level of the hatch for Hold No 3 - and of the superstructure, today there is only a confusing mass of bent, twisted and collapsed plating covered in coral, with a pair of lifeboat davits hanging over the starboard side.

Abaft the bridge, the devastated composite superstructure starts to slope off dramatically to where the whole aft part of the ship simply disappears, as though cut through by a huge knife and removed.

The sides of the ship at the break, where it has been cleaved in two, are peeled outwards with the expanding force of the explosion. That a ship can be torn apart, and almost vapourised like this, is extremely daunting. No one knows exactly what quantity of munitions were stored in the aft holds of *Sankisan Maru*, but no one on this part of the ship survived.

Where the ship ends abruptly, where she was torn apart, the seabed drops away dramatically down to where it flattens out at about 45 metres. As you follow the sloping seabed and descend towards the bottom, large sections of double bottoms, ship's plating, frames and general debris are strewn all around on the white sandy seabed.

About 60-70 metres away from the devastated bridge area, and your depth having dropped from 25 metres to 45 metres, divers will find the rudder and propeller sitting bolt upright on the sand – with only a small section of the keel attached. They lie directly underneath where the stern of the ship would have been when she was afloat, directly above you now.

Nuwa Paul leads the way down from the shallow section of wreck past scattered sections of ship towards the prop and rudder at 45 metres. (Courtesy Ewan Rowell)

The author beside the isolated prop and rudder in 45msw. (Courtesy Ewan Rowell)

33. *Sapporo Maru*
Motor trawler (1930)

IJN *Ippan Choyosen* Auxiliary Storeship (1943)

Combined Fleet Anchorage

Tonnage:	361-grt
Dimensions:	145-ft long; beam of 24-ft; draught of 14-ft
Launched:	24 October 1930
Sunk:	4 May 1944
Cause of loss:	Bombed by U.S. aircraft
Wreck location:	Combined Fleet Anchorage, north of Fefen Island
Depth to seabed:	25 metres – bow
	28 metres – stern
Least Depth:	16 metres – bow
	20 metres smokestack & wheelhouse
	24 metres - stern

The 361-ton deep-sea motor trawler *Sapporo Maru* was launched in 1930. She was strafed and eventually sunk in a follow up raid to Operation HAILSTONE on 4 May 1944.

The 361grt steel motor trawler *Sapporo Maru* was a sizable refrigerated deep-sea trawler built in Hikoshima by Mitsubishi Zosen Kaisha Ltd. for the fishing company Kyodyo Gyogyo K. K. Her keel was laid down on 9 August 1930.

Sapporo Maru was named after the city of Sapporo, which is the largest city on the northern main island of Hokkaido - and the fifth largest city in Japan. She was launched for fitting out on 24 October 1930 and completed on 25 November 1930. Power was delivered to her single screw by a diesel engine. *Sapporo Maru* was registered in Tobata on the southwest coast of Japan, immediately beside Hikoshima, where she was built.

At the time of her construction, Japan had one of the largest fishing industries in the world. In the early part of the 20th century, Japanese commercial fishing had mainly been dependent on the warm Japan Current that runs through the cold Pacific waters along Japan's southern and eastern coast, bringing essential nutrients and an abundant supply of fish. However, with advances in fishing boats and their technology, in the years following WWI,

Japanese trawlers had started to venture further afield. In April 1929, Kyodyo Gyogyo Kaisha sent its first trawlers to begin fishing in the Yellow Sea, the South China Sea and the Bering Sea.

The refrigerated deep-sea trawler *Sapporo Maru* entered service in late 1930 just as Kyodyo Gyogyo Kaisha was starting to work these distant waters. Five years later, in 1935, Kyodyo Gyogyo Kaisha started trawling in Mexico's Gulf of California and then in Argentine waters. In 1937 the company became part of Nippon Suisan K.K., which remains a major international maritime company today.

When Japan invaded China and began the 2nd Sino-Japanese war in 1937, *Sapporo Maru* was put to work replenishing naval vessels with fresh food around the Pearl River estuary in China.

On 24 May 1942, *Sapporo Maru* is listed as setting off in a northbound convoy of IJA and IJN transports from Tateyama in Tokyo Bay, escorted by the survey ship *Komahashi* and the minelayer *Ukishima*. The convoy was bound for Paramushiro, at the northernmost end of the Kurile Island chain, which stretches from the north of Japan to the Kamchatka Peninsula. Paramushiro had been developed by the Japanese into a strategically significant air and naval base for operations against Siberia and the Aleutian Islands.

On 5 December 1943, *Sapporo Maru* was requisitioned by the IJN and on 20 January 1944 she was registered as an auxiliary stores ship (*Otsu* category) attached to the Yokosuka Naval District and attached to the Fourth Fleet, based at Truk, as part of the Replenishment Force. There were two categories of such auxiliary vessels: *Ko* category had an IJN Captain whilst the *Otsu* category like *Sapporo Maru* did not.

Sapporo Maru is not a casualty of Operation HAILSTONE on 17/18 February 1944. But two months later, as part of the continued neutralisation of Truk, there were several bombing raids by American Consolidated B-24 Liberators on 4 and 5 April 1944. *Sapporo Maru* took a near miss from one bomb that damaged her engines and left her unnavigable.

The follow up Task Force 58 fast carrier raid to Operation HAILSTONE took place on 29-30 April 1944, three weeks after *Sapporo Maru* had been damaged by B-24 bombs. Whilst the Truk lagoon had thronged with large Japanese ships during Operation HAILSTONE, two months later in late April 1944 there were a relatively small number of small ships, tugs, harbour vessels and barges to attack. Still unnavigable following the B-24 bombing raid on 4/5 April 1944, *Sapporo Maru* was attacked by TF 58 aircraft and was an easy, almost defenceless, target. She was hit and two of her crew killed.

Sapporo Maru managed however to remain afloat – albeit temporarily. She is recorded as finally sinking a few days later, on 4 May 1944, north of Fefan Island. She now lies to the southwest of the large wreck of *Kiyosumi Maru*, sunk two months previously during HAILSTONE.

Immediately following the second fast carrier raids on 29/30 April 1944, the Japanese 4th Base Force HQ on Truk was demobilised and later that month, 71 aircraft were moved from Truk to Guam and Yap, leaving Truk as a neutralised naval base with no air power. Truk was effectively cut off from Japan and the local population and Japanese service personnel began to starve.

The deep-sea trawler *Sapporo Maru* today lies in 25-28 metres in an area of poor underwater visibility.

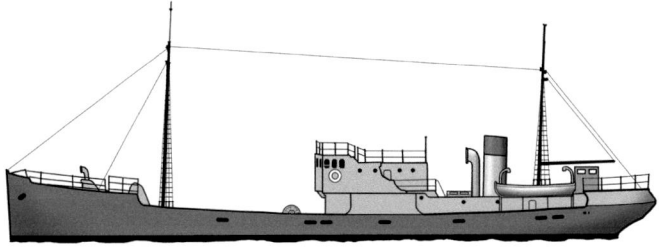

The Wreck today

The wreck of the IJN auxiliary stores ship *Sapporo Maru* is one of the most recent finds in the Truk lagoon - only being located close to the north of Fefan Island in 2002 after a determined search. She lies in an area of relatively poor visibility of about 10 metres on average.

The large motor trawler sits upright on her keel on a sloping bottom with a slight list to starboard. The depth to the seabed is 28 metres at the stern and 25 metres at the bow.

The hull and superstructure of the former auxiliary storeship remain fairly intact and the smokestack is still upright.

34. *Seiko Maru*
Cargo vessel (1940)
IJN *Ippan Choyosen* Auxiliary Transport Ship (1941)
U.S. Recognition Code: 45 MKMF

Fourth Fleet Anchorage

Tonnage:	5,385grt
Dimensions:	392.5-ft long; beam of 53-ft; draught of 30-ft
Launched:	14 May 1940
Sunk:	18 February 1944
Cause of loss:	Bombed by TF 58 aircraft during Operation HAILSTONE
Wreck location:	Fourth Fleet Anchorage north east of Eten Island
Depth to seabed:	52 metres
Least Depth:	29 metres - bridge
	40 metres - main deck

The large 5,385grt auxiliary transport ship *Seiko Maru* was launched in 1940 and requisitioned by the IJN in 1941. Constructed with her engines aft, she was misidentified during Operation HAILSTONE by U.S. pilots as an oiler.

The 5,385grt freighter *Seiko Maru* was laid down in 1939 at the Harima Zosensho K.K. shipyard in Aioi. She was named and launched on 14 May 1940 – the year before Japan initiated her Pacific war.

Seiko Maru was constructed with a raised fo'c'sle and two foredeck holds (No's 1&2) with the foremast rising up from a small masthouse between the hatches. Her bridge superstructure was set two thirds of the way forward whilst her machinery, her boiler and engine rooms etc, were set aft. With her engines aft and a slender amidships bridge superstructure, she looked very much like a conventional tanker – which always has its machinery at the stern. As a result, during Operation HAILSTONE a number of attacking U.S. aircraft misidentified her as an oiler.

Most of the aft ship was given over to large cargo holds – Hold No 3 was set directly abaft the amidships command bridge and had a goalpost pair of kingposts to work cargo.

The hatches for Hold No's 4&5 were set between the amidships bridge superstructure and the superstructure at the stern with the hatch for the aftmost Hold No 5 being at shelter deck level. The mainmast was positioned immediately in front of the stern superstructure, which covered the boiler and engine rooms below. On either side of the fireproof engine casing were cabins for crew accommodation. The steering gear was set at the very stern above the rudder. Lifeboats swung from davits on top of this deckhouse on either side of the smokestack.

Seiko Maru was fitted with two steam turbines DR geared to one shaft and a single screw. The turbines were manufactured by Ishikawajima Shipbuilding & Engineering Co of Tokyo. Steam for her two turbines was provided by coal - hence she sports the classic slender tall smokestack of a coal burning ship, designed to get the dirty smoke away from the sterncastle. In archive photos of the ship under way, clouds of black coal smoke billow from her smokestack. Her single screw gave her a service speed of 12 knots and a top speed of 14 knots. She could carry 800 tons of bunker coal that gave her a radius of 4,900 miles at 12 knots.

Following completion, *Seiko Maru* was registered in Dairen and on 17 July 1940 entered service with the large and prestigious Dairen Kisen K.K. The important trading port of Dairen (today known as Dalian - and known in the past as Port Arthur) was situated to the west of North Korea on the southern tip of the Liaodong peninsula, which projects out from the Chinese mainland into the north part of the East China Sea. *Seiko Maru* joined her sister ships *Shoko Maru,* and *Hokko Maru* already with Dairen Kisen K.K., which had international routes from Dairen to Tsingtao, Shanghai, Japan, America, Australia and Europe.

Following the Japanese attack on Pearl Harbor on 7 December 1941, *Seiko Maru* was requisitioned by the IJN as an *Ippan Choyosen* Auxiliary Transport, tasked with carrying war supplies from Japan to the Inner South Seas. In May 1942, she was in the Solomon Islands operating with *Kamikawa Maru* and *Nikkai Maru* to set up a seaplane base at Rekata Bay on the northern coast of Santa Isabel Island.

On 24 July 1943, *Seiko Maru* left Yokosuka, Japan, carrying a cargo of timber in an escorted convoy bound for Truk along with *Yamagiri Maru* and *Mogamigawa Maru*, which was carrying 700 troops along with torpedoes, A6M Zero fighter aircraft, spare aircraft engines, rice and general cargo.

Just before midnight on 31 July 1943, the convoy was attacked by the American submarine *Pogy* (SS-266) on its second war patrol. *Pogy* successfully torpedoed and sank *Mogamigawa Maru* with the loss of some 130 of the embarked troops. The kaibōkan *Fukue* counter-attacked, dropping depth charges and forcing *Pogy* deep as *Yamagiri Maru* and *Seiko Maru* used their speed to leave the area.

A few hours later *Fukue* and *Seiko Maru* returned to the scene in darkness and *Seiko Maru* began picking up some 600 survivors of the troops and crew who had been aboard *Mogamigawa Maru*. But at 0610, more than 200 nautical miles north east of Truk, *Seiko Maru* herself was torpedoed by the American submarine *Steelhead* (SS-280). Badly damaged, *Seiko Maru* was towed to Truk for repair before she once again assumed her transport duties.

On 17 February 1944, *Seiko Maru* was in the Truk lagoon, at anchor in the Fourth Fleet Anchorage about 1,000 metres north east of Eten Island, with *Hokuyo Maru* anchored just to her south east. After the initial fighter sweep by Hellcats had cleared the skies of Japanese fighters, the strikes by dive and torpedo bombers began.

Between 0630 and 0645, in the first bombing strike of the day, *Essex* Strike 2A torpedo bombers attacked what they believed was an oiler about two miles east of Dublon. It may well have been *Seiko Maru*, her engines aft configuration fooling U.S. aviators into thinking she was an oiler. They landed a 500-lb bomb aft of amidships before breaking off the attack.

For the second group strike of the day, TG 58.1 carrier *Enterprise* launched her Strike 1B aircraft between 0700-0710 for an assigned time at target of 0815-0830. 12 SBD Dauntless dive bombers roared into the air off her flight deck, along with seven TBF Avenger torpedo bombers and 10 escort Hellcats.

As the *Enterprise* Strike 1B aircraft headed for Truk, about 20-30 miles northwest of North Pass the TBF Avengers spotted and bombed the light cruiser *Katori*. The SBD Dauntlesses were then detached and entered the lagoon from the northeast around 0815. One division of SBD's attacked what they reported to be a tanker, north of Fefan. It was *Seiko Maru* – her engines aft configuration had again misled the U.S. aviators.

Bombs from the SBD Dauntlesses exploded on both sides of the aft hold. Large explosions were seen by the attacking aircraft to blow out the sides of the ship. A fierce fire started and a cloud of black smoke from burning fuel billowed upwards as the ship immediately started to settle by the stern. Her stern superstructure was soon submerged, her still buoyant bow being forced upwards. Meantime, torpedo planes were attacking the nearby *Hokuyo Maru*, a combat photograph taken at the time shows a torpedo running straight and true towards her stern on the starboard side.

Seiko Maru is ablaze and down by the stern in the centre of this combat photo of the 4th Fleet Anchorage. A torpedo streaks towards the stern of *Hokuyo Maru* as TF 58 planes are silhouetted as they range over the lagoon air space above. (National Archives)

Despite the serious damage, *Seiko Maru* was still apparently afloat on the second day of the raids when the group strikes ended. She had been so badly damaged at the stern, that I suspect, given she was almost 120 metres (392-ft) long with a draft of about 10 metres, that her stern was probably resting on the seabed in 50 metres of water, whilst her bow was still proud of the water.

She eventually succumbed to her wounds however - and sank to the bottom of the Fourth Fleet Anchorage.

The Wreck today

Today the wreck of the *Seiko Maru* sits upright on her keel with a very slight list to starboard in 52 metres of water with a least depth of 29 metres to the top of the bridge superstructure. The general depth to her fo'c'sle deck is about 35 metres and her weather deck at almost 40 metres.

The ship is largely intact from the bow to the aft pair of kingposts situated between Hold No's 3& 4. From Hold No 4 aft to the stern, there is clear evidence of the ferocity of

The wreck of *Seiko Maru*

Least depth: 29m (Bridge)
Depth to seabed: 52m

Mainmast

Lifeboat davits

Kingposts

Bridge superstructure:
two telegraphs and
helm in open water

Foremast

24-inch
Long Lance
torpedoes

Jury-rigged
filed artillery
bow gun

Pitched engine
room roof

Bomb damage; deck
bulges upwards and
hole in hull plating

Both anchor chains run out

Artist's impression of the large wreck of *Seiko Maru*, sitting upright
in the 4th Fleet Anchorage in just over 50 metres of water.

the attack and the damage caused by precise U.S. dive-bombing. Understandably, because of her machinery aft configuration, the returning U.S. pilots reported that they had attacked an oiler. It is no surprise therefore that the most significant damage is to the stern, where her machinery is situated. It has been a recurring feature of my diving Pacific WWII shipwrecks that tankers and oilers attacked by U.S. fast carrier planes are almost invariably hit at the stern - in the vast cathedral like spaces of the engine room compartments. As well as wrecking the engines and disabling the ship, these large spaces would fill with water and drag the ship down by the stern. It was known that with heavily compartmentalized oil tanks, a tanker or oiler could take several hits forward and remain afloat due to the buoyancy of many empty or half empty tanks.

At the imposing bow of *Seiko Maru*, the stem of which rises up some 15 metres from the seabed, both anchor chains run out from their hawse pipes to the sand. The starboard anchor chain is splayed slightly to starboard whilst the port chain runs out dead ahead.

Both anchor chains rise up through their hawse pipes to the fo'c'sle deck, at a depth of about 35 metres, where they lead back to the anchor windlass. There is a section of bulwark around the tip of the bow, but mostly the fo'c'sle deck was ringed by a guardrail that has now largely disintegrated and disappeared.

A vintage 75mm Type 90 field artillery field gun, originally with wooden wheels (an original horse drawn carriage style gun) had been jury-rig mounted on the fo'c'sle deck up near the bow. The Type 90 was unique amongst Japanese artillery pieces in that it had a muzzle brake at the end of the barrel that redirected propellant gases to counter recoil and reduce unwanted muzzle rise. The Type 90 was introduced to the IJA in 1930 in two forms, one with wooden wheels suitable to be horse drawn and the other with solid rubber tyres and a stronger suspension for towing by motor vehicles. The wooden wheels of this artillery piece are long gone, and its remains are now heavily encrusted with corals and sponges – making it virtually unrecognisable. A few spent shell casings lie nearby.

Moving aft from the bow and dropping down from the fo'c'sle deck to the well deck at a depth of just under 40 metres, the hatches for Hold No's 1&2 are found, separated by a small masthouse from which the foremast with its inverted crosstree rises high up towards the surface. On either side of the foremast stand short forced draft kingpost ventilators. The ventilator mushroom mouthpieces are turned to face inwards towards the foremast. Cargo handling booms run forward over Hold No 1 and aft over Hold No 2 from each kingpost.

Hold No 1 still has its athwartships hatch cover beams in place and has a number of 24-inch diameter Type 93 Long Lance torpedo bodies stored nose down in a vertical position - although some have fallen over. These 20-ft long Type 93 Long Lance torpedoes were at the time the best torpedoes in the world and were the result of Japan's attempts in the 1920's & 30's to compensate for the limitations on numbers of capital ships she was allowed in comparison to the Allies as a result of historic naval treaties, which did not apply to smaller warships such as destroyers.

The Type 93 torpedo design held a 1,080-lb warhead that was devastating against the thin steel shell plating of unarmoured merchant ships and could also punch through the underwater side protection systems of Allied capital ships. The Type 93 Long Lance torpedoes found in Hold No 1 had a range of 20,000 metres (12+ miles) at 48 knots and 40,000 metres (almost 25 miles) at 36 knots. They were powered by compressed oxygen, which produced less of a give-away bubble trail than conventional compressed air.

Continuing to move aft, most of the hatch cover beams for Hold No 2 are missing. The port cargo boom runs aft from its kingpost beside the foremast over Hold No 2 to rest its end on a cradle on the front bulkhead of the bridge superstructure. The starboard boom (which runs aft from the starboard kingpost on the masthouse), has been displaced to now run diagonally over Hold No 2 and rest its end on top of the port boom, on the bridge cradle. A descent into the depths of this hold reveals only a number of crushed 55-gallon drums.

Abaft Hold No 2, and well forward of amidships, stands the slim bridge superstructure, which runs from one side of the ship to the other and rises up three deck levels. A set of steps on either side of the well deck, at the lowest level, lead up from the well deck to walkways that run along either side of the bridge superstructure. As you swim aft along the walkway, the superstructure steps inboard and the shelter deck widens. The area above the walkway, abaft the bridge, is decked over to the side of the ship - creating an open boat deck where lifeboats swung in davits.

The topmost wooden level of the command bridge superstructure has rotted away or been burnt away to leave two engine order telegraphs and the helm, with rudder direction indicator pedestal, standing in open water at about 29 metres. The navigation compass lies nearby. The deck levels below held officers' accommodation in the higher levels and the ship's galley, mess area and radio room along with the crew's quarters, heads and tiled bathtubs at lower levels.

Moving aft from the command bridge, the depth increases as you drop down to the aft well deck at about 40 metres. Sets of steps lead down to the well deck from the walkways that run along either side of the bridge superstructure.

Set in the aft well deck, the hatches for Hold No's 3 & 4 are separated by a pair of goalpost kingposts, which are connected at the top by an intricately braced bridge. Two cargo booms run out, one from either kingpost forward over Hold No 3, which only has one cover beam in place and is largely empty. Two more cargo booms run aft out over Hold No 4.

The ship took bomb hits on either side towards the stern, the explosions causing much serious structural damage to the ship. The deck plates around Hold No 4 noticeably bulge upwards - and there are holes in the shell plating of the hull here on either side. The hatch cover beams have been blown away from the force of the explosions. The sides of the ship at the aft part of Hold No 4 are noticeably torn and displaced upwards.

Moving further aft from the seeming chaos at the aft end of Hold No 4, there is a rise to shelter deck level where the intact hatch for the aftmost Hold No 5 is found, with all its hatch cover beams still neatly in place. The hold is largely empty.

Short sets of steps lead up from the shelter deck to the open expanses of the deck above. The machinery superstructure here at the stern has the mainmast at its leading edge, with its inverted crosstree in place, flanked by short kingposts for cargo handling. The cargo booms are swung out to starboard.

Above the boiler room, at the front of this deckhouse, the tall imposing smokestack still rises vertically. There are two spare propeller blades secured to the sterncastle bulkhead immediately forward of the smokestack.

Immediately abaft the smokestack, the pitched roof of the engine room is flanked by mushroom shaped forced draft ventilators. Here, at either side of the smokestack on the Boat Deck, empty lifeboat davits are still in their stowed swung-in position – evidence that the crew had no time to lower the boats in this area as a result of the explosion and subsequent fierce fires. It was not uncommon for boats to be blown away or destroyed by bomb hits nearby.

Decked over walkways lead aft on either side of the sterncastle, where the crew would have been billeted in cabins inboard. The walkways lead to the very stern of the ship where the quarter deck has been violently uplifted by an explosion that must have taken place almost directly underneath.

Moving round the fantail and beginning to move forward on the starboard side, the quarter deck becomes even more mangled, until you arrive at a large athwartships tear in the deck where the ship has almost been cleaved in two by bomb explosions beneath. These have uplifted the whole stern section of the ship, stressed and fractured the deck and structure beneath.

If, as I suspect, she was resting with her damaged fantail on the seabed, whilst her bow was still proud of the water, then some of the damage we see today on the wreck will have been caused by weakened sections of the ship buckling with the great weight of the ship pressing down.

35. *Sinkoku Maru*
Merchant Tanker (1939)
Sinkoku Maru-class *Yusosen* Auxiliary oiler – *Ko* category (1941)
U.S. Recognition Code: MKMFK

Combined Fleet Anchorage

Tonnage:	10,020 grt
Dimensions:	503.3-ft long; beam of 65-ft; draught of 37.1-ft
Launched:	13 December 1939
Sunk:	18 February 1944
Cause of loss:	Bombed in radar guided night attack by *Enterprise* TBF's during Operation HAILSTONE
Wreck location:	Combined Fleet Anchorage
Depth to seabed:	40 metres
Least Depth:	12 metres - bridge
Other name:	*Shinkoku Maru*

———————————

The 10,020grt merchant tanker *Sinkoku Maru* was launched in 1939 and requisitioned as an auxiliary oiler by the IJN in 1941.

(For a discussion of the construction and layout of tankers, cf *Fujisan Maru*)

The 10,020grt merchant tanker *Sinkoku Maru* was laid down in October 1938 at the Kawasaki Dockyard Co. Ltd. in Kobe on the north shore of Osaka Bay, on the southern side of the main island of Honshū. The Romanized name registered at Lloyds, *Sinkoku Maru*, uses the old Kokutai spelling under the language system applicable at the time of construction. The Hepburn or Phonetic transliteration of Japanese words into English produces *Shi* where the Kokutai official system of the time produces *Si*. The significance of Kokutai diminished post 1945 and the vessel is more often referred to nowadays using the Hepburn system as *Shinkoku Maru*. But I feel that the spelling of her name in use at the time she was built and registered at Lloyds is probably the best to use to avoid difficulties in finding her in records of the time.

Sinkoku Maru was built for the Kobe Sanbashi K.K. Line to carry petroleum in bulk. She had a cruiser stern and her machinery aft. Propulsion was delivered by a single 2-stroke 8-cylinder diesel engine manufactured by the Kawasaki Dockyard Co that gave her a service

302

speed of 15 knots and a maximum speed of nearly 20 knots with an estimated operating radius of 18,500 miles at 15 knots. *Sinkoku Maru* would be the main large ship built for the Kobe Sanbashi K.K. Line - the others being tugs and tenders.

Such was Japan's need for fuel oil, to support her expansionist ambitions, that her civilian tanker fleet was steadily built up in the years before the war - and the Japanese government influenced their design and construction to allow use in any possible future conflict.

The tankers of the early part of the 20th century were basically a long steel box divided into a series of compartments or tanks, that gave exceptional strength and stability. Each cargo tank could be filled and emptied independently of the others so that different types of oil could be loaded into separate tanks and discharged without being cross contaminated. Each cargo tank was linked to a system of pipelines inside the ship that led to the ship's pumps. Another set of pipelines led up from the pumps up to the tanker's deck where they were conveniently located for connecting to shore pipelines for loading and discharging.

Pumps bring on the oil, and pumps force it off and bring ballast aboard. The pumps are operated from a Pump Control Room, housed deep inside the ship where a pumpman balanced the ship with oil cargo or with water to fill drained tanks. A vertical stairwell leads up from the control room to a small deckhouse on the weather deck. There could be several pump control rooms, one for the foreship usually set on just in front of the bridge superstructure, and another for the aft ship tanks. The ship's pumps were primarily used for pumping the cargo out of the ship to shore storage tanks - and for pumping ballast water in or out of the ship. Shore pumps were used for pumping oil aboard from the land to fill tanks.

The upper deck was a continuous weather deck only penetrated by small raised cargo hatches, one for each tank, which were fitted with watertight steel lids that were kept dogged down and sealed when the ship was loaded.

Sinkoku Maru was designed to carry some 93,300 barrels of oil in her tanks, where a barrel is 42 U.S. liquid gallons. This gave her a capacity to carry some 12,688-tons of crude oil.

Rising above the weather deck were three superstructures – the fo'c'sle, the bridge superstructure (forward of amidships) and the poop island or sterncastle where the engine machinery was situated, surrounded by the fireproof engine casing. Outwith the engine casing, the sterncastle provided accommodation for the rest of the ship's company, and often held the mess, galley, refrigerated space and steering gear.

Because of their strong heavy compartmentalized construction, tankers were constructed to sit deeper in the water than conventional merchant ships and in rough weather the weather deck would be continuously swept by seawater. A *flying bridge* catwalk walkway was set about 8 feet above the weather deck, allowing crew to pass safely to and from each of the three superstructures.

Fourteen months after her keel was laid, *Sinkoku Maru* was named and launched for fitting out afloat on 13 December 1939. She was completed on 28 February 1940, and the new *Sinkoku Maru* was chartered immediately by Kawasaki Kisen for oil transport services, with her first voyage being to the United States to collect oil.

On 18 August 1941, just one month after the final round of U.S. embargoes cut off oil supplies to Japan, with war now almost inevitable, the IJN requisitioned *Sinkoku Maru* and work began just days later at the Naniwa Dockyard in Osaka to convert her into a *Yusosen* auxiliary oiler. A 12cm/45-cal (4.7-inch) short naval gun was fitted on a gun platform on her foc'sle deck and another similar 12cm/45-cal gun was mounted at her stern. These were QF guns that could fire 8 rounds per minute, but their rate of elevation and traverse was too slow for effective use against aircraft.

The conversion work was completed on 24 September 1941, following which she was registered as an auxiliary oiler – *Ko* category, with IJN captain - and attached to the Kure Naval District with Kure as her home port.

In late October 1941, *Sinkoku Maru* and the oiler *Toho Maru* were assigned to the 1st Air Fleet and equipped for refuelling at sea. Some structural modifications were made and a heavy-duty tripod mast was fitted near her stern, abaft the smokestack, to support the heavy fuel lines used during replenishment-at-sea (RAS) operations with other vessels on both her port and starboard beams. Once the conversion was complete, she was tasked to proceed to Kagoshima Bay on Kyushu and en route, to conduct refueling exercises with the 1st Air Fleet *Kidō Butai* carriers and escort cruisers and destroyers in preparation for the forthcoming possible Pearl harbor strike.

The following month, on 18 November 1941, *Sinkoku Maru* and six other oilers, the *Kokuyo, Kenyo, Kyokuto, Toho, Nippon* and *Toei Maru's,* were tasked to take part in the Pearl Harbor raid and ordered to the Kuriles, which are a small group of islands in the Sea of Okhotsk, part of the chain of such islands that stretches down from the Kamchatka Peninsula, to the north of Japan. These oilers would operate as the Supply Group to provide fuel for Admiral Chūichi Nagumo's *Kidō Butai* Carrier Striking Force of the six fleet carriers *Akagi, Kaga, Hiryū, Sōryū, Shōkaku* and *Zuikaku* along with their Support Force of escort warships.

The *Kidō Butai* Carrier Striking Force of six fleet carriers, eight oilers and their screen of warships set sail from the Kuriles for Hawaii on 26 November 1941 under total secrecy. On 6 December 1941, the *Kidō Butai* carried out its final refuelling, after which, *Sinkoku Maru* along with the other 1st Supply Group oilers *Kenyo, Kokuyo* and *Kyokuto Maru's,* escorted by the destroyer *Kasumi* were detached and tasked to a designated rendezvous point to meet the *Kidō Butai* carriers on their return from Hawaii. Following the Pearl Harbor strike, *Sinkoku Maru* was discharged from refuelling operations on 16 December 1941.

On 8 January 1942, *Sinkoku Maru* left Kure bound for Truk with the oiler *Nippon Maru,* the two battleships *Kirishima* and *Hiei* and a number of escort destroyers. The naval squadron arrived at Truk on 14 January 1942, where *Sinkoku Maru* refueled the battleship *Hiei* before going on to refuel the fleet carrier *Zuikaku* and a destroyer.

Sinkoku Maru was then tasked to participate in the invasions of Rabaul and Kavieng that began on 20 January 1942. She again refueled the powerful Japanese aircraft carriers and other surface vessels, before briefly returning to Truk on 27 January 1942 before heading back to Japan.

After several more replenishment operations, *Sinkoku Maru* was assigned to Operation C for the raids into the Indian Ocean, refueling the IJN fleet carriers whose naval aircraft struck British naval bases at Colombo and Trincomalee in Ceylon (Sri Lanka) on 9 April

1942. After refueling the battleship *Hiei* on 15 April, *Sinkoku Maru* detached on 16 April 1942 and headed back to Kure in Japan.

On 27 May 1942, *Sinkoku Maru* departed Hashirajima as one of five oilers supporting Admiral Chūichi Nagumo's Carrier Striking Force for the invasion of Midway, that was designed to trap and destroy the remaining American carriers. By 3 June 1942, the Supply Group had concluded its refueling tasking and *Sinkoku Maru* was detached from the Carrier Strike Force and sent back to Japan. She arrived back at Yokosuka on 13 June 1942 and was then tasked to serve on general fuel duties, transporting heavy oil from Balikpapan, Borneo, Sumatra, Singapore and Malaya to the Combined Fleet Base at Truk.

On 17 August 1942, an escorted convoy with the two oilers *Sinkoku Maru* and *Nichiei Maru* was attacked by the American submarine *Gudgeon* (SS-211), northwest of Truk and almost midway between Guam and Truk. USS *Gudgeon* claimed three torpedo hits on *Sinkoku Maru* and two more on *Nichiei Maru* - but both oilers received only minor damage. The torpedoes were possibly duds, a common problem for the Americans at this point of the war.

The two fortunate oilers were able to proceed to Truk where they were quickly repaired and returned to duty, refueling warships off the eastern Solomons in late October before heading north to the IJN advance base at Truk.

Sinkoku Maru arrived at Truk on 31 October 1942 and immediately began refueling the heavy cruiser *Atago*, and in the days that followed, the destroyer *Kuroshio* and the light cruiser *Nagara*. *Sinkoku Maru* departed Truk on 9 November 1942 to rendezvous with the main battlefleet.

In early January 1943, *Sinkoku Maru* was sent to Saipan and then onwards to the oil fields of Balikpapan where she took on supplies of fuel before returning to Truk. After refueling naval units there, she was sent to Bougainville in the Solomons where she transferred fuel to the fleet oiler *Tsurumi* before heading back to Truk and then returning to Yokohama in Japan in March 1943.

After passages to Singapore, Korea, Moji and Taiwan, *Sinkoku Maru* departed Singapore on 30 June 1943, bound for Truk via the Philippines and Palau. During this passage, on July 7 1943, *Sinkoku Maru* was again torpedoed, this time by USS *Peto* (SS-265) to the south west of Truk, near Papua New Guinea. She took one hit in the bow - but was able to continue to Rabaul from where she was escorted to Seletar Naval Base, Singapore for final repair. She was operational again on 15 August 1943 and immediately set off on a refueling mission to Truk, arriving there on 11 September 1943. After refueling naval units, she set off from Truk on 27 September, bound for Japan via Palau.

In October 1943, *Sinkoku Maru* operated around Java in Indonesia - before calling at Singapore on 7 November 1943. She departed Singapore on 10 November, and arrived at Balikpapan on 14 November 1943, departing the same day for Truk carrying fuel oil in an escorted convoy with four other tankers and other auxiliaries. The fast tankers *Sinkoku Maru*, *Nippon Maru*, *Toa Maru* and *Nampo Maru* detached from the convoy at Palau, and were escorted by the two destroyers *Hibiki* and *Hamakaze* for the final leg of the voyage to Truk. The flotilla arrived at Truk on 22 November 1943, entering the lagoon via the South Channel.

Sinkoku Maru subsequently departed Truk on 7 December 1943 in an escorted convoy bound for Balikpapan, via Palau, to load fuel. The convoy arrived at Balikpapan on 19 December 1943 and *Sinkoku Maru* departed the next day under escort for Surabaya, a few hundred miles to the south in Indonesia, arriving there on 22 December 1943.

The next day, 24 December 1943, *Sinkoku Maru* departed Surabaya once again for Balikpapan, to load aviation fuel destined eventually for Rabaul, via Palau and Truk. With lading complete, *Sinkoku Maru* departed Balikpapan on 29 December 1943 in an escorted convoy for the long journey out through the Celebes Sea into the Pacific, to the first port of call, Palau, which lay almost 1,200 nautical miles away. With her in the convoy were the tankers *Akebono Maru* (subsequently sunk by TF 58 aircraft at Palau during Operation DESCRATE 1 in March 1944) and *Fujisan Maru* (a present day Truk wreck). The convoy arrived at Palau on 4 January 1944. Truk was still more than 1,000 nautical miles distant to the east.

Sinkoku Maru reached Truk safely on 10 January 1944 and departed once more on 19 January 1944 to pick up a cargo of fuel at Balikpapan. With her tanks once again full, she departed Balikpapan on 3 February 1944, arriving at Ulithi Atoll in the Carolines on 10 February 1944. She set off for Truk the next day – and arrived there on 14 February 1944. She immediately transferred oil to the auxiliary oiler *Tonan Maru No.3* before anchoring in the Combined Fleet Anchorage to the north of Fefan and west of Moen.

As Task Force 58 carrier aircraft began Operation HAILSTONE, just 3 days later on 17 February, tankers and oilers were valuable targets of high naval importance.

17 Helldivers, 8 TBF Avengers (carrying 500-lb, 1,000-lb and 1,600-lb bombs) were launched with four escort Hellcats between 0515 and 0530 for the first Strike 3A by Task Group 58.3 carrier *Bunker Hill*. The planes roared off the flight deck into the wind and then formed up aloft and climbed to 13,000-ft for the flight to Truk.

After about one hour of flight, the strike planes swept over the Truk lagoon for their allocated time over target between 0645 to 0700. The two preceding attacks, Strike 1A by Task Group 58.1 and Strike 2A TG 58.2 were just ending.

After coming in from the west and reporting heavy cloud cover, after attacking a warship that the pilots believed was an escort carrier, one Helldiver attacked a 4,000-ton oiler anchored northwest of Dublon – the pilot reporting a hit that started a fire. It is believed that this could only be *Sinkoku Maru*.

Around 1302, launching began aboard TG 58.1 *Yorktown* for Strike 1E. 13 SBD Dauntless dive-bombers, 6 TBF Avengers torpedo-bombers and 12 escort Hellcats were launched – and as the *Yorktown* planes arrived over Truk at about 1415, the Hellcats had a short engagement with Japanese fighters, shooting down three - before going on to strafe Eten airfield, an oiler, two freighters and a destroyer. The TBF's meanwhile attacked *Kiyosumi Maru,* north of Fefan, and then *Yamagiri Maru*, northwest of Fefan.

Several SBD's attacked *Yamagiri Maru,* and a transport at anchor east of Eten, before attacking a tanker northwest of Fefan –most likely *Sinkoku Maru*. The *Yorktown* SBD's hit the oiler amidships – but *Sinkoku Maru* remained afloat and survived the first day of the raid.

Just after 0200, during the darkness of the early hours of DOG-DAY, 18 February 1944, the first radar-guided night attack against Japanese shipping was launched by Torpedo 10 from *Enterprise,* which was steaming 100 nautical miles north east of Truk. All 12 TBF Avengers were equipped with radar - and armed with 500-lb bombs, they roared off the flight deck catapults into the pitch blackness of a tropical night that was lit only by a quarter moon. The TBF's vectored to Truk at an altitude of 500-ft on a compass bearing - Truk was detected on the radar screens when the group was 20 miles away. This radar-guided night raid would be extremely successful.

The 12 TBF's split into two groups and despite being detected as they crossed the barrier reef around the lagoon, triggering AA fire to open up, eight Japanese ships would be destroyed and five damaged. Some 60,000 tons of Japanese shipping went to the bottom of the lagoon for the loss of one TBF Avenger and several others damaged.

Sinkoku Maru was one of the ships targeted in this night radar attack. The TBF's scored a near miss, with a 500-lb delayed fuze bomb, on her port side towards the stern - abaft the smokestack. Despite being a near miss, the force of the explosion, transmitting through incompressible water, blew in her shell plating over a roughly circular area of about 25 feet in diameter – opening a vertical tear in her shell plating several metres high - directly into her cavernous engine room. Water flooded unchecked into this massive space, which rises up several deck levels, and she began to settle by the stern.

As the 11 surviving TBF's of Torpedo 10 returned towards their distant carriers, they saw the Hellcat fighters of the dawn initial fighter sweep inbound: the TBF's arrived over *Enterprise* at 0555, just as the sun was coming up.

Meanwhile, the rush of water into the cavernous machinery spaces at the stern of the great oiler caused her to settle by the stern, eventually pulling the rest of the ship under. 86 crew aboard had been killed.

Sinkoku Maru settled on the bottom of the lagoon, upright in about 40 metres of water. Given this depth - and her considerable size – even as she sat on the lagoon bottom, the topmost sections of her two masts protruded above the surface.

In subsequent years the top sections of her masts were cut away using explosives to minimize the hazard to other shipping.

The Wreck today

Today the wreck of the famous oiler *Sinkoku Maru* sits upright on her keel in 40 metres of water with a least depth to the top of her bridge superstructure of just over 10 metres. She is a big ship - the second largest in the lagoon.

Given her depth, a long dive starting at her deepest parts around the engine room at the stern, and ending with her shallowest bridge area, can be carried out with only minimal decompression. On most of the writer's dives we usually enter via the bomb hole near the seabed on her port side aft at a depth of about 38 metres. We often spend almost a full hour exploring the engine room, as we rise up through the various deck levels, before exiting the stern superstructure onto the boat deck at about 20 metres. Although we have incurred a significant decompression obligation by that time, we usually spend a further hour exploring

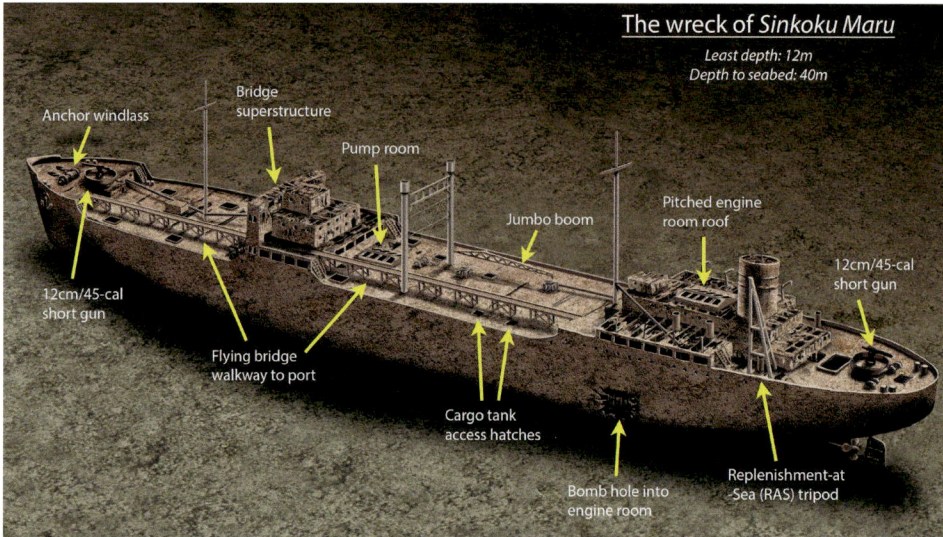

The wreck of *Sinkoku Maru*
Least depth: 12m
Depth to seabed: 40m

Anchor windlass

Bridge superstructure

Pump room

Jumbo boom

Pitched engine room roof

12cm/45-cal short gun

12cm/45-cal short gun

Flying bridge walkway to port

Cargo tank access hatches

Bomb hole into engine room

Replenishment-at -Sea (RAS) tripod

Sinkoku Maru was hit by a bomb on the port side aft at her machinery spaces during the night radar guided attack by Enterprise TBF's. She settled by the stern and came to rest on the seabed in 40 metres of water.

the remainder of this big ship, simultaneously and almost unnoticeably burning off our deco as we investigate the bridge superstructure and bow area - before a final ascent from a 2-hour dive with minimal final decompression.

Like all tankers and oilers of this period, *Sinkoku Maru* was constructed with her machinery aft. This configuration allows the most efficient use of aft compartments for oil tanks, without the complication of having a prop shaft tunnel running through them from an amidships engine.

The engine room of this wreck is one of the jewels of Truk lagoon, rising up for about five deck levels with crew quarters either side of the fireproof engine casing. But beware, the engine room spaces and adjacent compartments of the aft part of the ship are a maze of interconnecting passageways and machinery rooms and it is very easy to get disorientated. Great care should be taken if penetrating these spaces and this should not be attempted without an experienced local guide.

Entry to the engine room can be made in a number of ways. If you don't want to go deep down to the seabed and do serious penetration diving through the tight lower levels of the engine room, you can enter the upper engine room space through the large engine room skylights - or meander through the rooms of the upper level of the superstructure. In this way, you will stay shallower and enter directly into the upper level of the engine room, which is a large cathedral-like space with an athwartships catwalk running from side to side, high up. Piping, valves and gauges line the sides and bulkheads whilst broad shafts of sunlight from the skylights cut through the gloom bringing ambient light. Stairways lead down to the lower deck levels.

If diving with a local guide, then suitably experienced and trained divers can descend to the wreck, and then move aft along the port gunwale of the ship. As the divers approach the mainmast and then the stern superstructure, they drop over the port side of the ship, heading deep down the seemingly vertical wall of welded shell plating, forward of the stern.

As the divers almost reach the seabed, at a depth of just short of 40 metres, the vertical shell plating suddenly deforms - the plates are blown smoothly inwards, leaving a concave, almost circular depression in the hull about 25-ft, (8 metres) in diameter. In the middle of the concave depression, there is a vertical fissure, some 2-3 metres across, where the shell plates have been separated by the near miss 500-lb bomb exploding closeby in open water, the shockwave neatly parting the plates at the join.

This vertical fissure between shell plates allows divers access into the lower spaces of the engine machinery rooms. It is clear that the radar guided TBF Avengers were using delayed fuze bombs – this would be needed to allow the fatal bomb to get this far down the

Above: Detail of the stern of *Sinkoku Maru* showing bomb hole on her port side aft, her defensive stern gun and her aft deckhouse with pitched engine room roof just forward of the smokestack. The large RAS tripod for refuelling other ships under way at sea is on the port side.

Right: The author enters the wreck through the bomb hole on the port side aft at seabed level. (Courtesy Ewan Rowell)

Lower right: Near the very stern at the lowest level of the engine room, the author passes along a gangway beside the rockers of the steering or dock engine. (Courtesy Ewan Rowell)

side of the ship underwater, almost to the bilge keel, before detonating. This 500-lb bomb likely had a 2-second or 4-second delayed fuze, fairly common at this stage of the war.

Finning carefully through the vertical fissure, you enter the wreck into a sizeable area, where the lower deck is a few metres beneath you, mostly covered with heavy duty machinery. Thinner guardrails, stairways and fixtures here have been bent and deformed by the explosion – and such a big area, being torn open to the sea, would have let a vast amount of water flood into the ship, and search its way through corridors and up stairwells.

Pressing on into the ship, a vertical set of steps leads up to the deck above – it is striking how all the bulkheads and exposed metal are still blackened by wartime fires. Everything is heavily covered in fine silt, that is easily disturbed by careless finning – so exercise extreme caution with finning. You soon find yourself following the dive guide along corridors, up and down catwalks and drifting through the very innards of this vast ship.

Passing a long main switching panel bulkhead, divers can drop down a deck level via a stairwell to the very bottom of the ship, no doubt divers are now below the level of the seabed outside. Here you can swim along a catwalk that runs fore and aft beside the rockers of a long rectangular diesel engine. I have always assumed this to be the steering engine for turning the rudder, as well as providing power and electricity for the ship whilst tied up in port. At the end of the catwalk, it is possible to drop a further deck down past a wall of pipes, switches and gauges to a large space where a fuel transfer pump is situated with seemingly delicate glass inspection tubes still on top.

Pressing further into the ship and moving aft, the sides of the ship sweep together to form the very stern - with the prop shaft running along below you via thrust bearings to where it exits the ship at the stern gland.

Moving forward, deep down at the bottom of the engine room, divers move past the bases of the 8 cylinders of the diesel engine and then can pass athwartships, above a grated catwalk, past the rear of a large Scotch boiler - before turning to move forward once again along the side of the boiler. Another catwalk runs athwartships, from one longitudinal catwalk to a mirror image catwalk on the other side of the ship, forward of the boiler. Steam pipes coming from the boiler are still lagged in heat resistant material.

Filming the control panel in the cavernous aft engine room of *Sinkoku Maru*. Stairs lead up either side and cross the room high up. Light streams in through the open skylights at the very top. The large bolted cylinder tops of her engine are seen below. (Courtesy Ewan Rowell)

Moving up to the higher deck levels of the engine room, divers eventually reach the large space directly above the engine cylinders - the tops of the cylinders are found at a depth of about 32 metres, each with a number of large hexagonal nuts connecting the tops to the cylinders. Far above at a depth of about 20 metres at the top of this cathedral-like space, the engine room roof skylights allow shafts of light blue sunlight from outside to cut across the darkness and illuminate the space.

In this upper engine room, the iconic brass main fuel transfer pump for the ship's engine fuel can be found. There are three large rectangular inspection panels, now blue with contaminated fuel oil, on the main section frontage - and a smaller blue rectangular inspection panel on either side. High up, a gallery walkway runs from one side of the ship to the other across the space - and a doorway leads off on the port side to a workshop with a lathe and other heavy-duty fixtures.

Exiting from the engine room via the roof skylights onto the boat deck, empty lifeboat davits stand at either side of the ship, whilst the banded smokestack still stands upright.

Moving towards the stern of the ship, the 12cm/12-cal (4.7-inch) short naval gun still stands in position on its platform on the poop deck - almost completely covered in coral. A depth charge roll-off rack is located at the very tip of the stern. Looking over the fantail of the ship, the banded rudder and single screw are visible below.

Turning now to begin moving forward, on the port side, just abaft the smokestack, stands the tall tripod mast of the Replenishment-At-Sea (RAS) system. This would support the fuel transfer hoses that would be strung between the oiler and the vessel it was refueling abeam. Moving forward past the tripod mast, a set of steps leads up to the boat deck whilst walkways lead up along either side of the stern deckhouse at poop deck level. Crew cabins open off inboard from this walkway, each with a porthole. The tall mainmast still stands upright.

Moving forward from the aft deckhouse, past the mainmast, there is a drop down from the poop deck to the weather deck, which is a long flat expanse of open decking over the after oil tanks. The weather deck is peppered with small individual oil tank hatches, one for each tank - the lids are still dogged down.

The flying bridge walkway runs fore and aft, a few metres inboard of the port gunwale, and some 2-3 metres (8 feet) above the weather deck. The flying bridge offered a safe and dry way for crew to move between the poop island and the bridge superstructure. The flying bridge passes inboard of the port leg of the goal post kingposts situated abaft the bridge – a cargo boom lies on the deck on the starboard side. Forward of the kingposts, and abaft the bridge, a pitched roof similar to the engine room roof reveals where the Pump Control Room is situated below.

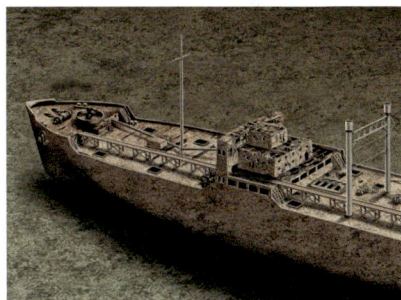

Detail of the forward section of *Sinkoku Maru* showing goalpost kingposts, amidships bridge superstructure, foremast and fo'c'sle with defensive gun platform. The flying bridge links all three islands and is about 8-feet above the weather deck on the port side.

Left: Divers pass aft beneath the amidships RAS masts of *Sinkoku Maru*. (Author)

Right: Engine order telegraph in the bridge of *Sinkoku Maru* (Courtesy Ewan Rowell)

Arriving at the bridge superstructure, the deckhouse steps upwards in several deck levels and has very noticeable slender bridge wings at the front. The navigation bridge at the highest level has long rectangular windows - and just inside, at the front, there are three engine order telegraphs, two close together just forward of the helm and rudder direction indicator pedestal - and a third, likely the revolutions telegraph, to the port side wing. A compass binnacle is attached to the front wall of the deckhouse on the centre line. Beneath this deck level, close to the bridge was the officers' quarters and on the deck level below, was the ship's infirmary, galley and mess.

The flying bridge continues forward from the bridge superstructure, again on the port side, connecting the bridge superstructure to the foc'sle deck. Some tankers and oilers had no flying bridge forward of the navigation bridge, whilst others had their flying bridge on the centre line of the vessel. Precise details like this allowed U.S. pilots, and analysts poring over reconnaissance photos, to identify which particular class of tanker was below them. There are several small oil tank hatches on the foredeck, spread around the foremast, which still stands upright. Doors at either side of the foc'sle bulkhead allow entry to the lamp room and other compartments inside.

Fixed steps lead up, either side of the foredeck, to the foc'sle deck where the 12cm/12-cal (4.7-inch) short naval gun can be found on its platform, heavily covered in corals due to the shallow depth of about 12 metres. Four boxes of ready-use shells sit on the aft portion of the gun platform.

A sturdy anchor windlass sits on deck in front of the bow gun. Chains lead up from their spurling pipes to the windlass and from there to a hawse pipe on either side of the deck. Both chains are run out to the seabed below.

The foc'sle rooms beneath are largely empty although more boxes of 12cm shells for the bow deck gun above can be found.

36. *Shotan Maru*
Standard Cargo vessel (1943)
U.S. Recognition Code: 23 MFM

Fourth Fleet Anchorage

Tonnage:	1,999-grt
Dimensions:	285-ft long (oa); beam of 43-ft; draught of 20 feet
Launched:	1943
Sunk:	18 February 1944.
Cause of loss:	Bombed by TF 58 aircraft during Operation HAILSTONE
Wreck location:	Fourth Fleet Anchorage – west of Fanamu Island
Depth to seabed:	51 metres
Least Depth:	39 metres – top of superstructure amidships
	45 metres – main deck
Other names:	*Matsutan Maru, Matsutani Maru, Syotan Maru*

The cargo steamship *Shotan Maru* was constructed during 1942 and launched in 1943 for Matsuoka Kisen K.K of Fuchu. The war was in full swing by this time and due to wartime secrecy, there is little direct information about her construction.

The 1,999-ton cargo ship *Shotan Maru* was launched during the war in 1943

There are rather confusingly a number of possible Romanized names for this vessel – a consequence of the fact that the kanji letters of her name can be Romanized as *Shotan* but also as *Matsutan* or *Matsutani*.

The ship was built during the war and was not registered in Lloyds Register under any of these Romanized names. She does not appear in the classified U.S. Naval Intelligence *Japanese Merchant Ships Recognition Manual*, which collated intelligence on all known Japanese ships at the time (O.N.I. 208-J (Revised)). There is reference to her as *Matsutani Maru* in the authoritative *Warships of the Imperial Japanese Navy 1869-1945* by Hansgeorg Jentschura, where she is listed as being sunk at Truk during Operation HAILSTONE. The *Dictionary of Disasters at Sea During the Age of Steam* lists her as *Shotan Maru*.

The established methods for transliteration of Japanese words into English spelling during the war were the Hepburn system (used by the U.S. Navy) and the wartime official Japanese Kokutai system. The Hepburn system is the most nearly phonetic rendering of spoken Japanese and produces her name as *Shotan Maru*. The wartime Kokutai system renders her name as *Syotan Maru*. The significance of Kokutai diminished post 1945 - and although you see her in places referred to as *Syotan Maru*, she is more often referred to nowadays as *Shotan Maru*. Despite the rather confusing possibilities, it is one and the same ship that is under consideration.

The name *Shotan Maru* has been the name commonly given to this wreck in Truk diving circles since it was rediscovered and subsequently identified after much original research and underwater measuring by the late Klaus Lindemann in 1980, who took the name from the list of ships lost in Truk compiled by the Japanese themselves after the war.

However, in the document *Japanese Naval and Merchant Shipping Losses During World War II by All Causes* prepared by the Joint Army-Navy Assessment Committee NAVEXOS P 468 dated February 1947, she is listed throughout as *Matsutan Maru* and nowhere is she called *Shotan Maru*. In Japanese wartime records she is more commonly called *Matsutan Maru*. For the purposes of this book and to avoid sewing endless confusion, despite the other names in usage, I have kept to the name *Shotan Maru* ascribed to the wreck since she was found by Klaus Lindemann in 1980.

The *Shotan Maru* was a Standard Type 1C steamship, built to a modest coastal three-island steamer standard design along with many other identical ships in much the same way as *standard ships* were built in large numbers for Great Britain in WWI.

Prior to 1941, Japan had no effective standardisation of ship building, the design was largely determined by shipping company requirements and by builders. In the six years before the war, approximately 330 ships over 1,000-tons were built in over 100 different classes.

With her sea lanes enormously extended soon after the outbreak of the Pacific war on 7 December 1941, and with the subsequent successful predation by American submarines already taking its toll, Japan belatedly realised her pressing need for merchant ships.

Japan began work on new modern *standard ship* designs in 1942, but with approximately two years required to design and start building new types of standard ship, construction of the newer designs of standard ships would only start in early 1944. In the interim, to boost her fleet of transport ships to service her far-flung Pacific garrisons, from 1941 Japan started a program of mass standard ship production using older, tried and tested, pre-war designs, which continued until July 1944. U.S. Intelligence also assessed that some 125 non-standard ships were built to a number of designs totaling some 430,000 gross tons of shipping.

The new standard ship designs would allow new ships to be quickly built, in quantity. Cargo capacity and speed of construction were ranked to be of paramount importance, with the performance of the ships themselves being sacrificed.

The new standard ship hull designs would have great angularity. They would have a broad beam in relation to length, producing a large cargo carrying capacity for a sacrifice of speed. The new standard ships would be an 'economy' type of ship that could be quickly built to a simple standard design, using simple flat surfaces instead of traditional smooth curved surfaces. Rapid production of these new standard ships would allow the continued transport of huge volumes of materials and supplies to the fight in the Pacific.

U.S. Intelligence allocated an identifying number to Japanese standard ships, which denoted the year of construction - with *Type 1* being a *1943* build, *Type 2* being *1944* and

Type 3 being *1945*. U.S. Intelligence identified nine standard classes, two being identical with pre-war design and classified them as Type, A, C, D, D (Modified), E, K, TL (Modified), TM and TM (Modified). The design of the individual types varied from year to year.

Constructed during 1942-43, the steamer *Shotan Maru* was thus built to an older pre-war design, as a standard three-island steamer classified by US Intelligence as a Type C design. Being launched in 1943, her designation was thus as a Type 1C vessel. She had a raised fo'c'sle, two foredeck holds, a composite superstructure with the boiler and engine rooms immediately abaft the bridge, two after deck holds and a poop island. She was fitted with a traditional coal-fired vertical triple expansion steam engine, her single screw giving her a service speed of 11 knots and a range of about 4,000 nautical miles. Being a coal burner, she had the classic tall narrow smokestack, in this case situated immediately abaft the bridge. Some 34 Type 1C ships were constructed in total.

On completion, on 2 September 1943, *Shotan Maru* departed Sasebo, Japan, for Kwajalein via Yokosuka and Truk. Later that month, she is listed (as *Matsutan Maru*) as completing the final leg of that voyage, departing Truk with *Seikai Maru* bound for Kwajalein on 30 September 1943, escorted by the Subchaser CH-31 and the auxiliary Subchasers *Kyo Maru No 6* and CHa-18. The convoy arrived at Kwajalein on 6 October 1943.

On 1 November 1943, *Matsutan Maru* left Kwajalein for a homeward trip to Sasebo in Japan, via Truk, in a convoy escorted by Subchasers CH-30 and CH-31, the torpedo boat *Hiyodori* and the auxiliary subchaser Cha-6. The convoy entered the Truk lagoon on 7 November 1943, departing thereafter for the long return voyage to Japan.

On 25 December 1943, *Matsutan Maru* set off at 0700 in an escorted convoy from Yokosuka, Japan with a cargo of belly tanks for Mitsubishi A6M Zero fighters in her holds. The present-day Truk wreck *Katsuragisan Maru* was also in the convoy. The convoy arrived at Truk on 6 January 1944 and she soon had offloaded her cargo and left the lagoon on other duties.

On 30 January 1944, *Matsutan Maru* departed Rabaul in an escorted convoy bound via Truk for Yokosuka, Japan, that was screened by the destroyers *Matsukaze* and *Fumizuki*, the latter being another present day Truk wreck.

The convoy was bombed by U.S. aircraft on 2 February and *Fumizuki* and the minesweeper W-21 were damaged. The beleaguered convoy arrived at Truk on 6 February 1944, and *Matsutan Maru* anchored in the Fourth Fleet Anchorage.

On the second day of Operation HAILSTONE, 18 February 1944, the initial dawn fighter sweep, VF-10 Hellcat fighters from *Enterprise* strafed all remaining aircraft or hulks and facilities on Moen, Eten and Param airfields and strafed targets of opportunity. Reports were sent back regarding possible targets – and one ship was observed running east of Moen and later Dublon, it was likely the *Matsutan Maru* (*Shotan Maru*).

Meantime, back on the carriers, some 100 miles distant, launching of Strike 1A aircraft on *Enterprise* and *Yorktown* had begun around 0500 in the half light of nautical dawn. Aboard *Enterprise,* 12 SBD dive bombers launched with eight Hellcats fighters as escorts with an allocated time over target of between 0615-0630.

The Strike 1A flight arrived over Truk before it was light enough to attack - and had to circle for about 10 minutes before the first division of 3 planes was able to push over for their attack on the 10,000-ton oiler *Fujisan Maru,* which was underway but slewed to a stop after 2-3 hits.

The second division dived on *Shotan Maru*, which was also underway, hitting her just aft of amidships, in her after hold. The devastation from the bomb hit was catastrophic, the structure of the aft part of the ship was destroyed. Fierce fires were started, which eventually destroyed all the woodwork of her amidships superstructure. As the *Enterprise* group turned to head back to their carrier, they strafed a 44-ft patrol boat, which caught fire and then blew up.

Burning fiercely and in sinking condition, the skipper of *Shotan Maru* steered his vessel towards the shore of nearby Fanamu Island, at the eastern periphery of the Fourth Fleet Anchorage, where he would try to beach his ship. But so great was the damage, that she foundered approximately 300 yards west of the island, her bows forlornly pointing directly towards Fanamu as she went under.

The Wreck today

Today, the structurally intact wreck of *Shotan Maru* sits on her keel with a very slight list - in 51 metres of water. Her bows, frozen in time as she tried to beach, still point towards the shallow reef structure around Fanamu Island to the east. Whereas on her starboard side at the stern, the seabed rises up towards the shallows quite steeply, the remainder of the ship sits on a relatively flat seabed that runs off gradually into greater depths. The least depth to the highest parts of the wreck is 39 metres and it is about 45 metres to the weather deck.

Being designed originally as a small coastal steamer, you will notice immediately when you arrive on the wreck, just how small and narrow of beam she appears in comparison to many of the larger Truk wrecks.

At the bow, the raised fo'c'sle deck is largely empty - the guardrails that once ringed around it are now gone. There is no bow gun, just an anchor windlass with two chains running from it to their hawse pipes. As she was underway and trying to beach, both anchors are still held tight in their hawse pipes. The ends of the two cargo booms, running neatly from short kingposts either side of the foremast, rest on the aft bulkhead of the fo'c'sle. Dropping down to the foredeck, two doors open forward into the fo'c'sle spaces.

On the foredeck, the hatches for Hold No's 1&2 are found – separated by a section of weather deck from which the foremast rises from a small masthouse, complete with crosstree and the remains of standing rigging. The foremast is flanked by short kingposts for cargo booms, two running forward and two aft. The top gallant section of foremast above the crosstree is no longer present, perhaps removed post war to reduce the hazard to shipping.

Hold No 1 still has all its hatch cover beams in place and is a single open space below deck with no tween deck space. Three construction trucks with small cranes mounted on their flatbeds had originally been stowed on top of the hatch cover beams. Two remained in place on the wreck when it was discovered, sitting side-by-side and facing port. However, over the years, as the trucks have corroded and degraded, they have broken apart and parts of them such as their axles with twin tyres either side, have fallen down into the hold. The third truck has gone over the port side of the ship as she sank and now rests upside down on the seabed leaning against the hull.

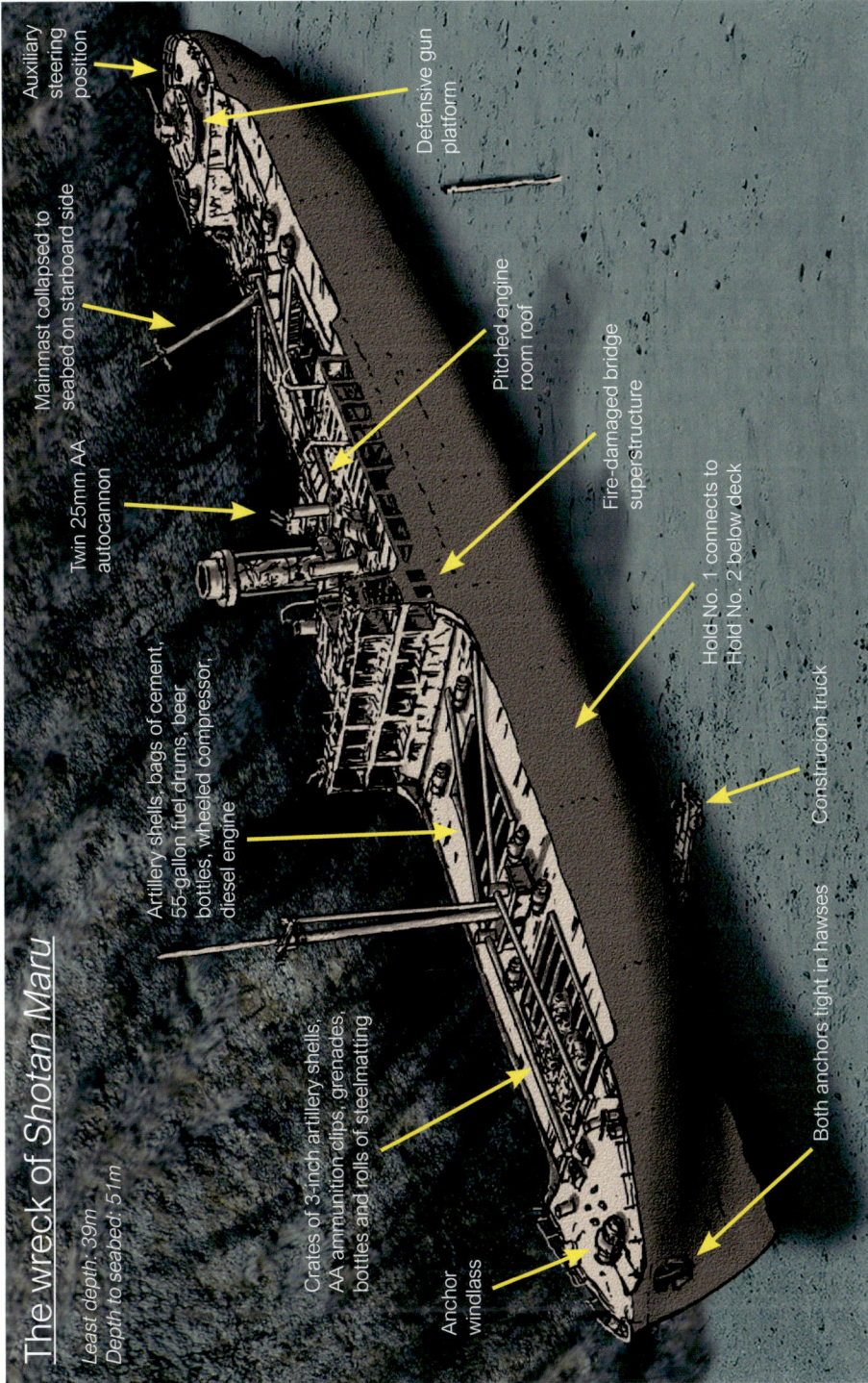

The wreck of *Shotan Maru*

Least depth: 39m
Depth to seabed: 51m

Auxiliary steering position

Defensive gun platform

Mainmast collapsed to seabed on starboard side

Twin 25mm AA autocannon

Pitched engine room roof

Fire-damaged bridge superstructure

Hold No. 1 connects to Hold No. 2 below deck

Artillery shells, bags of cement, 55-gallon fuel drums, beer bottles, wheeled compressor, diesel engine

Construcion truck

Crates of 3-inch artillery shells, AA ammunition clips, grenades, bottles and rolls of steelmatting

Anchor windlass

Both anchors tight in hawses

Shotan Maru took a number of bomb hits around her stern and sank into around 50 metres of water.

Dropping between the hatch cover beams down into the shallow hold, the axles and twin tyres of the two deck cargo trucks are found, with a large pile of beer bottles nearby. Masses of beer bottles are a common sight on nearly every Truk wreck, being a systematic attempt to give the service personnel a little something to ease the rigours of life in the tropics.

Hold No 1 contains 4-packs of 76mm (3-inch) naval gun shells, their wooden boxes rotted away. These were most likely for the aft 76mm (3-inch) short DEMS gun. Scattered around are small arms ammunition, machine gun clips for AA guns and grenades. Hold No 1 connects below decks to Hold No 2 - and divers can fin past the base of the foremast below deck.

Hold No 2 contains much of interest - there are many crushed 55-gallon fuel drums, more artillery shells, bags of cement now set hard and more beer bottles. Directly under the port side of the hatch stands a wheeled compressor - with a large diesel engine nearby and loose timber. Looking upwards, only one of the hatch cover beams for this hold is in place.

Rising up through the hatch onto the weather deck, the port cargo boom has swung to port – whilst the starboard boom has broken, with part of it now in the hold below.

Moving aft, divers now reach the amidships composite bridge superstructure, which appears to have been heavily damaged by fire with all wood and her upper decks being burnt away. Walkways led aft, at shelter deck level, along either side of the superstructure. Along either side of a central inner steel room, the wooden decking that made up the roof of the walkways has disappeared - leaving only the structural beams in place. In the rooms inside, fire-blackened crockery can sometimes be spotted.

The inner parts of her tall smokestack, so characteristic of a coal-burning steamer, still stand just abaft the navigation bridge, buckled and dented by fire and the carnage of her sinking. The thin metal outer shell of the smokestack has largely been blown away or rotted away, although parts around the base reveal the original full size.

Abaft the smokestack, the pitched roof of the engine room can be found. The skylights are closed and there are forced draft ventilators either side. The engine room can be accessed through the superstructure corridors.

Either side of the engine casing, just below the Boat Deck, a walkway leads along either side of the superstructure, with cabins opening off it inboard. With all the wooden decking burnt away, the structural beams of the roof of this deckhouse are now exposed.

A dual-mount 25mm AA autocannon is mounted on the starboard side of the aft boat deck, whilst a second dual-mount 25mm autocannon on the port side has fallen into the space below, after the deck gave way. On the starboard side of the Boat Deck, the lifeboat davits are in the swung-out position – the crew were able to abandon ship here and no doubt row to Fanamu Island nearby.

Moving aft, there is a drop down to the after well deck where two cargo holds are situated. The aft quarter of the ship lies up against the sandy slope that rises up to form the shallow reef around Fanamu Island (to the east).

The damage wrought by the bomb hit aft is very evident here – for about halfway along Hold No 3, the weather deck largely disappears. The ends of the deck plates are torn and curled, revealing the inner ribbed frames of the side of the ship down to the very bottom of the hold. A section of detached hatch coaming curls down to rest on the very bottom of the

Left: View of the fantail of *Shotan Maru* showing auxiliary steering position and defensive gun on its platform. (Courtesy Pete Mesley)

Middle: View of the starboard side aft showing mainmast fallen to rest its end on the seabed. In the distance, divers approach the aft gun platform. (Courtesy Pete Mesley)

Lower: Whilst the aft holds area is quite damaged, the composite superstructure (seen here from the starboard side) is undamaged. Lifeboat davits are swung out. (Author)

Right: The 76mm (3-inch) Type 41 defensive gun on its aft platform, with fixed ladder running up to the gun deck. (Author)

Middle: Looking from the fo'c'sle aft over the hatch for Hold No 1, which still has its cover beams in place. The foremast stands upright in the distance, with two cargo booms running from short kingposts on either side to rest their ends on cradles on the fo'c'sle. (Author)

Lower: The wheeled compressor in Hold No 2. (Author)

hold. The prop shaft tunnel running from the engine amidships towards the stern is visible at the bottom of this hold, on the centre line of the ship.

The section of weather deck, which supported the mainmast house, has collapsed down into the ship. Hold No 4 has largely been blown apart and collapsed, losing most of its depth, its bulkheads buckled and torn.

The mainmast has broken at its base and has fallen to starboard – its upper end now resting on the sandy sloping seabed. The starboard shell plating of the aft part of Hold No 4 has almost all been blown away – the damage wrought by the dive bombers was clearly catastrophic.

Despite the carnage around Hold No 4, the poop island at the very stern is largely intact. Rotted guardrails ring around the poop deck - and a short 76mm (3-inch) Type 41 gun sits on its raised circular platform pointing astern. These defensive Quick Fire (QF) guns were a design that originated before WWI and were often used on smaller auxiliaries as a DP gun against attack by aircraft - and by submarine on the surface. They could fire 15 rounds per minute.

Immediately abaft the 76mm stern gun, and directly above the rudder, is the auxiliary steering position with helm and telemotor. The spokes of the helm have rotted or been burnt away but the hub is still in place. The steering gear is housed below in the sterncastle.

37. *Taiho Maru*
Type 1C Standard Cargo vessel (1943)
IJN *Ippan Choyosen* Auxiliary Transport (1943)
U.S. Recognition Code: Unknown vessel - MFM

Sixth Fleet Anchorage

Tonnage:	2,827-grt
Dimensions:	320-ft long (oa); beam of 45-ft; draught of 21 feet
Launched:	May 1943
Sunk:	17 February 1944.
Cause of loss:	Bombed by TF 58 aircraft during Operation HAILSTONE
Wreck location:	Sixth Fleet Anchorage: south of Fefan, west of Uman.
Depth to seabed:	44 metres – amidships
	50 metres – at stern
Least depth:	30 metres

———————————————

The 2,827-grt coastal freighter *Taiho Maru* was one of 34 Type 1C standard steamships built between 1942-1944. She is thus of similar design to her sister Type 1C vessel *Shotan Maru* in the immediately preceding chapter. (For information on standard type nomenclature see that

Artist's impression of the requisitioned 2,827-grt IJN auxiliary transport ship *Taiho Maru*.

322

chapter). As with *Shotan Maru*, U.S. Naval Intelligence was unaware of the details of *Taiho Maru* and it does not appear in any wartime Recognition manuals.

The Type 1C standard ship *Taiho Maru* was a well-decked medium freighter with raised fo'c'sle, composite central superstructure housing navigation bridge, accommodation and machinery below - and a stern castle. The rest of the ship forward and aft of the composite superstructure was given over to cargo holds.

Taiho Maru was built by Osaka Shosen K.K. at the Hitachi Dockyard in Osaka. She was launched in May 1943 and requisitioned for war use shortly thereafter in October 1943, when a defensive gun was fitted at the stern. Osaka Shosen K.K. was renamed Hitachi Zosen Corporation the same year.

Although diesel engines were increasingly common by this time, being a standard ship built to an old pre-war design, *Taiho Maru* was fitted with a traditional vertical coal fired triple expansion engine that gave her a modest service speed of 10 knots.

Just over three months after being requisitioned, *Taiho Maru* arrived in Truk carrying mail, with her holds full of a cargo of bombs and 55-gallon drums of aviation gasoline. She anchored in the Sixth Fleet Anchorage south of Fefan Island and to the west of Uman Island - and work began to unload her cargo.

As the Operation HAILSTONE attacks began on 17 February, Strike 1D *Yorktown* planes had been tasked to attack Japanese shipping north east of Fefan in the Combined Fleet Anchorage, and south west of Dublon at the Sixth Fleet Anchorage. Between 1110 to 1122, 16 hellcats launched from *Yorktown* to provide escort for their more vulnerable TBF and SBD bombers also launching.

As the *Yorktown* flight arrived over Truk for an assigned time at target of 1215 to 1230, they encountered multiple Japanese Zero fighters. A series of dogfights broke out, in which one division of Hellcats was suddenly attacked by 10-15 Zekes, which swooped down out of the sun at about 20,000-ft. The Hellcats brought down six Zekes and damaged two others - as other divisions of Hellcats scrapped in dogfights as they fought to protect the bombers.

Despite the fierce attention by Zekes, the *Yorktown* TBF Avengers attacked a freighter at anchor east of Eten, then a freighter west of Eten. After attacking what was believed to be a submarine, the TBF Avengers then pressed home a mast head attack on a freighter west of Eten that was hit at the stern. Another transport ship was attacked south of Eten before a transport under way between Eten and Fefan was attacked.

Taiho Maru, still at anchor west of Uman and south of Fefan, was then attacked by the TBF's who scored two bomb hits - one on the bow and one amidships. The fore part of the ship caught fire and mortally wounded, she began to settle.

The fires spread – and eventually reached the freighter's volatile cargo of aviation fuel in 55-gallon drums in her foredeck holds. As happened to *Hoki Maru*, there was an enormous explosion of the drums of fuel in these forward holds that broke the ship in two just at the smokestack.

The forward part of the ship was destroyed and simply blown away. The shell plating and web frames were completely dispersed and flung some distance across the lagoon.

The stern section of the ship escaped destruction from about the smokestack aft. Holding some buoyancy and now free of her bow anchor, she drifted for a short period before eventually sinking and coming to rest on her port side some way away from the shattered remnants of the bow.

Only four of her crew were killed - the majority of her crew having been able to abandon ship safely as she burned after the attack.

The Wreck today

Diving on this wreck today most commonly focusses on the larger stern section, which was first located in the early 1970's. The secondary explosion of her cargo of fuel in the foredeck holds has blown apart the forward part of the ship - leaving only a tangled mass that is almost unrecognizable as the remains of a ship.

The explosion destroyed the bridge superstructure leaving bulkheads, decks and hull plating twisted and deformed and scattering sections of the ship around the seabed. A small 25-30-foot-long section of the very bow itself was located upside down about 20 years later in 1994, some 200 yards away from the remainder of the ship.

Close to the break, two landing craft are found on the seabed. These would have been being used as tenders to transport crew and cargo ashore – they would have been tied off to the ship when it exploded and dragged below as it sank.

The aft section of the ship lies well over on its port side on a sloping bottom that runs from about 45 metres amidships to 50 metres at the stern. The least depth over the starboard beam of the ship is about 27-30 metres.

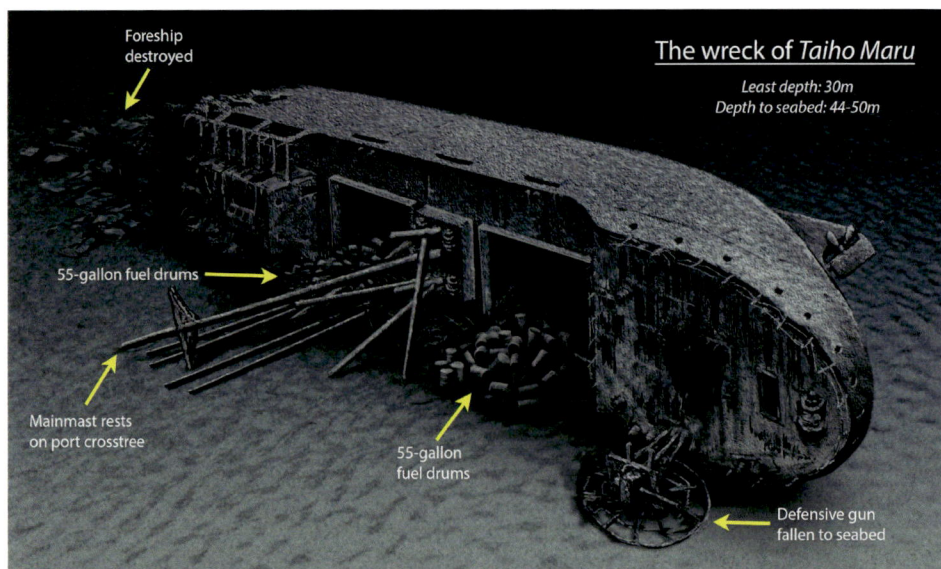

Foreship destroyed

The wreck of *Taiho Maru*

Least depth: 30m
Depth to seabed: 44-50m

55-gallon fuel drums

Mainmast rests on port crosstree

55-gallon fuel drums

Defensive gun fallen to seabed

Fires swept *Taiho Maru* after she was bombed during Operation HAILSTONE and ignited her cargo of 55-gallon drums of fuel in her foredeck holds. The forward part of the ship was destroyed in a catastrophic explosion.

A defensive 76mm (3-inch) Type 41 short naval gun (similar to the one on her sister Type 1C ship, *Shotan Maru*) was mounted on a firing pedestal atop a circular platform on the poop deck, on top of the sterncastle. This Dual-Purpose Quick Firing gun could fire some fifteen 76mm rounds per minute, both against aircraft and against surface targets. The gun has now fallen from its mount and is nowadays buried in the seabed.

There are traces of the lettering of the ship's name still visible around the fantail. The four-bladed propeller is still in place as is the large rectangular rudder, which now is angled down to the seabed.

The two aft holds contain hundreds of 55-gallon gasoline drums, many of which spilled out onto the seabed as the ship hit the bottom. Beware not to disturb any of these as some may well still contain aviation fuel which can cause nasty burns to diver's skin. The hatch beams are missing – perhaps they had been removed as part of the unloading process before the attack or perhaps they were blown away by the force of the blast. Alternatively, they may have simply tumbled off as the ship went over and 55-gallon fuel drums spilled onto the seabed.

At the bottom of the holds, the prop shaft tunnel leads aft to the stern gland from the destroyed engine room.

The mainmast with an inverted crosstree projects outwards diagonally from the masthouse between the hatches for Holds 3&4 and now rests its port crosstree on the seabed. The ends of the two forward and two aft cargo booms have fallen to rest on the seabed.

The ship ends where the fore part has been destroyed. Sections of the forward part of the ship are scattered around the seabed.

38. *Unkai Maru No 6*
(ex SS *Venus*)
Cargo Steamship (1905)
IJA *Rikugun Yusosen* (1937)
IJN *Ippan Choyosen* auxiliary transport vessel (1941)
U.S. Recognition Code: 38 MFMK

Sixth Fleet Anchorage

Tonnage:	3,217-grt
Dimensions:	331.0-ft long; beam of 49.2-ft; draught of 21.8 feet
Launched:	30 October 1905
Sunk:	18 February 1944.
Cause of loss:	Bombed by TF 58 aircraft during Operation HAILSTONE
Wreck location:	Sixth Fleet Anchorage: north of Uman Island.
Depth to seabed:	40 metres
Least depth:	25 metres - top of bridge superstructure

———————

The 3,217grt auxiliary transport *Unkai Maru No 6* is one of the oldest wrecks in the Truk lagoon. She was originally ordered for the Venus Steamship Co of Newcastle as the SS *Venus* and built by William Gray & Co Ltd. in West Hartlepool, England.

The 3,217grt merchant ship SS *Venus* was launched in 1905 in Britain. She was sold to Japanese interests in 1921 and renamed *Unkai Maru No 6*. She was an old ship by the time she was requisitioned by the IJN in 1941.

Her builders, the William Gray & Co Ltd shipbuilding business, had started out in 1839 and had grown rapidly in size. By 1878, the company held the British record for output with 18 ships being launched in a single year. By 1900, at the time the *SS Venus* was being designed, they had eleven slipways employing 3,000 men and by WWI had built 200 ships.

The SS *Venus* was built with a plumb stem and raised fo'c'sle, composite bridge superstructure (with machinery abaft and below) and a poop island. Her forward and after well decks both held two holds. She had a foremast, a tall slender smokestack abaft the bridge, a mainmast and a short pair of kingposts aft. Propulsion was delivered by a single screw powered by coal fed boilers and a 3-cylinder triple expansion steam engine constructed by

Blair & Co. Ltd of Stockton. This gave her a service speed of 8 ½ knots, a maximum speed of 10 knots and an operating radius of about 6,100 miles at 8 ½ knots.

Venus was launched on 30 October 1905 as Yard Number 714 and was completed that December for her first owners, the Cornhill Steamship Co Ltd of London, who sold her after eight years of service in 1913 to the Leander Steamship Co. Ltd of London. Seven years later in 1920, she was sold on to the Thompson Steamship Co. Ltd.

The following year, in 1921, she began her new life in the far east, when she was sold along with five other similar vessels, to the Japanese Nakamura Gumi K.K. line of Kinoye. She was renamed as *Unkai Maru No 6,* which means *'Sea of Clouds'* and registered in Hiroshima.

In 1937, her owners restyled the company as the Nakamura Kisen K.K. Line of Kinoye. In common with many merchant

Bow aspect of the SS *Venus* at Barry Docks.

ships, the *Unkai Maru No 6* was briefly requisitioned by the IJA in the 1930's during the invasion of China.

On 6 August 1941, just two months before the Pearl Harbor raid, she was requisitioned by the IJN as an *Ippan Choyosen* transport ship. She was soon at work carrying cargoes such as cement, for construction of fortifications, out to Japanese possessions such as Saipan and Tinian in the Marianas.

In September 1941, *Unkai Maru No 6* arrived at Palau, delivering cement to Peleliu where the important air base was being fortified. For the return journey to Japan, she loaded a cargo of bauxite ore on the main Palauan island of Babeldaob. Bauxite is primarily composed of aluminium oxide compounds that produce aluminium, vital for airplane manufacture. Arriving back in Japan on 16 October 1941, she unloaded her cargo of bauxite ore at Kobe and was then released back to her civilian owners.

By late 1943, the war was going badly for Japan, with significant losses of merchant ships to Allied planes and submarines. As losses of Japanese shipping intensified, on 5 January 1944, the 40-year-old ship was once again chartered by the IJN as an *Ippan Choyosen* transport ship - and assigned to the Yokosuka Naval District. By this time, she was fitted with an old British made 3-inch QF gun on her foc'sle.

Two weeks later, on 20 January 1944, she set off from Yokosuka, Japan, in a convoy bound for Truk, escorted by the kaibōkan *Oki*. Two other famous present day Truk wrecks were in the same convoy, *Hoki Maru* and *San Francisco Maru*.

After avoiding repeated submarine attacks en route that forced the convoy to divert to Saipan, the convoy arrived at Truk on 4 February 1944. As the convoy entered the lagoon, *Unkai Maru No 6* anchored with her port anchor in the Sixth Fleet Anchorage, two miles south of Eten Island and directly north of Uman Island.

On the first day of Operation HAILSTONE, 17 February 1944, *Unkai Maru No 6* was initially attacked at anchor by Strike 2B torpedo planes from *Essex* between 0830-0845. A bomb hit was scored on her port beam and then another on her port quarter. She began to list to starboard.

Later the same day, between 1215-1230, she was attacked at masthead level during Strike 1D by *Yorktown* TBF torpedo bombers, who scored another bomb hit. Around 1415-1430, she was again attacked, by Strike 1E *Yorktown* torpedo bombers and then around 1445-1500 by *Bunker Hill* Strike 3E dive-bombers. In amongst a number of near misses, one 1,000-lb bomb hit her aft of amidships. The explosion started a large fire and a cloud of thick black smoke billowed up. But despite the damage and the fires, *Unkai Maru No 6* managed to stay afloat throughout the rest of the day and into the night.

As dawn broke on the morning of the second day of the raids, 18 February 1944, the initial fighter sweep Hellcats swept across the lagoon to clear the way for the bombers. The beleaguered *Unkai Maru No 6* was still at anchor, burning and smoking from the previous day's attacks.

Strike 2B launched from *Essex* around 0715 – tasked to attack shipping in the Fourth Fleet Anchorage. The 10 SBD Dauntless dive bombers, four TBF Avengers and seven escort Hellcat fighters arrived an hour later over Truk between 0830-0845. The Hellcats headed for Eten Island to deal with any air opposition, but finding no Japanese fighters aloft, they shot up five fighters parked on the airfield.

With the Hellcats ensuring there was no air opposition, the SBD's attacked two transport ships nearby. The first ship was hit on the port quarter with three near misses that left the ship burning aft. A second ship was spotted anchored about two miles southwest of Eten Island – it was *Unkai Maru No 6*.

The SBD's pushed over for their dives, scoring two bomb hits near the bow and straddling the ship with three near misses. The explosions rocked the ship, lifting the bow upwards. The damage to her hull from these further attacks proved too much and she sank shortly thereafter.

The Wreck today

Today the wreck of *Unkai Maru No 6* sits on her keel in just over 40 metres of water some 600 metres north of Uman Island in the Sixth Fleet Anchorage with a depth just short of about 25 metres down to her fo'c'sle deck and the top of her bridge superstructure. She is a classic three island well deck cargo steamer, with a raised fo'c'sle, composite bridge and engine room superstructure amidships, and a stern castle.

The fo'c'sle deck is heavily covered with corals and still has sections of its guardrail in place around it. The wooden deck planking is all gone, perhaps consumed by the fires that swept the ship or perhaps by wood borer's – but in any event it is possible to look down through the structural beams into the fo'c'sle rooms below.

Near the very bow, the anchor windlass has both chains running from it across the deck to their hawse pipes. The starboard anchor is still held tight in its hawse whilst the port anchor rain is run out along the seabed dead ahead from the bow.

Immediately abaft the windlass stands a large skeletal circular gun platform with a small 3-inch naval gun still in place. Curious divers in the past have rubbed the encrusting coral

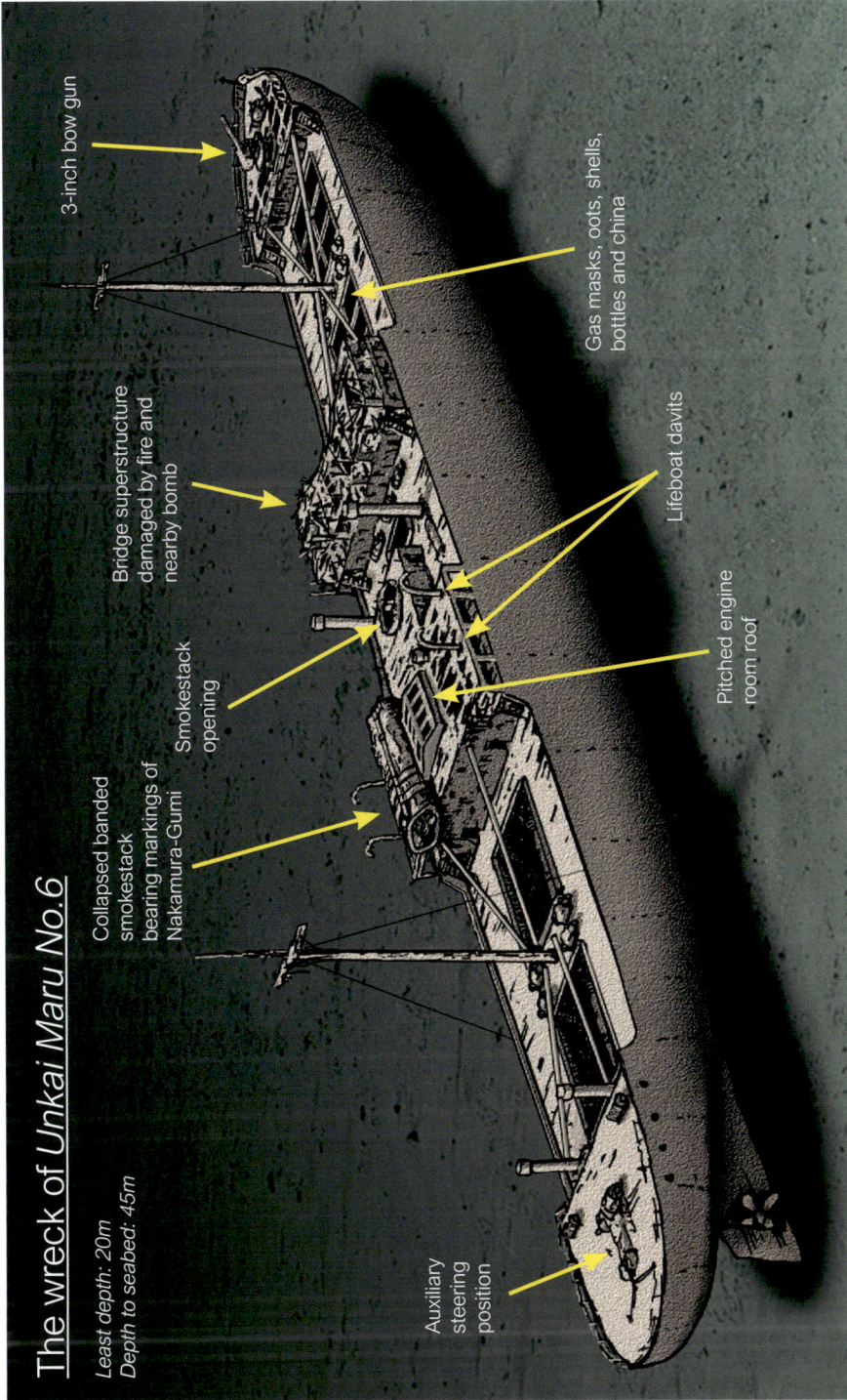

The wreck of *Unkai Maru No.6*

Least depth: 20m
Depth to seabed: 45m

3-inch bow gun

Gas masks, oots, shells, bottles and china

Bridge superstructure damaged by fire and nearby bomb

Lifeboat davits

Smokestack opening

Pitched engine room roof

Collapsed banded smokestack bearing markings of Nakamura-Gumi

Auxiliary steering position

Bombed and sunk by TF 58 aircraft in the Sixth Fleet Anchorage during Operation HAILSTONE, *Unkai Maru No 6* now rests in 40 metres of water.

of the brass plate on the breach and although the bore is indistinct, the plate is still clearly stamped with Q.F. No. 12360 and the year of manufacture, 1898. Some fired shell casings can be found around the fo'c'sle deck.

The fo'c'sle bulkhead on the well deck has three doors allowing access in to the fo'c'sle spaces. On either side of the well deck, a set of steps leads up onto the fo'c'sle deck. The Lamp Room is situated in the fo'c'sle on the starboard side and several 2-foot-high lamps are still in situ - with others having been lifted out by divers and placed on top of the fo'c'sle deck, beneath the deck gun.

Moving aft from the fo'c'sle on the well deck, the long narrow rectangular hatch for Hold No 1 has high coaming. The narrow hatch leaves a sizeable section of weather deck on either side. The hatch itself has old fashioned cover beams – different to the beams you see on most of the other ships in the lagoon. A central beam runs fore and aft, to which sturdy athwartships beams connect. At the bottom of the hold are gas masks, a pile of boots, shells for the bow gun, bottles and china.

Moving aft, the foremast with its crosstree still stands in place - with standing rigging still supporting it, and cargo winches set fore and aft. Hold No 2 has the same high coaming around the hatch but other than some timber, appears empty.

The front of the bridge superstructure rises up two deck levels from the well deck, where two forward facing open doors allow access into the lower rooms. Fixed steps lead up at either side of the well deck to walkways that ran along the sides of the bridge superstructure at shelter deck level.

The higher deck levels have largely disappeared, most likely largely wood on a skeletal framework that has been consumed by the fires that raged through the ship. Steel beams and bulkheads have been bent and buckled from the force of nearby bomb explosions – and sag from being weakened by wartime fires. The engine order telegraph and rudder direction indicator are still present. They would have been bolted to the floor but have now fallen onto their sides. A small hatch for loading bunker coal is situated abaft the bridge.

The tall slender smokestack of this coal burning steamer has fallen to lie fore and aft on the port side of the deckhouse above the boiler room and engine room, leaving its circular opening on the deck. Two 2-foot wide metal bands circle the upper section of the funnel, the markings of the Japanese civilian owners Nakamura-Gumi.

The lifeboat davits on the Boat deck are swung out and empty, left just as they were when the crew abandoned ship to row to nearby Uman. Two large forced draft ventilators, which would have stood either side of the smokestack, are collapsed to the deck. The steel beams of her structure here noticeably sag and are deformed, the result of the wartime fires that ravaged her.

The skylight hatches of the small pitched roof of the engine room are open and allow access down into the engine room - there are also open doors at either side. Entering the engine room, the vintage 3-cylinder triple expansion steam engine can be located at the very bottom along with a block and tackle (for lifting heavy pieces of engine room machinery), which ran on the steel beam that runs fore and aft across the upper void of the engine room.

An athwartships gallery catwalk crosses the engine room high up, and a flight of steps

Looking forward from the foremast over Hold No 1 to the fo'c'sle with gun platform on top. (Author)

A heavily encrusted 3-inch naval gun stands on a platform on the fo'c'sle. (Author)

Maker's plate on the breach of the bow gun with date 1898 stamped on it. (Author)

The smokestack has fallen to lie flat on the port side of the amidships composite superstructure. The adjacent lifeboat davits are swung out showing that the boats were lowered as she sank. (Author)

leads down to the lower engine room. There are a few panels with gauges and switches dotted around. This triple expansion engine has three cylinders (some triple expansion engines counterintuitively have four). Looking at a triple expansion steam engine, the small cylinder is the high-pressure cylinder where the HP steam first arrives from the boiler room, forward. Then comes the larger intermediate pressure cylinder and finally the largest low-pressure cylinder. If you ever find yourself disorientated in an engine room, you can tell which way is forward and which way aft just by looking at the cylinder sizes. Small is forward, large is aft. It is possible to get down past the cylinder tops and catwalks ringing around them to visit the lower engine room but watch your depth and bottom time, as you will be going beneath the level of the seabed outside at the very bottom.

Dropping down from the boat deck to the aft well-deck, the long narrow rectangular hatches for the two after holds can be found with the mainmast set in between and cargo winches, for operating the derricks, set fore and aft.

Two doors are set one on either side of the poop island deckhouse – only the starboard door is open. Three depth charges lie just inside on the starboard side with detonators nearby.

On the poop deck above, is an old-fashioned auxiliary steering apparatus with chains leading to the exposed steering quadrant. This is connected to the rudder directly below and was shackled in if steering control from the bridge was lost. A depth charge roll-off container sits at either side of the fantail, hence the depth charges nearby.

A large open square hatch on the poop deck allows divers to drop down a deck to see the innards of the poop island. Open doors lead back forward to the aft well deck.

Looking over the seemingly delicate fantail of the schooner stern, the propeller is still in situ forward of the rudder, protruding from the seabed at a depth of over 40 metres.

For all that this ship took a lot of punishment during Operation HAILSTONE, although it is evident that it has been swept by fire, there is surprisingly little obvious damage to the hull. There is no gaping bomb hole in her hull plating – although there is some deformation of plating at the stern.

The wartime pilot accounts speak of the bow being lifted up by the two hits claimed and three near misses. As there is no apparent damage to the higher parts of the hull at the bow, I suspect that this means that the delayed fuze of 2-4 seconds allowed the bombs to go deeper into the water before exploding. This would explain how the bow could be lifted - and suggests that any damage to the hull was low down and no doubt now concealed by the seabed.

The *Unkai Maru No 6* is not one of the glamour wrecks at Truk – and consequently isn't dived as much as the big names. But I love this delicate older steamship, it has so much to see and so much that is quite special.

39. *Yamagiri Maru*
Passenger-cargo vessel (1938)
IJN *Ippan Choyosen* auxiliary transport – *Ko* category (1941)
U.S. Recognition Code: 23A MKFMK

Repair Anchorage

Tonnage:	6,438-grt
Dimensions:	439.4-ft long; beam of 58.3-ft; draught of 32 feet
Launched:	13 May 1938
Sunk:	18 February 1944.
Cause of loss:	Bombed by TF 58 aircraft during Operation HAILSTONE
Wreck location:	Repair Anchorage.
Depth to seabed:	35 metres
Least depth:	15 metres – starboard side

The large passenger cargo ship *Yamagiri Maru* was laid down at the Mitsubishi Jukogyo K.K. shipyard in Yokohama for the Yamashita Kisen K.K. Line on 6 December 1937. She was named and launched on 13 May 1938 and fitting out afloat was completed on 2 July 1938 when she was registered in Tokyo.

This large ship was powered by a 2-stroke 6-cylinder diesel engine built by Mitsubishi Jukogyo K.K. that drove her single screw to give her a service speed of 14 knots and a top speed of 17 knots. She had a range of 47,000 miles at 14 knots.

Yamagiri Maru was built as a well deck vessel with a raised foc'sle and a tall composite central superstructure that rose some four deck levels above the shelter deck. The hull had two decks and a cruiser stern.

The large 6,438grt passenger cargo ship *Yamagiri Maru* was launched in 1938 and requisitioned by the IJN in 1941 as an auxiliary transport.

The foredeck held Hold No's 1 & 2; the two hatches in the weather deck being separated by a large masthouse from which the foremast rose with an inverted crosstree. Short kingposts either side of the foremast had cargo booms goosenecked to them - with two booms running forward over Hold No 1 and two running aft over Hold No 2. *Yamagiri Maru* was fitted with heavy lift gear for 60-ton lifts in No 2 hatch, and the jumbo boom for these lifts was stowed upright against the foremast when not in use (illustrated in archive photo above).

Immediately in front of the amidships composite superstructure, an extended section of superstructure contained Hold No 3, with its hatch at shelter deck level, one level above the weather deck. A tall goalpost pair of kingposts stood at the leading edge of the extended section of superstructure - with cargo booms goosenecked to it to work Hold No 3.

The amidships superstructure held the navigation bridge on the highest levels, with the large funnel directly abaft, surrounded by forced draft ventilator funnels and lifeboats swinging on davits.

The engine and machinery rooms were set at the lowest levels immediately abaft the bridge, whilst passenger accommodation along ran along either side of the fireproof engine casing. Two levels of promenade deck walkways ran along either side of the large superstructure.

Hold No 4 was set in a mirror image section of extended superstructure abaft the amidships superstructure, with Hold No's 5 & 6 in the after well deck, forward of the poop island. The mainmast rose from the shelter deck immediately abaft Hold No 4 with two cargo booms running forward over that hatch and two booms running aft over Hold No 5. The well deck hatches for Hold No's 5 & 6 were separated by a section of weather deck which accommodated a small deckhouse with forced draft ventilators rising from it.

At the very stern of the ship, a goalpost pair of kingposts rose from the poop island with cargo booms running forward over Hold No 6.

Some eight vessels were constructed to this Shinko Maru-class design at various shipping building yards in Japan between 1935 and 1939. With an eye on the future conflict, this class of ships was constructed to be able to mount 5-inch and 6-inch guns. All the ships in the class would be requisitioned as war erupted, three by the Army and five by Navy. On 23 July 1938, just a few weeks after completion, *Yamagiri Maru* departed Kobe on her maiden voyage to New York and South America.

After three years of civilian service, as Japan prepared for war in the Pacific, *Yamagiri Maru* was requisitioned on 5 September 1941 by the IJN for use as an auxiliary transport. She was registered in the IJN as a *Ko* category auxiliary transport (with IJN captain) and attached to the Sasebo Naval District on 20 September 1941. Conversion works began at the Mitsubishi Heavy Industries Shipyard in Yokohama, where she had been built, the works being completed by 15 October 1941.

On 3 November 1941, the month before the Pearl Harbor raid, she set off from Tokyo on her first transport run, arriving at Mili Atoll in the Marshall Islands later that month. After a couple of further supply runs from Japan to far flung Japanese South Seas possessions, *Yamagiri Maru* was attached to the naval force assembled for the invasion of Ambon Island, in the Dutch East Indies south of the Philippines, which took place between 29-31 January

1942. Ambon was deemed secure on 3 February 1942, allowing *Yamagiri Maru* to depart later that month, bound for Japan via Palau. In the following months of early 1942, she was busily engaged on supply passages around Japan and out to the Marshall Islands.

In the second half of 1942, she transported war materials locally to Taiwan, Hong Kong, Hainan Island and Indochina and also further afield to the Solomon's, the Caroline Islands, Saipan, Truk, Rabaul and Palau.

The first months of 1943 saw her making passages to Kwajalein in the Marshalls and Tarawa in the Gilberts and then out to Truk and Rabaul. After operating around Saipan, she departed for Yokosuka on 5 June 1943.

After a few weeks back in Yokosuka, she formed up in a large escorted convoy that departed for Truk on 24 July 1943. Another famous Truk wreck *Seiko Maru* was in the same convoy. Despite the attentions of American submarines en route, the convoy arrived at Truk on 2 August 1943. From there she moved on in convoy to Rabaul.

On 28 August 1943, she departed Rabaul for Palau in an escorted convoy that consisted of the auxiliary collier/tanker *Asakaze Maru*, *Nichiryo Maru* and IJA transports *Taisho Maru* and *Tacoma Maru* escorted by subchasers CH-38 and CH-39 and the minesweeper W-22. About 70 nautical miles west of Mussau Island, in the Bismarck Archipelago, the American submarine *Drum* (SS-228) intercepted the convoy - firing four torpedoes at one ship and two at another. One torpedo hit *Yamagiri Maru* in the starboard side between Hold No's 2 & 3 - opening a large hole in her hull. She remained afloat however and was able to turn to limp back towards Rabaul for emergency repairs, whilst the escorts searched for the submarine, dropping 27 depth charges. USS *Drum* however was able to leave the area unharmed to continue her patrol.

Yamagiri Maru managed to reach Rabaul safely – but by this time, Allied bombers had started attacking Rabaul on a daily basis. As a result, as soon as emergency repairs were carried out, she departed for Truk for permanent repair. Once repairs were complete there, she set off in convoy from Truk on 22 October 1943 for the first of two return trips to Ponape and then another to Rabaul - before returning once again to Truk on 5 December 1943.

On Dog-Day-Minus-One, 17 February 1944, as the fighters, dive bombers and torpedo planes of Task Force 58 readied for launch, *Yamagiri Maru* was swinging at anchor in the Repair Anchorage, north of Fefan Island.

After the initial Hellcat fighter sweep had achieved US air superiority, the waves of dive and torpedo bomber attacks began. A large valuable target, *Yamagiri Maru* was repeatedly attacked.

Aboard *Yorktown*, at about 1300, 12 Hellcats, 6 TBF Avengers and 13 SBD Dauntlesses launched for Strike 1E against shipping in the Repair Anchorage. The flight was over the lagoon by 1415-1430, the Hellcats soon tangling with and splashing three Japanese fighters before going on to strafe Eten Island airfield, an oiler, two freighters and a destroyer (which exploded amidships).

The *Yorktown* TBFs attacked *Kiyosumi Maru* near the north shore of Fefan and then attacked and missed *Yamagiri Maru*. The *Yorktown* SBD Dauntless dive -bombers then attacked *Yamagiri Maru* - and scored a hit and several near misses. At the same time Strike

1E planes from *Enterprise* attacked - and reported two bomb hits, one aft of amidships and one at the starboard stern. Despite the attention, *Yamagiri Maru* was still afloat as night fell.

The following day, Dog-Day, 18 February 1944, 23 planes launched from *Bunker Hill* for Strike 3B. Four hellcats escorted ten SB2C Helldivers armed with 500-lb and 1,000-lb bombs and 9 TBF Avengers carrying aerial torpedoes. After about an hour of flight, the strike planes arrived over the lagoon for their designated time over target between 0845-0900.

As the *Bunker Hill* flight arrived, most of the Hellcats went after a destroyer that had entered the lagoon through North Pass and was running south at speed – it was *Oite*. Five of the *Bunker Hill* TBF torpedo bombers joined in the attack up near North Pass, circling the scene below before making a coordinated attack once it became clear which way the speeding destroyer was making her evasive turn. *Oite* was hit by a torpedo amidships as she turned to starboard. The speeding destroyer broke into two pieces that jack-knifed and sank quickly.

Meanwhile, as two TBF Avengers attacked *Heian Maru* northwest of Dublon, four SB2C Helldiver dive bombers attacked *Yamagiri Maru*, dropping one 1,000-lb and six 500-lb bombs from 500 feet. Both the 1,000-lb bomb, and one of the 500-lb bombs, hit *Yamagiri Maru*.

One bomb appears to have blown out the bottom of Hold No 3 in a large explosion and another bomb appears to have hit the bridge forward of the funnel. The bridge was devastated – blown off almost down to the level of the extended superstructure of Hold No 3. Fires took hold and a plume of smoke rose up for thousands of feet - followed by a series of secondary explosions as munitions and fuel ignited. She had been mortally wounded and settled steadily into the water, listing to port. The *Bunker Hill* strike planes were back aboard their carrier by 1002.

By the time the raids of 18 February drew to a close, there was no sign of *Yamagiri Maru* in the Repair Anchorage. Only a large slick of oil above where she had been anchored, betrayed her presence below the surface of the lagoon.

The Wreck today

Today the wreck of the transport ship *Yamagiri Maru* lies on her port side in 35 metres of water about one mile from the north west shores of Fefan Island, with its bow facing towards Weno Island. At 439 feet in length, she is a big ship and yet with a beam of 49 feet, almost 20 metres, she is easily reached just 15 metres beneath the surface. She is structurally intact and wonderfully preserved - and is a favourite dive in the lagoon.

Yamagiri Maru was at anchor when she was attacked - and her starboard anchor chain today is still run out through its hawse pipe to drape over the stem and then hang down vertically to the seabed. A defensive gun is mounted on the raised foʼcʼsle deck and on the uppermost starboard side of the bow, the ship's name can be seen in Roman and kanji characters

Her foremast projects out horizontally from a masthouse set on the forward weather deck in between the hatches for Hold No's 1 & 2, and still has its inverted crosstree in place. A crosstree on a ship allows a much higher mast than would otherwise be possible. Standing

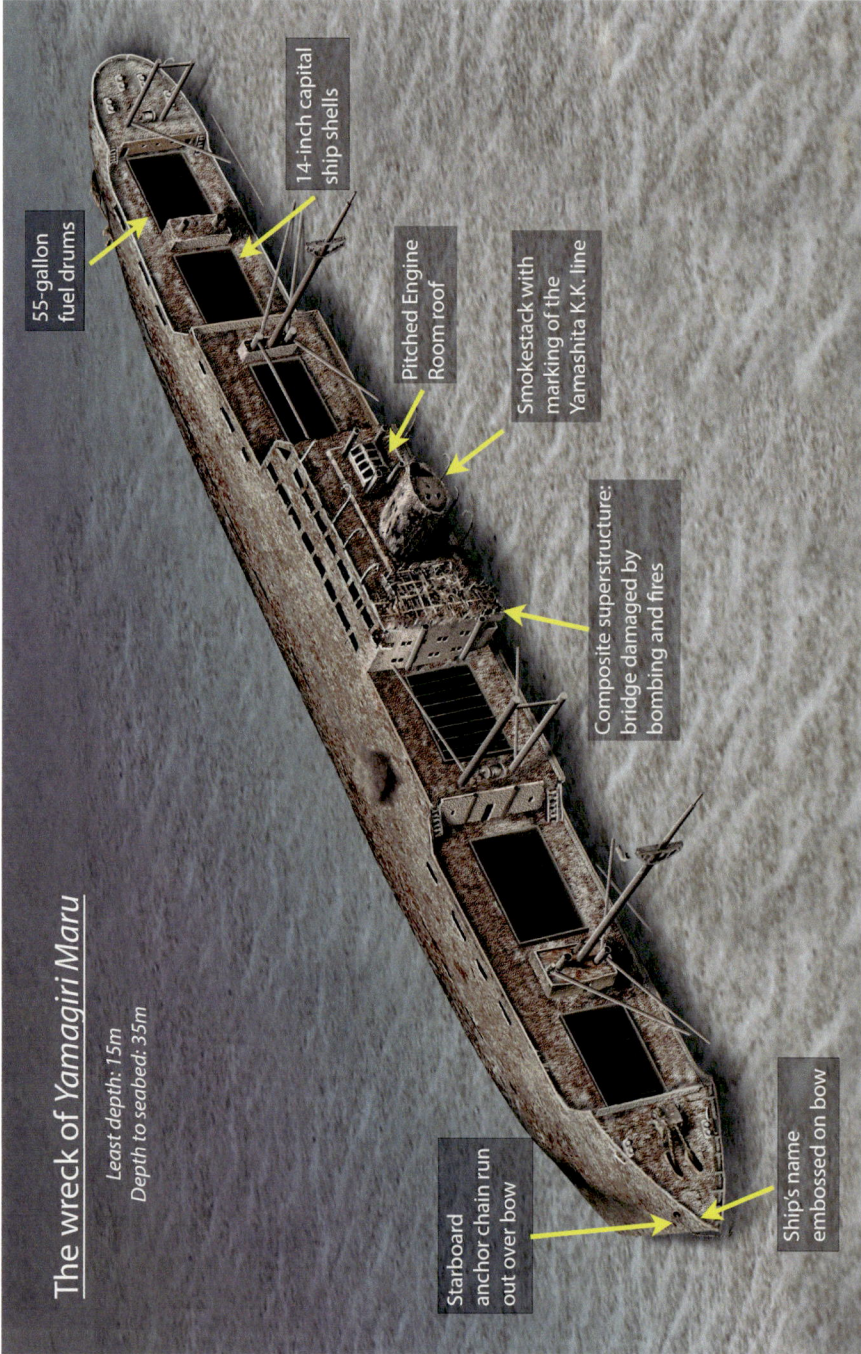

The wreck of *Yamagiri Maru*

Least depth: 15m
Depth to seabed: 35m

55-gallon fuel drums

14-inch capital ship shells

Pitched Engine Room roof

Smokestack with marking of the Yamashita K.K. line

Composite superstructure: bridge damaged by bombing and fires

Starboard anchor chain run out over bow

Ship's name embossed on bow

Artist's impression of the wreck of the 6,438grt auxiliary transport *Yamagiri Maru*, which now rests on her port side in 35 metres of water with a least depth of 15 metres. Hold No 5 contains 14-inch shells for the big guns of a battleship or battlecruiser.

rigging (or guy wires) run from the ends of the crosstree spars down to either side of the hull. When a ship is moving the mast is subjected to a powerful swaying motion. Guy wires or standing rigging share the load, essentially bracing the mast. But as ships have a narrow beam, this gives only a narrow angle for the guys to support the mast, making very tall masts unfeasible. The crosstree therefore serves as a fresh base to spread the next level of supporting rigging (guy wires) and provide support for another higher level of top mast. In early Japanese ships of this era, the crosstree was inverted – in later Japanese ships the crosstree supports were above the crosstree itself.

A short kingpost rises up from the masthouse on either side of the foremast with cargo handling booms running out from them, one forward across Hold No 1 and one aft across Hold No 2 from each kingpost. The forward booms are angled down to rest their ends on the seabed whilst the uppermost boom over Hold No 2 has detached and fallen to the seabed. The hatch cover beams for Hold No's 1 & 2 are not present and the two holds appear largely empty.

The hatch for Hold No 3 is set one deck higher, in the extended section of the superstructure projecting forward at the base of the bridge. A goalpost pair of kingposts stand at its forward edge with cargo handling booms running aft over the hatch. The starboard boom runs to a cradle on the front of the bridge superstructure whilst the port boom has dropped down to rest its far end on the seabed.

Hold No 3 still has its hatch cover beams in place. Looking into the now horizontal and apparently empty hold, divers can see a set of tween deck hatch beams and beyond them, daylight – where the hull shell plating was blown out. A gaping hole some 25-feet in diameter can be seen near the bottom of the hull. On the outer higher starboard side of the hull there is a large indentation of plating due to a near miss bomb.

Immediately abaft Hold No 3 is the composite superstructure with two large forced draft ventilator funnels rising up from the shelter deck either side its frontage. The superstructure only rises up for a couple of its original deck levels – as the top levels have been obliterated by a bomb hit or fire. The structural steel latticework of the remaining deck floor is evident – whilst the only trace of the higher levels of the bridge are torn and bent sections of the front of the bridge. Walkways on two deck levels, with cabins off, run along the side of the superstructure, bathed in light and now heavily covered in coral in just 15 metres of water. Empty lifeboat davits dot the edge of the Boat Deck.

The large smokestack is still in place projecting outwards just abaft the bridge. On most WWII era shipwrecks around the world the funnels are long gone – made of light steel they are usually some of the first structures to rust away and collapse. However here in the sheltered waters of the lagoon, with little current to bring oxygenated water coursing past it and accelerate rusting, the funnel remains intact – exhaust pipes projecting through its covered top. Either side of the funnel a large embossed "Y" can be found – the markings of the Yamashita Kisen Kaisha line. A large steam whistle is mounted on the forward side of the funnel and immediately abaft the funnel is the pitched Engine Room roof with its skylights.

The aft section of the ship is almost, but not quite, a mirror image of the forward section, the arrangement of mast and kingposts is different. Hold No 4 is set on the extended section

The author swims forward (left) from the stern alongside the now vertical deck. A short pair of goalpost kingposts projects outwards ahead. (Courtesy Ewan Rowell)

The author illuminates a cluster of 14-inch shells destined for a capital ship in the aft Holds of *Yamagiri Maru*. (Courtesy Ewan Rowell)

A diver's torch lights up the now horizontal cylinder heads inside the engine room of *Yamagiri Maru*. (Courtesy Ewan Rowell)

Looking down towards the hatch cover beams of Hold No 3 on the shelter deck section of extended superstructure in front of the bridge (to right of shot). Light can be seen streaming into the recesses of the hold from outside the ship through the hole blown in her keel by a dive bomber. (Courtesy Ewan Rowell)

of aft superstructure before two holds in the well deck. Hold No 4 is empty but it is possible to enter the Engine Room from the forward end of this hold - or through the Engine Room skylights. The engine room is a large cavernous space and the six now horizontal engine cylinders, with large hexagonal bolts securing the tops, are easily found – ringed by catwalk gratings. Large stairwells at the ends of the cylinders allow divers to swim horizontally deeper into the ship towards the lower section of the engine room.

The mainmast is set just aft of Hold No 4 on the extended section of superstructure and there is a small deckhouse between Hold No's 5 & 6, which has some forced draft ventilators rising out of it.

It is perhaps the contents of Hold No 5 that make this wreck one of the best known in the lagoon. For here in this hold are a large number of 3-4 foot long, 14-inch shells for the big guns of a battleship or battlecruiser.

Hold No 6 contains 55-gallon oil and gasoline drums, some of which have tumbled to the seabed. Looking aft from Hold No 6, the poop island bulkhead has a pair of open doors that allow access into the aft compartments, where the steering gear is located. A spare propeller is bolted to the aft deckhouse wall.

The sterncastle has its own small goalpost pair of kingposts for working Hold No 6. The boom from the starboard kingpost angles downwards to rest its end on the seabed, whilst the port boom has fallen to lie on the seabed.

The auxiliary steering position at the stern, directly above the steering gear, has the telemotor in situ and an engine order telegraph securely bolted to the deck on its starboard side.

Moving over the stern and then under the sweep of the fantail, the rudder and large propeller are still in place.

40. *Yubae Maru*
Cargo steamship (1919)
IJA *Rikugun Yusosen* auxiliary transport (1941)
U.S. Recognition Code: 38 MFM

Sixth Fleet Anchorage

Tonnage:	3,200-grt
Dimensions:	305.0-ft long; beam of 43.9-ft; draught of 27.3 feet
Launched:	1919
Sunk:	17 February 1944.
Cause of loss:	Torpedoed and bombed by TF 58 aircraft during Operation HAILSTONE
Wreck location:	Sixth Fleet Anchorage, north west of Uman Island
Depth to seabed:	36 metres – bow
	31 metres - stern
Least depth:	20 metres – at starboard side of propeller
Other name:	*Yuhai Maru*

The 3,200-grt well- deck steamer *Yubae Maru* was built in 5 months during 1919 by Ishikawajima Sanbashi of Tokyo, one of nine sister ships built to the same design by Ishikawajima Shipbuilding Co during 1918-1920. All sisters were built with two decks and a composite superstructure amidships that held the bridge, and immediately aft, the boiler and engine

Artist's impression of the 3,200grt cargo steamship *Yubae Maru* under way during the war.

rooms. The tall smokestack of a coal burning vessel rose up immediately abaft the bridge. Her forward and after decks housed two cargo holds each. She had a raised fo'c'sle at the bow and a poop island at the stern. Her sister ships were *Shinryu Maru, Dover Maru, Genchu Maru, Gozan Maru, Eastern Bell Maru, Eastern Maid Maru, Taizan Maru* and *Yakumo Maru*.

Propulsion was delivered by a 3-cylinder triple expansion engine (built by the same shipyard of Ishikawajima SB Co) that drove a single screw. She had a service speed of 10 knots and a top speed only marginally higher at 11 knots. She had an operating radius of 9,600 miles at 10 knots.

During the 1920's she was owned and operated by Kokusai Kisen K.K., a young company that had been established in Kobe in 1919 with government support to operate unsold stock boats from companies such as the large long established Kawasaki Group companies like Kawasaki Zosenjo and Kawasaki Kisen ("K" Line). These large Japanese ship building companies had expanded enormously during World War I but had been hit by the severe depression that followed the end of the war and left with a large stock of unsold ships. In 1931/32, Kokusai Kisen K.K. sold *Yubae Maru* on to Kuribayashi Shosen K.K. of Muroran.

Yubae Maru was a slow, old ship by the dawn of war in the Pacific, when she was requisitioned by the IJA on 22 September 1941, just a few months before hostilities began, as a Shinryu Maru-class auxiliary transport. She was put to work carrying war cargoes in the Philippine Island operations, forming part of the Manila Defence Force.

During 1943, she was based in Palau and was used extensively to move supplies around island garrisons from there. On 1 May 1943, she departed in convoy from Palau, arriving in Rabaul on 9 May. She then left Rabaul on 22 May in convoy back to Palau where, from 21 June to 2 July 1943 she was involved in moving units of the 20th IJA Division from Palau to Hansa Bay, New Guinea and back. Shortly thereafter, on 20 July 1943 she again departed Palau in an escorted convoy for Hansa Bay, New Guinea – arriving there on 25 July.

The following month she formed up in Palau again as part of a convoy for Wewak that included the *Nagano, Hankow, Aden* and *Shinyu Maru*'s. The convoy departed Palau on 20 August 1943 with the battleship *Nagato* escorting along with the subchasers CH-34 and CH-26. Three days into the voyage however, as a result of increasing American air activity over Wewak, the convoy was ordered back to Palau.

Yubae Maru's tasking was changed, and she set off the same day in a separate convoy bound for Kobe in Japan – arriving there on 13 September 1943. Later that month on 28 September 1943, she set off in convoy from the port of Mutsure in southern Japan bound for Takao on the west coast, arriving there on 3 October.

By 12 October 1943, she was in Manila, in the Philippines, loaded with stores and setting off south for Halmahera Island, north west of Papua New Guinea in convoy.

The following month, she departed Halmahera Island on 9 November 1943 in a convoy that was carrying the 2nd Field Airfield Construction Command and the 14th, 15th and 108th Field Airfield Construction Units bound for Manokwari, Papua New Guinea. By 3 December 1943, she was in Takao, Taiwan, setting off in a convoy bound for Mutsure, in southern Japan.

On 11 January 1944, she set off in convoy from the Japanese port of Moji bound once again for Takao, Taiwan. The old ship was working hard as the tide of war turned against Japan.

Just a month later, on 10 February 1944, *Yubae Maru* arrived in Truk in an escorted convoy that included the famous present day Truk wreck *Nippo Maru. Yubae Maru* anchored in the south part of the Sixth Fleet Anchorage, south east of Fefan and north west of Uman islands. On Dog-Day-Minus-One,17 February, she was spotted - riding high with her cargo apparently discharged – in close proximity to the *Sankisan Maru* and *Taiho Maru*.

Around midday, during Strike 3D-1, four torpedo planes from VT 17 of *Bunker Hill* attacked *Yubae Maru* scoring one, possibly two torpedo hits. She was also likely attacked by dive-bombers and hit by a 1,000-lb bomb, along with several near misses As the U.S. strike aircraft broke off their attack, she was left heavily damaged and starting to sink by the stern. Her stem was damaged, her shell plating abreast her superstructure was stove in and her keel was damaged near the stern.

As her cargo appears to have been earlier offloaded, she would have been *light* - her holds would have been large empty spaces, able to fill quickly with vast amounts of water. With so much damage, she went down quickly by the stern, the bow rising upwards, although her crew had sufficient time to take to the lifeboats. She rolled heavily to port, almost capsizing. Her masts hit the seabed, the foremast buckling with the weight of the ship above.

She was gone when the next waves of planes arrived over the lagoon.

The Wreck today

The ship rolled over heavily to port as it sank and landed on a gently shelving bottom with her bow coming to rest in deeper water of 36 metres and the stern in shallower water of about 31 metres. The wreck is well heeled over to port - almost capsized. As she hit the bottom, her superstructure was damaged and both masts and the tall funnel were broken off. The least depth down to her uppermost starboard side at the propeller is about 16 metres.

At the bow, her plumb stem, iconic of the era of her construction has both the starboard and port anchors run out from their hawse pipes. The anchor windlass is located on the raised fo'c'sle deck – however, immediately abaft, the bow gun platform has fallen from its mount to the seabed below. The 8cm (3-inch) gun is now mostly buried in the seabed and debris - but the breach and some of the splinter shield can be made out. The high front starboard hull of the fo'c'sle, at a depth of about 30 metres, is damaged - and the fo'c'sle deck itself seems to be separating from the hull. As differential corrosion turns its securing ties to dust, the fo'c'sle deck is beginning to follow the gun platform in a slow fall to the seabed.

Moving aft from the fo'c'sle, to the well deck, two doors in the fo'c'sle bulkhead allow access into the fo'c'sle spaces, now one large common space.

Hold No. 1 in the foredeck is empty, and it is possible to pass through the rotting bulkhead into Hold No. 2, which is also largely empty. Hold No 2 extends underneath the superstructure. Being a ship on its side, the structure of the wreck is rapidly decaying and much has fallen from above to leave the innards of this ship filled with a jumble of debris. Be very careful going under anything on this wreck.

The upper levels of the amidships superstructure have been crushed and collapsed. The engine order telegraph now lies on the seabed directly beneath where it had been located in the bridge, at a depth of about 34 metres. On the higher starboard side, promenade walkways

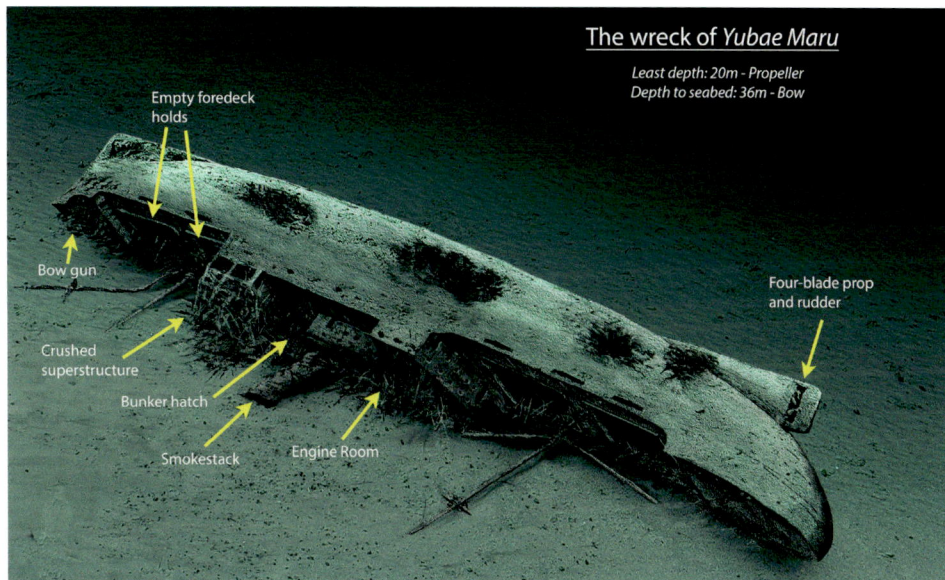

Artist's impression of the requisitioned IJA auxiliary transport *Yubae Maru*, which now rests on her port beam ends in just over 30 metres of water.

on two deck levels are visible leading along the side of the superstructure.

Abaft the bridge superstructure, in between the bridge and engine room, is a small hatch for the bunker hold for coal for the ship's boilers.

The tall slim smokestack of a coal burning ship has fallen from its mounts and now lies crumpled on the seabed. Immediately abaft of the circular smokestack base opening, is the pitched engine room roof with some of its skylights open allowing access into the inverted engine room. It is possible to explore the engine room and boiler room, forward. Here, at a depth of about 25 metres, the engine and its associated, catwalks and gauges, still filled with oil can be found. Large con rods connect from the engine to the crankshaft and the telegraph repeater with its white ceramic face lies amongst the debris. Crew accommodation cabins are located along either side of the engine casing.

Moving aft, the two after holds in the well deck are largely empty, and the mainmast has broken near its base as the mast took the weight of the ship as it rolled over.

The sterncastle houses the steering gear with the auxiliary steering position directly above the rudder. The brass circular section of the helm (that held the spokes of the wheel) is still present, although everything wooden has been burnt or rotted away. The chains necessary for turning the rudder from this steering position are still present.

Moving around the stern, the rudder and four-bladed propeller remain in place, the shallowest point of the wreck, at about 20 metres.

JAPANESE AIRCRAFT WRECKS
OF TRUK LAGOON

1. BETTY Bomber
2. EMILY Flying boat
3. JILL torpedo-bombers
4. MYRT reconnaissance plane
5. JUDY dive-bombers
6. ZEKE fighters (Zero)

Truk saw a bitter aerial contest during the initial Operation HAILSTONE attack by Task Force 58 on 17/18 February 1944 and in the follow up raids. More than 250 Japanese aircraft were shot down or destroyed at Truk - whilst 30 American planes were also shot down over the lagoon. The bottom of the Truk lagoon is scattered with aircraft wrecks – or parts of them – and more are rediscovered from time to time. The Project Recover team is dedicated to locating lost U.S. service personnel from the war and the wrecks of several U.S. planes have recently been located in the lagoon.

The Japanese plane wrecks listed here are the most common wrecks that divers today visit at Truk.

1. *Mitsubishi G4M Navy Type 1 Attack Bomber*
Allied reporting name: BETTY
Off Eten Island

The Mitsubishi G4M Navy Type 1 Attack Bomber was perhaps the most famous Japanese bomber of WWII. The 'G' stood for Attack Bomber, the '4' being the 4th in the attack bomber evolution, after the preceding G3M. The 'M' denotes it as a Mitsubishi plane. For ease of reporting, the Allies allocated shortened names to all Japanese aircraft, their reporting code name for the G4M bomber was BETTY – hence the famous Truk wreck is today simply called the Betty Bomber.

Mitsubishi G4M Navy Type 1 long range Attack Bomber. Allied reporting name: BETTY

Japanese Navy pilots called the G4M the *Hamaki* (Cigar) due to its cylindrical cigar like shape. With unprotected wing fuel tanks, when the Betty was hit by Allied planes or AA fire (even small arms), even with only slight damage they could explode or burst into flames. The sight of a large bomber on fire streaking across the sky earned the BETTY her unofficial Allied nickname, the *Flying Cigar*.

The G4M Navy Attack Bomber was intended as a replacement for the G3M Navy Type 96 Attack Bomber – Allied reporting name NELL. The G4M was a long-range, land based, twin-engine medium bomber designed by Mitsubishi Aircraft Company in 1939 that began production in 1940. The G4M would become the Navy's primary land-based bomber, operating either as a long-range reconnaissance aircraft or as a torpedo bomber or level bomber.

The G4M supplemented Japanese naval units operating in the Pacific theatre where the Japanese network of unsinkable aircraft carriers (their island air bases) were spread out. Practically all Japanese snooper aircraft were long range G4Ms. But once a G4M was sighted and attacked by Allied fighters, such as the F6F Hellcat, they were usually shot down very quickly, often before being able to make a radio distress call.

There were three versions of the G4M, Models 11, 22 & 24 - each of which was some 66 feet long with a wingspan of 82 feet and a crew of 6-7. They were powered by two Mitsubishi wing-mounted air-cooled radial engines, each driving a three-blade propeller and giving a service ceiling of about 27,890ft.

The G4M had very good performance for a medium bomber. The Model 11 had a maximum speed of just over 276mph, the Model 22 could make 325mph. Standard ranges for the three models, dependent on the load being carried, were 910 miles (Model 11), 1,370 miles (Model 22) and 2,630 miles (Model 24). The ferry range was about 3,100 miles.

The great speed and long-range capability of the G4M was gained by structural lightness of construction and fitments - and the omission of almost any protection for the crew by way of armour or self-sealing fuel tanks. Heavy losses of older Nell bombers in the war with China led to the development of a heavy escort version of the Betty, which was armed with four 7.7mm Type 92 machine guns, set one in her nose, one in her dorsal blister and two set one in each side blister. She also carried a heavy 20mm Type 99 cannon in her tail turret – a much heavier weapon than normally encountered with a bomber at the time and making an attack from behind the Betty very dangerous. This development allowed the use of the G4M Betty as a wingtip escort fighter with sufficient range to escort Nell bombers on raids deep into China.

The G4M could carry one 800kg (1,764-lb) bomb or four 250kg (550-lb) bombs – and it was G4M Betty bombers that attacked and bombed the U.S. Army base Clark Field in the Philippines on 8 December at the very beginning of the Pacific war.

The G4M could, alternatively, carry a single Type 91 aerial torpedo with a 235kg high explosive warhead and a range of about 2,000 metres. The Type 91 aerial torpedo had been developed by the Japanese as a shallow water torpedo for the attack on Pearl Harbor on 7 December 1941, where all eight American battleships present were sunk or damaged.

The same day as the Pearl raid, Japanese long-range Betty and Nell aircraft bombed Singapore. When reports arrived at British intelligence that the Japanese had started a land invasion 200 miles further north up the Malayan peninsula at Kota Bharu, Force Z, comprising the brand-new battleship HMS *Prince of Wales*, the modernised battlecruiser HMS *Repulse* and four escort destroyers set out to locate the invasion forces, if any, and attack them. It was a bold and daring plan that was reliant on monsoon rain and clouds to allow Force Z to arrive undetected with the element of surprise. They headed out into the South China Sea, hoping to surprise the Japanese forces at dawn on 10 December. But the Force was spotted.

As dawn on 10 December approached, long range Japanese reconnaissance aircraft were despatched from Saigon to sweep south in a large fan to locate the British Force. Once they were well on their way south, 85 bombers, Nakajima B5N Kate torpedo-bombers, Nells carrying bombs and Betty bombers carrying the Type 91 Revision 2 aerial torpedo took off from Saigon - following slowly and waiting for reports from the reconnaissance aircraft of Force Z's exact location. A Japanese reconnaissance aircraft spotted Force Z that morning, at the end of one of its sweeps, and the armada of 85 bombers was directed to attack. Whilst the older Nell G3M bombers attacked with high altitude bombs, the G4M Bettys hit home with their aerial torpedoes, sinking both *Prince of Wales* and *Repulse* with heavy loss of life. This was the first time in naval history that two modern capital ships had been sunk in action by air attack at sea, and the engagement is seen as defining the end of the era of the battleship.

In the build-up to the Pacific war, Japan stationed the G4M in Indochina and Formosa, and then as the war progressed, in the Dutch East Indies, New Guinea and the Solomon Islands – and this deployment allowed them to be used in the first long range bombing raids against Darwin, Australia on 19 February 1942.

Before long however, the lack of armour and unprotected fuel tanks was causing heavy losses of the Betty bombers in action. Admiral Isoroku Yamamoto, Commander in Chief of the IJN Combined Fleet, was killed on 18 April 1943 when the G4M1 he was being carried in was shot down by sixteen American P-38 Lightning fighters in Operation VENGEANCE.

The susceptibility of the G4M to ground AA fire was alleviated in later versions of the Betty where improved engines were developed that could carry the Betty above the effective ceiling for Allied light AA guns. Layers of rubber sheeting and sponge were added to protect the undersides of wings and fuselage tanks. Successive models were improved for fuel consumption and armament culminating late in 1944 with a version modified to carry the Yokosuka MXY-7 *Ohka* (Cherry Blossom) rocket-powered *kamikaze* piloted suicide plane.

The Betty bombers at Truk were based on the Moen No 1, Param and Eten airfields.

There were almost 2,500 G4M's produced by Japan and to the best of my knowledge no intact airworthy G4Ms survive today. A very few wrecks of downed G4Ms have been found in southeast Asia and on scattered Pacific islands.

The Wreck today

Depth: 15-20 metres

Today the wreck of the only known G4M Betty bomber in the Truk lagoon lies about 200 metres south west of Eten Island in 15-20 metres of water. During WWII, Eten Island was the primary Japanese fighter airfield defending Truk – when it was called the Takeshima Air Base.

Eten Island was one of the primary targets for the U.S. Hellcats during the dawn fighter sweep of the Truk lagoon. As the Hellcats commenced their dawn strafing runs on Eten they found a congestion of Japanese aircraft, which had been offloaded from transports such as the *Fujikawa Maru* - many of which had not yet been assembled. Japanese fighters were lined up wingtip to wingtip – easy prey for strafing. Many of the Japanese aircraft that started their motors and attempted to take off were shot up as they taxied along the runway or as they laboured into the sky after taking off. It is little wonder that today many of the significant aircraft wrecks are clustered around Eten. Today the jungle has largely reclaimed the island and from the sea there is little obvious evidence of its wartime role as an airfield.

This Betty appears to have crash-landed at speed on the water only 200 metres from the airstrip. She hit the water with such force that her two wing mounted Mitsubishi engines were ripped out of their mounts and now lie about 15 metres apart, more than 50 metres forward of the fuselage. The nose section of the plane is bent over to port as a result of the impact of hitting the water and the floor of the lagoon.

The corals that encrust any exposed ferrous metals on shipwrecks in the shallows don't like the taste of aluminium - and when you dive, you find that the aluminium is usually almost devoid of coral, with corals only clinging to any exposed ferrous parts. The skin of this Betty is now getting thin and fragile with age - and from the darkness inside the fuselage you can see light blue of the surroundings through the skin in places.

Barring the damage to the nose and cockpit of the plane, and the absence of the two engines, the rest of the fuselage is largely intact. The wings are still attached – with the tip of the starboard wing missing – perhaps torn off in the crash. The horizontal tail fins are still present, whilst the vertical tail fin has fallen over and now lies flat on the seabed behind.

The interior of the fuselage is open for inspection - and there is much to see inside. A grated deck runs most of the length of the interior - and halfway along either side, both side blisters are open and allow a diver to enter or exit with care. The dorsal blister is open, the hatch in the upright position.

A couple of the 7.7mm Type 92 machine guns used to be inside the wreck but have now been taken out and laid on the port side seabed. Inside the plane there are fire extinguishers and oxygen cylinders, the latter for altitude flying, and the radio.

The rear gunner's 20mm Type 99 cannon lies on the seabed near its tail gun location.

Left: Looking aft inside the BETTY bomber, the two side blisters can be seen (Courtesy Ewan Rowell)

Lower left: The Mitsubishi G4M BETTY bomber lies largely intact off Eten Island in 15-20 metres of water. (Courtesy Ewan Rowell)

Left: The engines were ripped from their wing mounts as the BETTY hit the water and the nose cone was destroyed. (Courtesy Ewan Rowell)

Lower left: The two engines lie isolated about 50 metres forward from the BETTY fuselage. (Courtesy Ewan Rowell)

Once you have explored the Betty fully, swim out forward directly from the front of the plane and some 50 metres or so away you will find the two engines ripped from their wing mounts as she hit the water.

Swimming out from the nose of the Betty, there are the very degraded remains of a couple of other downed aircraft. The first set of remains you come to are from an Aichi E13A long range reconnaissance seaplane, Allied reporting name JAKE.

The second set of remains are very small and widely dispersed but are believed to be from a Mitsubishi A6M fighter seaplane, Allied reporting name RUFE.

2. *Kawanishi H8K Navy Type 2 Flying Boat*
Allied reporting name: EMILY
North west of Eten Island

Kawanishi H8K flying boat.
Allied reporting name: EMILY

Development of a new large four-engined maritime monoplane reconnaissance flying boat, the H8K1, started in 1938 to replace the 210mph Kawanishi H6K Navy Flying Boat. The design specifications for the new H8K were for a much faster top speed of 290mph, a cruising speed of 207mph and a range of 4,440 nautical miles. The new aircraft would operate as bomber-reconnaissance or transport.

To meet the patrol range requirements, six large fuel tanks were built into the hull and eight smaller tanks installed in the wings. The fuel tanks in the hull were partially self-sealing with a carbon dioxide fire extinguishing system. The wing tanks were unprotected. All the fuel tanks were set up so that if a tank were ruptured the fuel could be drained into the bilges and then pumped back into undamaged tanks.

The H8K was 92-ft 3" long with a wingspan of 124-ft 7". Power was delivered by four wing mounted Mitsubishi 'Mars' Model engines, each driving a 4-blade propeller to give the aircraft a top speed as specified of 296mph and a range of 4,370 miles. The H8K carried a crew of 10.

The H8K was fitted with extensive heavy armour, which along with an impressive defensive armament, earned the Emily much respect from Allied pilots. Five powerful 20mm Type 99 cannons were set, one in the nose cone, one in each of the dorsal and tail turrets and one in each beam blister on both port and starboard sides. Four 7.7mm Type 97 machine guns were placed inside hatches and in the ventral position.

The H8K could carry 4,400-lb of bombs or depth charges. Alternatively, two aerial torpedoes could be carried under the wings.

The Emily was a *flying boat*, which differs from a *seaplane*, by floating with its hull in the water - with wingtip floats for stability. *Seaplanes*, such as the Mitsubishi A6M fighter (Allied reporting name *Rufe*), have floats that hold their fuselages above the water at all times.

The H8K1 entered production in 1941 and saw its first operational use during a second raid on Pearl Harbor on the night of 4 March 1942. Pearl Harbor lay outwith the H8K1's range - but the two Emily's rendezvoused en route with a Japanese supply submarine, landing on the water and refueling, some 550 miles north west of Hawaii, before continuing to attempt to bomb Pearl. Little damage was accomplished due to poor visibility.

Six days after the 2nd Pearl raid, an Emily was sent on a daylight photo-reconnaissance mission to photograph the strategically important American airbase at Midway Atoll. Marine

F2A Brewster Buffalo fighters were radar vectored to the Emily and shot it down with the loss of all the aircrew, including Lt Hashizume Hisao who had led the 2nd Pearl raid.

An improved model, the H8K2, came into production in 1943, which had more powerful engines, increased fuel capacity and armament. Later variations of the aircraft allowed her to carry 64 troops by the removal of her hull fuel tanks and some armament. In all, 131 of the bomber versions were constructed and 36 transport versions.

The H8K was the fastest and most heavily defended flying boat to serve in WWII and Allied fighter pilots considered the Emily a very difficult aircraft to shoot down – its performance being superior to the American Sikorsky and the British Short Sunderland flying boats.

This particular Emily lying in shallow water at Truk is believed to have been inbound from Palau to the Dublon Island Sea Plane Base carrying Japanese officers. She was attacked during the flight by U.S. aircraft and shot up – killing several of the passenger officers and the co-pilot. Shaking off her attackers in the clouds, she managed to limp on to Truk, where she eventually crashed into the sea.

The Wreck today

Depth: 12-15 metres

Today the wreck of the *Emily* Flying Boat is located several hundred yards off the south west tip of Tonoas Island (Dublon), and north west of Eten Island. Given the shallow depth and the proximity to the Betty bomber and the Zeke off Eten, it is common to roll all three planes into a single 'planes' afternoon of diving after a deeper morning dive.

The cockpit of the EMILY lies skewed to port and still has some cockpit glass in place. (Courtesy Ewan Rowell)

The Emily is essentially broken into three large sections:

a. The forward section of the fuselage is broken off just forward of the wings and lies canted to the left in an upright position. The nose cone is still identifiable with its glazed cockpit windows.

b. The wings are still attached to a large section of the fuselage, which lies upside down and crushed against the seabed. Both wing pontoon floats have become detached from the main support struts and lie alongside the wings.

c. The aft section of the fuselage, with the tail plane, is completely broken off from the main section and also lies upside down. The four large radial engines have fallen from the wings after supports gave way.

The EMILY flying boat lies in 12-15 metres between Eten and Tonoas Islands. (Courtesy Ewan Rowell)

Although the fuselage is upside down and broken into three pieces, the propeller blades are not bent from a crash landing on water under power at speed.

3. *Nakajima B6N Navy Tenzan Carrier-Borne Attack Plane*
Allied reporting name: JILL
Off Eten & Moen Islands

Nakajima B6N *Tenzan*, the IJN standard carrier-borne torpedo bomber. Allied reporting name: JILL

The Nakajima B6N1 and B6N2 Navy Carrier Attack Plane, Models 11 and 12 (Allied reporting name JILL) was the IJN standard carrier borne torpedo bomber and light bomber used to support ground forces during the final years of WWII. The B6N JILL was a successor to the B5N KATE.

The B5N Kate's weaknesses had become evident during Japan's invasion of China in 1937. The IJN began to look for a faster, longer-range aircraft and issued its specifications to Nakajima in 1939. The new B6N plane would carry a crew of three – the pilot, navigator/bombardier and radio operator/ gunner in an enclosed cockpit. It was to have a top speed of 299mph and a cruising speed of 207mph with a standard range of 1,084 nautical miles or 1,892 nautical miles on maximum overload on internal fuel tanks.

The B6N *Tenzan* (Heavenly Mountain) was 36 feet long with a wingspan of almost 49 feet and had a service ceiling of 29,660 feet. The plane was powered by a single radial engine driving a four-blade metal propeller. By the time the plane entered service, the Model 11 had a maximum speed of 300mph and a range of 2,300 miles, with the Model 12 achieving 310mph with a range of 1,600 miles.

Production of the majority of the B6N aircraft took place between June 1943 and August 1945 and the aircraft became well-known for its role in conventional and kamikaze attacks during the Okinawa campaign.

The B6N1 Jill was initially fitted with three 7.7mm Type 92 machine guns, one flexible rear firing MG at the rear of the triple cockpit, one flexible 7.7mm MG firing through a ventral tunnel at the rear of the cockpit and a 7.7mm Type 97 MG to the port wing. The wing MG was subsequently removed and the rear 7.7mm Type 92 MG was replaced with a heavier 13mm Type 2 machine gun in the B6N2a Model 12. The Jill could carry six 220-lb bombs or alternatively one 1,764-lb aerial torpedo.

The B6N Jill entered service with the IJN in August 1943 – but soon were prematurely committed to battle with devastating results. For when increased Allied activity in the Solomon Islands indicated a likely invasion of Bougainville, between 28 October 1943 and 1 November 1943, the IJN reinforced land-based aircraft at Rabaul with 173 carrier aircraft - including 40 B6N Jill's flown from carriers at Truk to airfields on Rabaul. The reinforcing carrier aircraft took heavy losses with only 52 of the original 173 aircraft making it back to Truk. Only six of the original 40 B6N Jill's returned to their carriers at Truk.

On 19-20 June 1944, the B6N Jill made its first carrier borne deployment to battle, at the Battle of the Philippine Sea being – deployed at a time when the US Navy had gained almost complete air superiority. The 300mph B6N Jill's took heavy losses to the U.S. Navy's new agile and powerfully armed 390mph Grumman F6F Hellcat fighter - whilst failing to inflict any significant damage on U.S. forces.

A new improved version of the B6N became available in mid-1944, but by then Japan had already lost most of its large fleet carriers and as a result of the high rate of attrition of its pilots, and failings in its pilot training system, was becoming desperately short of experienced carrier pilots. The vast majority of B6N sorties would subsequently take place from land bases - and would fail to achieve any great success.

The B6N Jill was used extensively at the Battle of Okinawa, which began in late March 1945 and lasted until 2 July - where they were also used for kamikaze missions for the first time. Just under 1,200 B6N Jill planes were produced during the war – and today only one B6N remains in existence, stored at the National Air & Space Museum in Washington, D.C.

The Wreck today

Nakajima B6N *Tenzan* torpedo bomber.

A B6N Jill sits upright in 36-38 metres on a sandy bottom some 300 yards off northeast Eten. Barring some bullet holes in the fuselage, the Jill is in fine intact condition with wings and vertical and horizontal tail fins still in place.

The cockpit still has the pilot seat in place, surrounded by control levers. The rear radio operator's seat is still in place, whilst the machine gun the radio operator used has been lifted out and put on top of the fuselage along with a number of circular ammo drums with the rounds exposed. The tips of the two, of her four propellers, that can be seen proud of the sand, are curled backwards indicating a high-speed crash landing.

4. *Nakajima C6N* Saiun *carrier borne Reconnaissance Plane*
Allied reporting name: MYRT
Off south west Moen

The Nakajima C6N *Saiun* carrier-based reconnaissance plane was the fastest naval aircraft that served with the IJN during WWII. Fitted with a single radial engine, it had a top speed of 380 mph, a long range of 2,500 nautical miles and a ceiling of just over 34,000 feet.

Nakajima C6N *Saiun* carrier-based reconnaissance aircraft. Allied reporting name: MYRT

The C6N Myrt was some 36'1" in length with a wingspan of 41-ft and carried a crew of three, who were housed in-line in a single long cockpit with a glazed canopy. Built for reconnaissance, and thus able to use her great speed to evade Allied fighters, to minimise weight, the plane was only lightly armed with a single flexibly mounted rearwards firing 7.92mm Type 2 machine gun.

The first prototype version of the C6N first flew in May 1943 and the final production model entered service in September 1944. Given that date, the Myrt off Moen is not a victim of Operation HAILSTONE.

On 17 November 1944, just a couple of months after the first C6N Myrt entered service, Allied bombers were close enough to begin strategic and urban area bombing of the Japanese home islands. Japan needed an effective night fighter – and the Myrt was certainly fast enough. Nakajima replaced the observer spot with two 20mm cannons but although this made the Myrt a powerful fast aircraft, fast enough to gain immunity from interception by Allied fighters, its effectiveness was hampered by the lack of air-to-air radar.

The Myrt is notable as being the last carrier-based aircraft to be shot down in WWII, on 15 August 1945, just minutes before all Japanese aircraft were grounded when Japan surrendered.

Just over 460 C6N Myrt aircraft were produced.

The wreck today
Depth: 15-17 metres.

The wreck of a Nakajima C6N Myrt sits upright and largely intact in 15-17 metres of water south west of Moen Island. This Myrt is often misidentified as being a 3-seat Nakaima B6N Jill torpedo bomber but the distinctive long glazed cockpit canopy, which provided excellent all-round visibility, is unmistakable and confirms the identification.

This plane appears to have hit the water hard as the engine has been ripped from its mounts. The complete fuselage and wings lie on a sand and coral seabed. The vertical and horizontal tail fins are still present.

5. *Yokosuka D4Y* Suisei *Navy Type 2 Reconnaissance Plane*
Allied reporting name: JUDY
Off Eten Island

Yokosuka D4Y *Susei* dive bomber.

The Japanese Navy developed the Yokosuka D4Y1 *Suisei* (Comet) as a single engine, two-seat catapult launched reconnaissance, carrier-borne dive-bomber. It was a low-mid-wing monoplane with a liquid cooled inverted V-12 in-line Aichi Atsuta engine. The D4Y1 was largely based on the German Heinkel He 118 V4 dive-bomber, although it was smaller and modified. The V-12 engine, which drove a 3-blade metal propeller, was a licenced copy of the German Daimler-Benz 601 engine. The D4Y was 34 feet long with a wingspan of 38 feet.

Development of the D4Y *Suisei* began in 1938, with the first prototype D4Y1 being completed in November 1940. Delays in development however slowed its entrance into theatre and kept its predecessor, the slower Aichi D3A2 (Allied reporting name: VAL) in service much longer than intended. When the D4Y did appear in the skies in mid-1942 it proved itself to be one of the fastest dive-bombers of the war with a top speed of 326mph for the Model 11, with a range of 2,500 miles. The subsequent Model 12 could make 361mph with a range of 1,320 miles, giving it superior performance to the delayed 295mph American SB2C Helldiver when it finally entered service in November 1943.

When the D4Y first entered service, it was utilised as a reconnaissance and dive bomber aircraft. Latterly, as the Allies advanced across the Pacific and closed on the Japanese home islands, the D4Y was used on kamikaze missions.

But fast though it may have been, the D4Y suffered from the same vulnerability as most Japanese WWII aircraft – as to achieve the IJN requirement for a long-range plane, weight was minimized by not fitting the D4Y with self-sealing fuel tanks or any pilot armour. This made the D4Y very vulnerable when attacked by an Allied fighter – often catching fire when hit.

The D4Y carried two forward facing 7.7mm machine guns mounted in the upper fuselage decking and one flexible rear firing 7.92mm Type 1 machine gun (selected for its rate of fire) manned by the rear seat radio operator. Latterly the 7.7mm machine guns were replaced with the 13mm Type 2 machine guns.

Whereas the Heinkel, on which it was based, carried its bombs externally, the D4Y could carry light bombs under its wings but also had an internal bomb bay able to carry a single 550-lb or 1,100-lb bomb. This payload was increased latterly for kamikaze missions to 1,764lb of bombs. The aircraft had a crew of two – the pilot and the rear gunner/radio operator, seated under a long, glazed canopy that provided good all-round visibility.

During development of the aircraft at Yokosuka, its performance and flight characteristics were initially promising. The D4Y had a much greater maximum speed and increased range in comparison to the older Nakajima B5N2 Kate dive bomber. However, during development, whilst simulating dive-bombing, the plane developed wing flutter and fatal cracking in its wing spars and airframe due to the increased stress of the dive. With these problems and the pressing need for carrier aircraft, the focus turned away from the D4Y being a dive-bomber to utilising its high speed and range to make it a carrier launched reconnaissance aircraft.

Pre-production models were built in 1942 and the D4Y took part in carrier reconnaissance during the attack on Midway Island. Meanwhile the Japanese continued to develop an improvement in the rigidity of the wings that would allow it to be used as a dive-bomber. In March 1943, the D4Y Model 11 was finally accepted as a dive-bomber.

The early versions of the D4Y proved difficult to keep operational because the Atsuta engines were unreliable and difficult to maintain in front line service. The aircraft was re-engined with the more reliable Mitsubishi MK8P *Kinsei* 62 radial engine, which gave a cruising speed of 265mph and a top speed of 343mph - making it the fastest carrier born dive bomber of WWII.

Whereas the D4Y's were adequate for 1943 - and faster than the Grumman F4F Wildcat - rapid advances in US aircraft development saw the introduction of the Grumman F6F Hellcat, which was faster and more agile than the D4Y. The Hellcats would soon be successfully exploiting that lack of armour and fuel protection.

Despite its shortcomings, the D4Y Judy did however cause considerable damage to American shipping - including the carrier *Franklin* (CV-13), which was almost sunk by a single D4Y in March 1945, with the loss of over 800 crew.

In June 1944, nine Japanese aircraft carriers set out to sea with 141 D4Y Judy dive-bombers, and 33 of the reconnaissance D4Y variant, to challenge the impending amphibious assaults on the Marianas chain of Islands. During the subsequent Battle of the Philippine Sea on 19-20 June 1944, the majority of the D4Y Judy's attempting to attack the TF 58 carriers were intercepted and shot down long before they reached the US carriers. Such was the great rate of attrition that the battle had soon been christened the *Great Marianas Turkey Shoot*, in which some 400 Japanese aircraft were shot down in a single day.

A modified version of the D4Y Judy was subsequently deployed against Allied operations in the Philippines. Despite heavy losses, the D4Y scored some successes, notably the sinking by a single bomb from a single D4Y of the light carrier USS *Princeton* (CVL-23) and hits on other U.S. carriers.

In late 1944, the D4Y4 model was designed for duty as a specialized suicide bomber with a single seat model being adapted to carry a single non-detachable 800kg bomb. When Task Force 58 approached southern Japan in March 1945 to strike military objectives in support of the invasion of Okinawa, the Japanese responded with massive kamikaze attacks using many D4Y's – installing rocket boosters on some kamikazes. The American carriers *Enterprise*, *Franklin* and *Yorktown* were all damaged by D4Y's and further hits on carriers by D4Y's continued until the end of the war.

The D4Y Judy was faster than the A6M Zero and so were employed as night fighters against the Boeing B-29 Superfortress bombers late in the war. The bomb equipment was removed and a 20mm Type 99 cannon with its barrel slanted upwards and forwards was installed in the rear cockpit. Some aircraft were fitted with 10cm air-to-air rockets under the wings. But lack of radar for night operations, an inadequate rate of climb and the B-29's high ceiling of almost 32,000 feet made them of little effective use as night fighters.

Some 2,319 Yokosuka D4Y aircraft were built during the war.

The Wreck today

Depth 3 metres

Today the wreck of a Yokosuka D4Y Judy, that appears to have been shot down just after take-off, can be found in easy snorkelling depth of 3 metres, about 100 metres from Eten Island just off the north east most end of the airstrip. The D4Y Judy lies about 50 metres from an upside-down Zeke, which has a propeller blade protruding from the water.

The Judy is aligned pointing to the east with the airstrip astern of it - indicating that it crashed just after taking off. Bullet holes can be found over the wings and down the fuselage. The Judy would have been at full revs and travelling at some speed during take-off. Once hit, it dived quickly, crashing with some violence into the sea and breaking into three sections. The heavy engine and attached propeller, still rotating, ripped out of the fuselage mountings as it hit the water. The fuselage with its two-seat cockpit came to rest upright - the cockpit canopy frame is in the slid-back position. The one-piece tail section lies about 5 metres behind the main fuselage.

Depth 8-10 metres

The wings and centre section of another Judy lie upside down amongst coral outcrops off Eten island in 8-10 metres. The engine also appears to have been ripped out of the plane and the section of fuselage from the wings aft is not present nearby.

The skin of the underside of the wings, now facing upwards, has disappeared in many places to reveal the lightweight lattice work of the structure. The wheel bays are empty, indicating that the wheels were down for landing or take off and not in the retracted position for flight.

6. *Mitsubishi A6M Navy Type O Carrier Fighter* - **Reisen *Zero***
Allied reporting name: ZEKE
Off Eten Island

The Mitsubishi A6M *Reisen* was a long-range fighter developed as a greatly improved successor to the Mitsubishi A5M fighter, which had entered service in 1937. Based on their immediate combat experiences of the A5M in China, in May 1937, the IJN sent out their requirements to Nakajima and Mitsubishi for a new carrier-based fighter with a speed of 370mph and a climb to 9,840 feet in 3.5 minutes. The fighter was to have drop tanks and six to eight hours flight at an economical cruising speed.

Mitsubishi A6M *Zero*, long range carrier-based fighter. Allied reporting name: ZEKE

The first prototype of the new improved A6M fighter was completed in March 1939. Fifteen were built and before testing had been completed, they were shipped to the war zone in China. They arrived in Manchuria in July 1940 and first saw combat in August 1940, proving to be almost untouchable for the Chinese fighters, the Polikarpov I-16's and I-153's that had been such a problem for the A5M's. In one clash thirteen A6M's shot down twenty-seven I-16's and I-153's in under three minutes - for no loss.

Flushed with this success, the IJN immediately ordered the A6M into production as the Type O Carrier Fighter. The 'A' stands for 'Carrier Fighter', the '6' denotes that it was the 6th to be designed by 'M' Mitsubishi. The final figure denotes the version of the plane – a further letter 'K' denotes a Trainer plane whilst 'N' denoted Fighter Seaplane, e.g. the A6M2-N, Allied reporting name RUFE, the seaplane version of the Zeke.

The A6M was usually referred to by its pilots as the "Zero-sen", zero being the last digit of the Imperial year 2600 (1940) when the Model 11 entered service with the Navy. The Allied Reporting Name during WWII for the A6M was ZEKE, although the use of ZERO was commonly adopted by the Allies later in the war.

The Zero was almost 29-ft 8" feet long with a wingspan of 39-ft 5". The A6M2 Model 11 was fitted with two 12.7 mm Type 97 machine guns in the upper fuselage decking (with 500 rounds per gun) and two wing-mounted 20mm Type 99-1 cannons (with 60 rounds per gun). The Zero could also carry two 132-lb bombs.

The Model 11 was fitted with a Nakajima 'Prosperity' engine that gave it a cruising speed of 230mph and a top speed of 328mph at 15,000 feet. The Model 11 had a range of 1,580 miles on internal fuel tanks, increasing to 1,929 with drop tanks. As in all Zekes, the wing was integral with the fuselage, saving weight and improving strength.

This plane's exceptional manoeuvrability and extraordinary range made it become the backbone of Japanese air power and it participated in the majority of naval actions - outmatching all Allied aircraft early in the Pacific war. It has become the iconic image of the Japanese WWII fighter.

In the British dependency of Malaya, the RAF had a handful of fighter squadrons but with a shortage of fighters due to the European war, these were equipped with American built Brewster F2A Buffalo fighter aircraft, which had a top speed of 323mph. The Brewster Buffalo had been rejected for service in Britain because of fuel starvation issues above 15,000 feet but, desperate for fighters for the Pacific and Asia, the RAF had ordered a number from America. The Buffalo would prove no match for the Zero in combat. The RAF in Malaya was almost wiped out during the first days of the Pacific War in December 1941.

After the delivery of only 65 A6M2 Model 11 aircraft by November 1940, a variant was developed, the A6M2 Type O Model 21, which had folding wing tips to allow them to be deployed more easily to aircraft carriers. The Model 21 would be the most common version produced during the war.

Nakajima A6M2-N Interceptor/Fighter Bomber. This floatplane fighter was developed from the Mitsubishi A6M Zero. Allied reporting name: RUFE.

The Nakajima A6M2-N (Navy Type 2 Interceptor/Fighter-Bomber) was a single-crew floatplane or seaplane deployed in 1942 that was based on the Mitsubishi A6M-2 Model 11 fuselage with added floats to enable seaborne operations. The Allied reporting name was RUFE.

Carrier based Zero fighters escorting Vals and Kates, spearheaded the surprise attacks on Pearl Harbor and the Philippines on 7 December 1941 and were involved in the attacks on Wake Island, Darwin and Ceylon. The Zeke was unstoppable during the first six months of the war emerging victorious over all Allied carrier and land-based aircraft it encountered.

With the introduction from 1942 onwards of modern Allied fighters in the Pacific theatre such as the Chance-Vought F4U Corsair, the Lockheed P-38 Lighting and the Supermarine Spitfire, the Zeke was unable to match their speed, armament and protection and began to take heavy losses in combat. The Zero could still hold its own in low altitude engagements but it was outclassed at higher altitudes and was no match for the new Allied fighters.

When heavy losses of aircraft and carriers at the Battle of Midway in June 1942 stopped the Japanese offensive advances, Japan was pushed onto the back foot. The Zero was forced to operate more in a defensive role for the rest of the war - where lack of armour and fuel tank protection made it very vulnerable. It was common for the Zero to catch fire when hit.

After further developments with the A6M3 and A6M4, in September 1943, the A6M5 Type O Model 52 was deployed – it is considered the most effective variant. The Model 52 carried heavier gauge skin, redesigned wings that were shorter and had rounded, not clipped tips and allowed the folding wing mechanism to be dispensed with. Either two 7.7mm machine guns or two 13.2mm guns were fitted in the fuselage plus two 20mm cannon mounted in the wings.

Although the same engine was retained, thrust augmentation exhaust stacks were added that increased the speed of the A6M5 Model 52 to 348mph with a range of 1,100 miles. It could now broadly match the Grumman F6F Hellcat for performance, but in fact faired poorly in combat with the Hellcat, which was faster, more strongly built and better protected. The Hellcat had a service ceiling of 37,300 feet compared to 33,000 feet for the Zero. The Zero was not very good in dives and had manoeuvrability limitations at speeds above 180mph.

By March 1944, other variants were introduced to improve on previous weaknesses with improved armament, armour glass for the cockpit and automatic fire extinguishers for fuel tanks. Even these later models were however outdated in comparison to the new American fighters and they suffered heavy losses to U.S. Navy Hellcats during the Great Marianas Turkey Shoot.

Towards the end of the war, the need to have as many fighters as possible to stave off the inexorable Allied advance towards Japan kept the by now obsolete A6M in production. From October 1944, when the Philippines came under assault by Allied forces, many Zeke's had no guns fitted but were equipped were with a single 1,000-lb bomb and/or two 132-lb bombs and used in kamikaze attacks against Allied shipping. The A6M7 was the last variant to see service.

In all, some 10,938 Zekes were manufactured, 6,215 of these by Nakajima.

The Wrecks today

Today there are two accessible Zeke aircraft wrecks close to Eten Island, which usually form part of any diving expedition to Truk. There is also a third Zeke in several pieces far out to the west of the lagoon, near the former airstrip at Param Island.

Eten Island

1. Depth: 2-3 metres

A fine example of the Zeke lies upside down about 100 metres off the north east most tip of Eten Island at the end of the former airstrip in just a few metres of water - and is an easy snorkel. Its landing gear is in the *gear down* position and lying directly off the end of the WWII airstrip it crashed or was shot down either on take-off or landing. Although the rubber tyres have disintegrated, the wheel structure just breaks the surface - as does one of the propeller blades. A 20mm Type 99 cannon protrudes from each wing.

2. Depth: 8 metres

The second Zeke is in slightly deeper water of 8 metres at the westmost tip of Eten Island – it also lies upside down. This one is the better Zeke to investigate and it is a modest snorkel down to see. For more time to investigate this virtually intact aircraft, it is often dived as an easy second or third dive of the day.

Like all the aluminium aircraft wrecks, the fuselage and wings are still clean and uncovered by coral - except for a few large brain corals that have managed to get a toehold. This Zeke appears to have been shot down from above given the exit bullet holes in the aluminium fabric of the uppermost underside of her wings. The 20mm Type 99 cannons still protrude from her wings. It is possible to duck under the upturned fuselage and see into the cockpit.

Param Island

The wreckage of a Zeke lies in shallow water about 500 yards off the end of the wartime airstrip on Param Island, well away to the west of the central islands of the lagoon. The Zeke appears to have impacted the water at speed as it has broken into several parts.

The remains of this aircraft are only rarely visited due to the distance involved.

Free diver above the upside down A6M Zero wreck off Eten Island. (Courtesy Ewan Rowell)

US TASK FORCE 58 STRIKE AIRCRAFT

1. *Dive Bombers*

a. Douglas SBD Dauntless

The Douglas Dauntless SBD (Scout Bomber Douglas) was the U.S. Navy's main carrier-borne scout plane and dive-bomber from 1940 to mid-1944. The SBD-1 went to the Marines in late 1940 and the SBD-2 to the Navy in early 1941, replacing the SBU Corsair and the Curtiss SBC Helldiver. In late 1944, the SBD Dauntless was superceded by the Curtiss SBC2 Helldiver.

The SBD, nicknamed *Slow But Deadly*, was a long range aircraft that was manoeuvrable and handled well with good diving characteristics from its perforated dive brakes on the trailing edges of its wings. The SBD was a low-wing cantilever configuration of all metal construction except for fabric covered flight controls. Its range of just over 1,100 nautical miles could be

Four armed SBD-5 dive bombers fly over the northern part of Eniwetok Atoll on 18 February 1944. (National Archives 80-G-218609)

extended with droppable tanks. It was well armed and rugged and could carry a potent bomb load – it could survive heavy battle damage and was much loved by its crews.

The roles of light bombers such as the SBD were still not well defined by 1943. Originally, during the 1920's, they had been designed as VS scout planes, where 'V' denotes heavier than air and 'S' denotes 'scout'.

After 1927, the VS scout type was adapted for dive bombing as the VSB scout bomber. With the advent of extensive bulky radio gear and airborne radar in 1942-43, the relatively compact VSB scout bomber could not fully perform both bombing roles and scouting missions - and after November 1943 it became a full-time dive-bomber, VB. In early 1944, the need for scout planes diminished when fighters could be equipped with a lightweight airborne radar set for reconnaissance missions.

The Douglas SBD Dauntless was just over 33-ft in length with a wingspan of 41ft 6in. It carried a crew of two, the pilot and a radio operator/rear gunner, in a two-man in-line tandem cockpit that was fitted with dual flight controls. It was more lightly armed than its successor the SB2C Helldiver, the SBD-1 carrying two 0.50-inch (12.7mm) forward-firing synchronized Browning M2 fixed machine guns in the engine cowling and twin 0.30-inch (7.62mm) flexible Browning machine guns mounted in a twin rearward firing mount at the rear of the cockpit. The

SBD-2 went to the Navy in early 1941 and by the time the most common SBD-5 variant entered production, the armament had been altered to a single forward firing 0.50-inch machine gun in the cowling and two rearward firing 0.30-inch machine guns in a twin mount. The SBD lacked the more powerful 20mm wing-mounted cannons of the SB2C Helldiver.

Compressibility had proved to be a major problem in the early development of dive bombers. During a dive, as the airplane approaches the sound barrier, shock waves can form on flight control surfaces causing tail buffeting. Excessive air loads on flight control surfaces can make them unusable and speed can build up very quickly. The airplane can go into an unrecoverable dive, be unable to pull up and impact the ground. Many pilots were lost in this way in the early days before compressibility was understood. The SBD had hydraulically actuated perforated split air brakes to control speed in the dive and reduce air frame stress.

The SBD had a maximum speed of 255mph at 14,000-feet – slow compared to the top speed of its 1944 successor the 295mph Curtiss SB2C Helldiver and the 390mph Grumman F6F Hellcat fighter. The SBD was also much slower than the 341mph of the Model 22 A6M Zero fighter.

The SBD-2s were retrofitted with self-sealing fuel tanks, whilst the SBD-3, which began manufacture in early 1941, was the first fully combat ready version with a total production of 585 planes. Flotation gear was removed, and armour and bullet-proof windscreen were added. The SBD could carry 2,250-lbs of bombs: one 1,000-lb fuselage bomb and two wing bombs.

The SBD Dauntless was the first U.S. Navy plane to sink an enemy vessel in action during WWII, sending the Japanese submarine I-70 to the bottom just three days after Pearl Harbor. The first real blooding of the SBD came on 7 May 1942 at the Battle of the Coral Sea where the SBD Dauntless and TBD Devastators sank the light carrier *Shōhō*, damaged *Shōkaku*, and badly depleted *Zuikaku*'s air group. At the Battle of Midway, just one month later in June 1942, as Grumman TBF Avengers and Devastators were shot down in numbers, 50 SBD's dived on the four Japanese fleet carriers *Akagi*, *Kaga*, *Sōryū* and *Hiryū*, leaving them as blazing hulks, and eventually sending all four to the bottom.

The SBD Dauntless would go on to be deployed during the Allied landings in North Africa and in the Battle of the Atlantic - and had the lowest rate of attrition amongst U.S. carrier aircraft due to its ability to absorb battle damage.

By 1944, the US Navy was replacing the SBD with the more powerful Curtiss SB2C Helldiver, which was faster and carried a greater bomb load. The Battle of the Philippine Sea off the Marianas in June 1944 was the last major engagement for the carrier-borne SBD Dauntless. The SBD Dauntless would continue to fly with Marine squadrons until the end of the war, finishing its wartime career as an anti-submarine bomber carrying depth charges and rockets.

The SBD Dauntless sank more enemy shipping in the Pacific than any other Allied bomber.

b. Curtiss SB2C Helldiver

In 1938, the Curtiss Wright Company designed a new dive bomber, the carrier launched two-person Scout Bomber 2, with the suffix 'C' denoting it as a Curtiss produced aircraft.

Initial development and production of the new SB2C Helldiver was plagued by delay – and when in the spring of 1943, the first SB2C Helldivers began to join the carriers for trials, the

Curtiss SB2C-4 Helldiver bomber in 1944 (Naval History & Heritage Command NH 95054-KN)

results were poor. Wing fold and arresting gear failed, fuselage and wing skin wrinkled, tail wheels collapsed, and hydraulic systems leaked. The Royal Navy and the Royal Australian Air Force cancelled substantial orders as a result. The SB2C's were returned by the carrier commanders to the factory for remedial work - incorporating almost 900 modifications. In the meantime, the carrier commanders continued to rely on the old rugged Douglas SBD Dauntless for dive bombing.

Modified SB2C's were finally deployed in limited numbers in November 1943 from *Bunker Hill* in an attack on the Japanese stronghold of Rabaul on New Britain. But it was still the rugged, old SBD Dauntlesses that would be instrumental in the great raid against Truk in February 1944 and then against Palau in March 1944, six weeks later.

Early opinions of the Helldiver in combat were very negative - due to its size, weight, electrical problems, poor stability, lack of power and reduced range compared to the Douglass SBD Dauntless that it was replacing. In June 1944, during the Battle of the Philippine Sea, after launching at extreme range to strike the Japanese carriers, 45 Helldivers were lost due to running out of fuel as they returned to their own carriers. The lack of power was finally corrected in 1944 with a change of engine.

The Helldiver was a larger aircraft than the Douglas SBD Dauntless it replaced, 36ft 8in long with a wingspan of 49ft 9in, compared to the 33ft length and 41.5-ft wingspan of the SBD. It was able to operate from the latest aircraft carriers and carry a considerable array of firepower in addition to having an internal bomb bay that reduced drag.

The SB2C had folding wings for storage and carried a crew of two, the pilot and radio operator/gunner. It had a top speed of 295mph (the SBD Dauntless was 255mph), and early variants had a range of 1,165 miles and a service ceiling of 29,100 feet, the range increasing to 1,420 miles with the SB2C-4 in November 1944. The SB2C-4 carried two 20mm wing mounted cannon and two 0.30 calibre 7.62mm Browning machine guns in the rear cockpit. It could carry two 1,000-lb bombs in its internal bomb bay or one aerial torpedo - in addition to 500-lb of bombs on each underwing hardpoint.

Despite the early problems, the SB2C Helldiver in the end proved to be a formidable aircraft and was flown during the last two years of the Pacific war. *Bunker Hill* was the only carrier to fly off SB2C planes during Operation HAILSTONE in February 1944, whilst the SBC2 went on to participate in the battles over the Marianas, the Philippines (where it was partly responsible for sinking the Japanese battleship *Musashi*), Taiwan, Iwo Jima and Okinawa.

The SB2C saw service in 1945 in strikes against the Ryuko Islands and then against the Japanese home island of Honshū in tactical attacks on airfields, communications and shipping as well as combat patrols at the time of the nuclear bombs being dropped. The advent of air to ground rockets ensured that the SB2C was the last purpose-built dive-bomber produced. Rockets allowed precision attacks against surface naval and land targets whilst avoiding the airframe stresses and aircraft vulnerability of near vertical dives close to the target.

2. *Torpedo Bomber*
Grumman TBF Avenger

Grumman TBF-1 Avenger torpedo bomber dropping a Mark XIII torpedo in October 1942. The torpedo is fitted with a plywood tail shroud to improve aerodynamic performance. (National Archives 80-G-19189)

The Grumman TBF Avenger was a U.S. Navy 3-seat torpedo-bomber that had its inaugural flight in August 1941, entered service in 1942 and first saw action during the Battle of Midway in June 1942. The suffix 'F' denotes a Grumman aircraft, the aircraft being designated TBM when manufactured by General Motors. The TBF Avenger was the successor to the Douglas TBD Devastator which had been the Navy's main torpedo-bomber since 1935 but which by the beginning of WWII had become relatively obsolete. The TBD Devastators would be decimated at the Battle of the Coral Sea in May 1942.

The TBF Avenger was the heaviest single-engined aircraft of World War II.

It was just over 40ft in length and had a wingspan of 54ft 2in. The crew of three sat in-line: pilot, rear-turret gunner, and radio operator who doubled as the ventral gunner and bombardier.

The early TBF's had a maximum speed of some 270mph, a service ceiling of 22,600 feet and depending on the payload being carried, a range of just over 900 miles. In early models the Avenger was fitted with one forward firing 0.30-in (7.62mm) nose mounted M1919 Browning machine gun along with one 0.50-in (12.7mm) M2 Browning machine gun in a rear-facing electrically powered dorsal turret for a dedicated rear turret machine gunner, and a 0.30-in (7.62mm) hand-fired M1919 Browning machine gun mounted under the tail in a rear facing ventral position for the bombardier, used to defend against fighters attacking from below and to the rear. Later models dispensed with the nose-mounted gun in favour of a 0.50-in wing mounted M2 Browning machine gun in each wing for better strafing ability. Later in the war, up to eight Forward Firing or High Velocity aircraft rockets were carried.

The TBF Avenger had a large bomb bay that could carry a Mark 13 aerial torpedo, depth charges and mines or a single 2,000lb bomb (or alternatively, up to four 500-lb bombs). This was a rugged and stable aircraft, well equipped, with good handling and a long range. The same folding wings as the Hellcat were fitted for use on carriers.

The Avenger's design role was to torpedo surface ships, they were ship-killers – and Avengers played an important role in several naval battles, such as in the Solomon Islands where they sank the Japanese light carrier *Ryūhō* in August 1942 and helped sink the crippled battleship *Hiei* at Guadalcanal in November 1942. In addition to surface shipping kills, Avengers claimed about 30 submarine kills and were the most effective submarine killers in the Pacific theatre.

In June 1943, future U.S. President George H.W. Bush was commissioned as one of the youngest naval aviators of the time, flying a TBF Avenger in the Pacific from the *San Jacinto* (CVL-30). On 2 September 1944, his Avenger was hit over the Pacific island of Chichi Jima and both his crewmates were killed. Bush managed to release his payload over the target before bailing out. Although he was subsequently picked up by the submarine *Finback* (SS-230), several other fellow aviators, shot down in the attack, were captured and executed. He was later awarded the Distinguished Flying Cross. The Hollywood actor Paul Newman flew as a rear-seat radioman and gunner in an Avenger during WWII.

By 1943, Grumman began to phase out production of the TBF Avenger to concentrate on producing F6F Hellcats, The Eastern Aircraft Division of General Motors took over production, their aircraft being designated TBM. The TBM-3 began production in mid-1944, with a more powerful engine and wing hard points for drop tanks and rockets.

Rugged and versatile, the TBF's acquired the nickname 'turkey'. The post-war disappearance of a flight of Avengers, known as Flight 19, in December 1945, added to the mystery of the Bermuda triangle.

3. *Fighters*
Grumman F6F Hellcat

Bogged down with the initial difficulties in carrier operations besetting the Vought F4U Corsair, and looking to
replace its aging F4F Wildcat fighter, the US Navy adopted
the new F6F Hellcat as its carrier fighter, with the first
Hellcats making their combat debut in September 1943.
Although the F6F Hellcat didn't have the performance of
the F4U Corsair, it had nevertheless been developed to

Grumman F6F Hellcat fighters
in 1943. (National Archives)

counter the strengths of the Mitsubishi A6M Zero and win
air superiority in the Pacific. The prefix 'F' denotes it as a fighter, whilst the suffix 'F' denotes
it as being manufactured by Grumman Aircraft Engineering Corporation.

Grumman had been working since 1938 on a successor to the 318mph F4F Wildcat, which
had entered service in 1940 but was now outperformed by the faster 328mph Mitsubishi A6M
Zero, which was more manoeuvrable and had a longer range. The intelligence breakthrough
came during the Midway campaign in June 1942 - when an A6M Zero from the carrier
Ryūhō, one of the two Japanese light carriers involved in the Japanese operation against the
Aleutian Islands, crash-landed on an isolated island.

The remains of the downed A6M Zero were recovered by American forces and shipped
to America for analysis. Bureau of Aeronautics flyers and engineers were stunned to find that
the A6M Zero's outstanding superior performance was achieved by a small 1,000-horsepower
engine – and that to lighten the aircraft and gain speed, Japanese designers incorporated every
possible weight saving measure they could into the design. There was no armour protection
for the pilot or for the engine and critical parts of the plane. The fuel tanks were vulnerable as
they were not self-sealing. High-altitude capability had also been sacrificed.

Now forearmed with this knowledge, Grumman engineers began an intensive effort to
produce a fighter that could counter the Zero's strengths and help gain command of the air
in the Pacific. Such are the pressures of war, that an experimental aircraft was produced in 3
months, the XF6F Hellcat. Although the final version of the F6F Hellcat resembled the F4F
Wildcat, it was a completely new design.

The F6F Hellcat was just over 33ft long with a wingspan of 42ft 10in. The wings could be
hydraulically or manually folded for use on carriers - with a folded stowage position parallel
to the fuselage with the leading edges pointing down.

A new 2,000-hp Pratt & Whitney R-2800 Double Wasp radial engine that had been
powering Vought's Corsair design since its beginnings in 1940 was installed. Grumman
redesigned and strengthened the F6F airframe to accommodate the new engine, which

369

drove a three-bladed Hamilton Standard propeller that gave later versions, such as the F6F-5 introduced in November 1944, a maximum speed of 380mph at 23,400 feet, 30mph faster than the 341mph Mitsubishi A6M Type O Model 22 Zero (introduced in December 1942).

The first production F6F-3 powered by the R-2800-10 flew on 3 October 1942, just three months after the A6M Zero had been downed in the Aleutians. The F6F Hellcat was faster at all altitudes and marginally outclimbed the Zero above 14,000-feet and rolled faster than the Zero above 235mph. The Zero however could outturn the Hellcat with ease at low speed and had a better rate of climb below 14,000-ft. The Zero was poorer than the Hellcat in dives and had manoeuvrability limitations at speeds above 180mph.

The first F6F Hellcat squadrons, untried in combat, began to arrive in Hawaii with newly constructed and commissioned carriers in late 1942 - and the class reached operational readiness on *Essex* in February 1943. The new plane was faster and could, with a service ceiling of 37,300-feet, operate several thousand feet higher than the 33,000-feet ceiling of the A6M Zero. The Hellcat could out dive and outclimb the Zero, whilst its heavier engine allowed for heavier guns.

Unlike the A6M Zero, the F6F Hellcat was designed to take damage and get the pilot safely back home. The new more powerful engine allowed for a bullet-resistant windshield, for 212-lb of cockpit armour to protect the pilot, and armour for the oil tank and oil cooler. The 250 US-gallon self-sealing fuel tank fitted in the fuselage was made of rubber encased in a canvas hammock to nullify the effect of bullet punctures. A centre-section hardpoint under the fuselage could carry a single 150 US-gallon disposable drop tank.

The extensive cockpit armour and fuel tank protection is in stark contrast to the almost complete lack of pilot and fuel protection in most Japanese combat aircraft. Just a few rounds striking a Japanese aircraft could be enough to set it on fire. The lack of pilot armour and fuel protection was a crucial flaw in the Zero and led to the early loss of a large percentage of their experienced front-line pilots.

The F6F was fitted with six 0.50 calibre M2 Browning air-cooled machine guns, three on each wing – and each had 400 rounds. This was a much more powerful punch than the A6M Zero's two 20mm cannon and two 7.7mm guns. The Browning M2 fired more than 1,000 0.5 cal rounds per minute and could pierce aircraft armour. With suspended containers, it could also carry more ammunition than its predecessor, the Wildcat. Later variations were equipped to carry bombs - with single bomb racks installed under each wing, inboard of the undercarriage bays. With these and the centre section hard point rack, late model F6F-3's could carry a total bomb load of more than 2,000-lbs. The Bureaus of Ordnance and Aeronautics were ordered in June 1943 to begin the development of a forward firing High Velocity 3.5-inch wing mounted rocket for fighters. Six High Velocity Aircraft Rockets (HVAR's) would eventually be carried, three under each wing.

The Hellcat was deployed in a variety of combat roles – as fighter, night-fighter, fighter-bomber and rocket platform. In all, more than 12,000 Hellcats would go on to be produced in two major variants. F6F Hellcats were credited with destroying 5,223 aircraft while in service with the U.S. Navy, U.S. Marine Corps and the British Royal Navy – more than shot down by all the other combat aircraft combined. They are the iconic U.S. Navy fighter of the Pacific War.

BIBLIOGRAPHY

1. Alden, Carroll Storrs, and Allan Westcott: *The United States Navy*, 2nd edition, revised, Philadelphia, Lippincott. (1945)
2. Alden, John D: *U.S. Submarine Attacks during WWII*. Naval Institute Press (1989)
3. Bailey, Dan. E:
    (i) *WWII Wrecks of the Kwajalein and Truk Lagoons*. North River Publications (1989)
    (ii) *World War II Wrecks of the Truk Lagoon*. North River Diver Publications (2000)
4. Blair, Clay Jr: *Silent Victory – The U.S. Submarine War Against Japan*. J.B. Lippincott Company (1975)
5. Buchanan, Lt A. R. USNR: *The United States and World War II*. New York (1964)
6. Buchanan, Lt A.R. USNR (ed) and the Aviation History Unit, *The Navy's Air War: A Mission Completed*, (New York, 1946),
7. Costello, John: *The Pacific War: 1941-1945*. William Morrow (1982)
8. Cressman, Robert J.: *Official Chronology of the U.S. Navy in World War II*. U.S. Naval Institute Press (1999)
9. Crowl, Phillip A. and Edmond F. Love: *The United States army in World War II – The War in the Pacific – Seizure of the Gilberts and Marshalls*. US Government Printing Office (1955)
10. Evans, David C. and Mark R. Peattie: *KAIGUN. Strategy, Tactics and Technology in the Imperial Japanese Nay 1887-1941*. Naval Institute Press (1997)
11. Francillon, R.J: *Japanese Aircraft of the Pacific War*. Funk & Wagnalls (1970)
12. Fukui, Shizuo: *Japanese Naval Vessels at the end of World War II*. Naval Institute Press (1987)
13. Green, William: *War Planes of the Second World War: Fighters, Vol 4*. Garden City (1961)
14. Grover, David H: *US Army Ships and Watercraft of World War II*. Naval Institute Press (1987)
15. Ito, Masanori: *The End of the Japanese Navy*. Norton Publishers (1962)
16. Jane, Fred T: *Janes Fighting Ships 1944-45*. David & Charles Ltd (1971)
17. Jensen, Lt. Oliver USNR: *Carrier War*. Pocket Books Inc (1945)
18. Jentschura, Hansgeorg: *Warships of the Imperial Japanese Navy 1869-1945*. Naval Institute Press (1976)
19. King, Fleet Admiral Ernest J.: *U.S. Navy at War, 1941-1945*. Washington (1945)
20. Leahy, Fleet Admiral William D., US: *I Was There*. New York (1950)
21. Lester, Robert E.: *U.S. Navy Action and Operational Reports from World War II. Part 3. Fifth Fleet and Fifth Fleet Carrier Task Forces*. University Publications of America. (1990)
22. Lindemann, Klaus: *Hailstorm Over Truk Lagoon*. Klaus, Pacific Press Publications (1989)
23. Lloyds of London: *Lloyds' Register of Shipping*. London
24. Macdonald, Rod: *Force Z Shipwrecks of the South China Sea – HMS Prince of Wales & HMS Repulse*. Whittles Publishing (2013)
25. Middlebrook, Martin: *The Sinking of the Prince of Wales & Repulse*. Allen Lane (1977)
26. Morison, Elting E., *Admiral Sims and the Modern American Navy*. Boston (1942)
27. Morison, Samuel E., *History of U.S. Naval Operations in World War II*.
    (i) Vol IV: *Coral Sea, Midway and Submarine Actions* (1949)
    (ii) Vol V: *The Struggle for Guadalcanal* (1949)
    (iii) Vol VI: *Breaking the Bismarcks Barrier* (1950)
    (iv) Vol VII; *Aleutians, Gilberts and Marshalls* (1957)
    (v) Vol VIII: *New Guinea and the Marianas* (1957)
    (vi) Vol XII: *Leyte* (1958)
    (vii) Vol XIII: *The Liberation of the Philippines* (1959)
    (viii) Vol XIV: *Victory in the Pacific* (1960). Little Brown & Co.

28. Morison, Samuel E.: *The Two Ocean War*. Boston (1963)
29. Odgers, George: *Air War against Japan 1943–1945*. Advertiser Printing Co. (1957)
30. Office of the Chief of Naval Operations – Division of Naval Intelligence. Government Printing Office:
    (a) *Japanese Merchant Ships Recognition Manual ONI 208-J – Restricted*. U.S. (1944)
    (b) *Standard Classes of Japanese Merchant Ships* ONI 208-J (Revised) Supplement 3. (1945)
    (c) *Far Eastern Small Craft* ONI 208-J Supplement 2. (1945)
    (d) *The Japanese Navy* ONI 222-J. (1945)
    (e) *Aerial Views of Japanese Naval Vessels* ONI 41–42. (1945)
31. Peattie, Mark R: *Nanyo – The Rise and Fall of the Japanese in Micronesia 1885-1945*. University of Hawaii Press (1988)
32. Prados, John: *Combined Fleet Decoded*. Random House (1995)
33. Reynolds, Clark G.: *The Fast Carriers – The Forging of an Air Navy*. Naval Institute Press (1968)
34. Rosenberg, Phillip Alan: *Shipwrecks of Truk*. Philip Alan Rosenberg (1981)
35. Sherrod, Robert: *History of Marine Corps Aviation in WW II*. Combat Forces Press (1952)
36. Smallpage, Roy: *TRUK The Ultimate Wreck Site*. Underwater Publications (1994)
37. Spector, Ronald H., *Eagle Against the Sun: The American War with Japan*. Random House (1992)
38. Stewart, William H: *Ghost Fleet of the Truk Lagoon*. Pictorial Histories Publishing Co. (1986)
39. Stille, Mark:
    (a) *Imperial Japanese Navy Destroyers 1919-45 (1)*. Osprey Publishing (2013)
    (b) *Imperial Japanese Navy Destroyers 1919-45 (2)*. Osprey Publishing (2013)
40. Symonds, Craig L.: *The Battle of Midway (Pivotal Moments in American History)*. Oxford University press (2013)
41. Taylor, Theodore: *The Magnificent Mitscher*. Norton (1954)
42. Tillman, Barrett: *Hellcats Over Truk*. US Naval Institute Proceedings (1977)
43. Tillman, Barrett & Lawson Robert: *U.S. Navy Dive and Torpedo Bombers of World War II*. Motorbooks Int (2001)
44. Toll, Ian W.:
    (i) *Pacific Crucible: War at Sea in the Pacific, 1941-1943*. W.W. Norton & Co (2012)
    (ii) *The Conquering Tide: War in the Pacific Islands, 1942-1944*. W.W. Norton & Co (2020)
45. US Joint Army-Navy Assessment Committee: *Japanese Naval and Merchant Shipping Losses During World War II by All Causes*. US Government Printing Office (1947)
46. U.S. Marine Corps Historical Branch, G-3 Division: *History of U.S. Marine Corps Operations in WWII. Central Pacific Drive*. U.S. Government Printing Office (1966)
47. U.S. Navy Action and Operational Reports from World War II. Pacific Theater. Part 3. Fifth Fleet and Fifth Fleet Carrier Task Forces, University Publications of America, (1990)
48. Wagner, Ray: *American Combat Planes*. Garden City (1960)
49. Watts, A.J: Japanese Warships of World War II. Doubleday & Co Inc. (1966)
50. Wooldridge, E.T., *Carrier Warfare in the Pacific – An Oral History Collection*. Smithsonian Institution Press (1993)

Websites referred to:

Although too numerous to list, of particular assistance were the following websites:

    (a) www.combinedfleet.com

Nihon Kaigun: The authors of this website have carried out a vast amount of original work and research. It is an amazing resource which I recommend highly for anyone interested in the Imperial Japanese Navy.

    (b) www.history.navy.mil

The U.S. History & Heritage Command – it is a vast source of online documentary & photographic resources

    (c) www.archives.gov

U.S. National Archives and Records Administration

    (d) www.southampton.spydus.co.uk

This site gives online access to Lloyd's Register of Ships

INDEX

Agano, IJN light cruiser 21, 41/2, 188, 242/3, 267,

Aikoku Maru xxiv, 21/22, 31/2,35/6, **51-60**, 61-65 (wreck), 67, 149, 151, 157, 198, 202, 214, 227, 261

Akagi, IJN carrier 8, 10, 93, 95, 172, 203, 304, 365

Akashi, IJN Repair Ship 32, 83, 110, 157, 165, 187/8, 205, 251, 267

Akebono Maru 96, 203, 306

Alf Reconnaissance Seaplane 53-56, 203

Amagisan Maru 35, **66-70**, 70-74 (wreck), 96, 287/8

Amatsukaze, IJN Escort Vessel 165, 251

Asakaze Maru, auxiliary tanker 336

Aspro, USS/M 24

Atago, IJN 305

B-17 Flying Fortress bomber xix, 95, 133, 203

B-24 Liberator bomber xviii, xix, 20, 46, 95, 109, 116, 133, 187, 204, 213, 294

B-25, USAAF bomber xix, 116, 119, 157, 220

B-29 Super Fortress bomber xix, 12, 46, 359

Balao, USS/M 205

Belleau Wood, USS 15, 23, 25/6, 37

Bengal, HMIS 56

Betty bomber 25, 28, **347-349**, 349-351 (wreck)

Bradford, USS 24, 37

Buenos Aires Maru 264

Bunker Hill, USS 15, 23, 26, 30, 32-37, 39-42, 69/70, 84, 97, 120, 125/6, 134/5, 145, 150, 158, 161, 187-189, 205, 213, 226, 242/3,
267, 277, 287/8, 306, 328, 337, 344, 366

Burmeister & Wain diesel engines 52, 66, 141, 180, 191

Burns, USS 24, 37

Burrfish, USS/M 24

Bush, President George H.W., 368

Cabot, USS 14, 15, 23, 26, 37, 40, 43, 145

CHa-18, IJN auxiliary Sub Chaser 315

Coral Sea, Battle of 9, 10, 164, 241, 250/1, 365, 367

Cowpens, USS 15, 23, 26, 33, 37, 41, 187/8

Curtiss SB2C Helldiver 26, 30, 35, 213, 188, **365-366**

Dace, USS/M 24, 134

Darter, USS/M 24

Douglas SBD Dauntless dive-bomber xix, 26, 30, 32, 34, 40, 58, 70, 132/3, 157, 164, 188, 205, 207, 226/7, 298, 306, 328, 336, **364-366**

Douglas TBD Devastator torpedo-bomber xix, 133/4, 365, 367

Drum, USS/M 336

Elysia, SS 55

Enterprise, USS 26/7, 30, 32/3, 37/8/9, 40, 43/4, 97/8, 110/111, 133/4/5, 166, 187/8, 203, 205/6, 226, 261, 298, 302, 307/8, 315/6, 337, 358

Essex, USS, 11, 13, 15, 23/4, 26, 29, 30, 32/3/4, 36, 38/9, 40, 44, 58, 150, 157/8, 161, 187/8, 213, 220, 226/7, 261, 267, 277, 298, 327/8, 370

Export Control Act 1940, U.S., 6

Franklin, USS 358

Fujikawa Maru vii, **81-84**, 84-91 (wreck), 349

Fujisan Maru 28, 40, 68, **92-98**, 98-102 (wreck), 306, 316

Fukue, IJN Escort Vessel 119, 198, 212, 287, 298

Fumizuki, IJN 22, **103-111**, 111-114 (wreck), 187, 240, 245, 253, 315

Futagami, IJN Rescue Tug 76, 78, **115-116**, 116-117 (wreck), 175, 249

Fusō, IJN 19, 24, 165

Gato, USS/M 24, 68

Genota, SS 55

Genyo Maru 165

Gokoku Maru 53

Gosei Maru **118-120**, 120-123 (wreck), 157

Grumman TBF Avenger torpedo-bomber 30, 33/4/5/6, 39/40, 58/9, 70, 84, 126, 135/6, 150, 157/8, 161, 187-9, 205, 213, 226, 243, 243, 261, 277, 288, 298, 305-7, 309, 323, 328, 336/7, **367/8**

Grumman F4F Wildcat 241, 358, 369/70

Grumman F6F Hellcat xv, 26-44 (HAILSTONE), 69/70, 157, 347, 356, 358, 362, 365, **369-379**

Gudgeon, USS/M 305

Haddock, USS/M 165, 167

Halibut, USS/M 57

Halsey, Admiral William 14, 133

Hamaguchi, Minister Osachi 3

Hammann, USS 10, 171, 203

Hanagawa Maru 41, **123-126**, 126-130 (wreck), 260

Hankow Maru 343,

Hara, Vice Admiral Chiuchi 47

Harima Shipyard, Hyogo 92, 115, 265, 284, 296

Harusame, IJN destroyer 68, 96, 251

Hatakaze, IJN destroyer 287
Hauraki, SS 36, 55/6, 147-151
Heian Maru 22, 32, 39/40, 109, **131-135**, 135-142 (wreck), 174, 189, 337
Herring, USS/M 260
Hie Maru 131/2
Hikawa Maru, IJN Hospital ship 131
Hikawa Maru No 2 134
Hino Maru No 2 43, **143-145**, 145/6
Hinode Maru 287
Hirado, IJN Kaibōkan 125, 180, 187
Hiryu, IJN carrier xxii, 8, 10, 95, 172, 203, 304, 365
Hisajima Maru 156
Hiyoshi Maru 197, 212
Hoki Maru 31, 36, 56, **147-151**, 151-154 (wreck), 157, 277, 323, 327
Hokko Maru 297
Hokoku Maru 53-57, 149, 151, 202
Hokusho Maru 156
Hokuyo Maru 31, 40, **155-158**, 158-161 (wreck), 297/8
Hoyo Maru 32, 110, **162-166**, 166-169 (wreck), 187, 250
Ikazuchi, IJN destroyer 187
Intrepid, USS 15, 23, 26, 28, 30-44 (HAILSTONE), 59, 97, 158, 187/8, 226, 242, 261
I-1 95
I-2 95
I-3 95
I-8 267
I-10 54
I-16 54
I-18 54
I-20 54
I-23 164
I-30 54
I-33 225/6
I-59 265
I-60 265
I-62 265
I-64 265
I-65 265
I-66 265
I-68 171/2
I-70 171/2, 365
I-71 171/2
I-72 171/2
I-73 171/2
I-168 171

I-169 116, **170-175**, 175-177 (wreck)
Iowa, USS 24, 37, 44, 107
Ishizaki, IJN Minelayer 144
Isokaze, IJN destroyer 204
Isoroku, Admiral Yamamoto 172, 203, 349
Isuzu, IJN light cruiser 83, 204
Kaga, IJN carrier 8, 10, 93, 95, 172, 203, 304, 365
Kagu Maru 265
Kaibōkan 125, 134, 150, 180, 187, 198, 212, 260, 277, 287, 297, 327
Kaidai Type 6A 170-173, 175
Kaiten suicide torpedo xiii, xviii, 19/20
Kaizyo Maru 162
Kamikawa Maru 109, 297
Kano Maru 145, 197
Kasagisan Maru 179, 180
Kasuga Maru, Repair Ship 266
Kasugasan Maru 179, 180
Kasumi, IJN destroyer 304
Katori, IJN cruiser 21, 33, 37, 133, 164, 298
Katori Maru 83, 213
Katsuragisan Maru xvii, 179-182, 182-184 (wreck), 261, 315
Kawanishi Type 94 E7K twin-float *Alf* reconnaissance seaplane 53-56, 203
Kawanishi H8K *Emily* Flying-Boat xix, 34, **352-353**
Kawanishi H6K *Mavis* Flying-Boat xx, 34
Kawasaki Kisen Kaisha 124, 186, 195/6, 211, 303, 343
Kazan Maru 125
Keinan Maru 287
Kensyo Maru ix, 32, 110, 165, **185-189**, 189-194 (wreck), 205, 213
Kikukawa Maru 76, **195-198**, 199-200 (wreck), 211/2, 249, 251/2
Kirikawa Maru 195-197, 212
Kiyosumi Maru 21, 32, 53, 110, 165, 187-189, **201-206**, 206-208 (wreck), 294, 306, 336
Koboyashi, Vice Admiral, Commander Fourth Fleet, IJN 25
Koga, Admiral Mineichi, IJN xiv, 19, 21, 165
Kogi Maru 119
Komahashi, IJN survey ship 294
Koshin Maru 68
Kure Naval Arsenal 54, 57, 95, 115,

132/3, 163/4, 171, 174, 202/3, 226, 256, 265, 267, 304/5
Kyo Maru No 6, IJN auxiliary Sub Chaser 315
Kyoei Maru No 2 220
Kyokuto Maru 304
Lindemann, Klaus xvi, 181/2, 189, 237, 314
Lingayen Gulf 108
Lockheed P-38 Lightning fighter 119, 157, 220, 361
Long Lance torpedo 42, **106/7**, 113, 138/9, 240, 277, 284, 299, 300
Maikaze, IJN destroyer 22, 33, 37
Maizuru Navy Yard 67/8, 83, 249
Malama, SS 54
Matsukawa Maru 197, 212
Matsukaze, IJN destroyer 111, 315
Matsutan Maru 180, 313-315
Matsutani Maru 313
Matukawa Maru 212, 224
Midway, Battle of 10, 95, 144, 171, 173, 203, 256, 361, 365, 367
Minazuki, IJN destroyer 204
Minneapolis, USS 24, 37
Mitscher, Admiral Mark, USN 13, 14, 19, 23, 26
Mitsubishi A6M3 fighter – *Hamp* xx, 157
Mitsubishi A6M *Reisen* fighter *Zero - Zeke* xv, xx, 20/1, 28-30, 36, 83, 119, 157, 297, 315, 323, **360-363**
Mitsubishi F1M Observation Seaplane – *Pete* xx
Mitsubishi G3M Navy Type 96 Attack Bomber – *Nell* xx, 347/8
Mitsubishi G4M Navy Type 1 Attack Bomber – *Betty* 25, 28, **347-349**, 349-351 (wreck)
Mitsubishi-Sulzer diesel engine 202, 208
Mogamigawa Maru 297
Momokawa Maru 31, 187, 196/7, **211-214**, 214-217 (wreck), 223
Monterey, USS 15, 23, 26, 37, 42, 84, 120, 188, 205
Musashi, IJN xiv, 16, 19, 20/1, 23, 165, 204, 366
Nagano Maru 31, 58, **218-220**, 220-223 (wreck), 343
Nagara, IJN 83, 165, 305
Nagato, IJN xxii, 19, 24, 165, 343
Nagumo, Admiral Chūichi, IJN 172
Naka, IJN light cruiser 21, 33, 83, 165, 204/5

Nakajima A6M2 *Rufe* seaplane fighter xx, 21, 28, 30, 351/2, **360/1**

Nakajima B5N Navy Carrier Attack torpedo bomber – *Kate* 30, 38, 348, 354, 358, 361

Nakajima B6N Navy Carrier Attack Bomber *Tenzan* – *Jill* xx, 36, 83, **354/5**

Nakajima C6N Navy Carrier Reconnaissance plane – *Myrt* **356**

Nakajima Ki-44 *Tojo* xx, 28

Nampo Maru 305

Nanei Maru 150

Nasami, IJN minelayer 58

New Jersey, USS 23/4, 37, 44

New Orleans, USS 24, 37

Nichiryo Maru 336

Nikkai Maru 297

Nimitz, Admiral Chester, CINCPAC – CINCPOA, USN 13, 21, 43

Nippo Maru 31, 158, 196, 212, **224-227**, 227-237 (wreck), 280, 282, 344

Nowake, IJN 22

Oite, IJN xvii, xxii, 22, 41/2, 96, 104, 111, 135, 188/9, **238-243**, 243-248 (wreck), 253, 337

Ojima, IJN 76, 185, 198, **249-251**, 242 (wreck)

Oki, IJN 134, 198, 327

Okikaze, IJN 180

Okitsu Maru 226

Ondina, SS 56/7

Operation CATCHPOLE (U.S Eniwetok Invasion) 13, 15, 30

Operation FLINTLOCK (U.S. Invasion of the Marshall Islands) 13/ 58

Operation HAILSTONE (U.S. strike against Truk) xv-xviii, **12-43**

Ose, IJN 55

Oyodo, IJN light cruiser 205

Ozawa, Admiral Jisaburō IJN 259

Panay, U.S. Navy gunboat 4

Pargo, USS/M 287

Patrol Boat No 34 (ex-*Susuki*) 104, **253-256**, 256/7 (wreck)

PB4Y *Liberator*, U.S. Navy recon aircraft xiii, xix, 20-22, 174

PBY-5 *Catalina* Flying Boat xix, 203

Permit, USS/M 24, 83, 156, 213

Peto, USSM 305

Pogy, USS/M 297

Princeton, USS 15, 23, 358

Reiyo Maru xvii, 31, 58, 125, **258-261**, 261-263 (wreck)

Rio de Janeiro Maru vii, 22, **264-267**, 267-274 (wreck)

Roosevelt, President Franklin D., 5, 132

Sakagami, Lt Shinji 45, 47

San Francisco Maru 22, 31, 42, 150, 157/8, 214, 231, 233, **275-278**, 278-284 (wreck), 327

Sanae, IJN destroyer 287

Sankisan Maru 35, 70, 126, 151, 198, 261, **284-288**, 288-292 (wreck), 344

Sanyo Maru, IJN oiler 251

Sapporo Maru xvii, 43, **293-295**

Sasebo Naval Arsenal 108, 144, 197, 213, 225, 241, 265, 335

Sea Raven, USS/M 24

Seiha Maru 265

Seiko Maru 31, 40, 157/8, **296-298**, 298-301 (wreck), 336

Sinkoku Maru 39, 40, 68, 93, 96, 168, 206, **302-307**, 307-312 (wreck)

Shiretoko, IJN 83, 168, 213

Shōhō, IJN 10, 164, 251, 365

Shōkaku, IJN 8, 10, 165, 172, 251, 304, 365

Shoko Maru 297

Shonan Maru No 15 33, 37

Shotan Maru 40, 98, 180, **313-316**, 316-321 (wreck), 322/3, 325

Shunko Maru 197, 212

Sixth Fleet, IJN (Submarines) 55, 119, 120, 132/3/4, 171, 174

Sixth Fleet Anchorage 32, 66, 68, 95, 118, 120, 143, 178, 188, 205, 209, 261, 264, 267, 277, 285, 287, 322/3, 326/7/7, 342

Skipjack, USS/M 22

Snapper, USS/M 260

Skate, USS/M 24, 41, 242

Sōryū, IJN 8, 10, 95, 172, 203, 304, 365

Spearfish, USS/M 125, 260, 267

Spruance, Admiral Raymond, USN 13, 14, 15, 23, 37

Stack, USS 46

Standard Ships, general, nomenclature 16, **124-125**, 275, 286, **314/5**, 323

Steelhead, USS/M 297

Sumikawa, Rear Admiral Michio, IJN 42

Sunfish, USS/M 24

Susuki, IJN second-class destroyer (Patrol Boat No 34) 104, **253-256**, 256/7 (wreck)

Suzukaze, IJN destroyer 226

Swordfish, USS/M 266

Tachikaze, IJN *xvii, 22, 96*

Tachi Maru xvii

Tacoma Maru 336

Taiho Maru 151, **322-324**, 324-325 (wreck), 344

Taisho Maru 336

Takagi, Admiral Takeo, IJN 134

Takunan Maru No 6, auxiliary Sub Chaser 287

Tang, USS/M 24, 38

Tanikaze, IJN destroyer 205

Tanner, USS 189

Tatsufuku Maru 266

Toa Maru, IJN 93, 95/6, 164, 305

Toei Maru 212

Toho Maru, oiler 212, 304

Tōjō, Army Minister, General Hideki 5, 7

Tonan Maru No 3 xviii, 32, 110, 165, 187, 306

Trigger, USS/M 58, 157

Type 1B Standard Ship 41, 124/5

Type 1C Standard Ship 314/5, 322/3, 325

Ukishima, IJN 144/5/6, 294

Unkai Maru No 6 120, 150, 158, 277, **326-328**, 328-333 (wreck)

Urakami Maru, IJN Auxiliary Repair Ship 32, 134, 225

Urakaze, IJN destroyer 251

Venus, SS 326/7

Vincent, SS 53/4

Wahoo, USS/M 251

Wake Island 8, 165, 173, 186, 241, 361

W-22, IJN minesweeper 205, 336

Yakaze, IJN Minekaze-class destroyer (target ship) 165, 256

Yamabiko Maru, Repair Ship 266

Yamagiri Maru 40, 135, 188, 205, 297, 306, **334-337**, 337-341 (wreck)

Yamato, IJN xiv, xxii, 16, 19, 165, 203/4

Yasukuni Maru 58, 133, 164

Yokosuka D4Y *Suisei* dive-bomber – *Judy* xx, **357-359**

Yokosuka Naval Arsenal,
    Japan 109, 132, 145, 149, 186,
    287, 294, 327
Yorktown (CV-10) USS 23-42
    (HAILSTONE), 83, 134, 150,
    158, 166, 171, 187/8, 203, 205,
    207, 213, 226, 261, 267, 277,
    306, 315, 323, 328, 336, 358
Yoshida Maru 187
Yubae Maru 69, **342-344**, 344-345
    (wreck)
Yubari, IJN 204, 241

Yura, IJN 266
Yuzuki, IJN 267
Zuikaku, IJN 8, 10, 165, 172, 251,
    304